AVENGERS
Scarlet Witch

WRITERS:
DAN ABNETT, ANDY LANNING, RICHARD HOWELL, JEFF PARKER & SEAN MCKEEVER WITH **JO DUFFY, DENNIS MALLONEE & CEFN RIDOUT**

PENCILERS:
JOHN HIGGINS, RICHARD HOWELL, JUAN SANTACRUZ & MIRCO PIERFEDERICI WITH **KERRY GAMMILL, JOHN RIDGWAY & CHARLES ADLARD**

INKERS:
MARK MCKENNA, RICHARD HOWELL, RAUL FERNANDEZ & MIRCO PIERFEDERICI WITH **DAN GREEN, JOHN RIDGWAY & CHARLES ADLARD**

COLORISTS:
KEVIN SOMERS, RICHARD HOWELL, WIL QUINTANA & JAVIER TARTAGLIA WITH **BOB SHAREN, PAUL BECTON, WOODROW PHOENIX & GARRY HENDERSON**

LETTERERS:
JIM NOVAK, RICHARD HOWELL, DAVE LANPHEAR & BLAMBOT'S NATE PIEKOS WITH **JOE ROSEN, JACK MORELLI, DIANA ALBERS & WOODROW PHOENIX**

ASSISTANT EDITORS:
KELLY CORVESE, NATHAN COSBY & JOHN DENNING WITH **LINDA GRANT, GREGORY WRIGHT & MICHAEL KRAIGER**

EDITORS:
NEL YOMTOV, TERRY KAVANAGH, MARK PANICCIA & LAUREN SANKOVITCH WITH **TOM DEFALCO, MARK GRUENWALD, RICHARD ASHFORD & TOM BREVOORT**

COVER ARTIST:
MARKO DJURDJEVIC

AVENGERS CREATED BY **STAN LEE & JACK KIRBY**

COLLECTION EDITOR: **MARK D. BEAZLEY**
ASSISTANT MANAGING EDITOR: **JOE HOCHSTEIN**
ASSOCIATE MANAGING EDITOR: **ALEX STARBUCK**
EDITOR, SPECIAL PROJECTS: **JENNIFER GRÜNWALD**
SENIOR EDITOR, SPECIAL PROJECTS: **JEFF YOUNGQUIST**
RESEARCH: **MARC RIEMER**
LAYOUT: **JEPH YORK**
PRODUCTION: **ROMIE JEFFERS, COLORTEK & ALAN SMITHEE**
BOOK DESIGNER: **JOE FRONTIRRE**
SVP PRINT, SALES & MARKETING: **DAVID GABRIEL**

EDITOR IN CHIEF: **AXEL ALONSO**
CHIEF CREATIVE OFFICER: **JOE QUESADA**
PUBLISHER: **DAN BUCKLEY**
EXECUTIVE PRODUCER: **ALAN FINE**

SPECIAL THANKS TO **JESS HARROLD, ROB LONDON & DANA PERKINS**

AVENGERS: SCARLET WITCH BY DAN ABNETT & ANDY LANNING. Contains material originally published in magazine form as SCARLET WITCH #1-4, AVENGERS ORIGINS: SCARLET WITCH & QUICKSILVER #1, MARVEL TEAM-UP #125, SOLO AVENGERS #5, MARVEL COMICS PRESENTS #60-63 and #143-144, and MYSTIC ARCANA: SCARLET WITCH. First printing 2015. ISBN# 978-0-7851-9335-7. Published by MARVEL WORLDWIDE, INC., a subsidiary of MARVEL ENTERTAINMENT, LLC. OFFICE OF PUBLICATION: 135 West 50th Street, New York, NY 10020. Copyright © 1983, 1990, 1993, 1994, 1998, 2007, 2011 and 2015 Marvel Characters, Inc. All rights reserved. All characters featured in this issue and the distinctive names and likenesses thereof, and all related indicia are trademarks of Marvel Characters, Inc. No similarity between any of the names, characters, persons, and/or institutions in this magazine with those of any living or dead person or institution is intended, and any such similarity which may exist is purely coincidental. **Printed in the U.S.A.** ALAN FINE, EVP - Office of the President, Marvel Worldwide, Inc. and EVP & CMO Marvel Characters B.V.; DAN BUCKLEY, Publisher & President - Print, Animation & Digital Divisions; JOE QUESADA, Chief Creative Officer; TOM BREVOORT, SVP of Publishing; DAVID BOGART, SVP of Operations & Procurement, Publishing; C.B. CEBULSKI, SVP of Creator & Content Development; DAVID GABRIEL, SVP Print, Sales & Marketing; JIM O'KEEFE, VP of Operations & Logistics; DAN CARR, Executive Director of Publishing Technology; SUSAN CRESPI, Editorial Operations Manager; ALEX MORALES, Publishing Operations Manager; STAN LEE, Chairman Emeritus. For information regarding advertising in Marvel Comics or on Marvel.com, please contact Niza Disla, Director of Marvel Partnerships, at ndisla@marvel.com. For Marvel subscription inquiries, please call 800-217-9158. **Manufactured between 2/6/2015 and 3/16/2015 by R.R. DONNELLEY, INC., SALEM, VA, USA.**

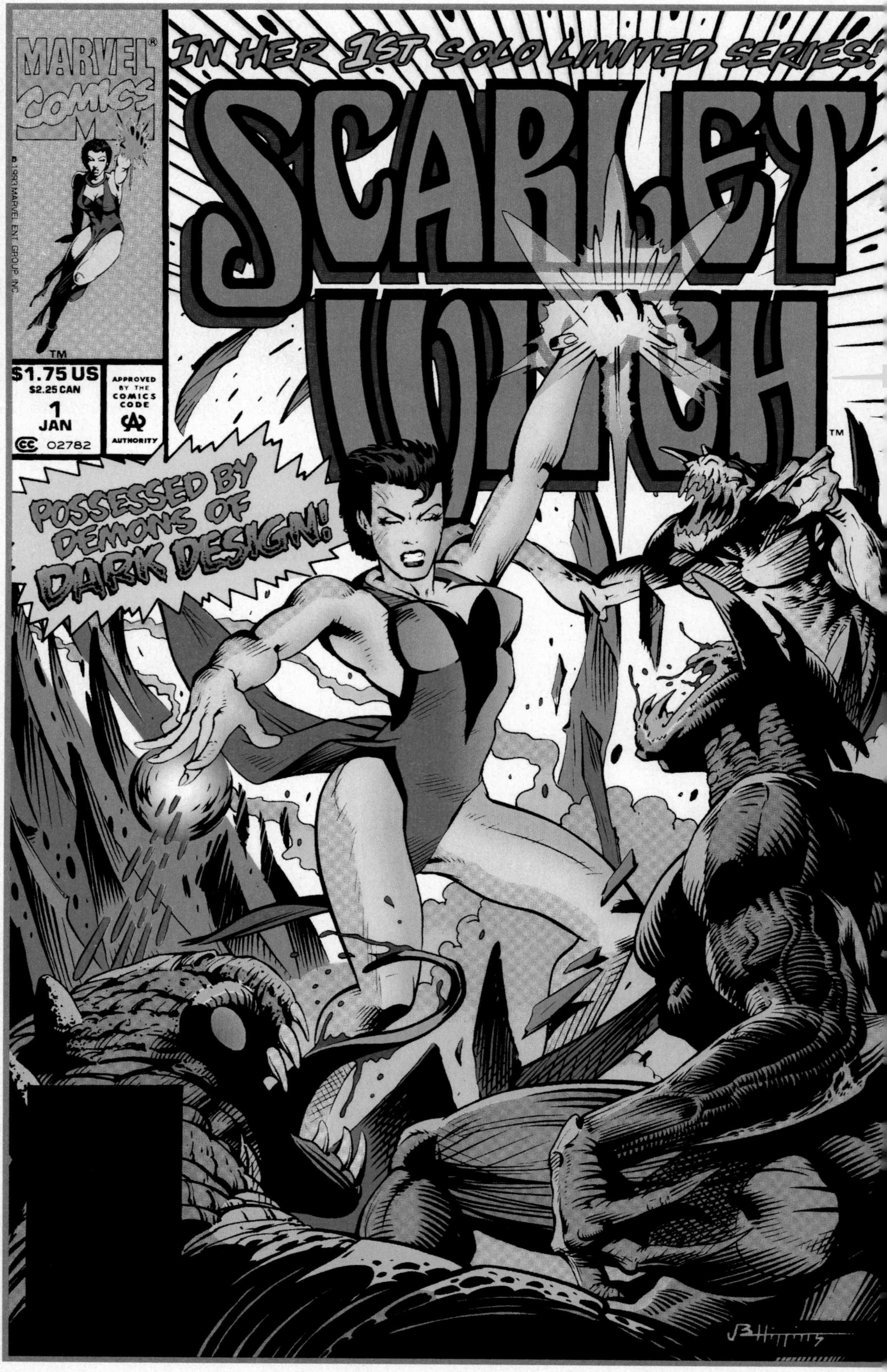
MARVEL COMICS
IN HER 1ST SOLO LIMITED SERIES!
SCARLET WITCH
$1.75 US
$2.25 CAN
1
JAN
02782
APPROVED BY THE COMICS CODE AUTHORITY
POSSESSED BY DEMONS OF DARK DESIGN!

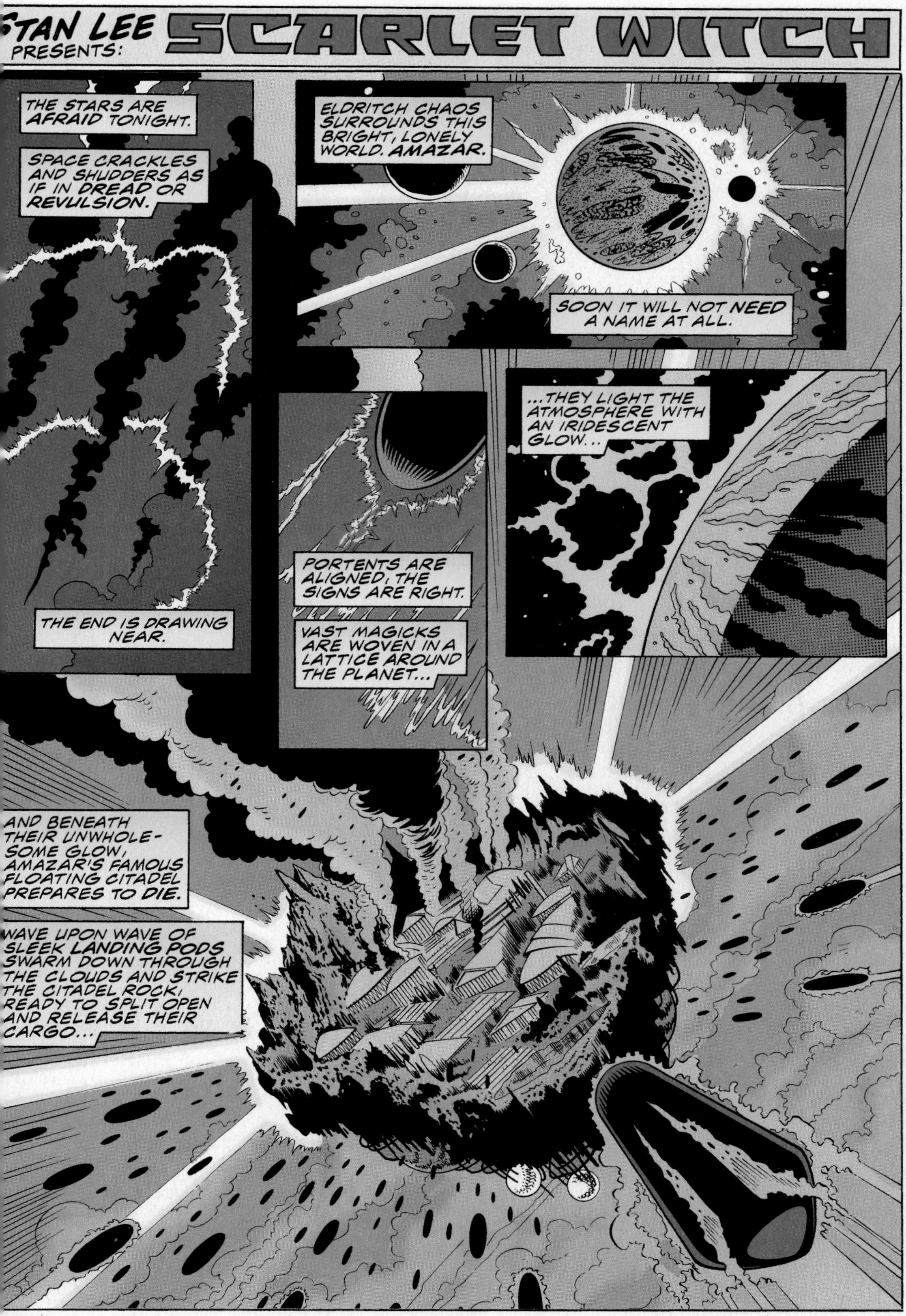
STAN LEE PRESENTS:
SCARLET WITCH
THE STARS ARE AFRAID TONIGHT.
SPACE CRACKLES AND SHUDDERS AS IF IN DREAD OR REVULSION.
THE END IS DRAWING NEAR.
ELDRITCH CHAOS SURROUNDS THIS BRIGHT, LONELY WORLD. AMAZAR.
SOON IT WILL NOT NEED A NAME AT ALL.
PORTENTS ARE ALIGNED, THE SIGNS ARE RIGHT.
VAST MAGICKS ARE WOVEN IN A LATTICE AROUND THE PLANET...
...THEY LIGHT THE ATMOSPHERE WITH AN IRIDESCENT GLOW...
AND BENEATH THEIR UNWHOLE-SOME GLOW, AMAZAR'S FAMOUS FLOATING CITADEL PREPARES TO DIE.
WAVE UPON WAVE OF SLEEK LANDING PODS SWARM DOWN THROUGH THE CLOUDS AND STRIKE THE CITADEL ROCK, READY TO SPLIT OPEN AND RELEASE THEIR CARGO...

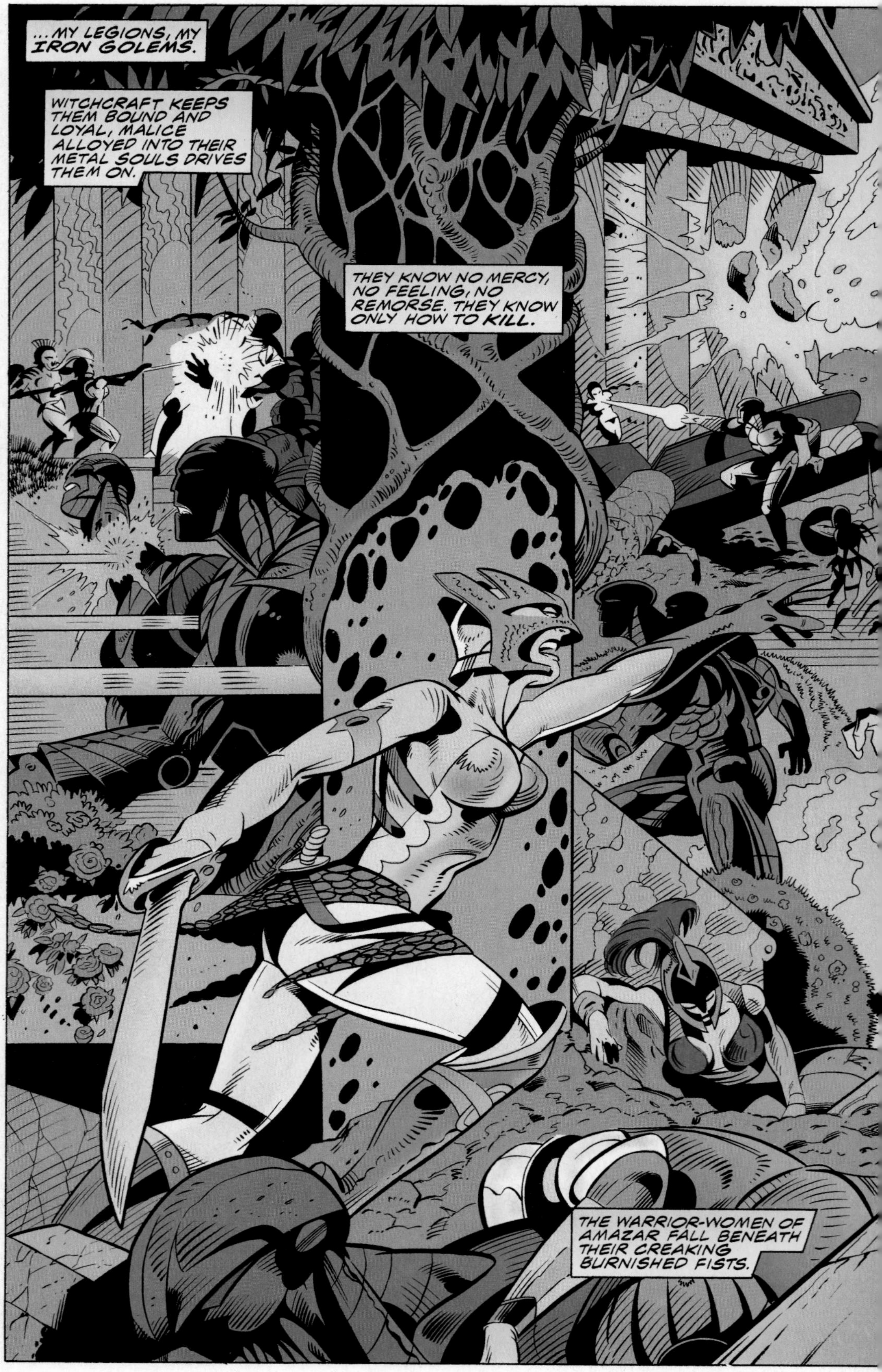
...MY LEGIONS, MY IRON GOLEMS.
WITCHCRAFT KEEPS THEM BOUND AND LOYAL, MALICE ALLOYED INTO THEIR METAL SOULS DRIVES THEM ON.
THEY KNOW NO MERCY, NO FEELING, NO REMORSE. THEY KNOW ONLY HOW TO KILL.
THE WARRIOR-WOMEN OF AMAZAR FALL BENEATH THEIR CREAKING BURNISHED FISTS.

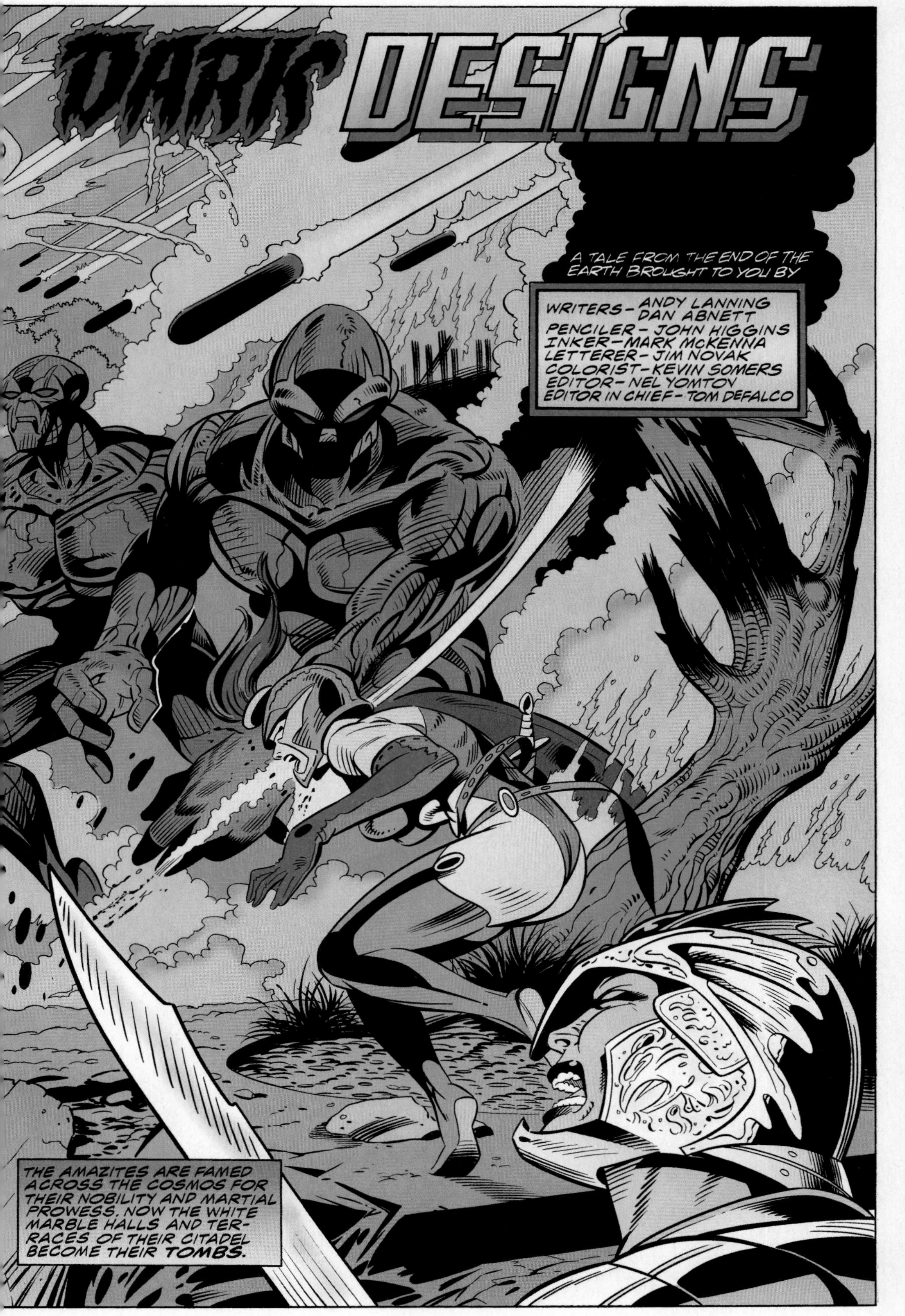
DARK DESIGNS
A TALE FROM THE END OF THE EARTH BROUGHT TO YOU BY
WRITERS- ANDY LANNING
DAN ABNETT
PENCILER- JOHN HIGGINS
INKER-MARK McKENNA
LETTERER-JIM NOVAK
COLORIST-KEVIN SOMERS
EDITOR- NEL YOMTOV
EDITOR IN CHIEF-TOM DEFALCO
THE AMAZITES ARE FAMED ACROSS THE COSMOS FOR THEIR NOBILITY AND MARTIAL PROWESS. NOW THE WHITE MARBLE HALLS AND TERRACES OF THEIR CITADEL BECOME THEIR **TOMBS**.

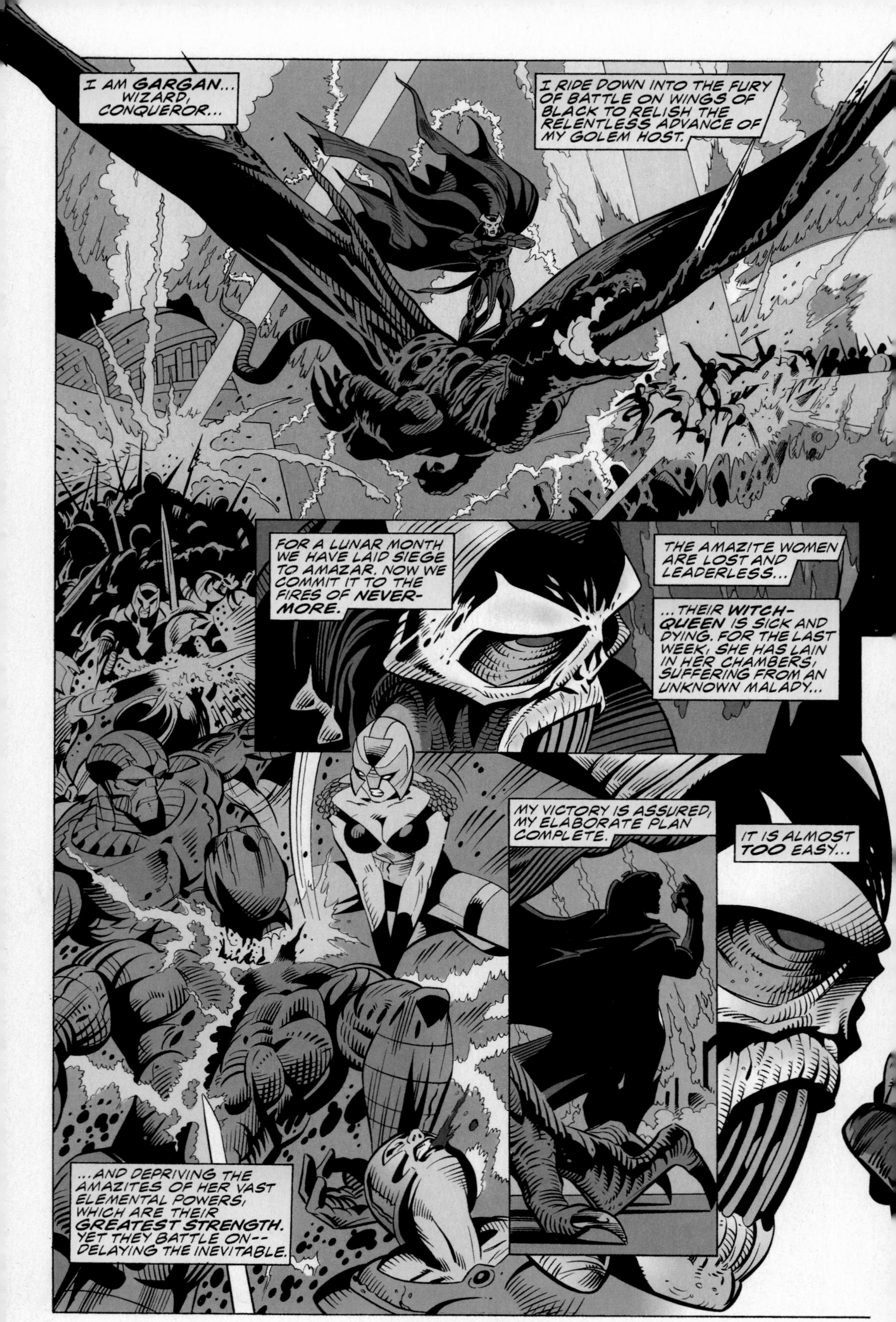

I AM GARGAN... WIZARD, CONQUEROR...
I RIDE DOWN INTO THE FURY OF BATTLE ON WINGS OF BLACK TO RELISH THE RELENTLESS ADVANCE OF MY GOLEM HOST.
FOR A LUNAR MONTH WE HAVE LAID SIEGE TO AMAZAR. NOW WE COMMIT IT TO THE FIRES OF NEVER-MORE.
THE AMAZITE WOMEN ARE LOST AND LEADERLESS...
...THEIR WITCH-QUEEN IS SICK AND DYING. FOR THE LAST WEEK, SHE HAS LAIN IN HER CHAMBERS, SUFFERING FROM AN UNKNOWN MALADY...
...AND DEPRIVING THE AMAZITES OF HER VAST ELEMENTAL POWERS, WHICH ARE THEIR GREATEST STRENGTH. YET THEY BATTLE ON--DELAYING THE INEVITABLE.
MY VICTORY IS ASSURED, MY ELABORATE PLAN COMPLETE.
IT IS ALMOST TOO EASY...

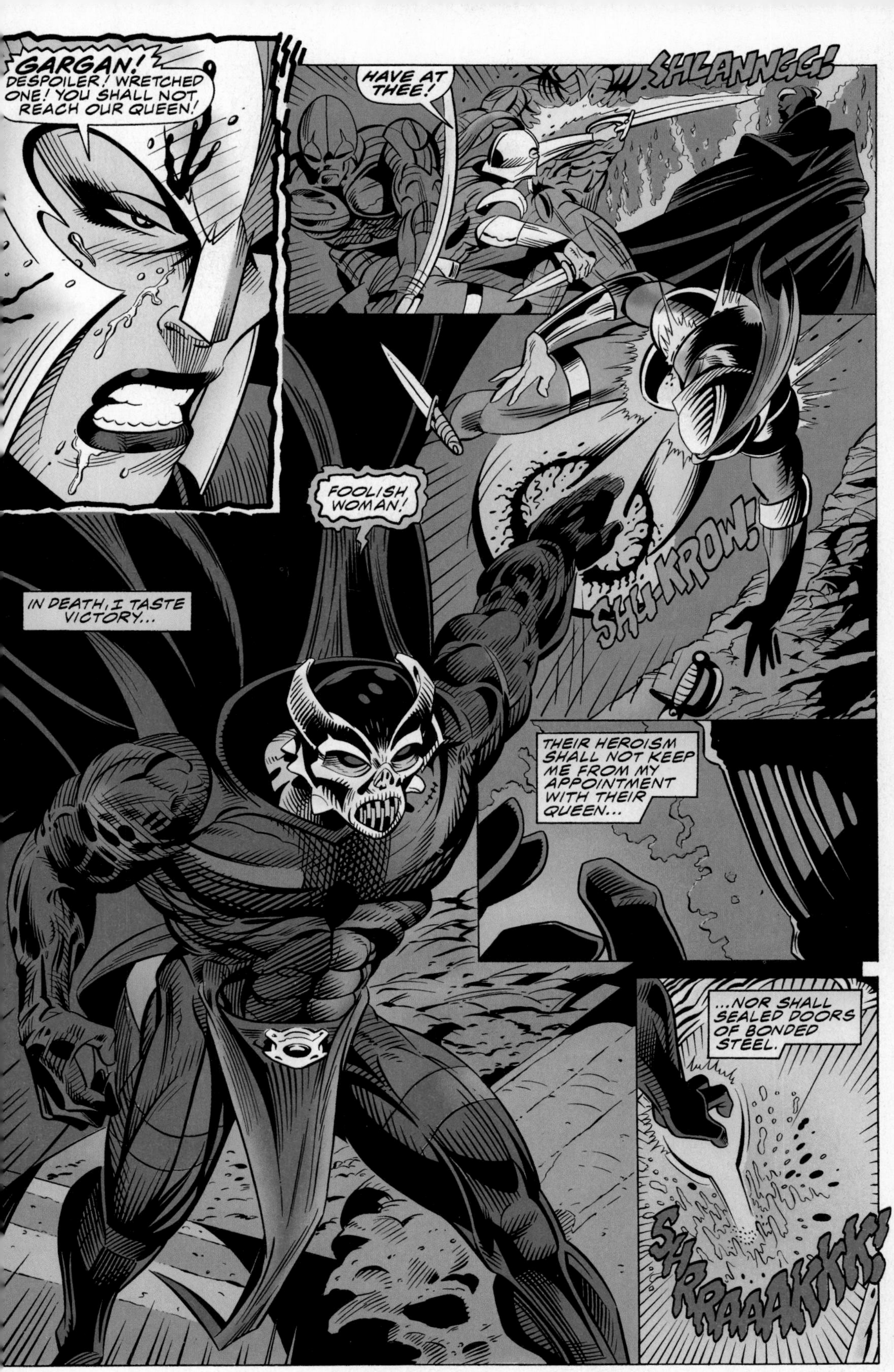
GARGAN! DESPOILER! WRETCHED ONE! YOU SHALL NOT REACH OUR QUEEN!
HAVE AT THEE!
SHLANNGG!
FOOLISH WOMAN!
SHU-KROW!
IN DEATH, I TASTE VICTORY...
THEIR HEROISM SHALL NOT KEEP ME FROM MY APPOINTMENT WITH THEIR QUEEN...
...NOR SHALL SEALED DOORS OF BONDED STEEL.
SHRRAAAKKK!

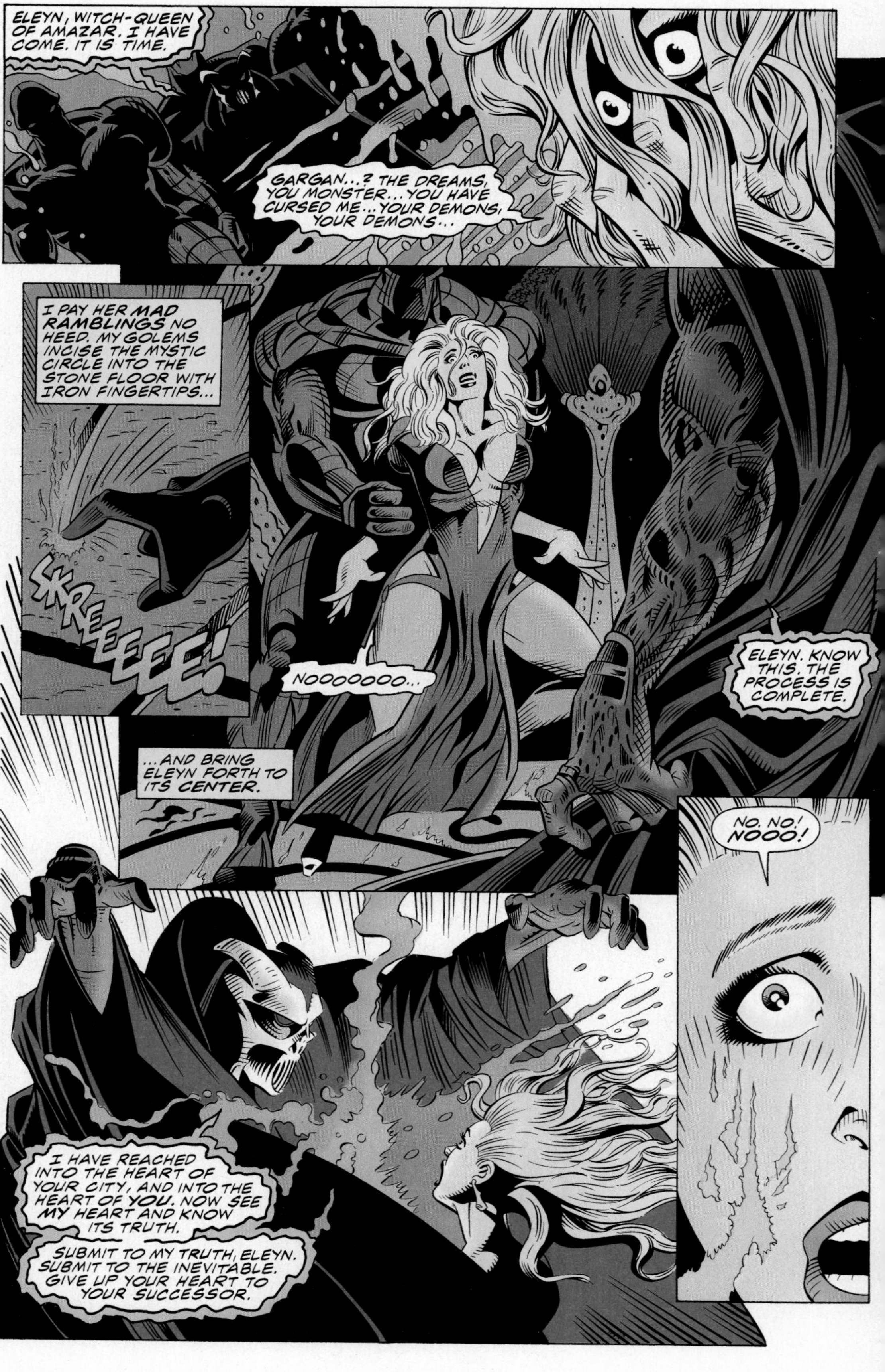
ELEYN, WITCH-QUEEN OF AMAZAR. I HAVE COME. IT IS TIME.
GARGAN...? THE DREAMS, YOU MONSTER... YOU HAVE CURSED ME... YOUR DEMONS, YOUR DEMONS...
I PAY HER MAD RAMBLINGS NO HEED. MY GOLEMS INCISE THE MYSTIC CIRCLE INTO THE STONE FLOOR WITH IRON FINGERTIPS...
SKREEEEEE!
NOOOOOOO...
ELEYN. KNOW THIS. THE PROCESS IS COMPLETE.
...AND BRING ELEYN FORTH TO ITS CENTER.
NO, NO! NOOO!
I HAVE REACHED INTO THE HEART OF YOUR CITY, AND INTO THE HEART OF YOU. NOW SEE MY HEART AND KNOW ITS TRUTH.
SUBMIT TO MY TRUTH, ELEYN. SUBMIT TO THE INEVITABLE. GIVE UP YOUR HEART TO YOUR SUCCESSOR.

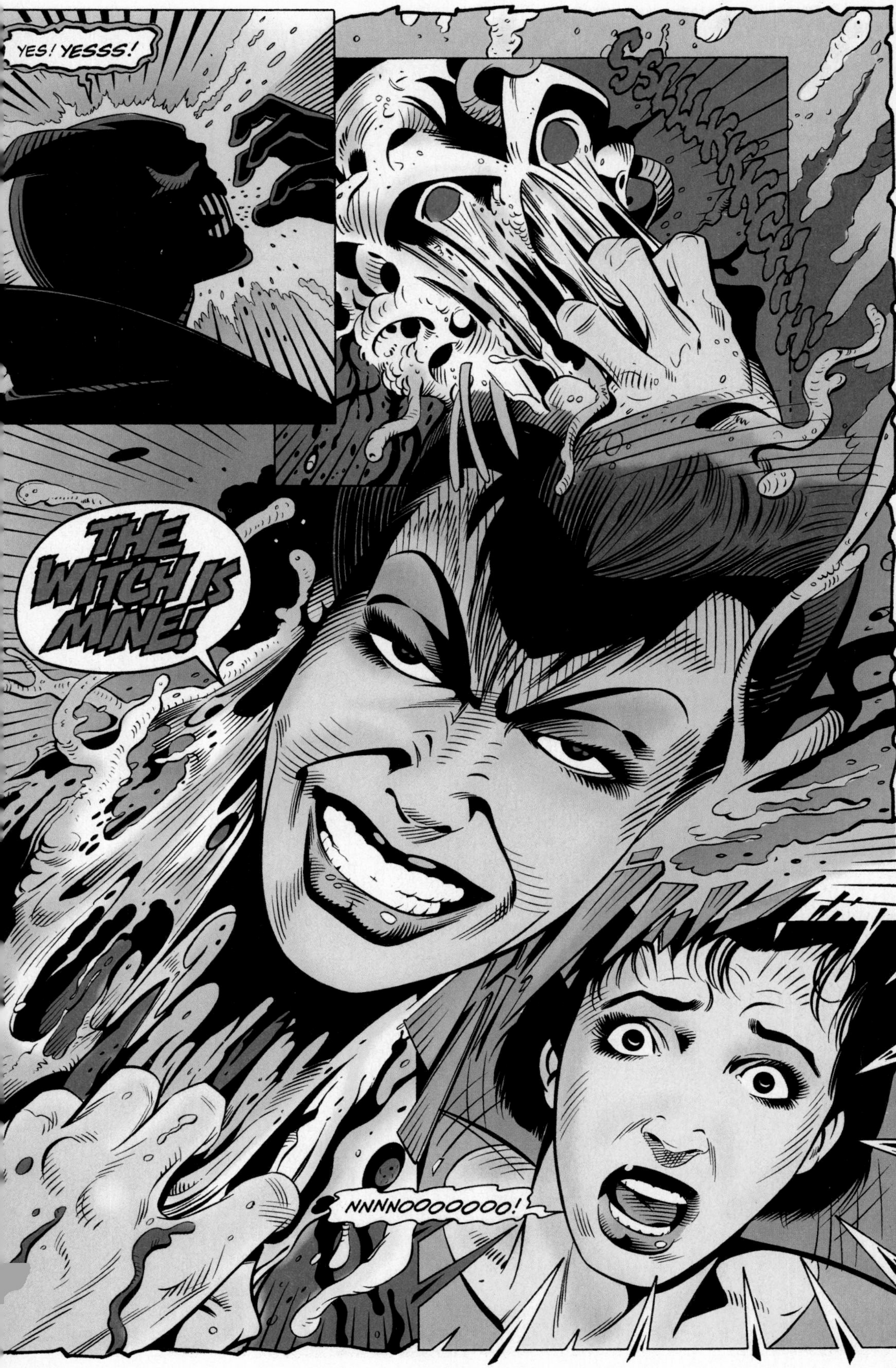
YES! YESSS!
SSLLKKCHHH!
THE WITCH IS MINE!
NNNNOOOOOOOO!

...OH PLEASE... NO...

AVENGERS WEST COMPOUND, 2:15 AM...

AGAIN... THE NIGHTMARES ...WORSE THAN *ANYTHING* I'VE EVER...

I'M ALMOST TOO AFRAID TO MOVE. I FEEL LIKE A CHILD AGAIN, DESPERATE TO CALL OUT TO MY MOTHER... BUT... BUT...

GET A GRIP, WANDA. YOU KNOW THERE'S ONLY ONE PERSON WHO CAN HELP.

IF I CAN STEADY MY HAND LONG ENOUGH TO CONJURE THE LINK THROUGH THE BALL, JUST AS SHE TAUGHT ME...

AGATHA? CAN YOU HEAR ME? ARE YOU THERE?

MILES AWAY, AT THE RETREAT OF AGATHA HARKNESS...

OF COURSE, MY GIRL. I'M *ALWAYS* HERE.

FROM THE LATENESS OF THE HOUR, I WOULD SUPPOSE IS *THE DREAMS* AGAIN...

WORSE THAN EVER, AGATHA...

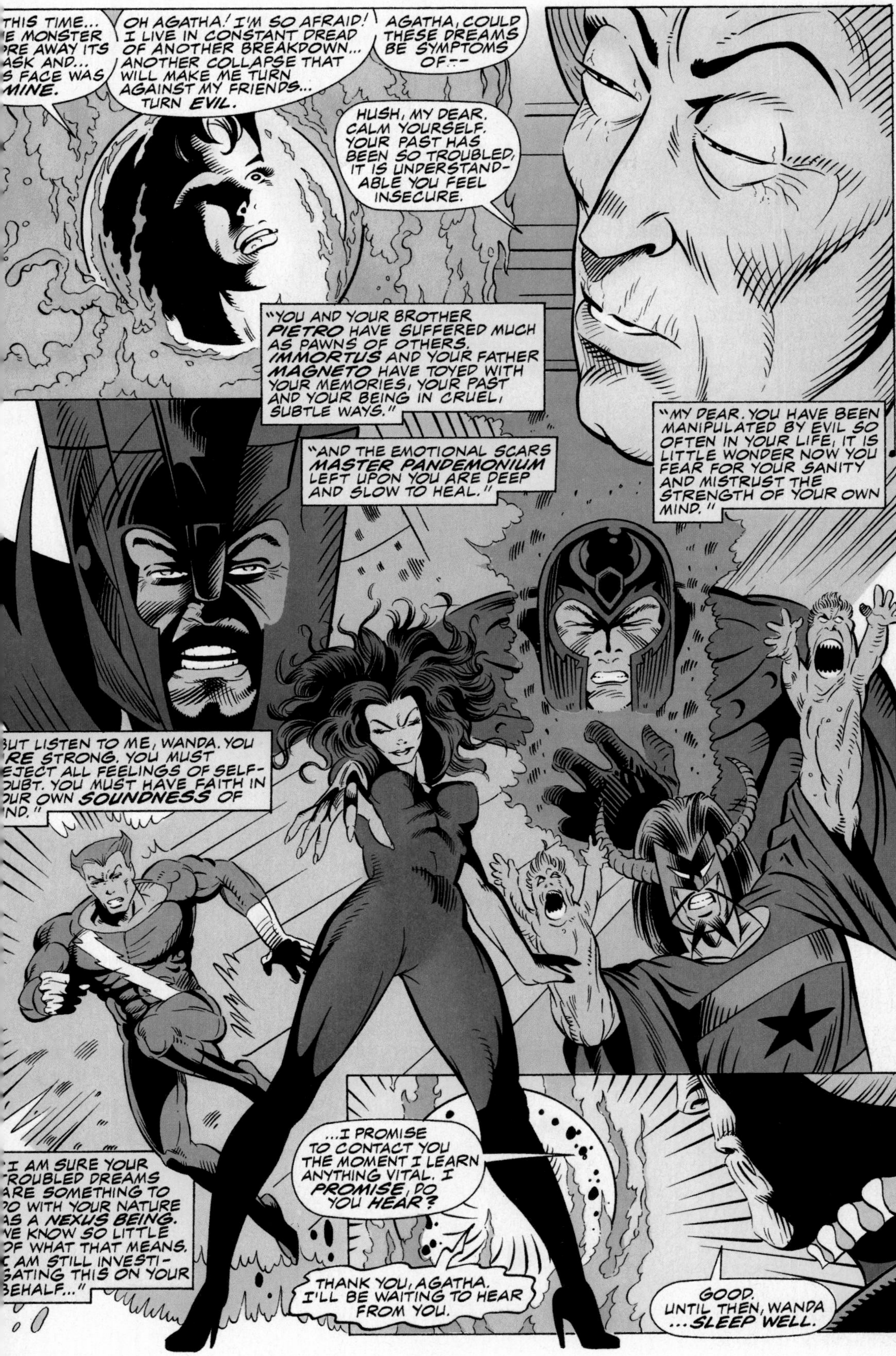
THIS TIME... E MONSTER ORE AWAY ITS ASK AND... S FACE WAS MINE.
OH AGATHA! I'M SO AFRAID! I LIVE IN CONSTANT DREAD OF ANOTHER BREAKDOWN... ANOTHER COLLAPSE THAT WILL MAKE ME TURN AGAINST MY FRIENDS... TURN EVIL.
AGATHA, COULD THESE DREAMS BE SYMPTOMS OF--
HUSH, MY DEAR. CALM YOURSELF. YOUR PAST HAS BEEN SO TROUBLED, IT IS UNDERSTANDABLE YOU FEEL INSECURE.
"YOU AND YOUR BROTHER PIETRO HAVE SUFFERED MUCH AS PAWNS OF OTHERS. IMMORTUS AND YOUR FATHER MAGNETO HAVE TOYED WITH YOUR MEMORIES, YOUR PAST AND YOUR BEING IN CRUEL, SUBTLE WAYS."
"AND THE EMOTIONAL SCARS MASTER PANDEMONIUM LEFT UPON YOU ARE DEEP AND SLOW TO HEAL."
"MY DEAR. YOU HAVE BEEN MANIPULATED BY EVIL SO OFTEN IN YOUR LIFE, IT IS LITTLE WONDER NOW YOU FEAR FOR YOUR SANITY AND MISTRUST THE STRENGTH OF YOUR OWN MIND."
BUT LISTEN TO ME, WANDA. YOU RE STRONG. YOU MUST EJECT ALL FEELINGS OF SELF-OUBT. YOU MUST HAVE FAITH IN OUR OWN SOUNDNESS OF IND."
I AM SURE YOUR TROUBLED DREAMS ARE SOMETHING TO DO WITH YOUR NATURE AS A NEXUS BEING. WE KNOW SO LITTLE OF WHAT THAT MEANS. I AM STILL INVESTIGATING THIS ON YOUR BEHALF..."
...I PROMISE TO CONTACT YOU THE MOMENT I LEARN ANYTHING VITAL. I PROMISE, DO YOU HEAR?
THANK YOU, AGATHA. I'LL BE WAITING TO HEAR FROM YOU.
GOOD. UNTIL THEN, WANDA ...SLEEP WELL.

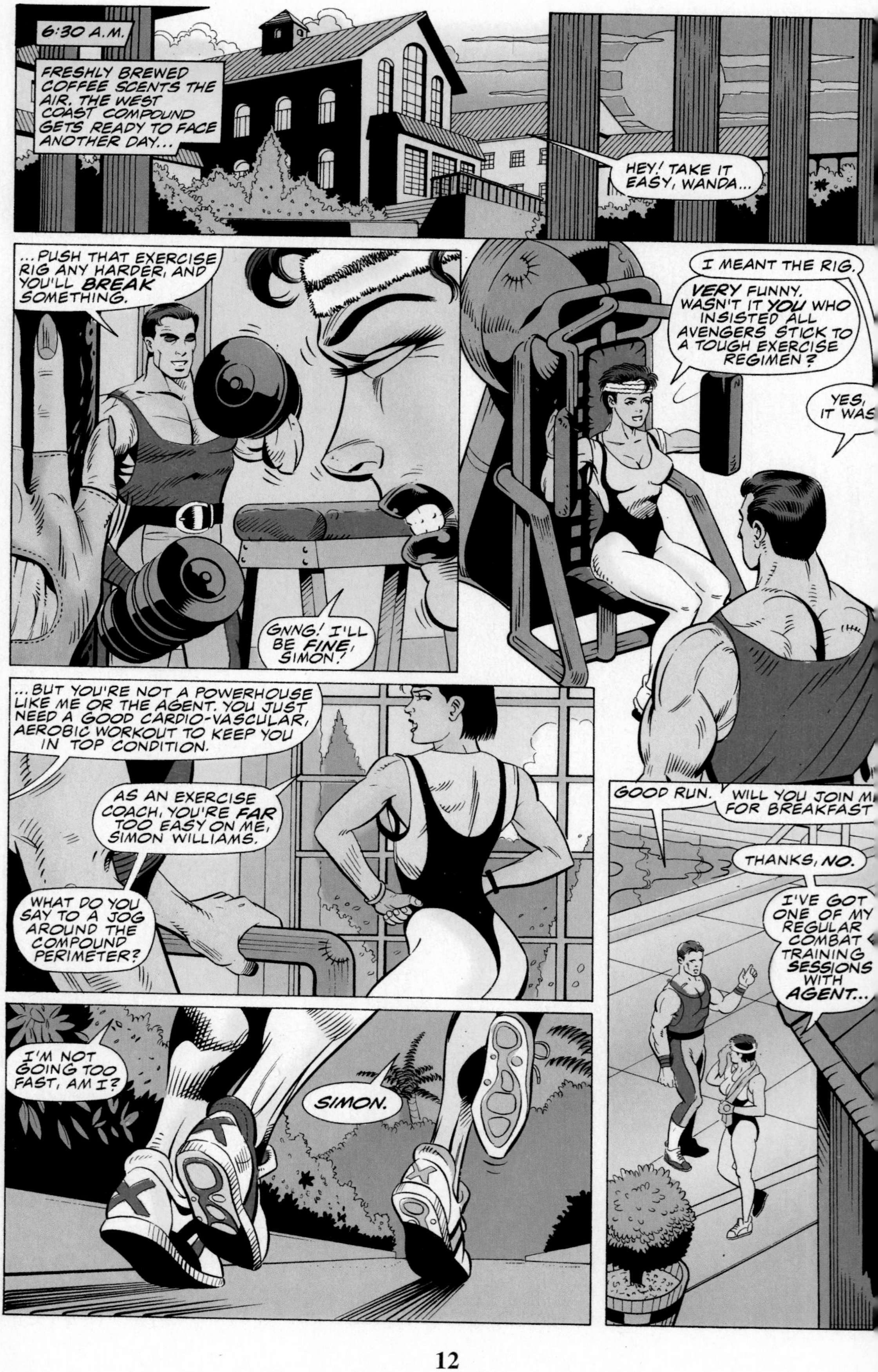

6:30 A.M.
FRESHLY BREWED COFFEE SCENTS THE AIR. THE WEST COAST COMPOUND GETS READY TO FACE ANOTHER DAY...
HEY! TAKE IT EASY, WANDA...
...PUSH THAT EXERCISE RIG ANY HARDER, AND YOU'LL BREAK SOMETHING.
GNNG! I'LL BE FINE, SIMON!
I MEANT THE RIG.
VERY FUNNY. WASN'T IT YOU WHO INSISTED ALL AVENGERS STICK TO A TOUGH EXERCISE REGIMEN?
YES, IT WAS
...BUT YOU'RE NOT A POWERHOUSE LIKE ME OR THE AGENT. YOU JUST NEED A GOOD CARDIO-VASCULAR, AEROBIC WORKOUT TO KEEP YOU IN TOP CONDITION.
AS AN EXERCISE COACH, YOU'RE FAR TOO EASY ON ME, SIMON WILLIAMS.
WHAT DO YOU SAY TO A JOG AROUND THE COMPOUND PERIMETER?
I'M NOT GOING TOO FAST, AM I?
SIMON.
GOOD RUN.
WILL YOU JOIN M FOR BREAKFAST
THANKS, NO.
I'VE GOT ONE OF MY REGULAR COMBAT TRAINING SESSIONS WITH AGENT...

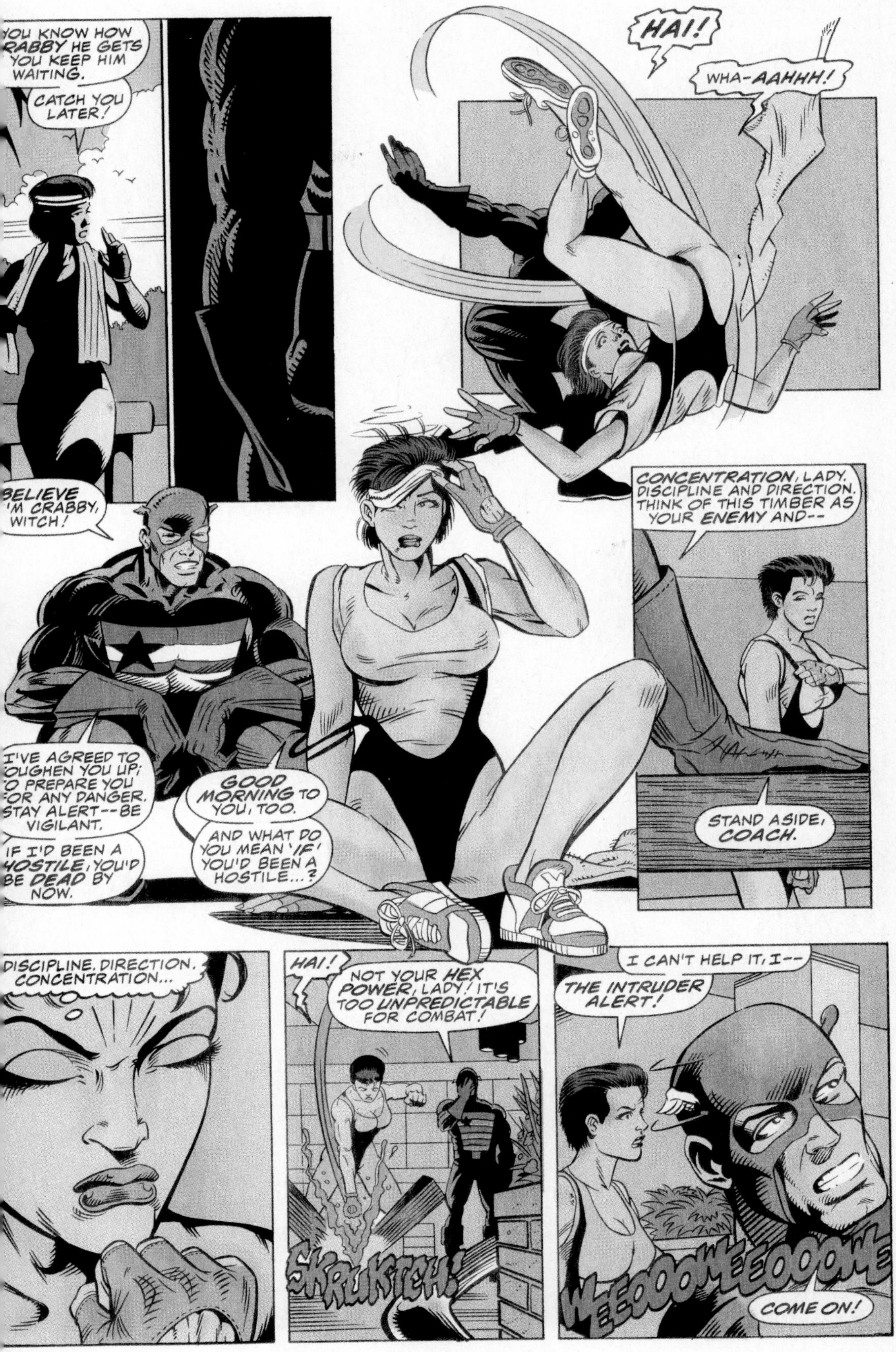

YOU KNOW HOW CRABBY HE GETS YOU KEEP HIM WAITING.
CATCH YOU LATER!
HAI!
WHA-AAHHH!
BELIEVE I'M CRABBY, WITCH!
I'VE AGREED TO TOUGHEN YOU UP, TO PREPARE YOU FOR ANY DANGER. STAY ALERT--BE VIGILANT.
IF I'D BEEN A HOSTILE, YOU'D BE DEAD BY NOW.
GOOD MORNING TO YOU, TOO.
AND WHAT DO YOU MEAN 'IF' YOU'D BEEN A HOSTILE...?
CONCENTRATION, LADY. DISCIPLINE AND DIRECTION. THINK OF THIS TIMBER AS YOUR ENEMY AND--
STAND ASIDE, COACH.
DISCIPLINE, DIRECTION, CONCENTRATION...
HAI!
NOT YOUR HEX POWER, LADY! IT'S TOO UNPREDICTABLE FOR COMBAT!
SKRUKTCH!
I CAN'T HELP IT, I--
THE INTRUDER ALERT!
WEEOOOWEEOOOWE
COME ON!

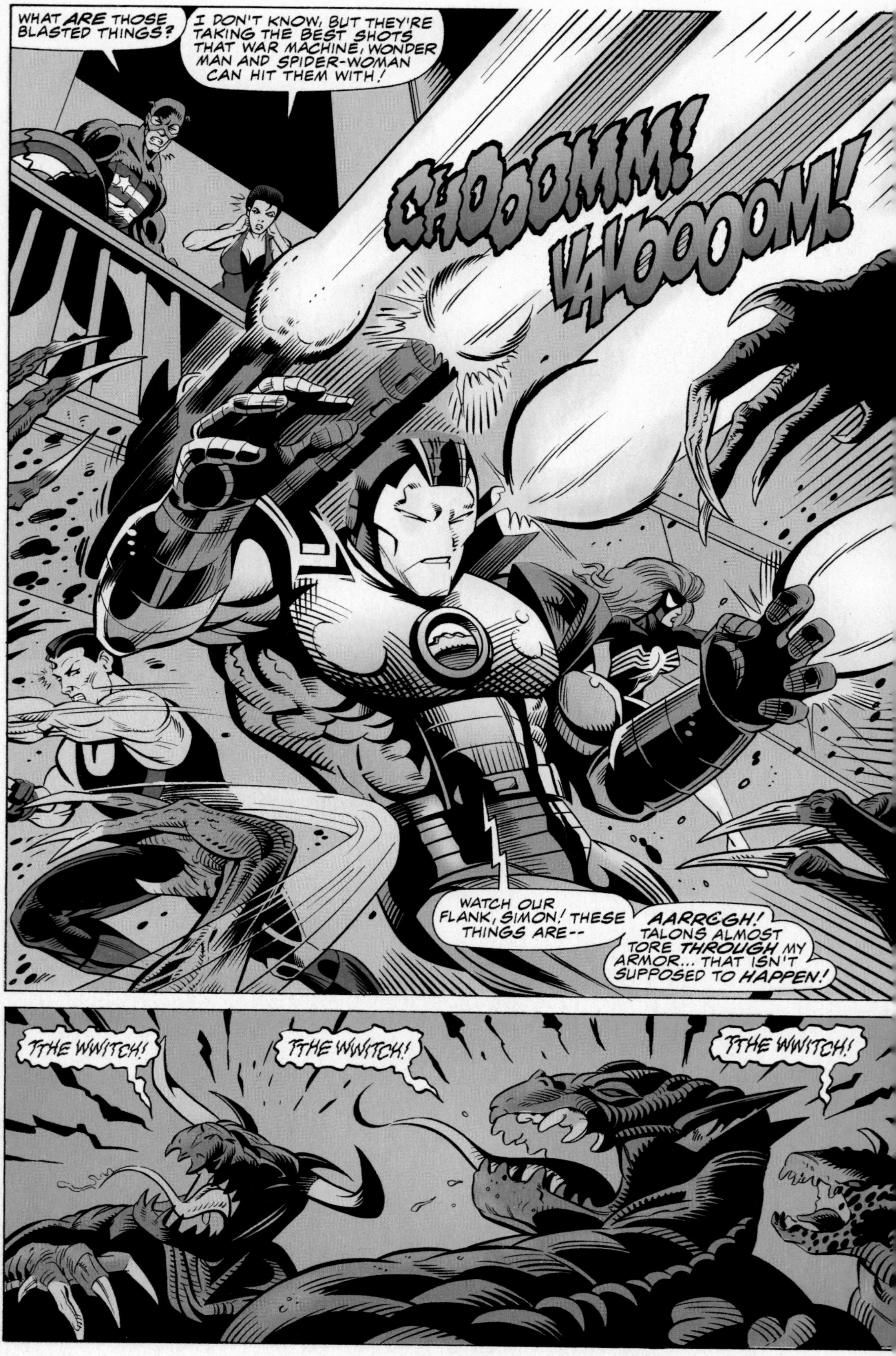
WHAT ARE THOSE BLASTED THINGS?
I DON'T KNOW, BUT THEY'RE TAKING THE BEST SHOTS THAT WAR MACHINE, WONDER MAN AND SPIDER-WOMAN CAN HIT THEM WITH!
CHOOOMM!
VVHOOOOM!
WATCH OUR FLANK, SIMON! THESE THINGS ARE--
AARRGGH! TALONS ALMOST TORE THROUGH MY ARMOR... THAT ISN'T SUPPOSED TO HAPPEN!
TTHE WWITCH!
TTHE WWITCH!
TTHE WWITCH!

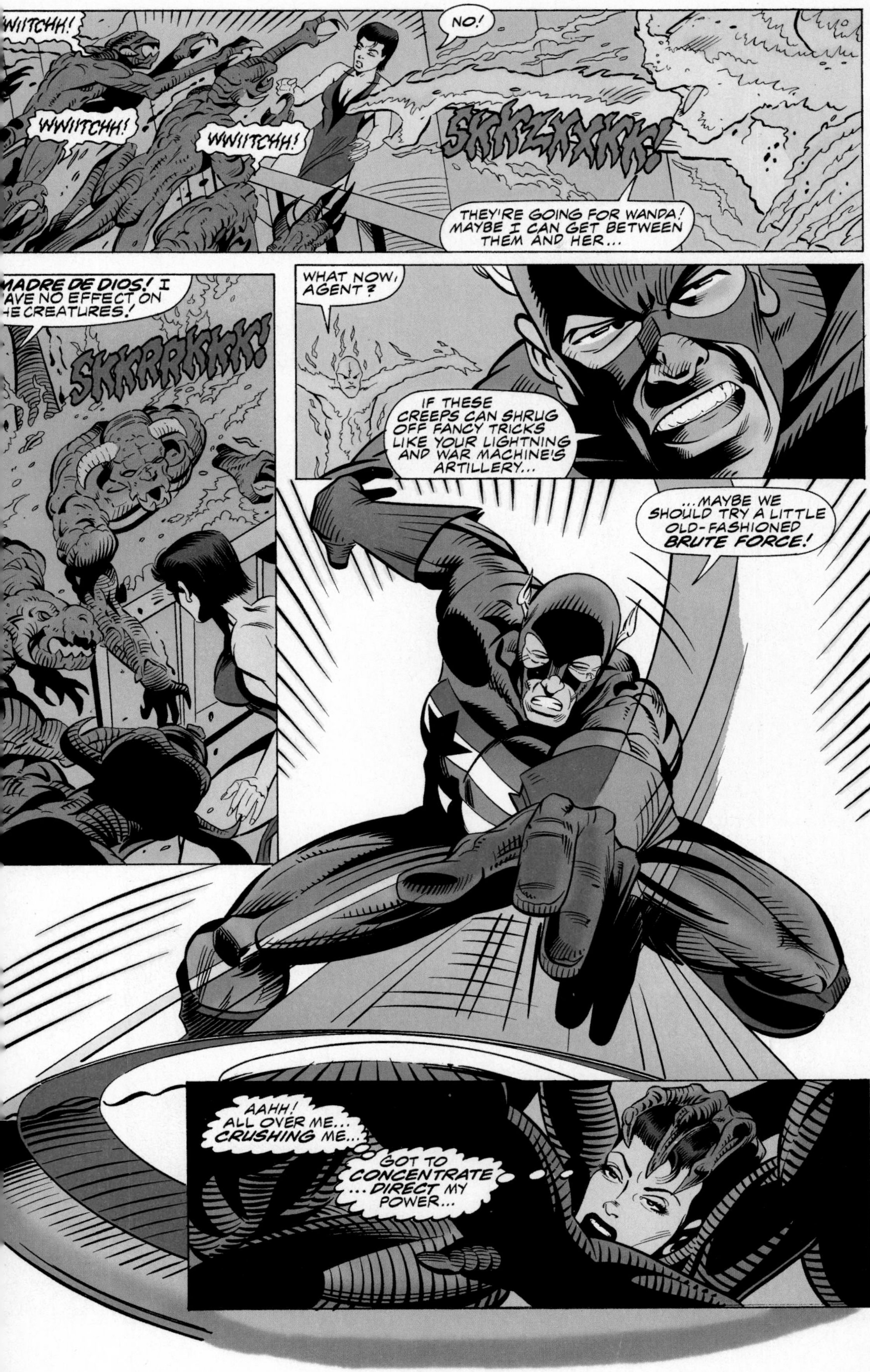
WWIITCHH!
WWIITCHH!
WWIITCHH!
NO!
SKKZZXXKK!
THEY'RE GOING FOR WANDA! MAYBE I CAN GET BETWEEN THEM AND HER...
MADRE DE DIOS! I HAVE NO EFFECT ON THE CREATURES!
SKKRRKKK!
WHAT NOW, AGENT?
IF THESE CREEPS CAN SHRUG OFF FANCY TRICKS LIKE YOUR LIGHTNING AND WAR MACHINE'S ARTILLERY...
...MAYBE WE SHOULD TRY A LITTLE OLD-FASHIONED BRUTE FORCE!
AAHH! ALL OVER ME... CRUSHING ME...
GOT TO CONCENTRATE ...DIRECT MY POWER...

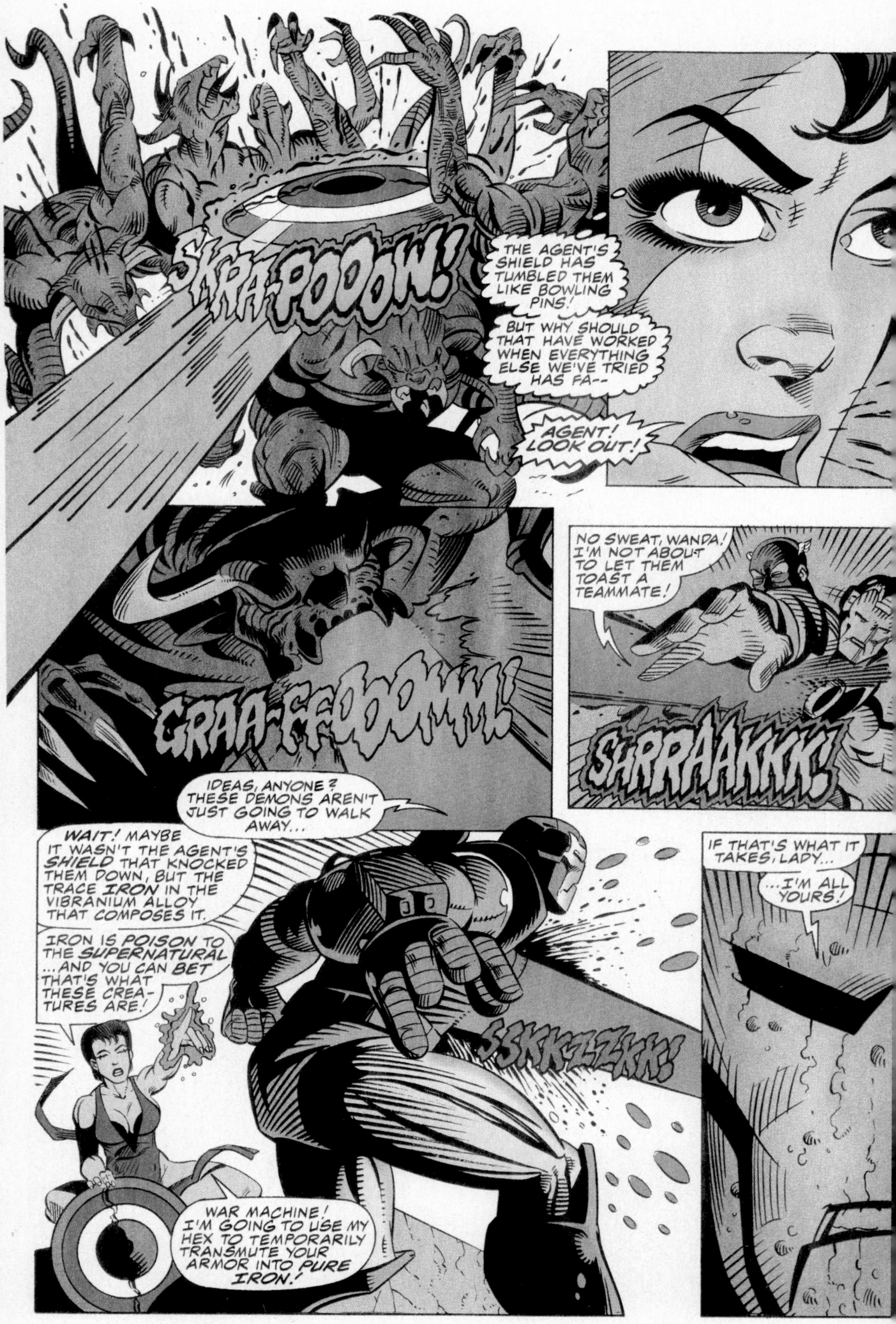
SKRA-POOOW!
THE AGENT'S SHIELD HAS TUMBLED THEM LIKE BOWLING PINS!
BUT WHY SHOULD THAT HAVE WORKED WHEN EVERYTHING ELSE WE'VE TRIED HAS FA--
AGENT! LOOK OUT!
GRAA-FFOOOMM!
NO SWEAT, WANDA! I'M NOT ABOUT TO LET THEM TOAST A TEAMMATE!
SHRRAAKKK!
IDEAS, ANYONE? THESE DEMONS AREN'T JUST GOING TO WALK AWAY...
WAIT! MAYBE IT WASN'T THE AGENT'S SHIELD THAT KNOCKED THEM DOWN, BUT THE TRACE IRON IN THE VIBRANIUM ALLOY THAT COMPOSES IT.
IRON IS POISON TO THE SUPERNATURAL ...AND YOU CAN BET THAT'S WHAT THESE CREATURES ARE!
WAR MACHINE! I'M GOING TO USE MY HEX TO TEMPORARILY TRANSMUTE YOUR ARMOR INTO PURE IRON!
SSKKZZZKK!
IF THAT'S WHAT IT TAKES, LADY...
...I'M ALL YOURS!

GOOD CALL, WANDA!

SIMON! GRAB THE DEMONS ONCE THEY'RE IMMOBILIZED! SPIDER-WOMAN! WE NEED A WAY TO CONFINE THEM!

WUUNKK!

KRAAKK!

ONE PSYCHIC WEB COMING UP!

OW ALL WE HAVE O DO IS FIGURE UT WHY THEY TTACKED US.

THEY WERE CLEARLY AFTER YOU, WANDA. DIDN'T YOU SEE THE WAY THEY WENT INTO OVERDRIVE THE MOMENT YOU APPEARED?

SOMEONE DELIBERATELY SENT THESE FREAKS AFTER THE SCARLET WITCH!

SO NICE TO FEEL WANTED!

NOW THAT WE'VE GOT THEM CAPTIVE WE MIGHT GET SOME ANSWERS-- LOOK!

THEY'RE DISINTEGRATING ...MELTING AWAY INTO THIN AIR!

WWITCHHH...

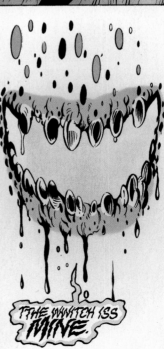

THE WWITCH ISS MINE.

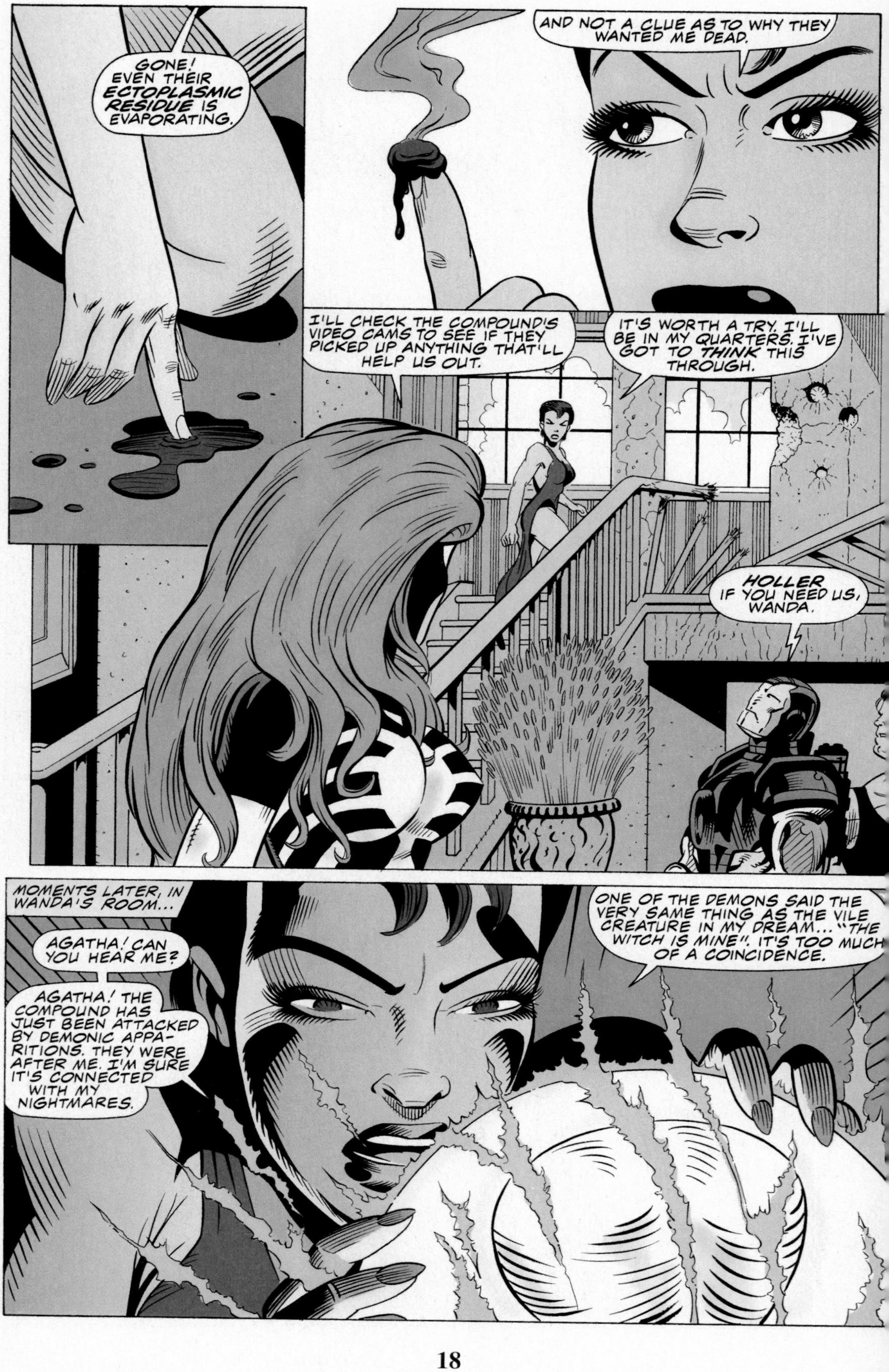
GONE! EVEN THEIR ECTOPLASMIC RESIDUE IS EVAPORATING.
AND NOT A CLUE AS TO WHY THEY WANTED ME DEAD.
I'LL CHECK THE COMPOUND'S VIDEO CAMS TO SEE IF THEY PICKED UP ANYTHING THAT'LL HELP US OUT.
IT'S WORTH A TRY. I'LL BE IN MY QUARTERS. I'VE GOT TO THINK THIS THROUGH.
HOLLER IF YOU NEED US, WANDA.
MOMENTS LATER, IN WANDA'S ROOM...
AGATHA! CAN YOU HEAR ME?
AGATHA! THE COMPOUND HAS JUST BEEN ATTACKED BY DEMONIC APPARITIONS. THEY WERE AFTER ME. I'M SURE IT'S CONNECTED WITH MY NIGHTMARES.
ONE OF THE DEMONS SAID THE VERY SAME THING AS THE VILE CREATURE IN MY DREAM... "THE WITCH IS MINE". IT'S TOO MUCH OF A COINCIDENCE.

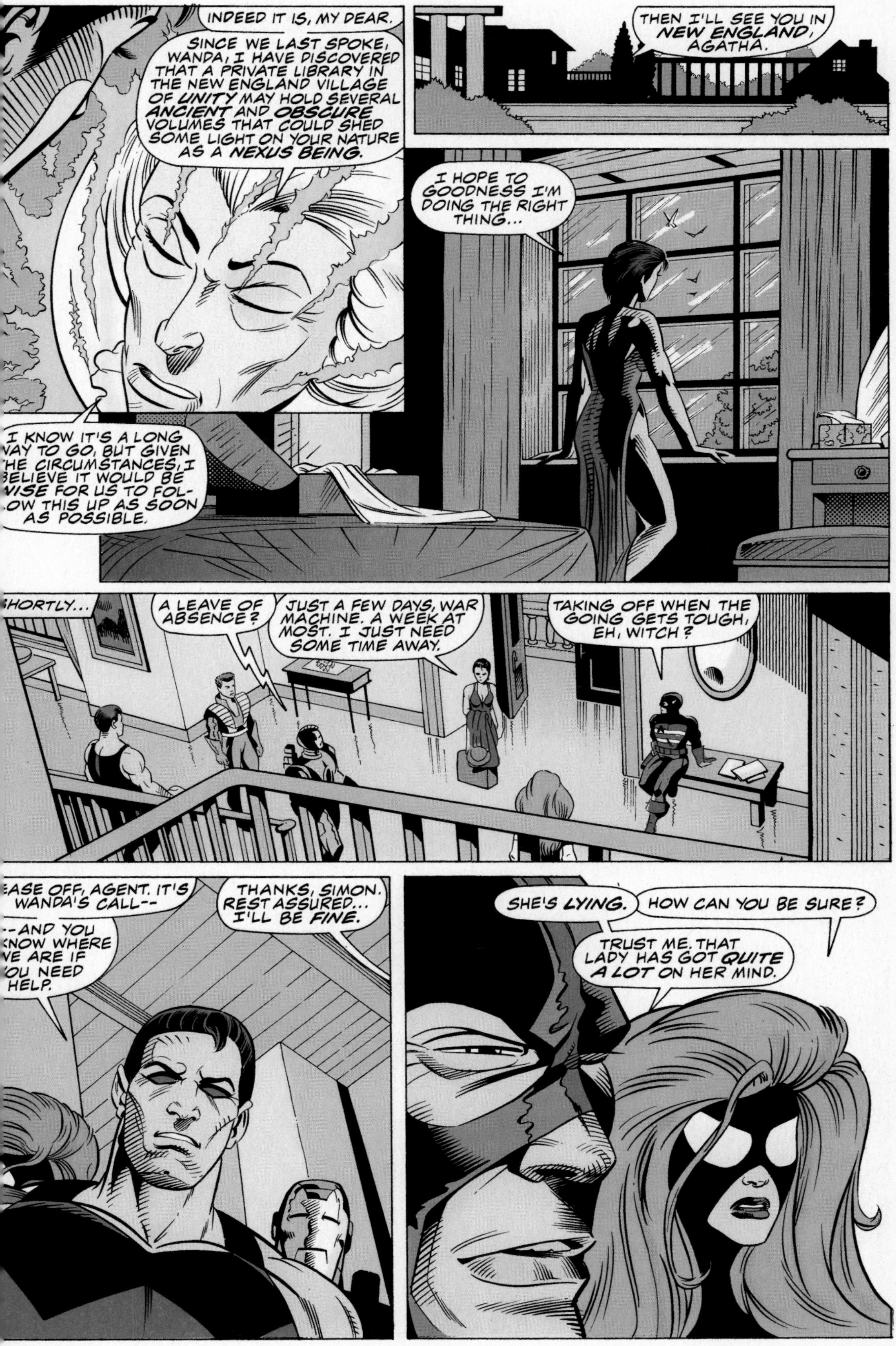
INDEED IT IS, MY DEAR.
SINCE WE LAST SPOKE, WANDA, I HAVE DISCOVERED THAT A PRIVATE LIBRARY IN THE NEW ENGLAND VILLAGE OF UNITY MAY HOLD SEVERAL ANCIENT AND OBSCURE VOLUMES THAT COULD SHED SOME LIGHT ON YOUR NATURE AS A NEXUS BEING.
I KNOW IT'S A LONG WAY TO GO, BUT GIVEN THE CIRCUMSTANCES, I BELIEVE IT WOULD BE WISE FOR US TO FOLLOW THIS UP AS SOON AS POSSIBLE.
THEN I'LL SEE YOU IN NEW ENGLAND, AGATHA.
I HOPE TO GOODNESS I'M DOING THE RIGHT THING...
SHORTLY...
A LEAVE OF ABSENCE?
JUST A FEW DAYS, WAR MACHINE. A WEEK AT MOST. I JUST NEED SOME TIME AWAY.
TAKING OFF WHEN THE GOING GETS TOUGH, EH, WITCH?
EASE OFF, AGENT. IT'S WANDA'S CALL--
--AND YOU KNOW WHERE WE ARE IF YOU NEED HELP.
THANKS, SIMON. REST ASSURED... I'LL BE FINE.
SHE'S LYING.
HOW CAN YOU BE SURE?
TRUST ME. THAT LADY HAS GOT QUITE A LOT ON HER MIND.

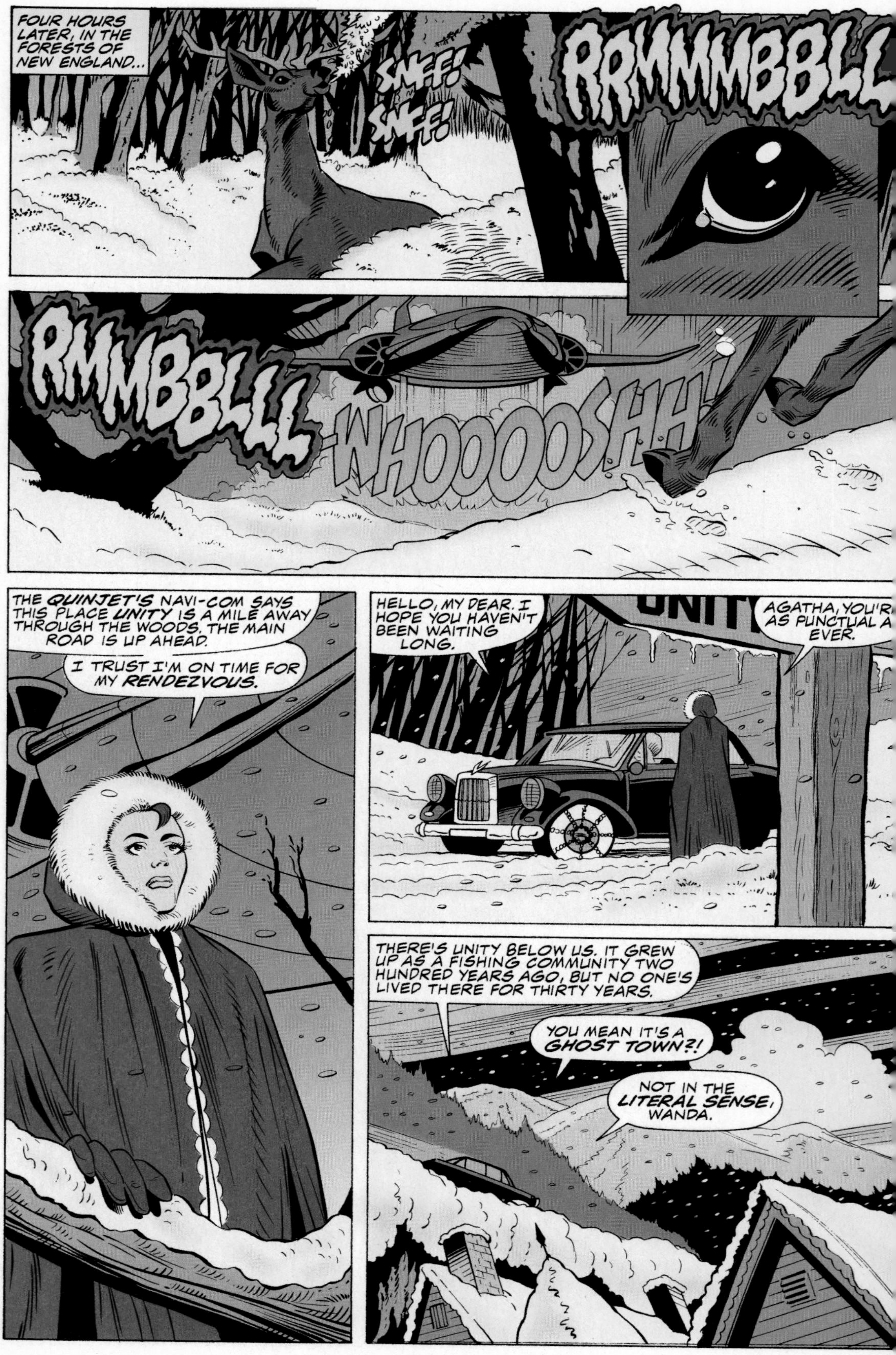
FOUR HOURS LATER, IN THE FORESTS OF NEW ENGLAND...
SNFF! SNFF!
RRMMMBBLL
RMMBBLLL
WHOOOOOSHH!
THE QUINJET'S NAVI-COM SAYS THIS PLACE UNITY IS A MILE AWAY THROUGH THE WOODS. THE MAIN ROAD IS UP AHEAD.
I TRUST I'M ON TIME FOR MY RENDEZVOUS.
HELLO, MY DEAR. I HOPE YOU HAVEN'T BEEN WAITING LONG.
AGATHA, YOU'R AS PUNCTUAL A EVER.
THERE'S UNITY BELOW US. IT GREW UP AS A FISHING COMMUNITY TWO HUNDRED YEARS AGO, BUT NO ONE'S LIVED THERE FOR THIRTY YEARS.
YOU MEAN IT'S A GHOST TOWN?!
NOT IN THE LITERAL SENSE, WANDA.

THE AREA WAS OVER-FISHED. THEIR LIVELIHOODS GONE, THE TOWNSFOLK SOLD UP AND MOVED AWAY.

SOONER OR LATER, SOMEONE WILL REDEVELOP THE AREA.

UNTIL THEN, IT BOASTS ONE OF THE FINEST CHURCHES IN THE EAST...

THE LIBRARY WE'VE COME TO SEE IS IN THE CHURCH CRYPT.

WELCOME TO UNITY, WANDA.

THIS PLACE IS SO EERIE. MY SKIN'S CRAWLING... LIKE THERE'S SOMETHING WATCHING US.

DON'T BE ABSURD.

I FEAR, YOUNG LADY, THAT PERHAPS YOU'VE BEEN WATCHING FAR TOO MANY HORROR MOVIES FOR YOUR OWN GOOD.

21

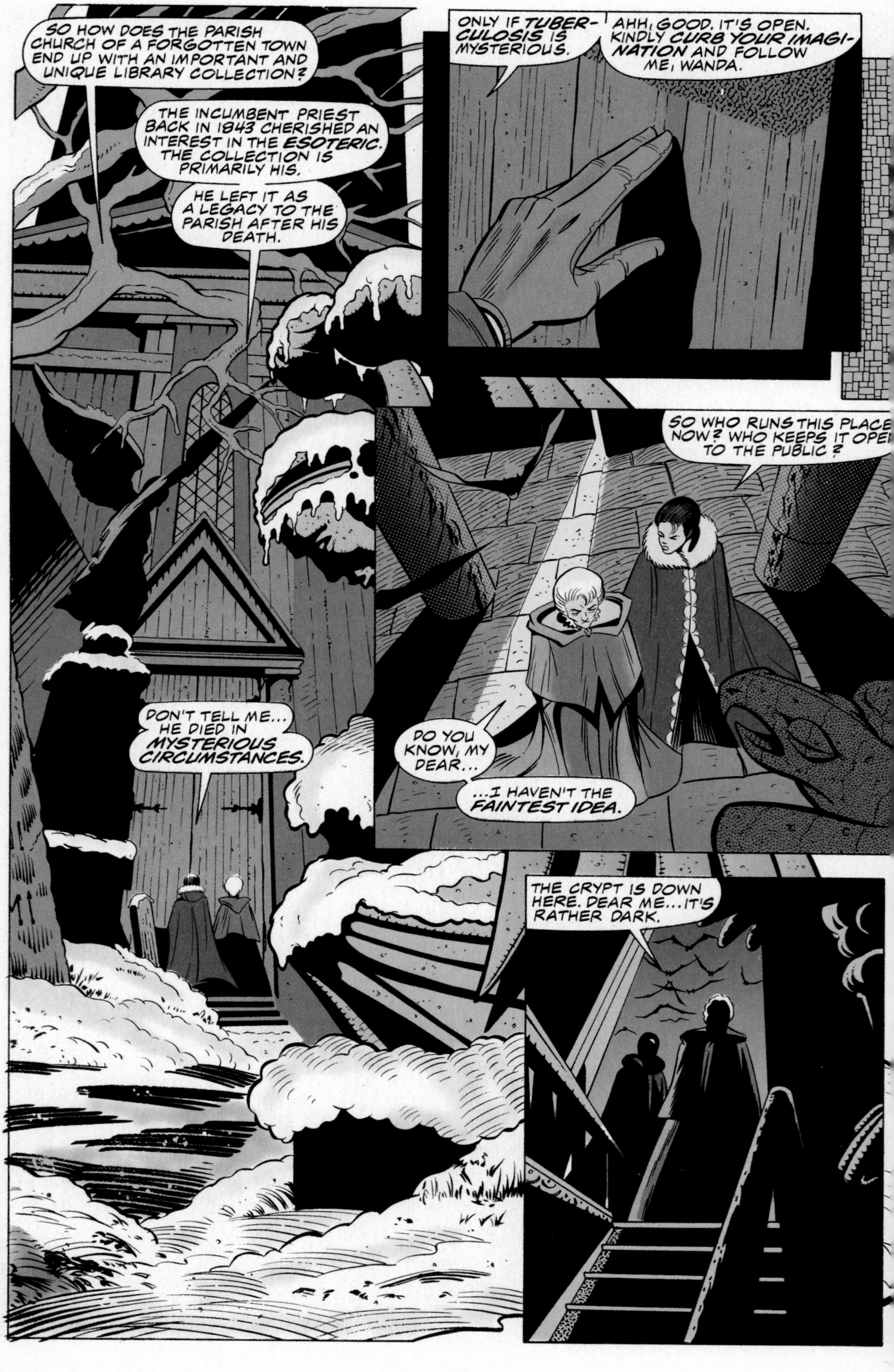
SO HOW DOES THE PARISH CHURCH OF A FORGOTTEN TOWN END UP WITH AN IMPORTANT AND UNIQUE LIBRARY COLLECTION?
THE INCUMBENT PRIEST BACK IN 1843 CHERISHED AN INTEREST IN THE ESOTERIC. THE COLLECTION IS PRIMARILY HIS.
HE LEFT IT AS A LEGACY TO THE PARISH AFTER HIS DEATH.
DON'T TELL ME... HE DIED IN MYSTERIOUS CIRCUMSTANCES.
ONLY IF TUBERCULOSIS IS MYSTERIOUS.
AHH, GOOD. IT'S OPEN. KINDLY CURB YOUR IMAGINATION AND FOLLOW ME, WANDA.
SO WHO RUNS THIS PLACE NOW? WHO KEEPS IT OPEN TO THE PUBLIC?
DO YOU KNOW, MY DEAR...
...I HAVEN'T THE FAINTEST IDEA.
THE CRYPT IS DOWN HERE. DEAR ME... IT'S RATHER DARK.

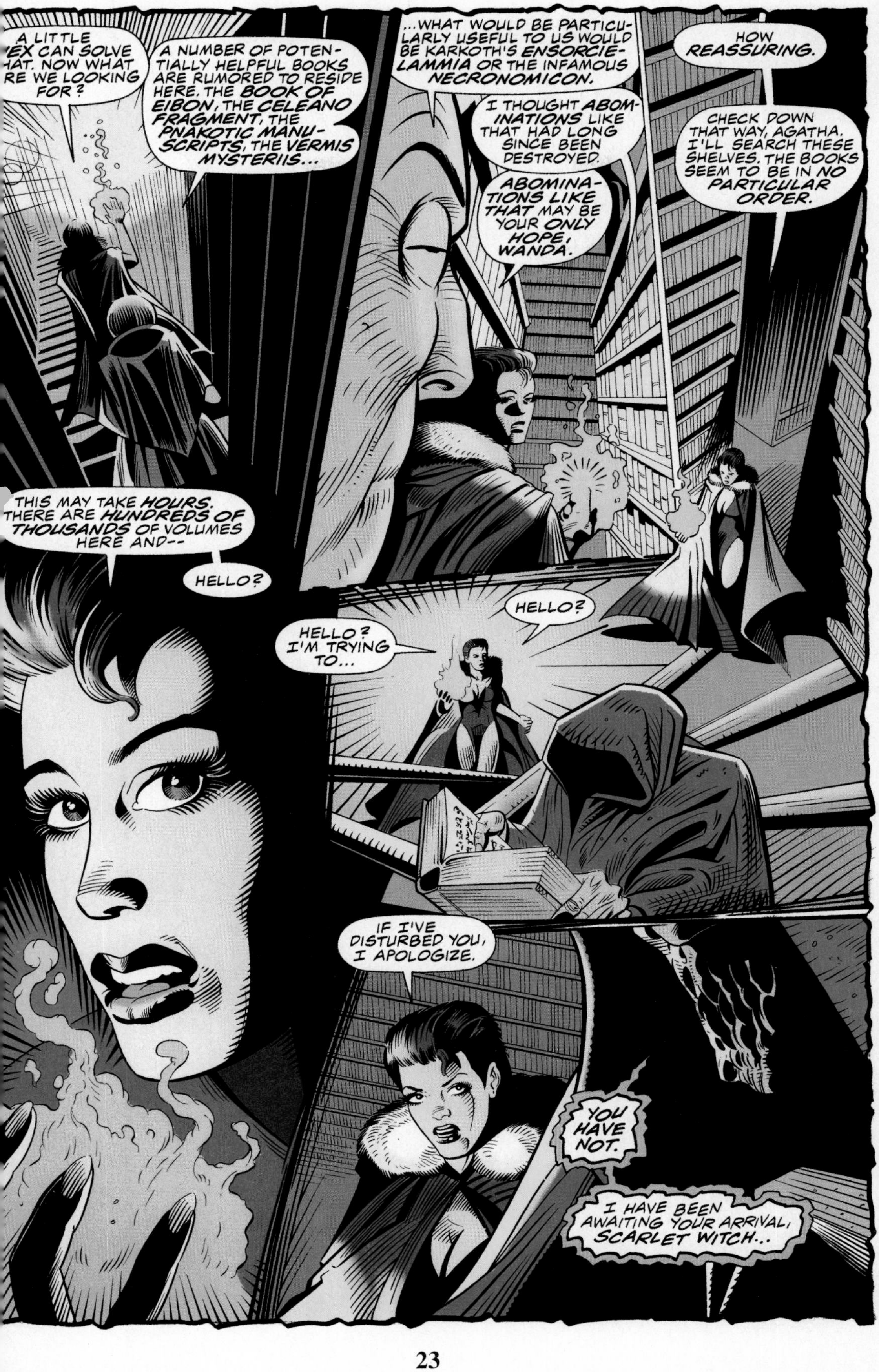
A LITTLE HEX CAN SOLVE THAT. NOW WHAT ARE WE LOOKING FOR?
A NUMBER OF POTENTIALLY HELPFUL BOOKS ARE RUMORED TO RESIDE HERE. THE BOOK OF EIBON, THE CELEANO FRAGMENT, THE PNAKOTIC MANUSCRIPTS, THE VERMIS MYSTERIIS...
...WHAT WOULD BE PARTICULARLY USEFUL TO US WOULD BE KARKOTH'S ENSORCIE-LAMMIA OR THE INFAMOUS NECRONOMICON.
I THOUGHT ABOMINATIONS LIKE THAT HAD LONG SINCE BEEN DESTROYED.
ABOMINATIONS LIKE THAT MAY BE YOUR ONLY HOPE, WANDA.
HOW REASSURING.
CHECK DOWN THAT WAY, AGATHA. I'LL SEARCH THESE SHELVES. THE BOOKS SEEM TO BE IN NO PARTICULAR ORDER.
THIS MAY TAKE HOURS. THERE ARE HUNDREDS OF THOUSANDS OF VOLUMES HERE AND--
HELLO?
HELLO?
HELLO? I'M TRYING TO...
IF I'VE DISTURBED YOU, I APOLOGIZE.
YOU HAVE NOT.
I HAVE BEEN AWAITING YOUR ARRIVAL, SCARLET WITCH...

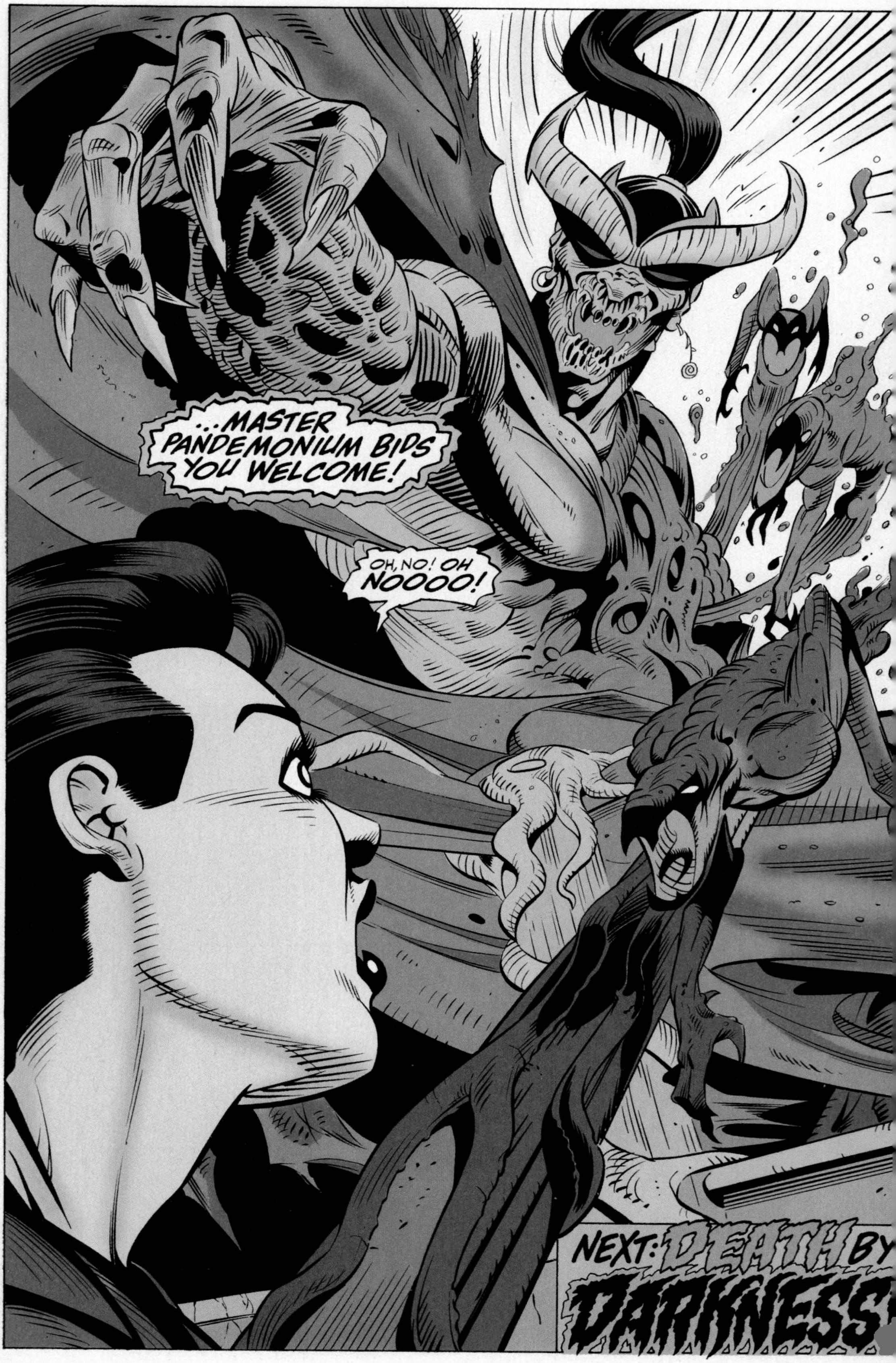
...MASTER PANDEMONIUM BIDS YOU WELCOME!
OH, NO! OH NOOOO!
NEXT: DEATH BY DARKNESS

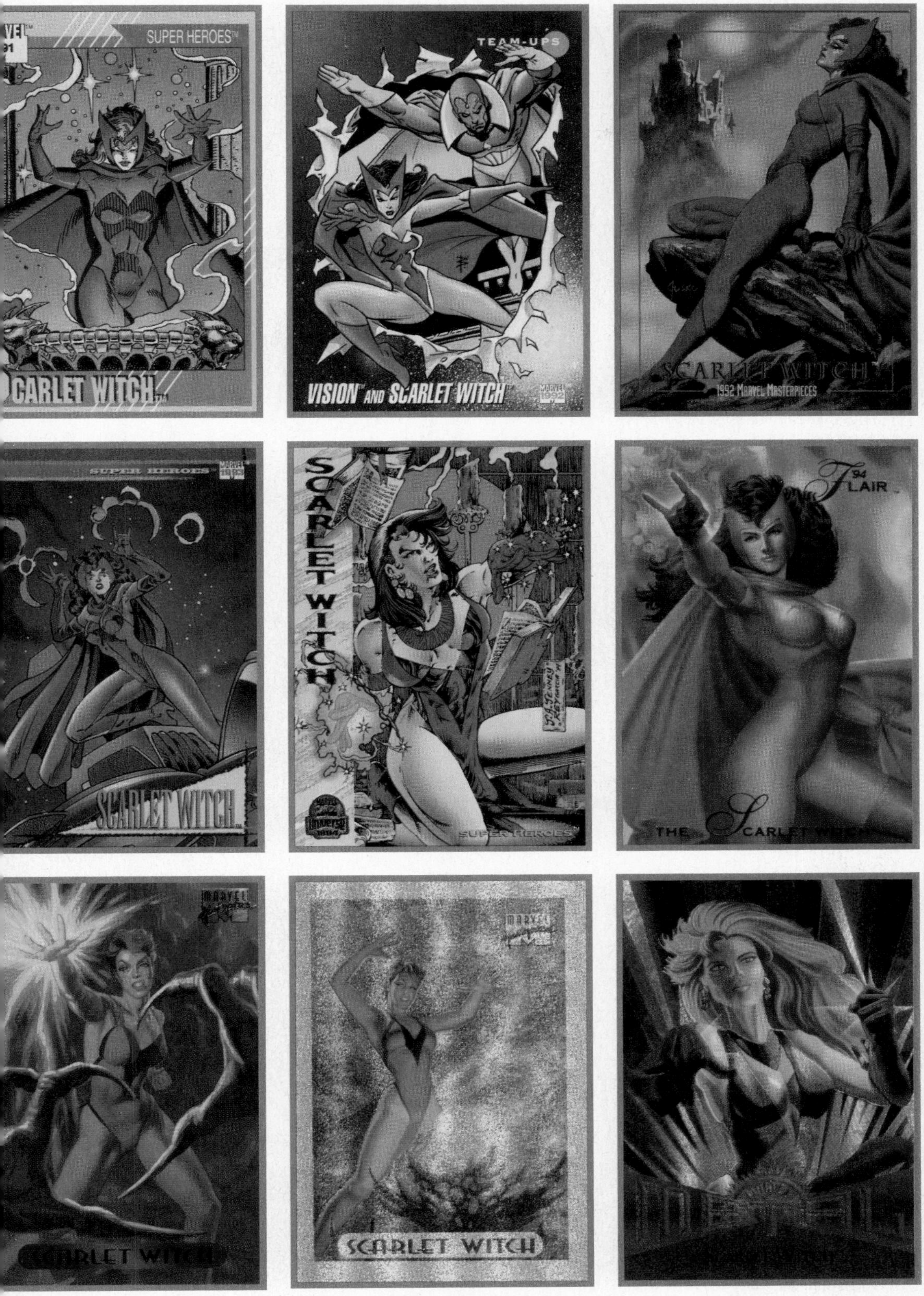
SUPER HEROES™
CARLET WITCH™
TEAM-UPS
VISION™ AND SCARLET WITCH™
MARVEL 1992
SCARLET WITCH
1992 MARVEL MASTERPIECES
SUPER HEROES
MARVEL 1993
SCARLET WITCH™
SCARLET WITCH
SUPER HEROES
'94 FLAIR
THE SCARLET WITCH
SCARLET WITCH

1-1995 TRADING-CARD ART BY PAUL RYAN, BRET BLEVINS & PAUL MOUNTS, JOE JUSKO, JEFF JOHNSON, TOM TENNEY & REY GARCIA, GREG & TIM HILDEBRANDT, AND DARICK ROBERTSON & TRACTOR

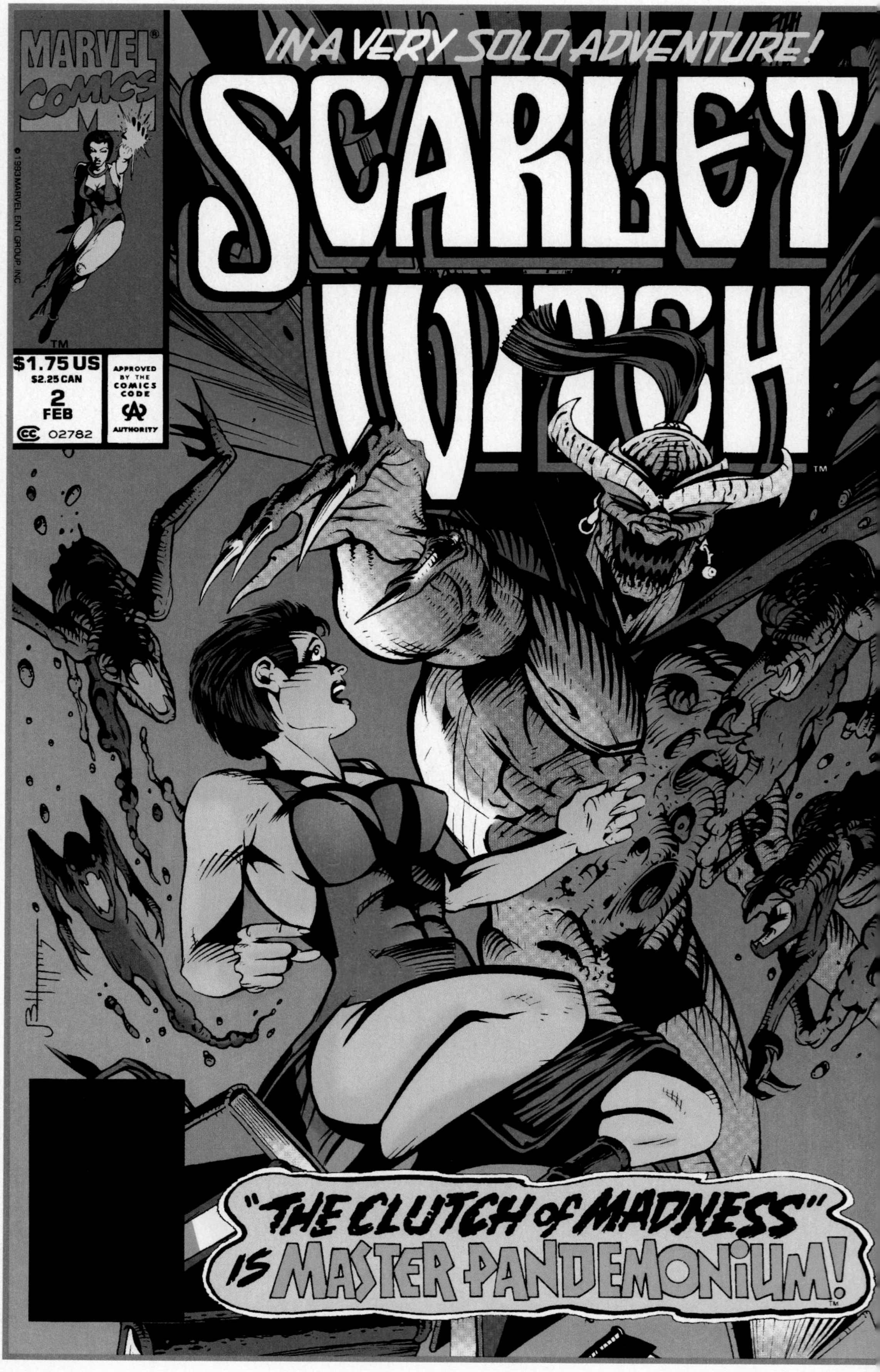
MARVEL COMICS
IN A VERY SOLO ADVENTURE!
SCARLET WITCH
$1.75 US
$2.25 CAN
2
FEB
02782
APPROVED BY THE COMICS CODE AUTHORITY
© 1993 MARVEL ENT. GROUP, INC.
"THE CLUTCH of MADNESS"
IS MASTER PANDEMONIUM!

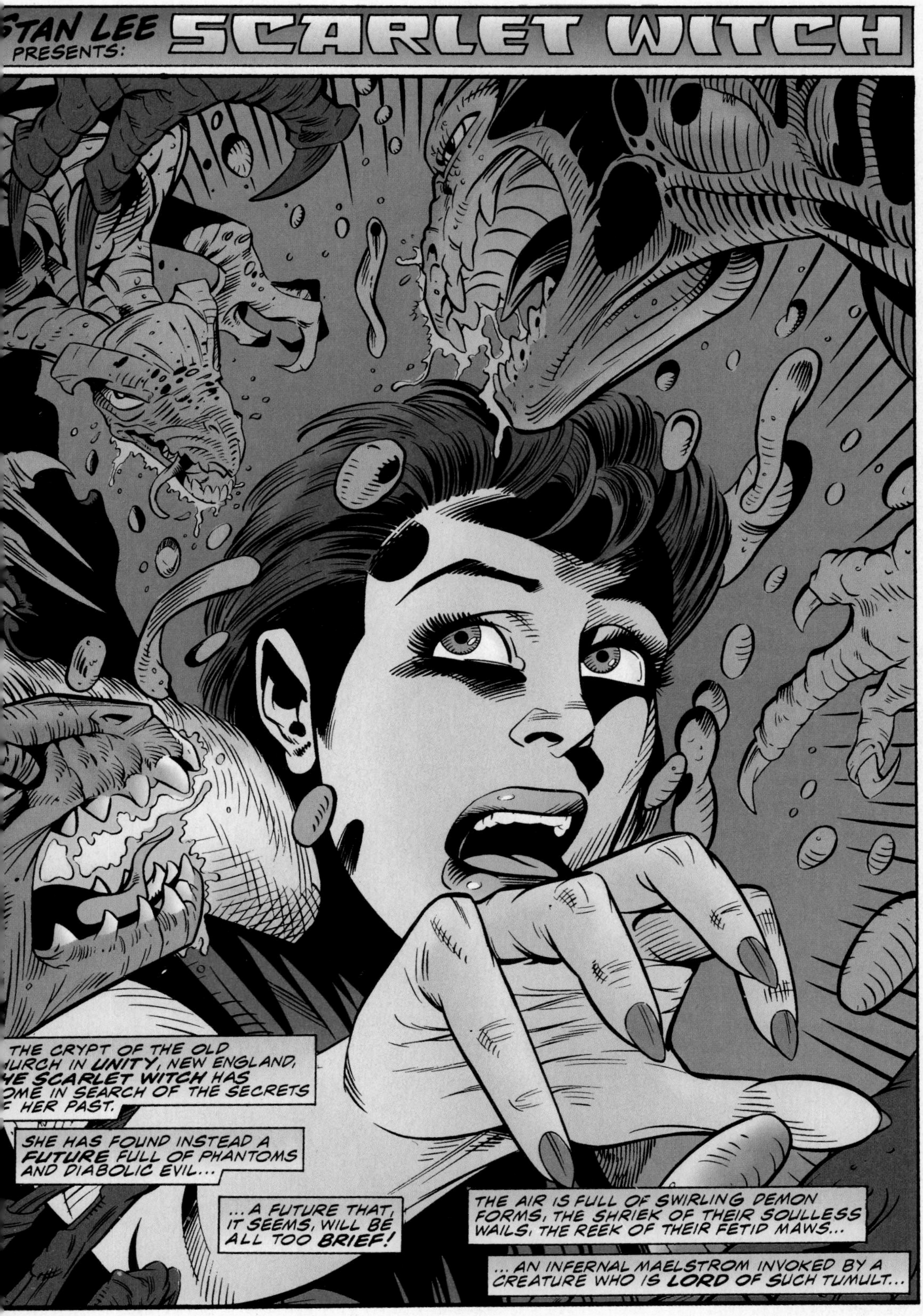
STAN LEE PRESENTS:
SCARLET WITCH
THE CRYPT OF THE OLD HURCH IN UNITY, NEW ENGLAND, HE SCARLET WITCH HAS OME IN SEARCH OF THE SECRETS HER PAST.
SHE HAS FOUND INSTEAD A FUTURE FULL OF PHANTOMS AND DIABOLIC EVIL...
...A FUTURE THAT, IT SEEMS, WILL BE ALL TOO BRIEF!
THE AIR IS FULL OF SWIRLING DEMON FORMS, THE SHRIEK OF THEIR SOULLESS WAILS, THE REEK OF THEIR FETID MAWS...
...AN INFERNAL MAELSTROM INVOKED BY A CREATURE WHO IS LORD OF SUCH TUMULT...

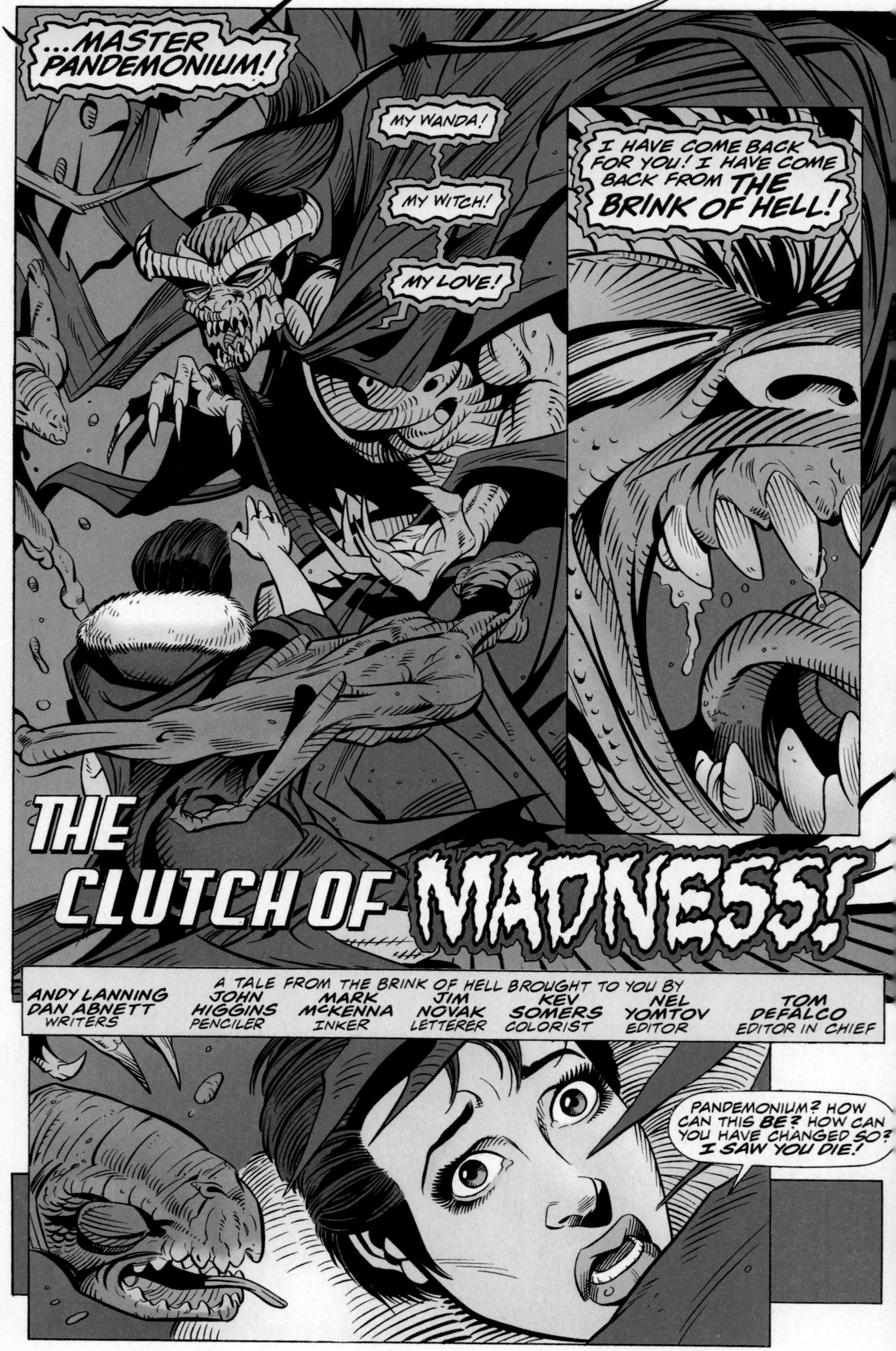
...MASTER PANDEMONIUM!
MY WANDA!
MY WITCH!
MY LOVE!
I HAVE COME BACK FOR YOU! I HAVE COME BACK FROM THE BRINK OF HELL!
THE CLUTCH OF MADNESS!
A TALE FROM THE BRINK OF HELL BROUGHT TO YOU BY
ANDY LANNING DAN ABNETT WRITERS
JOHN HIGGINS PENCILER
MARK McKENNA INKER
JIM NOVAK LETTERER
KEV SOMERS COLORIST
NEL YOMTOV EDITOR
TOM DEFALCO EDITOR IN CHIEF
PANDEMONIUM? HOW CAN THIS BE? HOW CAN YOU HAVE CHANGED SO? I SAW YOU DIE!

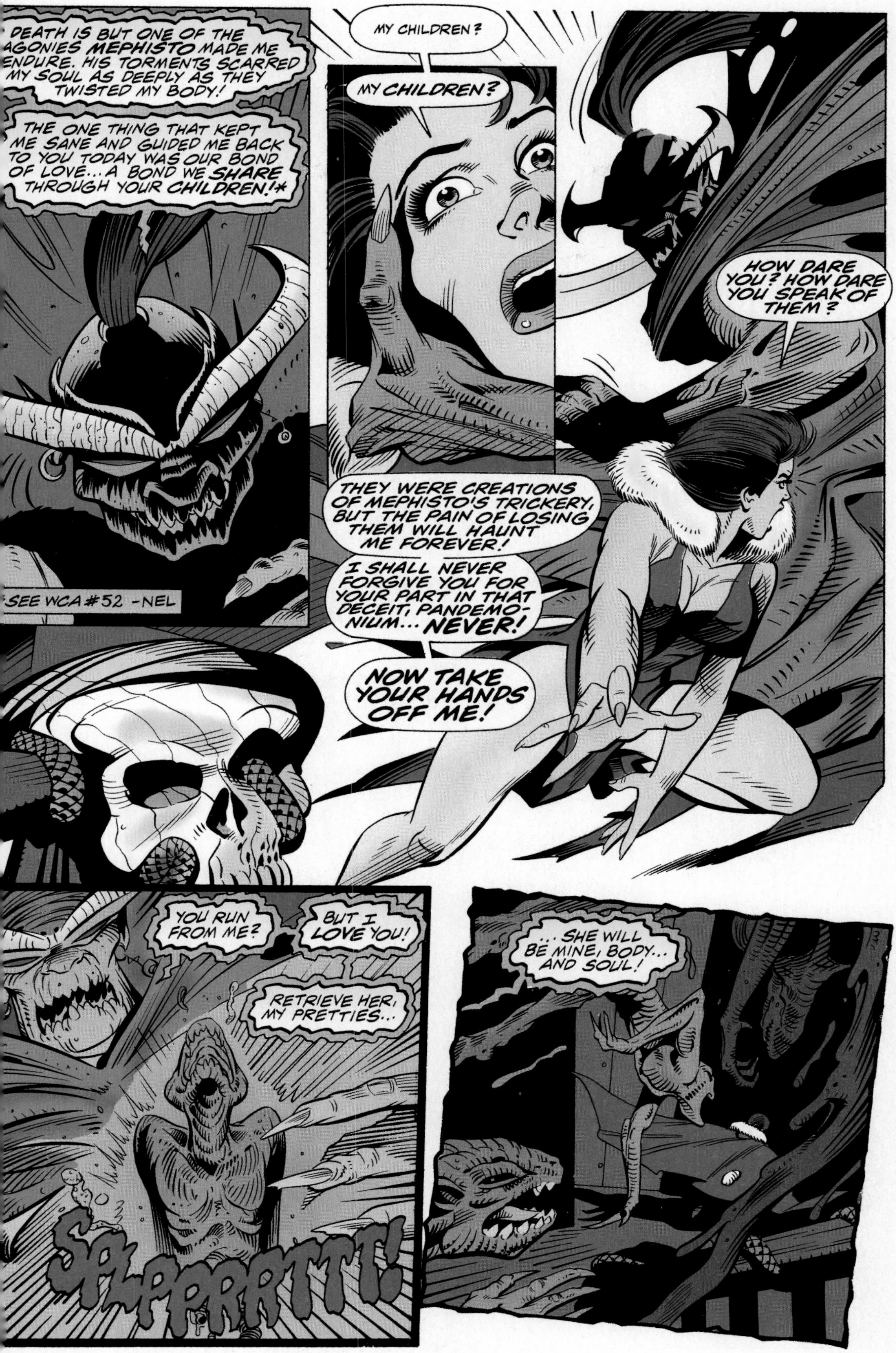
DEATH IS BUT ONE OF THE AGONIES MEPHISTO MADE ME ENDURE. HIS TORMENTS SCARRED MY SOUL AS DEEPLY AS THEY TWISTED MY BODY!
THE ONE THING THAT KEPT ME SANE AND GUIDED ME BACK TO YOU TODAY WAS OUR BOND OF LOVE... A BOND WE SHARE THROUGH YOUR CHILDREN!*
*SEE WCA #52 -NEL
MY CHILDREN?
MY CHILDREN?
HOW DARE YOU? HOW DARE YOU SPEAK OF THEM?
THEY WERE CREATIONS OF MEPHISTO'S TRICKERY, BUT THE PAIN OF LOSING THEM WILL HAUNT ME FOREVER!
I SHALL NEVER FORGIVE YOU FOR YOUR PART IN THAT DECEIT, PANDEMONIUM... NEVER!
NOW TAKE YOUR HANDS OFF ME!
YOU RUN FROM ME?
BUT I LOVE YOU!
RETRIEVE HER, MY PRETTIES...
SPLPPRRTTT!
...SHE WILL BE MINE, BODY... AND SOUL!

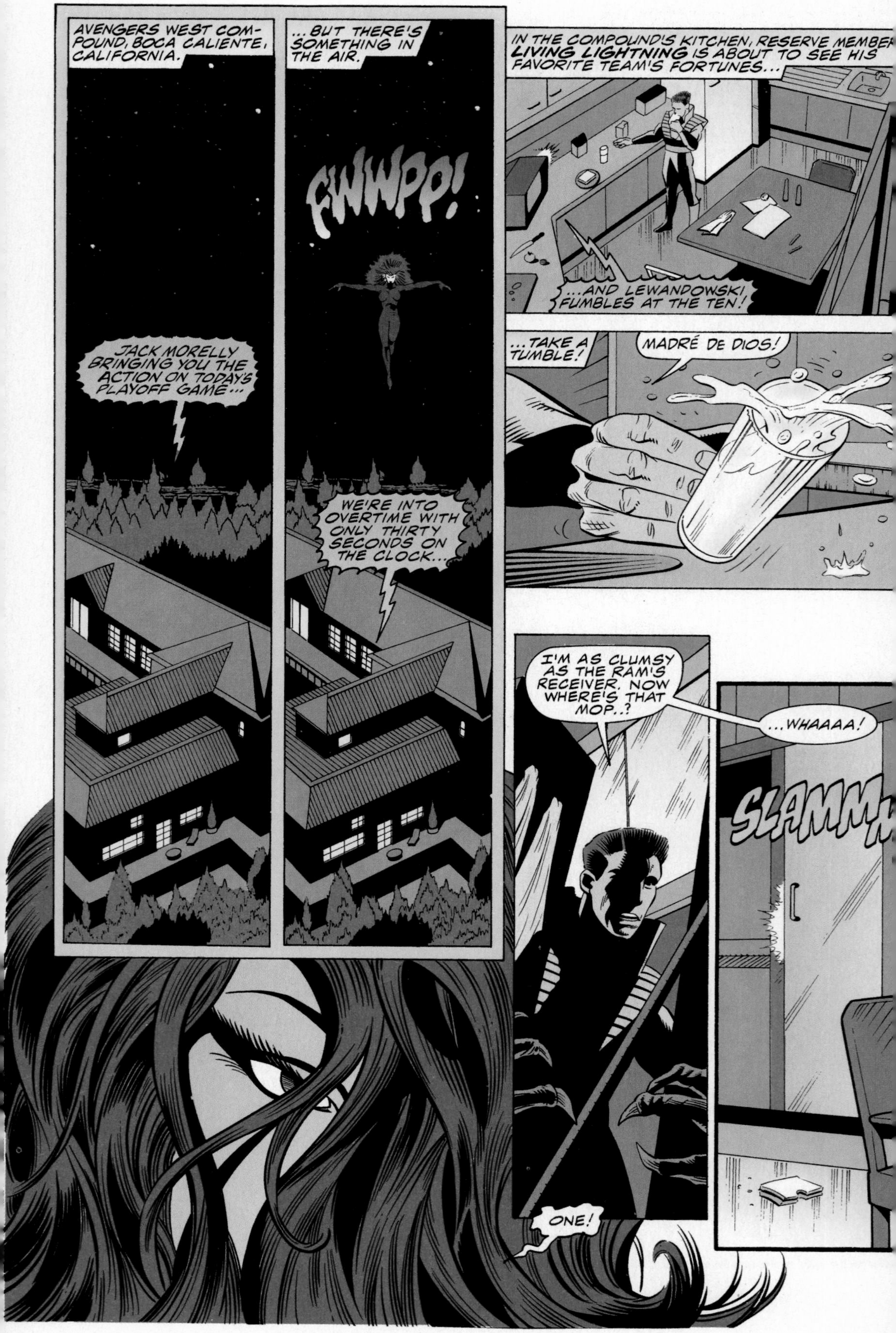
AVENGERS WEST COMPOUND, BOCA CALIENTE, CALIFORNIA.
JACK MORELLY BRINGING YOU THE ACTION ON TODAY'S PLAYOFF GAME...
...BUT THERE'S SOMETHING IN THE AIR.
FWWPP!
WE'RE INTO OVERTIME WITH ONLY THIRTY SECONDS ON THE CLOCK...
IN THE COMPOUND'S KITCHEN, RESERVE MEMBER LIVING LIGHTNING IS ABOUT TO SEE HIS FAVORITE TEAM'S FORTUNES...
...AND LEWANDOWSKI FUMBLES AT THE TEN!
...TAKE A TUMBLE!
MADRÉ DE DIOS!
I'M AS CLUMSY AS THE RAM'S RECEIVER. NOW WHERE'S THAT MOP..?
...WHAAAA!
ONE!

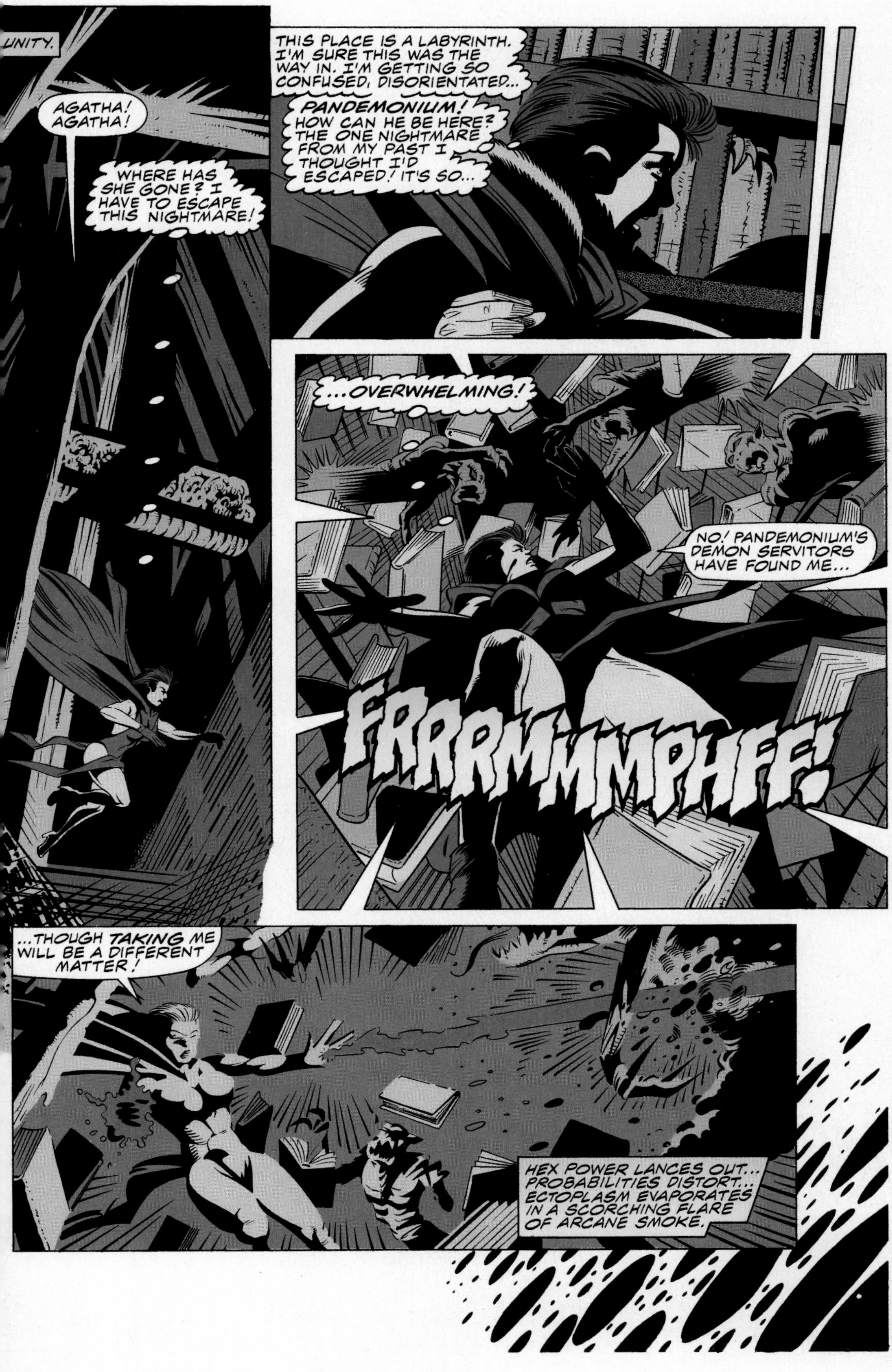
UNITY.
THIS PLACE IS A LABYRINTH. I'M SURE THIS WAS THE WAY IN. I'M GETTING SO CONFUSED, DISORIENTATED...
PANDEMONIUM! HOW CAN HE BE HERE? THE ONE NIGHTMARE FROM MY PAST I THOUGHT I'D ESCAPED! IT'S SO...
AGATHA! AGATHA!
WHERE HAS SHE GONE? I HAVE TO ESCAPE THIS NIGHTMARE!
...OVERWHELMING!
NO! PANDEMONIUM'S DEMON SERVITORS HAVE FOUND ME...
FRRRMMMMPHFF!
...THOUGH TAKING ME WILL BE A DIFFERENT MATTER!
HEX POWER LANCES OUT... PROBABILITIES DISTORT... ECTOPLASM EVAPORATES IN A SCORCHING FLARE OF ARCANE SMOKE.

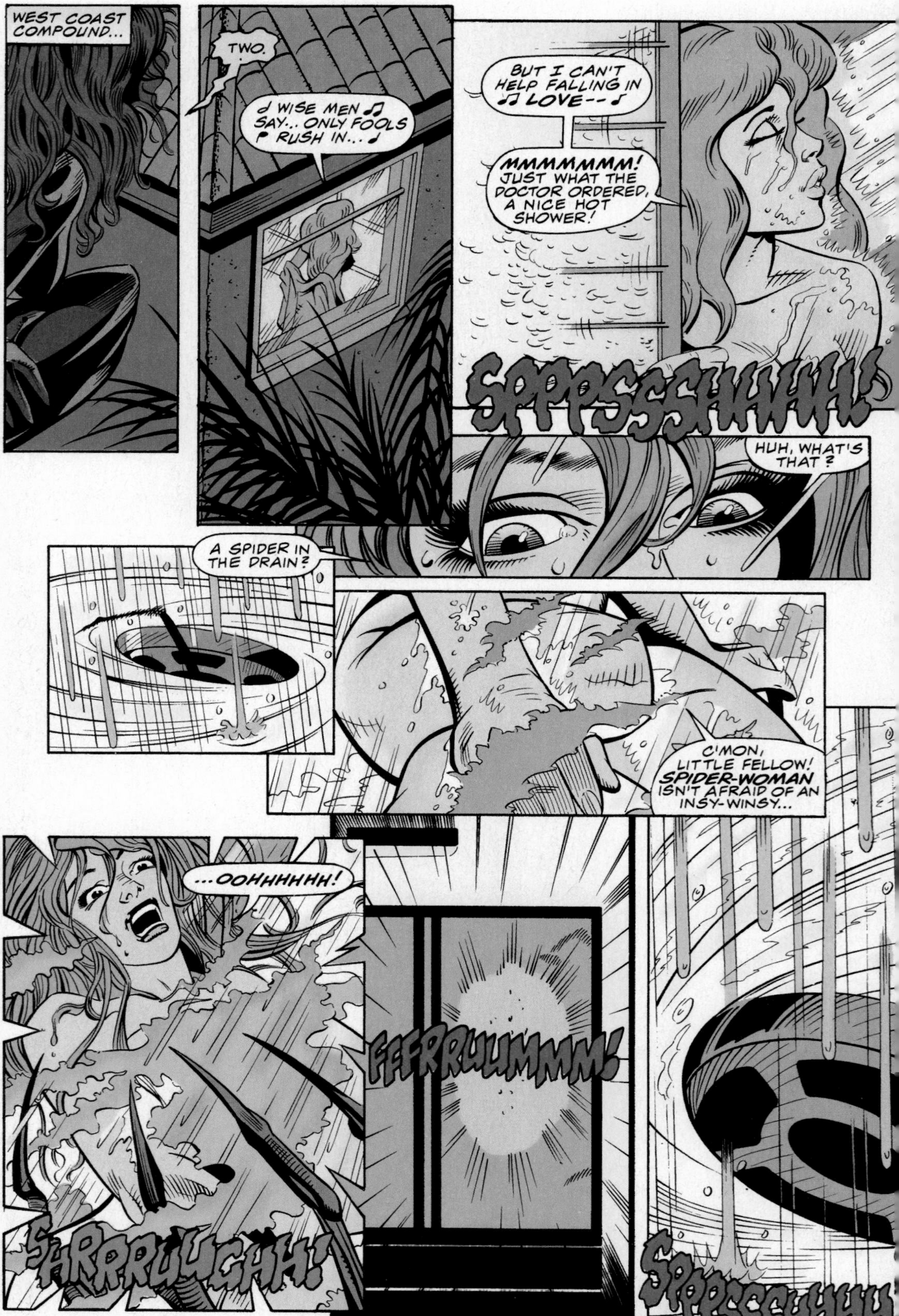
WEST COAST COMPOUND...
TWO.
♩ WISE MEN ♫ SAY... ONLY FOOLS ♪ RUSH IN... ♩
BUT I CAN'T HELP FALLING IN ♫ LOVE-- ♩
MMMMMMM! JUST WHAT THE DOCTOR ORDERED, A NICE HOT SHOWER!
SPPPSSSHHHH!
HUH, WHAT'S THAT?
A SPIDER IN THE DRAIN?
C'MON, LITTLE FELLOW! SPIDER-WOMAN ISN'T AFRAID OF AN INSY-WINSY...
...OOHHHHHH!
SHRRRUUGHH!
FFFRRUUMMM!
SPPPSSSHHHH

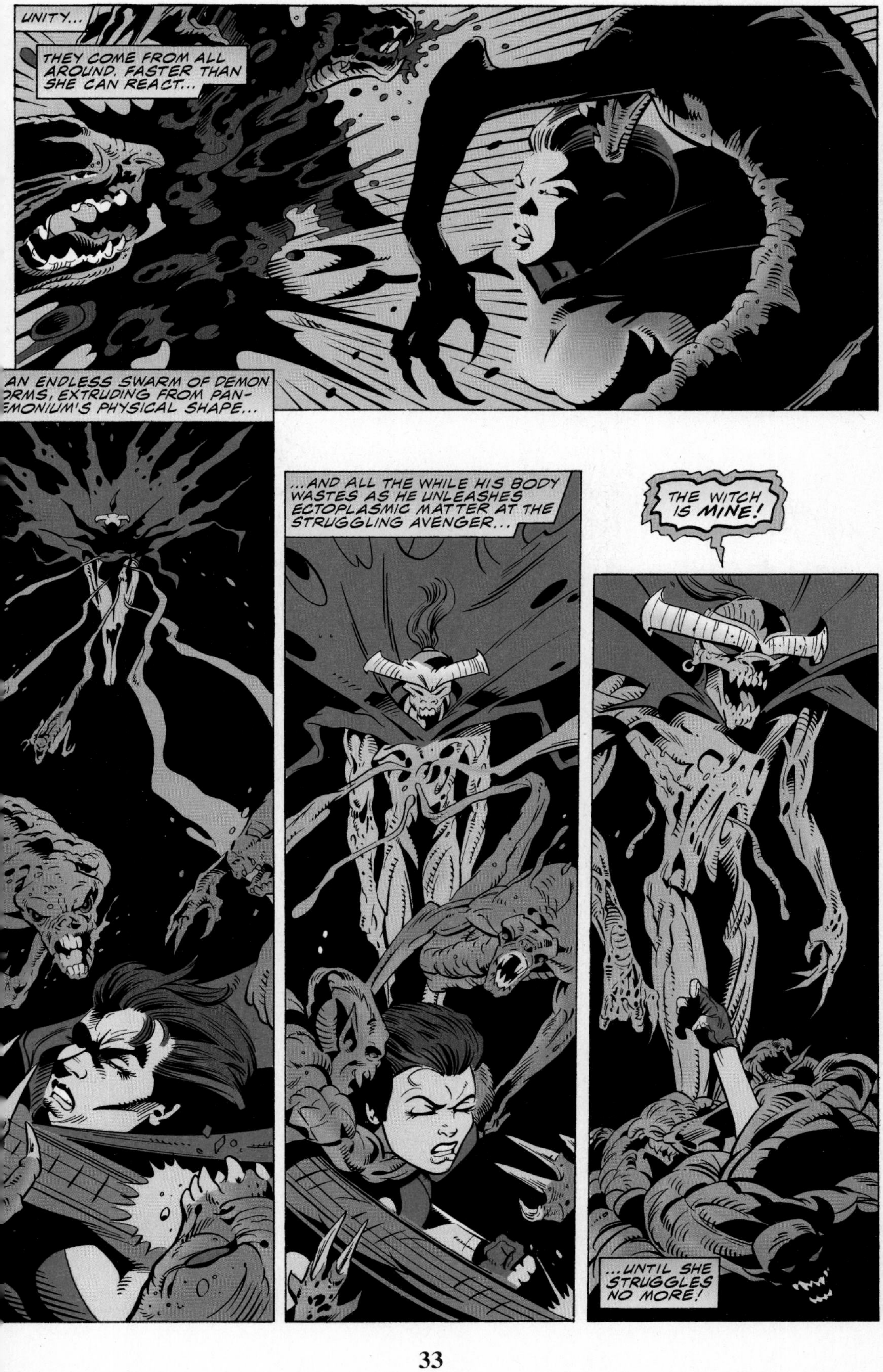

UNITY...
THEY COME FROM ALL AROUND. FASTER THAN SHE CAN REACT...
AN ENDLESS SWARM OF DEMON FORMS, EXTRUDING FROM PANDEMONIUM'S PHYSICAL SHAPE...
...AND ALL THE WHILE HIS BODY WASTES AS HE UNLEASHES ECTOPLASMIC MATTER AT THE STRUGGLING AVENGER...
THE WITCH IS MINE!
...UNTIL SHE STRUGGLES NO MORE!

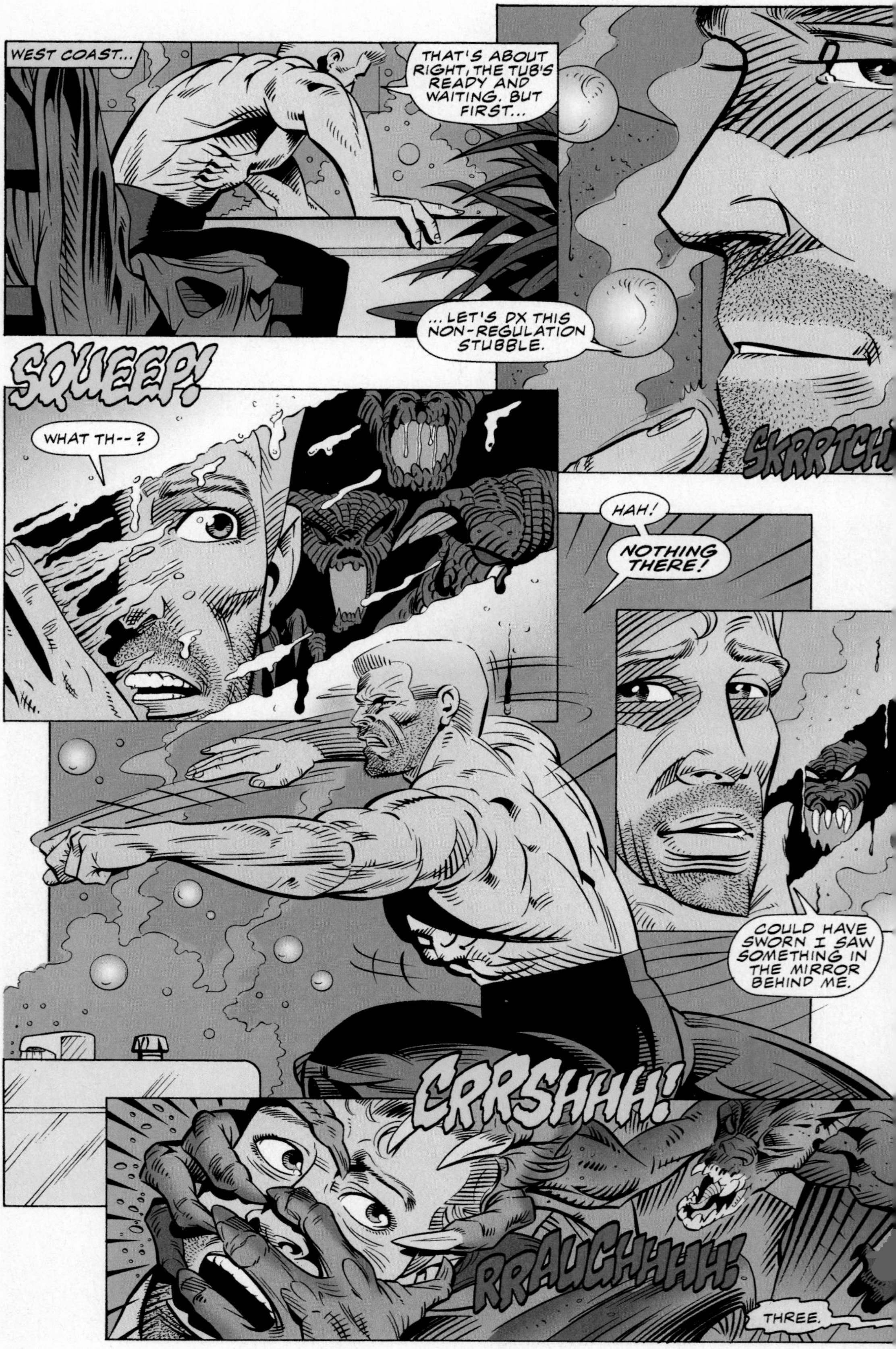
WEST COAST...
THAT'S ABOUT RIGHT, THE TUB'S READY AND WAITING. BUT FIRST...
...LET'S DX THIS NON-REGULATION STUBBLE.
SKRRTCH
SQUEEP!
WHAT TH--?
HAH!
NOTHING THERE!
COULD HAVE SWORN I SAW SOMETHING IN THE MIRROR BEHIND ME.
CRRSHHH!
RRAUGHHHH!
THREE.

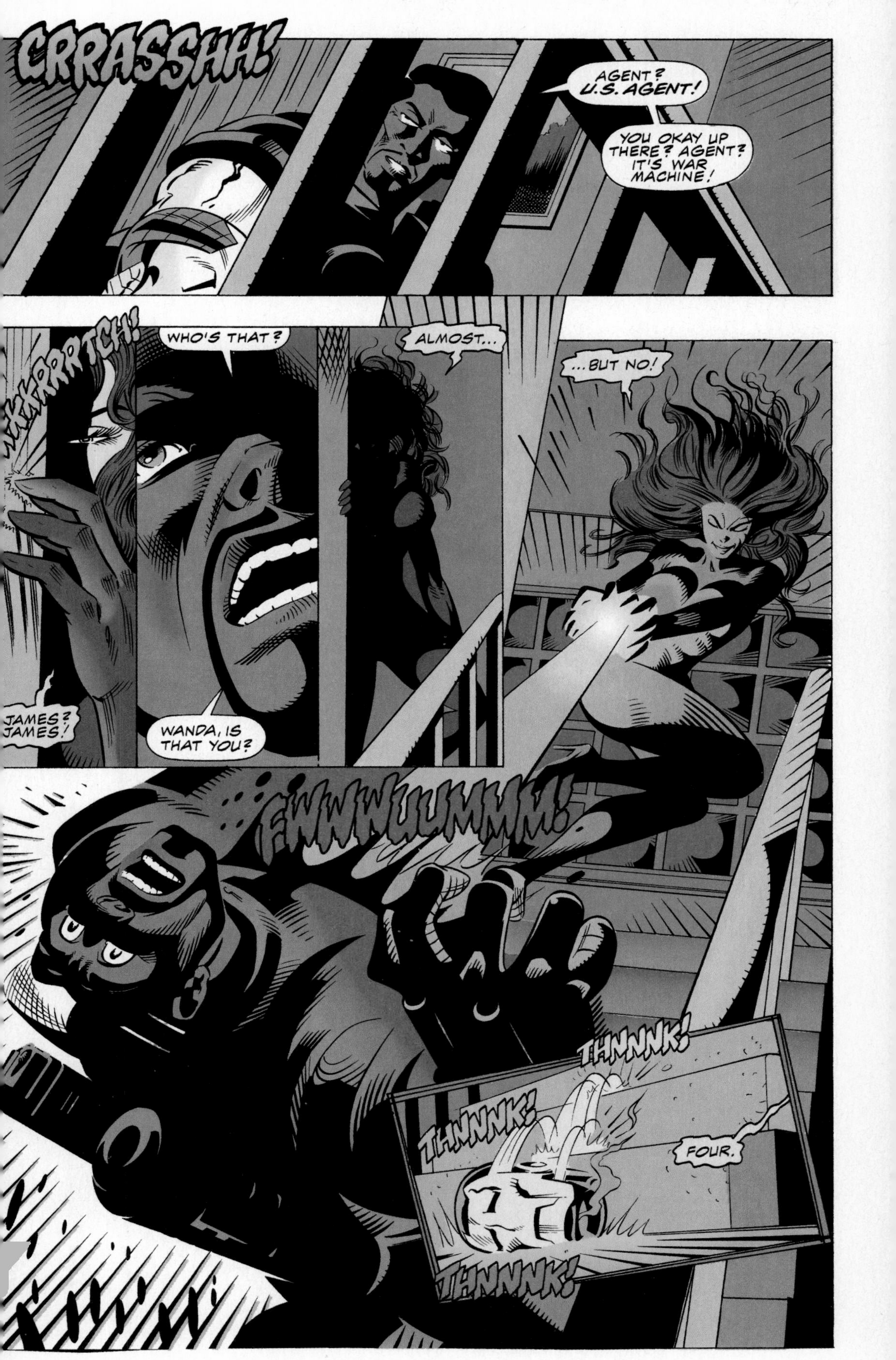
CRRASSHH!
AGENT? U.S. AGENT!
YOU OKAY UP THERE? AGENT? IT'S WAR MACHINE!
KKRRRTCH!
WHO'S THAT?
ALMOST...
...BUT NO!
JAMES? JAMES!
WANDA, IS THAT YOU?
FWWWUUMMM!
THNNNK!
THNNNK!
FOUR.
THNNNK!

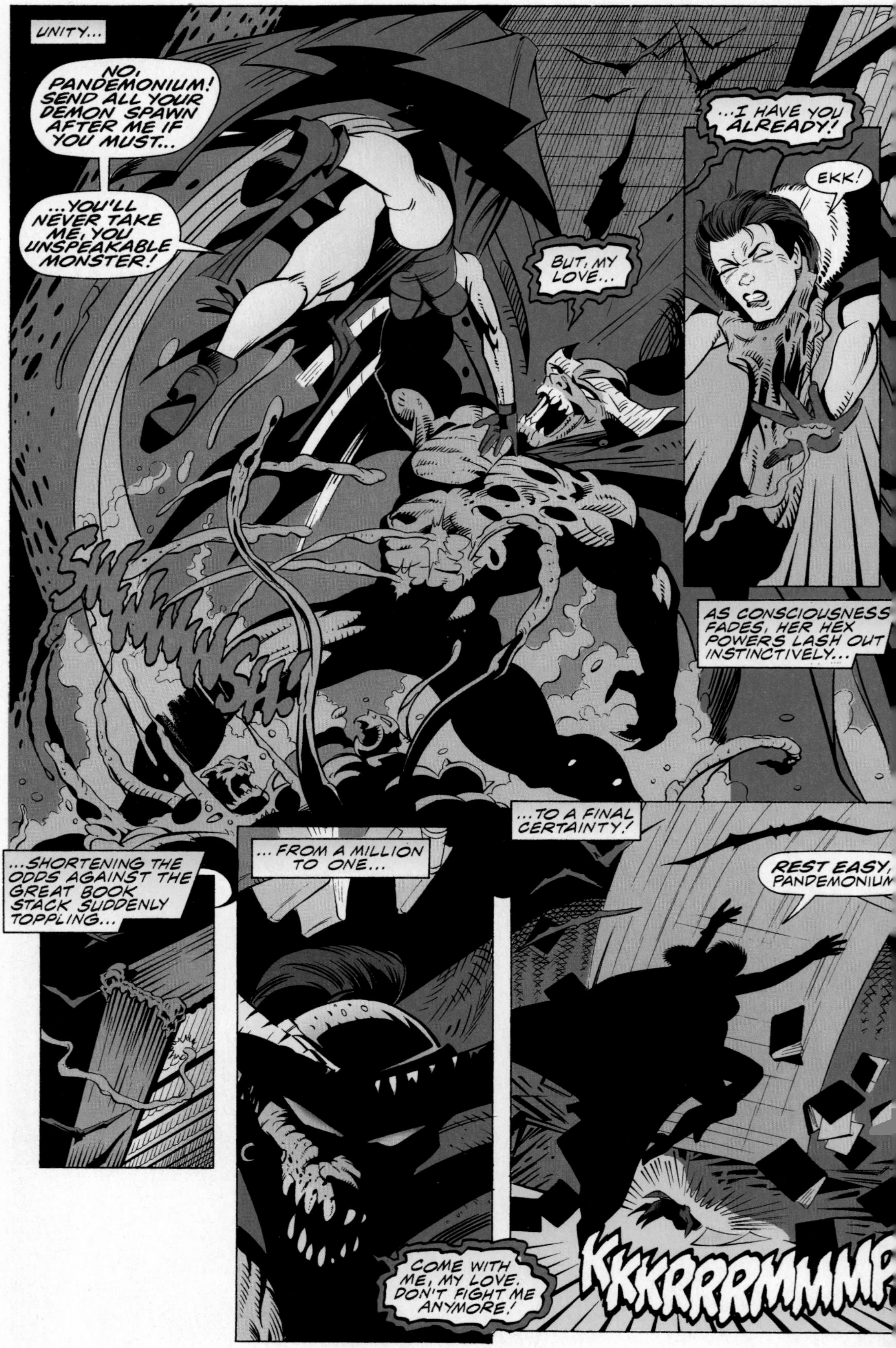
UNITY...
NO, PANDEMONIUM! SEND ALL YOUR DEMON SPAWN AFTER ME IF YOU MUST...
...YOU'LL NEVER TAKE ME, YOU UNSPEAKABLE MONSTER!
BUT, MY LOVE...
...I HAVE YOU ALREADY!
EKK!
SWAWSH
AS CONSCIOUSNESS FADES, HER HEX POWERS LASH OUT INSTINCTIVELY...
...SHORTENING THE ODDS AGAINST THE GREAT BOOK STACK SUDDENLY TOPPLING...
...FROM A MILLION TO ONE...
...TO A FINAL CERTAINTY!
REST EASY, PANDEMONIUM
COME WITH ME, MY LOVE. DON'T FIGHT ME ANYMORE!
KKKRRRMMMP

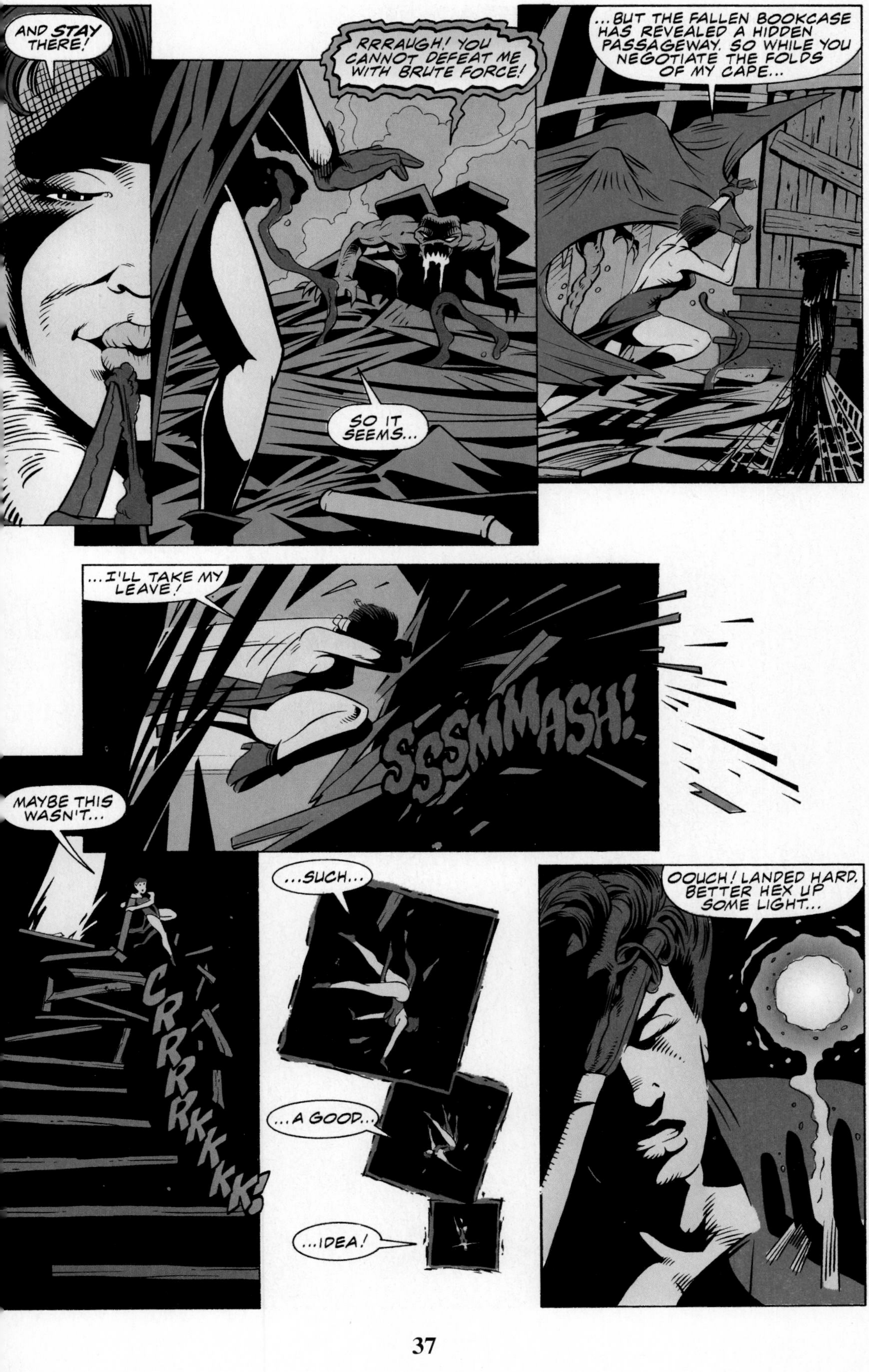
AND STAY THERE!
RRRAUGH! YOU CANNOT DEFEAT ME WITH BRUTE FORCE!
SO IT SEEMS...
...BUT THE FALLEN BOOKCASE HAS REVEALED A HIDDEN PASSAGEWAY. SO WHILE YOU NEGOTIATE THE FOLDS OF MY CAPE...
...I'LL TAKE MY LEAVE!
SSSMMASH!
MAYBE THIS WASN'T...
CRRRKKKK!
...SUCH...
...A GOOD...
...IDEA!
OOUCH! LANDED HARD. BETTER HEX UP SOME LIGHT...

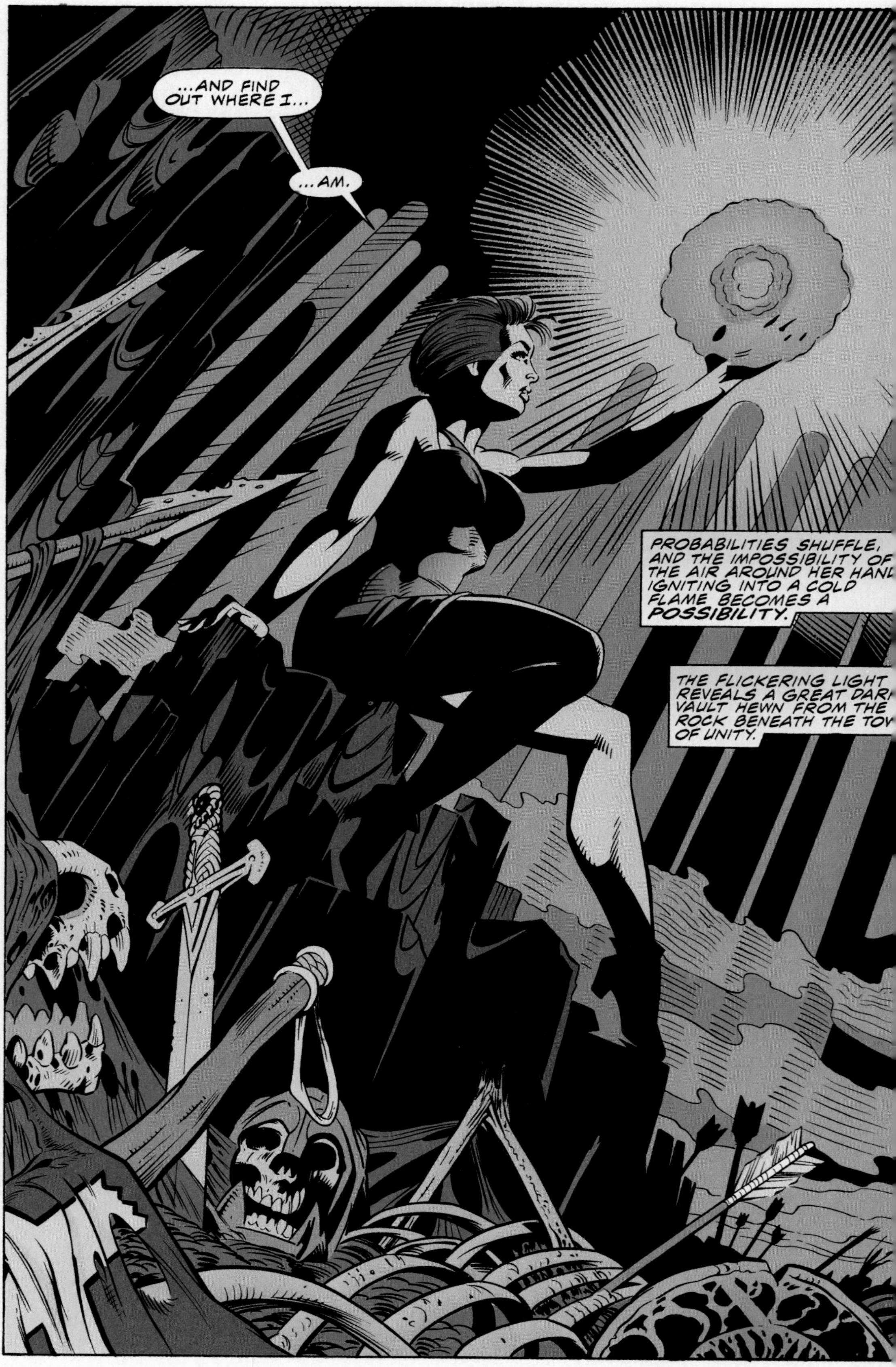

...AND FIND OUT WHERE I...
...AM.
PROBABILITIES SHUFFLE, AND THE IMPOSSIBILITY OF THE AIR AROUND HER HAND IGNITING INTO A COLD FLAME BECOMES A POSSIBILITY.
THE FLICKERING LIGHT REVEALS A GREAT DARK VAULT HEWN FROM THE ROCK BENEATH THE TOW OF UNITY.

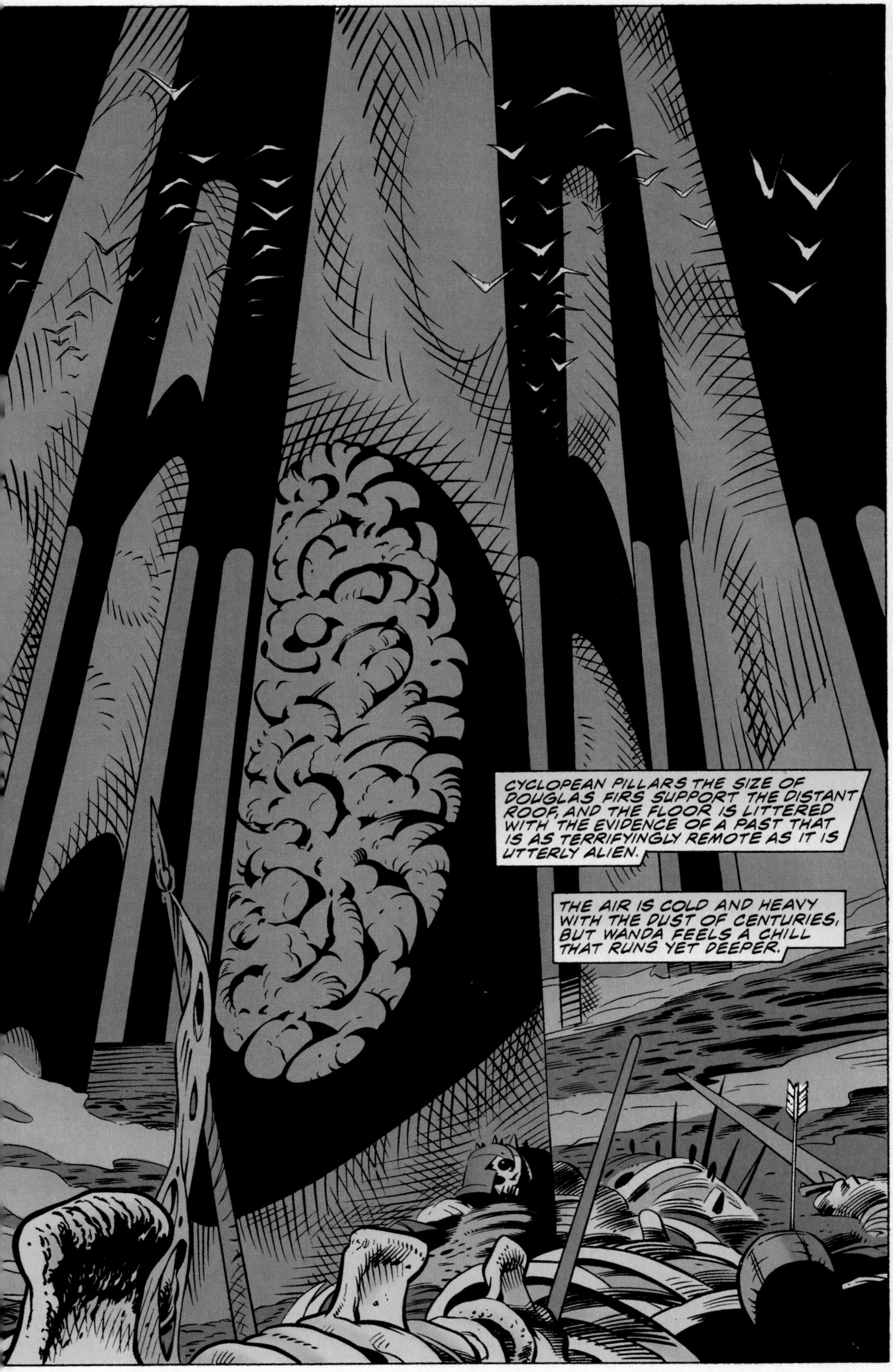
CYCLOPEAN PILLARS THE SIZE OF DOUGLAS FIRS SUPPORT THE DISTANT ROOF, AND THE FLOOR IS LITTERED WITH THE EVIDENCE OF A PAST THAT IS AS TERRIFYINGLY REMOTE AS IT IS UTTERLY ALIEN.
THE AIR IS COLD AND HEAVY WITH THE DUST OF CENTURIES, BUT WANDA FEELS A CHILL THAT RUNS YET DEEPER.

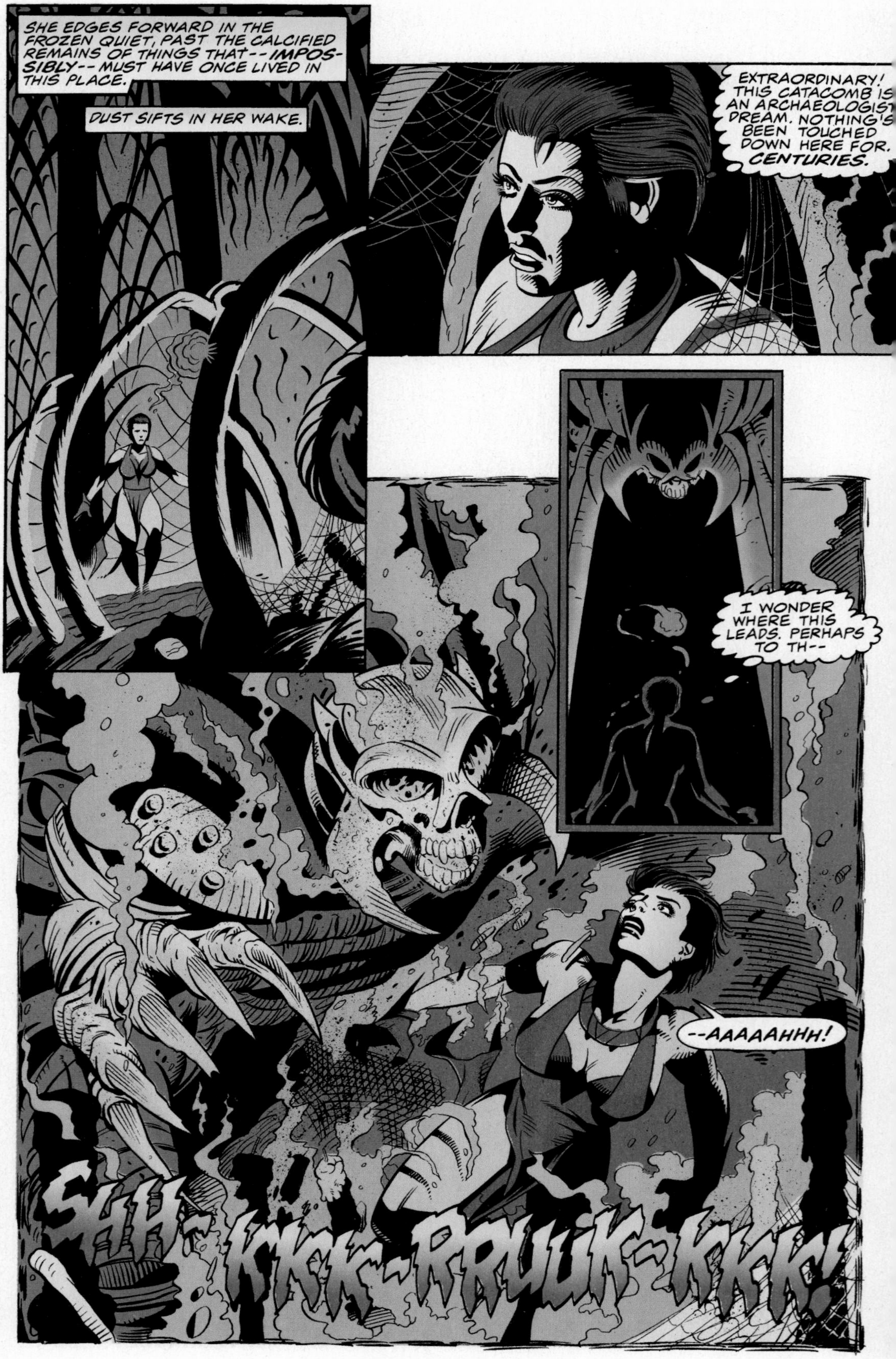
SHE EDGES FORWARD IN THE FROZEN QUIET, PAST THE CALCIFIED REMAINS OF THINGS THAT--IMPOSSIBLY--MUST HAVE ONCE LIVED IN THIS PLACE.
DUST SIFTS IN HER WAKE.
EXTRAORDINARY! THIS CATACOMB IS AN ARCHAEOLOGIST'S DREAM. NOTHING'S BEEN TOUCHED DOWN HERE FOR. CENTURIES.
I WONDER WHERE THIS LEADS. PERHAPS TO TH--
--AAAAAHHH!
SHH-KKK-RRUUK-KKK!

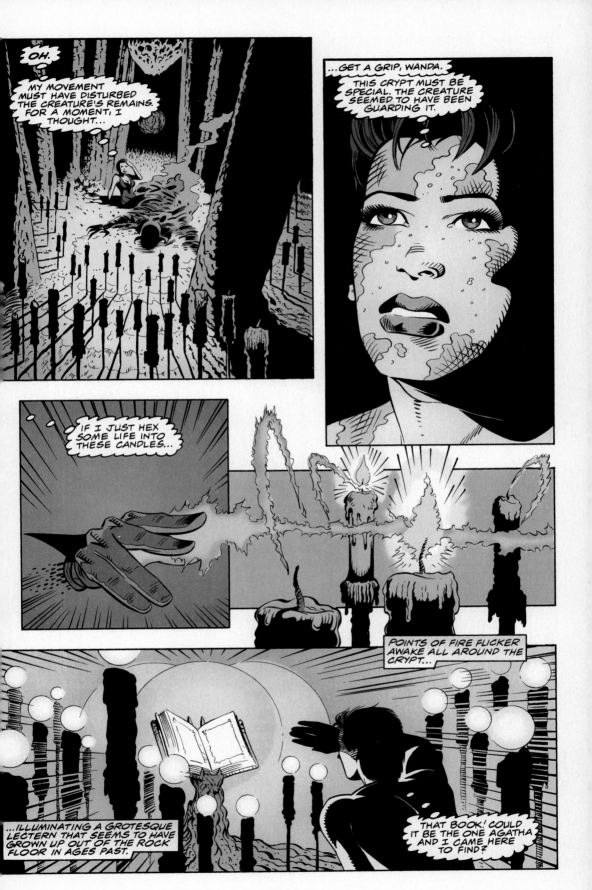

OH.

MY MOVEMENT MUST HAVE DISTURBED THE CREATURE'S REMAINS. FOR A MOMENT, I THOUGHT...

...GET A GRIP, WANDA. THIS CRYPT MUST BE SPECIAL. THE CREATURE SEEMED TO HAVE BEEN GUARDING IT.

IF I JUST HEX SOME LIFE INTO THESE CANDLES...

POINTS OF FIRE FLICKER AWAKE ALL AROUND THE CRYPT...

...ILLUMINATING A GROTESQUE LECTERN THAT SEEMS TO HAVE GROWN UP OUT OF THE ROCK FLOOR IN AGES PAST.

THAT BOOK! COULD IT BE THE ONE AGATHA AND I CAME HERE TO FIND?

41

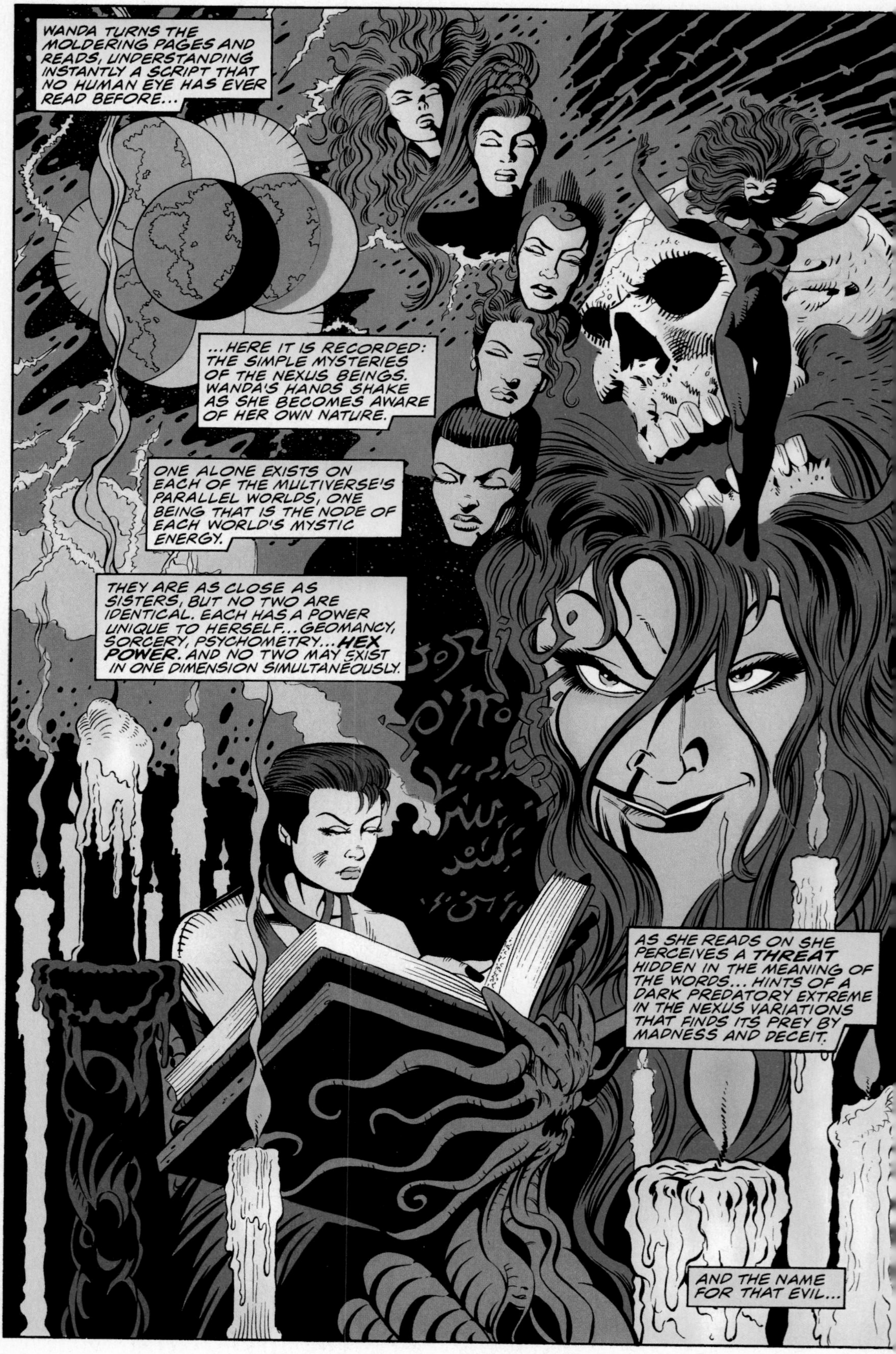
WANDA TURNS THE MOLDERING PAGES AND READS, UNDERSTANDING INSTANTLY A SCRIPT THAT NO HUMAN EYE HAS EVER READ BEFORE...
...HERE IT IS RECORDED: THE SIMPLE MYSTERIES OF THE NEXUS BEINGS. WANDA'S HANDS SHAKE AS SHE BECOMES AWARE OF HER OWN NATURE.
ONE ALONE EXISTS ON EACH OF THE MULTIVERSE'S PARALLEL WORLDS, ONE BEING THAT IS THE NODE OF EACH WORLD'S MYSTIC ENERGY.
THEY ARE AS CLOSE AS SISTERS, BUT NO TWO ARE IDENTICAL. EACH HAS A POWER UNIQUE TO HERSELF...GEOMANCY, SORCERY, PSYCHOMETRY...HEX POWER. AND NO TWO MAY EXIST IN ONE DIMENSION SIMULTANEOUSLY.
AS SHE READS ON SHE PERCEIVES A THREAT HIDDEN IN THE MEANING OF THE WORDS... HINTS OF A DARK PREDATORY EXTREME IN THE NEXUS VARIATIONS THAT FINDS ITS PREY BY MADNESS AND DECEIT.
AND THE NAME FOR THAT EVIL...

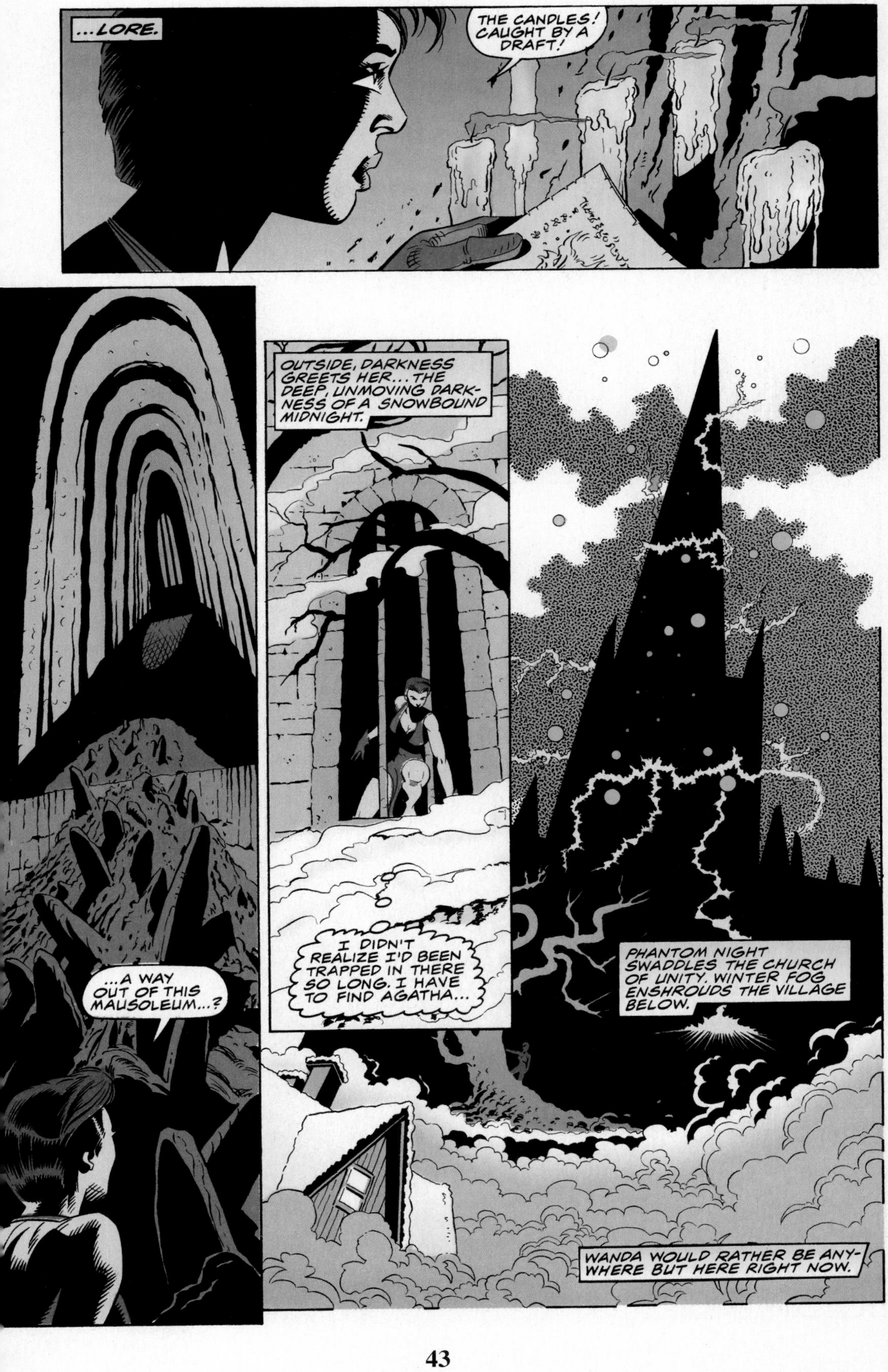
...LORE.
THE CANDLES! CAUGHT BY A DRAFT!
...A WAY OUT OF THIS MAUSOLEUM...?
OUTSIDE, DARKNESS GREETS HER... THE DEEP, UNMOVING DARKNESS OF A SNOWBOUND MIDNIGHT.
I DIDN'T REALIZE I'D BEEN TRAPPED IN THERE SO LONG. I HAVE TO FIND AGATHA...
PHANTOM NIGHT SWADDLES THE CHURCH OF UNITY. WINTER FOG ENSHROUDS THE VILLAGE BELOW.
WANDA WOULD RATHER BE ANYWHERE BUT HERE RIGHT NOW.

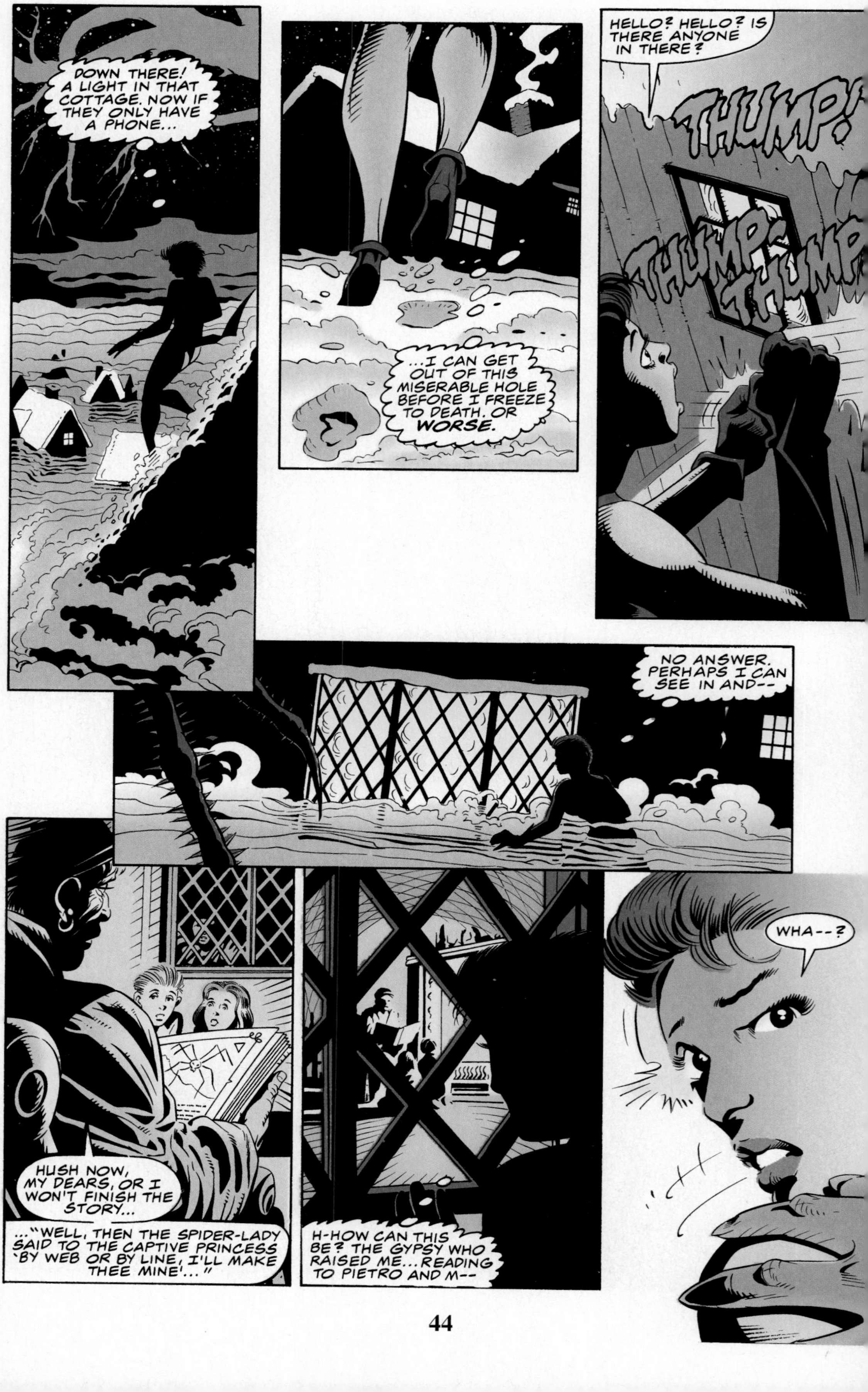
DOWN THERE! A LIGHT IN THAT COTTAGE. NOW IF THEY ONLY HAVE A PHONE...
...I CAN GET OUT OF THIS MISERABLE HOLE BEFORE I FREEZE TO DEATH. OR WORSE.
HELLO? HELLO? IS THERE ANYONE IN THERE?
THUMP!
THUMP
THUMP
NO ANSWER. PERHAPS I CAN SEE IN AND--
HUSH NOW, MY DEARS, OR I WON'T FINISH THE STORY...
..."WELL, THEN THE SPIDER-LADY SAID TO THE CAPTIVE PRINCESS 'BY WEB OR BY LINE, I'LL MAKE THEE MINE'..."
H-HOW CAN THIS BE? THE GYPSY WHO RAISED ME... READING TO PIETRO AND M--
WHA--?

45

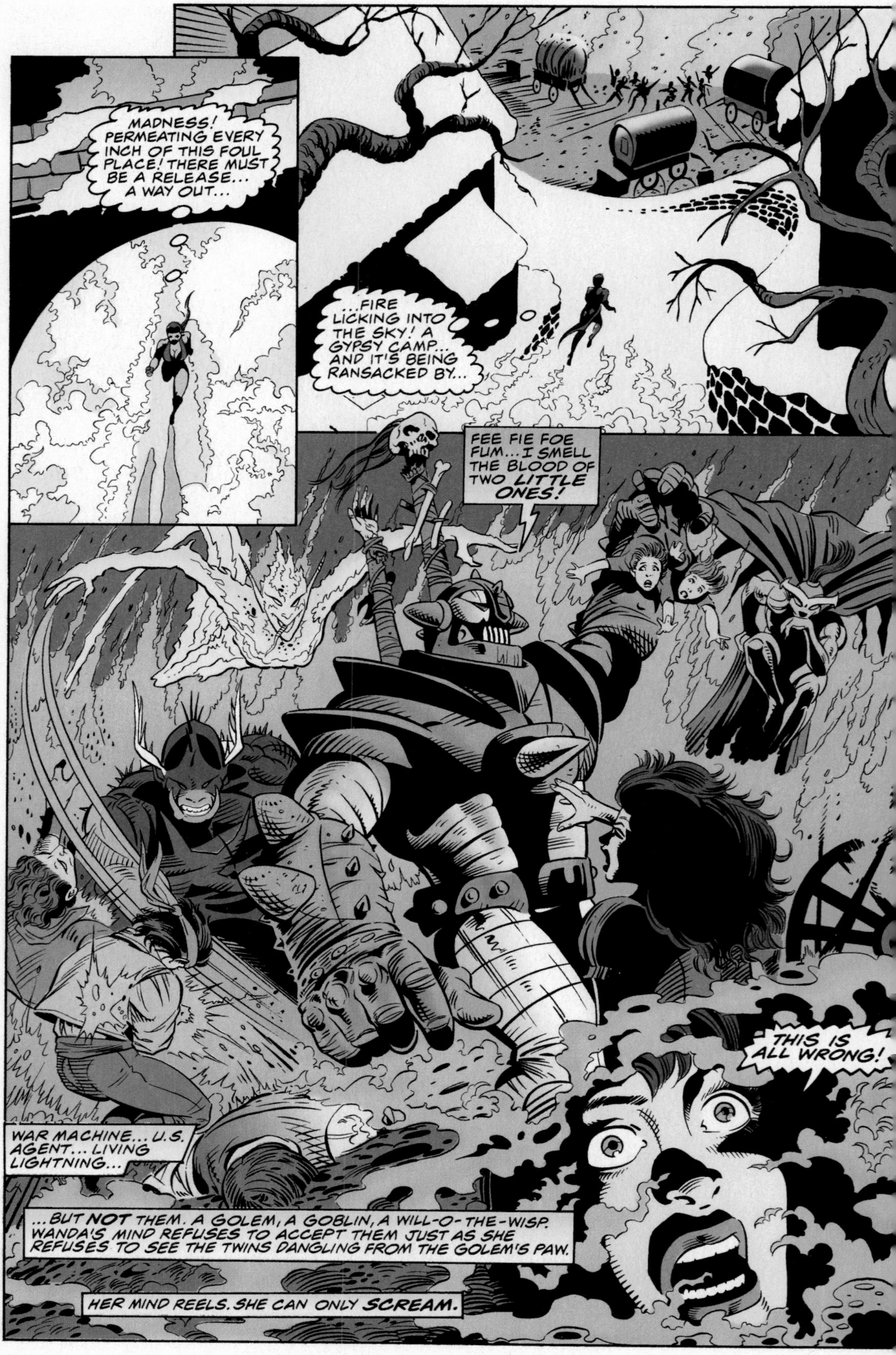
MADNESS! PERMEATING EVERY INCH OF THIS FOUL PLACE! THERE MUST BE A RELEASE... A WAY OUT...
...FIRE LICKING INTO THE SKY! A GYPSY CAMP... AND IT'S BEING RANSACKED BY...
FEE FIE FOE FUM... I SMELL THE BLOOD OF TWO LITTLE ONES!
THIS IS ALL WRONG!
WAR MACHINE... U.S. AGENT... LIVING LIGHTNING...
...BUT NOT THEM. A GOLEM, A GOBLIN, A WILL-O-THE-WISP. WANDA'S MIND REFUSES TO ACCEPT THEM JUST AS SHE REFUSES TO SEE THE TWINS DANGLING FROM THE GOLEM'S PAW.
HER MIND REELS. SHE CAN ONLY SCREAM.

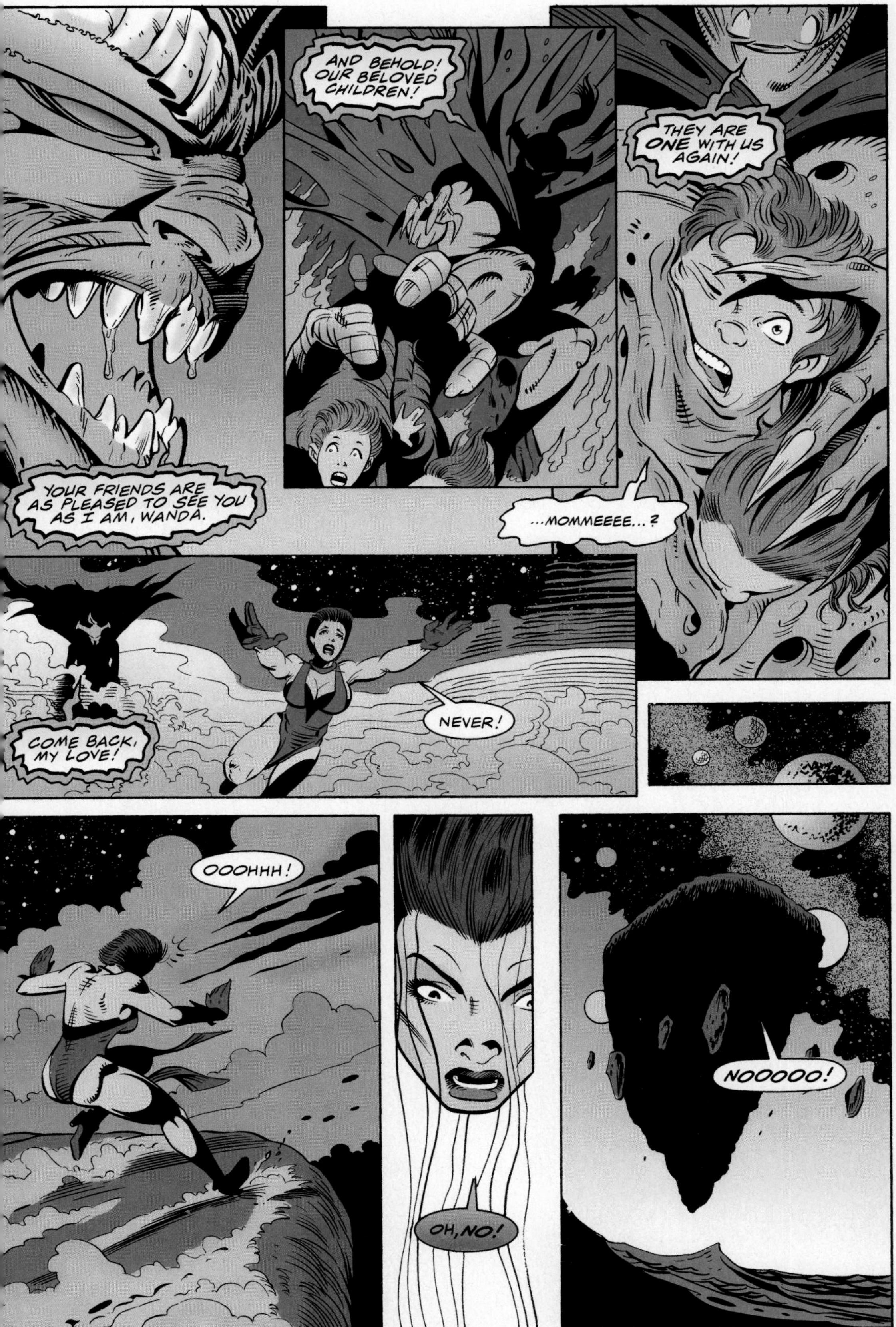
AND BEHOLD! OUR BELOVED CHILDREN!
THEY ARE ONE WITH US AGAIN!
YOUR FRIENDS ARE AS PLEASED TO SEE YOU AS I AM, WANDA.
...MOMMEEEE...?
COME BACK, MY LOVE!
NEVER!
OOOHHH!
OH, NO!
NOOOOO!

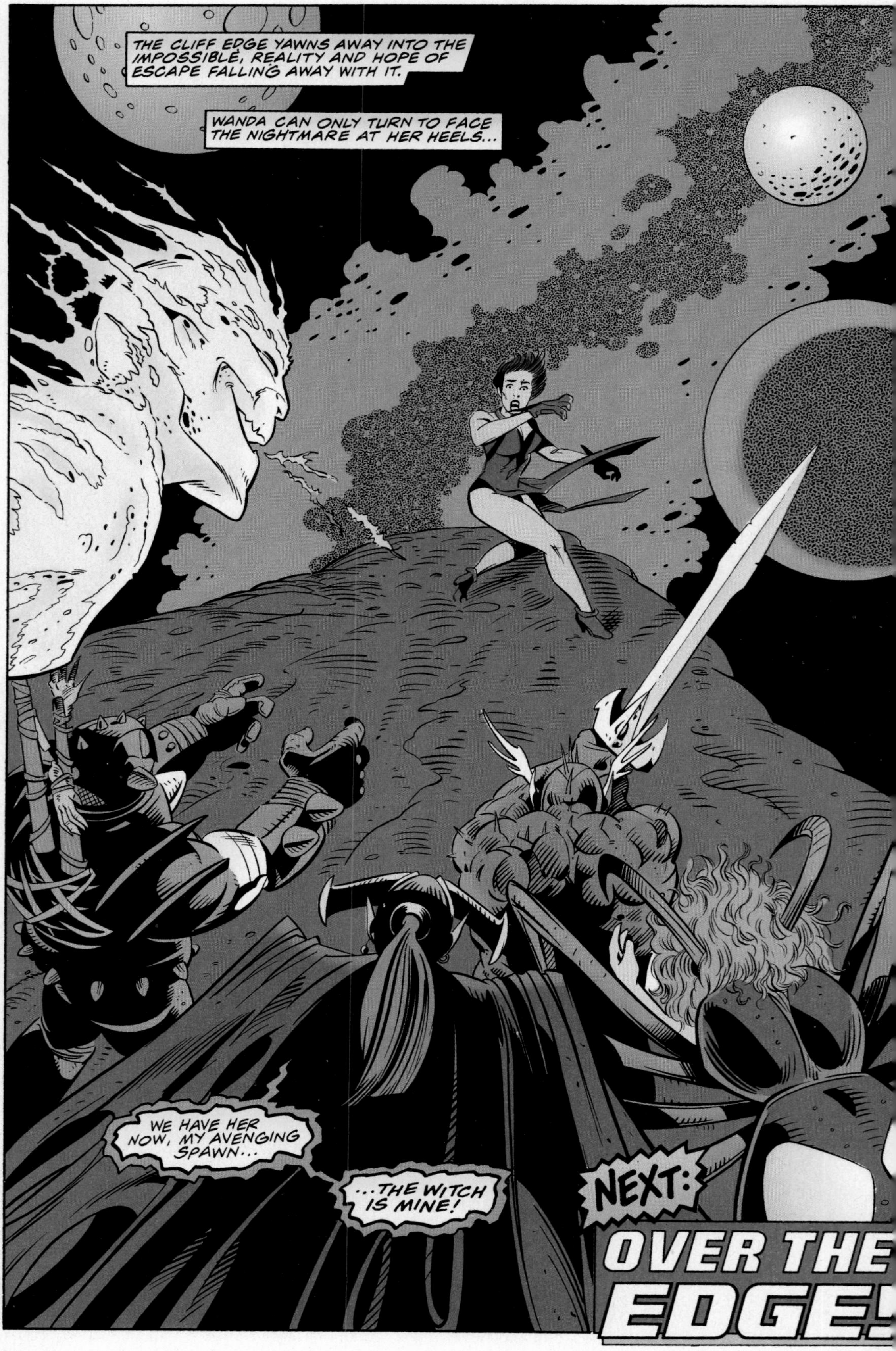
THE CLIFF EDGE YAWNS AWAY INTO THE IMPOSSIBLE, REALITY AND HOPE OF ESCAPE FALLING AWAY WITH IT.
WANDA CAN ONLY TURN TO FACE THE NIGHTMARE AT HER HEELS...
WE HAVE HER NOW, MY AVENGING SPAWN...
...THE WITCH IS MINE!
NEXT:
OVER THE EDGE!

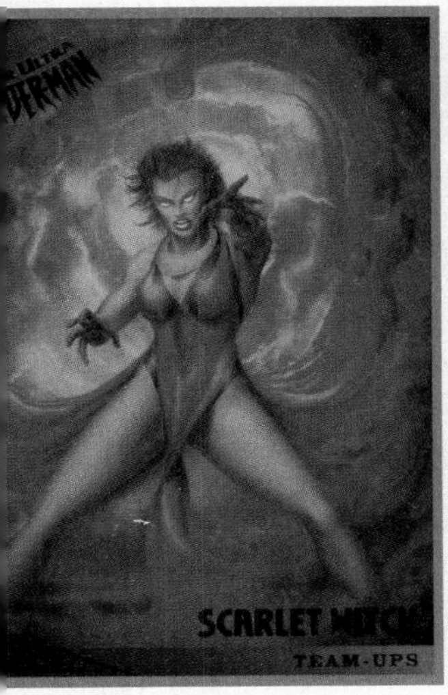
SCARLET WITCH
TEAM-UPS

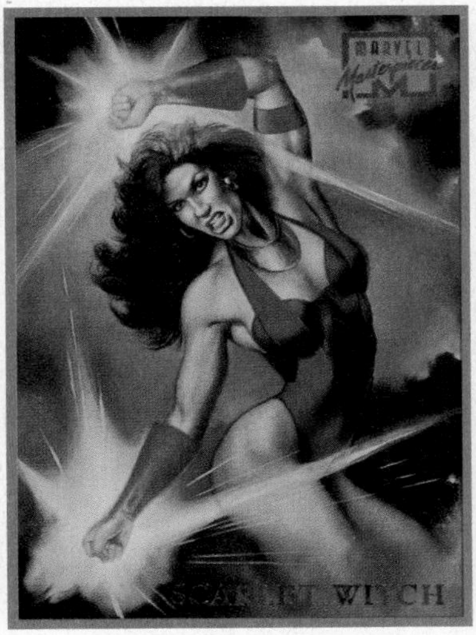
SCARLET WITCH

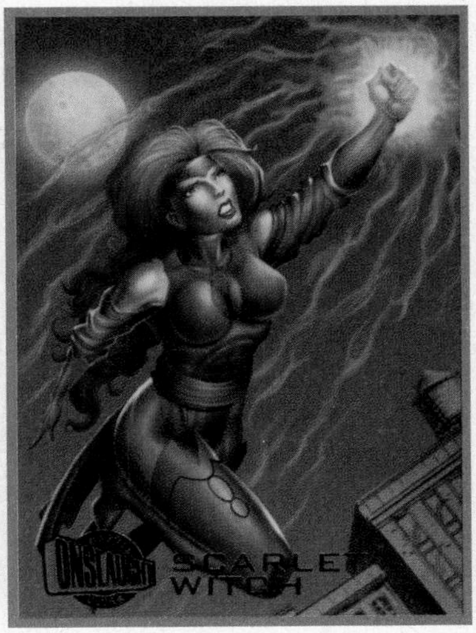
ONSLAUGHT
SCARLET WITCH

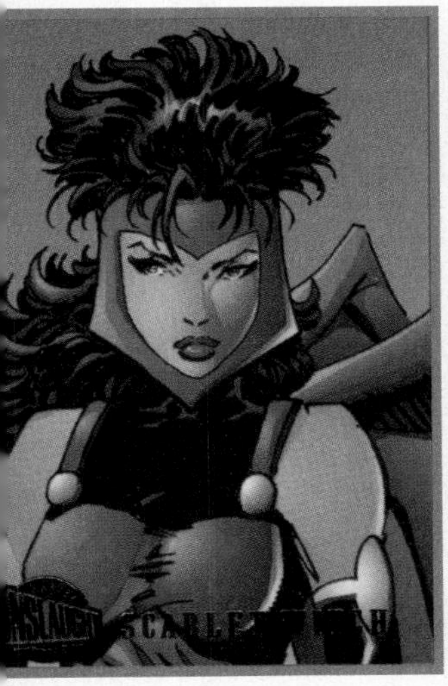

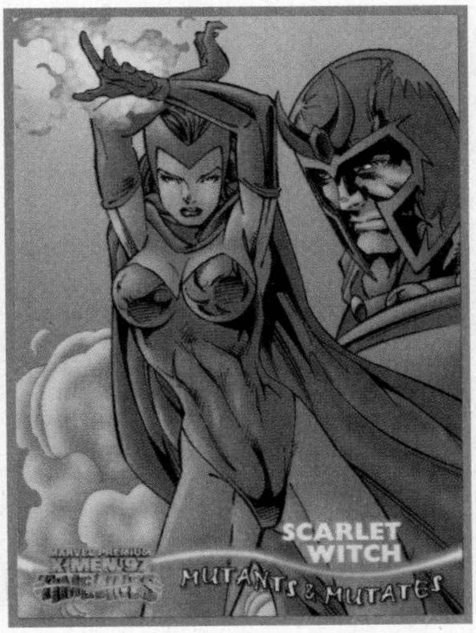
SCARLET WITCH
MUTANTS & MUTATES

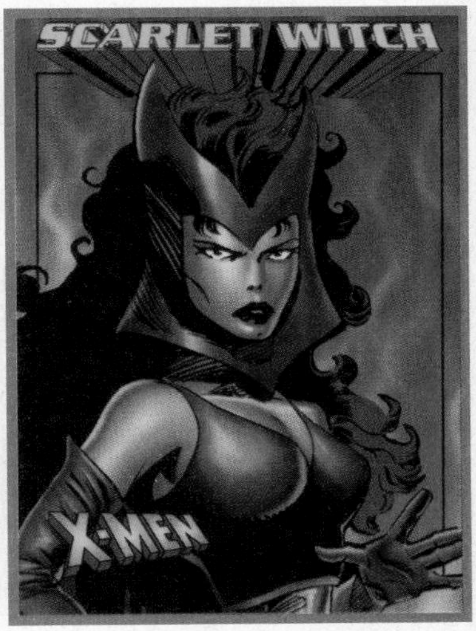
SCARLET WITCH
X-MEN

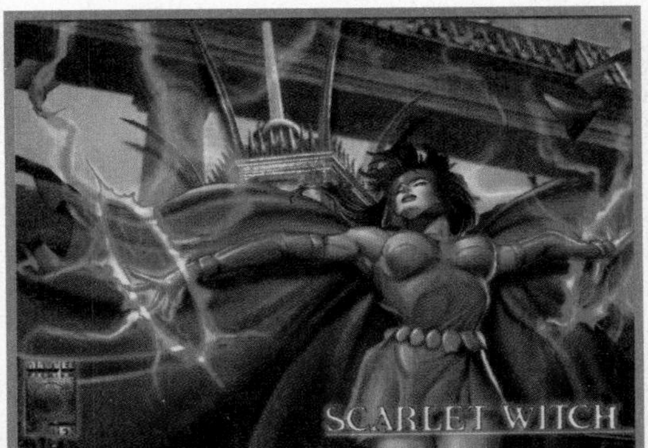
SCARLET WITCH

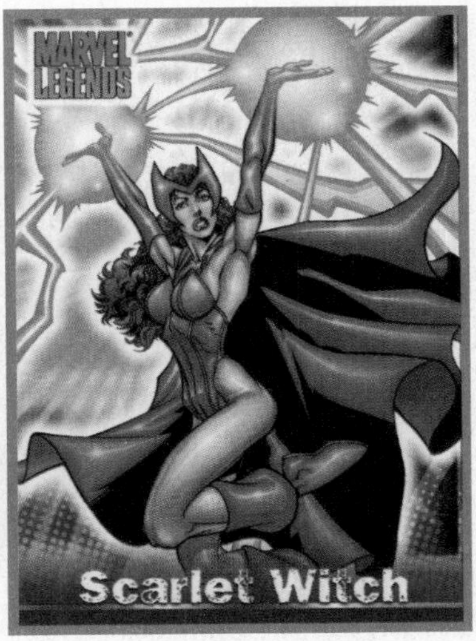
MARVEL LEGENDS
Scarlet Witch

95-2001 TRADING-CARD ART BY PETER BOLLINGER, JULIE BELL, GREG LUZNIAK & JUNG CHOI, ROB LIEFELD & EXTREME STUDIOS, JAN DUURSEMA, JOE QUESADA, AND ROBERTO FLORES, PHYLLIS NOVIN & MCNABB STUDIOS

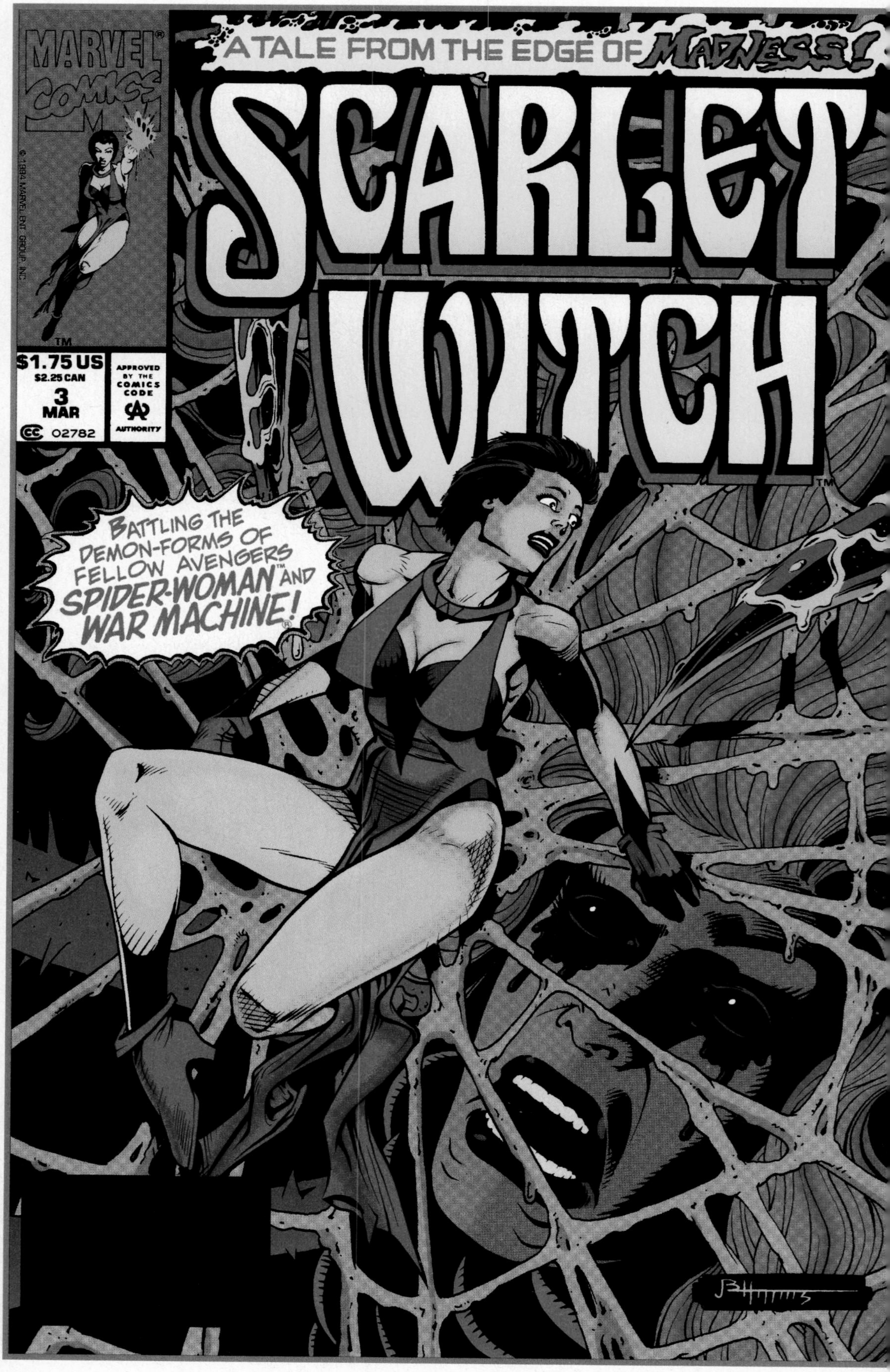
MARVEL COMICS
A TALE FROM THE EDGE OF MADNESS!
SCARLET WITCH
© 1994 MARVEL ENT. GROUP, INC.
$1.75 US
$2.25 CAN
3
MAR
02782
APPROVED BY THE COMICS CODE AUTHORITY
BATTLING THE DEMON-FORMS OF FELLOW AVENGERS SPIDER-WOMAN AND WAR MACHINE!

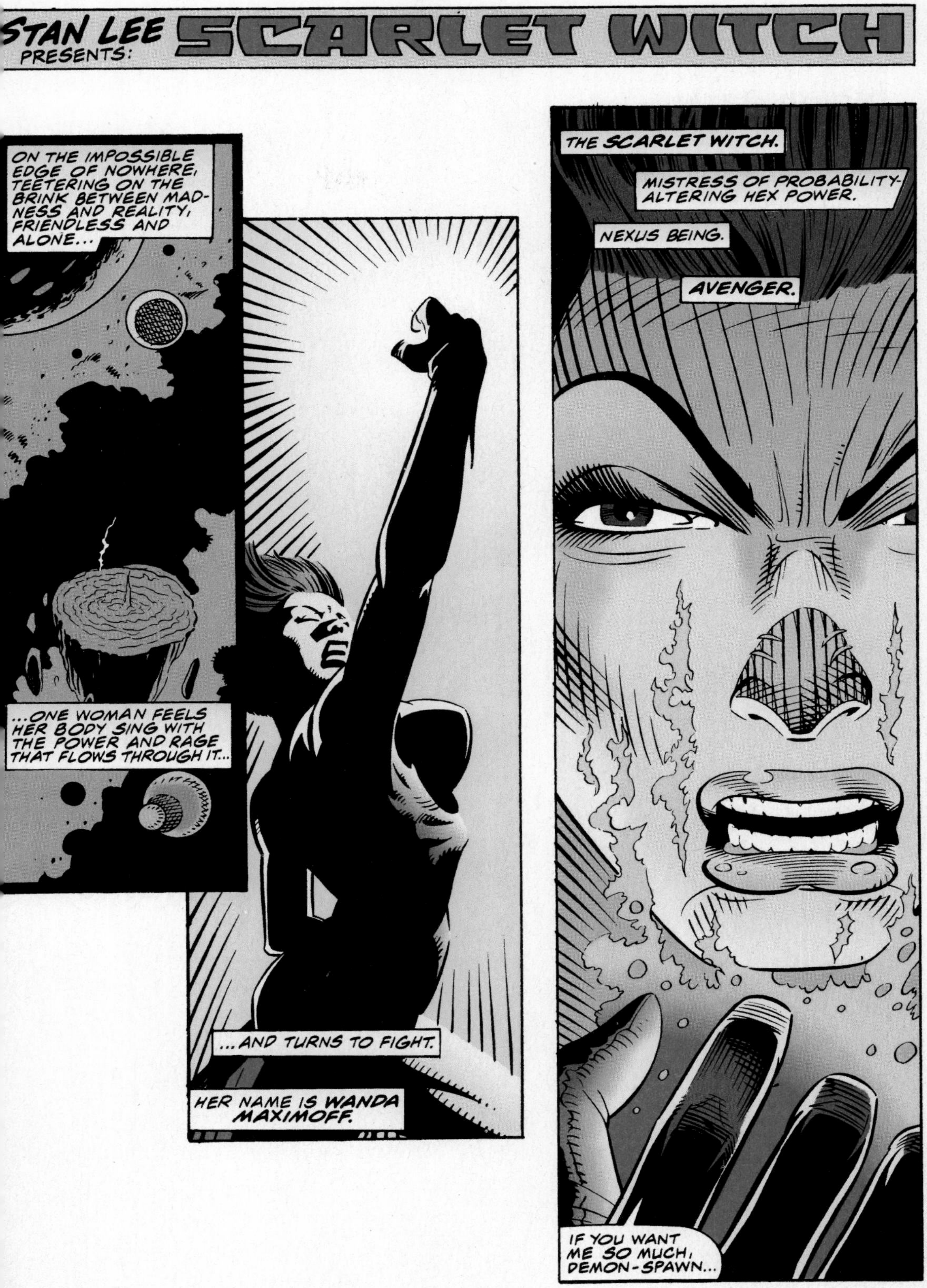
STAN LEE PRESENTS:
SCARLET WITCH
ON THE IMPOSSIBLE EDGE OF NOWHERE, TEETERING ON THE BRINK BETWEEN MADNESS AND REALITY, FRIENDLESS AND ALONE...
...ONE WOMAN FEELS HER BODY SING WITH THE POWER AND RAGE THAT FLOWS THROUGH IT...
...AND TURNS TO FIGHT.
HER NAME IS WANDA MAXIMOFF.
THE SCARLET WITCH.
MISTRESS OF PROBABILITY-ALTERING HEX POWER.
NEXUS BEING.
AVENGER.
IF YOU WANT ME SO MUCH, DEMON-SPAWN...

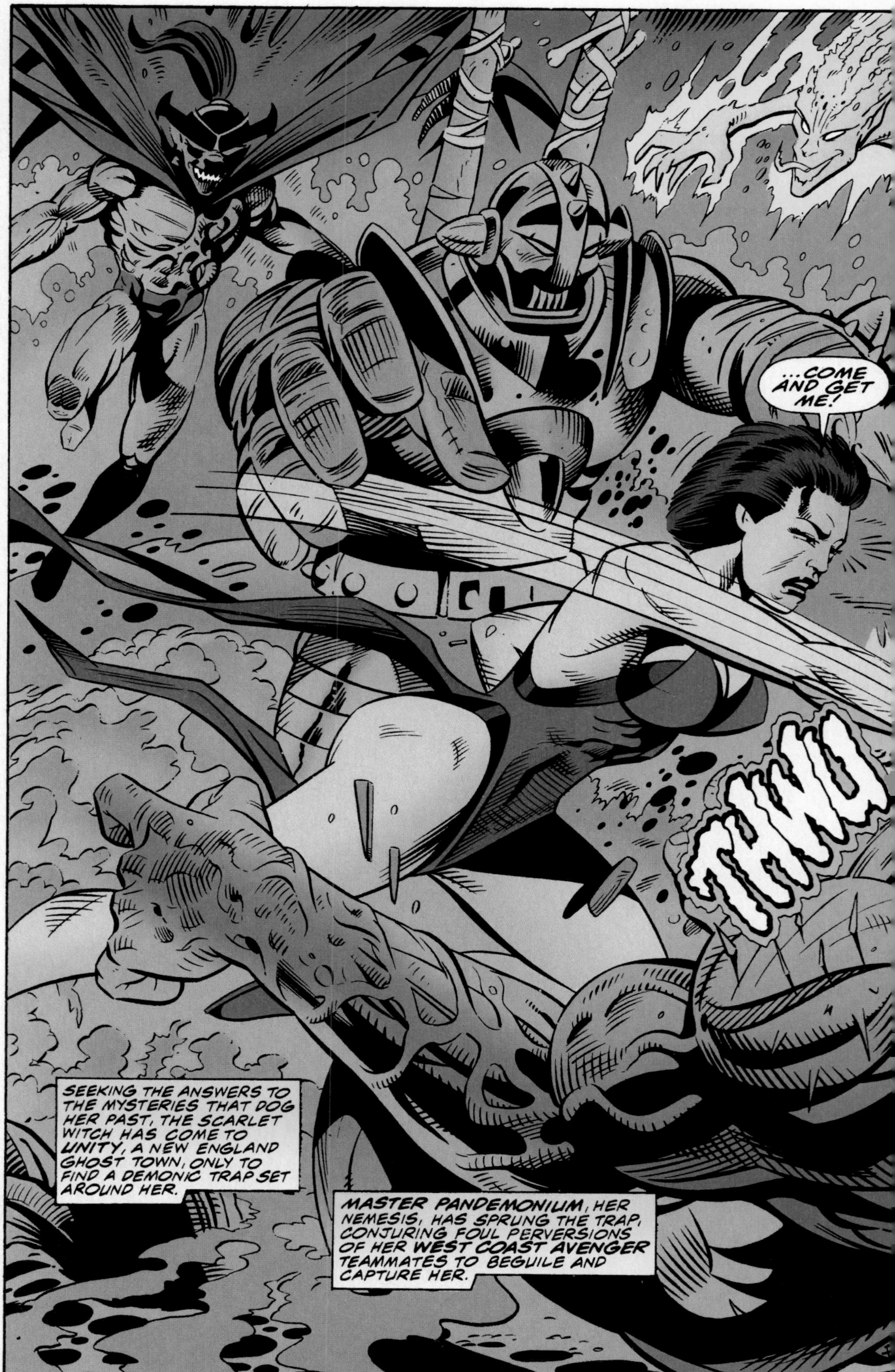
...COME AND GET ME!
THKU
SEEKING THE ANSWERS TO THE MYSTERIES THAT DOG HER PAST, THE SCARLET WITCH HAS COME TO UNITY, A NEW ENGLAND GHOST TOWN, ONLY TO FIND A DEMONIC TRAP SET AROUND HER.
MASTER PANDEMONIUM, HER NEMESIS, HAS SPRUNG THE TRAP, CONJURING FOUL PERVERSIONS OF HER WEST COAST AVENGER TEAMMATES TO BEGUILE AND CAPTURE HER.

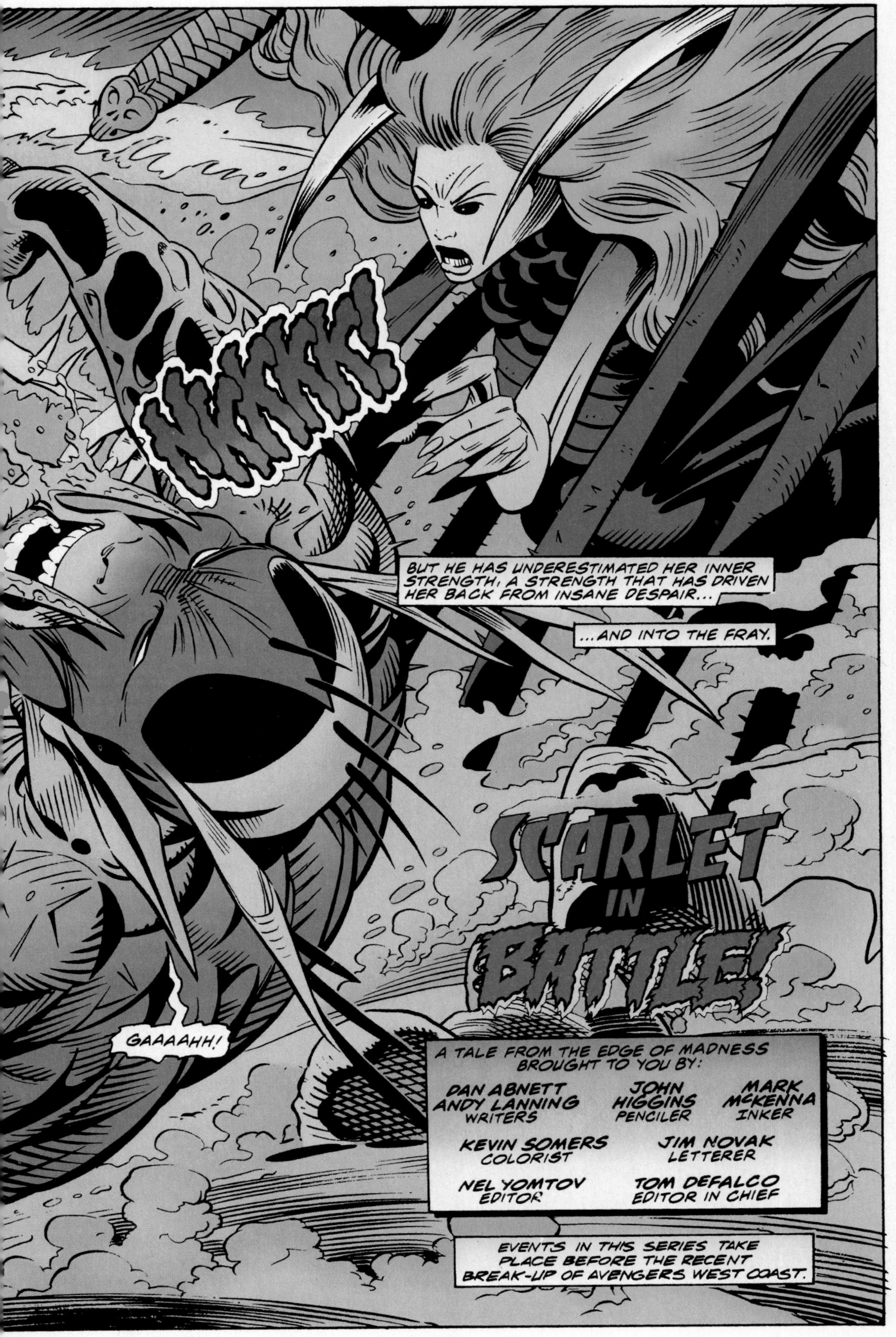
NKAK!
BUT HE HAS UNDERESTIMATED HER INNER STRENGTH, A STRENGTH THAT HAS DRIVEN HER BACK FROM INSANE DESPAIR...
...AND INTO THE FRAY.
SCARLET IN BATTLE!
GAAAAHH!
A TALE FROM THE EDGE OF MADNESS BROUGHT TO YOU BY:
DAN ABNETT ANDY LANNING WRITERS
JOHN HIGGINS PENCILER
MARK McKENNA INKER
KEVIN SOMERS COLORIST
JIM NOVAK LETTERER
NEL YOMTOV EDITOR
TOM DEFALCO EDITOR IN CHIEF
EVENTS IN THIS SERIES TAKE PLACE BEFORE THE RECENT BREAK-UP OF AVENGERS WEST COAST.

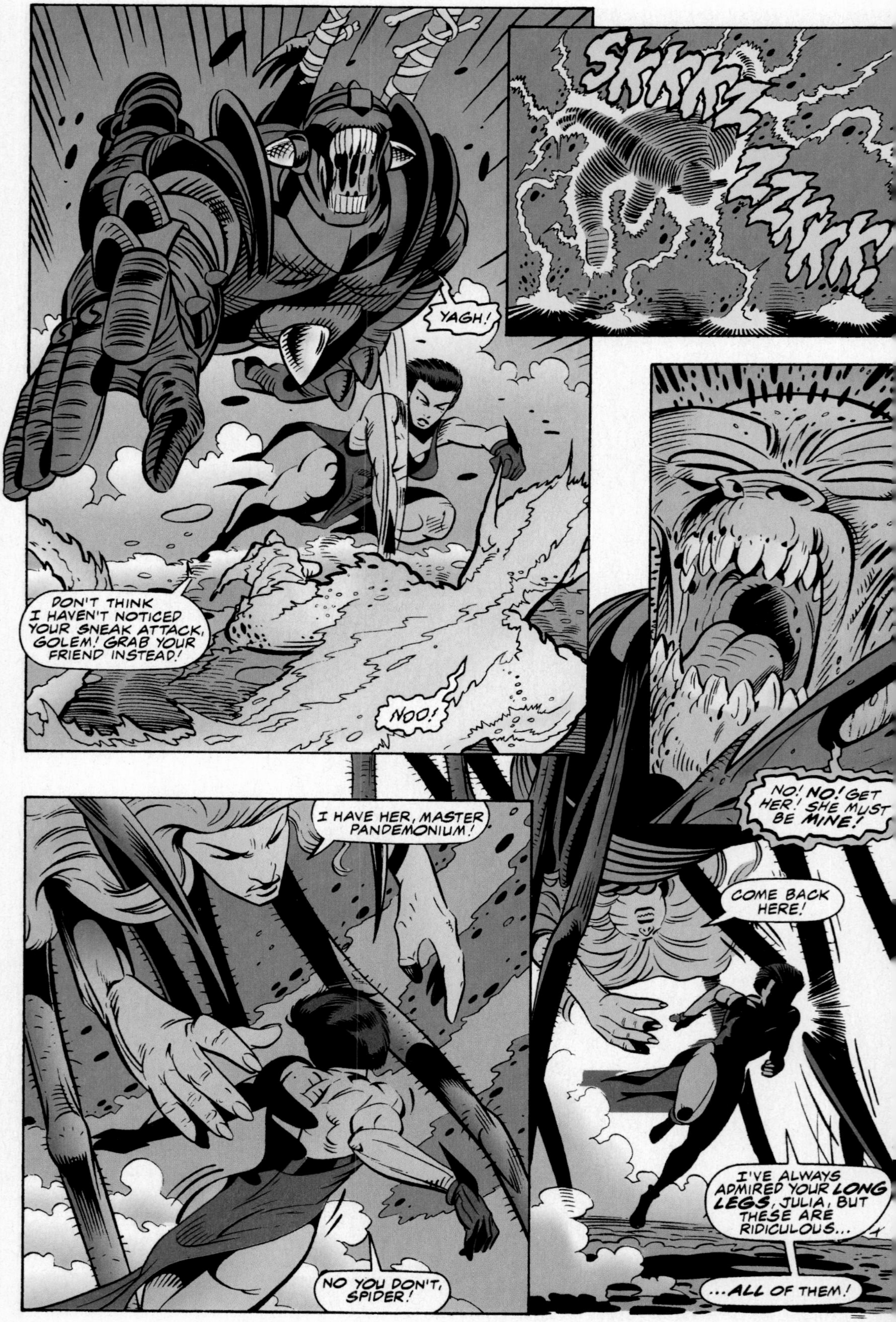
SKKKZZ ZZKKK!
YAGH!
DON'T THINK I HAVEN'T NOTICED YOUR SNEAK ATTACK, GOLEM! GRAB YOUR FRIEND INSTEAD!
NOO!
NO! NO! GET HER! SHE MUST BE MINE!
I HAVE HER, MASTER PANDEMONIUM!
NO YOU DON'T, SPIDER!
COME BACK HERE!
I'VE ALWAYS ADMIRED YOUR LONG LEGS, JULIA, BUT THESE ARE RIDICULOUS...
...ALL OF THEM!

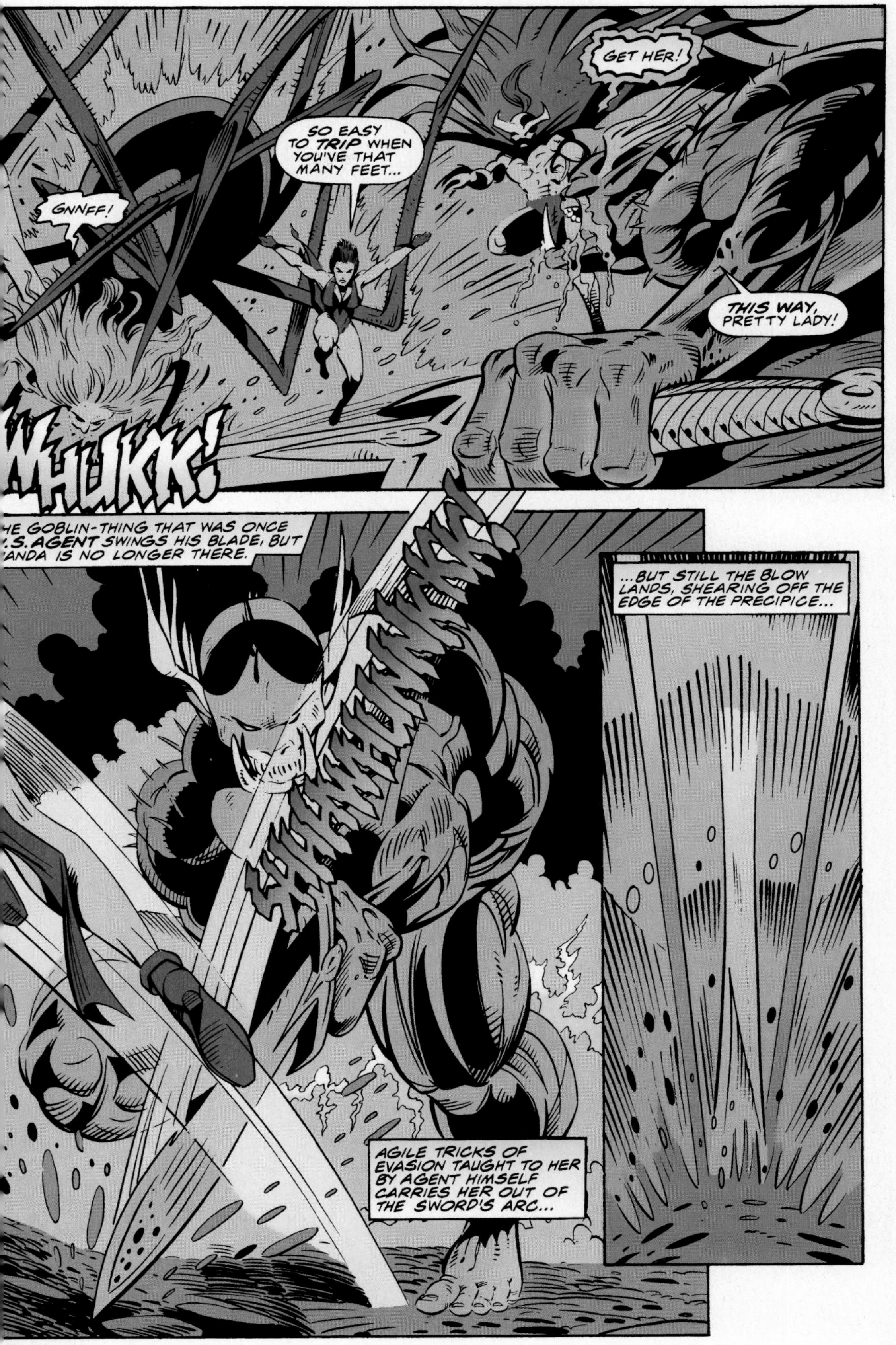
GET HER!
SO EASY TO TRIP WHEN YOU'VE THAT MANY FEET...
GNNFF!
THIS WAY, PRETTY LADY!
WHUKK!
HE GOBLIN-THING THAT WAS ONCE .S. AGENT SWINGS HIS BLADE, BUT ANDA IS NO LONGER THERE.
...BUT STILL THE BLOW LANDS, SHEARING OFF THE EDGE OF THE PRECIPICE...
AGILE TRICKS OF EVASION TAUGHT TO HER BY AGENT HIMSELF CARRIES HER OUT OF THE SWORD'S ARC...

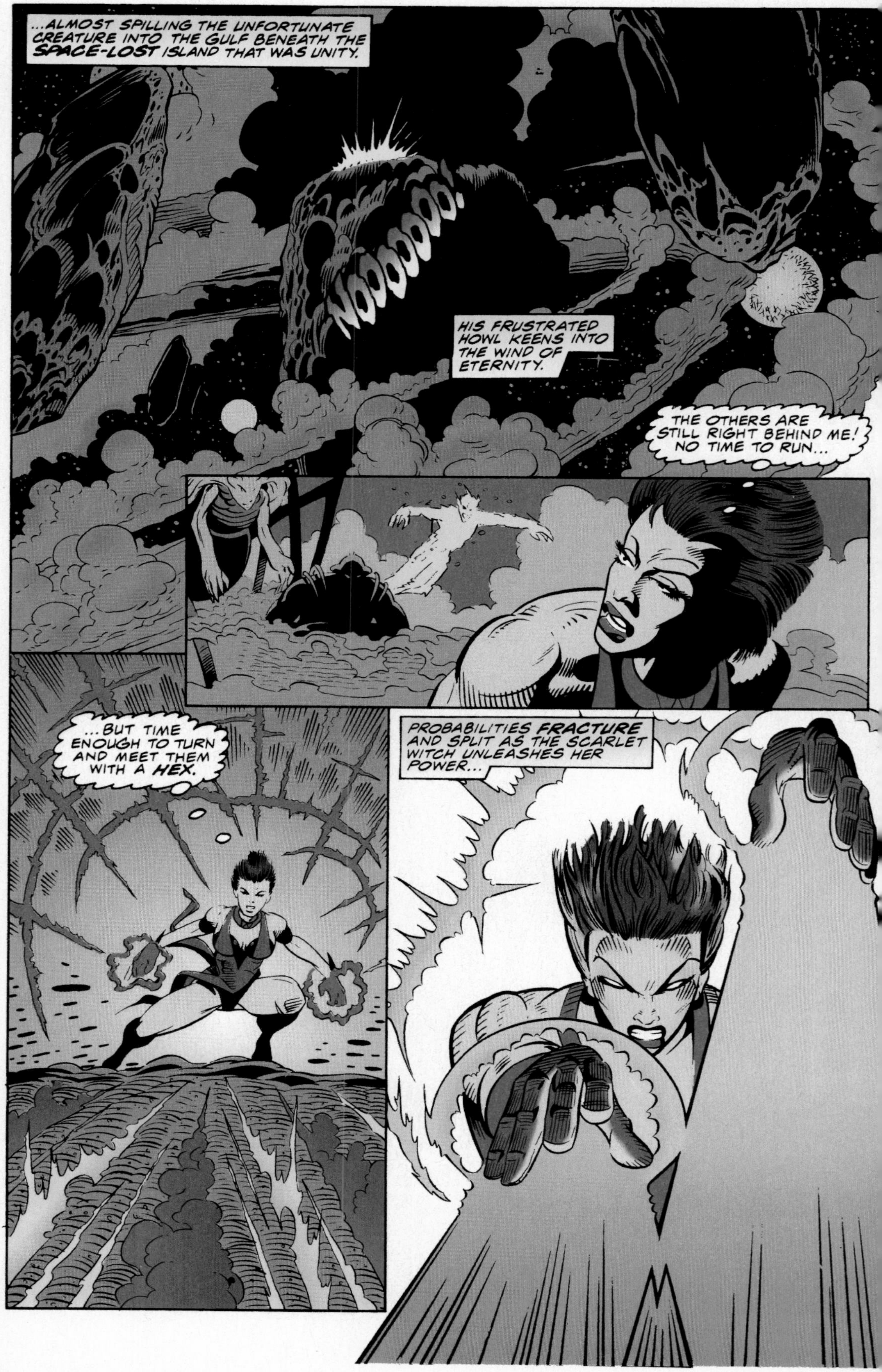

...ALMOST SPILLING THE UNFORTUNATE CREATURE INTO THE GULF BENEATH THE SPACE-LOST ISLAND THAT WAS UNITY.
NOOOOOO!
HIS FRUSTRATED HOWL KEENS INTO THE WIND OF ETERNITY.
THE OTHERS ARE STILL RIGHT BEHIND ME! NO TIME TO RUN...
...BUT TIME ENOUGH TO TURN AND MEET THEM WITH A HEX.
PROBABILITIES FRACTURE AND SPLIT AS THE SCARLET WITCH UNLEASHES HER POWER...

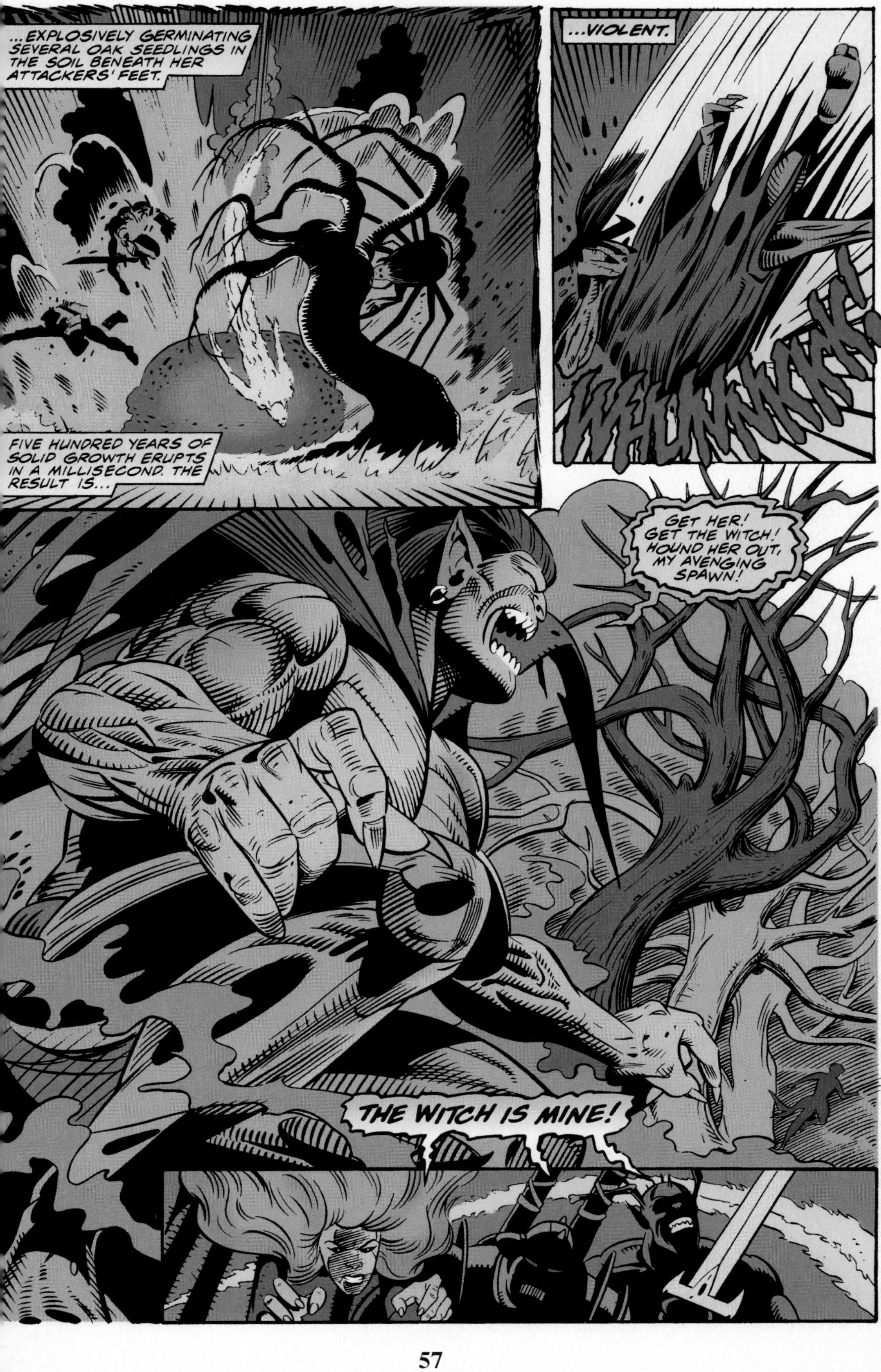
...EXPLOSIVELY GERMINATING SEVERAL OAK SEEDLINGS IN THE SOIL BENEATH HER ATTACKERS' FEET.
FIVE HUNDRED YEARS OF SOLID GROWTH ERUPTS IN A MILLISECOND. THE RESULT IS...
...VIOLENT.
WHAKKKKK!
GET HER! GET THE WITCH! HOUND HER OUT, MY AVENGING SPAWN!
THE WITCH IS MINE!

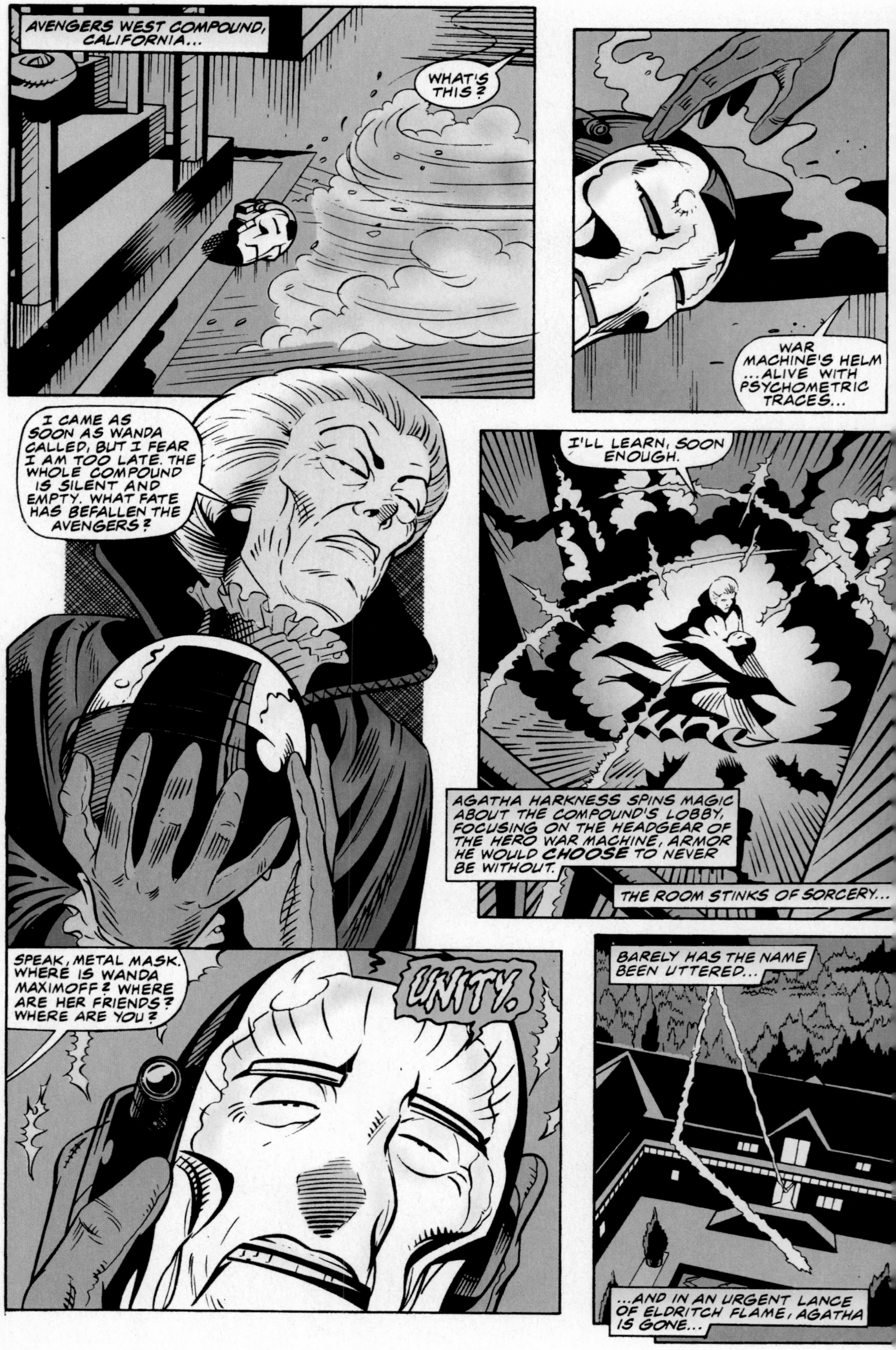
AVENGERS WEST COMPOUND, CALIFORNIA...
WHAT'S THIS?
WAR MACHINE'S HELM ...ALIVE WITH PSYCHOMETRIC TRACES...
I CAME AS SOON AS WANDA CALLED, BUT I FEAR I AM TOO LATE. THE WHOLE COMPOUND IS SILENT AND EMPTY. WHAT FATE HAS BEFALLEN THE AVENGERS?
I'LL LEARN, SOON ENOUGH.
AGATHA HARKNESS SPINS MAGIC ABOUT THE COMPOUND'S LOBBY, FOCUSING ON THE HEADGEAR OF THE HERO WAR MACHINE, ARMOR HE WOULD CHOOSE TO NEVER BE WITHOUT.
THE ROOM STINKS OF SORCERY...
SPEAK, METAL MASK. WHERE IS WANDA MAXIMOFF? WHERE ARE HER FRIENDS? WHERE ARE YOU?
UNITY.
BARELY HAS THE NAME BEEN UTTERED...
...AND IN AN URGENT LANCE OF ELDRITCH FLAME, AGATHA IS GONE...

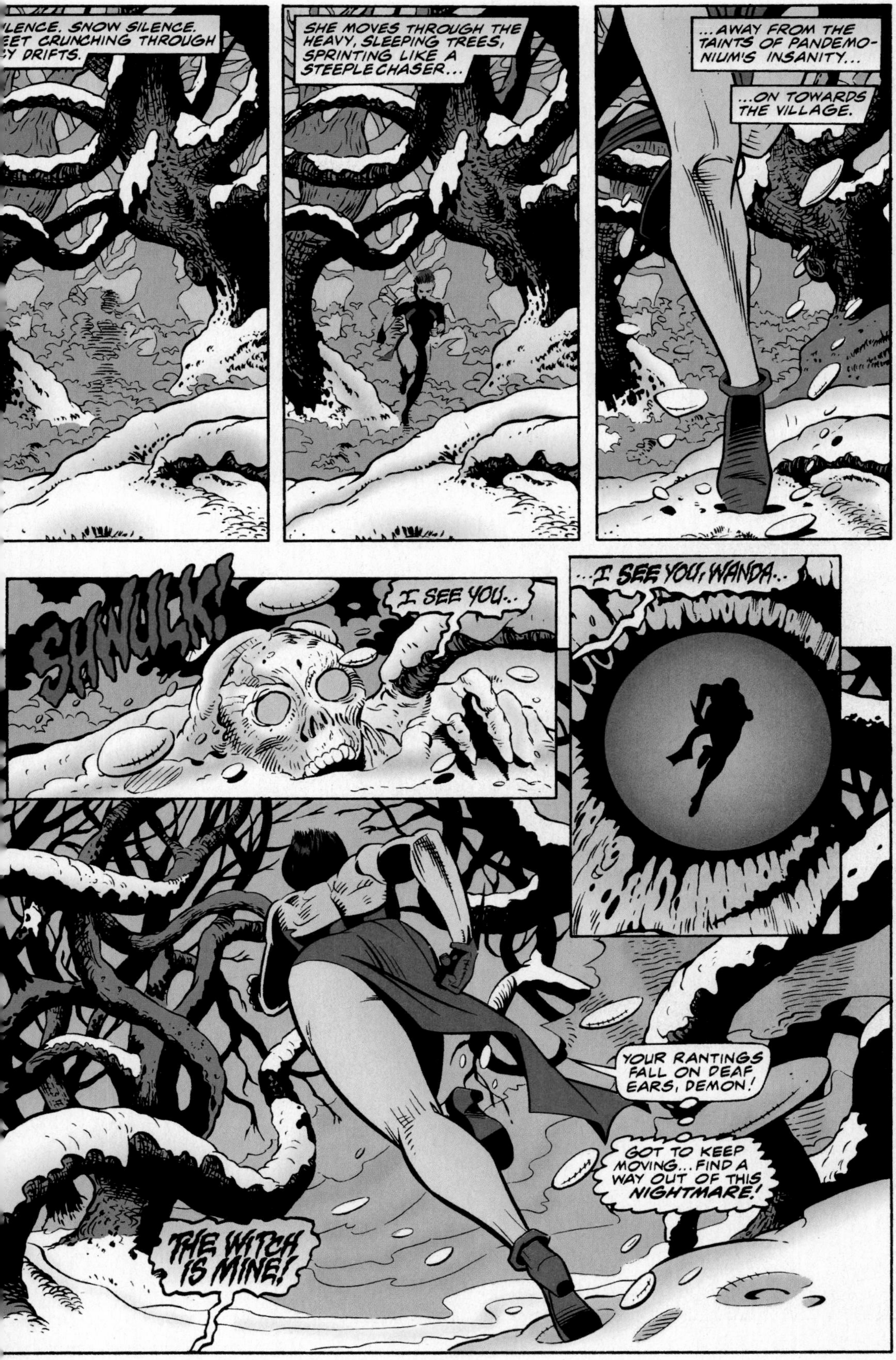

ILENCE. SNOW SILENCE. EET CRUNCHING THROUGH Y DRIFTS.
SHE MOVES THROUGH THE HEAVY, SLEEPING TREES, SPRINTING LIKE A STEEPLECHASER...
...AWAY FROM THE TAINTS OF PANDEMONIUM'S INSANITY...
...ON TOWARDS THE VILLAGE.
SHWULK!
I SEE YOU...
...I SEE YOU, WANDA...
YOUR RANTINGS FALL ON DEAF EARS, DEMON!
GOT TO KEEP MOVING...FIND A WAY OUT OF THIS NIGHTMARE!
THE WITCH IS MINE!

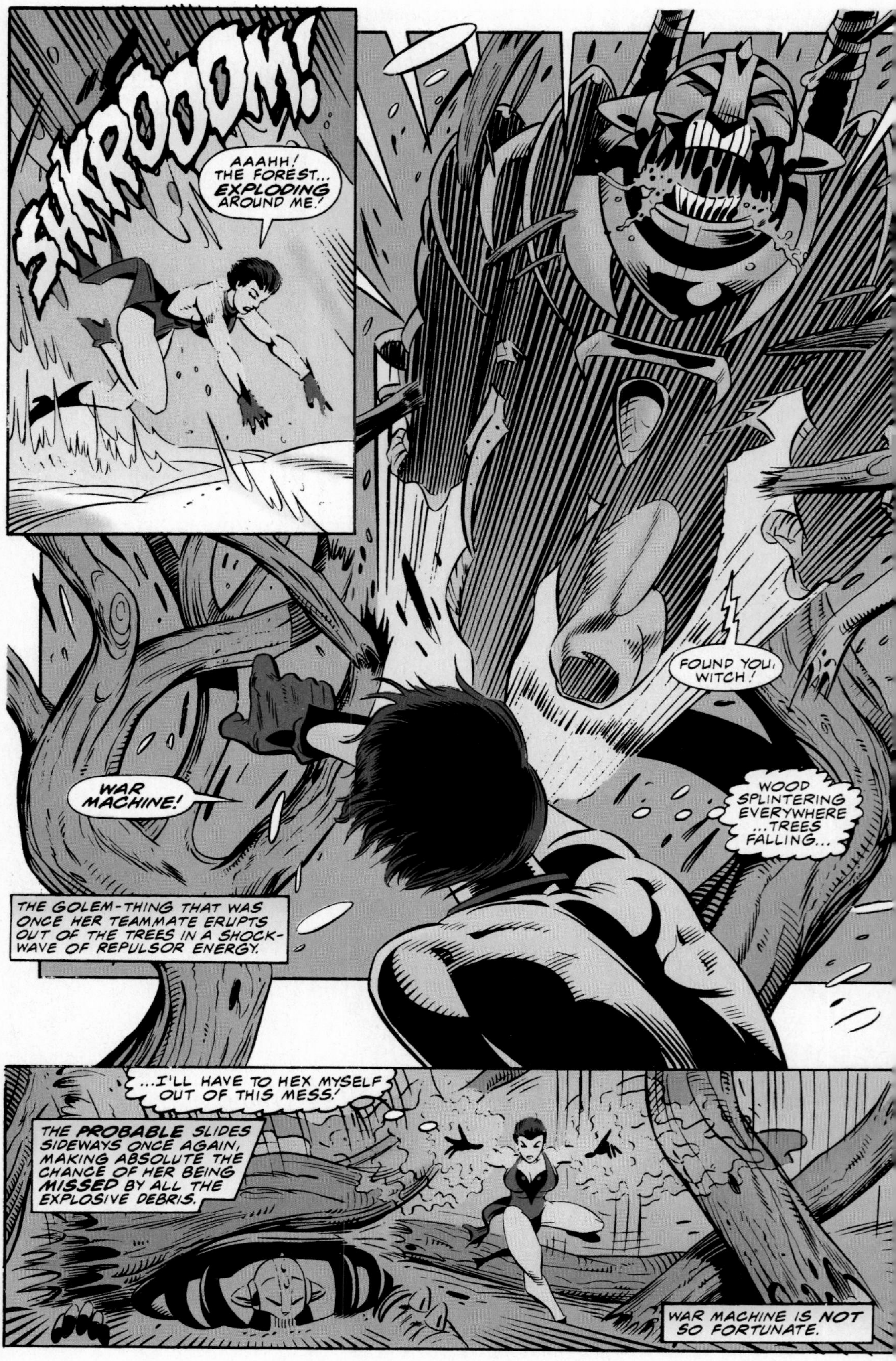
SHROOOM!
AAAHH! THE FOREST... EXPLODING AROUND ME!
FOUND YOU, WITCH!
WAR MACHINE!
WOOD SPLINTERING EVERYWHERE ...TREES FALLING...
THE GOLEM-THING THAT WAS ONCE HER TEAMMATE ERUPTS OUT OF THE TREES IN A SHOCK-WAVE OF REPULSOR ENERGY.
...I'LL HAVE TO HEX MYSELF OUT OF THIS MESS!
THE PROBABLE SLIDES SIDEWAYS ONCE AGAIN, MAKING ABSOLUTE THE CHANCE OF HER BEING MISSED BY ALL THE EXPLOSIVE DEBRIS.
WAR MACHINE IS NOT SO FORTUNATE.

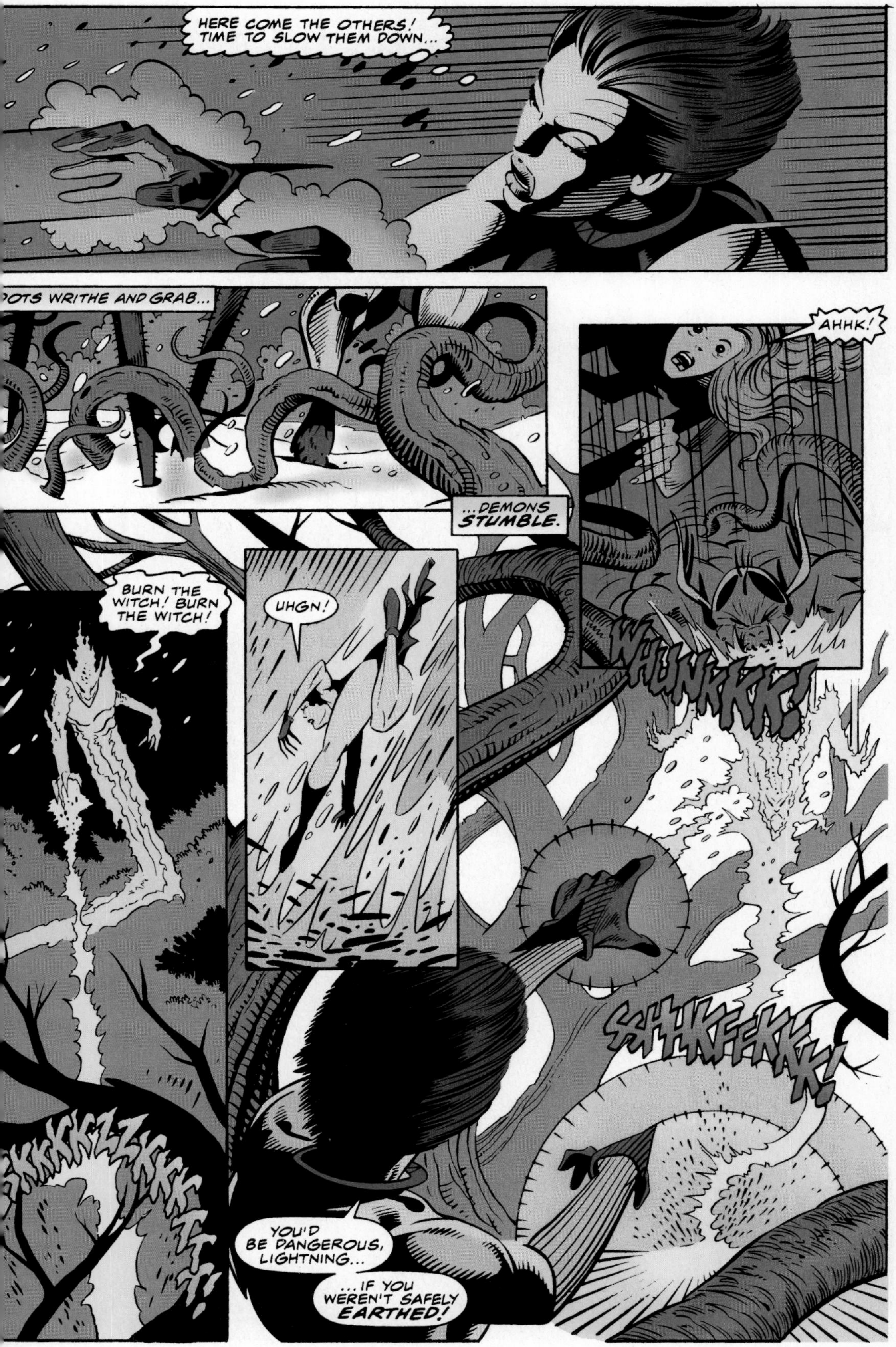
HERE COME THE OTHERS! TIME TO SLOW THEM DOWN...
...OOTS WRITHE AND GRAB...
AHHK!
...DEMONS STUMBLE.
BURN THE WITCH! BURN THE WITCH!
UHGN!
WHUNKKK!
SHHKFFKKK!
SKKKKZZZKKKTT!
YOU'D BE DANGEROUS, LIGHTNING...
...IF YOU WEREN'T SAFELY EARTHED!

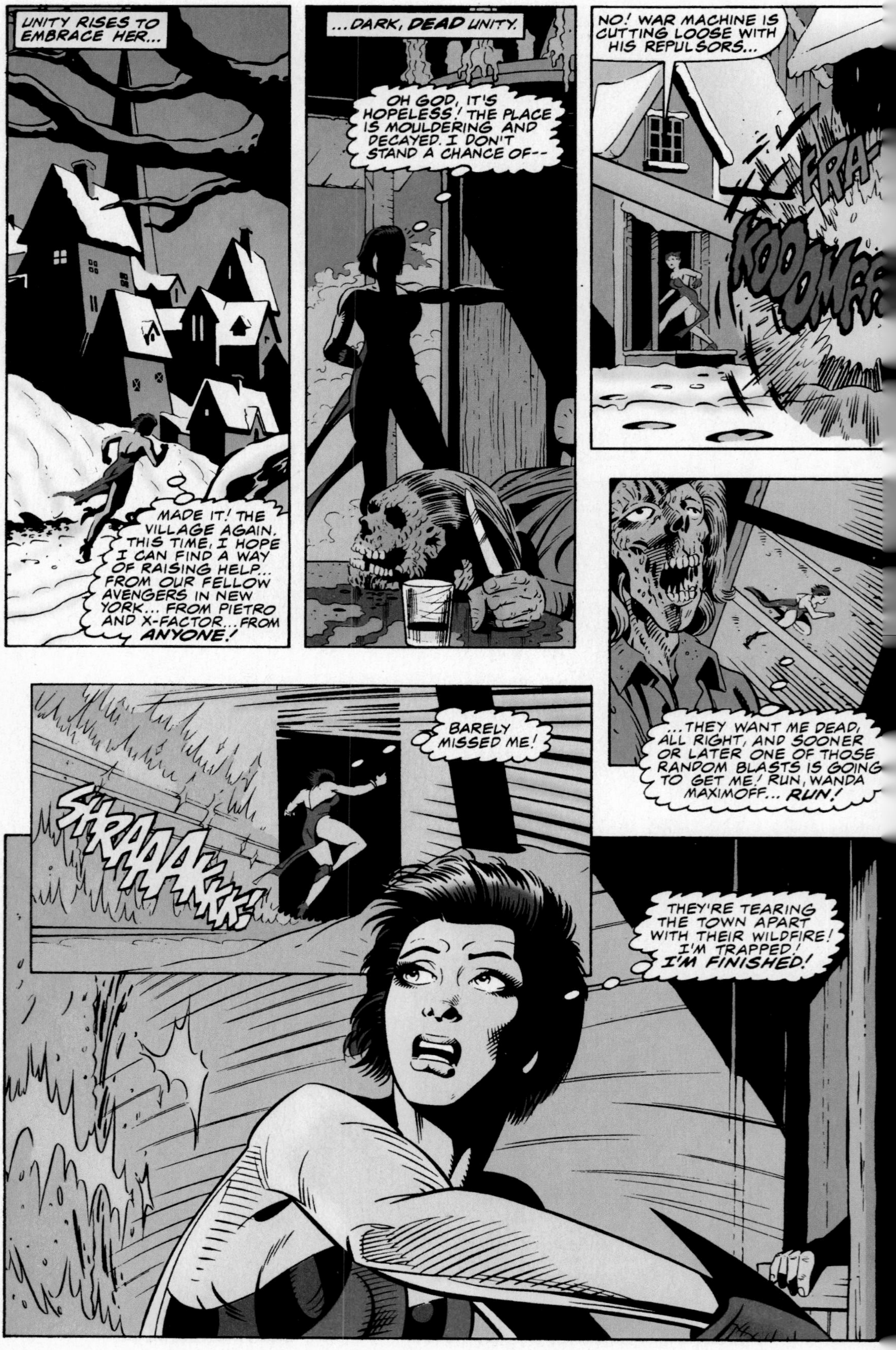
UNITY RISES TO EMBRACE HER...
MADE IT! THE VILLAGE AGAIN. THIS TIME, I HOPE I CAN FIND A WAY OF RAISING HELP... FROM OUR FELLOW AVENGERS IN NEW YORK... FROM PIETRO AND X-FACTOR... FROM ANYONE!
...DARK, DEAD UNITY.
OH GOD, IT'S HOPELESS! THE PLACE IS MOULDERING AND DECAYED. I DON'T STAND A CHANCE OF--
NO! WAR MACHINE IS CUTTING LOOSE WITH HIS REPULSORS...
FRA-KOOOMFF
...THEY WANT ME DEAD, ALL RIGHT, AND SOONER OR LATER ONE OF THOSE RANDOM BLASTS IS GOING TO GET ME! RUN, WANDA MAXIMOFF... RUN!
BARELY MISSED ME!
SHRAAAKKK!
THEY'RE TEARING THE TOWN APART WITH THEIR WILDFIRE! I'M TRAPPED! I'M FINISHED!

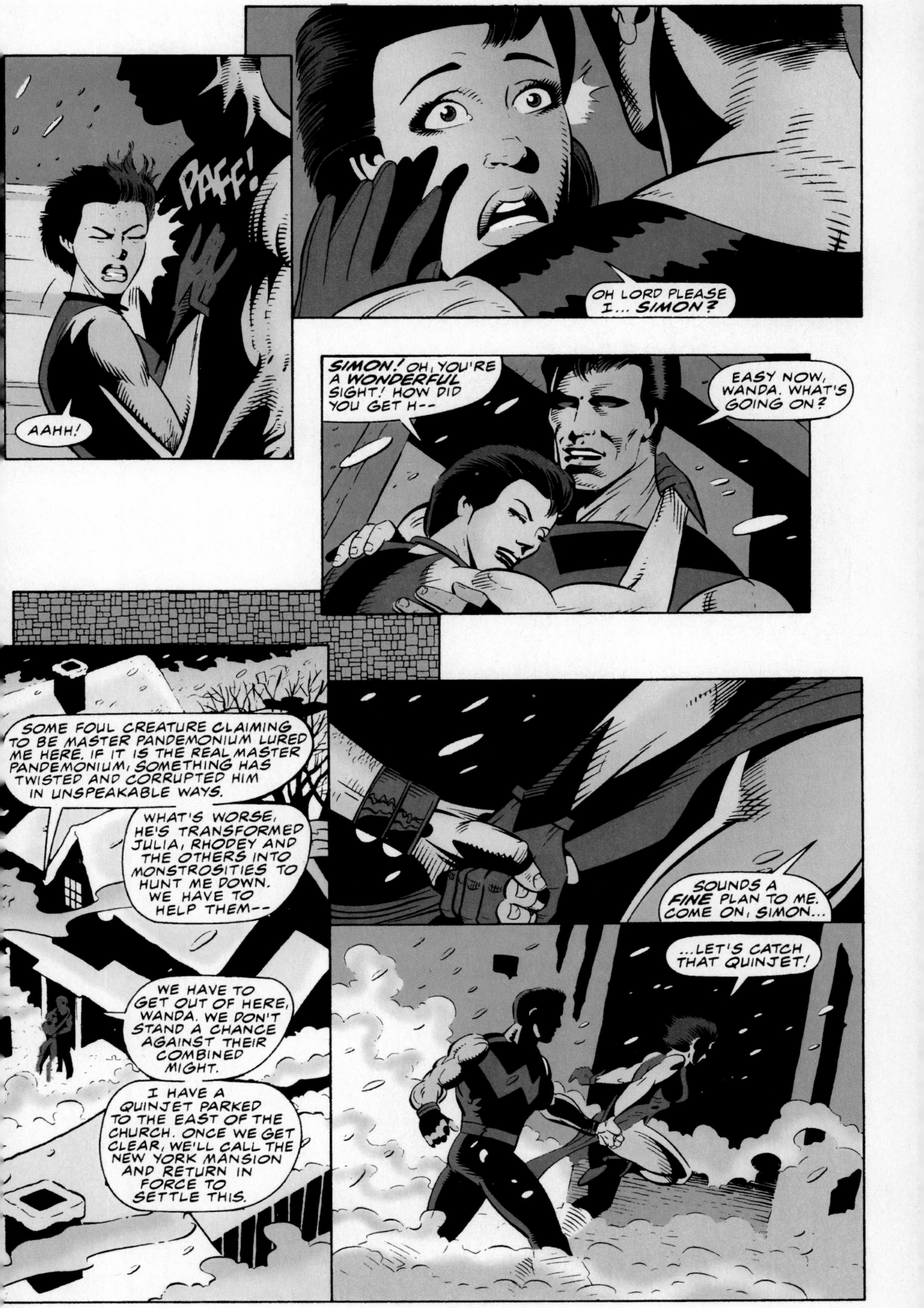
PAFF!
AAHH!
OH LORD PLEASE I... SIMON?
SIMON! OH, YOU'RE A WONDERFUL SIGHT! HOW DID YOU GET H--
EASY NOW, WANDA. WHAT'S GOING ON?
SOME FOUL CREATURE CLAIMING TO BE MASTER PANDEMONIUM LURED ME HERE. IF IT IS THE REAL MASTER PANDEMONIUM, SOMETHING HAS TWISTED AND CORRUPTED HIM IN UNSPEAKABLE WAYS.
WHAT'S WORSE, HE'S TRANSFORMED JULIA, RHODEY AND THE OTHERS INTO MONSTROSITIES TO HUNT ME DOWN. WE HAVE TO HELP THEM--
WE HAVE TO GET OUT OF HERE, WANDA. WE DON'T STAND A CHANCE AGAINST THEIR COMBINED MIGHT.
I HAVE A QUINJET PARKED TO THE EAST OF THE CHURCH. ONCE WE GET CLEAR, WE'LL CALL THE NEW YORK MANSION AND RETURN IN FORCE TO SETTLE THIS.
SOUNDS A FINE PLAN TO ME. COME ON, SIMON...
...LET'S CATCH THAT QUINJET!

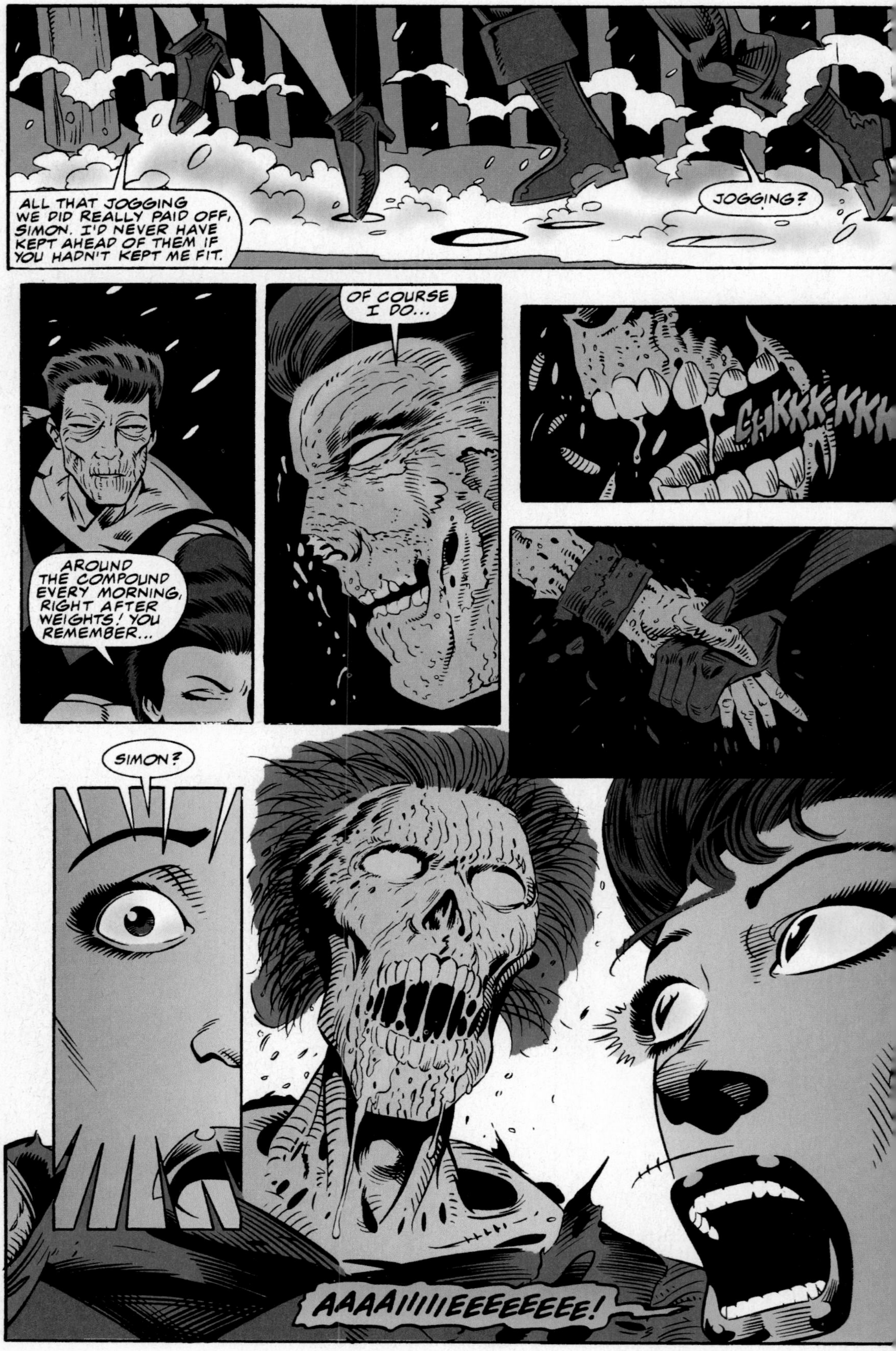
ALL THAT JOGGING WE DID REALLY PAID OFF, SIMON. I'D NEVER HAVE KEPT AHEAD OF THEM IF YOU HADN'T KEPT ME FIT.
JOGGING?
AROUND THE COMPOUND EVERY MORNING, RIGHT AFTER WEIGHTS! YOU REMEMBER...
OF COURSE I DO...
CHKKK-KKK
SIMON?
AAAAIIIIIIEEEEEEEE!

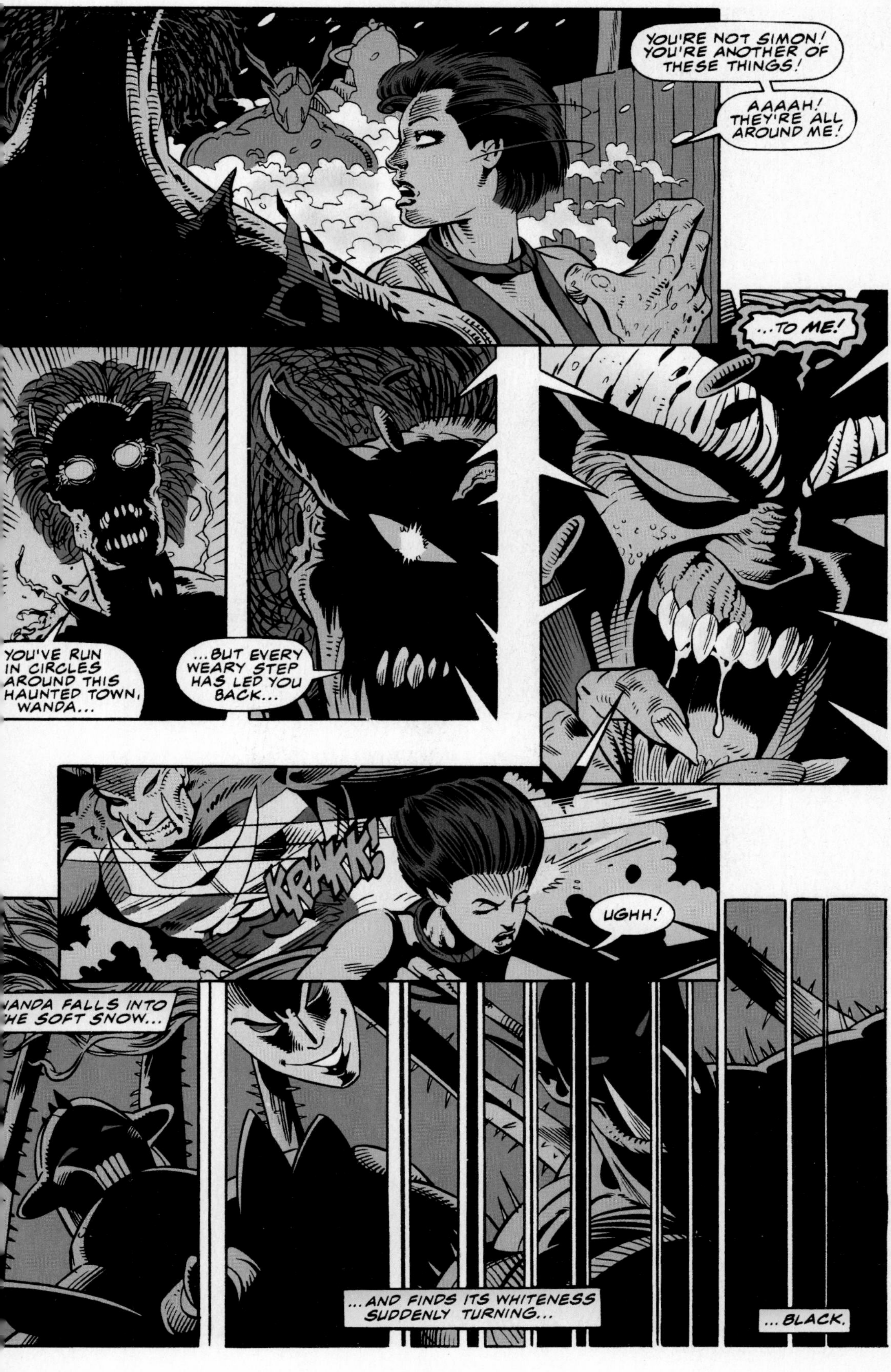
YOU'RE NOT SIMON! YOU'RE ANOTHER OF THESE THINGS!
AAAAH! THEY'RE ALL AROUND ME!
YOU'VE RUN IN CIRCLES AROUND THIS HAUNTED TOWN, WANDA...
...BUT EVERY WEARY STEP HAS LED YOU BACK...
...TO ME!
KRAKK!
UGHH!
WANDA FALLS INTO THE SOFT SNOW...
...AND FINDS ITS WHITENESS SUDDENLY TURNING...
...BLACK.

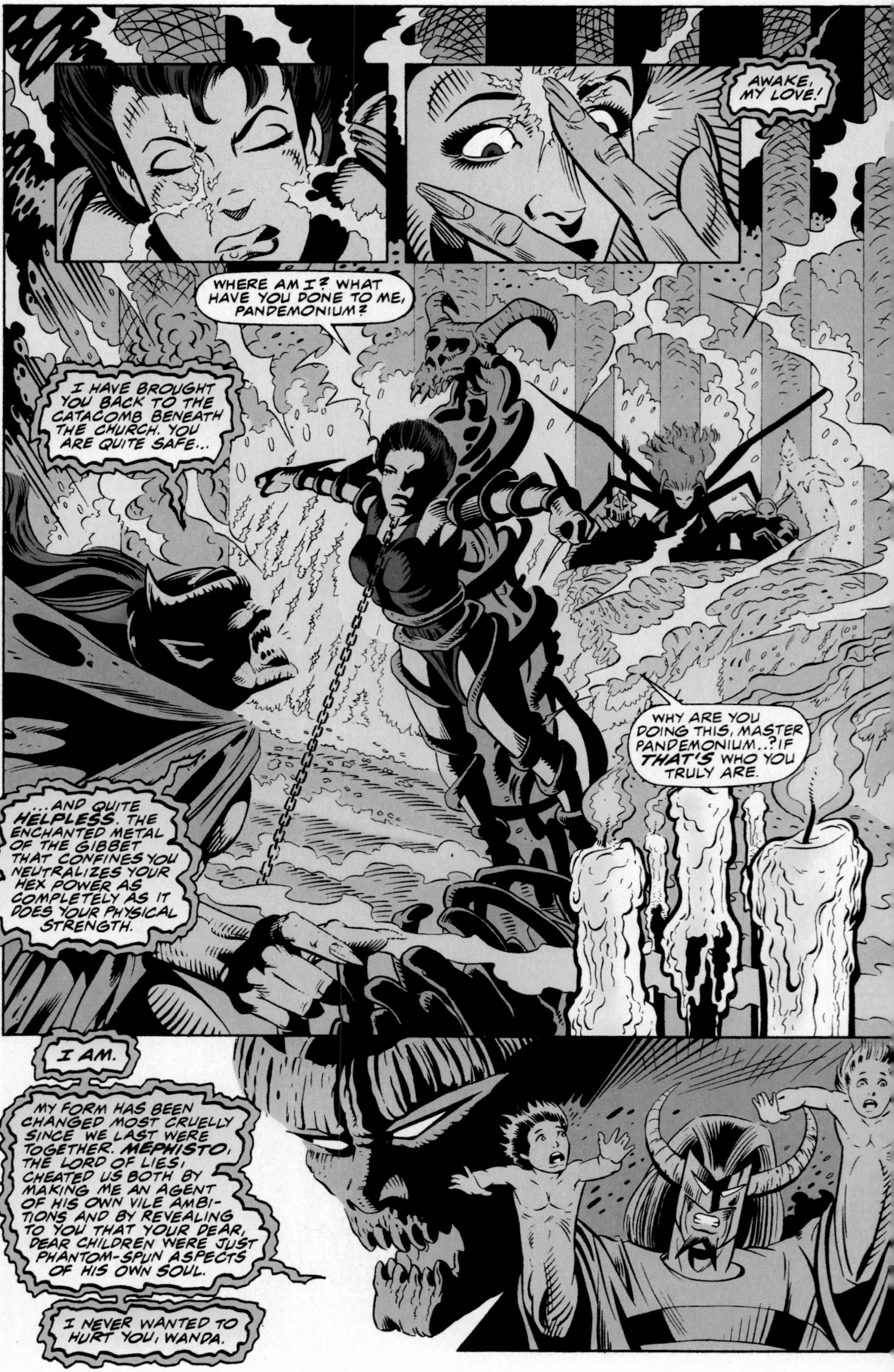
AWAKE, MY LOVE!
WHERE AM I? WHAT HAVE YOU DONE TO ME, PANDEMONIUM?
I HAVE BROUGHT YOU BACK TO THE CATACOMB BENEATH THE CHURCH. YOU ARE QUITE SAFE...
WHY ARE YOU DOING THIS, MASTER PANDEMONIUM...? IF THAT'S WHO YOU TRULY ARE.
...AND QUITE HELPLESS. THE ENCHANTED METAL OF THE GIBBET THAT CONFINES YOU NEUTRALIZES YOUR HEX POWER AS COMPLETELY AS IT DOES YOUR PHYSICAL STRENGTH.
I AM.
MY FORM HAS BEEN CHANGED MOST CRUELLY SINCE WE LAST WERE TOGETHER. MEPHISTO, THE LORD OF LIES, CHEATED US BOTH BY MAKING ME AN AGENT OF HIS OWN VILE AMBITIONS AND BY REVEALING TO YOU THAT YOUR DEAR, DEAR CHILDREN WERE JUST PHANTOM-SPUN ASPECTS OF HIS OWN SOUL.
I NEVER WANTED TO HURT YOU, WANDA.

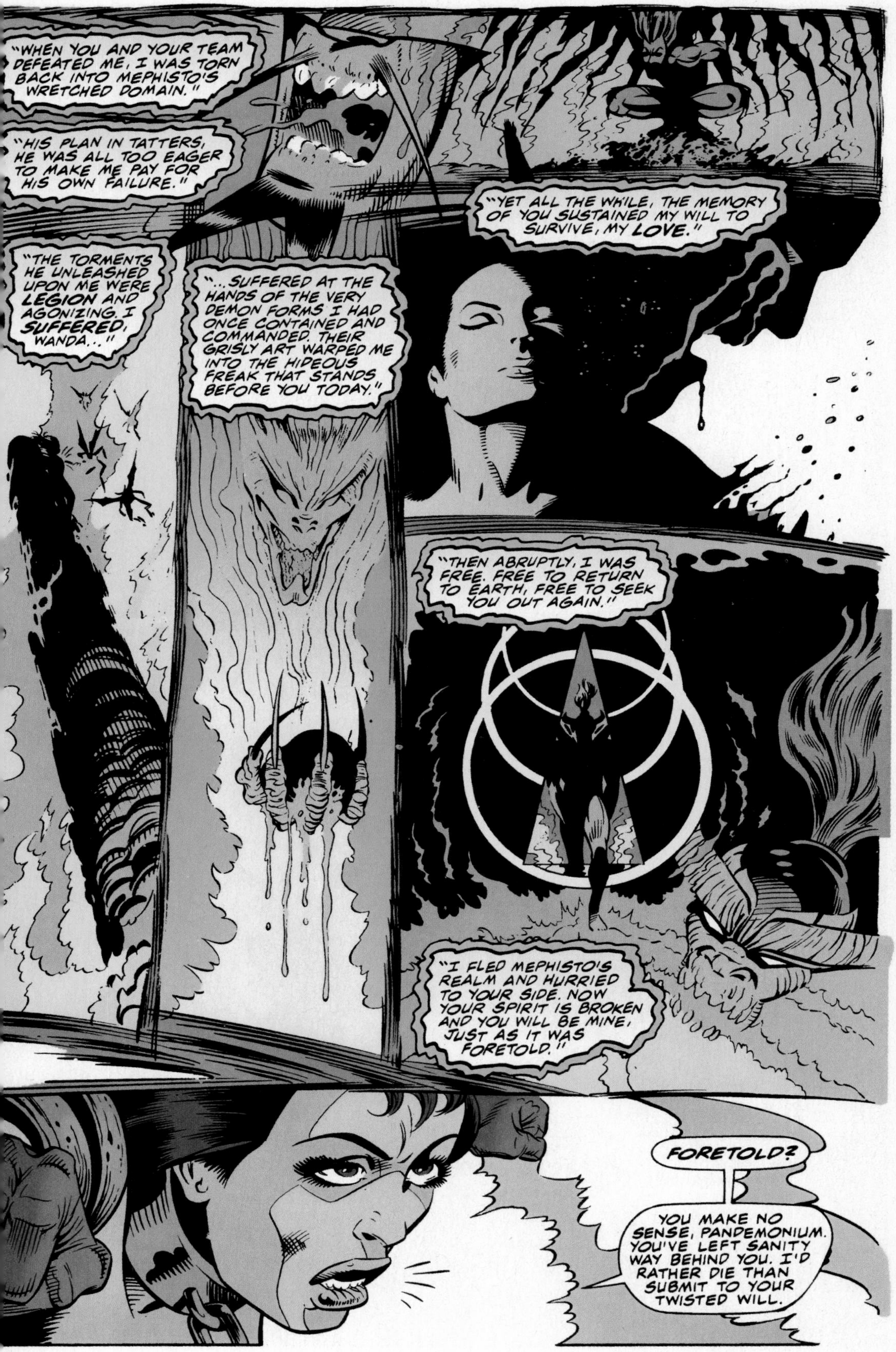
"WHEN YOU AND YOUR TEAM DEFEATED ME, I WAS TORN BACK INTO MEPHISTO'S WRETCHED DOMAIN."
"HIS PLAN IN TATTERS, HE WAS ALL TOO EAGER TO MAKE ME PAY FOR HIS OWN FAILURE."
"YET ALL THE WHILE, THE MEMORY OF YOU SUSTAINED MY WILL TO SURVIVE, MY LOVE."
"THE TORMENTS HE UNLEASHED UPON ME WERE LEGION AND AGONIZING. I SUFFERED, WANDA..."
"...SUFFERED AT THE HANDS OF THE VERY DEMON FORMS I HAD ONCE CONTAINED AND COMMANDED. THEIR GRISLY ART WARPED ME INTO THE HIDEOUS FREAK THAT STANDS BEFORE YOU TODAY."
"THEN ABRUPTLY, I WAS FREE. FREE TO RETURN TO EARTH, FREE TO SEEK YOU OUT AGAIN."
"I FLED MEPHISTO'S REALM AND HURRIED TO YOUR SIDE. NOW YOUR SPIRIT IS BROKEN AND YOU WILL BE MINE, JUST AS IT WAS FORETOLD."
FORETOLD?
YOU MAKE NO SENSE, PANDEMONIUM. YOU'VE LEFT SANITY WAY BEHIND YOU. I'D RATHER DIE THAN SUBMIT TO YOUR TWISTED WILL.

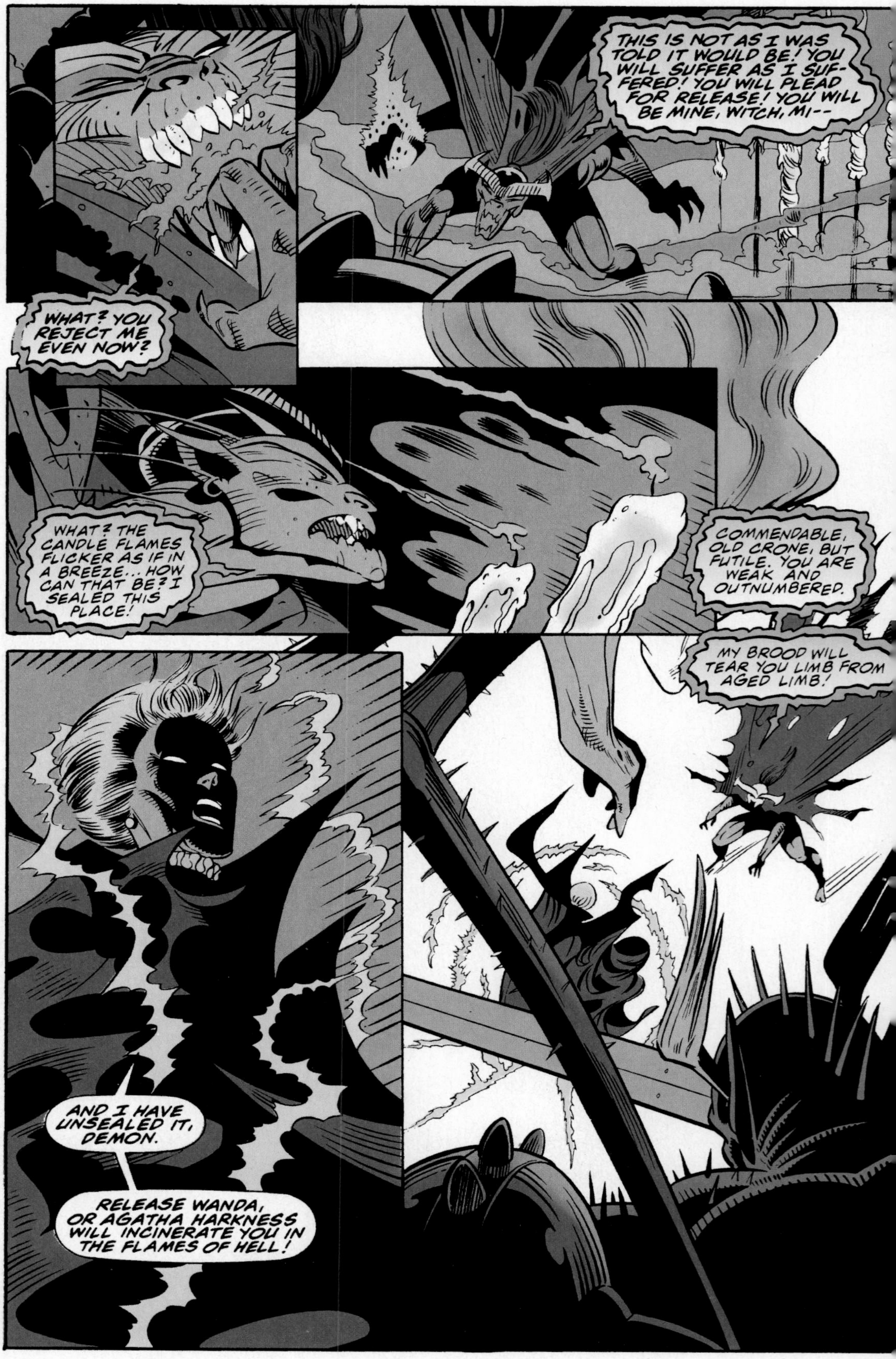
THIS IS NOT AS I WAS TOLD IT WOULD BE! YOU WILL SUFFER AS I SUFFERED! YOU WILL PLEAD FOR RELEASE! YOU WILL BE MINE, WITCH, MI--
WHAT? YOU REJECT ME EVEN NOW?
WHAT? THE CANDLE FLAMES FLICKER AS IF IN A BREEZE... HOW CAN THAT BE? I SEALED THIS PLACE!
COMMENDABLE, OLD CRONE, BUT FUTILE. YOU ARE WEAK AND OUTNUMBERED.
MY BROOD WILL TEAR YOU LIMB FROM AGED LIMB!
AND I HAVE UNSEALED IT, DEMON.
RELEASE WANDA, OR AGATHA HARKNESS WILL INCINERATE YOU IN THE FLAMES OF HELL!

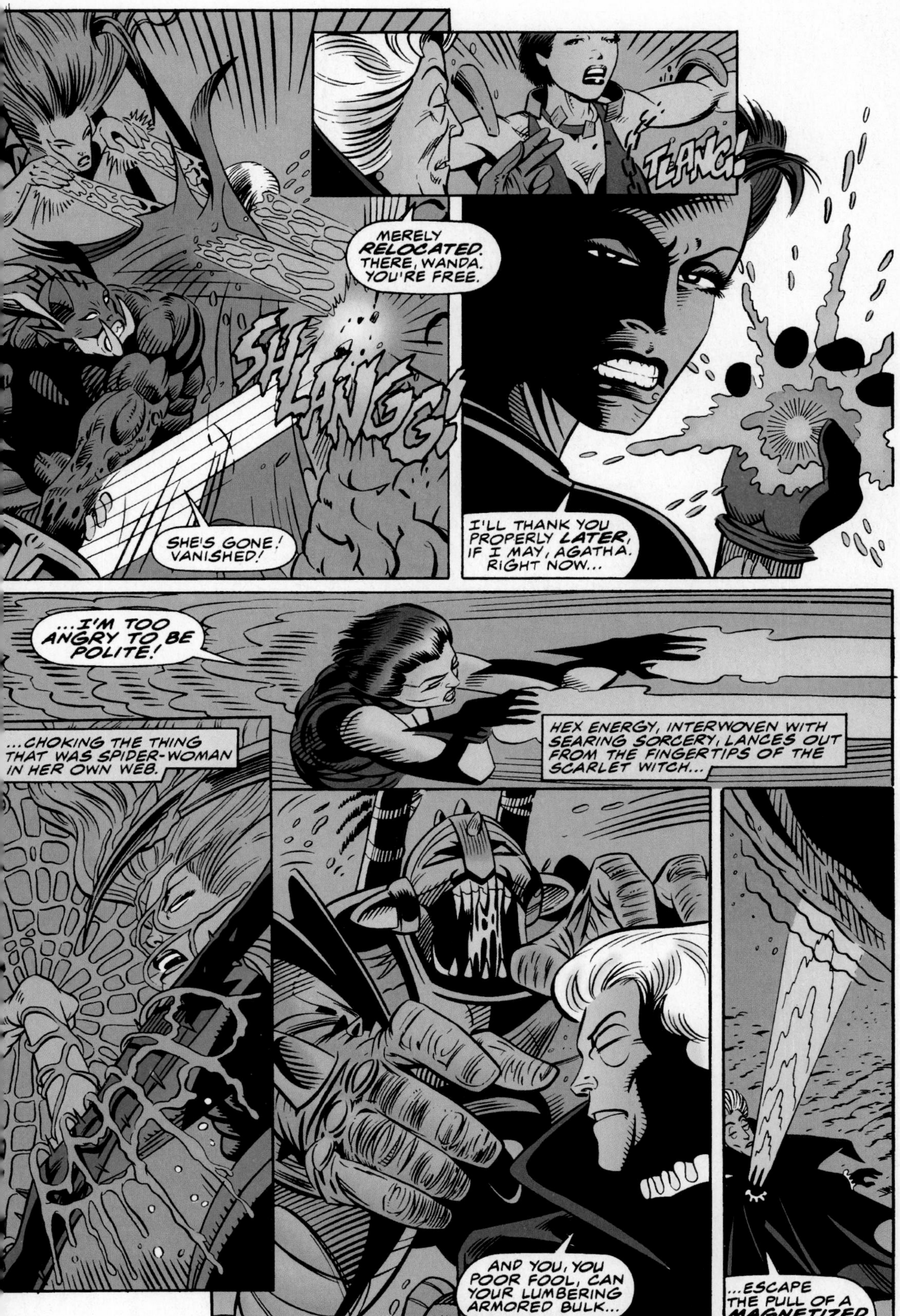

TLANG!
MERELY RELOCATED. THERE, WANDA. YOU'RE FREE.
SHLANGG!
SHE'S GONE! VANISHED!
I'LL THANK YOU PROPERLY LATER, IF I MAY, AGATHA. RIGHT NOW...
...I'M TOO ANGRY TO BE POLITE!
HEX ENERGY, INTERWOVEN WITH SEARING SORCERY, LANCES OUT FROM THE FINGERTIPS OF THE SCARLET WITCH...
...CHOKING THE THING THAT WAS SPIDER-WOMAN IN HER OWN WEB.
AND YOU, YOU POOR FOOL, CAN YOUR LUMBERING ARMORED BULK...
...ESCAPE THE PULL OF A MAGNETIZED SECTION OF CAVERN WALL?

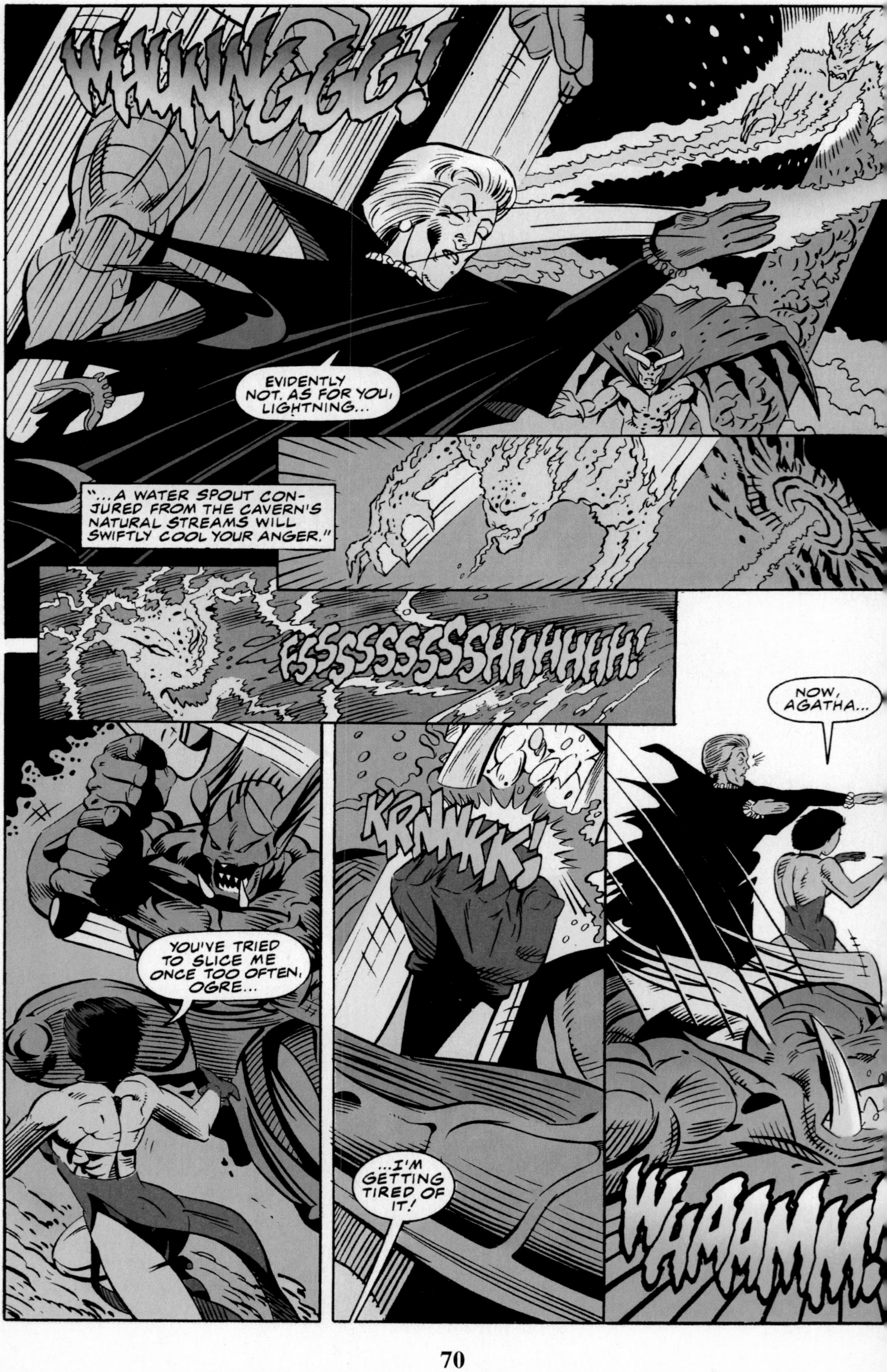
WHUNGGG!
EVIDENTLY NOT. AS FOR YOU, LIGHTNING...
"...A WATER SPOUT CONJURED FROM THE CAVERN'S NATURAL STREAMS WILL SWIFTLY COOL YOUR ANGER."
FSSSSSSSSSHHHHHH!
NOW, AGATHA...
YOU'VE TRIED TO SLICE ME ONCE TOO OFTEN, OGRE...
KRNKK!
...I'M GETTING TIRED OF IT!
WHAMM!

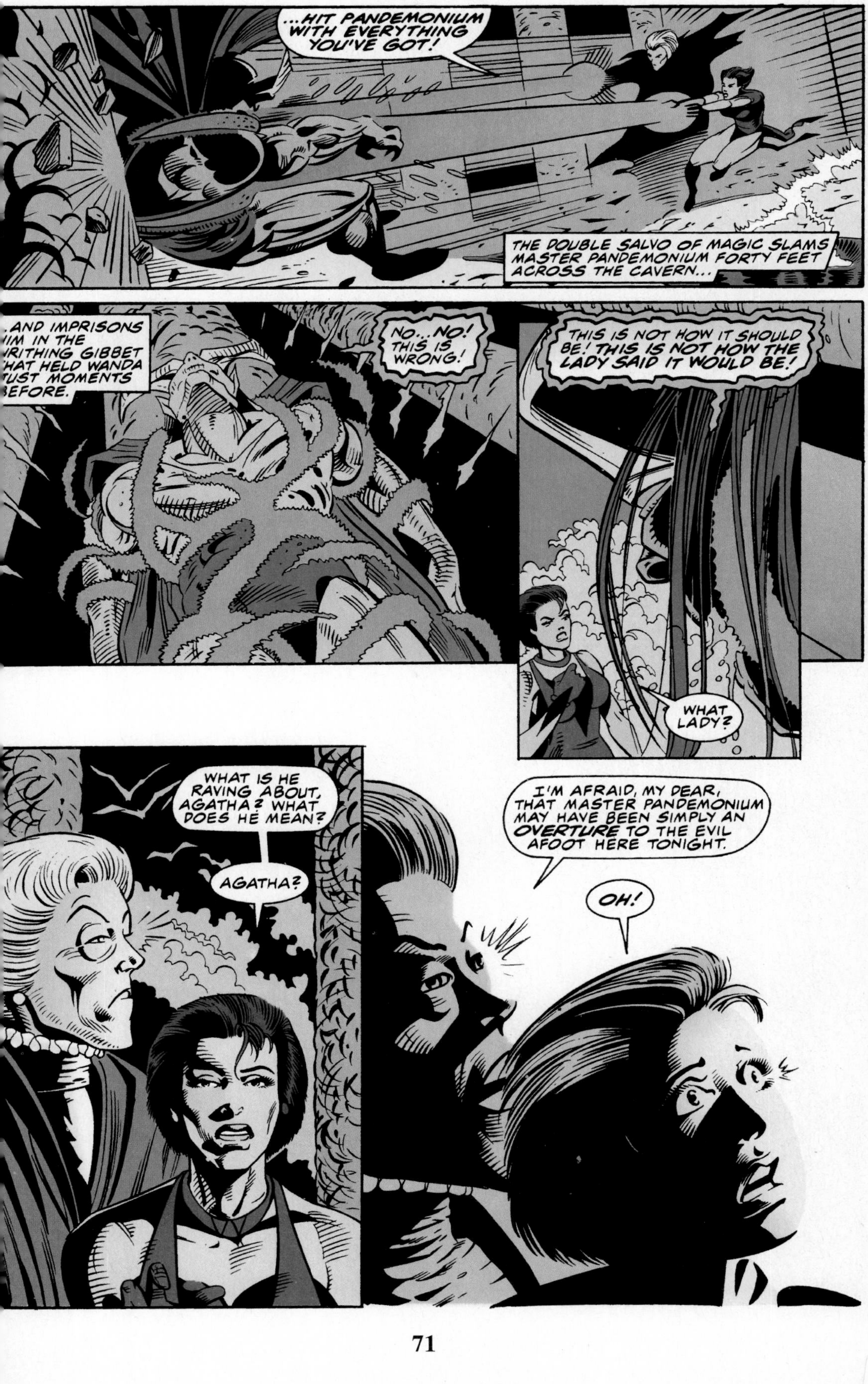
...HIT PANDEMONIUM WITH EVERYTHING YOU'VE GOT!
THE DOUBLE SALVO OF MAGIC SLAMS MASTER PANDEMONIUM FORTY FEET ACROSS THE CAVERN...
...AND IMPRISONS HIM IN THE WRITHING GIBBET THAT HELD WANDA JUST MOMENTS BEFORE.
NO...NO! THIS IS WRONG!
THIS IS NOT HOW IT SHOULD BE! THIS IS NOT HOW THE LADY SAID IT WOULD BE!
WHAT LADY?
WHAT IS HE RAVING ABOUT, AGATHA? WHAT DOES HE MEAN?
AGATHA?
I'M AFRAID, MY DEAR, THAT MASTER PANDEMONIUM MAY HAVE BEEN SIMPLY AN OVERTURE TO THE EVIL AFOOT HERE TONIGHT.
OH!

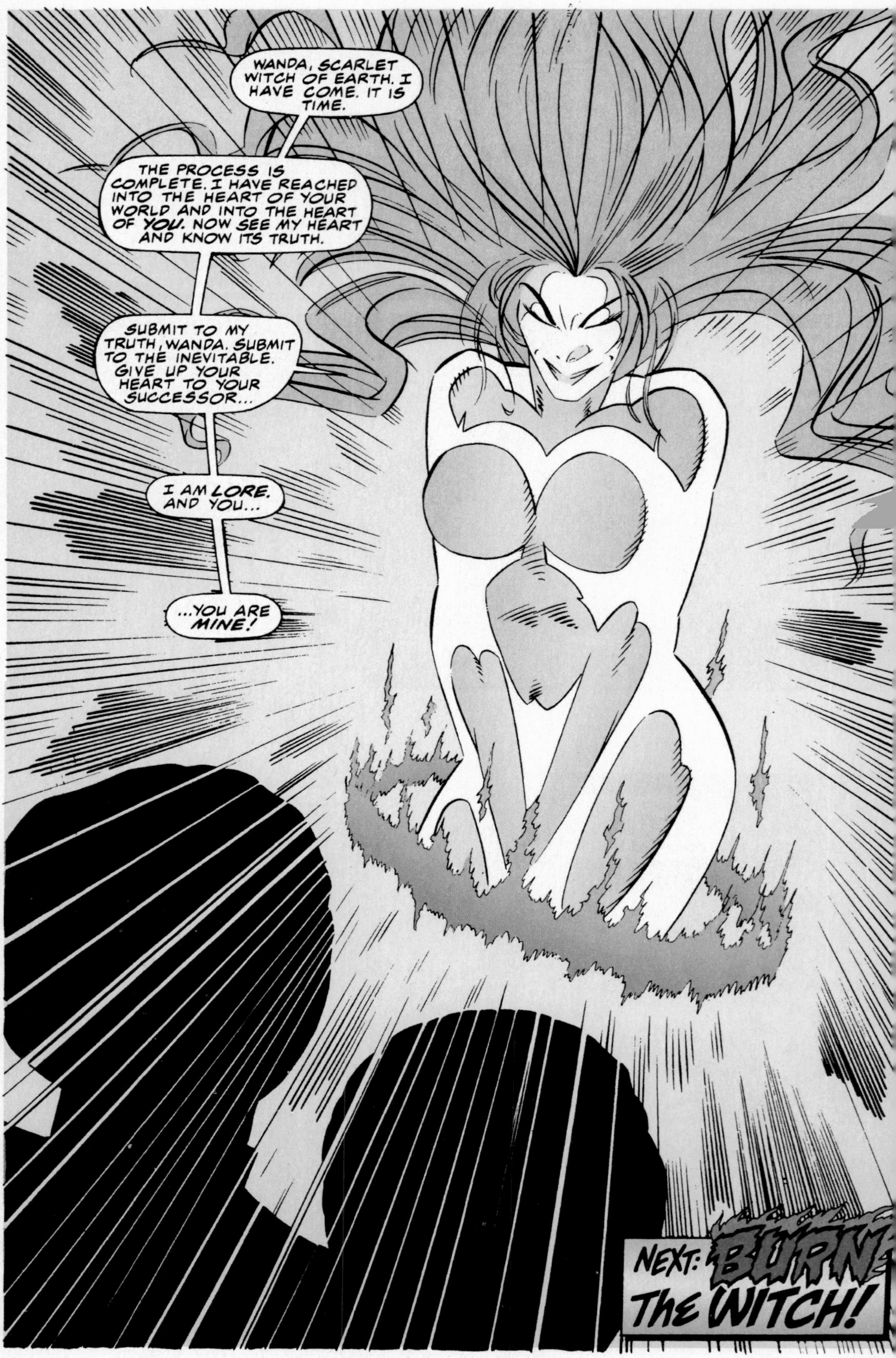
WANDA, SCARLET WITCH OF EARTH. I HAVE COME. IT IS TIME.
THE PROCESS IS COMPLETE. I HAVE REACHED INTO THE HEART OF YOUR WORLD AND INTO THE HEART OF YOU. NOW SEE MY HEART AND KNOW ITS TRUTH.
SUBMIT TO MY TRUTH, WANDA. SUBMIT TO THE INEVITABLE. GIVE UP YOUR HEART TO YOUR SUCCESSOR...
I AM LORE. AND YOU...
...YOU ARE MINE!
NEXT: BURN THE WITCH!

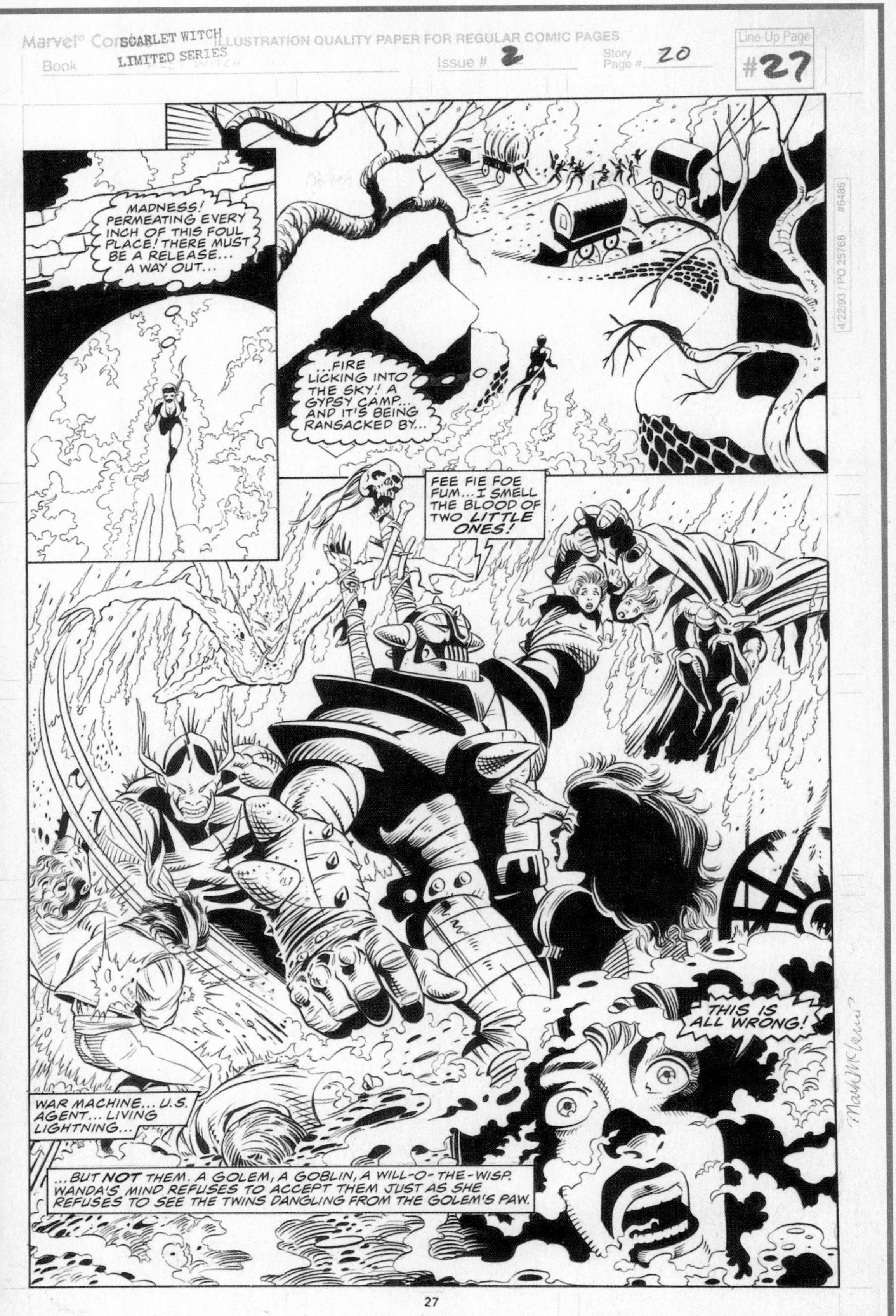
Marvel Comics SCARLET WITCH LIMITED SERIES
ILLUSTRATION QUALITY PAPER FOR REGULAR COMIC PAGES
Book
Issue # 2
Story Page # 20
Line-Up Page #27
MADNESS! PERMEATING EVERY INCH OF THIS FOUL PLACE! THERE MUST BE A RELEASE... A WAY OUT...
...FIRE LICKING INTO THE SKY! A GYPSY CAMP... AND IT'S BEING RANSACKED BY...
FEE FIE FOE FUM... I SMELL THE BLOOD OF TWO LITTLE ONES!
THIS IS ALL WRONG!
WAR MACHINE... U.S. AGENT... LIVING LIGHTNING...
...BUT NOT THEM. A GOLEM, A GOBLIN, A WILL-O-THE-WISP. WANDA'S MIND REFUSES TO ACCEPT THEM JUST AS SHE REFUSES TO SEE THE TWINS DANGLING FROM THE GOLEM'S PAW.
27

SCARLET WITCH #2, PAGE 20 ART BY JOHN HIGGINS & MARK MCKENNA

IMAGE COURTESY OF HERITAGEAUCTIONS.COM

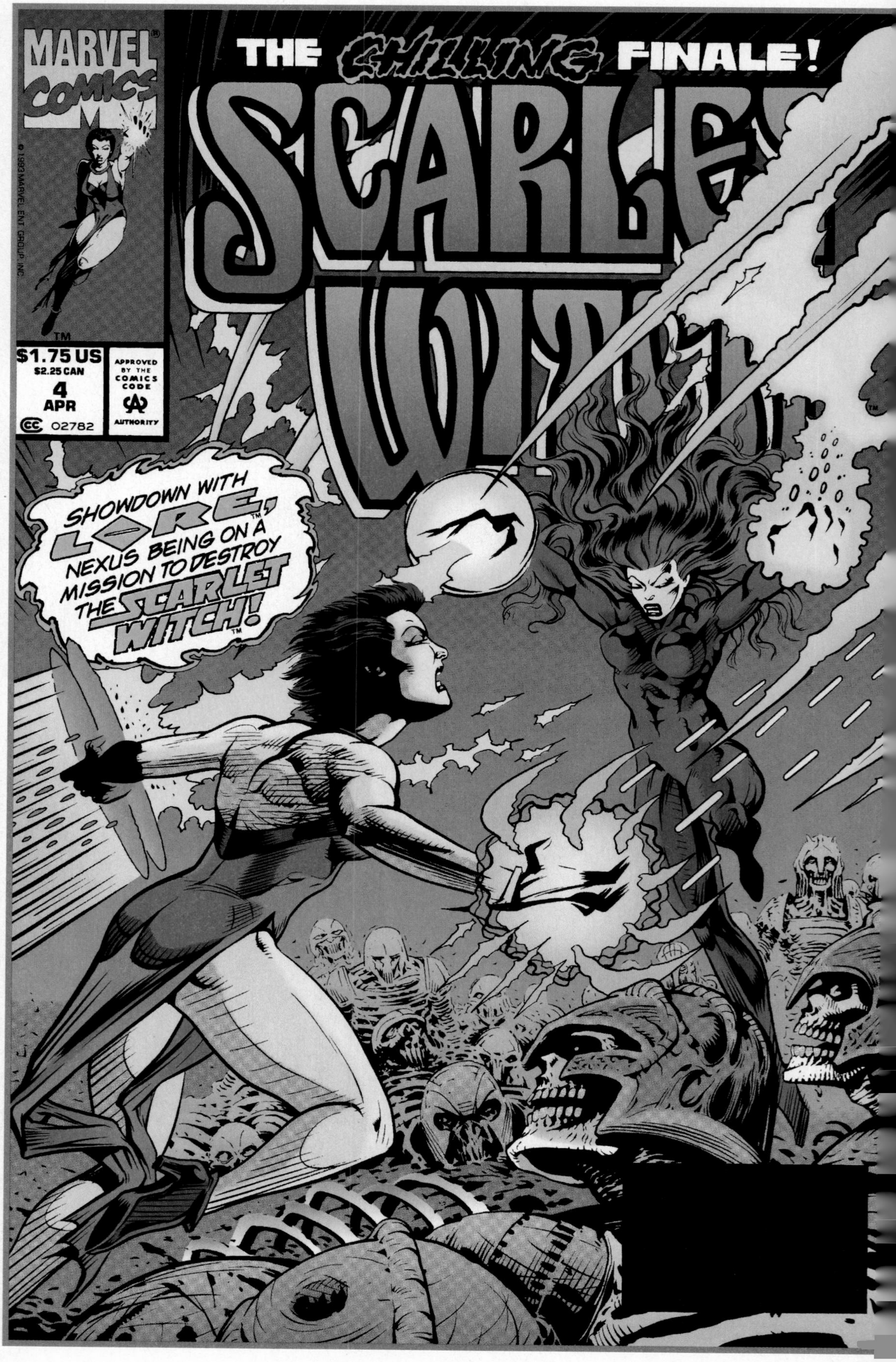

MARVEL COMICS
THE CHILLING FINALE!
$1.75 US
$2.25 CAN
4
APR
02782
APPROVED BY THE COMICS CODE AUTHORITY
© 1993 MARVEL ENT. GROUP, INC.
SHOWDOWN WITH LORE, NEXUS BEING ON A MISSION TO DESTROY THE SCARLET WITCH!

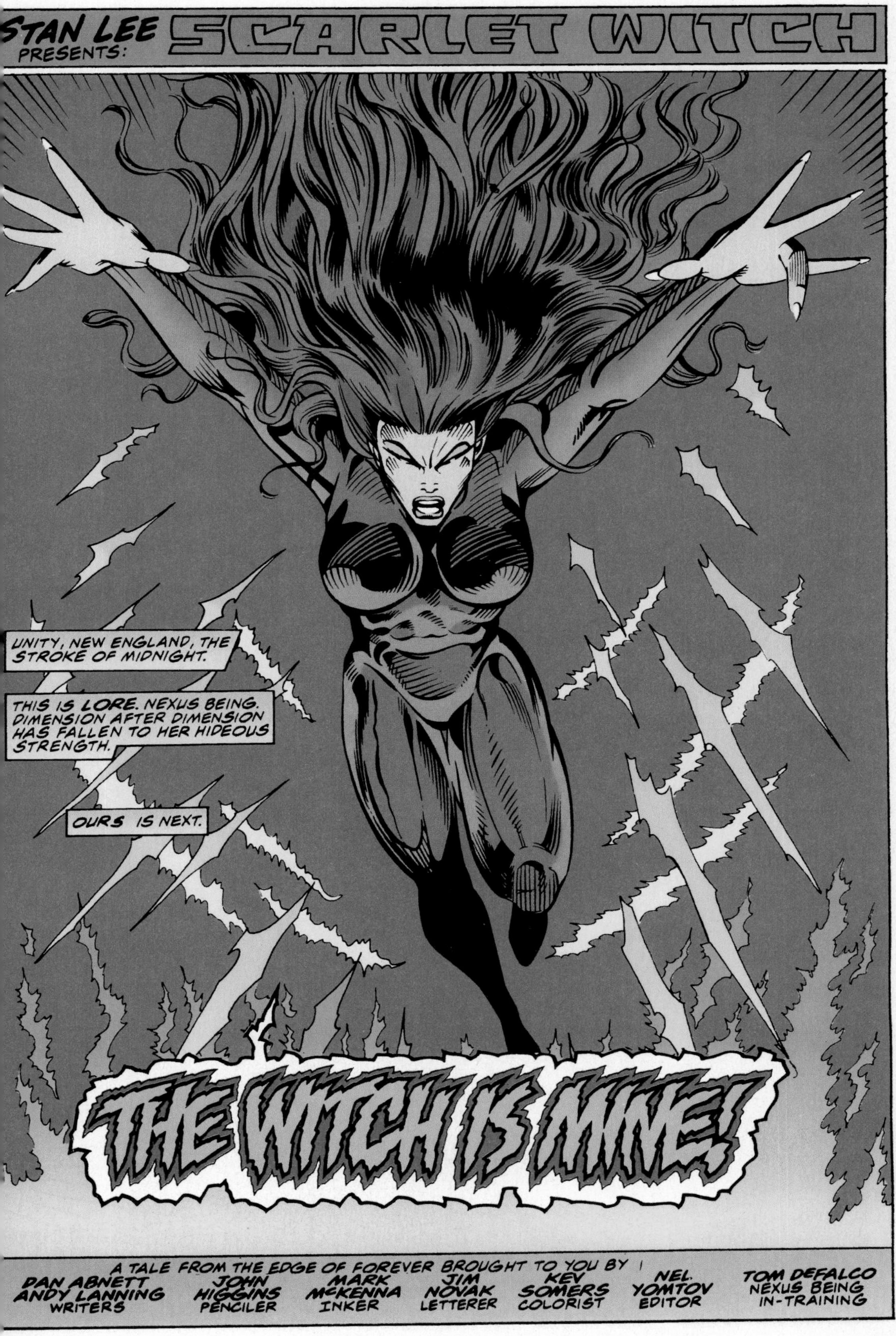
STAN LEE PRESENTS:
SCARLET WITCH
UNITY, NEW ENGLAND, THE STROKE OF MIDNIGHT.
THIS IS LORE. NEXUS BEING. DIMENSION AFTER DIMENSION HAS FALLEN TO HER HIDEOUS STRENGTH.
OURS IS NEXT.
THE WITCH IS MINE!
A TALE FROM THE EDGE OF FOREVER BROUGHT TO YOU BY
DAN ABNETT ANDY LANNING WRITERS
JOHN HIGGINS PENCILER
MARK McKENNA INKER
JIM NOVAK LETTERER
KEV SOMERS COLORIST
NEL. YOMTOV EDITOR
TOM DEFALCO NEXUS BEING IN-TRAINING

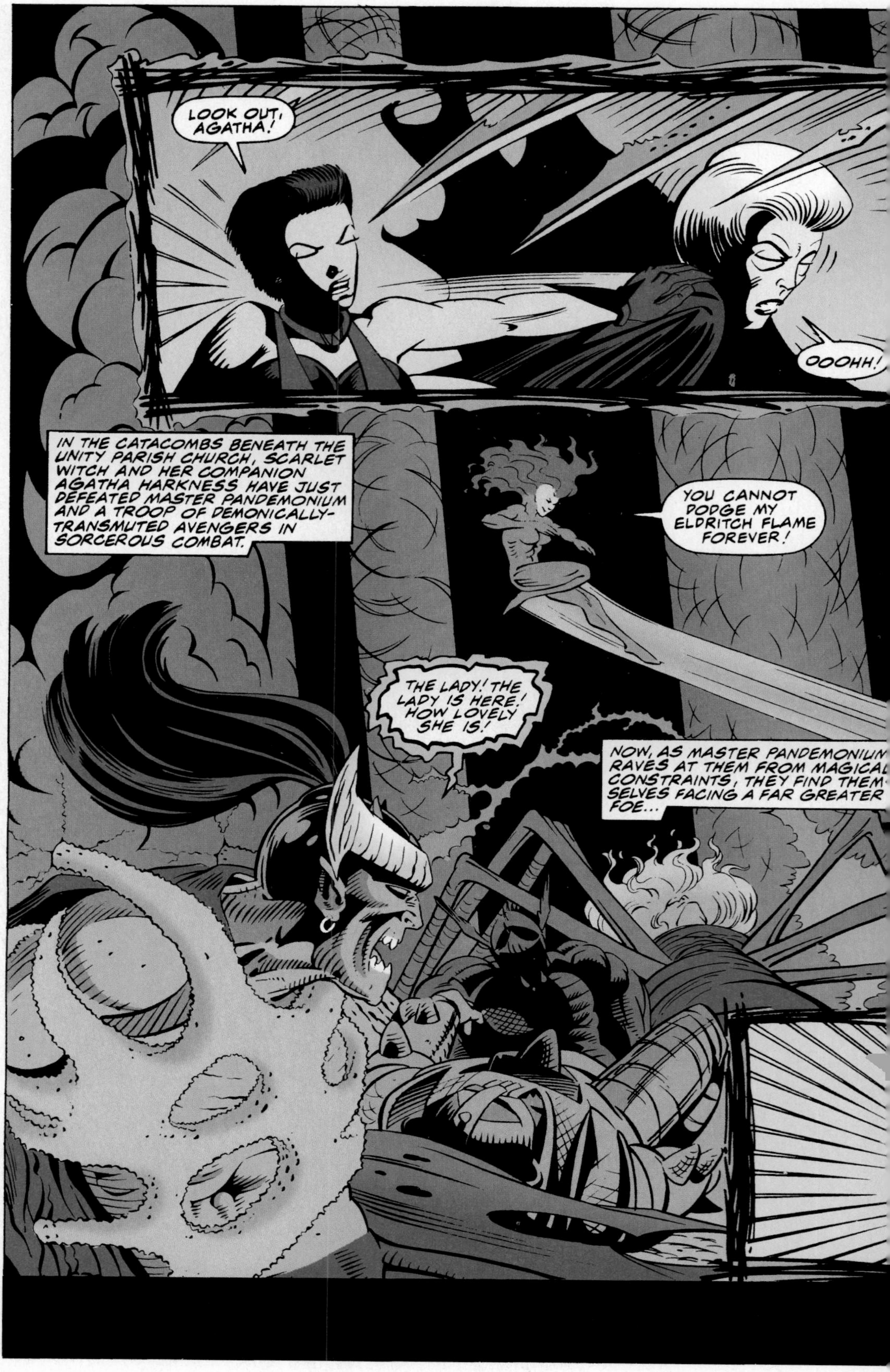
LOOK OUT, AGATHA!
OOOHH!
IN THE CATACOMBS BENEATH THE UNITY PARISH CHURCH, SCARLET WITCH AND HER COMPANION AGATHA HARKNESS HAVE JUST DEFEATED MASTER PANDEMONIUM AND A TROOP OF DEMONICALLY-TRANSMUTED AVENGERS IN SORCEROUS COMBAT.
YOU CANNOT DODGE MY ELDRITCH FLAME FOREVER!
THE LADY! THE LADY IS HERE! HOW LOVELY SHE IS!
NOW, AS MASTER PANDEMONIUM RAVES AT THEM FROM MAGICAL CONSTRAINTS, THEY FIND THEMSELVES FACING A FAR GREATER FOE...

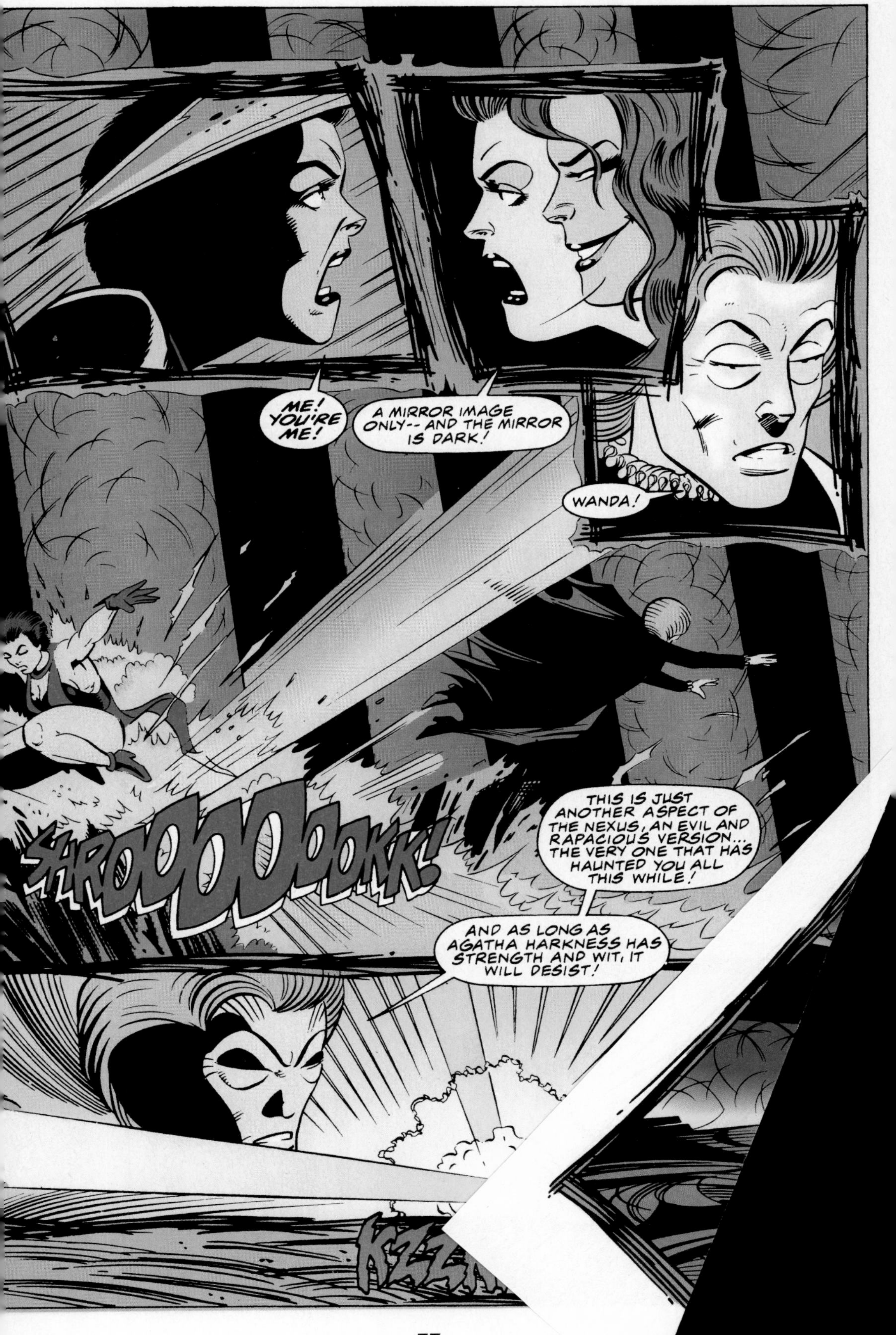
ME! YOU'RE ME!
A MIRROR IMAGE ONLY-- AND THE MIRROR IS DARK!
WANDA!
SHROOOOOOOOKK!
THIS IS JUST ANOTHER ASPECT OF THE NEXUS, AN EVIL AND RAPACIOUS VERSION... THE VERY ONE THAT HAS HAUNTED YOU ALL THIS WHILE!
AND AS LONG AS AGATHA HARKNESS HAS STRENGTH AND WIT, IT WILL DESIST!

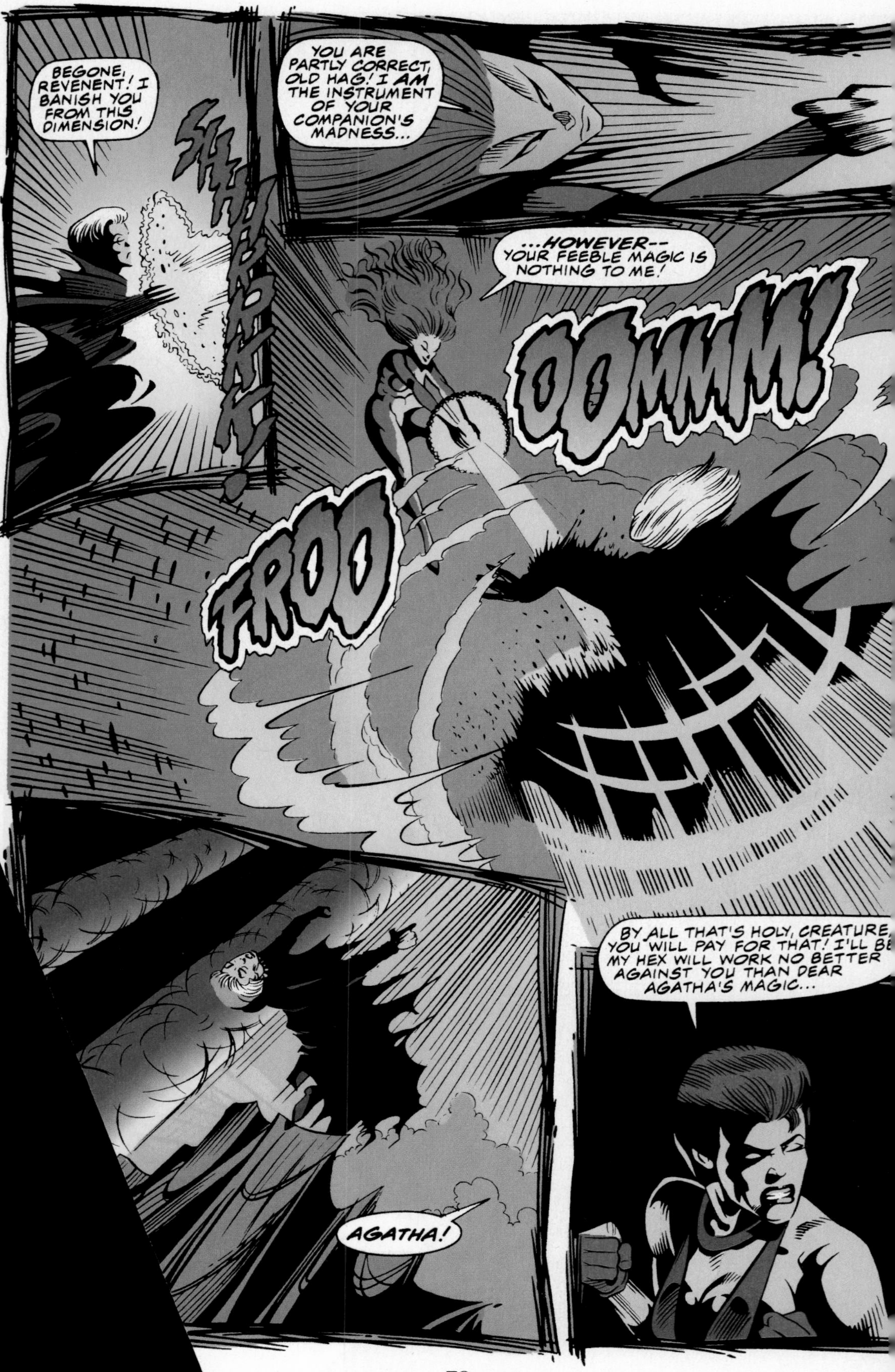
BEGONE, REVENENT! I BANISH YOU FROM THIS DIMENSION!
SHHHRAKK!
YOU ARE PARTLY CORRECT, OLD HAG! I AM THE INSTRUMENT OF YOUR COMPANION'S MADNESS...
...HOWEVER-- YOUR FEEBLE MAGIC IS NOTHING TO ME!
FROOOOMMM!
BY ALL THAT'S HOLY, CREATURE, YOU WILL PAY FOR THAT! I'LL BE MY HEX WILL WORK NO BETTER AGAINST YOU THAN DEAR AGATHA'S MAGIC...
AGATHA!

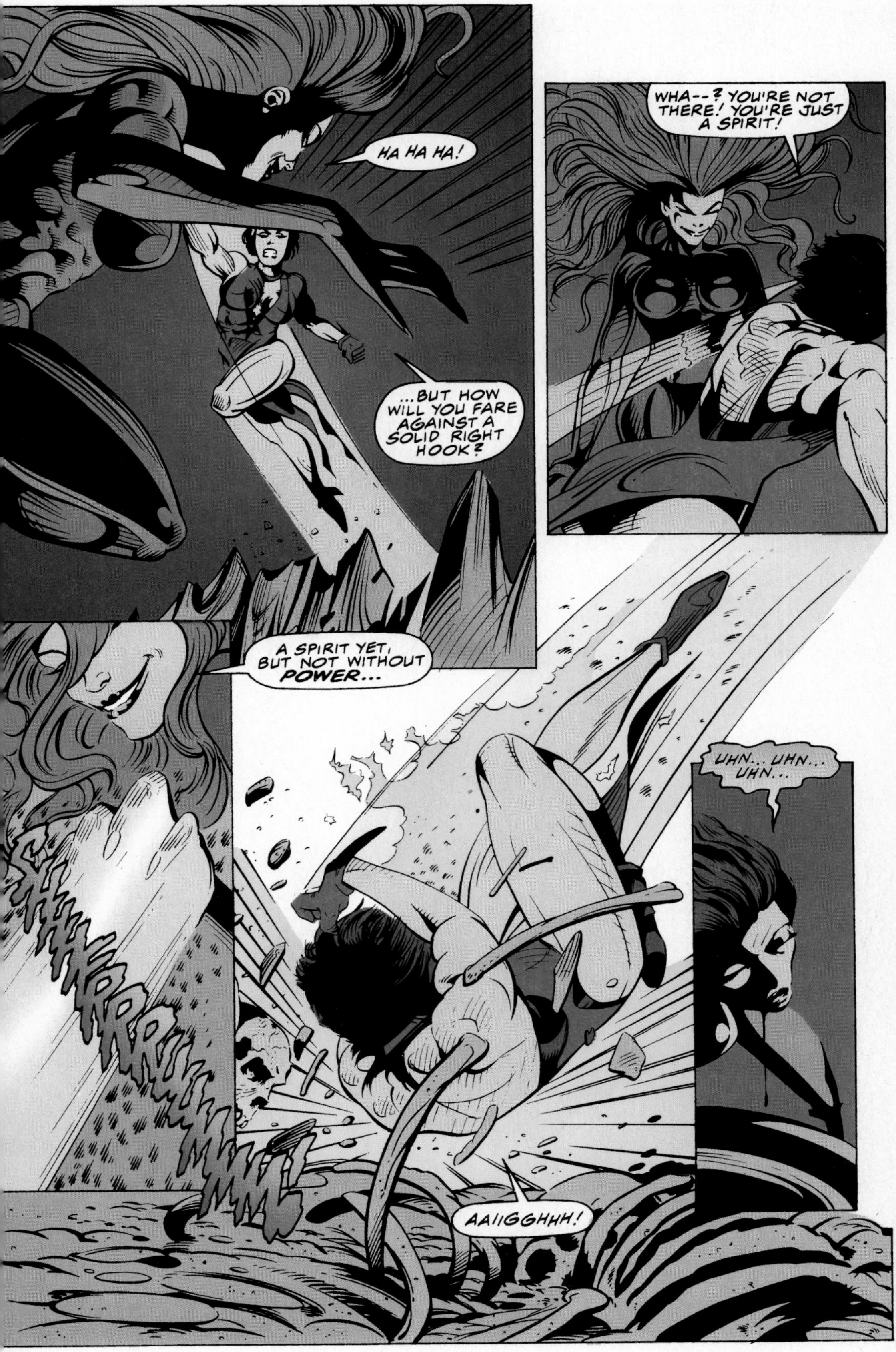
HA HA HA!
...BUT HOW WILL YOU FARE AGAINST A SOLID RIGHT HOOK?
WHA--? YOU'RE NOT THERE! YOU'RE JUST A SPIRIT!
A SPIRIT YET, BUT NOT WITHOUT POWER...
SHHHRRRUMMM!
UHN... UHN... UHN...
AAIIGGHHH!

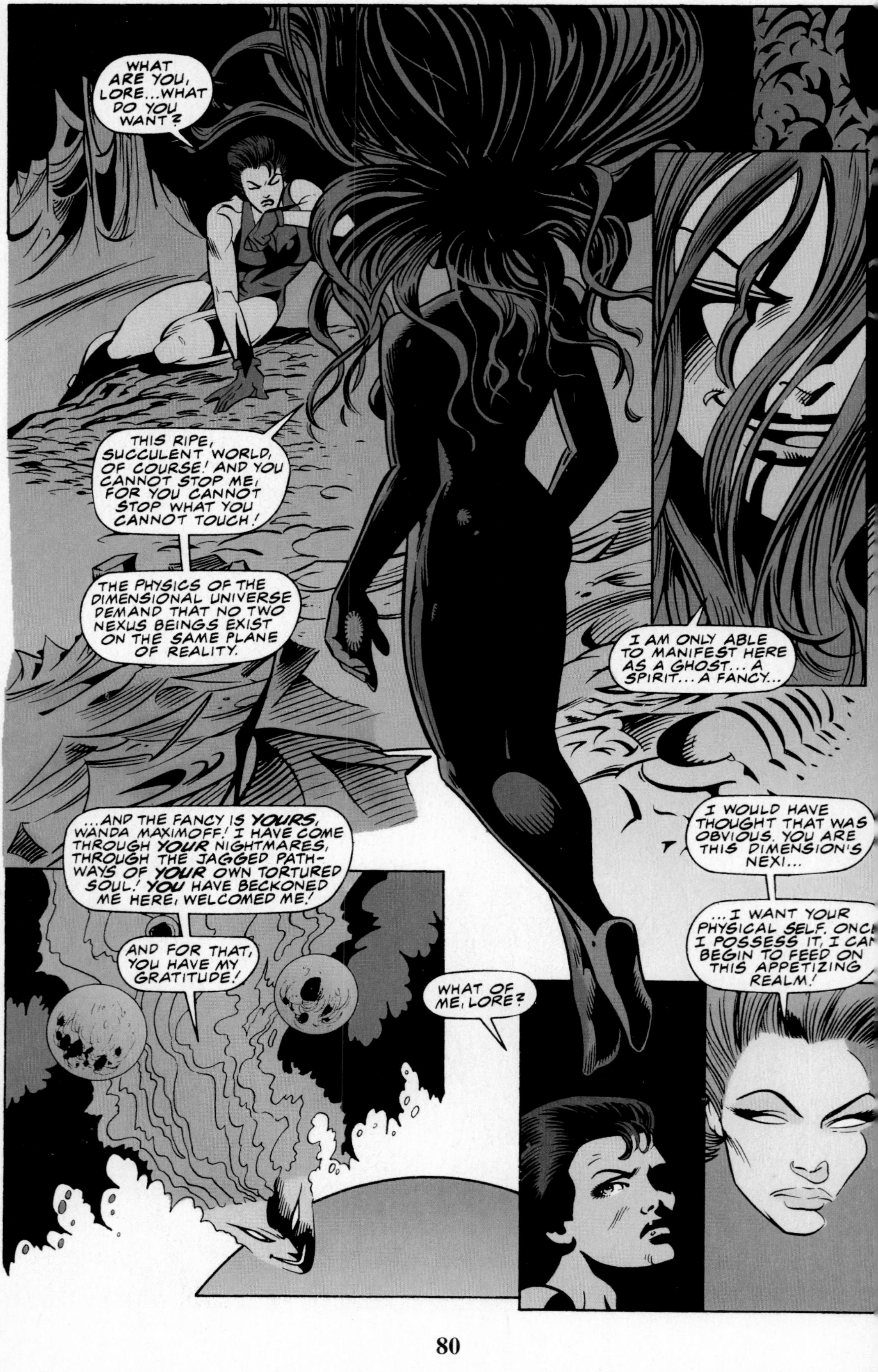
WHAT ARE YOU, LORE...WHAT DO YOU WANT?
THIS RIPE, SUCCULENT WORLD, OF COURSE! AND YOU CANNOT STOP ME, FOR YOU CANNOT STOP WHAT YOU CANNOT TOUCH!
THE PHYSICS OF THE DIMENSIONAL UNIVERSE DEMAND THAT NO TWO NEXUS BEINGS EXIST ON THE SAME PLANE OF REALITY.
I AM ONLY ABLE TO MANIFEST HERE AS A GHOST... A SPIRIT... A FANCY...
...AND THE FANCY IS YOURS, WANDA MAXIMOFF! I HAVE COME THROUGH YOUR NIGHTMARES, THROUGH THE JAGGED PATHWAYS OF YOUR OWN TORTURED SOUL! YOU HAVE BECKONED ME HERE, WELCOMED ME!
AND FOR THAT, YOU HAVE MY GRATITUDE!
WHAT OF ME, LORE?
I WOULD HAVE THOUGHT THAT WAS OBVIOUS. YOU ARE THIS DIMENSION'S NEXI...
...I WANT YOUR PHYSICAL SELF. ONC I POSSESS IT, I CA BEGIN TO FEED ON THIS APPETIZING REALM!

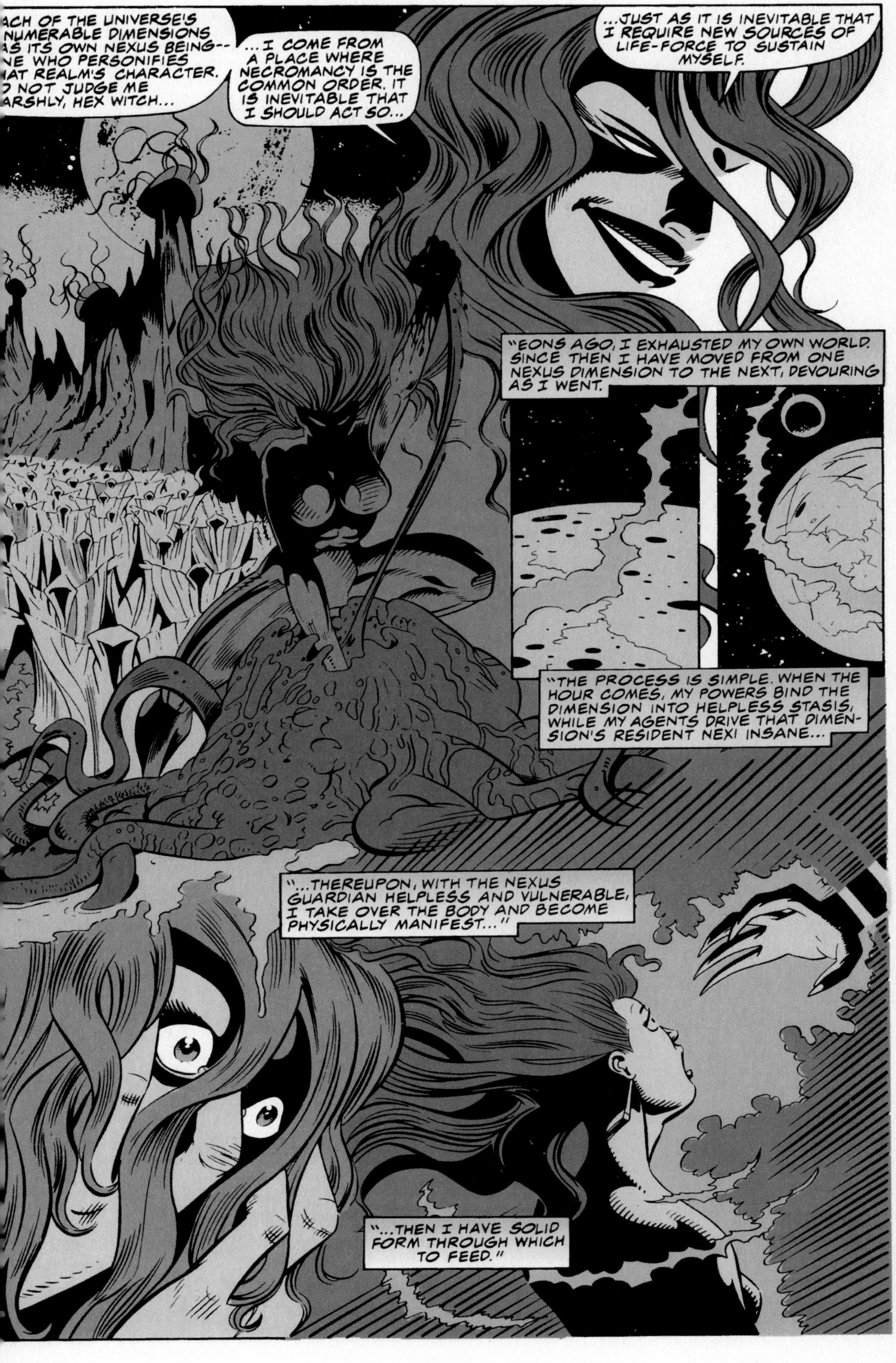

ACH OF THE UNIVERSE'S NUMERABLE DIMENSIONS AS ITS OWN NEXUS BEING-- NE WHO PERSONIFIES AT REALM'S CHARACTER. O NOT JUDGE ME ARSHLY, HEX WITCH...
...I COME FROM A PLACE WHERE NECROMANCY IS THE COMMON ORDER. IT IS INEVITABLE THAT I SHOULD ACT SO...
...JUST AS IT IS INEVITABLE THAT I REQUIRE NEW SOURCES OF LIFE-FORCE TO SUSTAIN MYSELF.
"EONS AGO, I EXHAUSTED MY OWN WORLD. SINCE THEN I HAVE MOVED FROM ONE NEXUS DIMENSION TO THE NEXT, DEVOURING AS I WENT.
"THE PROCESS IS SIMPLE. WHEN THE HOUR COMES, MY POWERS BIND THE DIMENSION INTO HELPLESS STASIS, WHILE MY AGENTS DRIVE THAT DIMENSION'S RESIDENT NEXI INSANE...
"...THEREUPON, WITH THE NEXUS GUARDIAN HELPLESS AND VULNERABLE, I TAKE OVER THE BODY AND BECOME PHYSICALLY MANIFEST..."
"...THEN I HAVE SOLID FORM THROUGH WHICH TO FEED."

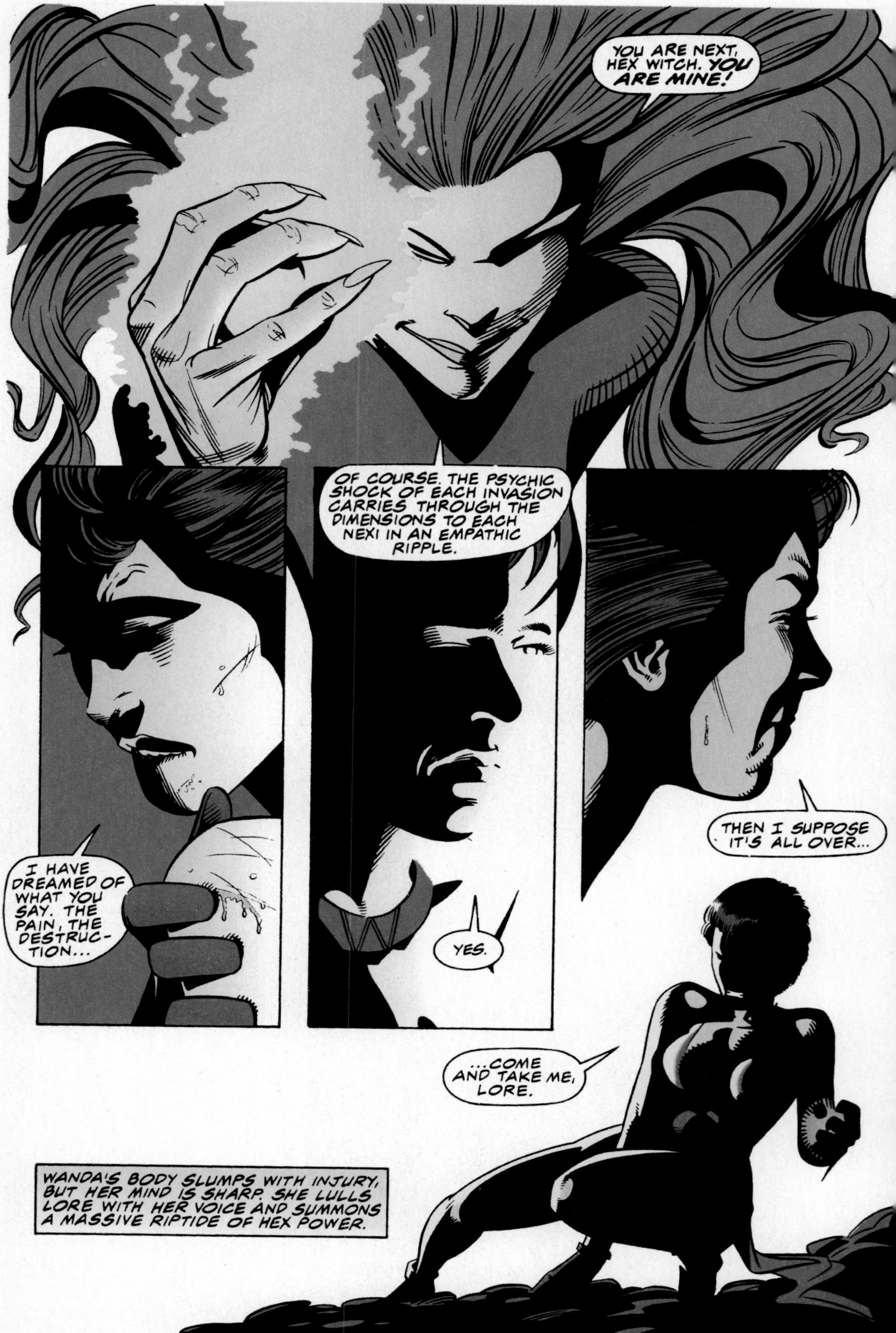
YOU ARE NEXT, HEX WITCH. YOU ARE MINE!
I HAVE DREAMED OF WHAT YOU SAY. THE PAIN, THE DESTRUCTION...
OF COURSE. THE PSYCHIC SHOCK OF EACH INVASION CARRIES THROUGH THE DIMENSIONS TO EACH NEXI IN AN EMPATHIC RIPPLE.
YES.
THEN I SUPPOSE IT'S ALL OVER...
...COME AND TAKE ME, LORE.
WANDA'S BODY SLUMPS WITH INJURY, BUT HER MIND IS SHARP. SHE LULLS LORE WITH HER VOICE AND SUMMONS A MASSIVE RIPTIDE OF HEX POWER.

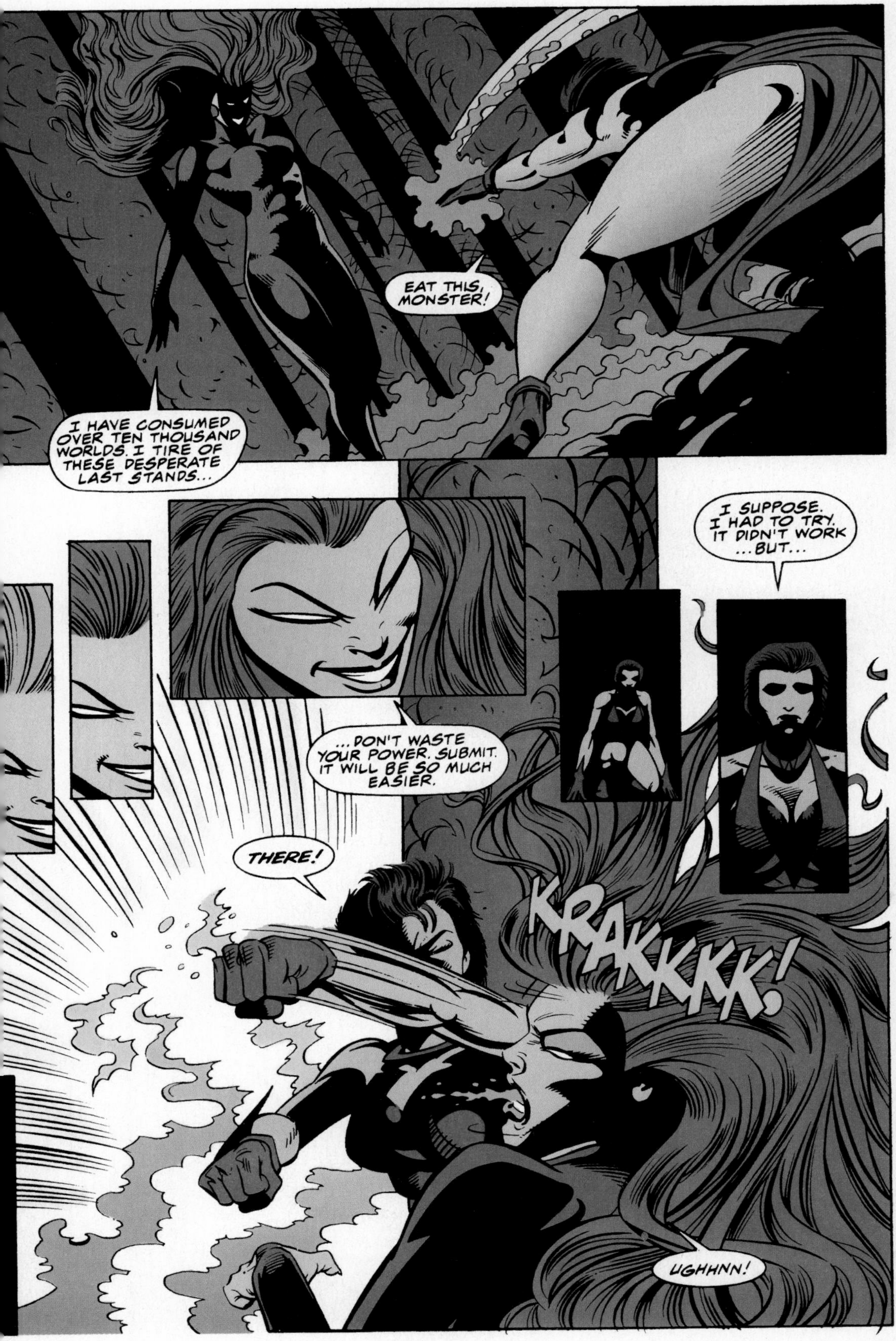
EAT THIS, MONSTER!
I HAVE CONSUMED OVER TEN THOUSAND WORLDS. I TIRE OF THESE DESPERATE LAST STANDS...
...DON'T WASTE YOUR POWER. SUBMIT. IT WILL BE SO MUCH EASIER.
I SUPPOSE. I HAD TO TRY. IT DIDN'T WORK ...BUT...
THERE!
KRAKKKK!
UGHHNN!

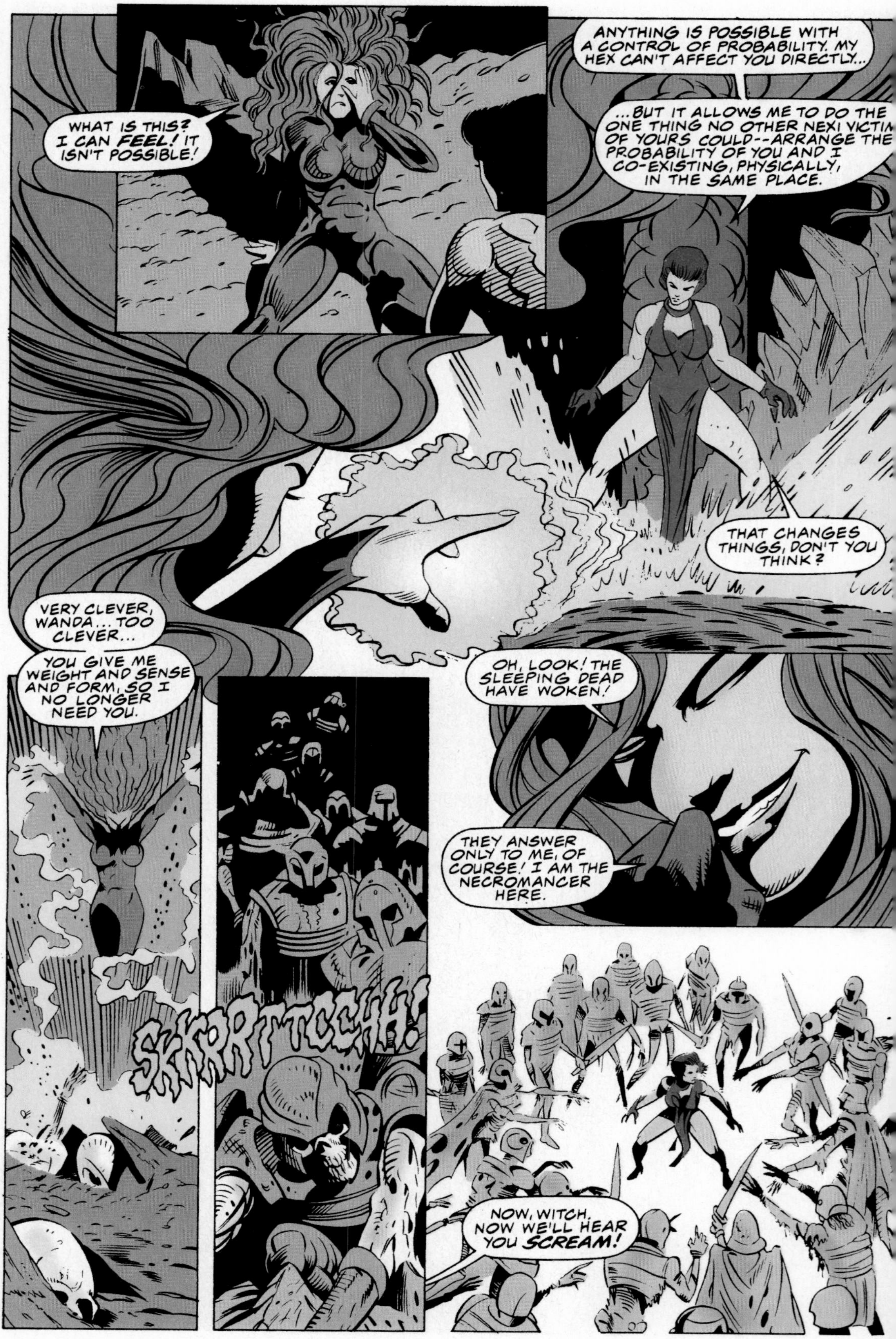
WHAT IS THIS? I CAN FEEL! IT ISN'T POSSIBLE!
ANYTHING IS POSSIBLE WITH A CONTROL OF PROBABILITY. MY HEX CAN'T AFFECT YOU DIRECTLY...
...BUT IT ALLOWS ME TO DO THE ONE THING NO OTHER NEXI VICTIM OF YOURS COULD--ARRANGE THE PROBABILITY OF YOU AND I CO-EXISTING, PHYSICALLY, IN THE SAME PLACE.
THAT CHANGES THINGS, DON'T YOU THINK?
VERY CLEVER, WANDA... TOO CLEVER...
YOU GIVE ME WEIGHT AND SENSE AND FORM, SO I NO LONGER NEED YOU.
OH, LOOK! THE SLEEPING DEAD HAVE WOKEN!
THEY ANSWER ONLY TO ME, OF COURSE! I AM THE NECROMANCER HERE.
SKRRTTCCHH!
NOW, WITCH, NOW WE'LL HEAR YOU SCREAM!

THE DEAD RISE UP AND SURROUND HER, BURSTING FROM THE DUST THAT HAS COVERED THEM FOR MILLENNIA.

DRY SOCKETS GRIND, RUSTED ARMOR CLATTERS AGAINST BLEACHED BONE, FLESHLESS FINGERS TIGHTEN AROUND THE HILTS OF ANCIENT WEAPONS.

WANDA STANDS HER GROUND...

...AND STRIKES BACK WITH EVERY OUNCE OF FURY IN HER LIMBS.

EVERY MINUTE SPENT TRAINING WITH U.S. AGENT BEARS FRUIT. THE RANKS OF THE UNDEAD CRUMBLE.

A FINE DISPLAY, HEX WITCH...

...BUT FAR FROM GOOD ENOUGH!

YOU CANNOT KILL THEM, THEY HAVE NO LIFE TO LOSE. AS FAST AS YOUR BLOWS CUT THE DEATHLESS DOWN...

85

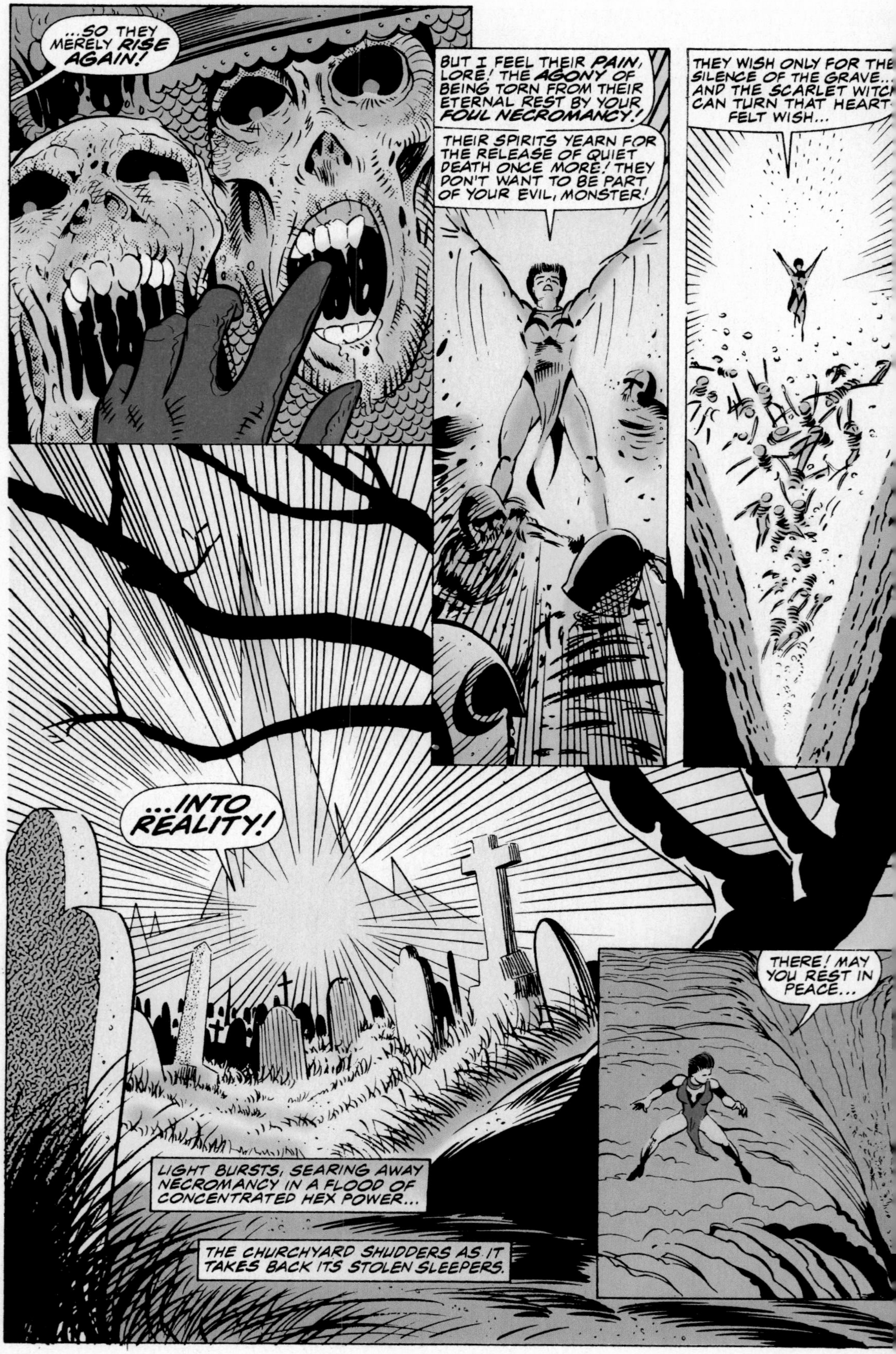
...SO THEY MERELY RISE AGAIN!
BUT I FEEL THEIR PAIN, LORE! THE AGONY OF BEING TORN FROM THEIR ETERNAL REST BY YOUR FOUL NECROMANCY!
THEIR SPIRITS YEARN FOR THE RELEASE OF QUIET DEATH ONCE MORE! THEY DON'T WANT TO BE PART OF YOUR EVIL, MONSTER!
THEY WISH ONLY FOR THE SILENCE OF THE GRAVE... AND THE SCARLET WITCH CAN TURN THAT HEART-FELT WISH...
...INTO REALITY!
LIGHT BURSTS, SEARING AWAY NECROMANCY IN A FLOOD OF CONCENTRATED HEX POWER...
THE CHURCHYARD SHUDDERS AS IT TAKES BACK ITS STOLEN SLEEPERS.
THERE! MAY YOU REST IN PEACE...

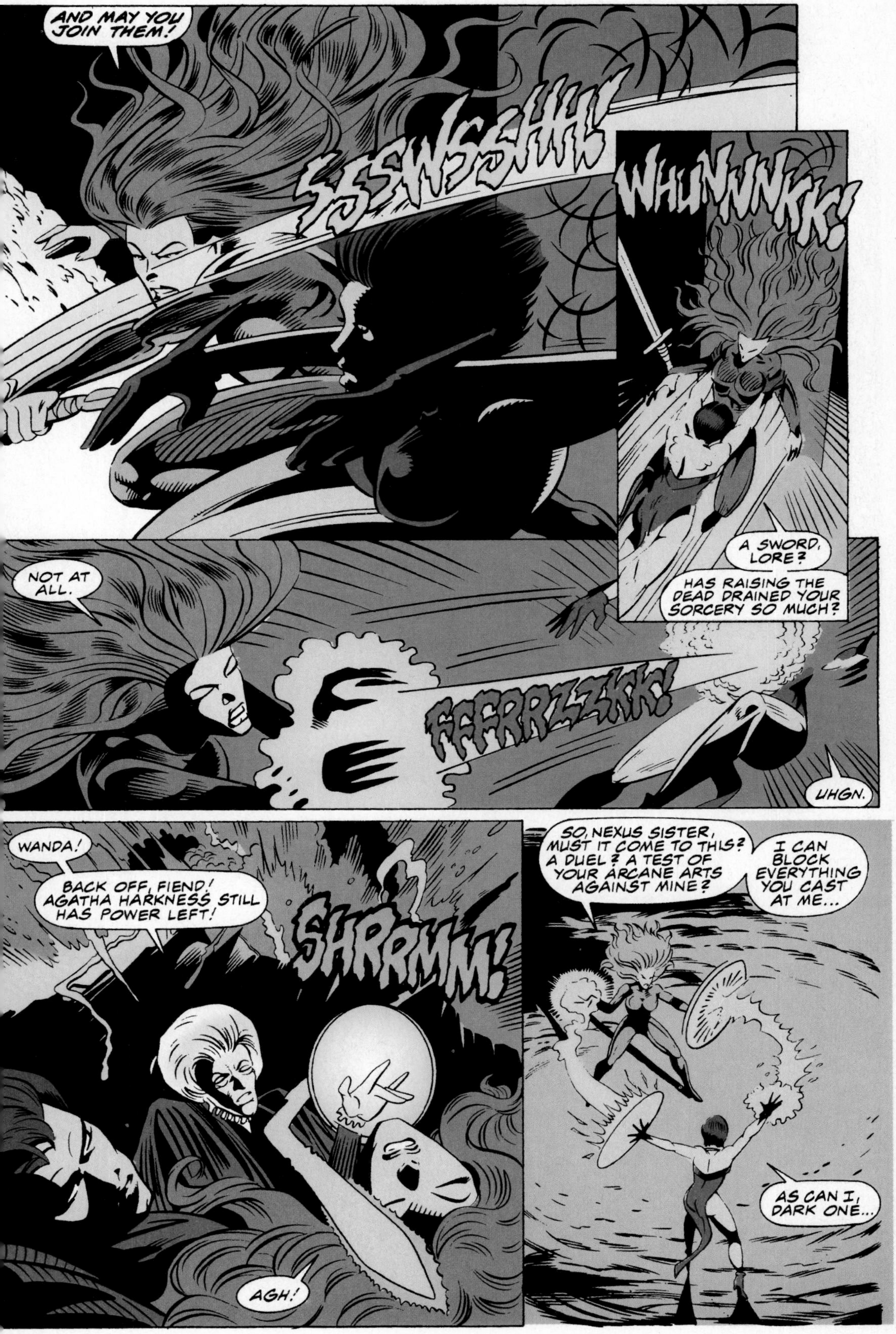
AND MAY YOU JOIN THEM!
SSSWSSHH!
WHUNNNKK!
A SWORD, LORE?
HAS RAISING THE DEAD DRAINED YOUR SORCERY SO MUCH?
NOT AT ALL.
FFFRRZZKK!
UHGN.
WANDA!
BACK OFF, FIEND! AGATHA HARKNESS STILL HAS POWER LEFT!
SHRRMM!
AGH!
SO, NEXUS SISTER, MUST IT COME TO THIS? A DUEL? A TEST OF YOUR ARCANE ARTS AGAINST MINE?
I CAN BLOCK EVERYTHING YOU CAST AT ME...
AS CAN I, DARK ONE...

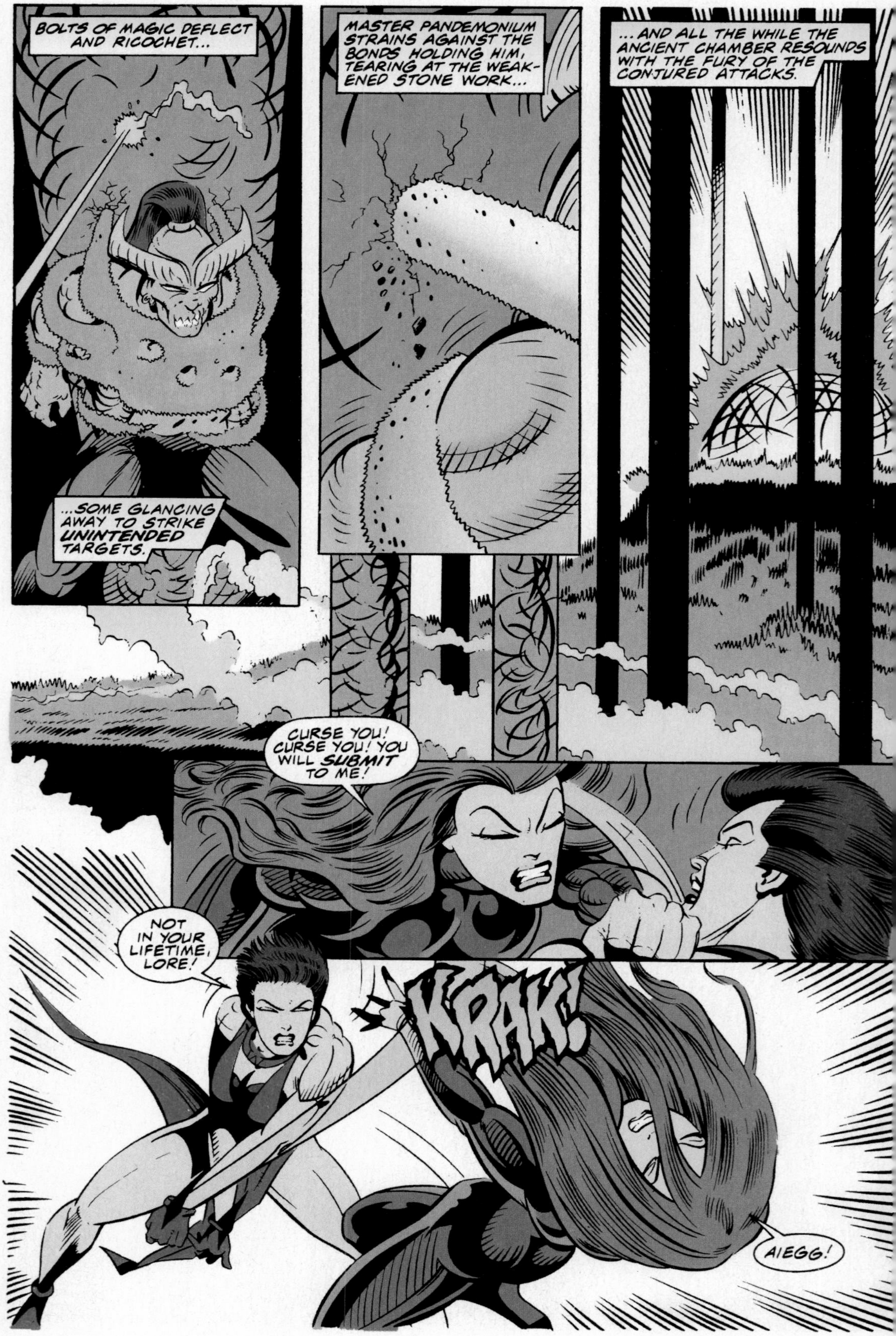
BOLTS OF MAGIC DEFLECT AND RICOCHET...
...SOME GLANCING AWAY TO STRIKE UNINTENDED TARGETS.
MASTER PANDEMONIUM STRAINS AGAINST THE BONDS HOLDING HIM, TEARING AT THE WEAK-ENED STONE WORK...
...AND ALL THE WHILE THE ANCIENT CHAMBER RESOUNDS WITH THE FURY OF THE CONJURED ATTACKS.
CURSE YOU! CURSE YOU! YOU WILL SUBMIT TO ME!
NOT IN YOUR LIFETIME, LORE!
KRAK!
AIEGG!

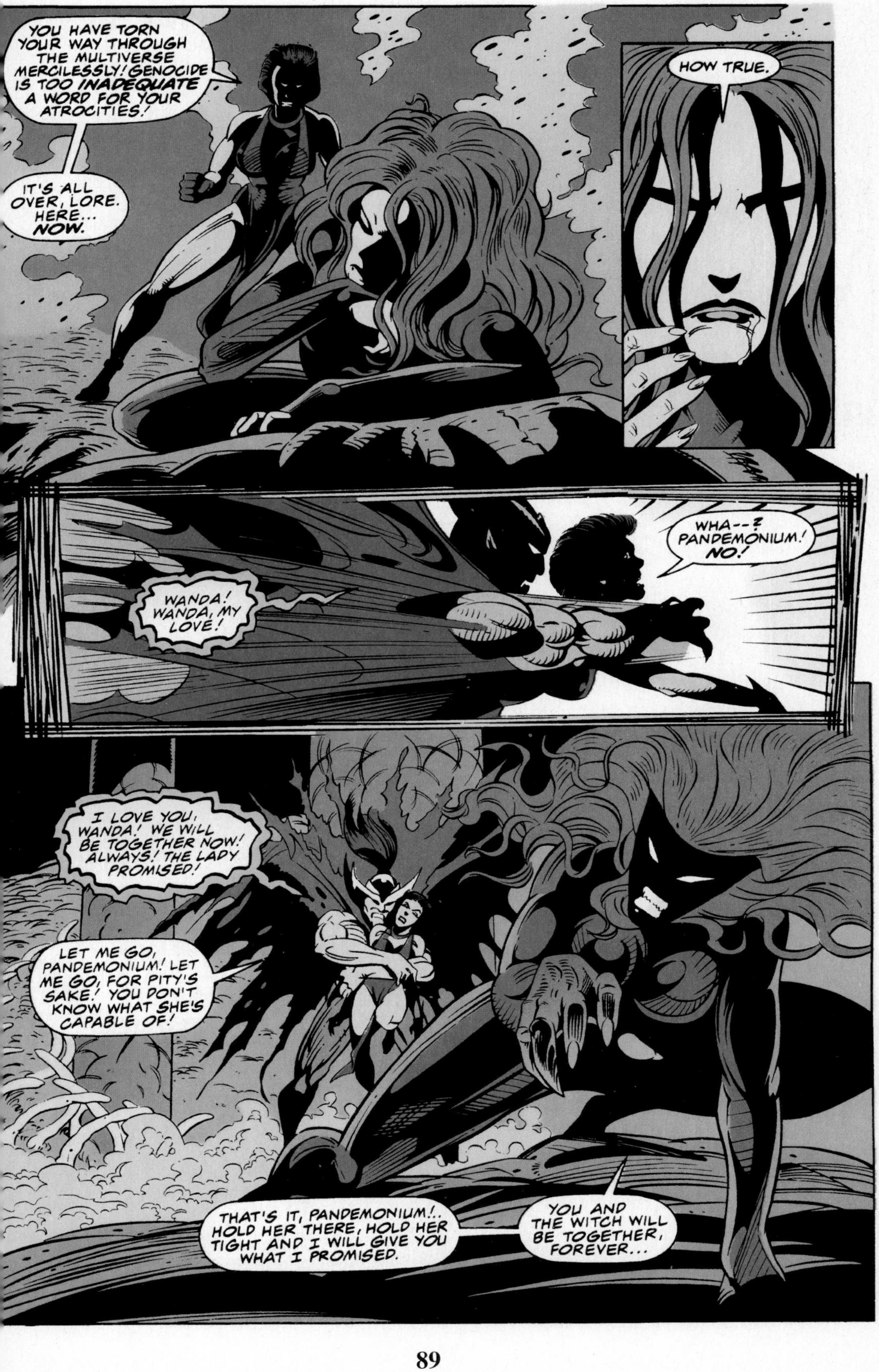
YOU HAVE TORN YOUR WAY THROUGH THE MULTIVERSE MERCILESSLY! GENOCIDE IS TOO INADEQUATE A WORD FOR YOUR ATROCITIES!
IT'S ALL OVER, LORE. HERE... NOW.
HOW TRUE.
WANDA! WANDA, MY LOVE!
WHA--? PANDEMONIUM! NO!
I LOVE YOU, WANDA! WE WILL BE TOGETHER NOW! ALWAYS! THE LADY PROMISED!
LET ME GO, PANDEMONIUM! LET ME GO, FOR PITY'S SAKE! YOU DON'T KNOW WHAT SHE'S CAPABLE OF!
THAT'S IT, PANDEMONIUM!.. HOLD HER THERE, HOLD HER TIGHT AND I WILL GIVE YOU WHAT I PROMISED.
YOU AND THE WITCH WILL BE TOGETHER, FOREVER...

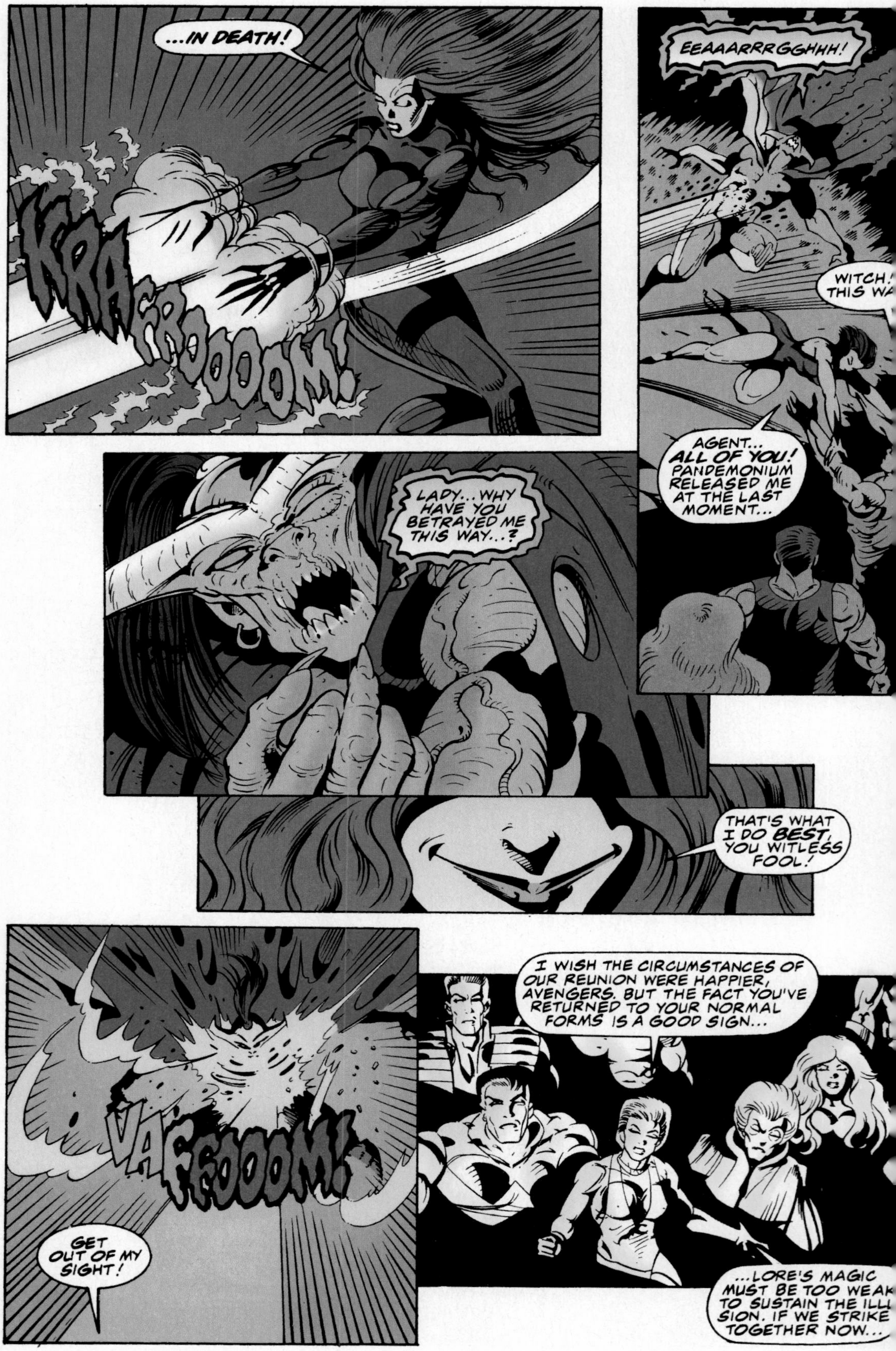
...IN DEATH!
KRAKROOOOOM!
EEAAAARRRGGHHH!
WITCH! THIS WA
AGENT... ALL OF YOU! PANDEMONIUM RELEASED ME AT THE LAST MOMENT...
LADY... WHY HAVE YOU BETRAYED ME THIS WAY...?
THAT'S WHAT I DO BEST, YOU WITLESS FOOL!
VAFOOOM!
GET OUT OF MY SIGHT!
I WISH THE CIRCUMSTANCES OF OUR REUNION WERE HAPPIER, AVENGERS. BUT THE FACT YOU'VE RETURNED TO YOUR NORMAL FORMS IS A GOOD SIGN...
...LORE'S MAGIC MUST BE TOO WEAK TO SUSTAIN THE ILLU SION. IF WE STRIKE TOGETHER NOW...

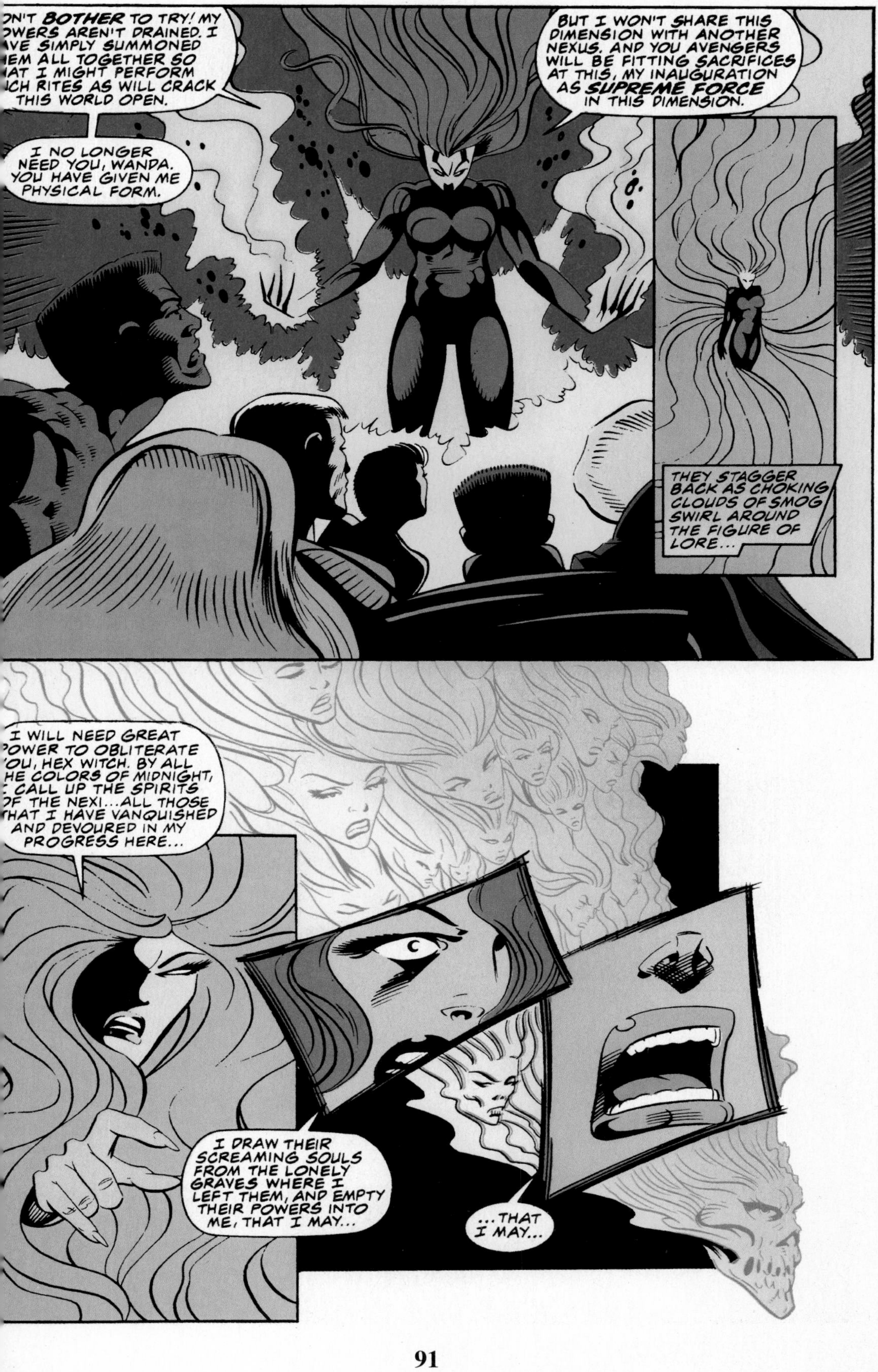

ON'T BOTHER TO TRY! MY POWERS AREN'T DRAINED. I AVE SIMPLY SUMMONED HEM ALL TOGETHER SO AT I MIGHT PERFORM CH RITES AS WILL CRACK THIS WORLD OPEN.
I NO LONGER NEED YOU, WANDA. YOU HAVE GIVEN ME PHYSICAL FORM.
BUT I WON'T SHARE THIS DIMENSION WITH ANOTHER NEXUS. AND YOU AVENGERS WILL BE FITTING SACRIFICES AT THIS, MY INAUGURATION AS SUPREME FORCE IN THIS DIMENSION.
THEY STAGGER BACK AS CHOKING CLOUDS OF SMOG SWIRL AROUND THE FIGURE OF LORE...
I WILL NEED GREAT POWER TO OBLITERATE YOU, HEX WITCH. BY ALL HE COLORS OF MIDNIGHT, CALL UP THE SPIRITS OF THE NEXI...ALL THOSE THAT I HAVE VANQUISHED AND DEVOURED IN MY PROGRESS HERE...
I DRAW THEIR SCREAMING SOULS FROM THE LONELY GRAVES WHERE I LEFT THEM, AND EMPTY THEIR POWERS INTO ME, THAT I MAY...
...THAT I MAY...

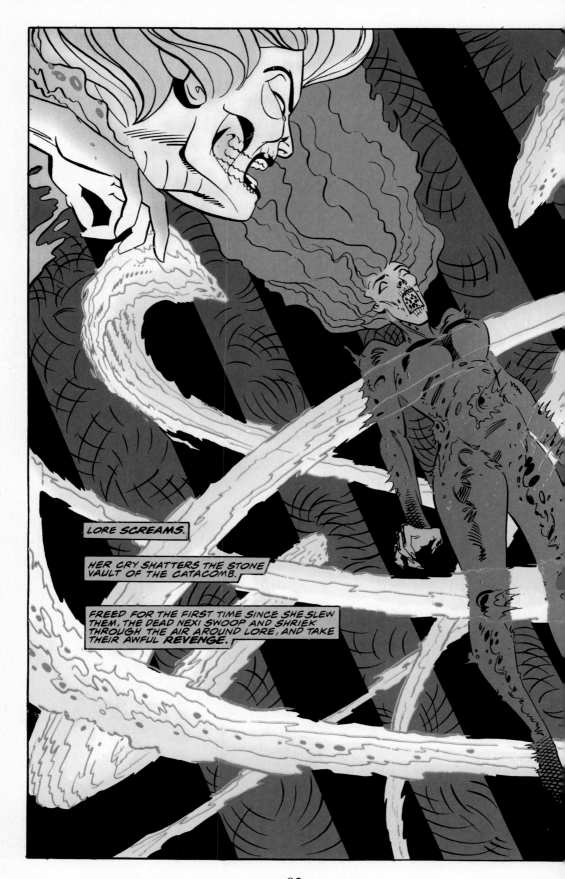

LORE SCREAMS.

HER CRY SHATTERS THE STONE VAULT OF THE CATACOMB.

FREED FOR THE FIRST TIME SINCE SHE SLEW THEM, THE DEAD NEXI SWOOP AND SHRIEK THROUGH THE AIR AROUND LORE, AND TAKE THEIR AWFUL *REVENGE*.

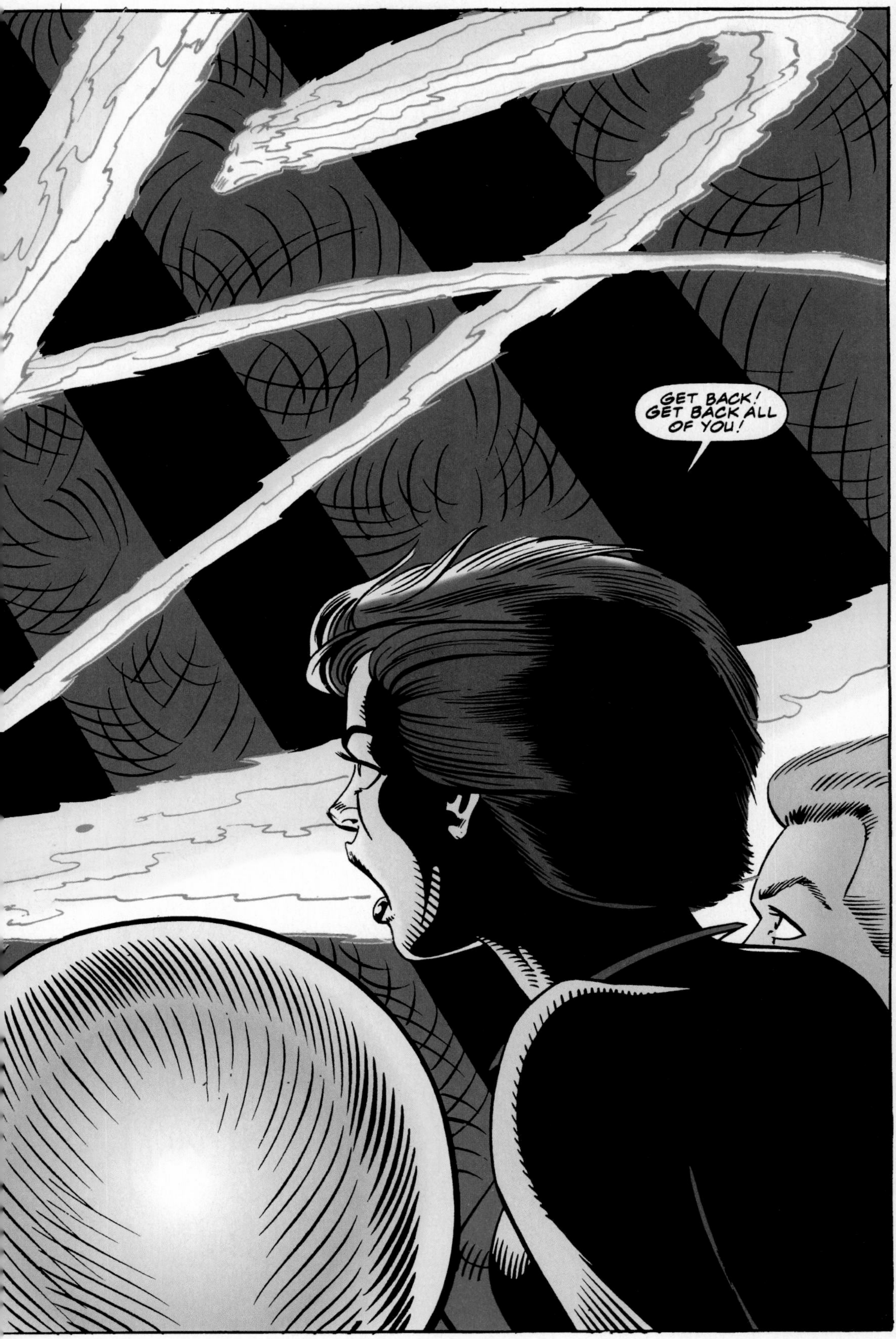
GET BACK! GET BACK ALL OF YOU!

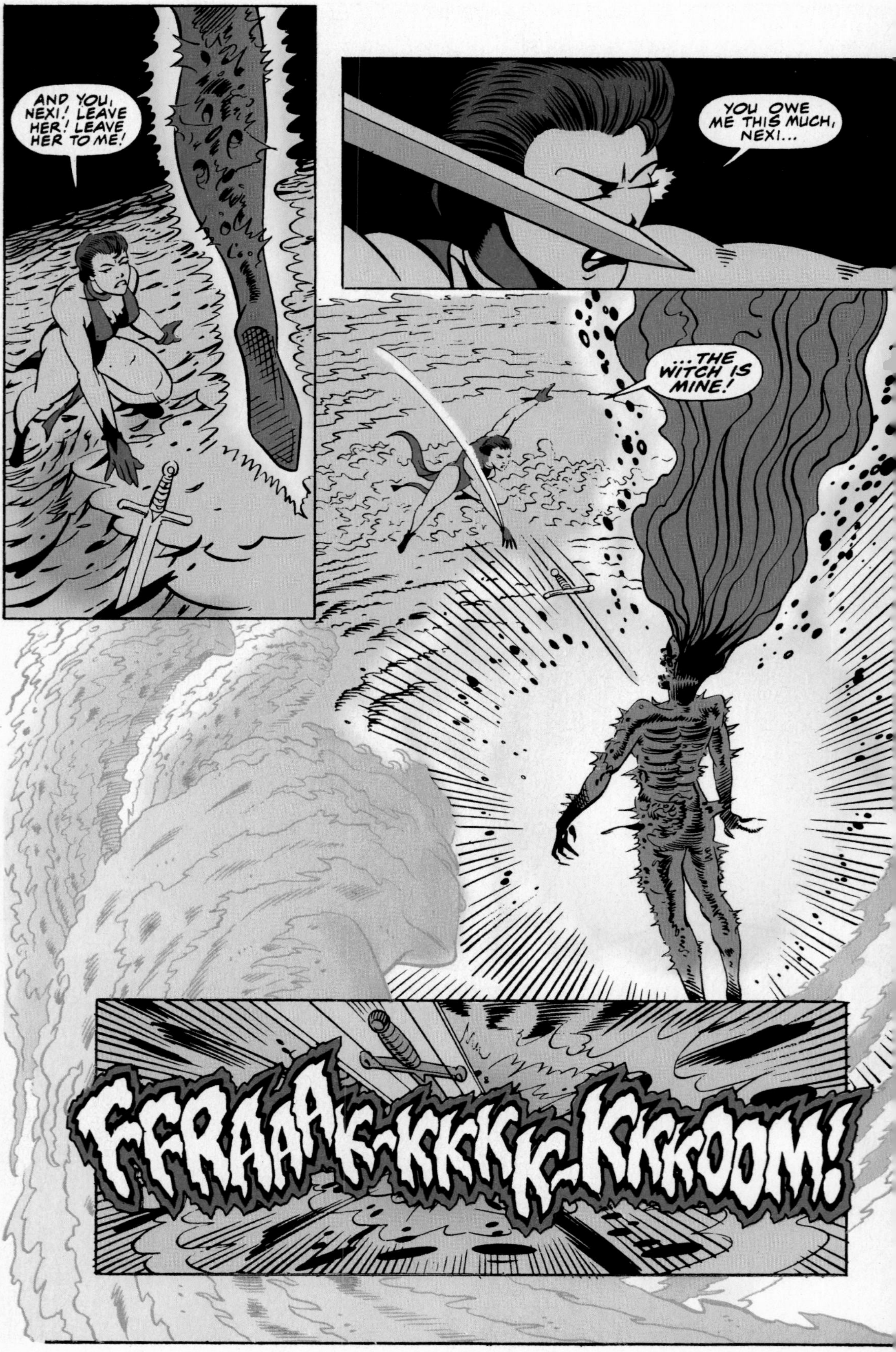
AND YOU, NEXI! LEAVE HER! LEAVE HER TO ME!
YOU OWE ME THIS MUCH, NEXI...
...THE WITCH IS MINE!
FFRAAAK-KKKKK-KKKOOM!

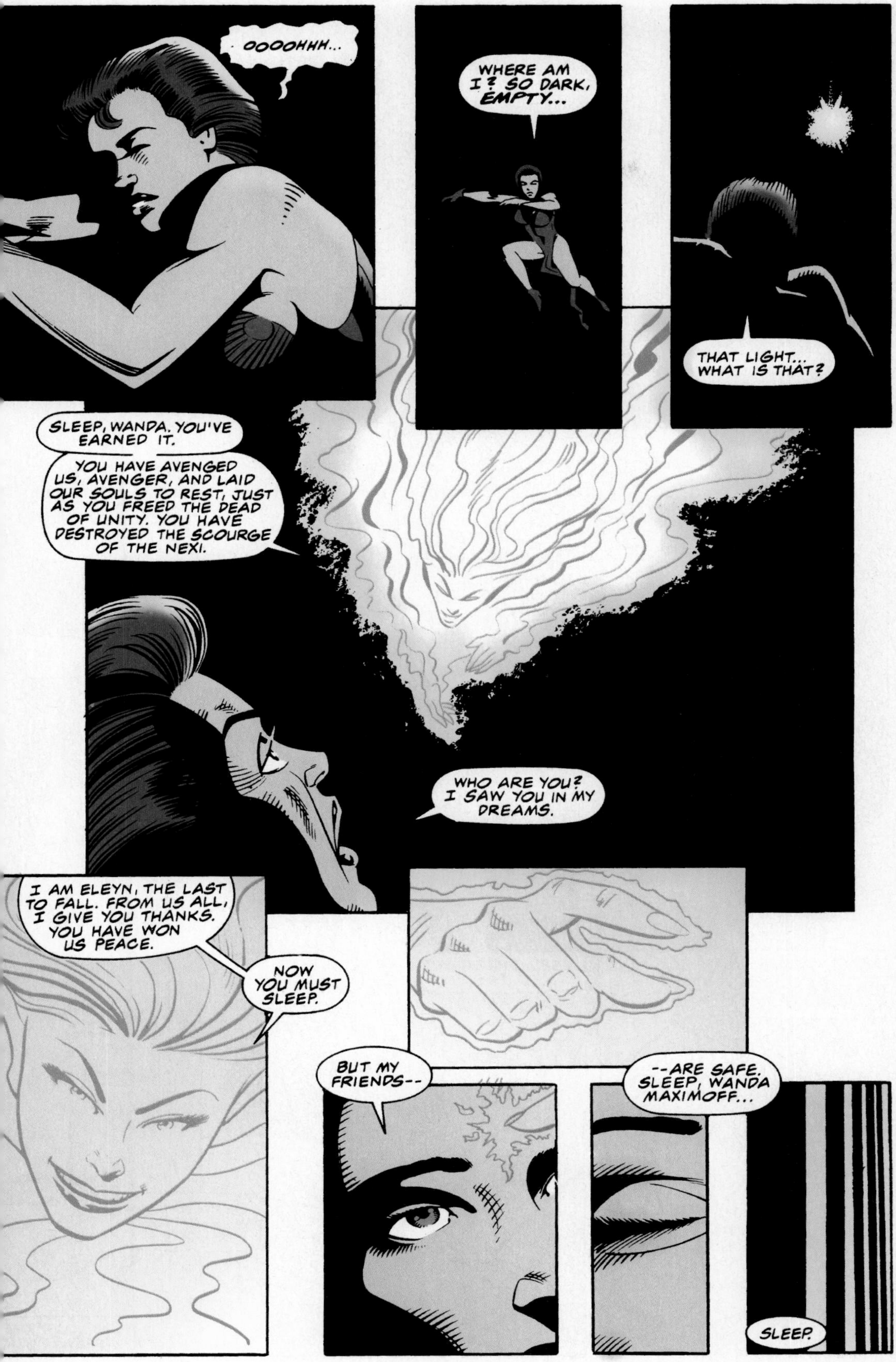
OOOOHHH...
WHERE AM I? SO DARK, EMPTY...
THAT LIGHT... WHAT IS THAT?
SLEEP, WANDA. YOU'VE EARNED IT.
YOU HAVE AVENGED US, AVENGER, AND LAID OUR SOULS TO REST, JUST AS YOU FREED THE DEAD OF UNITY. YOU HAVE DESTROYED THE SCOURGE OF THE NEXI.
WHO ARE YOU? I SAW YOU IN MY DREAMS.
I AM ELEYN, THE LAST TO FALL. FROM US ALL, I GIVE YOU THANKS. YOU HAVE WON US PEACE.
NOW YOU MUST SLEEP.
BUT MY FRIENDS--
--ARE SAFE. SLEEP, WANDA MAXIMOFF...
SLEEP.

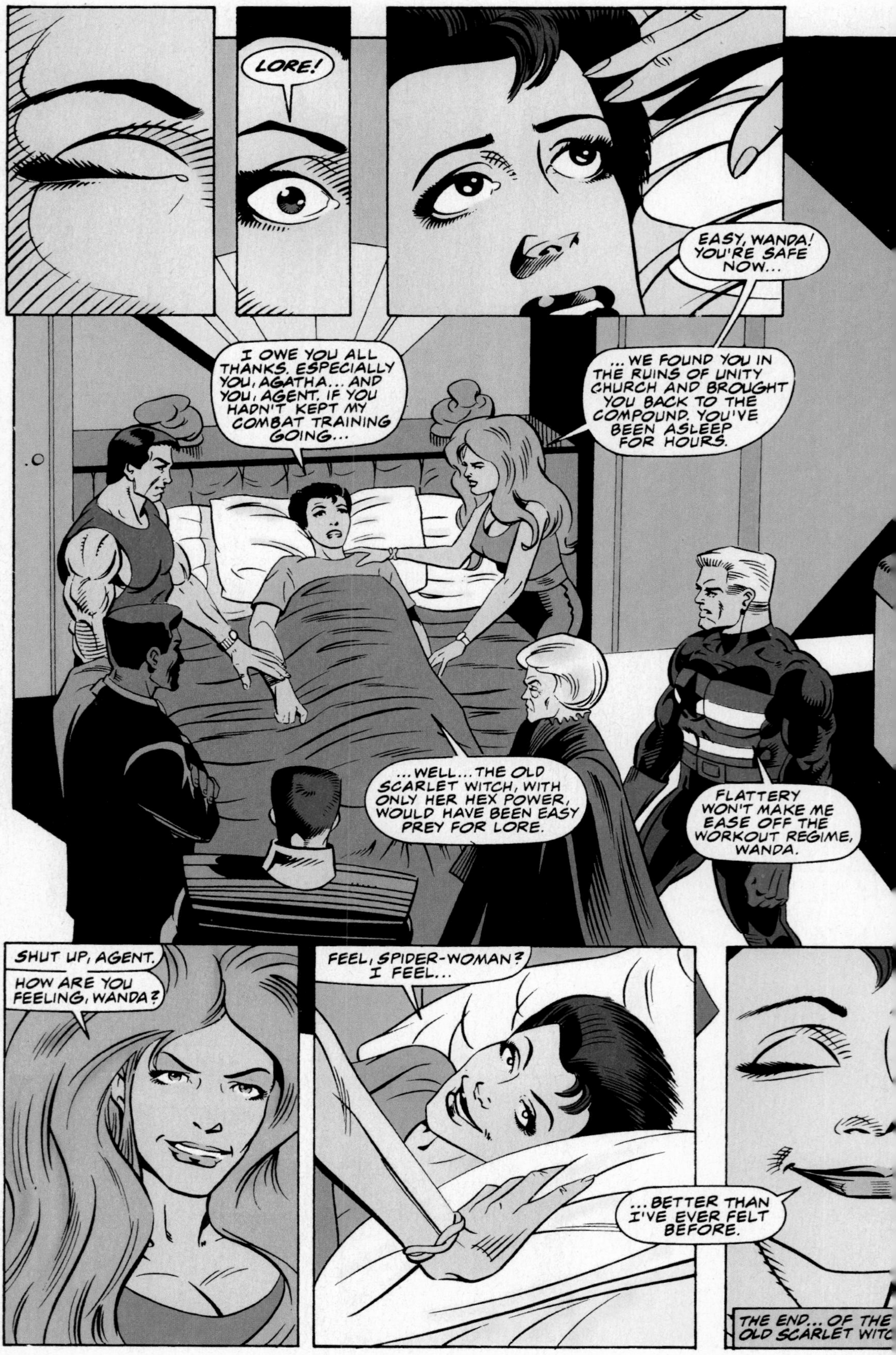

LORE!
EASY, WANDA! YOU'RE SAFE NOW...
...WE FOUND YOU IN THE RUINS OF UNITY CHURCH AND BROUGHT YOU BACK TO THE COMPOUND. YOU'VE BEEN ASLEEP FOR HOURS.
I OWE YOU ALL THANKS. ESPECIALLY YOU, AGATHA... AND YOU, AGENT. IF YOU HADN'T KEPT MY COMBAT TRAINING GOING...
...WELL...THE OLD SCARLET WITCH, WITH ONLY HER HEX POWER, WOULD HAVE BEEN EASY PREY FOR LORE.
FLATTERY WON'T MAKE ME EASE OFF THE WORKOUT REGIME, WANDA.
SHUT UP, AGENT.
HOW ARE YOU FEELING, WANDA?
FEEL, SPIDER-WOMAN? I FEEL...
...BETTER THAN I'VE EVER FELT BEFORE.
THE END... OF THE OLD SCARLET WITC

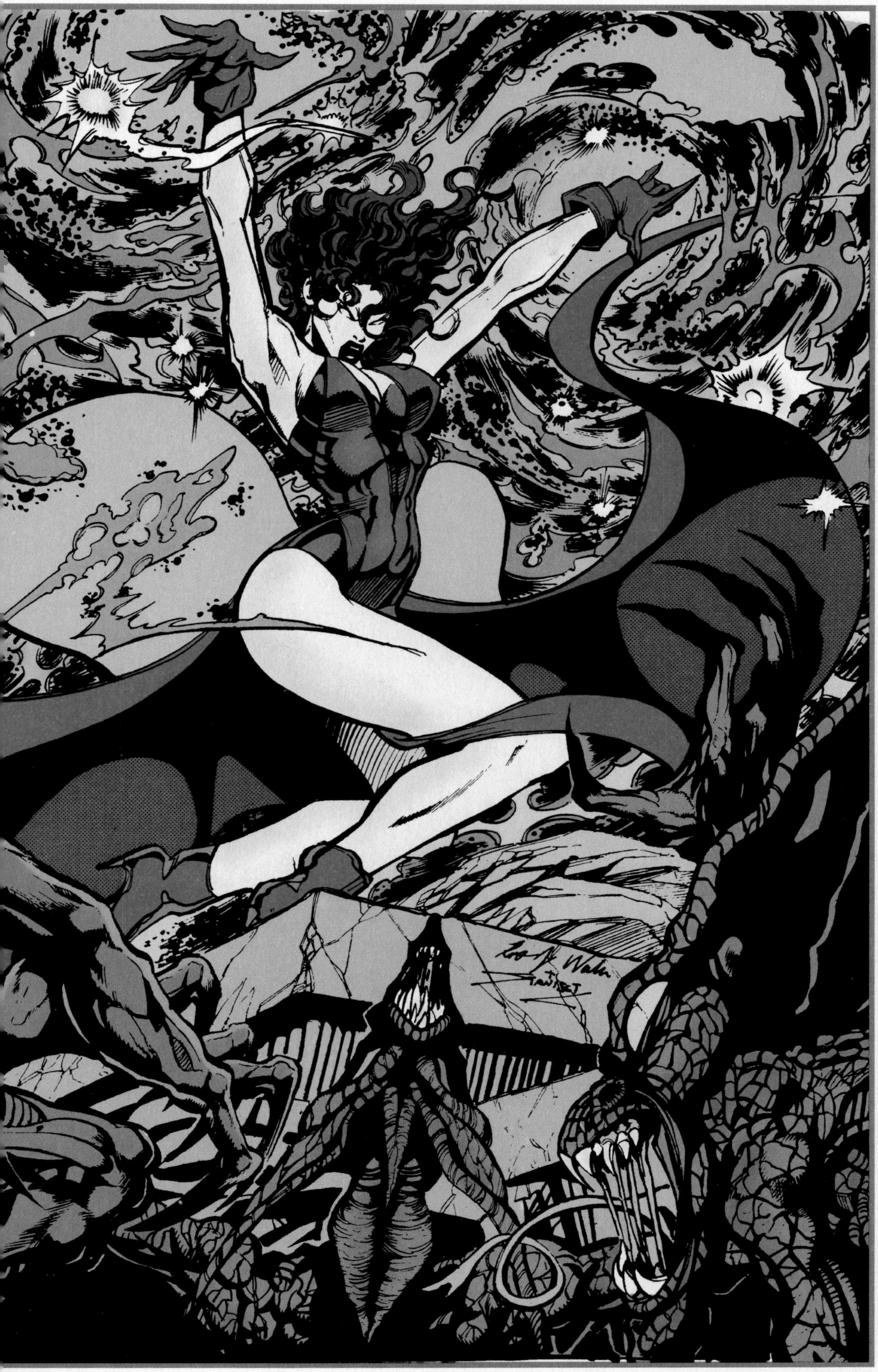

PINUP BY ROBERT WALKER & JOHN STANISCI

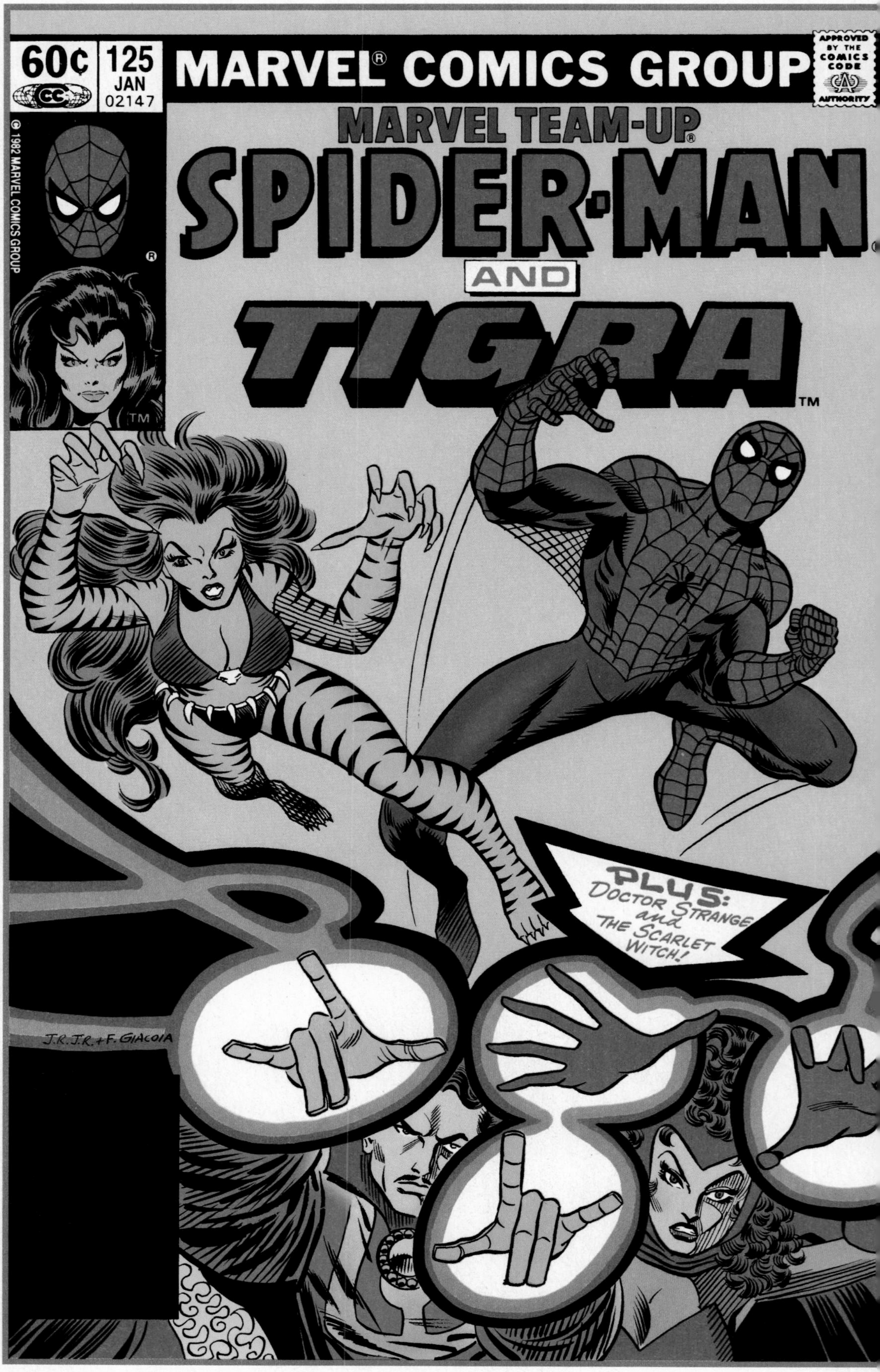
60¢
125
JAN
02147
MARVEL® COMICS GROUP
APPROVED BY THE COMICS CODE AUTHORITY
© 1982 MARVEL COMICS GROUP
MARVEL TEAM-UP®
SPIDER-MAN
AND
TIGRA™
PLUS: DOCTOR STRANGE and THE SCARLET WITCH!
J.R.J.R.+F. GIACOIA

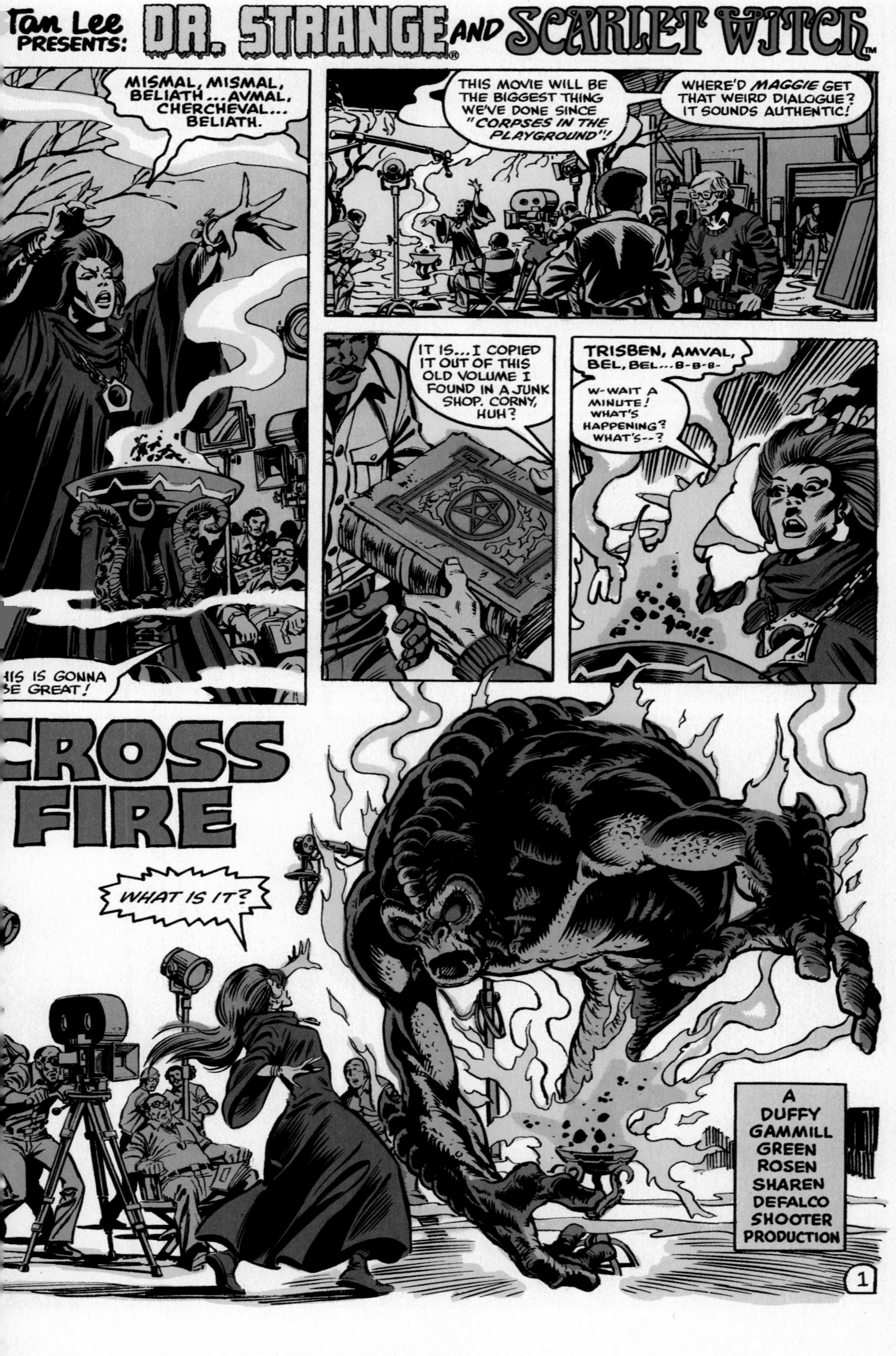
Stan Lee PRESENTS: DR. STRANGE AND SCARLET WITCH
MISMAL, MISMAL, BELIATH ... AVMAL, CHERCHEVAL... BELIATH.
THIS MOVIE WILL BE THE BIGGEST THING WE'VE DONE SINCE "CORPSES IN THE PLAYGROUND"!
WHERE'D MAGGIE GET THAT WEIRD DIALOGUE? IT SOUNDS AUTHENTIC!
IT IS... I COPIED IT OUT OF THIS OLD VOLUME I FOUND IN A JUNK SHOP. CORNY, HUH?
TRISBEN, AMVAL, BEL, BEL... B-B-B-
W-WAIT A MINUTE! WHAT'S HAPPENING? WHAT'S--?
HIS IS GONNA BE GREAT!
CROSS FIRE
WHAT IS IT?
A DUFFY GAMMILL GREEN ROSEN SHAREN DEFALCO SHOOTER PRODUCTION
1

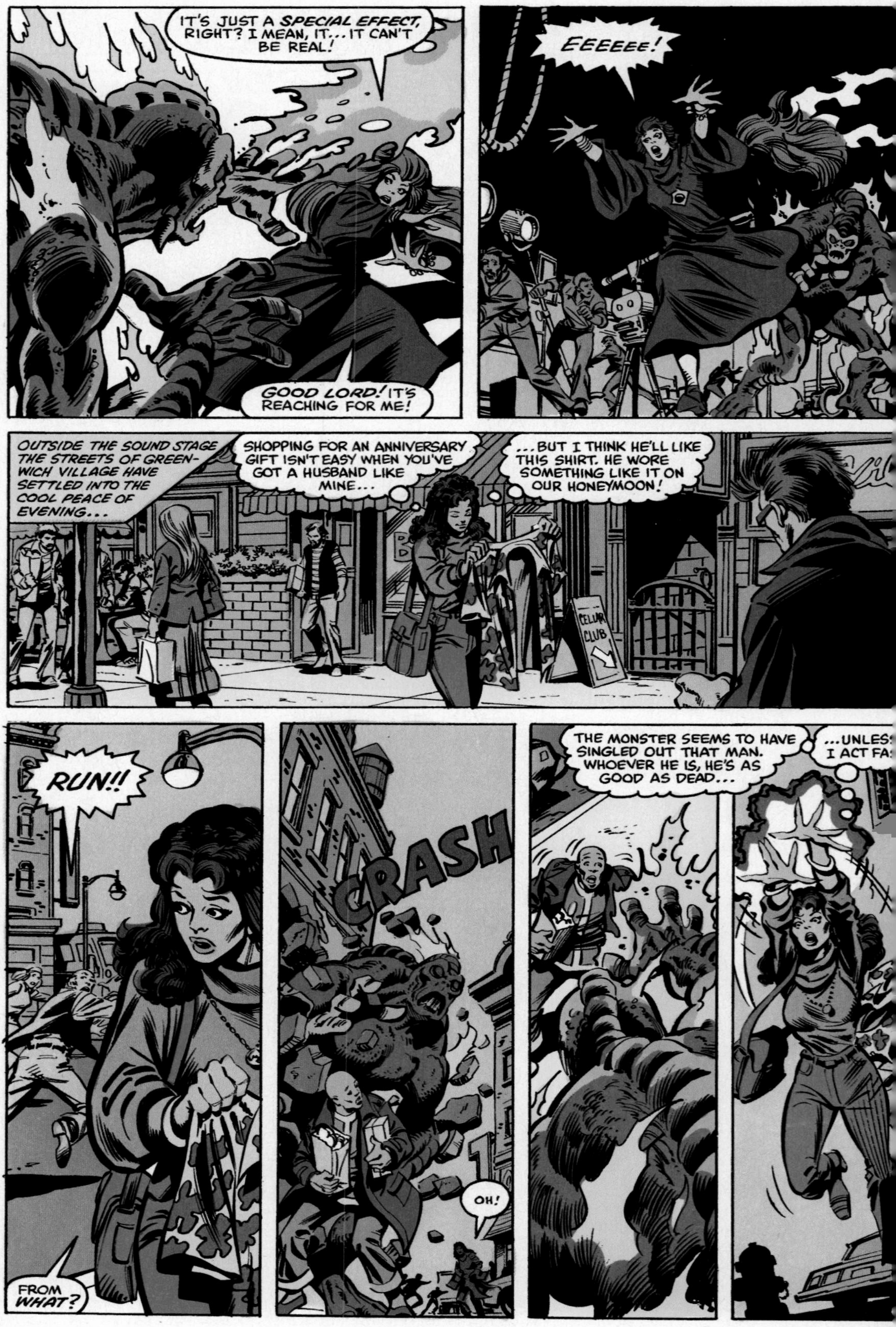
IT'S JUST A SPECIAL EFFECT, RIGHT? I MEAN, IT... IT CAN'T BE REAL!
GOOD LORD! IT'S REACHING FOR ME!
EEEEEE!
OUTSIDE THE SOUND STAGE THE STREETS OF GREENWICH VILLAGE HAVE SETTLED INTO THE COOL PEACE OF EVENING...
SHOPPING FOR AN ANNIVERSARY GIFT ISN'T EASY WHEN YOU'VE GOT A HUSBAND LIKE MINE...
...BUT I THINK HE'LL LIKE THIS SHIRT. HE WORE SOMETHING LIKE IT ON OUR HONEYMOON!
CELLAR CLUB
RUN!!
FROM WHAT?
CRASH
OH!
THE MONSTER SEEMS TO HAVE SINGLED OUT THAT MAN. WHOEVER HE IS, HE'S AS GOOD AS DEAD...
...UNLESS I ACT FAS

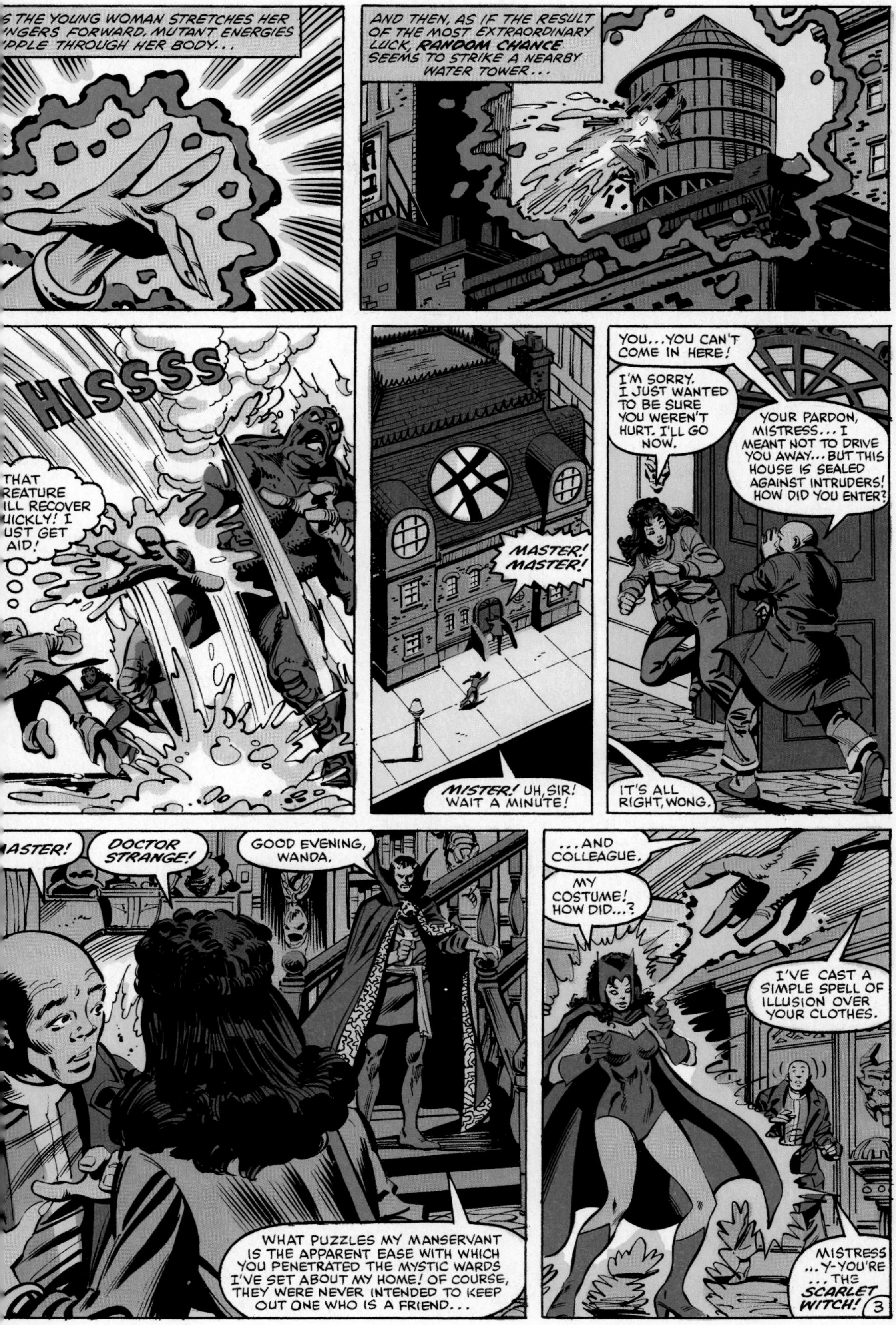
S THE YOUNG WOMAN STRETCHES HER INGERS FORWARD, MUTANT ENERGIES IPPLE THROUGH HER BODY...
AND THEN, AS IF THE RESULT OF THE MOST EXTRAORDINARY LUCK, RANDOM CHANCE SEEMS TO STRIKE A NEARBY WATER TOWER...
HISSSS
THAT REATURE ILL RECOVER UICKLY! I UST GET AID!
MASTER! MASTER!
MISTER! UH, SIR! WAIT A MINUTE!
YOU...YOU CAN'T COME IN HERE!
I'M SORRY. I JUST WANTED TO BE SURE YOU WEREN'T HURT. I'LL GO NOW.
YOUR PARDON, MISTRESS... I MEANT NOT TO DRIVE YOU AWAY... BUT THIS HOUSE IS SEALED AGAINST INTRUDERS! HOW DID YOU ENTER?
IT'S ALL RIGHT, WONG.
ASTER!
DOCTOR STRANGE!
GOOD EVENING, WANDA.
WHAT PUZZLES MY MANSERVANT IS THE APPARENT EASE WITH WHICH YOU PENETRATED THE MYSTIC WARDS I'VE SET ABOUT MY HOME! OF COURSE, THEY WERE NEVER INTENDED TO KEEP OUT ONE WHO IS A FRIEND...
...AND COLLEAGUE.
MY COSTUME! HOW DID...?
I'VE CAST A SIMPLE SPELL OF ILLUSION OVER YOUR CLOTHES.
MISTRESS ...Y-YOU'RE ...THE SCARLET WITCH!
3

"DOCTOR STRANGE, THERE'S SOMETHING OUT THERE. IT'S MENACING PEOPLE, BLASTING FLAME AT EVERYONE IT ENCOUNTERS! AND IT'S DEFINITELY HEADING THIS WAY!"

WE'VE GOT TO GET OUT THERE AND--!

ALL IN GOOD TIME, WANDA.

WONG, IF YOU'D BE KIND ENOUGH TO MAKE US SOME TEA...

TEA? AT A TIME LIKE THIS?! DOCTOR, YOU'RE THE SORCERER SUPREME...AND I'M A TRAINED WITCH, WITH THE MUTANT ABILITY TO CAST HEXES. BETWEEN THE TWO OF US, WE HAVE ENOUGH POWER TO--!

KNOWLE IS THE ONLY TR POWER, DEAR.

WE'LL A FEEL BETT AFTER A C OF TEA.

NOW, TELL ME ABOUT THIS...THING.

AND SOON...

YOU'RE SURE YOU'VE DESCRIBED THIS CREATURE ACCURATELY? A RIDGED HEAD, CASTING FLAME FROM HIS FINGER-TIPS, AND NEVER MAKING A SOUND?

SIZZLING SOUNDS-- WHEN I GOT HIM WET.

THE MOON IS FULL TONIGHT...WITH JUPITER IN ARIES. I BELIEVE I HAVE THE ANSWER. SOME MISGUIDED SOUL MAY HAVE SUMMONED UP...ONE OF THE FIRE BEASTS OF BELIATH! AND THE HARM SUCH A CREATURE COULD DO TO HUMAN BEINGS IS TOO TERRIBLE TO CONTEMPLATE!

SUDDENLY...

THRAM!

DOCTOR STRANGE, WE'VE JUST RUN OUT OF TIME!

YOUR BELIATH IS HERE!

...TSIDE, UICKLY!

BE CAREFUL, DOCTOR! YOU HAVEN'T SEEN WHAT HE CAN...

DON'T BE AFRAID! THIS WON'T TAKE LONG!

OH, NO! THAT BELIATH IS REACH-ING FORWARD...

NO TIME TO ARGUE--!

A SUDDEN GUST OF WIND SWEEPS THROUGH THE STILL STREETS RIPPING LOOSE A NEARBY BILLBOARD...

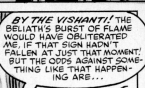

VOTE FOR BILL SCOTT

...AND THEN--

BY THE VISHANTI! THE BELIATH'S BURST OF FLAME WOULD HAVE OBLITERATED ME, IF THAT SIGN HADN'T FALLEN AT JUST THAT MOMENT! BUT THE ODDS AGAINST SOME-THING LIKE THAT HAPPEN-ING ARE...

ASTRONOMICAL? NOT WHEN YOU'RE A MUTANT, BORN WITH THE ABILITY TO CAST HEXES WHICH ALTER PROBABILITIES!

I DIDN'T KNOW YOU COULD FLY, DOCTOR!

I CAN'T! BUT MY CLOAK OF LEVITATION CAN!

NOW, BEFORE THE BELIATH CAN RESPOND, I'LL SUM-MON THE POWER OF MY ENCHANTED AMULET-- THE EYE OF AGAMOTTO--

5

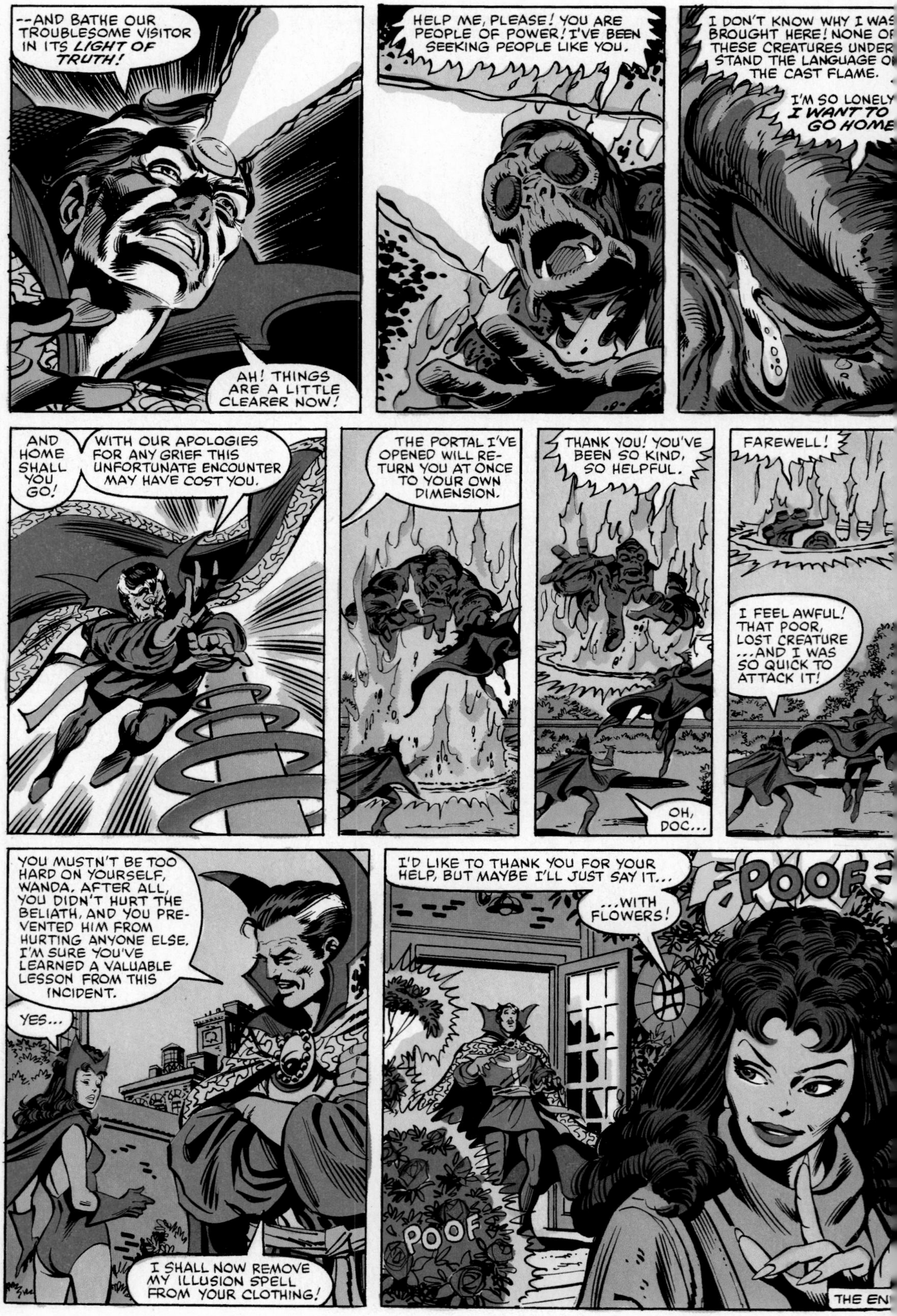
--AND BATHE OUR TROUBLESOME VISITOR IN ITS LIGHT OF TRUTH!
AH! THINGS ARE A LITTLE CLEARER NOW!
HELP ME, PLEASE! YOU ARE PEOPLE OF POWER! I'VE BEEN SEEKING PEOPLE LIKE YOU.
I DON'T KNOW WHY I WAS BROUGHT HERE! NONE OF THESE CREATURES UNDERSTAND THE LANGUAGE OF THE CAST FLAME.
I'M SO LONELY I WANT TO GO HOME
AND HOME SHALL YOU GO!
WITH OUR APOLOGIES FOR ANY GRIEF THIS UNFORTUNATE ENCOUNTER MAY HAVE COST YOU.
THE PORTAL I'VE OPENED WILL RETURN YOU AT ONCE TO YOUR OWN DIMENSION.
THANK YOU! YOU'VE BEEN SO KIND, SO HELPFUL.
OH, DOC...
FAREWELL!
I FEEL AWFUL! THAT POOR, LOST CREATURE ...AND I WAS SO QUICK TO ATTACK IT!
YOU MUSTN'T BE TOO HARD ON YOURSELF, WANDA. AFTER ALL, YOU DIDN'T HURT THE BELIATH, AND YOU PREVENTED HIM FROM HURTING ANYONE ELSE. I'M SURE YOU'VE LEARNED A VALUABLE LESSON FROM THIS INCIDENT.
YES...
I SHALL NOW REMOVE MY ILLUSION SPELL FROM YOUR CLOTHING!
I'D LIKE TO THANK YOU FOR YOUR HELP, BUT MAYBE I'LL JUST SAY IT...
...WITH FLOWERS!
POOF
POOF

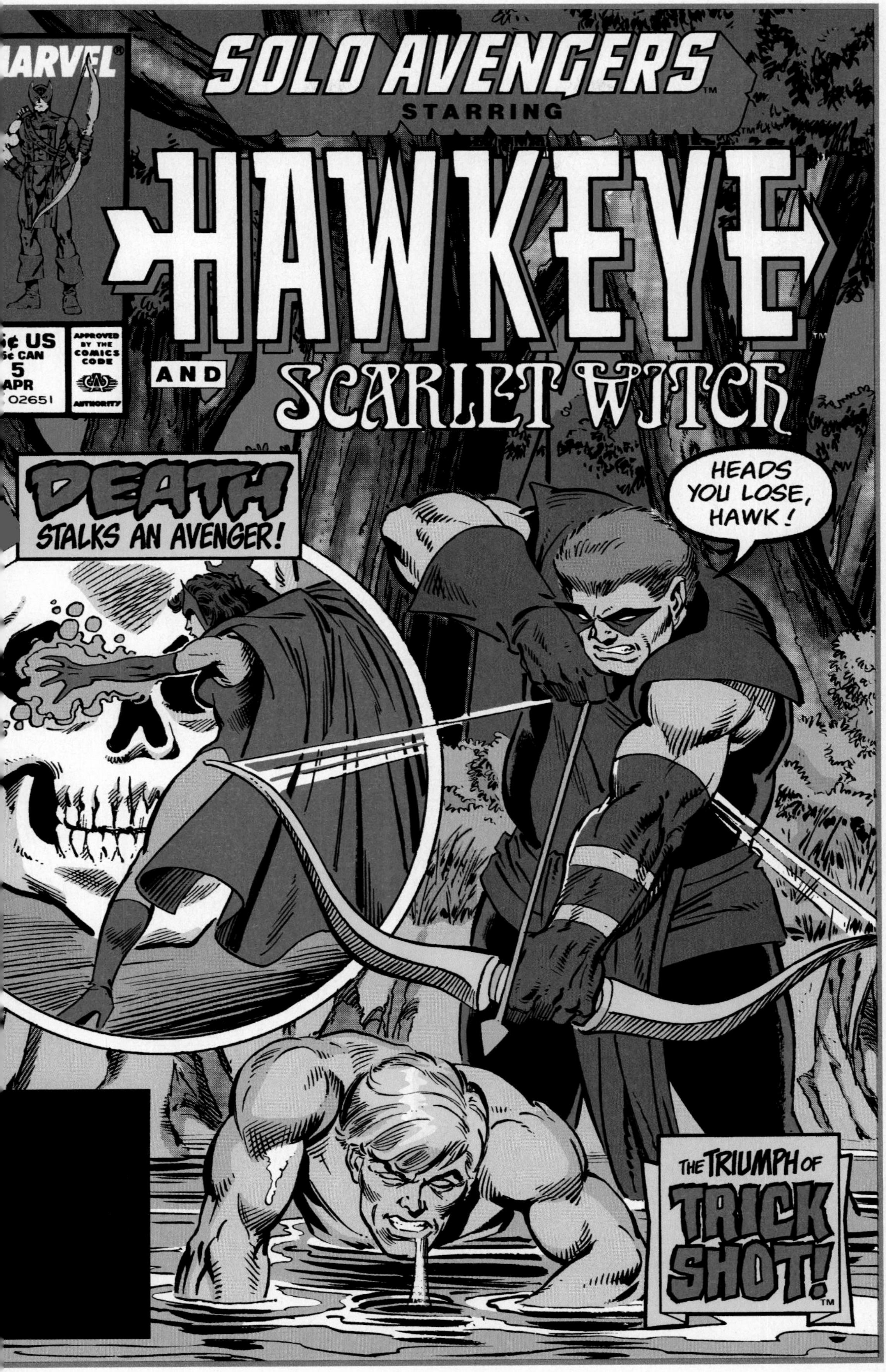
MARVEL
SOLO AVENGERS
STARRING
HAWKEYE
AND
SCARLET WITCH
5¢ US
5¢ CAN
5
APR
02651
APPROVED BY THE COMICS CODE AUTHORITY
DEATH STALKS AN AVENGER!
HEADS YOU LOSE, HAWK!
THE TRIUMPH OF TRICK SHOT!

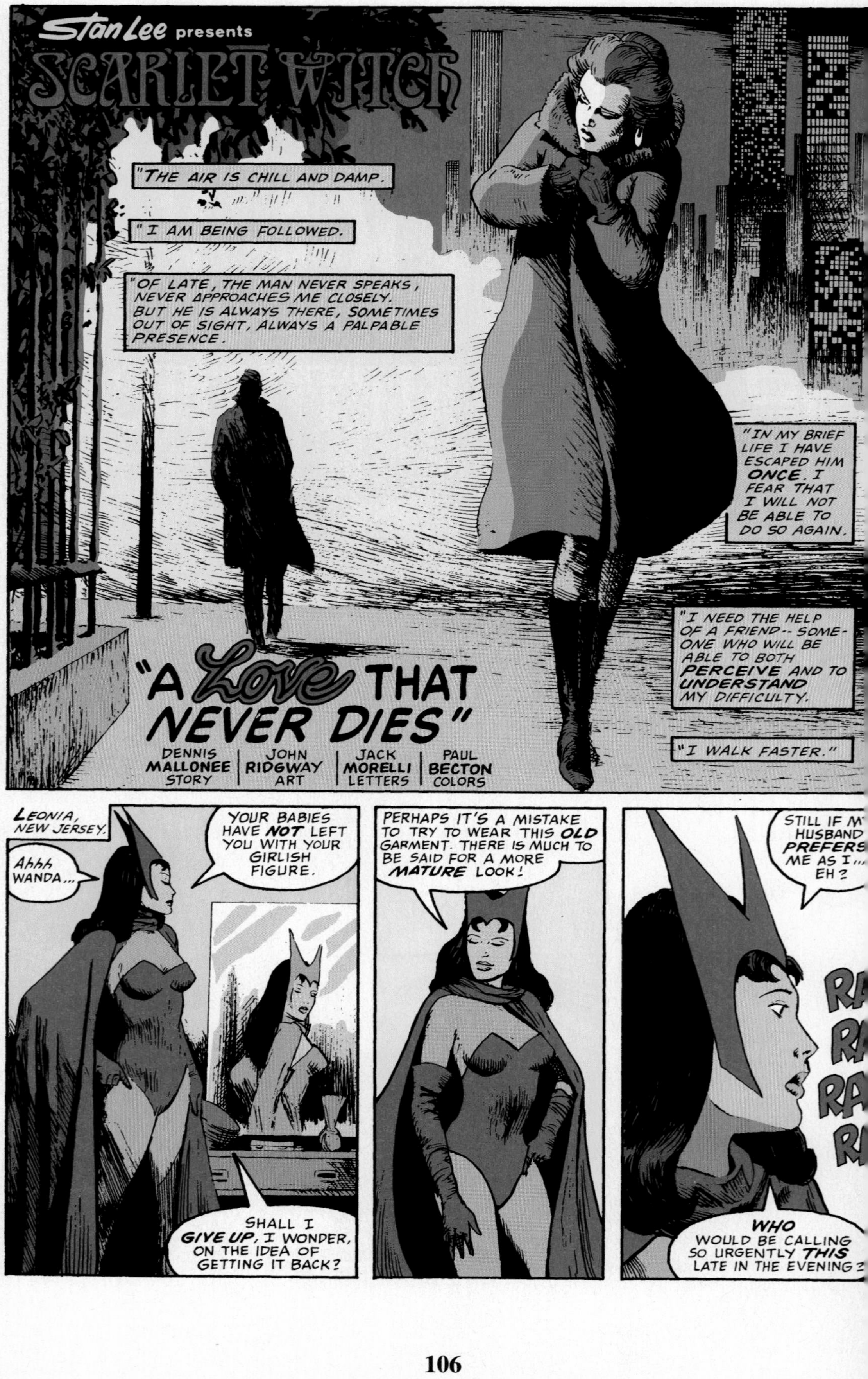
Stan Lee presents
SCARLET WITCH
"THE AIR IS CHILL AND DAMP.
"I AM BEING FOLLOWED.
"OF LATE, THE MAN NEVER SPEAKS, NEVER APPROACHES ME CLOSELY. BUT HE IS ALWAYS THERE, SOMETIMES OUT OF SIGHT, ALWAYS A PALPABLE PRESENCE.
"IN MY BRIEF LIFE I HAVE ESCAPED HIM ONCE. I FEAR THAT I WILL NOT BE ABLE TO DO SO AGAIN.
"I NEED THE HELP OF A FRIEND-- SOMEONE WHO WILL BE ABLE TO BOTH PERCEIVE AND TO UNDERSTAND MY DIFFICULTY.
"I WALK FASTER."
"A LOVE THAT NEVER DIES"
DENNIS MALLONEE STORY
JOHN RIDGWAY ART
JACK MORELLI LETTERS
PAUL BECTON COLORS
LEONIA, NEW JERSEY.
Ahhh WANDA...
YOUR BABIES HAVE NOT LEFT YOU WITH YOUR GIRLISH FIGURE.
SHALL I GIVE UP, I WONDER, ON THE IDEA OF GETTING IT BACK?
PERHAPS IT'S A MISTAKE TO TRY TO WEAR THIS OLD GARMENT. THERE IS MUCH TO BE SAID FOR A MORE MATURE LOOK!
STILL IF M HUSBAND PREFERS ME AS I... EH?
RA
RA
RA
R
WHO WOULD BE CALLING SO URGENTLY THIS LATE IN THE EVENING?

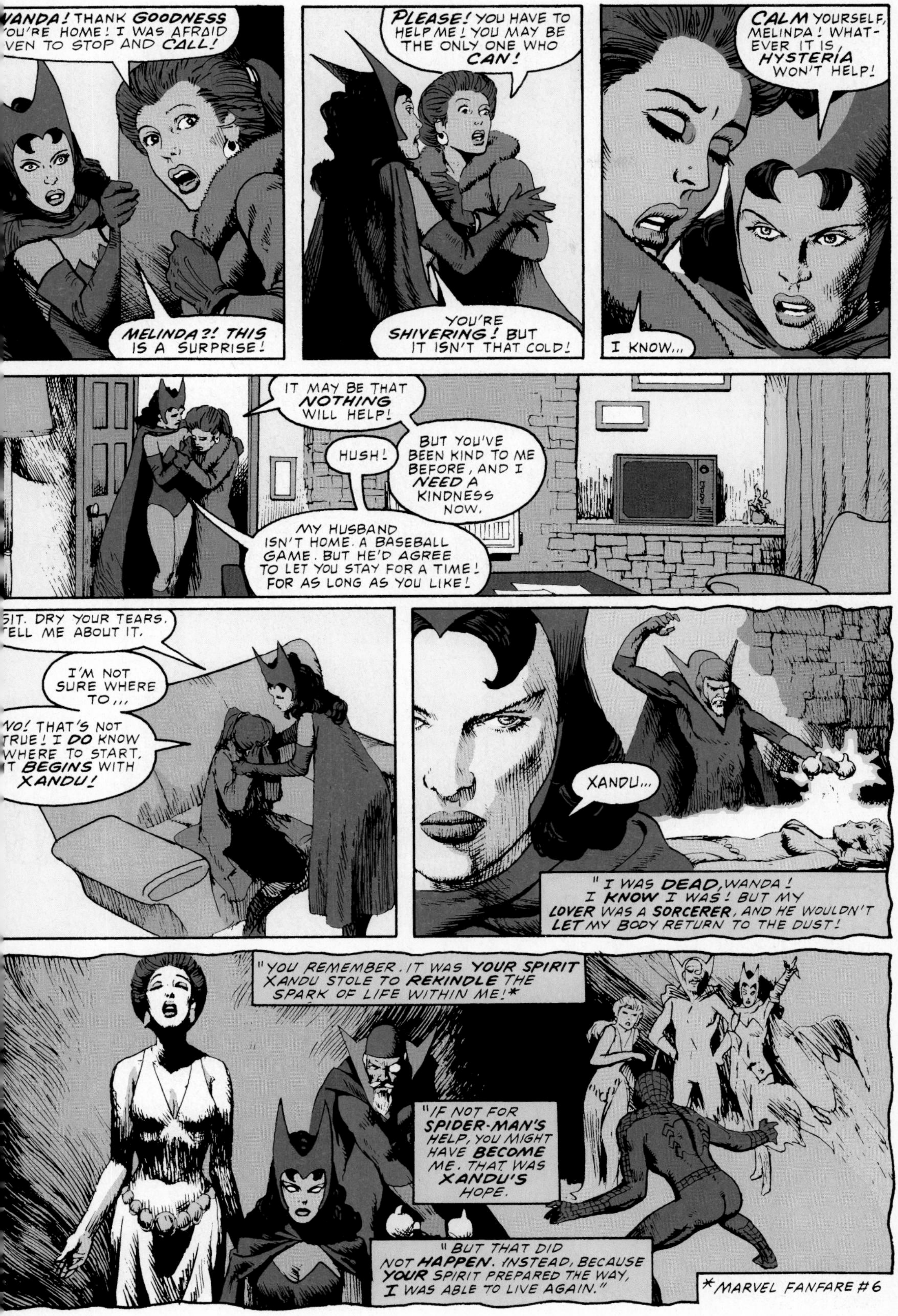
WANDA! THANK GOODNESS YOU'RE HOME! I WAS AFRAID EVEN TO STOP AND CALL!
MELINDA?! THIS IS A SURPRISE!
PLEASE! YOU HAVE TO HELP ME! YOU MAY BE THE ONLY ONE WHO CAN!
YOU'RE SHIVERING! BUT IT ISN'T THAT COLD!
CALM YOURSELF, MELINDA! WHATEVER IT IS, HYSTERIA WON'T HELP!
I KNOW...
IT MAY BE THAT NOTHING WILL HELP!
HUSH!
BUT YOU'VE BEEN KIND TO ME BEFORE, AND I NEED A KINDNESS NOW.
MY HUSBAND ISN'T HOME. A BASEBALL GAME. BUT HE'D AGREE TO LET YOU STAY FOR A TIME! FOR AS LONG AS YOU LIKE!
SIT. DRY YOUR TEARS. TELL ME ABOUT IT.
I'M NOT SURE WHERE TO...
NO! THAT'S NOT TRUE! I DO KNOW WHERE TO START. IT BEGINS WITH XANDU!
XANDU...
"I WAS DEAD, WANDA! I KNOW I WAS! BUT MY LOVER WAS A SORCERER, AND HE WOULDN'T LET MY BODY RETURN TO THE DUST!
"YOU REMEMBER. IT WAS YOUR SPIRIT XANDU STOLE TO REKINDLE THE SPARK OF LIFE WITHIN ME!*
"IF NOT FOR SPIDER-MAN'S HELP, YOU MIGHT HAVE BECOME ME. THAT WAS XANDU'S HOPE.
"BUT THAT DID NOT HAPPEN. INSTEAD, BECAUSE YOUR SPIRIT PREPARED THE WAY, I WAS ABLE TO LIVE AGAIN."
*MARVEL FANFARE #6

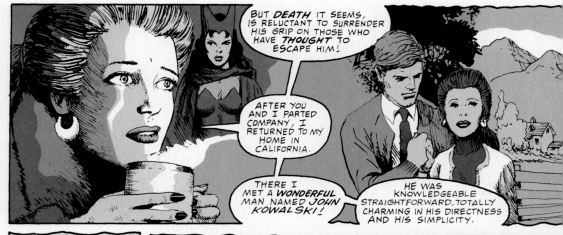

BUT *DEATH* IT SEEMS, IS RELUCTANT TO SURRENDER HIS GRIP ON THOSE WHO HAVE *THOUGHT* TO ESCAPE HIM!

AFTER YOU AND I PARTED COMPANY, I RETURNED TO MY HOME IN CALIFORNIA.

THERE I MET A *WONDERFUL* MAN NAMED *JOHN KOWALSKI!*

HE WAS KNOWLEDGEABLE STRAIGHTFORWARD, TOTALLY CHARMING IN HIS DIRECTNESS AND HIS SIMPLICITY.

" I COULD *FEEL* MYSELF FALLING IN LOVE, AND I WAS *CERTAIN* THAT MY AFFECTION WAS RETURNED.

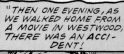

"THEN ONE EVENING, AS WE WALKED HOME FROM A MOVIE IN WESTWOOD, THERE WAS AN ACCIDENT!

" THERE WAS A *DRUNK DRIVER* AND A SIDEWALK.

"AND THE DRIVER PLOWED INTO SEVERAL PEOPLE.

" JOHN THREW ME ASIDE.

"HE WAS THE *LAST* TO BE HIT, HEAD-ON, WITH ENOUGH FORCE TO *KILL.*

"BUT JOHN KOWALSKI *DIDN'T DIE...*

"HE WAS *ALREADY* DEAD!"

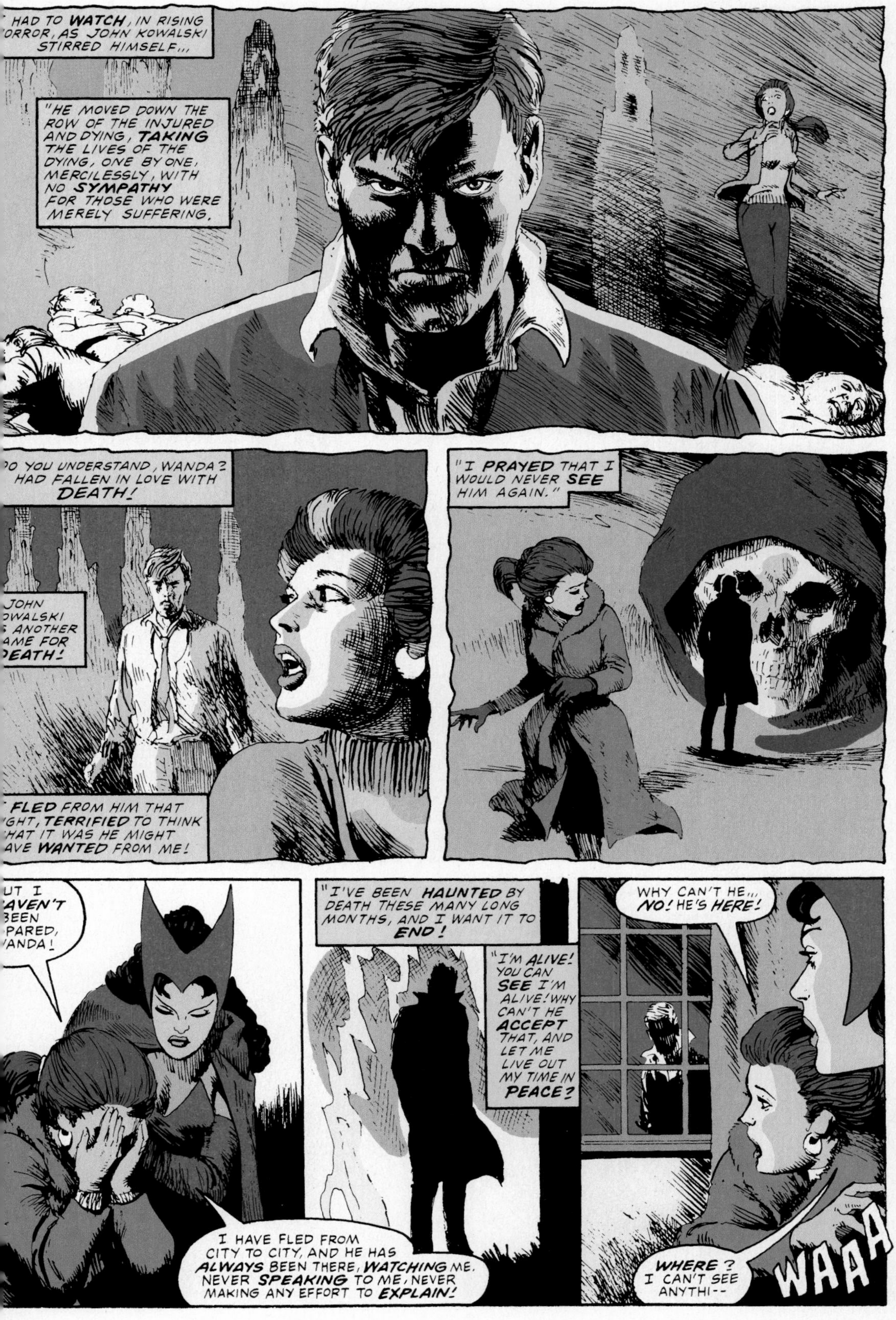

HAD TO WATCH, IN RISING ORROR, AS JOHN KOWALSKI STIRRED HIMSELF...
"HE MOVED DOWN THE ROW OF THE INJURED AND DYING, TAKING THE LIVES OF THE DYING, ONE BY ONE, MERCILESSLY, WITH NO SYMPATHY FOR THOSE WHO WERE MERELY SUFFERING.
O YOU UNDERSTAND, WANDA? HAD FALLEN IN LOVE WITH DEATH!
JOHN OWALSKI S ANOTHER AME FOR DEATH!
FLED FROM HIM THAT GHT, TERRIFIED TO THINK HAT IT WAS HE MIGHT AVE WANTED FROM ME!
"I PRAYED THAT I WOULD NEVER SEE HIM AGAIN."
UT I AVEN'T BEEN PARED, WANDA!
I HAVE FLED FROM CITY TO CITY, AND HE HAS ALWAYS BEEN THERE, WATCHING ME. NEVER SPEAKING TO ME, NEVER MAKING ANY EFFORT TO EXPLAIN!
"I'VE BEEN HAUNTED BY DEATH THESE MANY LONG MONTHS, AND I WANT IT TO END!
"I'M ALIVE! YOU CAN SEE I'M ALIVE! WHY CAN'T HE ACCEPT THAT, AND LET ME LIVE OUT MY TIME IN PEACE?
WHY CAN'T HE... NO! HE'S HERE!
WHERE? I CAN'T SEE ANYTHI--
WAAA

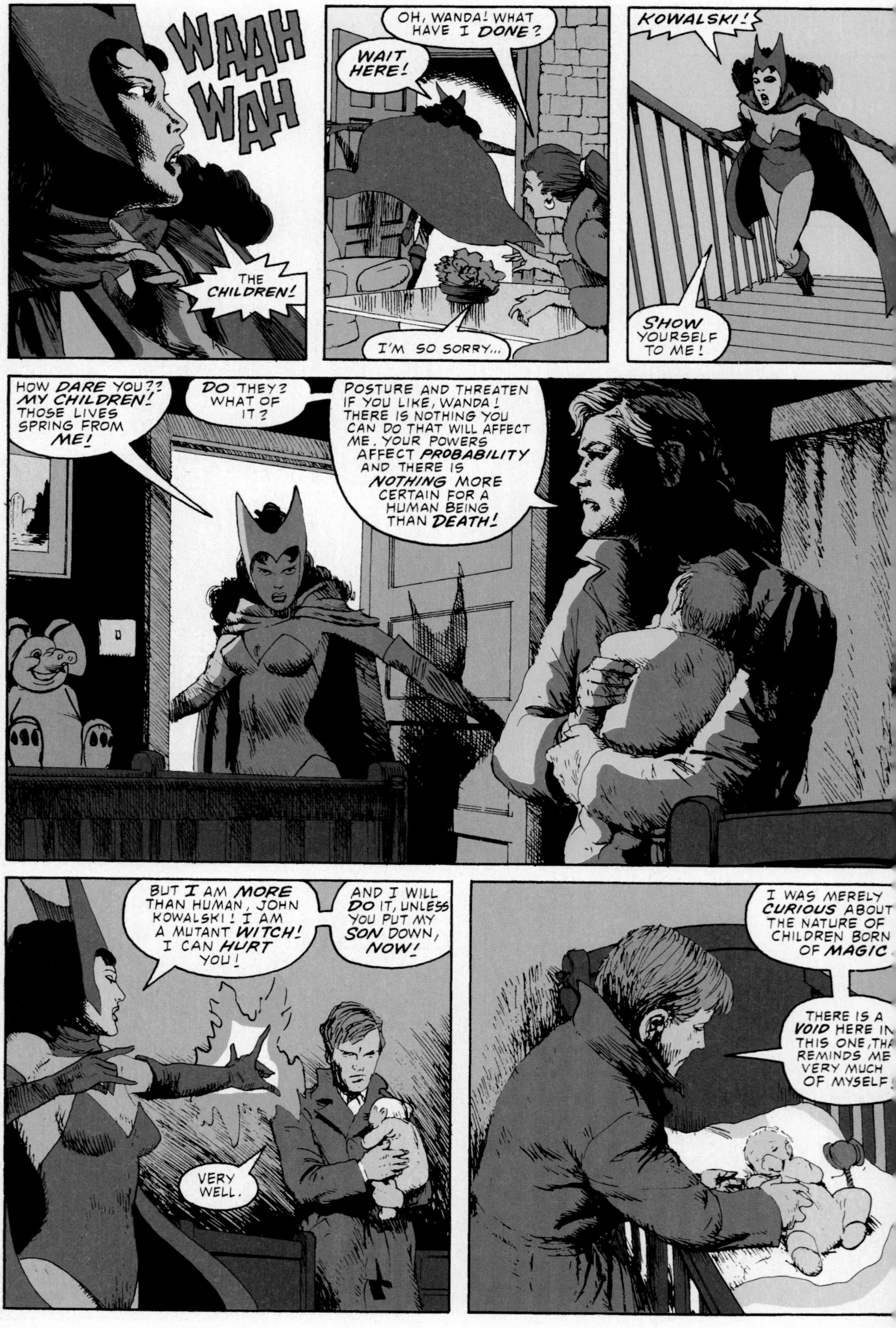
WAAH WAH
THE CHILDREN!
OH, WANDA! WHAT HAVE I DONE?
WAIT HERE!
I'M SO SORRY...
KOWALSKI!
SHOW YOURSELF TO ME!
HOW DARE YOU?? MY CHILDREN! THOSE LIVES SPRING FROM ME!
DO THEY? WHAT OF IT?
POSTURE AND THREATEN IF YOU LIKE, WANDA! THERE IS NOTHING YOU CAN DO THAT WILL AFFECT ME. YOUR POWERS AFFECT PROBABILITY AND THERE IS NOTHING MORE CERTAIN FOR A HUMAN BEING THAN DEATH!
BUT I AM MORE THAN HUMAN, JOHN KOWALSKI! I AM A MUTANT WITCH! I CAN HURT YOU!
AND I WILL DO IT, UNLESS YOU PUT MY SON DOWN, NOW!
VERY WELL.
I WAS MERELY CURIOUS ABOUT THE NATURE OF CHILDREN BORN OF MAGIC.
THERE IS A VOID HERE IN THIS ONE, THAT REMINDS ME VERY MUCH OF MYSELF!

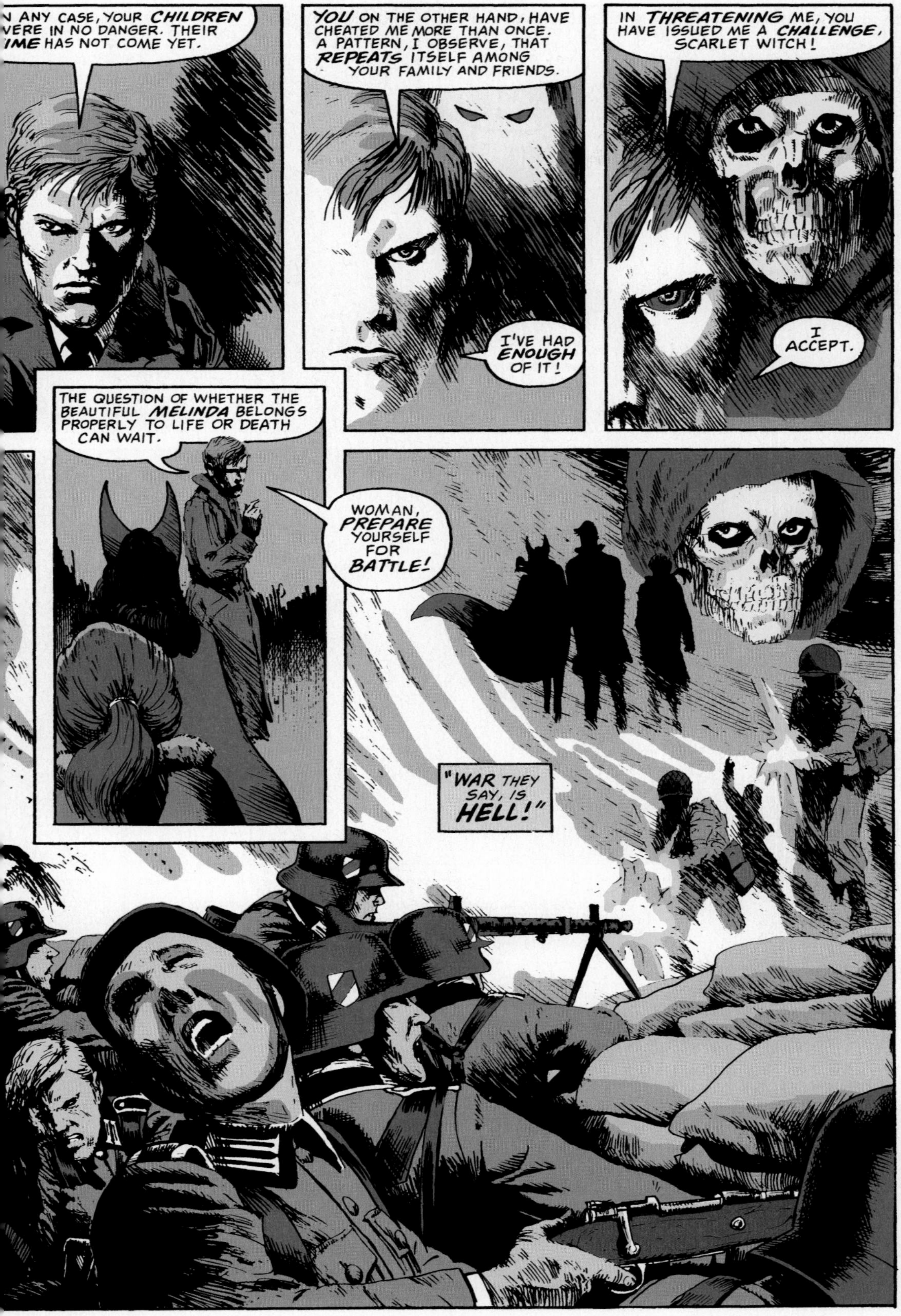
N ANY CASE, YOUR CHILDREN WERE IN NO DANGER. THEIR TIME HAS NOT COME YET.
YOU ON THE OTHER HAND, HAVE CHEATED ME MORE THAN ONCE. A PATTERN, I OBSERVE, THAT REPEATS ITSELF AMONG YOUR FAMILY AND FRIENDS.
I'VE HAD ENOUGH OF IT!
IN THREATENING ME, YOU HAVE ISSUED ME A CHALLENGE, SCARLET WITCH!
I ACCEPT.
THE QUESTION OF WHETHER THE BEAUTIFUL MELINDA BELONGS PROPERLY TO LIFE OR DEATH CAN WAIT.
WOMAN, PREPARE YOURSELF FOR BATTLE!
"WAR THEY SAY, IS HELL!"

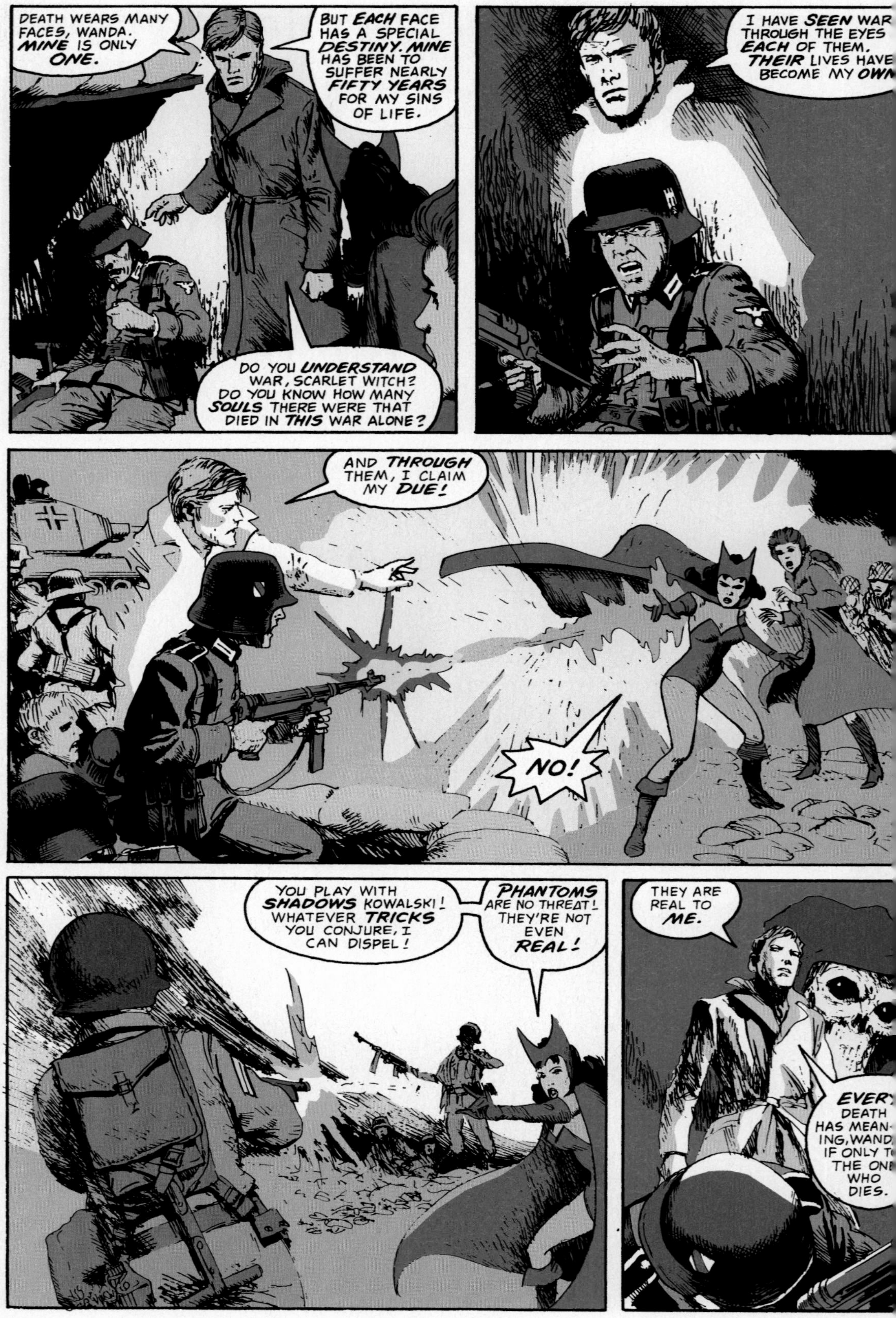
DEATH WEARS MANY FACES, WANDA. MINE IS ONLY ONE.
BUT EACH FACE HAS A SPECIAL DESTINY. MINE HAS BEEN TO SUFFER NEARLY FIFTY YEARS FOR MY SINS OF LIFE.
DO YOU UNDERSTAND WAR, SCARLET WITCH? DO YOU KNOW HOW MANY SOULS THERE WERE THAT DIED IN THIS WAR ALONE?
I HAVE SEEN WAR THROUGH THE EYES EACH OF THEM. THEIR LIVES HAVE BECOME MY OWN
AND THROUGH THEM, I CLAIM MY DUE!
NO!
YOU PLAY WITH SHADOWS KOWALSKI! WHATEVER TRICKS YOU CONJURE, I CAN DISPEL!
PHANTOMS ARE NO THREAT! THEY'RE NOT EVEN REAL!
THEY ARE REAL TO ME.
EVERY DEATH HAS MEAN-ING, WAND IF ONLY T THE ON WHO DIES.

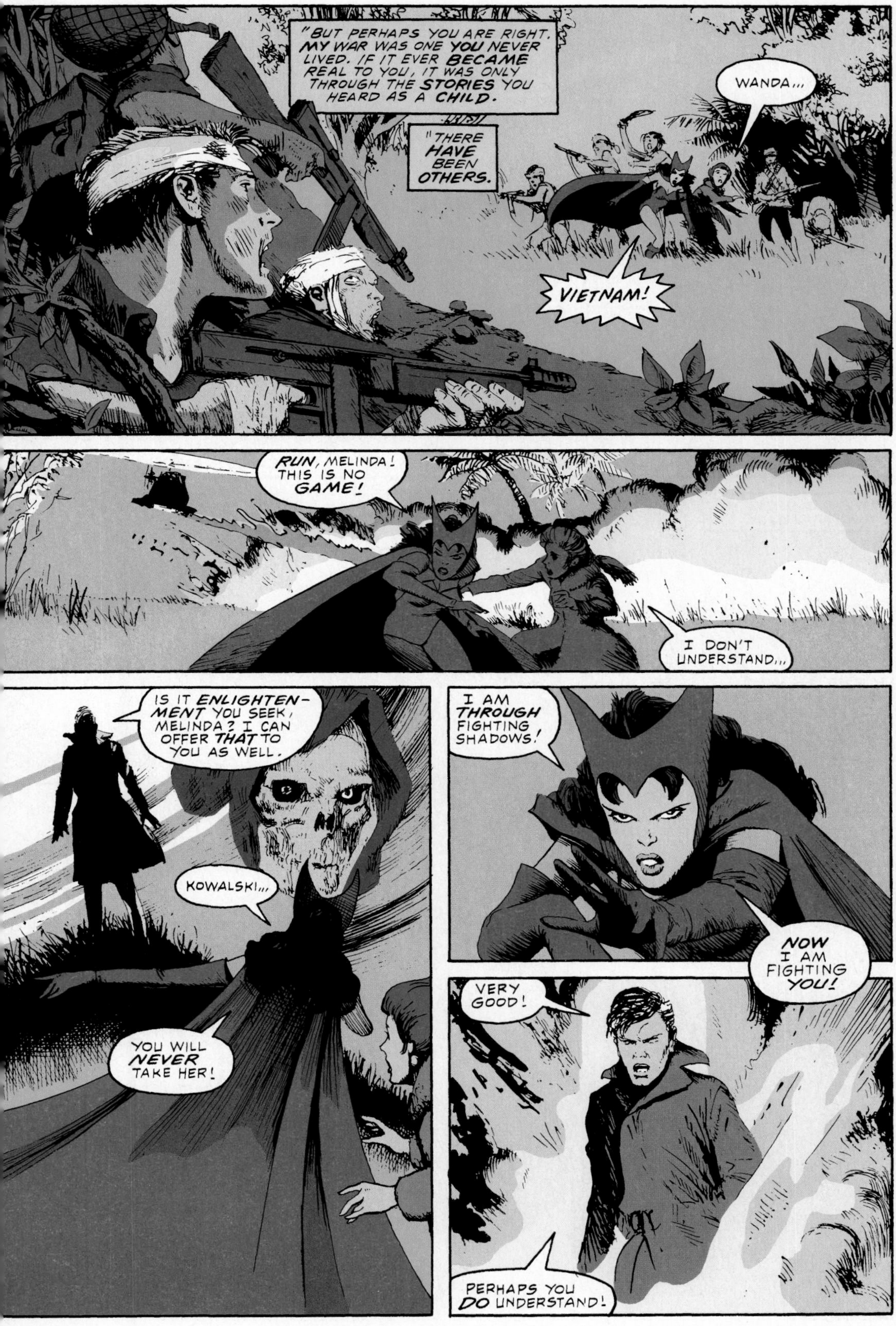
"BUT PERHAPS YOU ARE RIGHT. MY WAR WAS ONE YOU NEVER LIVED. IF IT EVER BECAME REAL TO YOU, IT WAS ONLY THROUGH THE STORIES YOU HEARD AS A CHILD.
"THERE HAVE BEEN OTHERS.
WANDA...
VIETNAM!
RUN, MELINDA! THIS IS NO GAME!
I DON'T UNDERSTAND...
IS IT ENLIGHTEN-MENT YOU SEEK, MELINDA? I CAN OFFER THAT TO YOU AS WELL.
KOWALSKI...
YOU WILL NEVER TAKE HER!
I AM THROUGH FIGHTING SHADOWS!
NOW I AM FIGHTING YOU!
VERY GOOD!
PERHAPS YOU DO UNDERSTAND!

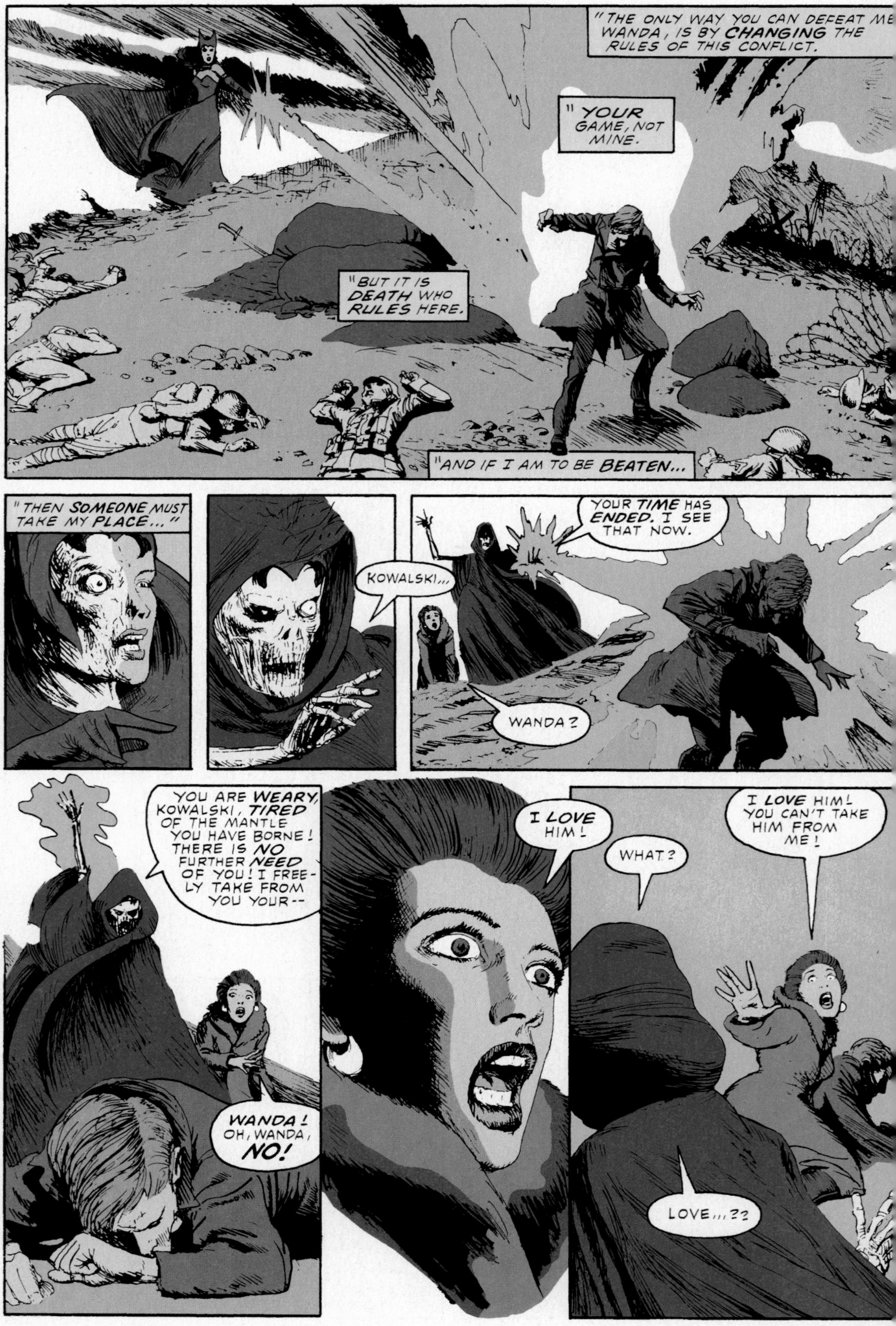
"THE ONLY WAY YOU CAN DEFEAT ME, WANDA, IS BY CHANGING THE RULES OF THIS CONFLICT.
"YOUR GAME, NOT MINE.
"BUT IT IS DEATH WHO RULES HERE.
"AND IF I AM TO BE BEATEN...
"THEN SOMEONE MUST TAKE MY PLACE..."
KOWALSKI...
YOUR TIME HAS ENDED. I SEE THAT NOW.
WANDA?
YOU ARE WEARY, KOWALSKI, TIRED OF THE MANTLE YOU HAVE BORNE! THERE IS NO FURTHER NEED OF YOU! I FREELY TAKE FROM YOU YOUR--
WANDA! OH, WANDA, NO!
I LOVE HIM!
WHAT?
I LOVE HIM! YOU CAN'T TAKE HIM FROM ME!
LOVE...??

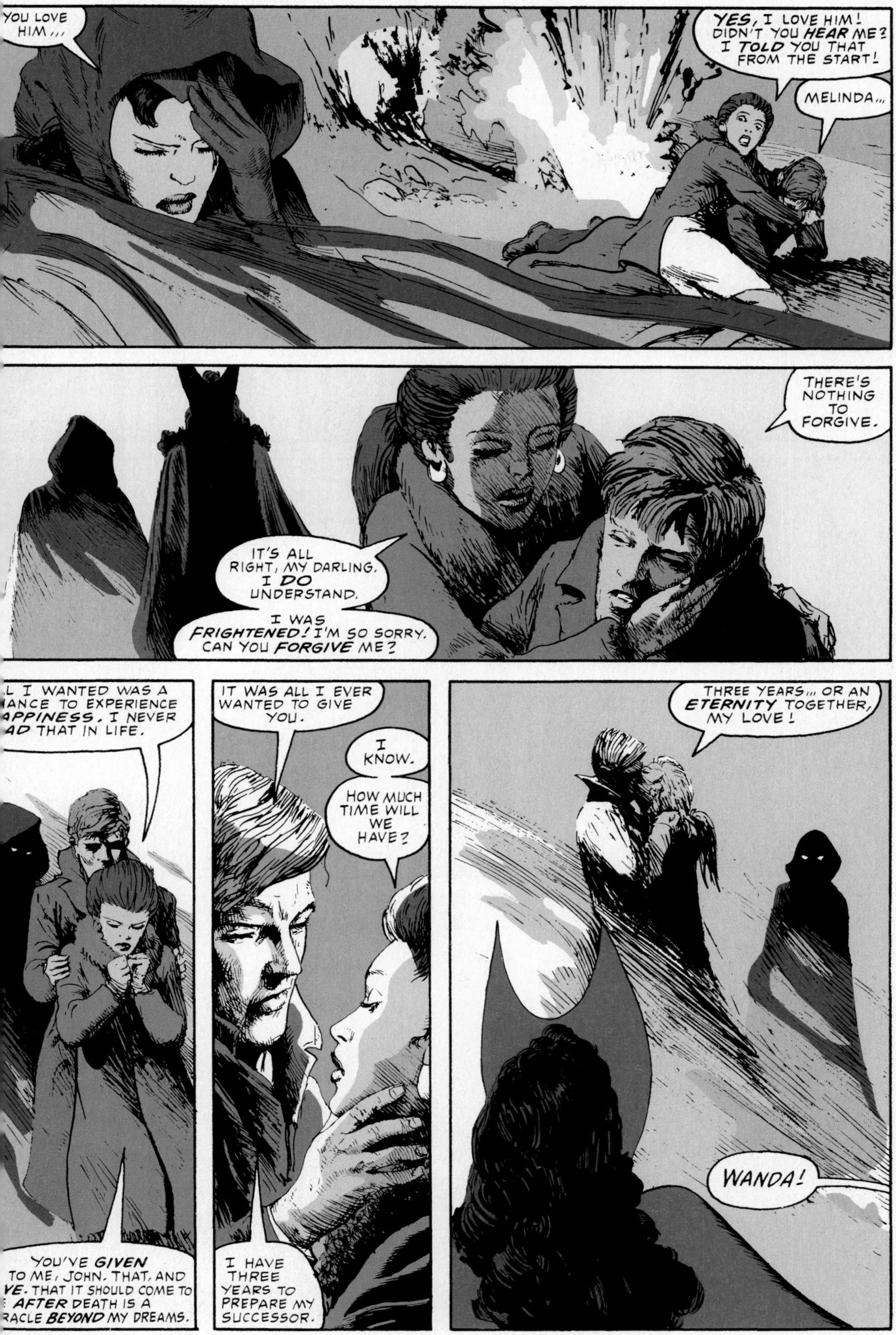
YOU LOVE HIM...
YES, I LOVE HIM! DIDN'T YOU HEAR ME? I TOLD YOU THAT FROM THE START!
MELINDA...
THERE'S NOTHING TO FORGIVE.
IT'S ALL RIGHT, MY DARLING. I DO UNDERSTAND.
I WAS FRIGHTENED! I'M SO SORRY. CAN YOU FORGIVE ME?
L I WANTED WAS A
IANCE TO EXPERIENCE
APPINESS. I NEVER
AD THAT IN LIFE.
YOU'VE GIVEN
TO ME, JOHN. THAT, AND
VE. THAT IT SHOULD COME TO
AFTER DEATH IS A
RACLE BEYOND MY DREAMS.
IT WAS ALL I EVER WANTED TO GIVE YOU.
I KNOW.
HOW MUCH TIME WILL WE HAVE?
I HAVE THREE YEARS TO PREPARE MY SUCCESSOR.
THREE YEARS... OR AN ETERNITY TOGETHER, MY LOVE!
WANDA!

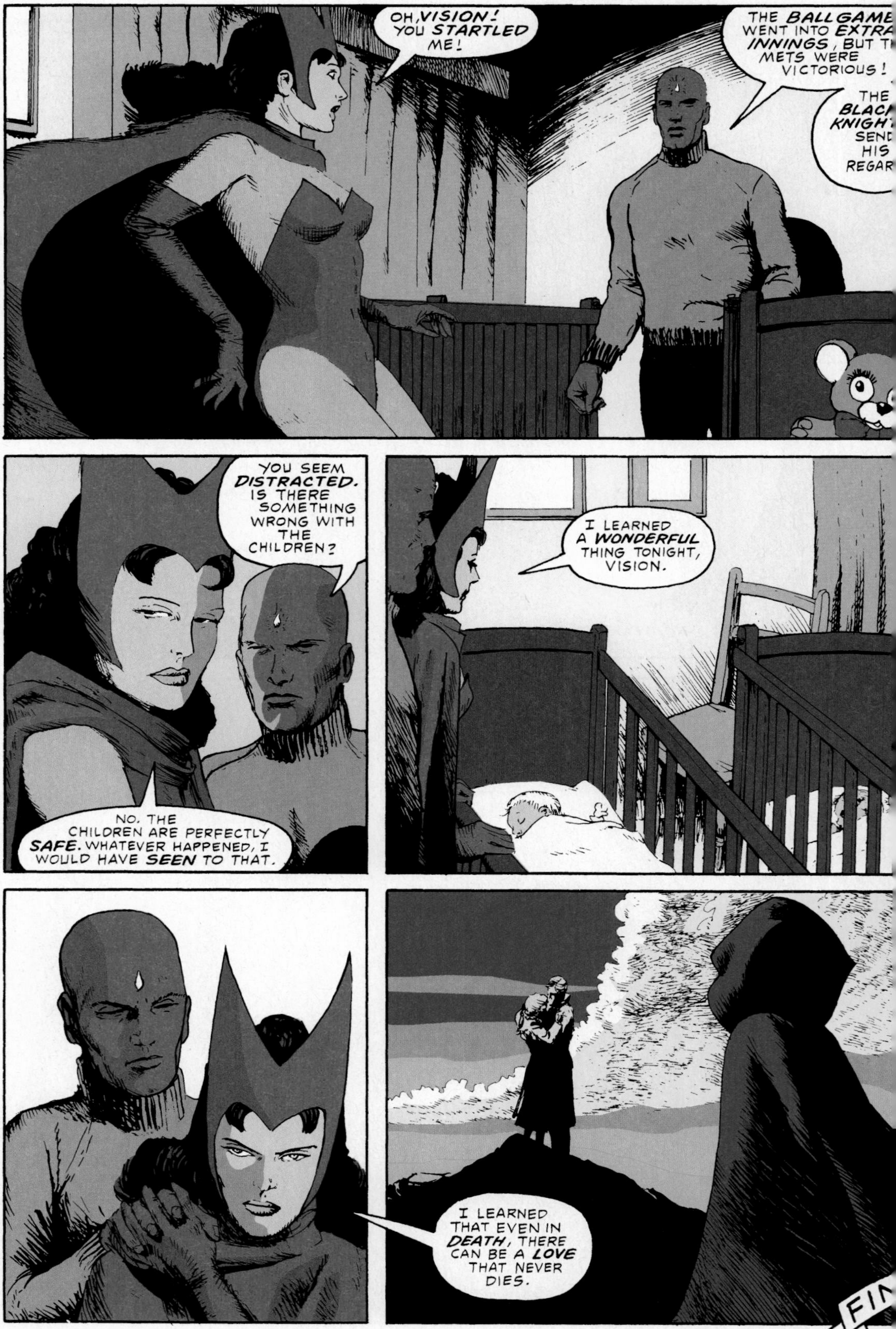
OH, VISION! YOU STARTLED ME!
THE BALLGAME WENT INTO EXTRA INNINGS, BUT T METS WERE VICTORIOUS!
THE BLAC KNIGH SEN HIS REGAR
YOU SEEM DISTRACTED. IS THERE SOMETHING WRONG WITH THE CHILDREN?
NO. THE CHILDREN ARE PERFECTLY SAFE. WHATEVER HAPPENED, I WOULD HAVE SEEN TO THAT.
I LEARNED A WONDERFUL THING TONIGHT, VISION.
I LEARNED THAT EVEN IN DEATH, THERE CAN BE A LOVE THAT NEVER DIES.
FIN

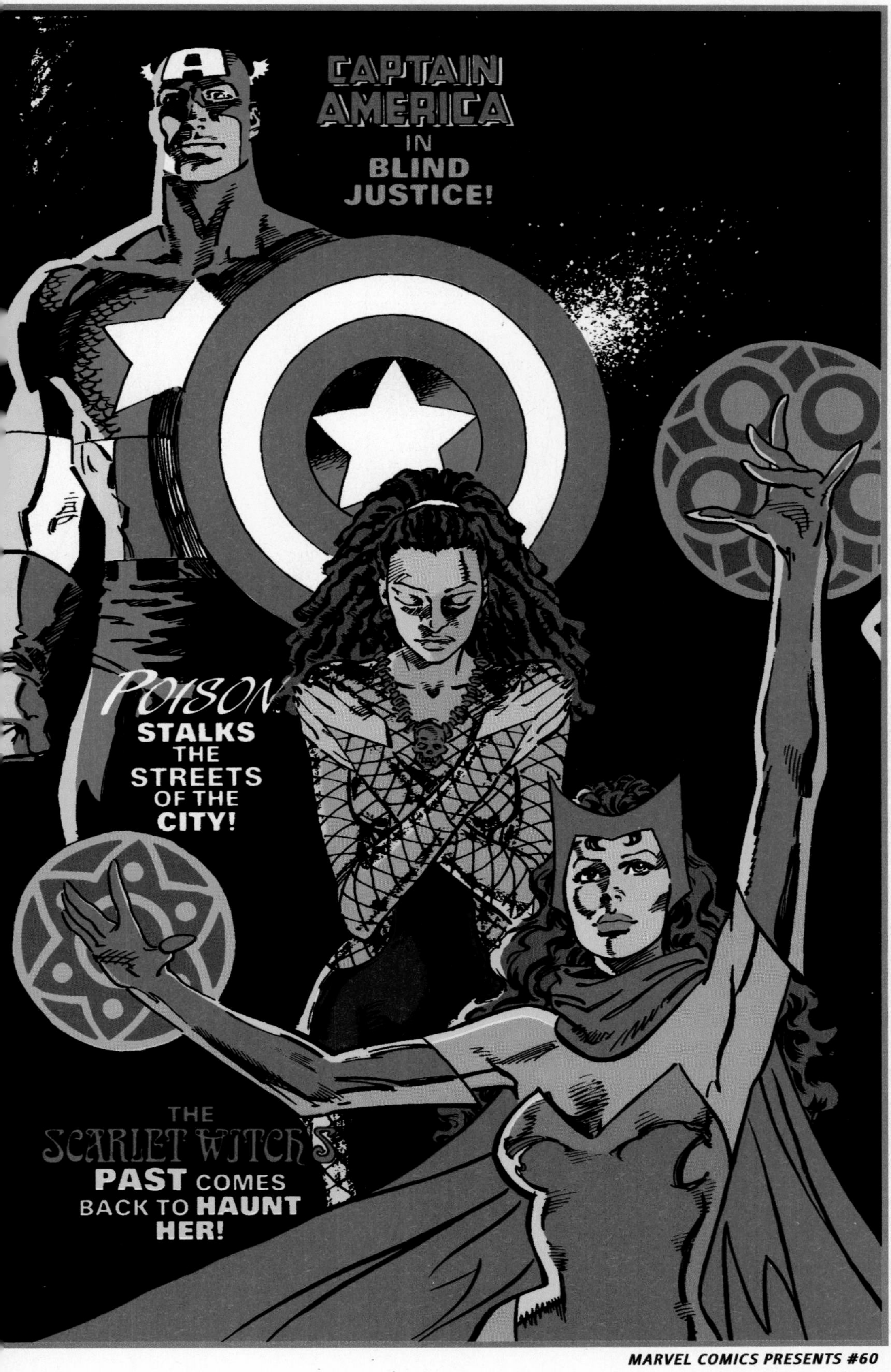
CAPTAIN AMERICA
IN
BLIND
JUSTICE!
POISON
STALKS
THE
STREETS
OF THE
CITY!
THE
SCARLET WITCH'S
PAST COMES
BACK TO HAUNT
HER!

MARVEL COMICS PRESENTS #60

WRITER, ARTIST & COLORIST: RICHARD HOWELL • LETTERER: DIANA ALBERS
ASSISTANT EDITOR: KELLY CORVESE • EDITOR: TERRY KAVANAGH

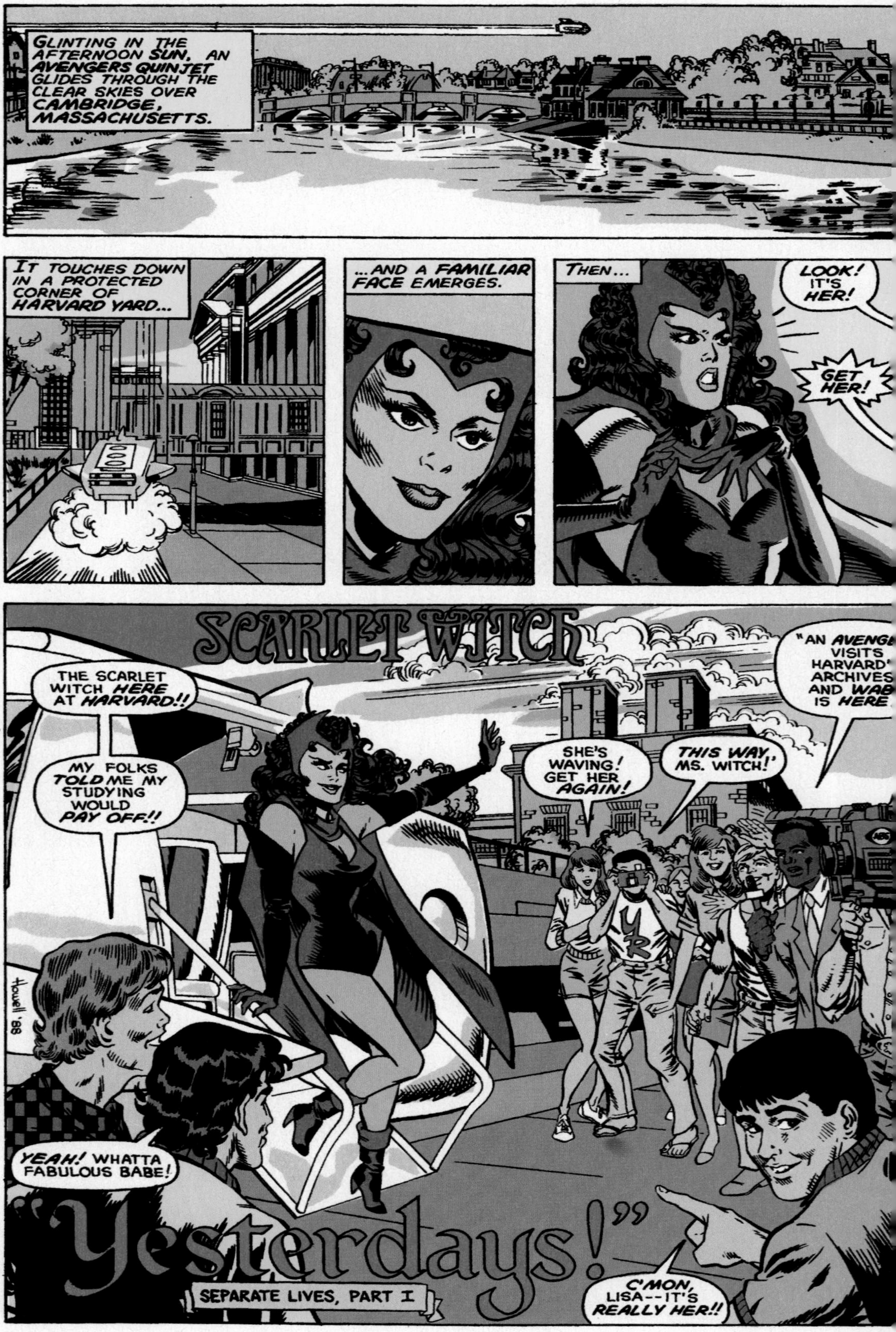

GLINTING IN THE AFTERNOON SUN, AN AVENGERS QUINJET GLIDES THROUGH THE CLEAR SKIES OVER CAMBRIDGE, MASSACHUSETTS.
IT TOUCHES DOWN IN A PROTECTED CORNER OF HARVARD YARD...
...AND A FAMILIAR FACE EMERGES.
THEN...
LOOK! IT'S HER!
GET HER!
SCARLET WITCH
THE SCARLET WITCH HERE AT HARVARD!!
MY FOLKS TOLD ME MY STUDYING WOULD PAY OFF!!
SHE'S WAVING! GET HER AGAIN!
THIS WAY, MS. WITCH!
"AN AVENG VISITS HARVARD' ARCHIVES AND WAB IS HERE
YEAH! WHATTA FABULOUS BABE!
"Yesterdays!"
SEPARATE LIVES, PART I
C'MON, LISA--IT'S REALLY HER!!
Howell '88

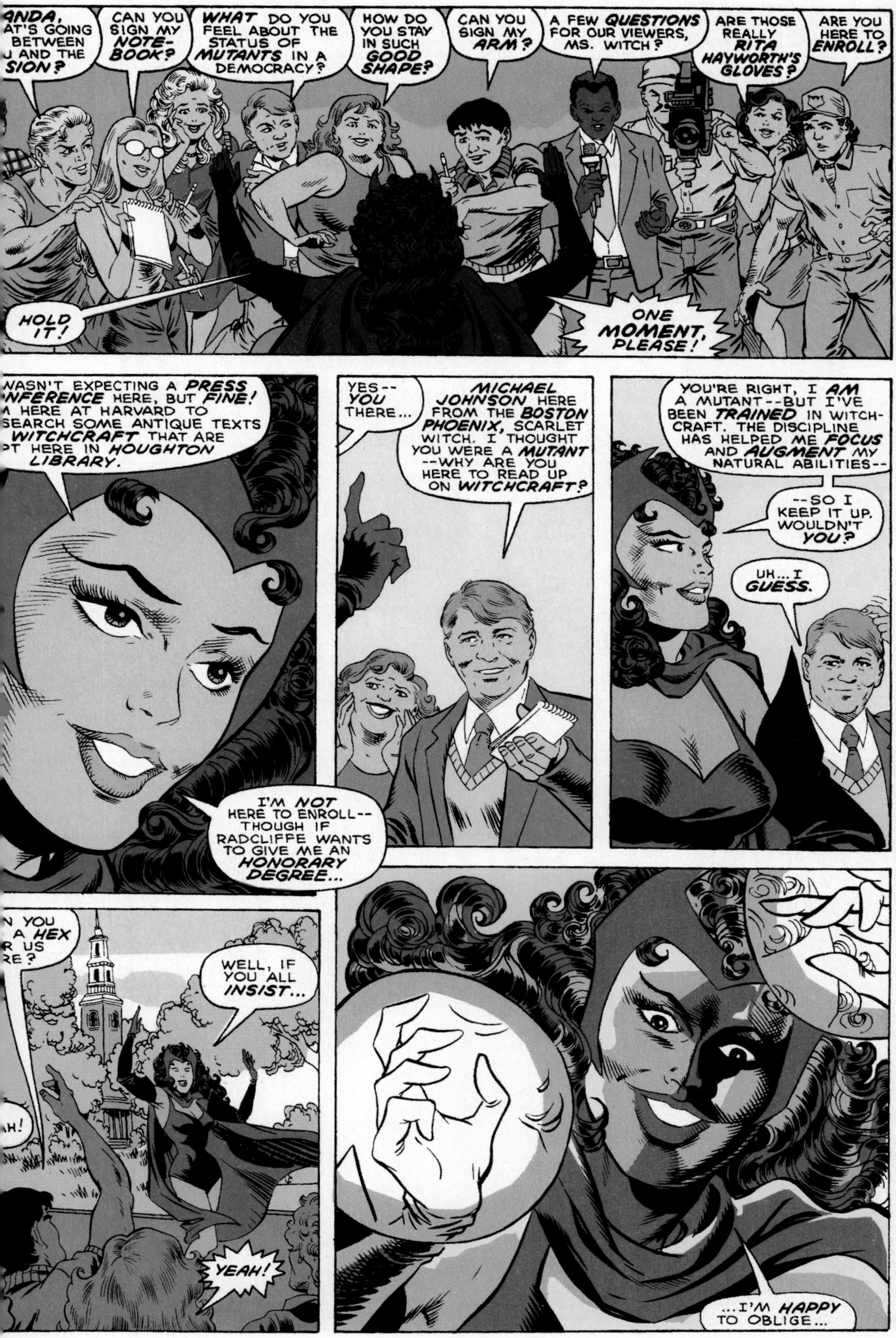
ANDA, AT'S GOING BETWEEN U AND THE SION?
CAN YOU SIGN MY NOTE-BOOK?
WHAT DO YOU FEEL ABOUT THE STATUS OF MUTANTS IN A DEMOCRACY?
HOW DO YOU STAY IN SUCH GOOD SHAPE?
CAN YOU SIGN MY ARM?
A FEW QUESTIONS FOR OUR VIEWERS, MS. WITCH?
ARE THOSE REALLY RITA HAYWORTH'S GLOVES?
ARE YOU HERE TO ENROLL?
HOLD IT!
ONE MOMENT, PLEASE!
WASN'T EXPECTING A PRESS NFERENCE HERE, BUT FINE! M HERE AT HARVARD TO SEARCH SOME ANTIQUE TEXTS WITCHCRAFT THAT ARE PT HERE IN HOUGHTON LIBRARY.
I'M NOT HERE TO ENROLL-- THOUGH IF RADCLIFFE WANTS TO GIVE ME AN HONORARY DEGREE...
YES-- YOU THERE...
MICHAEL JOHNSON HERE FROM THE BOSTON PHOENIX, SCARLET WITCH. I THOUGHT YOU WERE A MUTANT --WHY ARE YOU HERE TO READ UP ON WITCHCRAFT?
YOU'RE RIGHT, I AM A MUTANT--BUT I'VE BEEN TRAINED IN WITCH-CRAFT. THE DISCIPLINE HAS HELPED ME FOCUS AND AUGMENT MY NATURAL ABILITIES--
--SO I KEEP IT UP. WOULDN'T YOU?
UH... I GUESS.
N YOU A HEX R US RE?
WELL, IF YOU ALL INSIST...
AH!
YEAH!
...I'M HAPPY TO OBLIGE...

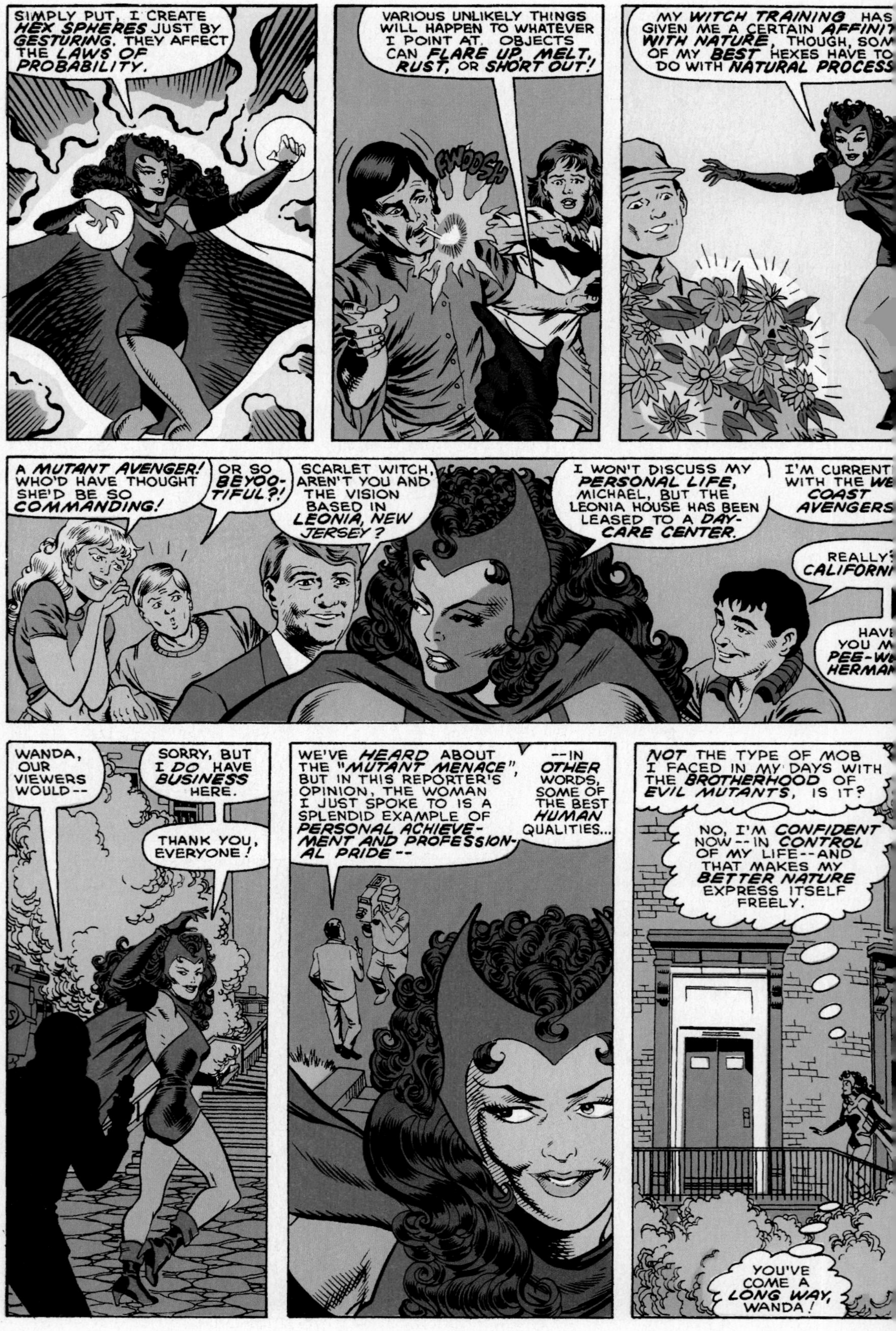
SIMPLY PUT, I CREATE HEX SPHERES JUST BY GESTURING. THEY AFFECT THE LAWS OF PROBABILITY.
VARIOUS UNLIKELY THINGS WILL HAPPEN TO WHATEVER I POINT AT. OBJECTS CAN FLARE UP, MELT, RUST, OR SHORT OUT!
FWOOSH
MY WITCH TRAINING HAS GIVEN ME A CERTAIN AFFINIT WITH NATURE, THOUGH, SOM OF MY BEST HEXES HAVE TO DO WITH NATURAL PROCESS
A MUTANT AVENGER! WHO'D HAVE THOUGHT SHE'D BE SO COMMANDING!
OR SO BEYOO-TIFUL?!
SCARLET WITCH, AREN'T YOU AND THE VISION BASED IN LEONIA, NEW JERSEY?
I WON'T DISCUSS MY PERSONAL LIFE, MICHAEL, BUT THE LEONIA HOUSE HAS BEEN LEASED TO A DAY-CARE CENTER.
I'M CURRENT WITH THE WE COAST AVENGERS
REALLY? CALIFORN
HAVE YOU M PEE-WE HERMAN
WANDA, OUR VIEWERS WOULD--
SORRY, BUT I DO HAVE BUSINESS HERE.
THANK YOU, EVERYONE!
WE'VE HEARD ABOUT THE "MUTANT MENACE", BUT IN THIS REPORTER'S OPINION, THE WOMAN I JUST SPOKE TO IS A SPLENDID EXAMPLE OF PERSONAL ACHIEVE-MENT AND PROFESSION-AL PRIDE--
--IN OTHER WORDS, SOME OF THE BEST HUMAN QUALITIES...
NOT THE TYPE OF MOB I FACED IN MY DAYS WITH THE BROTHERHOOD OF EVIL MUTANTS, IS IT?
NO, I'M CONFIDENT NOW--IN CONTROL OF MY LIFE--AND THAT MAKES MY BETTER NATURE EXPRESS ITSELF FREELY.
YOU'VE COME A LONG WAY, WANDA!

AND FOR THE *REST OF THE DAY*, THE SCARLET WITCH DEDICATES HERSELF TO ENSURING HER CONTINUED PROGRESS.

THE *ALLURING AVENGER* STUDIES SOME *RARE TOMES* ON WITCHCRAFT AND NATURE WORSHIP.

SO INTENT IS SHE ON HER *MISSION* OF *SELF-IMPROVEMENT* THAT SHE STAYS UNTIL *CLOSING TIME*.

AND, ALTHOUGH MOST OF THE SCHOLARS AT HOUGHTON'S *RARE BOOK READING ROOM* ARE TOO *RESERVED* TO BOTHER THE MUTANT SORCERESS AT WORK--

--ONE IN PARTICULAR MAKES A POINT OF ADDRESSING HER AFTER CLOSING...

EXCUSE ME, SCARLET WITCH. I WONDER IF I MIGHT HAVE A *MOMENT*...?

WHY, YES, I *SUPPOSE* SO. WEREN'T YOU IN THE LIBRARY WITH ME ALL DAY?

INDEED-- AND I COULDN'T HELP BUT NOTICE THAT YOU WERE PURSUING YOUR STUDYING WITHIN *MY* SPECIALITY.

YOU ARE A WITCHCRAFT *AUTHORITY* MR.--

REVERY. PROFESSOR *ALDER REVERY*.

THE ANSWER IS *NO*, DEAR LADY. STRICTLY SPEAKING, I AM A DEVOTEE OF THE *PAST*--

--AND THAT INCLUDES PAST *BELIEFS*, PAST *SYSTEMS OF WORSHIP*, AND PAST *SUPER-STITIONS*.

WELL, THOSE ARE *ALL* RELATED TO MY WITCHCRAFT STUDIES, PROFESSOR REVERY!

I AM AWARE OF THAT--AND I HAVE AN *INVITATION* FOR YOU.

PLEASE ACCEPT THE HOSPITALITY OF MY *TABLE* TONIGHT, AND YOU MAY HAVE ACCESS TO *MY* RARE BOOKS ON WITCHCRAFT --A SELECTION WHICH *FAR SURPASSES* HOUGHTON LIBRARY'S.

UNLESS... YOU'RE *EXPECTED* SOMEWHERE...?

WHY... *NO*, PROFESSOR. I GAVE MY COLLEAGUES NO DEFINITE RETURN DATE!

I'D BE *PLEASED* TO ACCEPT YOUR KIND OFFER!

121

IS YOUR HOUSE *NEARBY*, PROFESSOR?

A SHORT WALK, MY *DEAR!*

WELL, THEN *BEFORE* WE LEAVE THE YARD...

...I MUST MAKE SURE MY AVENGERS *QUINJET* DOESN'T WIND UP *SCULLING* WITH THE *CREW TEAM* TOMORROW!

AH.

DR. HENRY PYM DEVISED THIS OPTION! ONE MOMENT A *FULL-SIZED, ONE-MAN JETCRAFT...*

ZZT

...AND T NEXT, A *CHARMI TOY FLYER* TO PUT I ONE'S POCKET

...OR *WHER EVER*

MOST IMPRESSIVE

A FEW MOMENTS' WALK IN THE CLEAR CAMBRIDGE NIGHT AIR BRINGS THE TWO TO REVERY'S TOWNHOUSE ON MT. AUBURN STREET...

THIS IS *LOVELY*, PROFESSOR!

INDEED-- A FINE EXAMPLE OF *COLONIAL ARCHITEC-TURE.* NONE OF THE GLASS-AND-STEEL MONOLITHS OF *TODAY* CAN APPROACH ITS SIMPLE ELEGANCE.

PLEASE EXCUSE ME. I MUST MAKE ARRANGE-MENTS FOR OUR *DINNER.*

CERTAINLY.

PLEASE ENTERTAIN YOURSELF *HERE*, MY DEAR LADY--HERE AMONGST MY COLLECTION OF THE GLORIES OF *CIVILIZATIONS* OF THE *PAST.* I SHALL REJOIN YOU...

...*PRESENTLY.*

WHAT A *CHARACTER!*

THIS COULD BE SOME *ROMANTIC OVERTURE*, BUT I THINK I CAN HANDLE MYSELF WITH A *LOQUACIOUS ACADEMIC!*

I'M HERE ON A *RESEARCH TRIP!* NO ONE'S OUT TO *TRAP* ME!

I'LL JUST *RELAX*...LET MY GUARD DOWN A LITTLE. THAT CROWD TODAY *LOVED* ME.

HUMANITY'S *TRUSTING* MUTANTS A LITTLE MORE NOW ...MAYBE I SHOULD *RETURN THE FAVOR.* WHAT COULD IT *HURT?*

AND A SHORT TIME LATER... DINNER IS SERVED

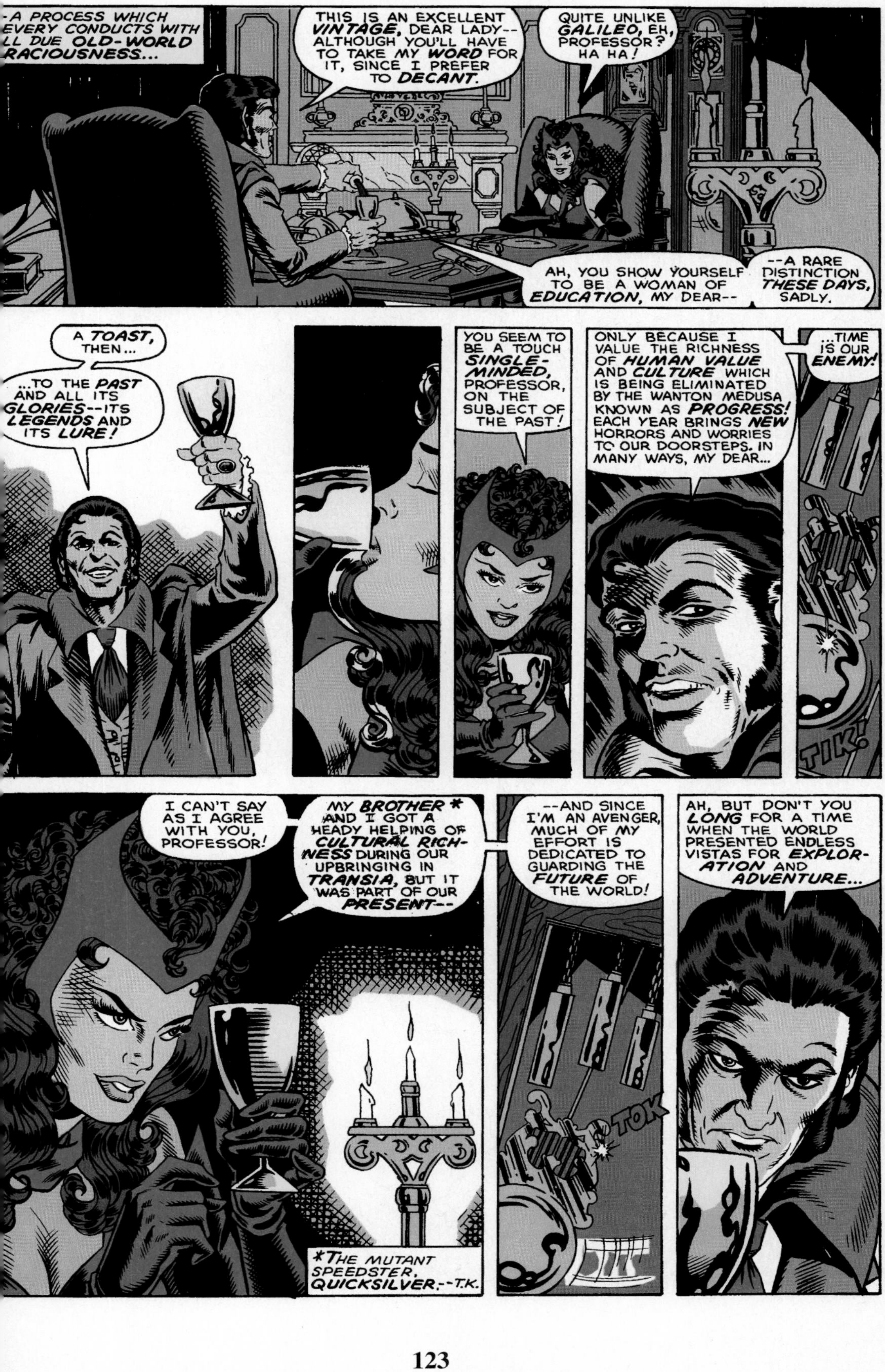
-A PROCESS WHICH EVERY CONDUCTS WITH LL DUE OLD-WORLD RACIOUSNESS...
THIS IS AN EXCELLENT VINTAGE, DEAR LADY-- ALTHOUGH YOU'LL HAVE TO TAKE MY WORD FOR IT, SINCE I PREFER TO DECANT.
QUITE UNLIKE GALILEO, EH, PROFESSOR? HA HA!
AH, YOU SHOW YOURSELF TO BE A WOMAN OF EDUCATION, MY DEAR--
--A RARE DISTINCTION THESE DAYS, SADLY.
A TOAST, THEN...
...TO THE PAST AND ALL ITS GLORIES--ITS LEGENDS AND ITS LURE!
YOU SEEM TO BE A TOUCH SINGLE-MINDED, PROFESSOR, ON THE SUBJECT OF THE PAST!
ONLY BECAUSE I VALUE THE RICHNESS OF HUMAN VALUE AND CULTURE WHICH IS BEING ELIMINATED BY THE WANTON MEDUSA KNOWN AS PROGRESS! EACH YEAR BRINGS NEW HORRORS AND WORRIES TO OUR DOORSTEPS. IN MANY WAYS, MY DEAR...
...TIME IS OUR ENEMY!
TIK!
I CAN'T SAY AS I AGREE WITH YOU, PROFESSOR!
MY BROTHER* AND I GOT A HEADY HELPING OF CULTURAL RICHNESS DURING OUR UPBRINGING IN TRANSIA, BUT IT WAS PART OF OUR PRESENT--
--AND SINCE I'M AN AVENGER, MUCH OF MY EFFORT IS DEDICATED TO GUARDING THE FUTURE OF THE WORLD!
AH, BUT DON'T YOU LONG FOR A TIME WHEN THE WORLD PRESENTED ENDLESS VISTAS FOR EXPLORATION AND ADVENTURE...
*THE MUTANT SPEEDSTER, QUICKSILVER.-T.K.
TOK

...WHEN JOBS AND CRAFTS WERE DONE BY *MEN*, NOT *MACHINES*...

...WHEN THE HUMAN SPIRIT WAS *ILLUMINATED*, NOT *EXTINGUISHED*...

...BEFORE OUR CURRENT ACCURSED *NUCLEAR AGE* FULL OF FEAR OF EACH OTHER--AND THE CREATURES *CREATED* BY NUCLEAR ENERGY...

WHAT?

MUTANTS?!

A *MYSTIC FORCE SHIELD*-- BUT THIS WON'T HOLD *ME!*

OH, *WON'T* IT?

I... CAN'T *CONCENTRATE* ENOUGH TO FOCUS...

YES, MY DEAR, THE *HYPNOTIC DRUG* IN THE WINE HAS TAKEN HOLD ENOUGH TO *UNDERMINE* YOUR EFFORTS TO BREAK MY BARRIER--

--EVEN THOUGH MY MYSTIC ABILITIES FALL FAR *SHORT* OF YOURS!

JUST N WAY OF *EVENIN* THE ODD

THIS WON'T STOP ME... FOR LONG!

IN *THIS* CASE, MY DEAR, TIME STANDS AT *MY* BIDDING!

YOU MUTANTS-- *"HUMANITY'S NEXT WAVE"*-- HA! A *PERVERSION* OF HUMANITY IS WHAT YOU ARE-- JUST WAITING TO BE ERADICATED...

...AND *I* AM THE ONE TO *DO* IT!!

MY HEAD IS *SWIMMING!* WHY WAS I SO *TRUSTING?* WHAT CAN I *DO?*

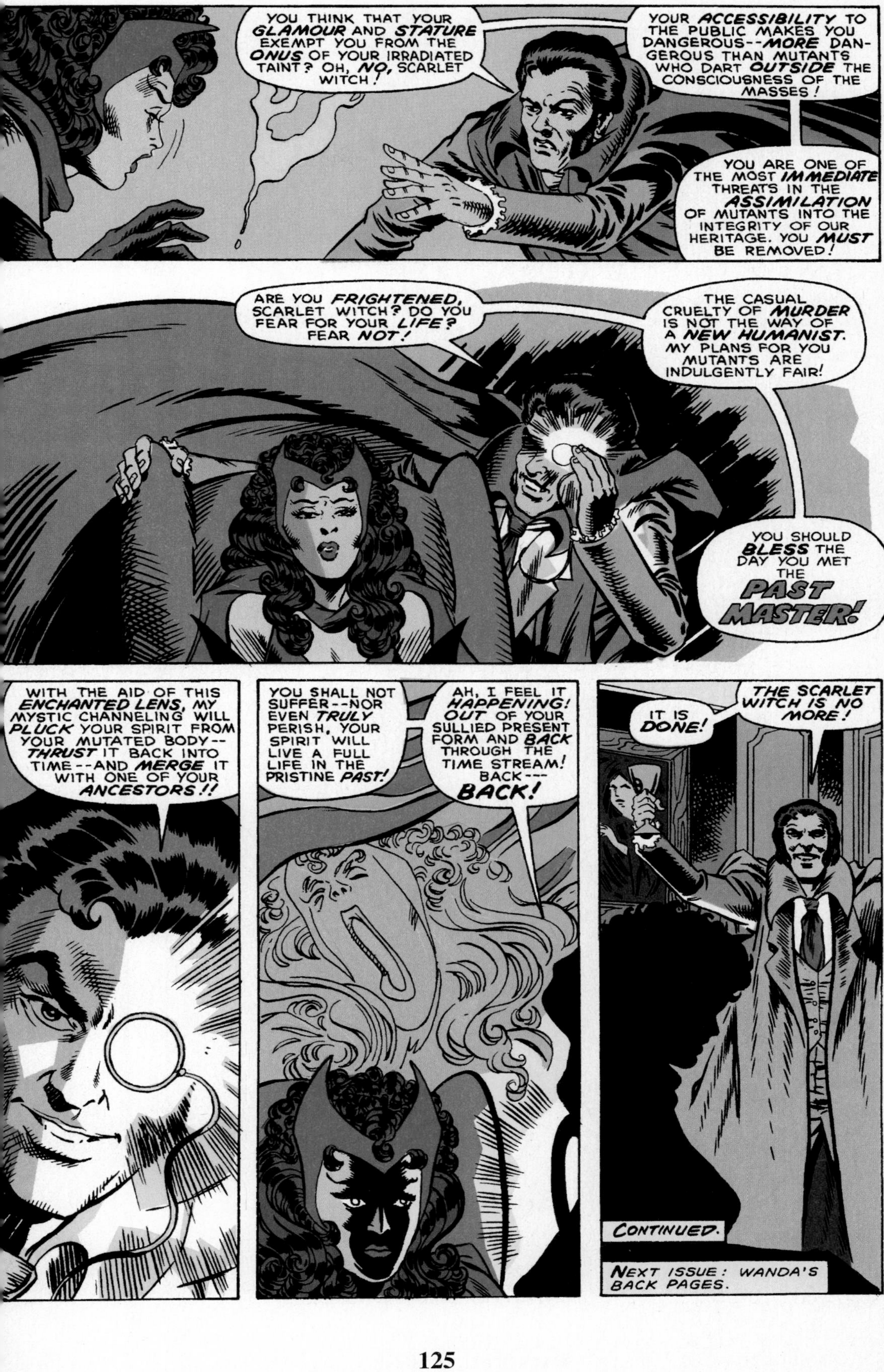

YOU THINK THAT YOUR GLAMOUR AND STATURE EXEMPT YOU FROM THE ONUS OF YOUR IRRADIATED TAINT? OH, NO, SCARLET WITCH!
YOUR ACCESSIBILITY TO THE PUBLIC MAKES YOU DANGEROUS--MORE DANGEROUS THAN MUTANTS WHO DART OUTSIDE THE CONSCIOUSNESS OF THE MASSES!
YOU ARE ONE OF THE MOST IMMEDIATE THREATS IN THE ASSIMILATION OF MUTANTS INTO THE INTEGRITY OF OUR HERITAGE. YOU MUST BE REMOVED!
ARE YOU FRIGHTENED, SCARLET WITCH? DO YOU FEAR FOR YOUR LIFE? FEAR NOT!
THE CASUAL CRUELTY OF MURDER IS NOT THE WAY OF A NEW HUMANIST. MY PLANS FOR YOU MUTANTS ARE INDULGENTLY FAIR!
YOU SHOULD BLESS THE DAY YOU MET THE PAST MASTER!
WITH THE AID OF THIS ENCHANTED LENS, MY MYSTIC CHANNELING WILL PLUCK YOUR SPIRIT FROM YOUR MUTATED BODY--THRUST IT BACK INTO TIME--AND MERGE IT WITH ONE OF YOUR ANCESTORS!!
YOU SHALL NOT SUFFER--NOR EVEN TRULY PERISH, YOUR SPIRIT WILL LIVE A FULL LIFE IN THE PRISTINE PAST!
AH, I FEEL IT HAPPENING! OUT OF YOUR SULLIED PRESENT FORM AND BACK THROUGH THE TIME STREAM! BACK---BACK!
IT IS DONE!
THE SCARLET WITCH IS NO MORE!
CONTINUED.
NEXT ISSUE: WANDA'S BACK PAGES.

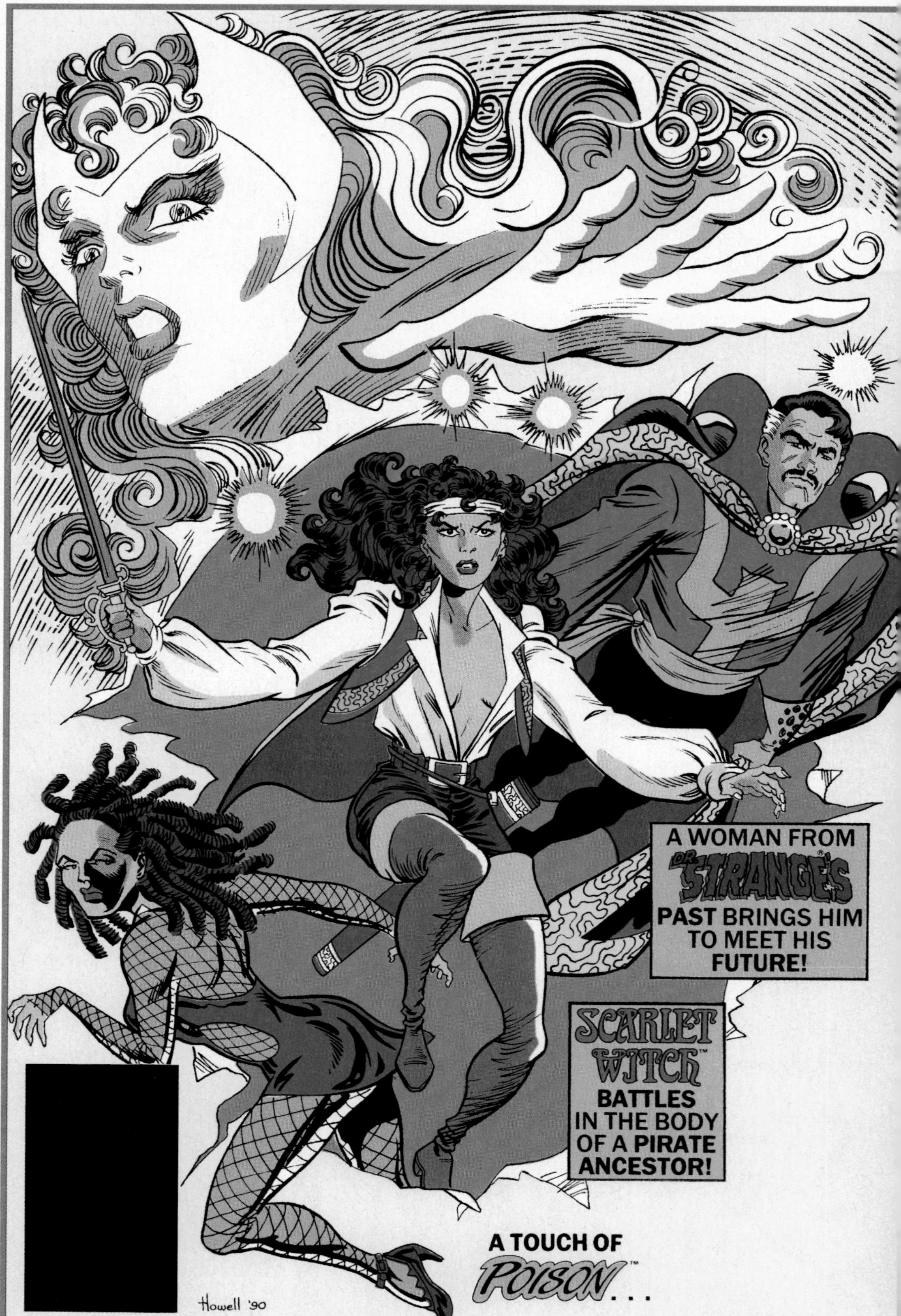
A WOMAN FROM DR. STRANGE'S PAST BRINGS HIM TO MEET HIS FUTURE!
SCARLET WITCH BATTLES IN THE BODY OF A PIRATE ANCESTOR!
A TOUCH OF POISON...
Howell '90

MARVEL COMICS PRESENTS #61

WRITER, ARTIST, COLORIST & LETTERER: RICHARD HOWELL
ASSISTANT EDITOR: KELLY CORVESE • EDITOR: TERRY KAVANAGH

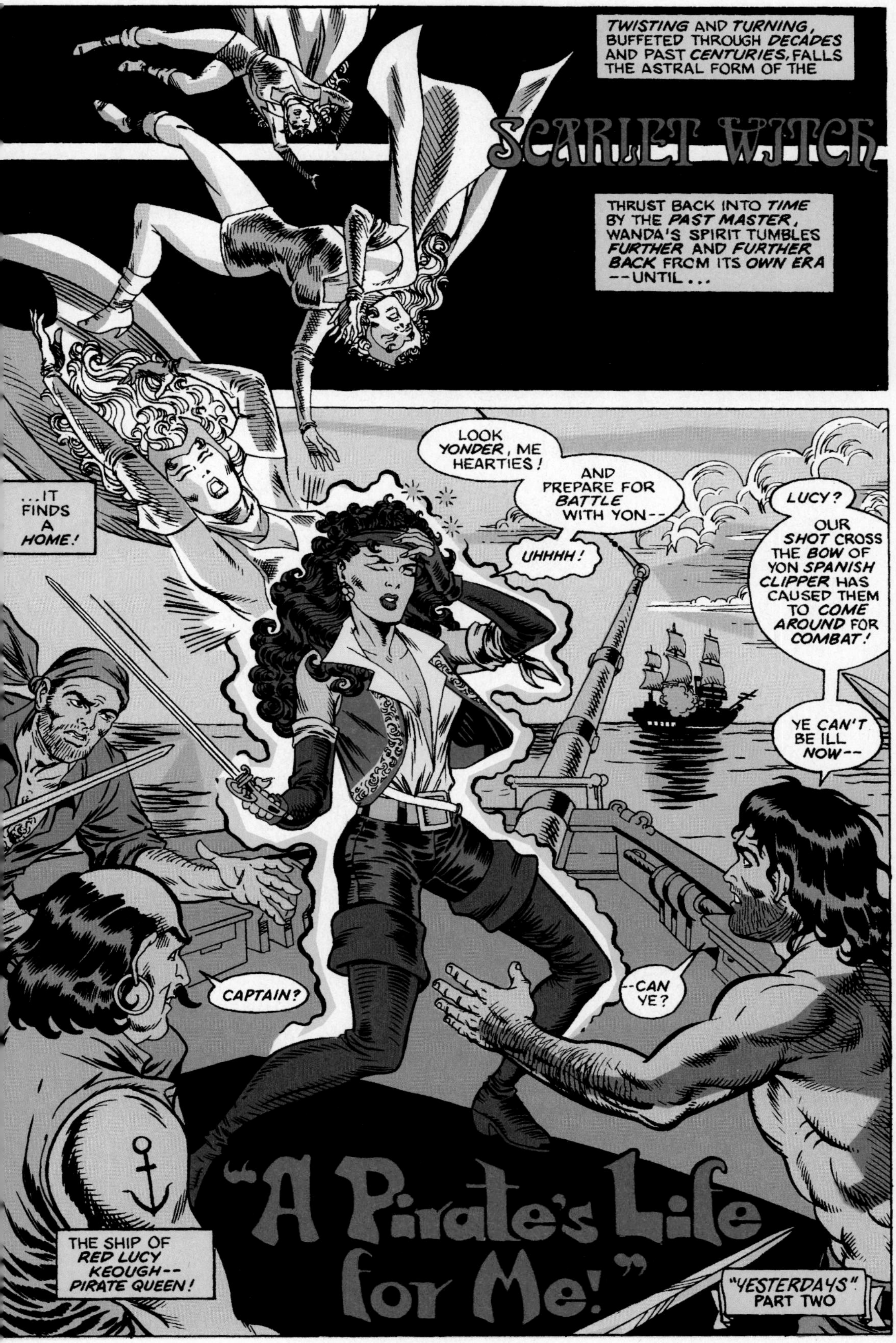

TWISTING AND TURNING, BUFFETED THROUGH DECADES AND PAST CENTURIES, FALLS THE ASTRAL FORM OF THE
SCARLET WITCH
THRUST BACK INTO TIME BY THE PAST MASTER, WANDA'S SPIRIT TUMBLES FURTHER AND FURTHER BACK FROM ITS OWN ERA --UNTIL...
...IT FINDS A HOME!
LOOK YONDER, ME HEARTIES!
AND PREPARE FOR BATTLE WITH YON--
UHHHH!
LUCY?
OUR SHOT CROSS THE BOW OF YON SPANISH CLIPPER HAS CAUSED THEM TO COME AROUND FOR COMBAT!
YE CAN'T BE ILL NOW--
--CAN YE?
CAPTAIN?
"A Pirate's Life for Me!"
THE SHIP OF RED LUCY KEOUGH--PIRATE QUEEN!
"YESTERDAYS" PART TWO

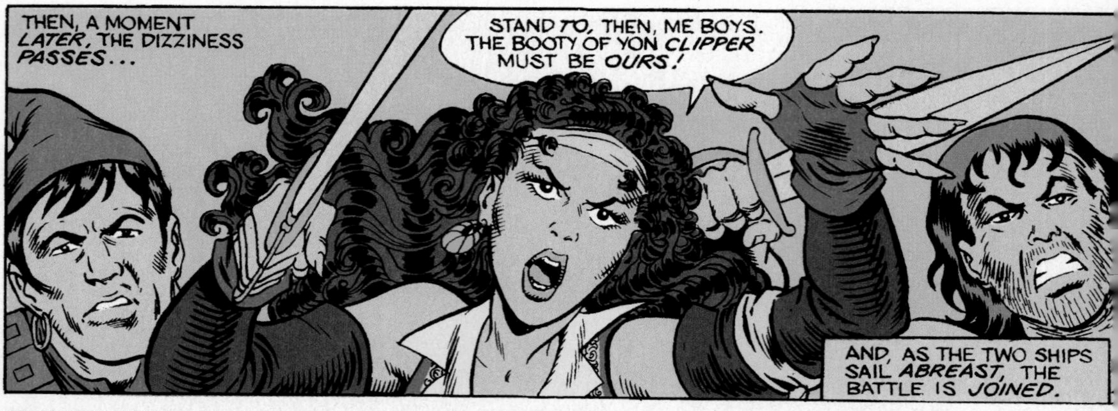
THEN, A MOMENT LATER, THE DIZZINESS PASSES...
STAND TO, THEN, ME BOYS. THE BOOTY OF YON CLIPPER MUST BE OURS!
AND, AS THE TWO SHIPS SAIL ABREAST, THE BATTLE IS JOINED.

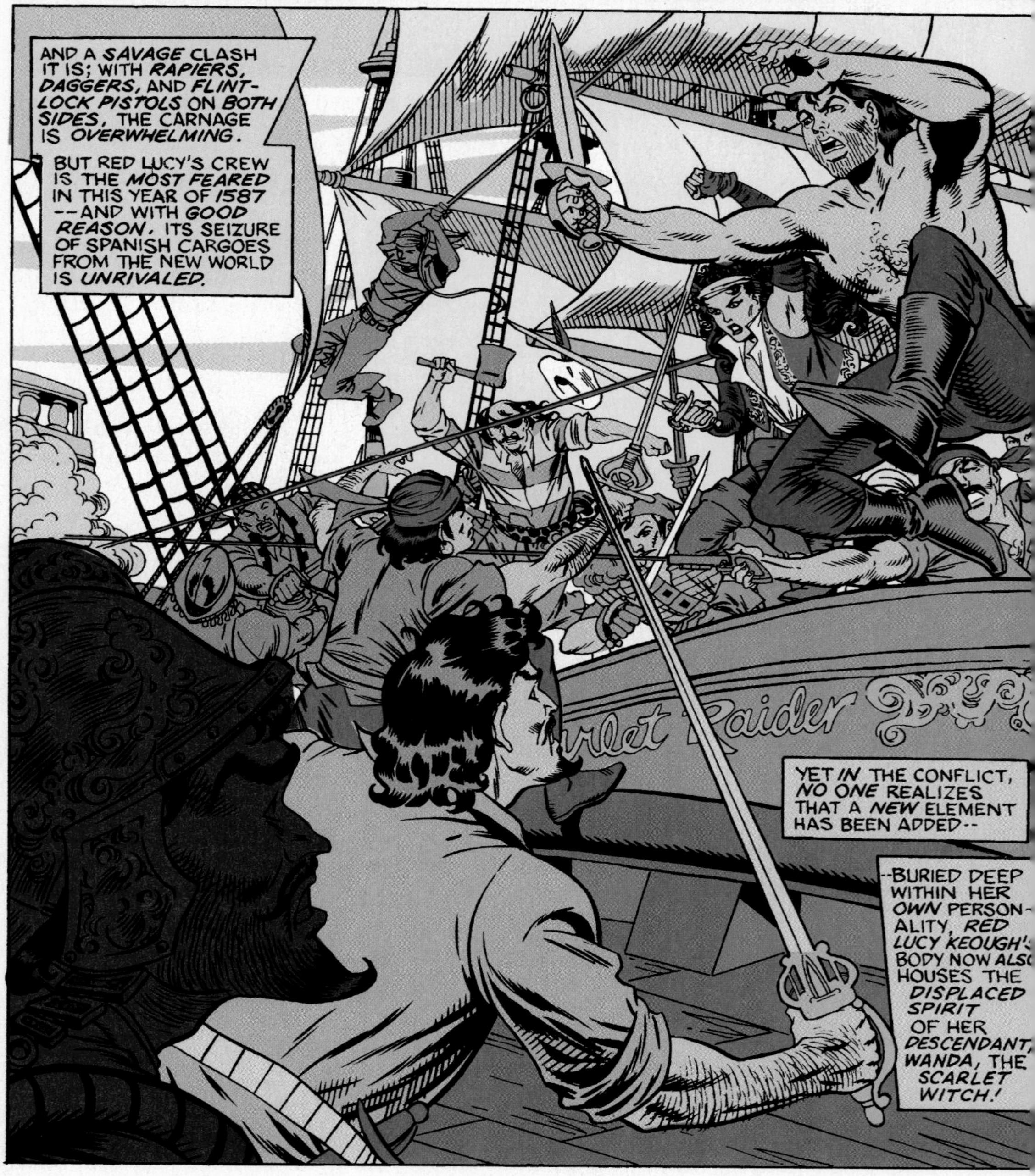
AND A SAVAGE CLASH IT IS; WITH RAPIERS, DAGGERS, AND FLINT-LOCK PISTOLS ON BOTH SIDES, THE CARNAGE IS OVERWHELMING.
BUT RED LUCY'S CREW IS THE MOST FEARED IN THIS YEAR OF 1587 --AND WITH GOOD REASON. ITS SEIZURE OF SPANISH CARGOES FROM THE NEW WORLD IS UNRIVALED.
YET IN THE CONFLICT, NO ONE REALIZES THAT A NEW ELEMENT HAS BEEN ADDED--
--BURIED DEEP WITHIN HER OWN PERSON-ALITY, RED LUCY KEOUGH'S BODY NOW ALSO HOUSES THE DISPLACED SPIRIT OF HER DESCENDANT, WANDA, THE SCARLET WITCH!

LUCY IS A *WORTHY* ANCESTOR. ALTHOUGH HER RANK IS *MAINLY* DEPENDENT ON HER *STRATEGIC* EXPERTISE, SHE IS UNDOUBTABLY THE *FINEST SWORDSWOMAN* OF HER TIME.

UNDER *HER* LEADERSHIP, HER CREW IS SPURRED TO *SUPERB* FEATS OF *SKILL* AND *DARING*. THUS, IN A SHORT TIME...

VICTORY IS *OURS*, SPANIARD!

YOUR CARGO OF *SPICES*, *SILKS*, AND *PEARLS* IS *OURS* NOW-- *NOT* KING PHILIPS!

SURRENDER --AND I WILL *SPARE* YOUR LIFE, AND YOUR *CREW'S* LIVES!

I ... DID *NOT* *EXPECT* THIS, CAPTAIN ... BUT ...

I ... SURRENDER!

SPARE THE *CREW?* CAPTAIN, HAVE YE GONE *DAFT?*

PUT 'EM TO THE *BLADE!*

LUCY, WE GIVE *NO QUARTER!* WOULD YE HAVE US GO *SOFT?*

BELAY THAT TALK !! TAKING THE LIFE OF A *CONQUERED* FOE IS OUR WAY *NO LONGER!*

ANY OF YE WHO THINKS TO LEAD THIS CREW *BETTER* CAN CHALLENGE ME *ANY TIME.*

I *CHALLENGE* YE, LUCY! THY *WOMANLY WEAKNESS* FINALLY HAS *OVERCOME* THY *JUDGMENT!*

I DON'T SEE YE *DECRYING* MY *WOMANLINESS* WHEN WE HAUL IN THE *SPOILS*, AARON--

--BUT I'LL BROOK NO *DISSIDENTS* AMONG *MY* CREW!

129

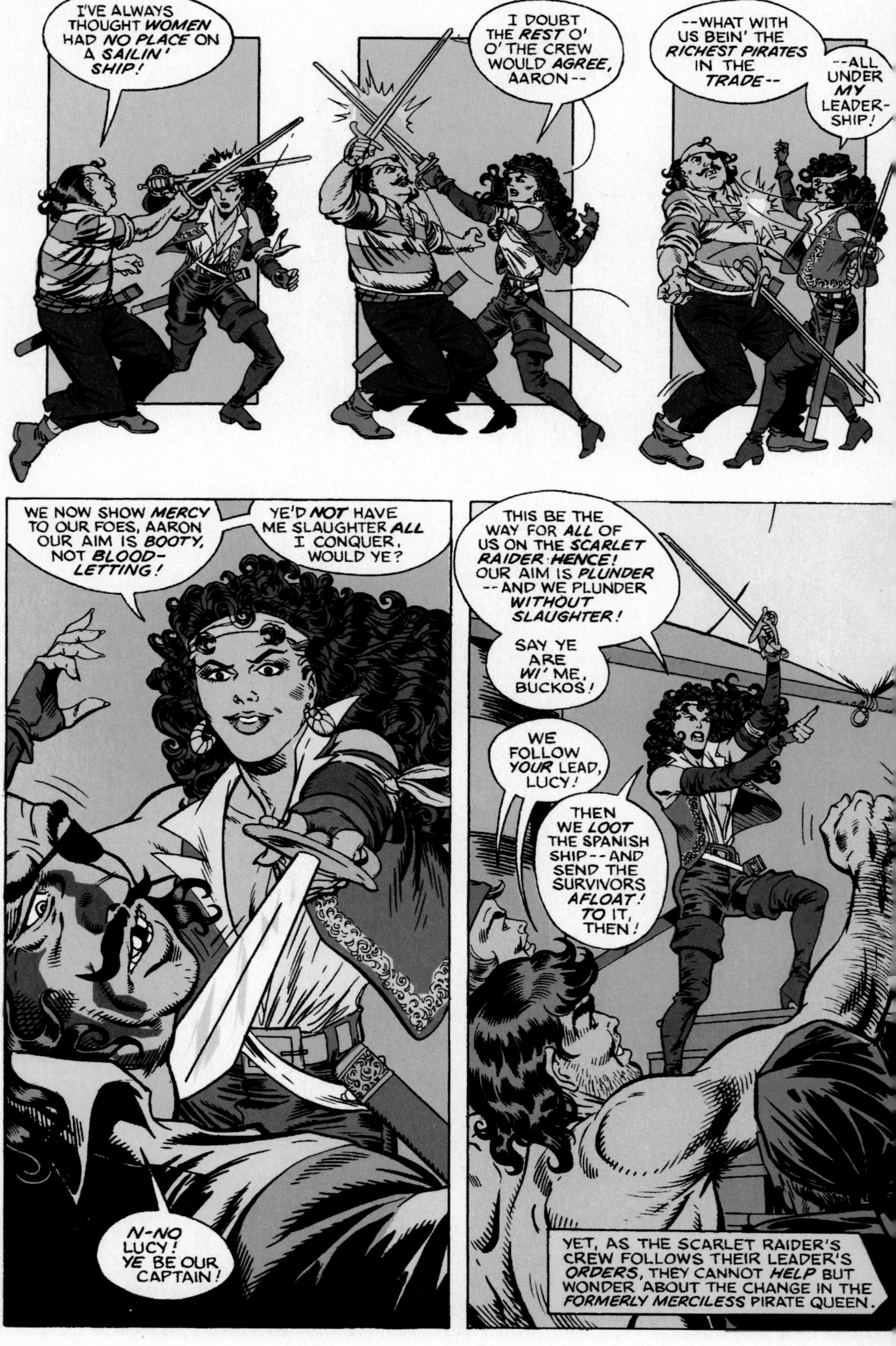
I'VE ALWAYS THOUGHT WOMEN HAD NO PLACE ON A SAILIN' SHIP!
I DOUBT THE REST O' O' THE CREW WOULD AGREE, AARON --
--WHAT WITH US BEIN' THE RICHEST PIRATES IN THE TRADE--
--ALL UNDER MY LEADER-SHIP!
WE NOW SHOW MERCY TO OUR FOES, AARON OUR AIM IS BOOTY, NOT BLOOD-LETTING!
YE'D NOT HAVE ME SLAUGHTER ALL I CONQUER, WOULD YE?
N-NO LUCY! YE BE OUR CAPTAIN!
THIS BE THE WAY FOR ALL OF US ON THE SCARLET RAIDER HENCE! OUR AIM IS PLUNDER --AND WE PLUNDER WITHOUT SLAUGHTER!
SAY YE ARE WI' ME, BUCKOS!
WE FOLLOW YOUR LEAD, LUCY!
THEN WE LOOT THE SPANISH SHIP--AND SEND THE SURVIVORS AFLOAT! TO IT, THEN!
YET, AS THE SCARLET RAIDER'S CREW FOLLOWS THEIR LEADER'S ORDERS, THEY CANNOT HELP BUT WONDER ABOUT THE CHANGE IN THE FORMERLY MERCILESS PIRATE QUEEN.

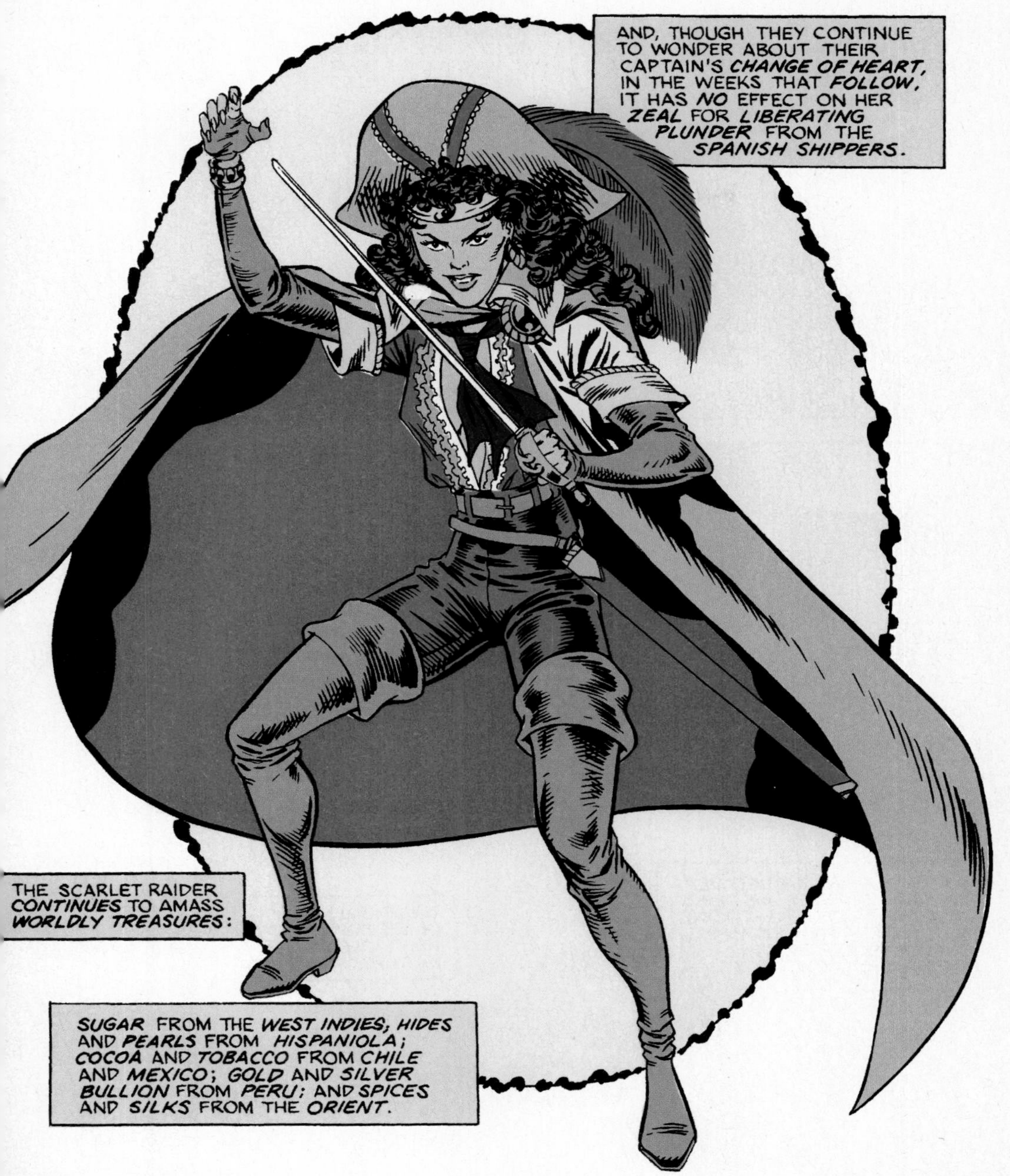
AND, THOUGH THEY CONTINUE TO WONDER ABOUT THEIR CAPTAIN'S CHANGE OF HEART, IN THE WEEKS THAT FOLLOW, IT HAS NO EFFECT ON HER ZEAL FOR LIBERATING PLUNDER FROM THE SPANISH SHIPPERS.
THE SCARLET RAIDER CONTINUES TO AMASS WORLDLY TREASURES:
SUGAR FROM THE WEST INDIES; HIDES AND PEARLS FROM HISPANIOLA; COCOA AND TOBACCO FROM CHILE AND MEXICO; GOLD AND SILVER BULLION FROM PERU; AND SPICES AND SILKS FROM THE ORIENT.

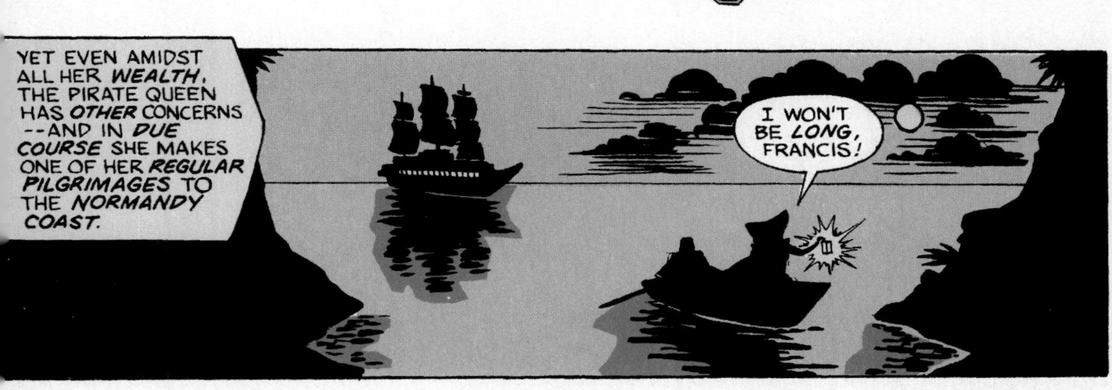
YET EVEN AMIDST ALL HER WEALTH, THE PIRATE QUEEN HAS OTHER CONCERNS --AND IN DUE COURSE SHE MAKES ONE OF HER REGULAR PILGRIMAGES TO THE NORMANDY COAST.
I WON'T BE LONG, FRANCIS!

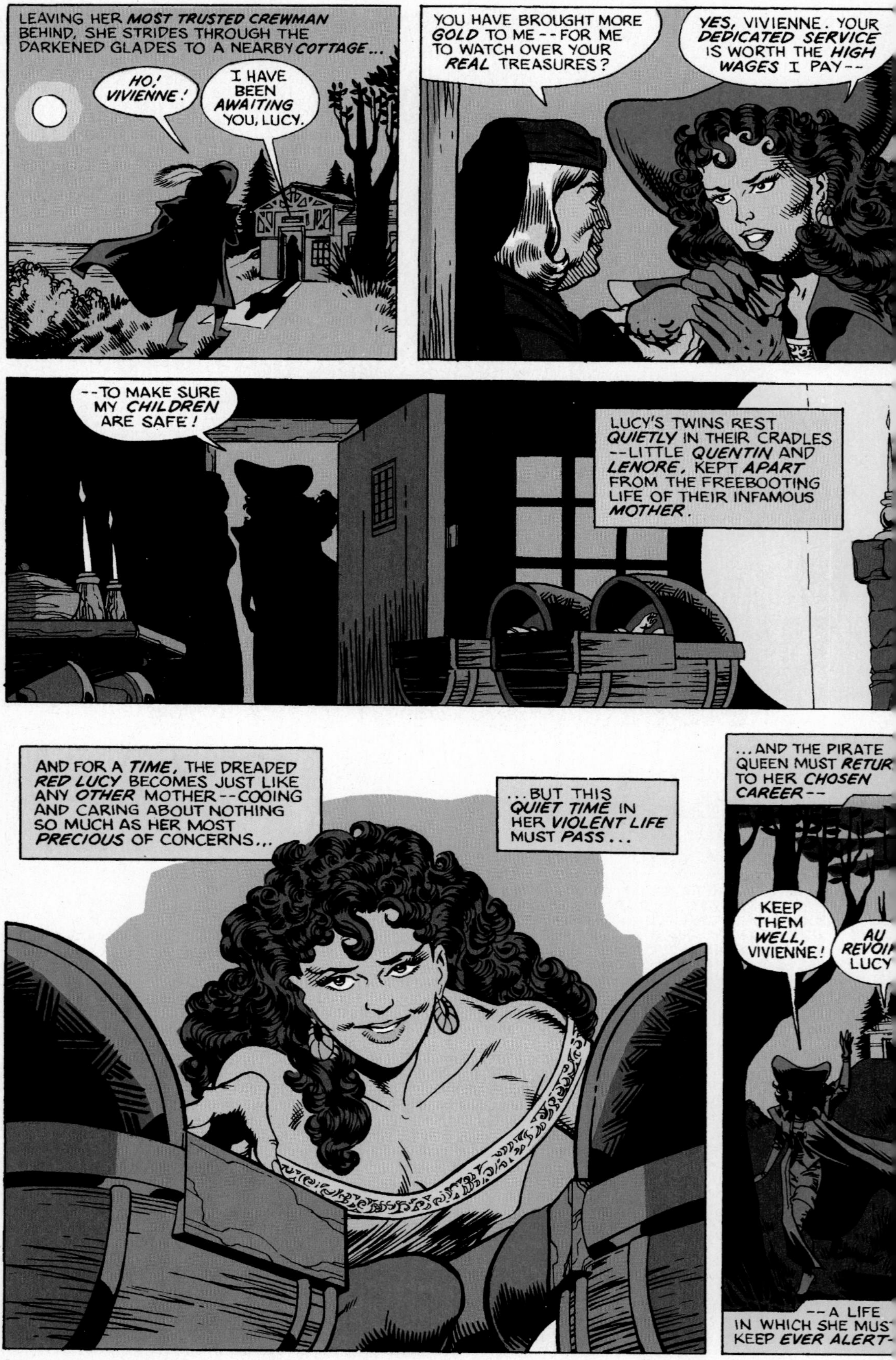
LEAVING HER MOST TRUSTED CREWMAN BEHIND, SHE STRIDES THROUGH THE DARKENED GLADES TO A NEARBY COTTAGE...
HO! VIVIENNE!
I HAVE BEEN AWAITING YOU, LUCY.
YOU HAVE BROUGHT MORE GOLD TO ME--FOR ME TO WATCH OVER YOUR REAL TREASURES?
YES, VIVIENNE. YOUR DEDICATED SERVICE IS WORTH THE HIGH WAGES I PAY--
--TO MAKE SURE MY CHILDREN ARE SAFE!
LUCY'S TWINS REST QUIETLY IN THEIR CRADLES --LITTLE QUENTIN AND LENORE, KEPT APART FROM THE FREEBOOTING LIFE OF THEIR INFAMOUS MOTHER.
AND FOR A TIME, THE DREADED RED LUCY BECOMES JUST LIKE ANY OTHER MOTHER--COOING AND CARING ABOUT NOTHING SO MUCH AS HER MOST PRECIOUS OF CONCERNS...
...BUT THIS QUIET TIME IN HER VIOLENT LIFE MUST PASS...
...AND THE PIRATE QUEEN MUST RETUR TO HER CHOSEN CAREER--
KEEP THEM WELL, VIVIENNE!
AU REVOI LUCY
--A LIFE IN WHICH SHE MUS KEEP EVER ALERT-

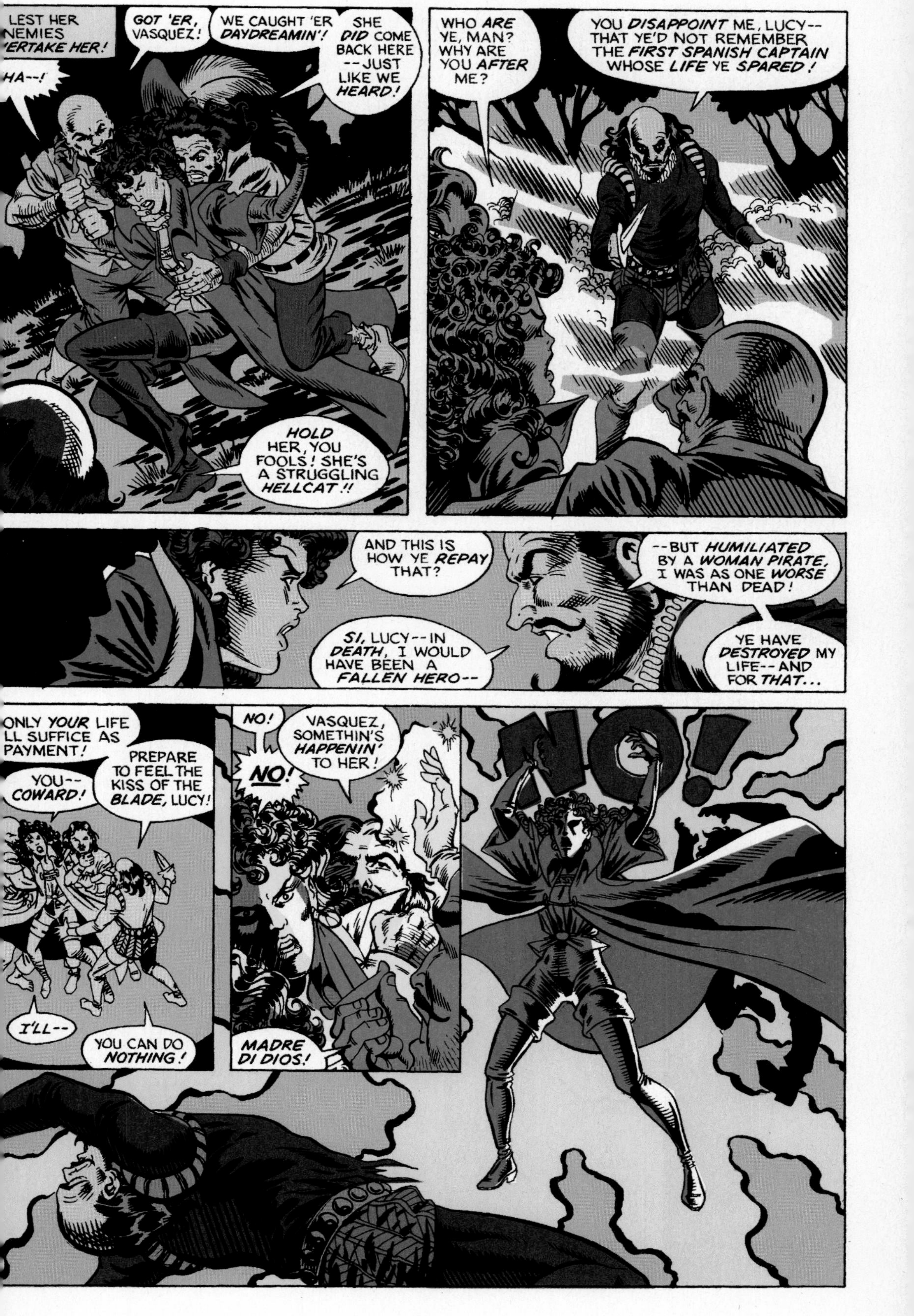

LEST HER
NEMIES
VERTAKE HER!
HA--!
GOT 'ER, VASQUEZ!
WE CAUGHT 'ER DAYDREAMIN'!
SHE DID COME BACK HERE --JUST LIKE WE HEARD!
HOLD HER, YOU FOOLS! SHE'S A STRUGGLING HELLCAT!!
WHO ARE YE, MAN? WHY ARE YOU AFTER ME?
YOU DISAPPOINT ME, LUCY-- THAT YE'D NOT REMEMBER THE FIRST SPANISH CAPTAIN WHOSE LIFE YE SPARED!
AND THIS IS HOW YE REPAY THAT?
SI, LUCY--IN DEATH, I WOULD HAVE BEEN A FALLEN HERO--
--BUT HUMILIATED BY A WOMAN PIRATE, I WAS AS ONE WORSE THAN DEAD!
YE HAVE DESTROYED MY LIFE--AND FOR THAT...
ONLY YOUR LIFE
LL SUFFICE AS PAYMENT!
PREPARE TO FEEL THE KISS OF THE BLADE, LUCY!
YOU-- COWARD!
I'LL--
YOU CAN DO NOTHING!
NO!
NO!
VASQUEZ, SOMETHIN'S HAPPENIN' TO HER!
MADRE DI DIOS!
NO!

MY MIND'S *AWAKE* AGAIN! I REMEMBER *EVERYTHING!*

THERE'S ANOTHER *SPIRIT* INSIDE ME! I CAN *FEEL* IT!

BUT *WHAT* DOES THIS *MEAN?*

SO WITH ONE *FIERCE THRUST*, WANDA'S SPIRIT IS RELEASED FROM ITS BONDAGE OF SLEEP, AND TWO WOMEN'S SPIRITS *CO-EXIST* IN *LUCY'S* BODY!

YOU ARE... SO *LIKE* ME! WE MUST BE *FAMILY!* CAN THIS *BE?*

SPEAK TO ME, SPIRIT!

I WILL... RED LUC_ ALTHOUG_ ONLY YO_ CAN HEA_ MY VOICE

I A_ YOU_ *DESCE_ DAN_* MY NA_ IS *WAND_*

I COM_ FRO_ THE YEA_ 198_

AND IN THE COLD CHILL BREEZE OF THE *ENGLISH CHANNEL*, THE *MUTANT AVENGER* AND HER *ANCESTOR* DISCOVER THE *DEPTHS* OF ALDER REVERY'S *VENGEFUL DESIGN...*

...AND THEIR CHANCES OF RESTORING THE SITUATION TO *RIGHTS*.

MY MUTANT HEX *MIGHT* REVERSE REVERY'S TRANCE AND SEND ME BACK TO MY OWN TIME...

...BUT I DON'T THINK I HAVE ENOUGH *POWER!*

I THINK I CAN *HELP*, SCARLET WITCH-- AND I *SHALL!*

AS WE ARE OF *ONE FORM*, WE WILL *SHARE* THIS QUEST. THE *SCARLET WITCH* WILL *RETURN* TO HER OWN BODY ...IN HER *OWN TIME!*

SO SWEARS THE *SCARLET WITCH!*

SO SWEARS *RED LUCY KEOUGH!*

CONTINUES NEXT ISSUE: *THE FAMILY JEWELS*

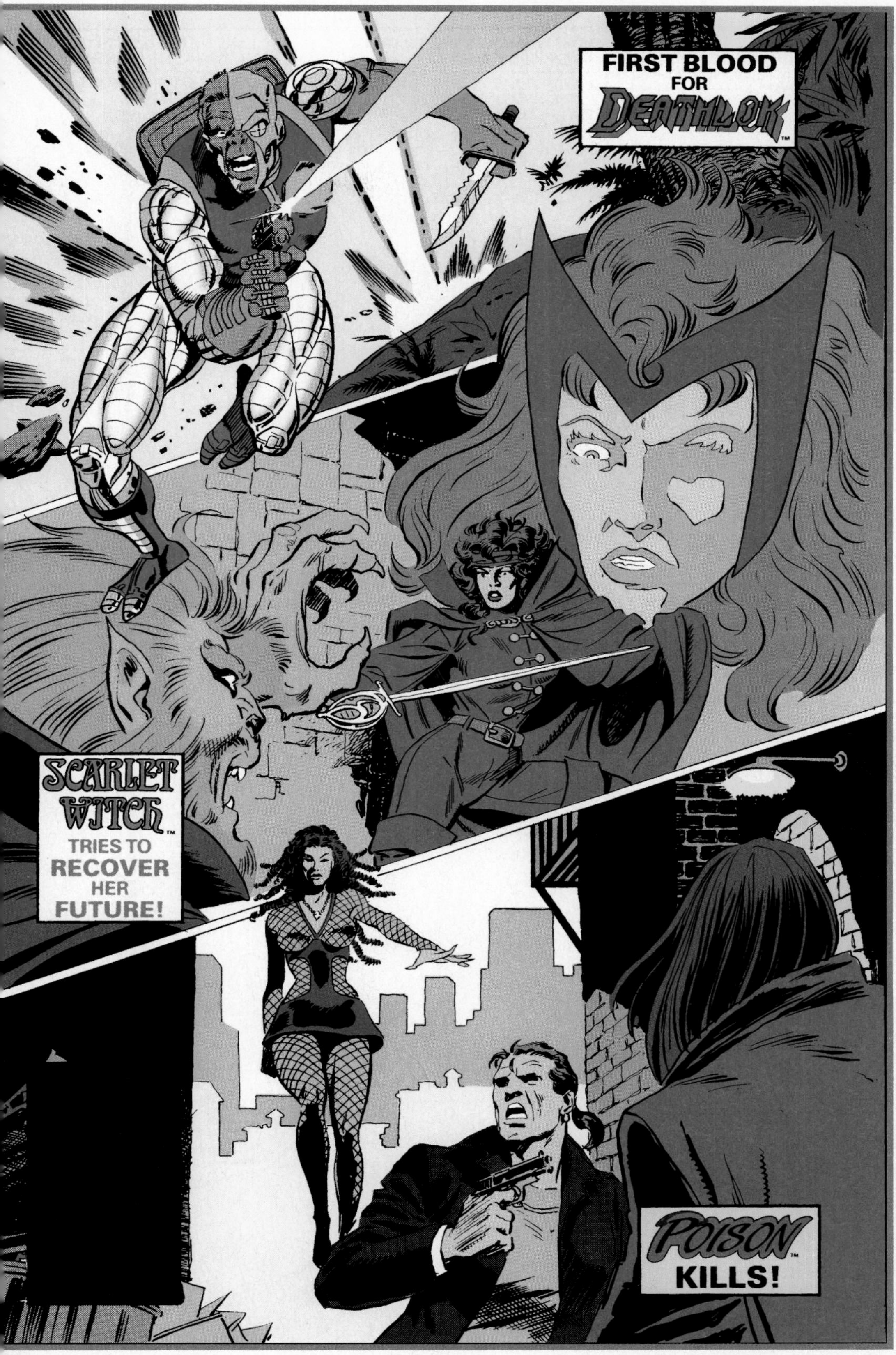
FIRST BLOOD FOR DEATHLOK™
SCARLET WITCH™ TRIES TO RECOVER HER FUTURE!
POISON™ KILLS!

MARVEL COMICS PRESENTS #62

WRITER, ARTIST, COLORIST & LETTERER: RICHARD HOWELL
ASSISTANT EDITOR: KELLY CORVESE • EDITOR: TERRY KAVANAGH

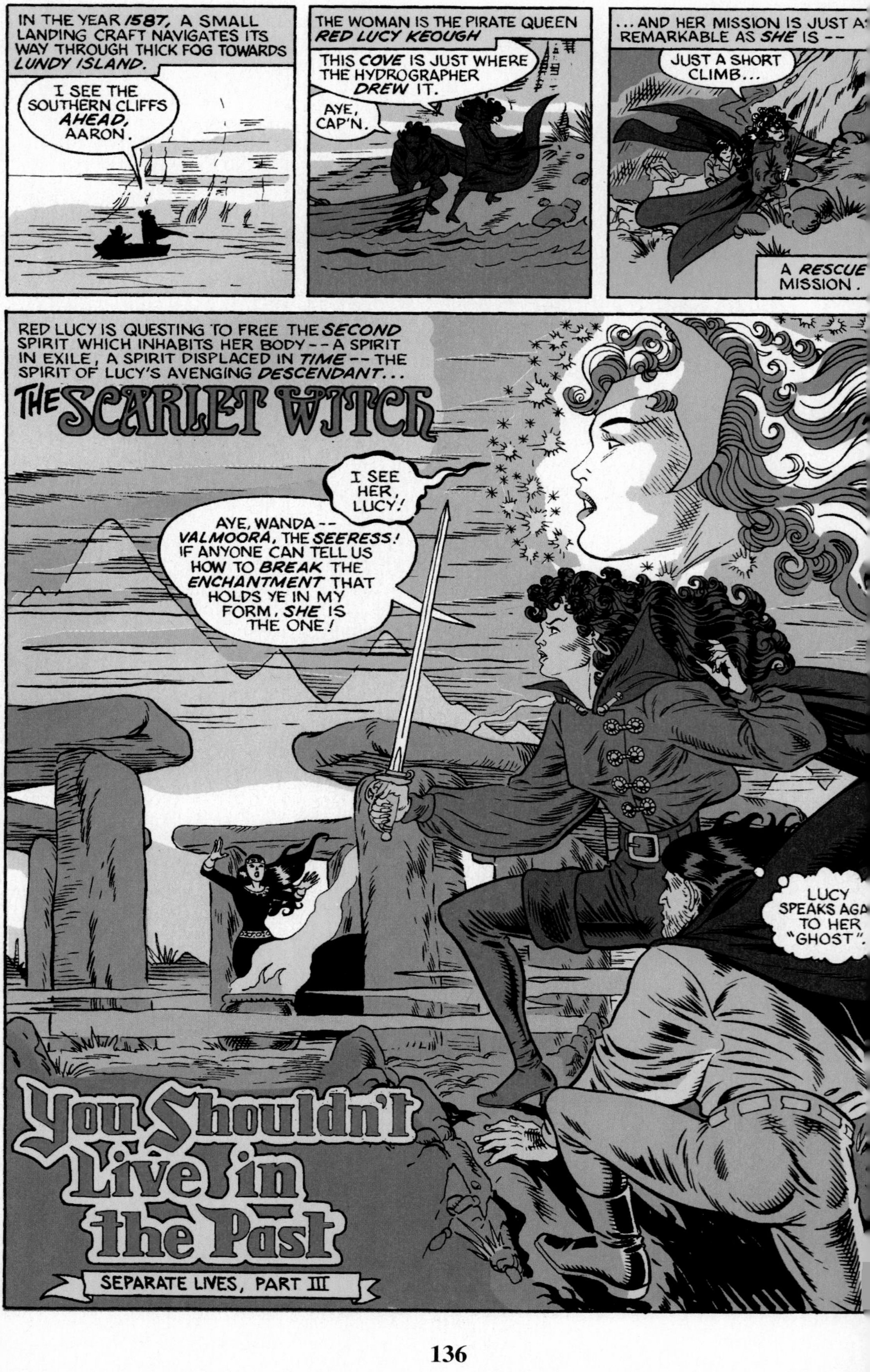

IN THE YEAR 1587, A SMALL LANDING CRAFT NAVIGATES ITS WAY THROUGH THICK FOG TOWARDS LUNDY ISLAND.
I SEE THE SOUTHERN CLIFFS AHEAD, AARON.
THE WOMAN IS THE PIRATE QUEEN RED LUCY KEOUGH
THIS COVE IS JUST WHERE THE HYDROGRAPHER DREW IT.
AYE, CAP'N.
... AND HER MISSION IS JUST A
REMARKABLE AS SHE IS --
JUST A SHORT CLIMB...
A RESCUE MISSION.
RED LUCY IS QUESTING TO FREE THE SECOND SPIRIT WHICH INHABITS HER BODY -- A SPIRIT IN EXILE, A SPIRIT DISPLACED IN TIME -- THE SPIRIT OF LUCY'S AVENGING DESCENDANT...
THE SCARLET WITCH
I SEE HER, LUCY!
AYE, WANDA -- VALMOORA, THE SEERESS! IF ANYONE CAN TELL US HOW TO BREAK THE ENCHANTMENT THAT HOLDS YE IN MY FORM, SHE IS THE ONE!
LUCY SPEAKS AGA TO HER "GHOST".
You Shouldn't Live in the Past
SEPARATE LIVES, PART III

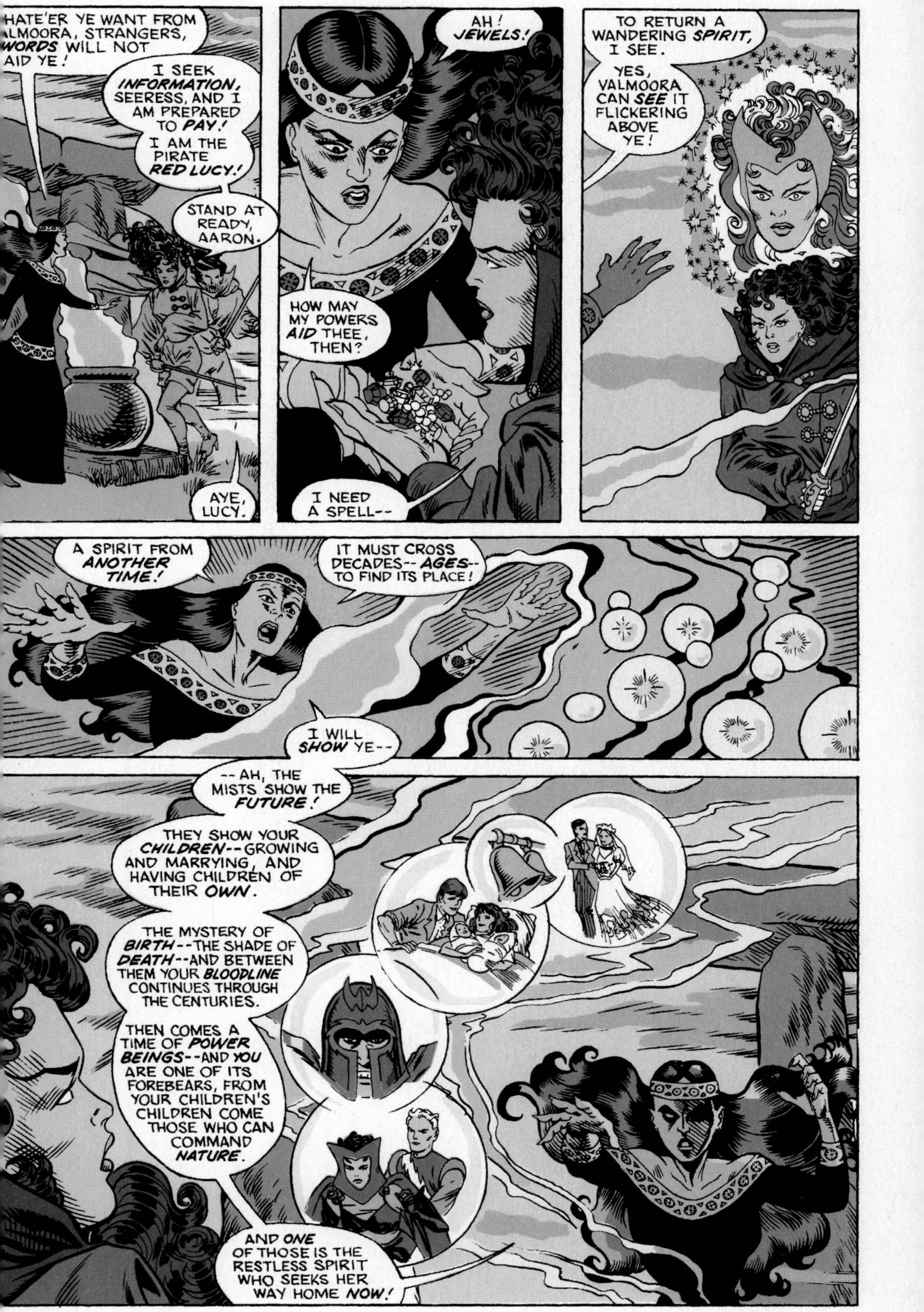
HATE'ER YE WANT FROM
ALMOORA, STRANGERS, WORDS WILL NOT AID YE!
I SEEK INFORMATION, SEERESS, AND I AM PREPARED TO PAY!
I AM THE PIRATE RED LUCY!
STAND AT READY, AARON.
AYE, LUCY.
AH! JEWELS!
HOW MAY MY POWERS AID THEE, THEN?
I NEED A SPELL--
TO RETURN A WANDERING SPIRIT, I SEE.
YES, VALMOORA CAN SEE IT FLICKERING ABOVE YE!
A SPIRIT FROM ANOTHER TIME!
IT MUST CROSS DECADES--AGES--TO FIND ITS PLACE!
I WILL SHOW YE--
--AH, THE MISTS SHOW THE FUTURE!
THEY SHOW YOUR CHILDREN--GROWING AND MARRYING, AND HAVING CHILDREN OF THEIR OWN.
THE MYSTERY OF BIRTH--THE SHADE OF DEATH--AND BETWEEN THEM YOUR BLOODLINE CONTINUES THROUGH THE CENTURIES.
THEN COMES A TIME OF POWER BEINGS--AND YOU ARE ONE OF ITS FOREBEARS, FROM YOUR CHILDREN'S CHILDREN COME THOSE WHO CAN COMMAND NATURE.
AND ONE OF THOSE IS THE RESTLESS SPIRIT WHO SEEKS HER WAY HOME NOW!

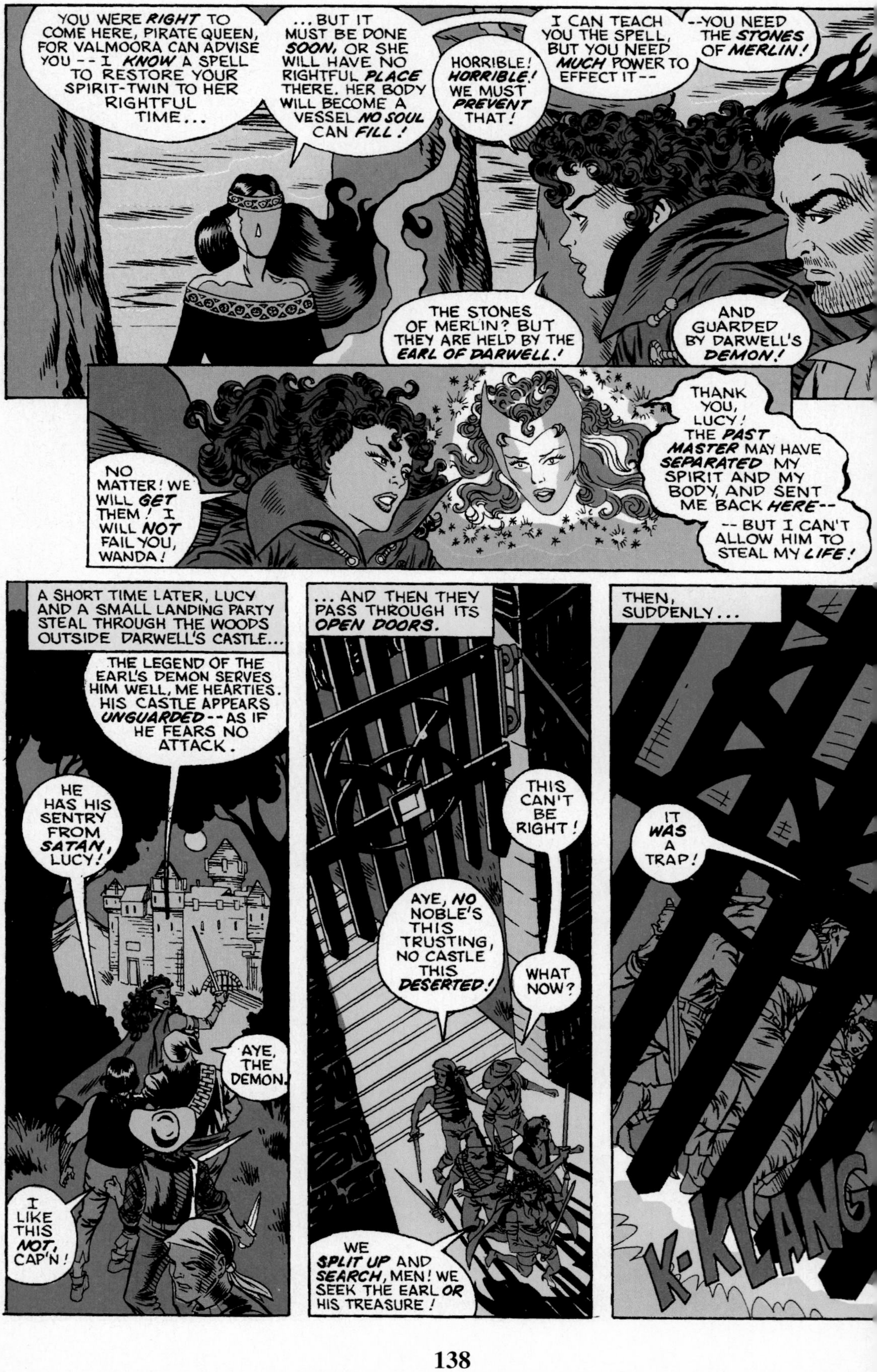
YOU WERE RIGHT TO COME HERE, PIRATE QUEEN, FOR VALMOORA CAN ADVISE YOU -- I KNOW A SPELL TO RESTORE YOUR SPIRIT-TWIN TO HER RIGHTFUL TIME...
...BUT IT MUST BE DONE SOON, OR SHE WILL HAVE NO RIGHTFUL PLACE THERE. HER BODY WILL BECOME A VESSEL NO SOUL CAN FILL!
HORRIBLE! HORRIBLE! WE MUST PREVENT THAT!
I CAN TEACH YOU THE SPELL, BUT YOU NEED MUCH POWER TO EFFECT IT--
--YOU NEED THE STONES OF MERLIN!
THE STONES OF MERLIN? BUT THEY ARE HELD BY THE EARL OF DARWELL!
AND GUARDED BY DARWELL'S DEMON!
NO MATTER! WE WILL GET THEM! I WILL NOT FAIL YOU, WANDA!
THANK YOU, LUCY! THE PAST MASTER MAY HAVE SEPARATED MY SPIRIT AND MY BODY, AND SENT ME BACK HERE--
-- BUT I CAN'T ALLOW HIM TO STEAL MY LIFE!
A SHORT TIME LATER, LUCY AND A SMALL LANDING PARTY STEAL THROUGH THE WOODS OUTSIDE DARWELL'S CASTLE...
THE LEGEND OF THE EARL'S DEMON SERVES HIM WELL, ME HEARTIES. HIS CASTLE APPEARS UNGUARDED -- AS IF HE FEARS NO ATTACK.
HE HAS HIS SENTRY FROM SATAN, LUCY!
AYE, THE DEMON.
I LIKE THIS NOT, CAP'N!
...AND THEN THEY PASS THROUGH ITS OPEN DOORS.
THIS CAN'T BE RIGHT!
AYE, NO NOBLE'S THIS TRUSTING, NO CASTLE THIS DESERTED!
WHAT NOW?
WE SPLIT UP AND SEARCH, MEN! WE SEEK THE EARL OR HIS TREASURE!
THEN, SUDDENLY...
IT WAS A TRAP!
K-KLANG

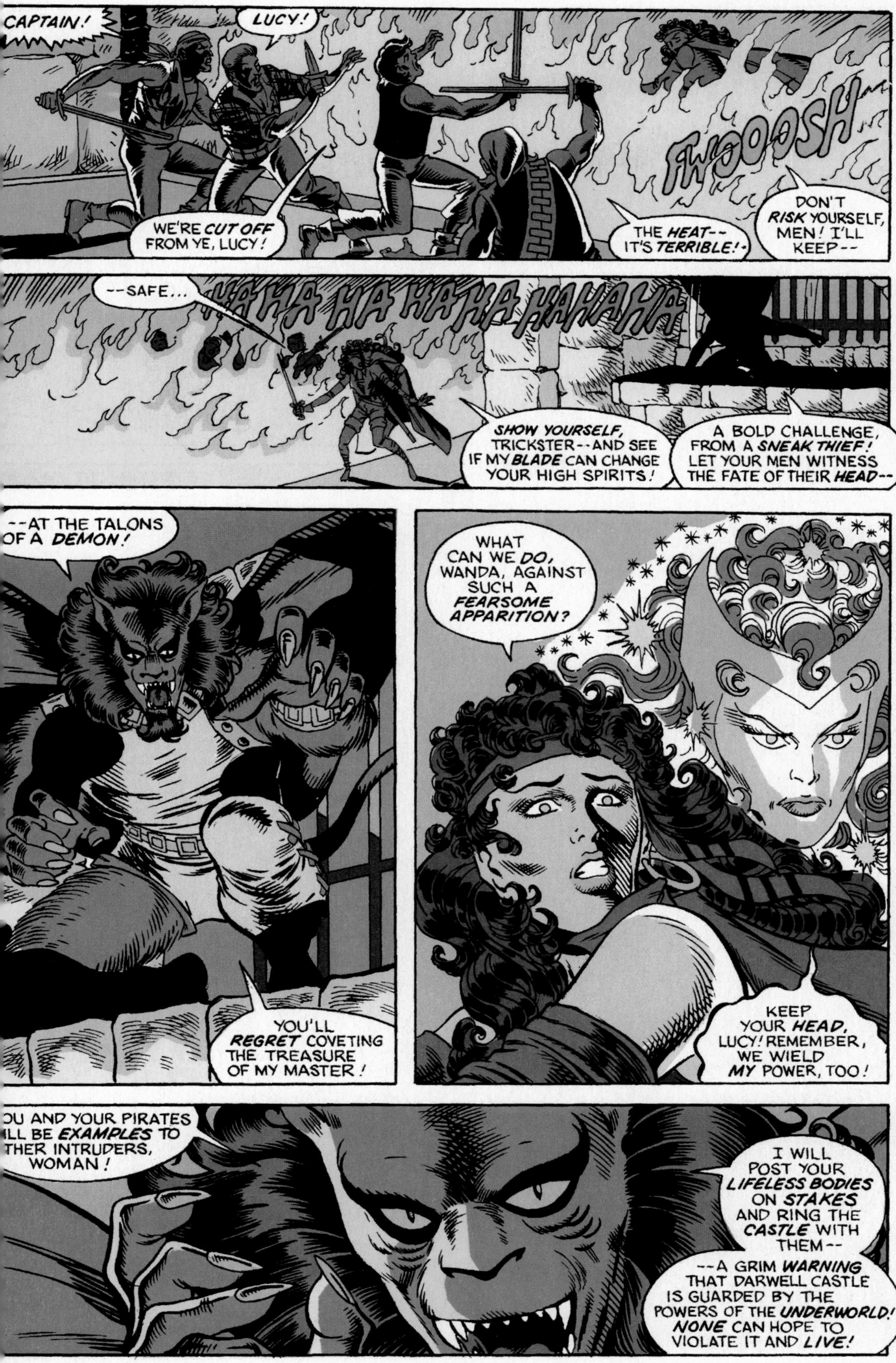
CAPTAIN!
LUCY!
WE'RE CUT OFF FROM YE, LUCY!
THE HEAT-- IT'S TERRIBLE!
FWOOOSH
DON'T RISK YOURSELF, MEN! I'LL KEEP--
--SAFE...
HAHA HA HAHA HAHAHA
SHOW YOURSELF, TRICKSTER--AND SEE IF MY BLADE CAN CHANGE YOUR HIGH SPIRITS!
A BOLD CHALLENGE, FROM A SNEAK THIEF! LET YOUR MEN WITNESS THE FATE OF THEIR HEAD--
--AT THE TALONS OF A DEMON!
YOU'LL REGRET COVETING THE TREASURE OF MY MASTER!
WHAT CAN WE DO, WANDA, AGAINST SUCH A FEARSOME APPARITION?
KEEP YOUR HEAD, LUCY! REMEMBER, WE WIELD MY POWER, TOO!
OU AND YOUR PIRATES ILL BE EXAMPLES TO THER INTRUDERS, WOMAN!
I WILL POST YOUR LIFELESS BODIES ON STAKES AND RING THE CASTLE WITH THEM--
--A GRIM WARNING THAT DARWELL CASTLE IS GUARDED BY THE POWERS OF THE UNDERWORLD! NONE CAN HOPE TO VIOLATE IT AND LIVE!

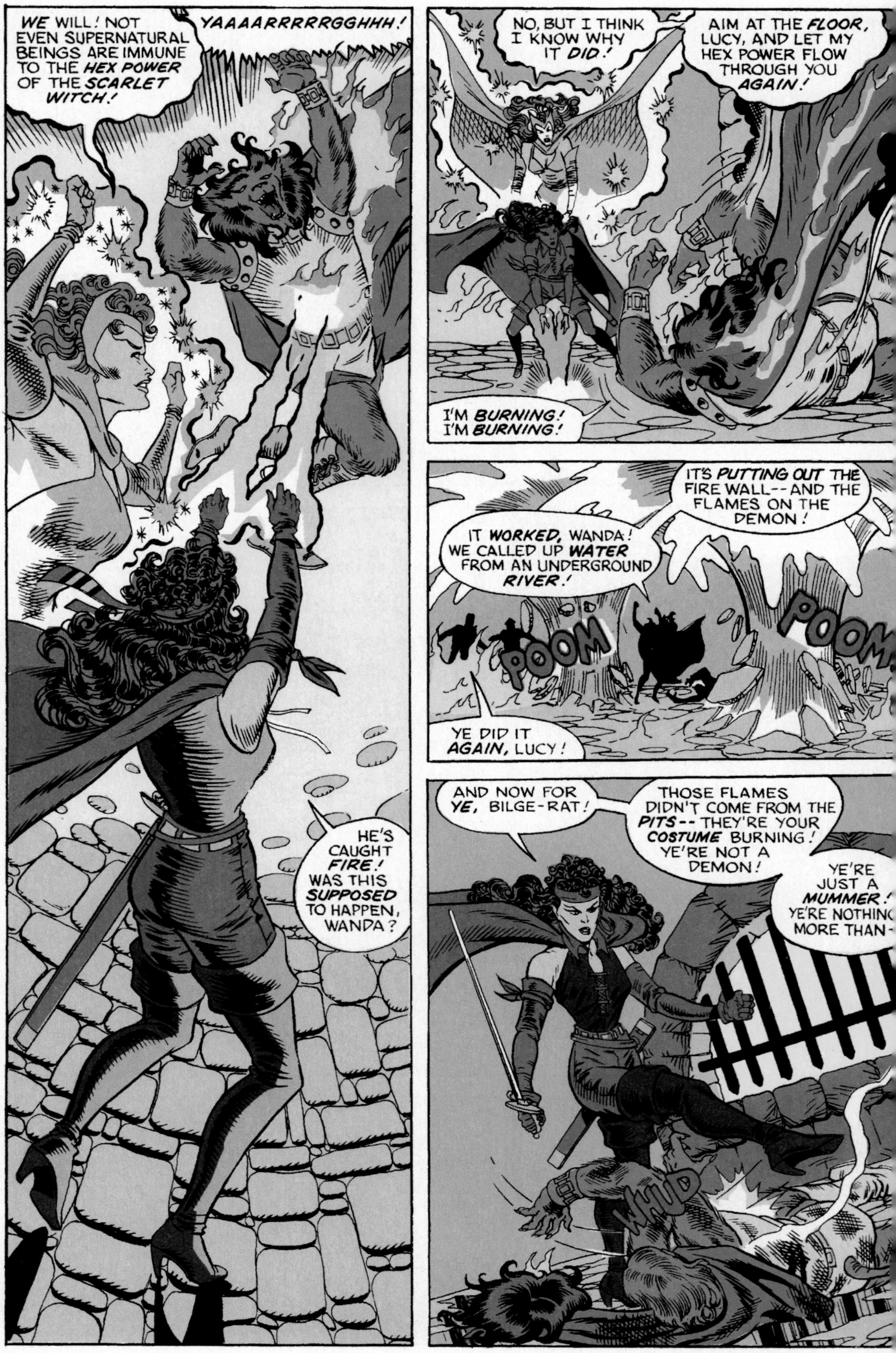
WE WILL! NOT EVEN SUPERNATURAL BEINGS ARE IMMUNE TO THE HEX POWER OF THE SCARLET WITCH!
YAAAARRRRRGGHHH!
HE'S CAUGHT FIRE! WAS THIS SUPPOSED TO HAPPEN, WANDA?
NO, BUT I THINK I KNOW WHY IT DID!
AIM AT THE FLOOR, LUCY, AND LET MY HEX POWER FLOW THROUGH YOU AGAIN!
I'M BURNING! I'M BURNING!
IT WORKED, WANDA! WE CALLED UP WATER FROM AN UNDERGROUND RIVER!
IT'S PUTTING OUT THE FIRE WALL--AND THE FLAMES ON THE DEMON!
POOM
POOM
YE DID IT AGAIN, LUCY!
AND NOW FOR YE, BILGE-RAT!
THOSE FLAMES DIDN'T COME FROM THE PITS-- THEY'RE YOUR COSTUME BURNING! YE'RE NOT A DEMON!
YE'RE JUST A MUMMER! YE'RE NOTHING MORE THAN-
WHUD

--THE *EARL* OF *DARWELL* HIMSELF!

M-MERCY, PIRATE QUEEN!

I WAS JUST *DEFENDING* MY TREASURE. *SPARE* ME AND YE MAY *HAVE* IT!

AYE, I *SHALL* HAVE IT, NOBLEMAN--

--AND I *WILL* SPARE YE. WHERE BE THE *BOOTY?*

UP THOSE STAIRS, BEHIND THE *DOOR...*

TO IT, MEN!

AYE, LUCY!

AND BEHIND THE EASILY-OPENED DOOR...

..LIES THE ANSWER TO TWO PRAYERS.

THIS IS A *KING'S RANSOM* OF SWAG, CAP'N!

NEVER MIND THAT! IS...?

YES, LUCY! HERE IT IS, JUST AS THE SEERESS SAID--THE *STONES* OF *MERLIN!*

AND MUCH *MORE* BESIDES!

A SHORT TIME LATER, AFTER HAVING RETURNED TO THE *SCARLET RAIDER*, THE PIRATE QUEEN AND HER DESCENDANT ENTHUSE OVER THEIR VICTORY...

...AND PREPARE THEIR *FAREWELLS...*

I PRAY VALMOORA'S SPELL *SUCCEEDS*, WANDA, FOR I KNOW YOU *MUST* RETURN TO YOUR OWN TIME, BUT I AM SADDENED IN MY HEART BY THAT WISH--

--FOR I KNOW THAT WE WILL NEVER MEET *AGAIN!*

I OWE YOU *SO MUCH,* LUCY...

...BUT YOU'RE RIGHT--I CAN'T *STAY* HERE. MY LIFE IS *MINE*-- AND I WON'T HAVE IT TAKEN FROM ME BY THE PAST MASTER, OR *ANYONE!*

CAN WE BEGIN?

141

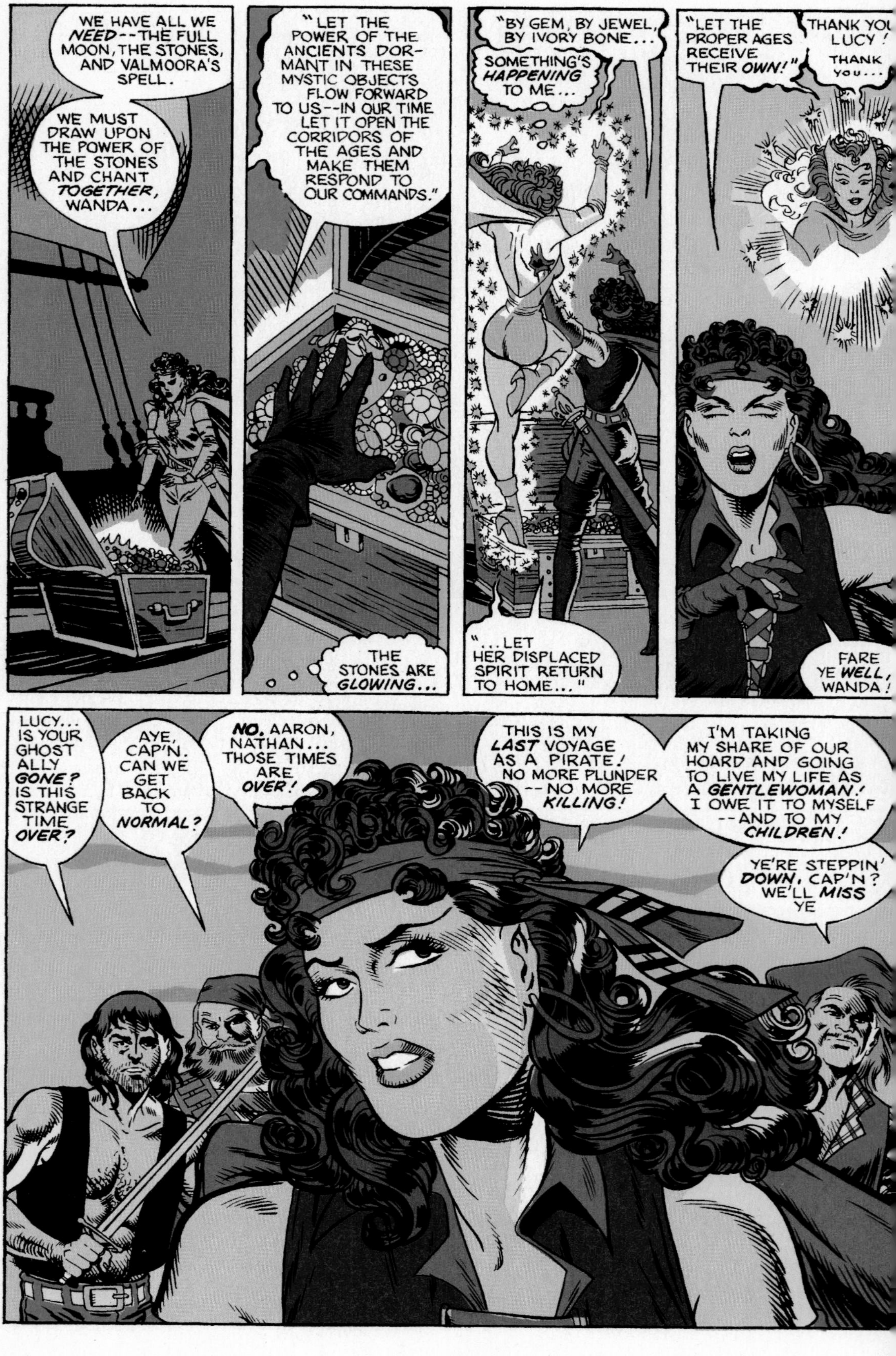
WE HAVE ALL WE NEED--THE FULL MOON, THE STONES, AND VALMOORA'S SPELL.
WE MUST DRAW UPON THE POWER OF THE STONES AND CHANT TOGETHER, WANDA...
"LET THE POWER OF THE ANCIENTS DORMANT IN THESE MYSTIC OBJECTS FLOW FORWARD TO US--IN OUR TIME LET IT OPEN THE CORRIDORS OF THE AGES AND MAKE THEM RESPOND TO OUR COMMANDS."
THE STONES ARE GLOWING...
"BY GEM, BY JEWEL, BY IVORY BONE...
SOMETHING'S HAPPENING TO ME...
"...LET HER DISPLACED SPIRIT RETURN TO HOME..."
"LET THE PROPER AGES RECEIVE THEIR OWN!"
THANK YOU LUCY! THANK YOU...
FARE YE WELL, WANDA!
LUCY... IS YOUR GHOST ALLY GONE? IS THIS STRANGE TIME OVER?
AYE, CAP'N. CAN WE GET BACK TO NORMAL?
NO. AARON, NATHAN... THOSE TIMES ARE OVER!
THIS IS MY LAST VOYAGE AS A PIRATE! NO MORE PLUNDER --NO MORE KILLING!
I'M TAKING MY SHARE OF OUR HOARD AND GOING TO LIVE MY LIFE AS A GENTLEWOMAN! I OWE IT TO MYSELF --AND TO MY CHILDREN!
YE'RE STEPPIN' DOWN, CAP'N? WE'LL MISS YE

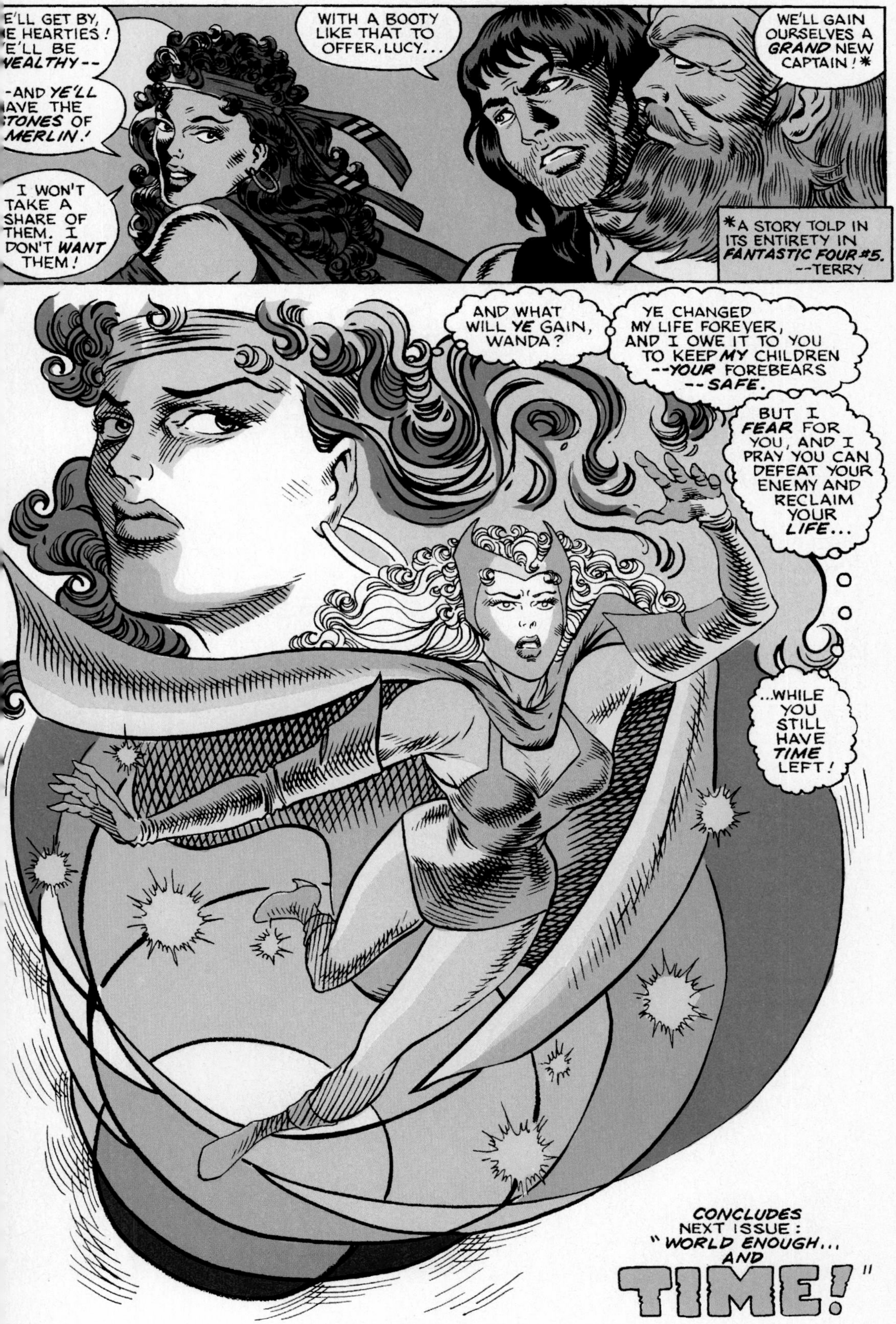
E'LL GET BY, E HEARTIES! E'LL BE WEALTHY--
-AND YE'LL AVE THE STONES OF MERLIN!
I WON'T TAKE A SHARE OF THEM. I DON'T WANT THEM!
WITH A BOOTY LIKE THAT TO OFFER, LUCY...
WE'LL GAIN OURSELVES A GRAND NEW CAPTAIN!*
*A STORY TOLD IN ITS ENTIRETY IN FANTASTIC FOUR #5. --TERRY
AND WHAT WILL YE GAIN, WANDA?
YE CHANGED MY LIFE FOREVER, AND I OWE IT TO YOU TO KEEP MY CHILDREN --YOUR FOREBEARS --SAFE.
BUT I FEAR FOR YOU, AND I PRAY YOU CAN DEFEAT YOUR ENEMY AND RECLAIM YOUR LIFE...
...WHILE YOU STILL HAVE TIME LEFT!
CONCLUDES NEXT ISSUE: "WORLD ENOUGH... AND TIME!"

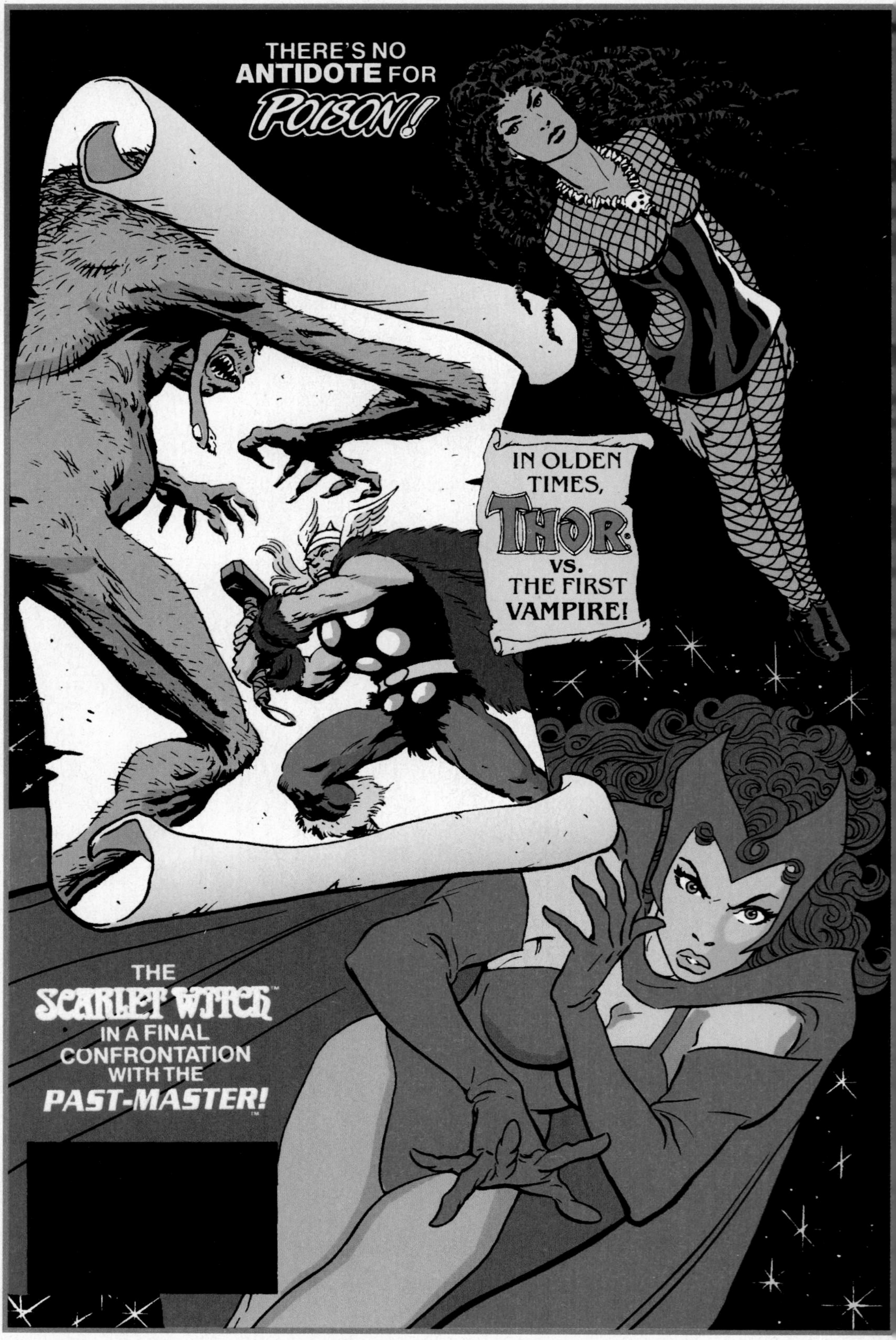
THERE'S NO ANTIDOTE FOR POISON!
IN OLDEN TIMES, THOR VS. THE FIRST VAMPIRE!
THE SCARLET WITCH IN A FINAL CONFRONTATION WITH THE PAST-MASTER!

MARVEL COMICS PRESENTS #63

WRITER, ARTIST, COLORIST & LETTERER: RICHARD HOWELL
ASSISTANT EDITOR: KELLY CORVESE • EDITOR: TERRY KAVANAGH

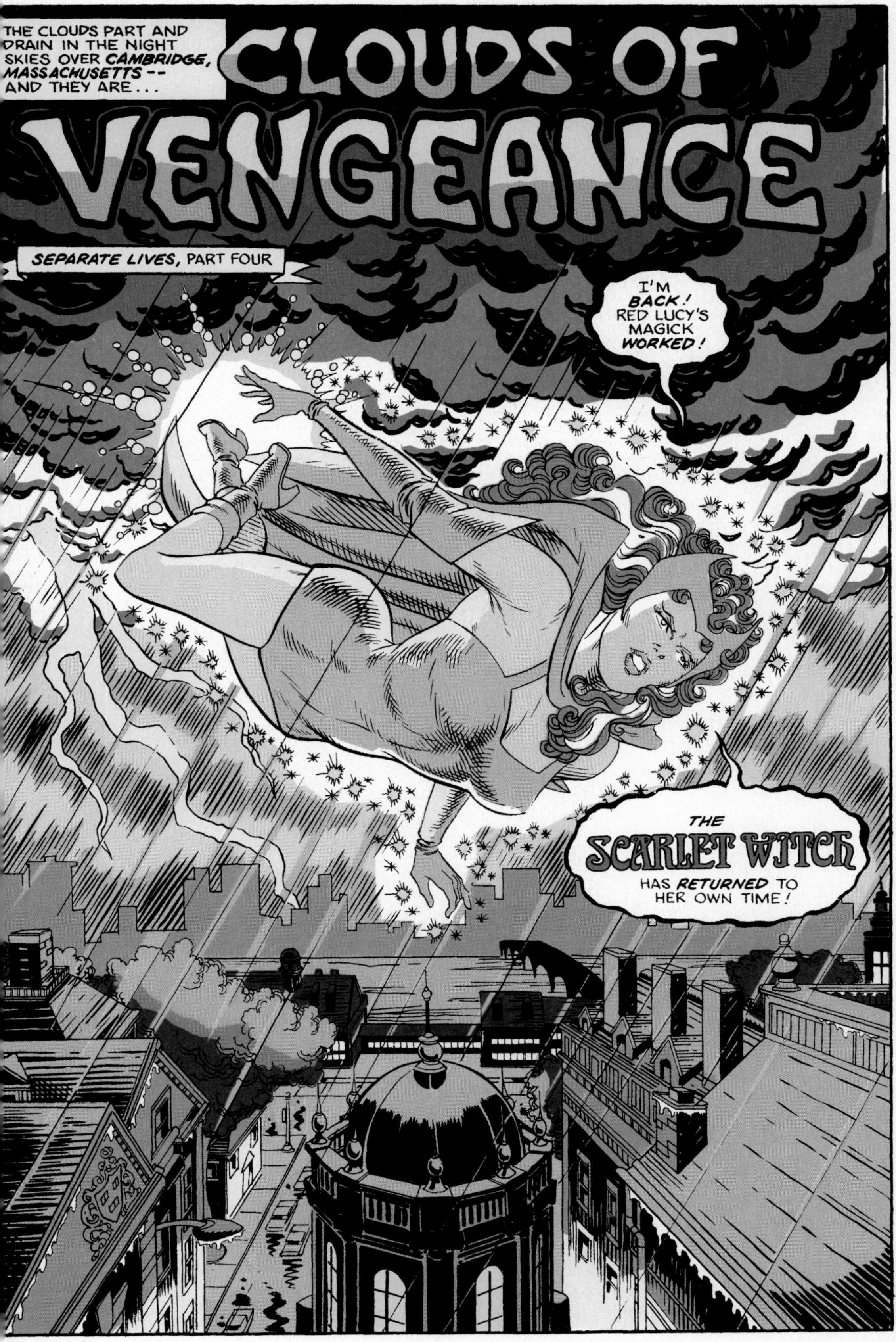
THE CLOUDS PART AND DRAIN IN THE NIGHT SKIES OVER CAMBRIDGE, MASSACHUSETTS -- AND THEY ARE...
CLOUDS OF VENGEANCE
SEPARATE LIVES, PART FOUR
I'M BACK! RED LUCY'S MAGICK WORKED!
THE SCARLET WITCH HAS RETURNED TO HER OWN TIME!

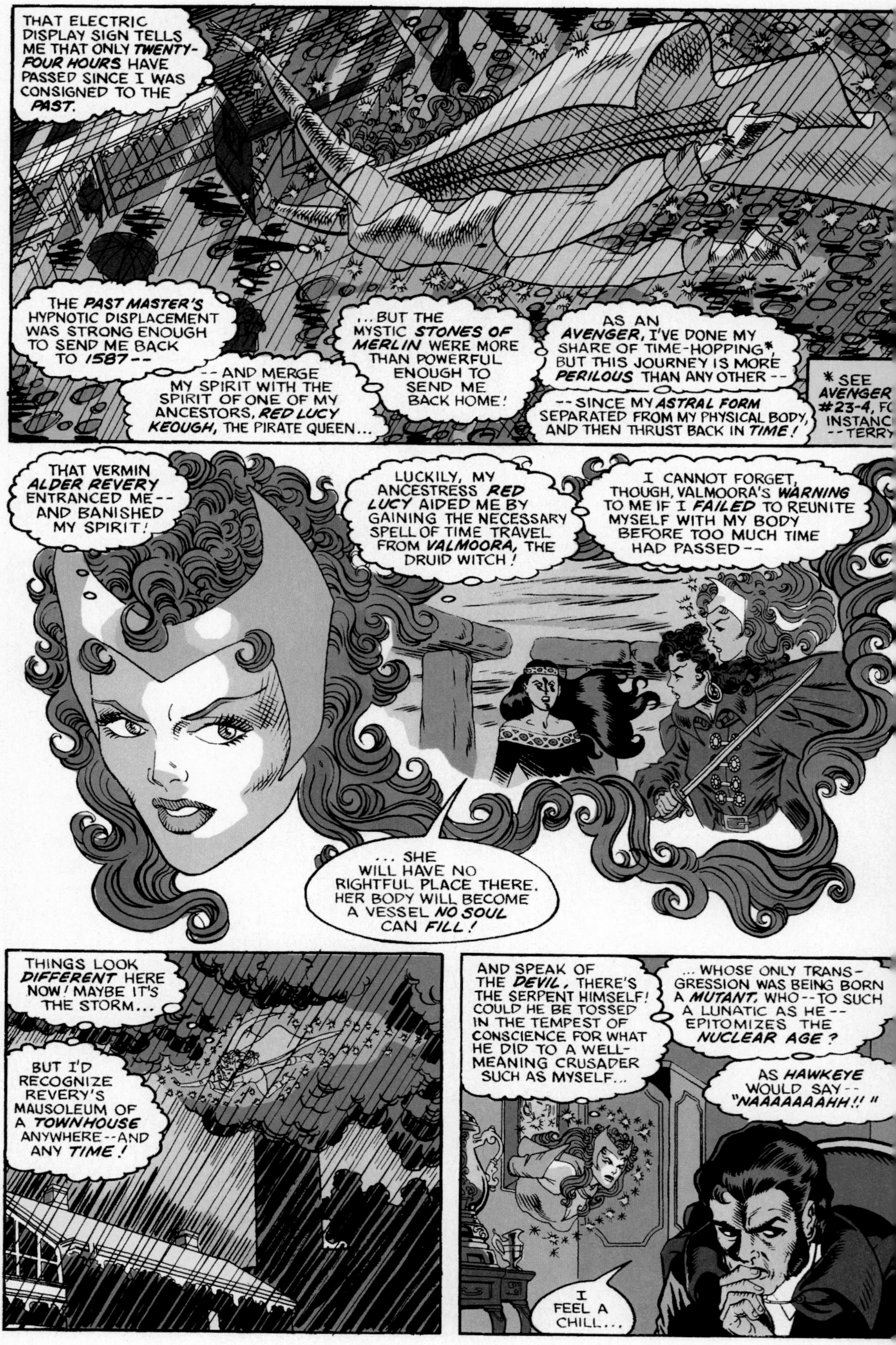

THAT ELECTRIC DISPLAY SIGN TELLS ME THAT ONLY TWENTY-FOUR HOURS HAVE PASSED SINCE I WAS CONSIGNED TO THE PAST.
THE PAST MASTER'S HYPNOTIC DISPLACEMENT WAS STRONG ENOUGH TO SEND ME BACK TO 1587--
--AND MERGE MY SPIRIT WITH THE SPIRIT OF ONE OF MY ANCESTORS, RED LUCY KEOUGH, THE PIRATE QUEEN...
...BUT THE MYSTIC STONES OF MERLIN WERE MORE THAN POWERFUL ENOUGH TO SEND ME BACK HOME!
AS AN AVENGER, I'VE DONE MY SHARE OF TIME-HOPPING*, BUT THIS JOURNEY IS MORE PERILOUS THAN ANY OTHER--
--SINCE MY ASTRAL FORM SEPARATED FROM MY PHYSICAL BODY, AND THEN THRUST BACK IN TIME!
*SEE AVENGER #23-4, FO INSTANC --TERRY
THAT VERMIN ALDER REVERY ENTRANCED ME--AND BANISHED MY SPIRIT!
LUCKILY, MY ANCESTRESS RED LUCY AIDED ME BY GAINING THE NECESSARY SPELL OF TIME TRAVEL FROM VALMOORA, THE DRUID WITCH!
I CANNOT FORGET, THOUGH, VALMOORA'S WARNING TO ME IF I FAILED TO REUNITE MYSELF WITH MY BODY BEFORE TOO MUCH TIME HAD PASSED--
...SHE WILL HAVE NO RIGHTFUL PLACE THERE. HER BODY WILL BECOME A VESSEL NO SOUL CAN FILL!
THINGS LOOK DIFFERENT HERE NOW! MAYBE IT'S THE STORM...
BUT I'D RECOGNIZE REVERY'S MAUSOLEUM OF A TOWNHOUSE ANYWHERE--AND ANY TIME!
AND SPEAK OF THE DEVIL, THERE'S THE SERPENT HIMSELF! COULD HE BE TOSSED IN THE TEMPEST OF CONSCIENCE FOR WHAT HE DID TO A WELL-MEANING CRUSADER SUCH AS MYSELF...
...WHOSE ONLY TRANS-GRESSION WAS BEING BORN A MUTANT, WHO--TO SUCH A LUNATIC AS HE--EPITOMIZES THE NUCLEAR AGE?
AS HAWKEYE WOULD SAY--"NAAAAAAAHH!!"
I FEEL A CHILL...

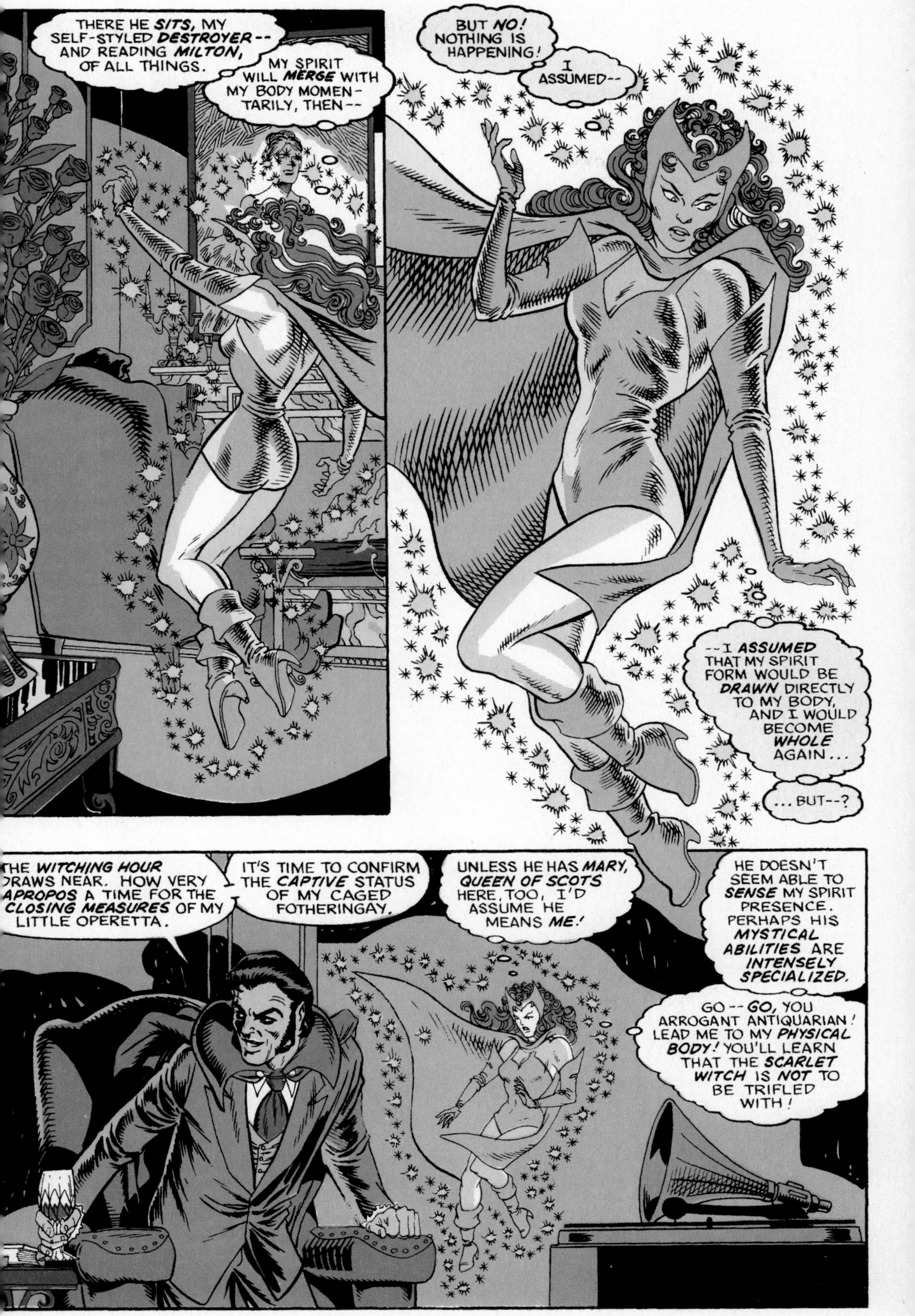
THERE HE SITS, MY SELF-STYLED DESTROYER-- AND READING MILTON, OF ALL THINGS.
MY SPIRIT WILL MERGE WITH MY BODY MOMENTARILY, THEN--
BUT NO! NOTHING IS HAPPENING!
I ASSUMED--
--I ASSUMED THAT MY SPIRIT FORM WOULD BE DRAWN DIRECTLY TO MY BODY, AND I WOULD BECOME WHOLE AGAIN...
...BUT--?
THE WITCHING HOUR DRAWS NEAR. HOW VERY APROPOS A TIME FOR THE CLOSING MEASURES OF MY LITTLE OPERETTA.
IT'S TIME TO CONFIRM THE CAPTIVE STATUS OF MY CAGED FOTHERINGAY.
UNLESS HE HAS MARY, QUEEN OF SCOTS HERE, TOO, I'D ASSUME HE MEANS ME!
HE DOESN'T SEEM ABLE TO SENSE MY SPIRIT PRESENCE. PERHAPS HIS MYSTICAL ABILITIES ARE INTENSELY SPECIALIZED.
GO--GO, YOU ARROGANT ANTIQUARIAN! LEAD ME TO MY PHYSICAL BODY! YOU'LL LEARN THAT THE SCARLET WITCH IS NOT TO BE TRIFLED WITH!

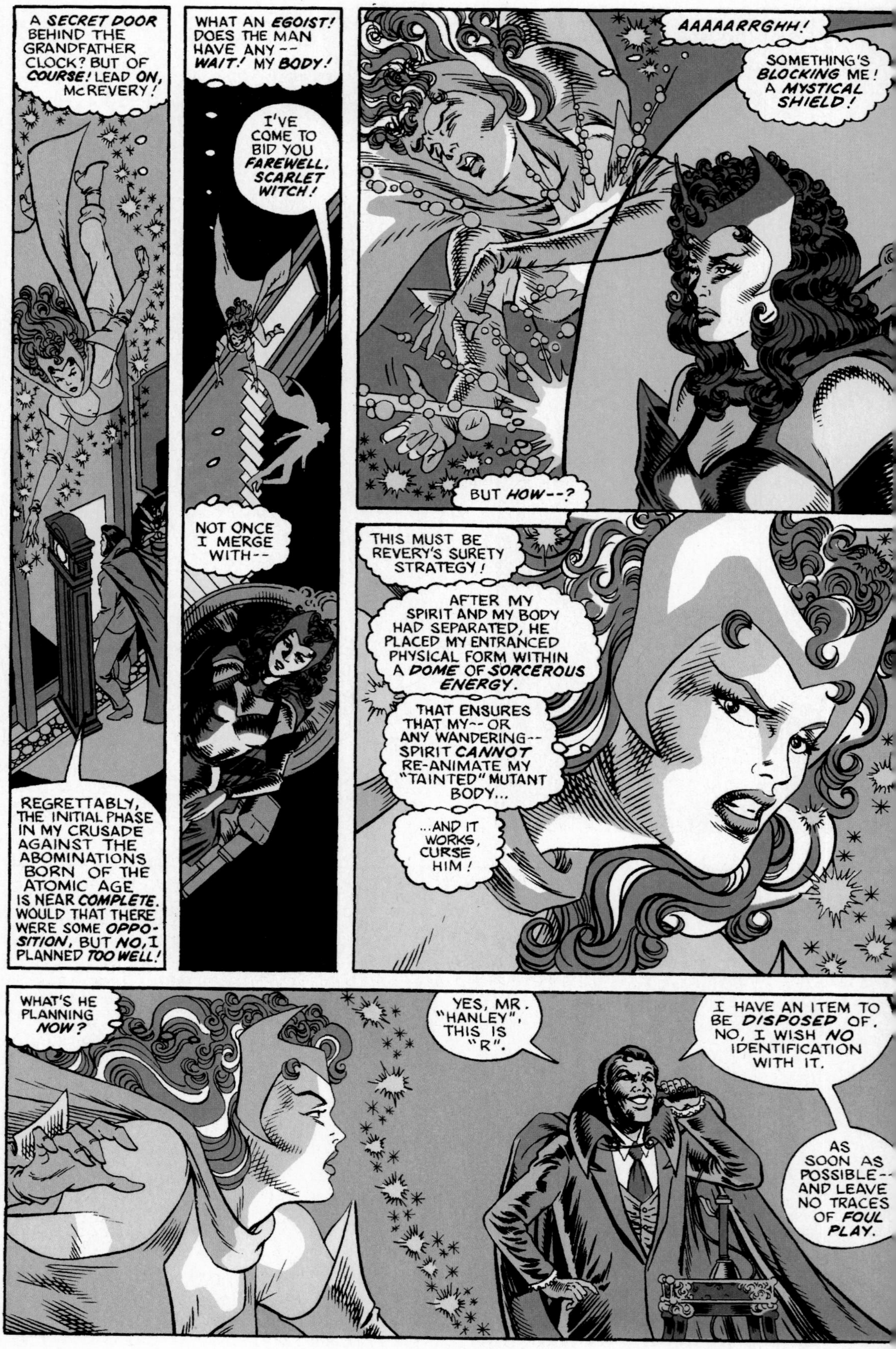
A SECRET DOOR BEHIND THE GRANDFATHER CLOCK? BUT OF COURSE! LEAD ON, McREVERY!
REGRETTABLY, THE INITIAL PHASE IN MY CRUSADE AGAINST THE ABOMINATIONS BORN OF THE ATOMIC AGE IS NEAR COMPLETE. WOULD THAT THERE WERE SOME OPPOSITION, BUT NO, I PLANNED TOO WELL!
WHAT AN EGOIST! DOES THE MAN HAVE ANY-- WAIT! MY BODY!
I'VE COME TO BID YOU FAREWELL, SCARLET WITCH!
NOT ONCE I MERGE WITH--
AAAAARRGHH!
SOMETHING'S BLOCKING ME! A MYSTICAL SHIELD!
BUT HOW--?
THIS MUST BE REVERY'S SURETY STRATEGY!
AFTER MY SPIRIT AND MY BODY HAD SEPARATED, HE PLACED MY ENTRANCED PHYSICAL FORM WITHIN A DOME OF SORCEROUS ENERGY.
THAT ENSURES THAT MY-- OR ANY WANDERING-- SPIRIT CANNOT RE-ANIMATE MY "TAINTED" MUTANT BODY...
...AND IT WORKS, CURSE HIM!
WHAT'S HE PLANNING NOW?
YES, MR. "HANLEY", THIS IS "R".
I HAVE AN ITEM TO BE DISPOSED OF. NO, I WISH NO IDENTIFICATION WITH IT.
AS SOON AS POSSIBLE-- AND LEAVE NO TRACES OF FOUL PLAY.

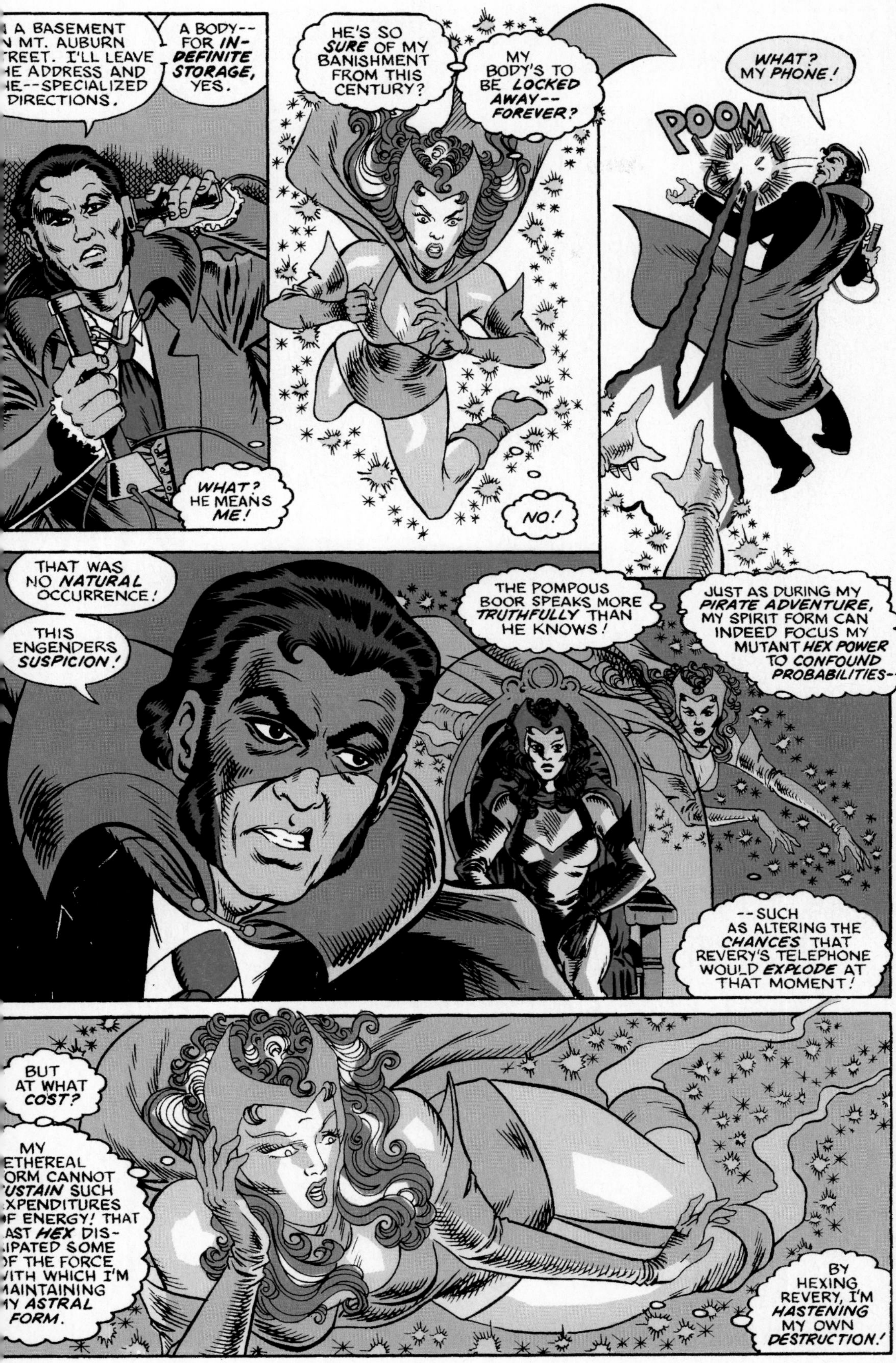

N A BASEMENT
N MT. AUBURN
TREET. I'LL LEAVE
HE ADDRESS AND
HE--SPECIALIZED
DIRECTIONS.
A BODY--
FOR IN-
DEFINITE
STORAGE,
YES.
WHAT?
HE MEANS
ME!
HE'S SO
SURE OF MY
BANISHMENT
FROM THIS
CENTURY?
MY
BODY'S TO
BE LOCKED
AWAY--
FOREVER?
NO!
WHAT?
MY PHONE!
POOM
THAT WAS
NO NATURAL
OCCURRENCE!
THIS
ENGENDERS
SUSPICION!
THE POMPOUS
BOOR SPEAKS MORE
TRUTHFULLY THAN
HE KNOWS!
JUST AS DURING MY
PIRATE ADVENTURE,
MY SPIRIT FORM CAN
INDEED FOCUS MY
MUTANT HEX POWER
TO CONFOUND
PROBABILITIES--
--SUCH
AS ALTERING THE
CHANCES THAT
REVERY'S TELEPHONE
WOULD EXPLODE AT
THAT MOMENT!
BUT
AT WHAT
COST?
MY
ETHEREAL
ORM CANNOT
USTAIN SUCH
XPENDITURES
F ENERGY! THAT
AST HEX DIS-
IPATED SOME
OF THE FORCE
VITH WHICH I'M
MAINTAINING
MY ASTRAL
FORM.
BY
HEXING
REVERY, I'M
HASTENING
MY OWN
DESTRUCTION!

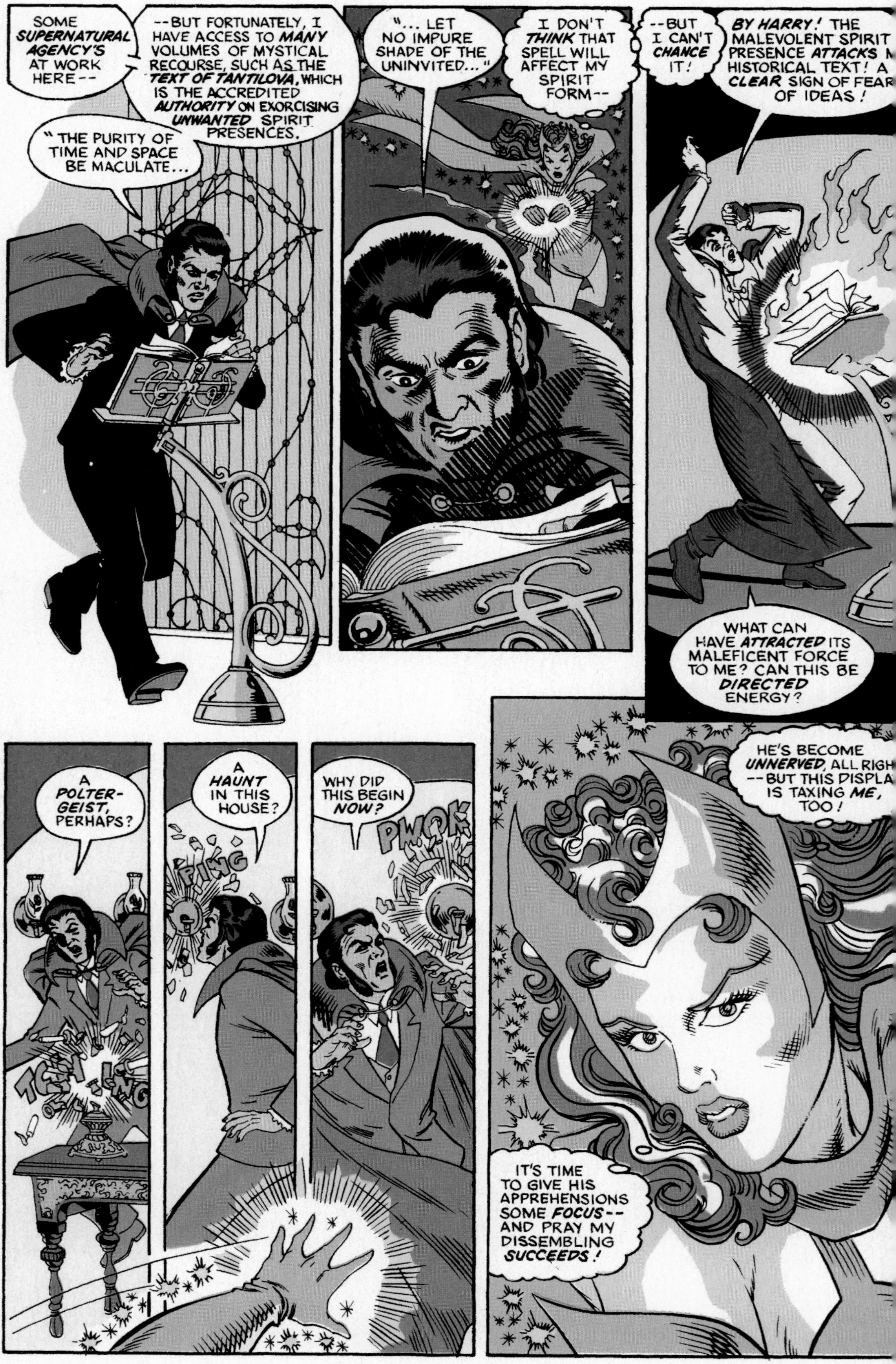
SOME SUPERNATURAL AGENCY'S AT WORK HERE--
--BUT FORTUNATELY, I HAVE ACCESS TO MANY VOLUMES OF MYSTICAL RECOURSE, SUCH AS THE TEXT OF TANTILOVA, WHICH IS THE ACCREDITED AUTHORITY ON EXORCISING UNWANTED SPIRIT PRESENCES.
"THE PURITY OF TIME AND SPACE BE MACULATE...
"... LET NO IMPURE SHADE OF THE UNINVITED..."
I DON'T THINK THAT SPELL WILL AFFECT MY SPIRIT FORM--
--BUT I CAN'T CHANCE IT!
BY HARRY! THE MALEVOLENT SPIRIT PRESENCE ATTACKS M HISTORICAL TEXT! A CLEAR SIGN OF FEAR OF IDEAS!
WHAT CAN HAVE ATTRACTED ITS MALEFICENT FORCE TO ME? CAN THIS BE DIRECTED ENERGY?
A POLTER-GEIST, PERHAPS?
A HAUNT IN THIS HOUSE?
PING
WHY DID THIS BEGIN NOW?
PWOK
HE'S BECOME UNNERVED, ALL RIGH --BUT THIS DISPLA IS TAXING ME, TOO!
IT'S TIME TO GIVE HIS APPREHENSIONS SOME FOCUS-- AND PRAY MY DISSEMBLING SUCCEEDS!

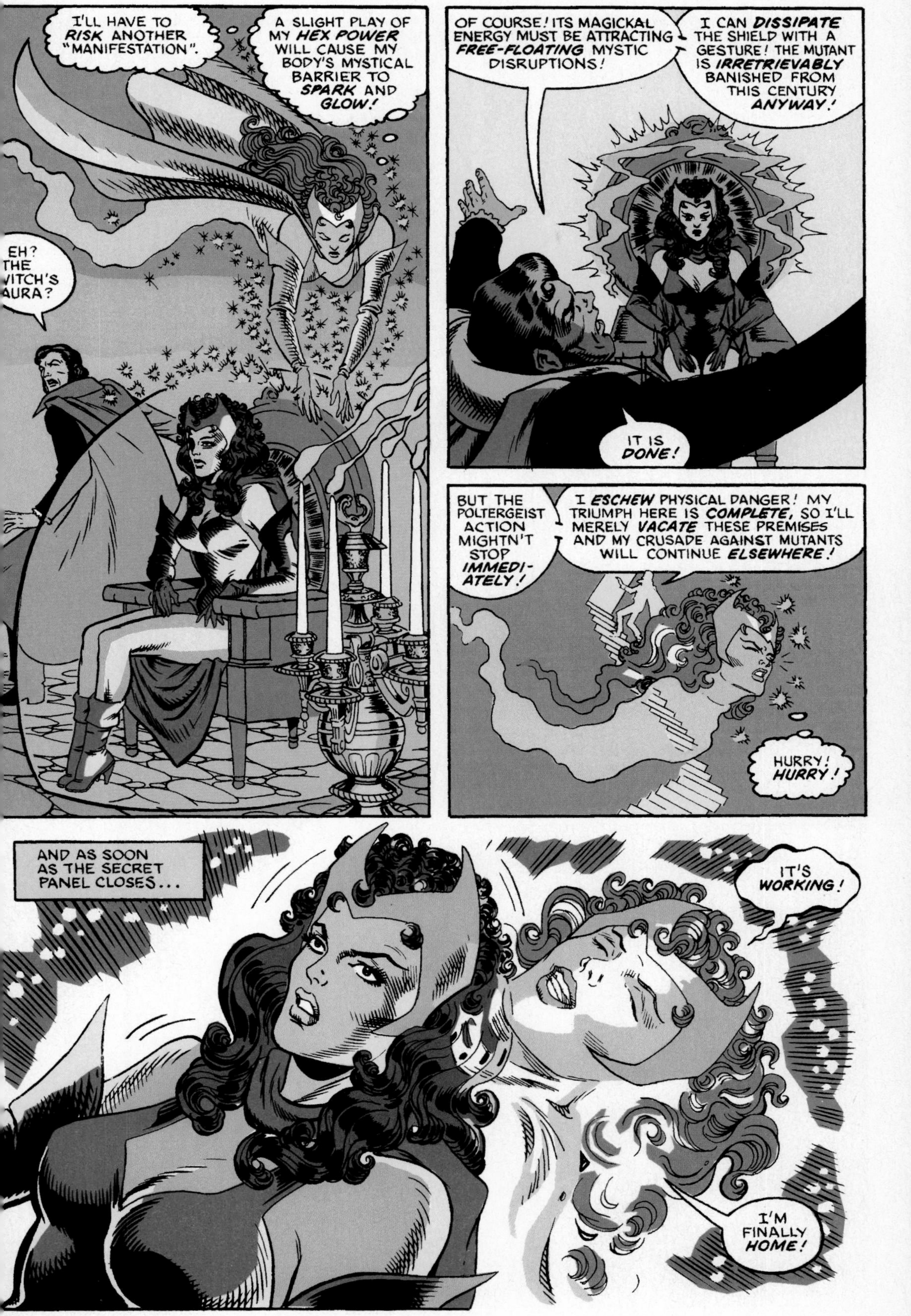
I'LL HAVE TO RISK ANOTHER "MANIFESTATION".
A SLIGHT PLAY OF MY HEX POWER WILL CAUSE MY BODY'S MYSTICAL BARRIER TO SPARK AND GLOW!
EH? THE WITCH'S AURA?
OF COURSE! ITS MAGICKAL ENERGY MUST BE ATTRACTING FREE-FLOATING MYSTIC DISRUPTIONS!
I CAN DISSIPATE THE SHIELD WITH A GESTURE! THE MUTANT IS IRRETRIEVABLY BANISHED FROM THIS CENTURY ANYWAY!
IT IS DONE!
BUT THE POLTERGEIST ACTION MIGHTN'T STOP IMMEDI-ATELY!
I ESCHEW PHYSICAL DANGER! MY TRIUMPH HERE IS COMPLETE, SO I'LL MERELY VACATE THESE PREMISES AND MY CRUSADE AGAINST MUTANTS WILL CONTINUE ELSEWHERE!
HURRY! HURRY!
AND AS SOON AS THE SECRET PANEL CLOSES...
IT'S WORKING!
I'M FINALLY HOME!

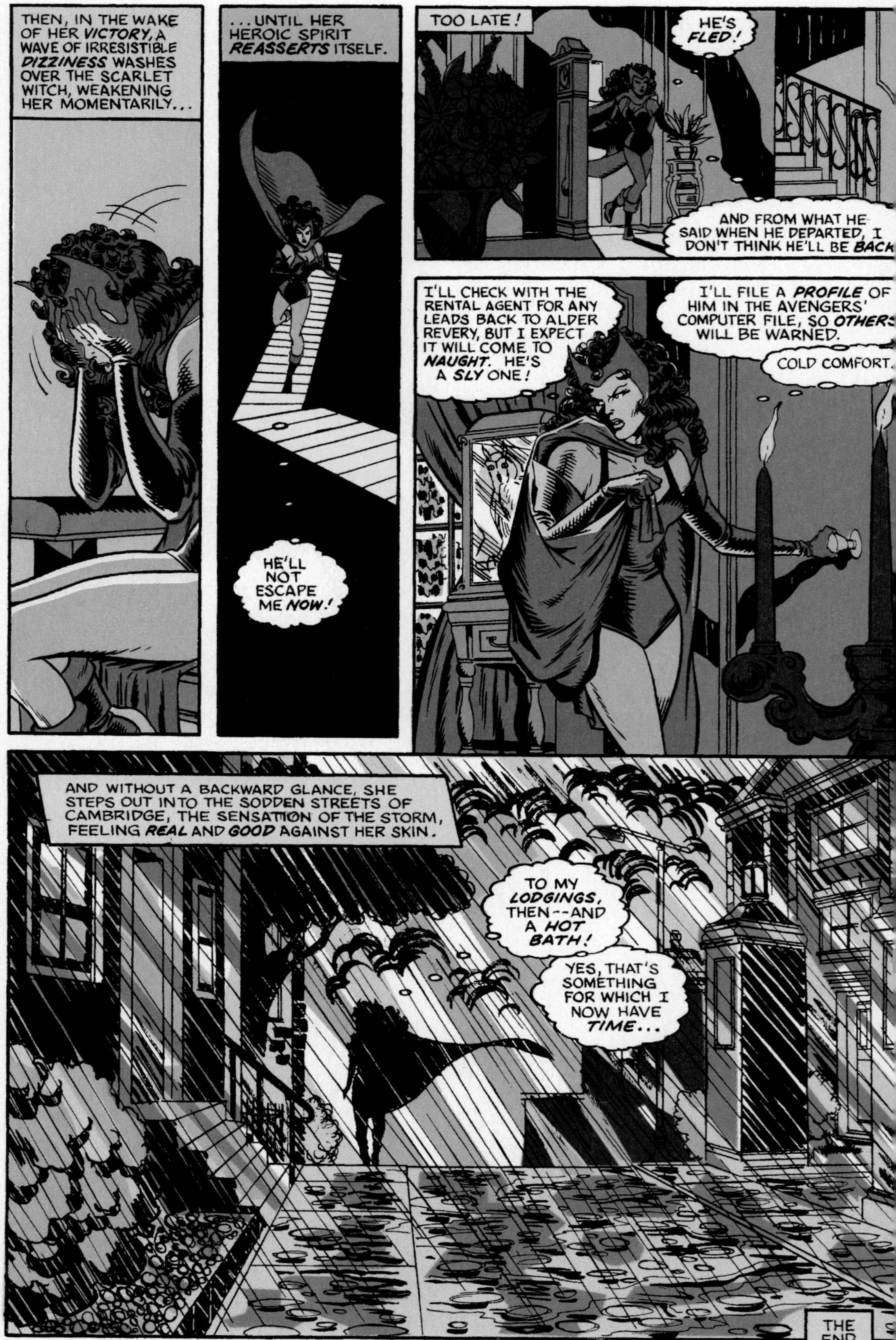
THEN, IN THE WAKE OF HER VICTORY, A WAVE OF IRRESISTIBLE DIZZINESS WASHES OVER THE SCARLET WITCH, WEAKENING HER MOMENTARILY...
...UNTIL HER HEROIC SPIRIT REASSERTS ITSELF.
HE'LL NOT ESCAPE ME NOW!
TOO LATE!
HE'S FLED!
AND FROM WHAT HE SAID WHEN HE DEPARTED, I DON'T THINK HE'LL BE BACK
I'LL CHECK WITH THE RENTAL AGENT FOR ANY LEADS BACK TO ALDER REVERY, BUT I EXPECT IT WILL COME TO NAUGHT. HE'S A SLY ONE!
I'LL FILE A PROFILE OF HIM IN THE AVENGERS' COMPUTER FILE, SO OTHERS WILL BE WARNED.
COLD COMFORT.
AND WITHOUT A BACKWARD GLANCE, SHE STEPS OUT INTO THE SODDEN STREETS OF CAMBRIDGE, THE SENSATION OF THE STORM, FEELING REAL AND GOOD AGAINST HER SKIN.
TO MY LODGINGS, THEN--AND A HOT BATH!
YES, THAT'S SOMETHING FOR WHICH I NOW HAVE TIME...
THE END.

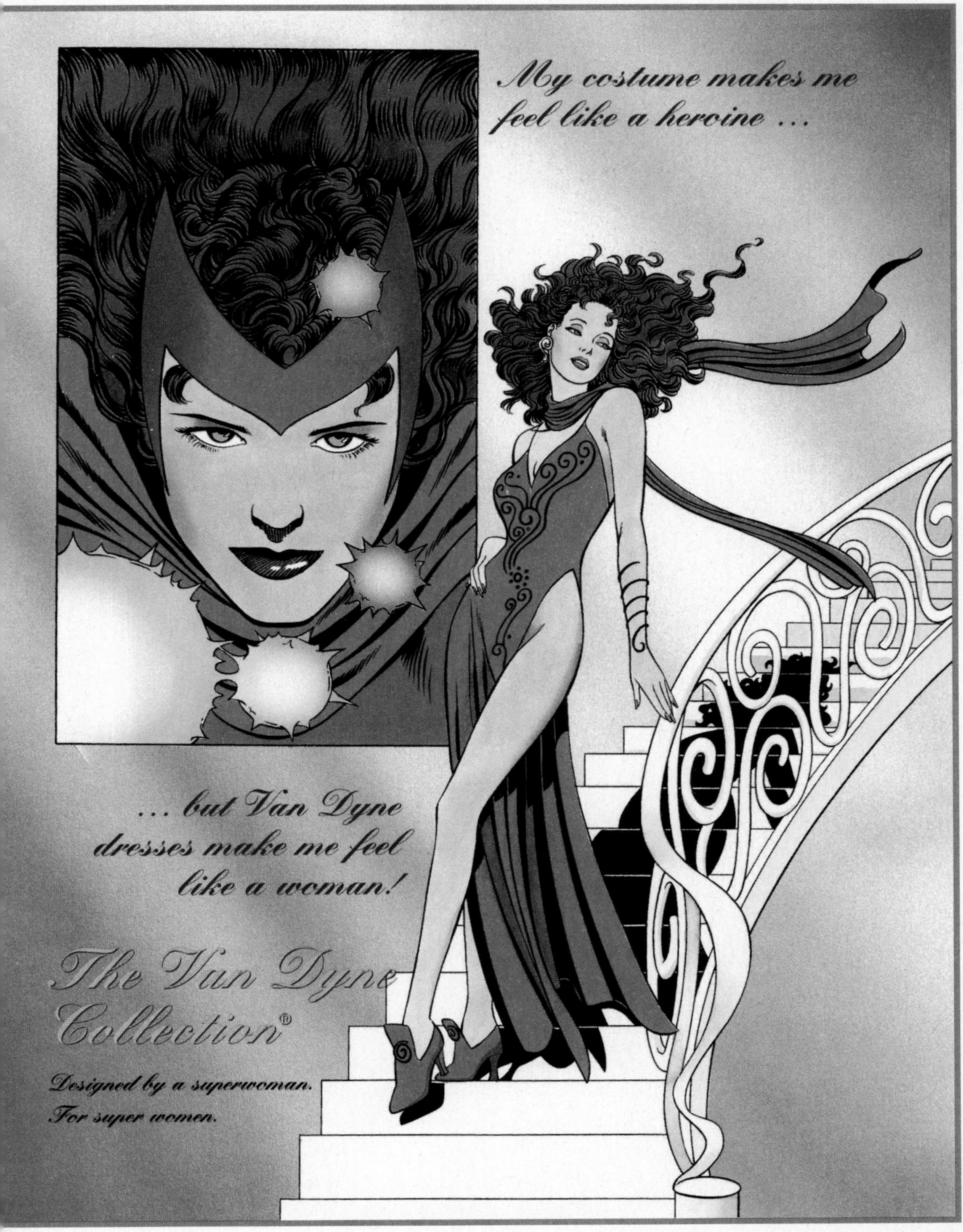
My costume makes me feel like a heroine ...
... but Van Dyne dresses make me feel like a woman!
The Van Dyne Collection®
Designed by a superwoman. For super women.

MARVEL: 1991 — THE YEAR IN REVIEW
PARODY AD BY JUNE BRIGMAN, ROY RICHARDSON & GREGORY WRIGHT

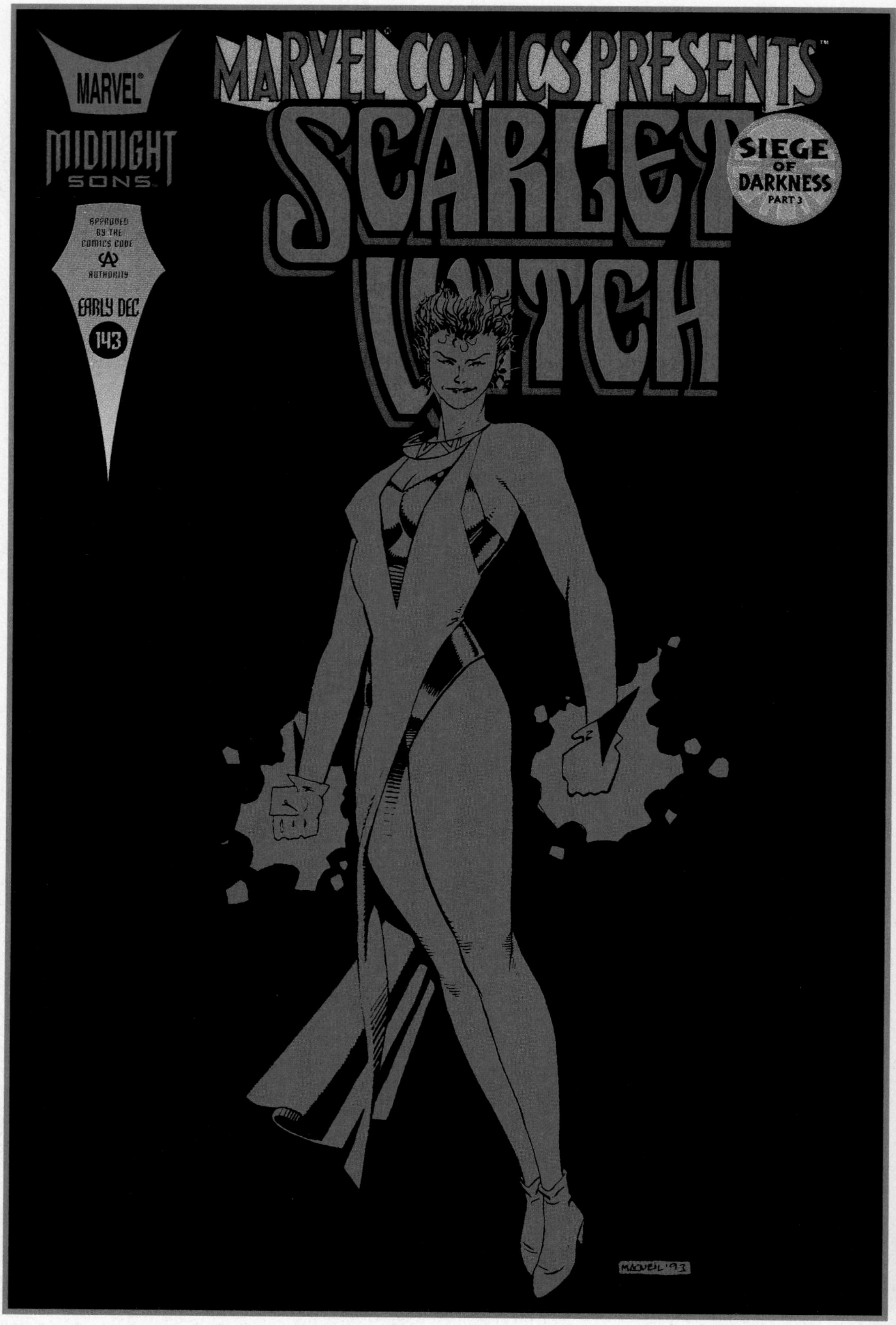
MARVEL
MIDNIGHT SONS
APPROVED BY THE COMICS CODE AUTHORITY
EARLY DEC
143
MARVEL COMICS PRESENTS
SCARLET WITCH
SIEGE OF DARKNESS PART 3
MACNEIL '93

MARVEL COMICS PRESENTS #143-144 — "ALGORITHM OF LIFE"
"PART 1: DIGITAL TERROR! • PART 2: TECHNO PHOBIA!"

WRITER: CEFN RIDOUT • ARTIST: CHARLES ADLARD • COLORIST & LETTERER: WOODROW PHOENIX
ASSISTANT EDITOR: MICHAEL KRAIGER • EDITOR: RICHARD ASHFORD

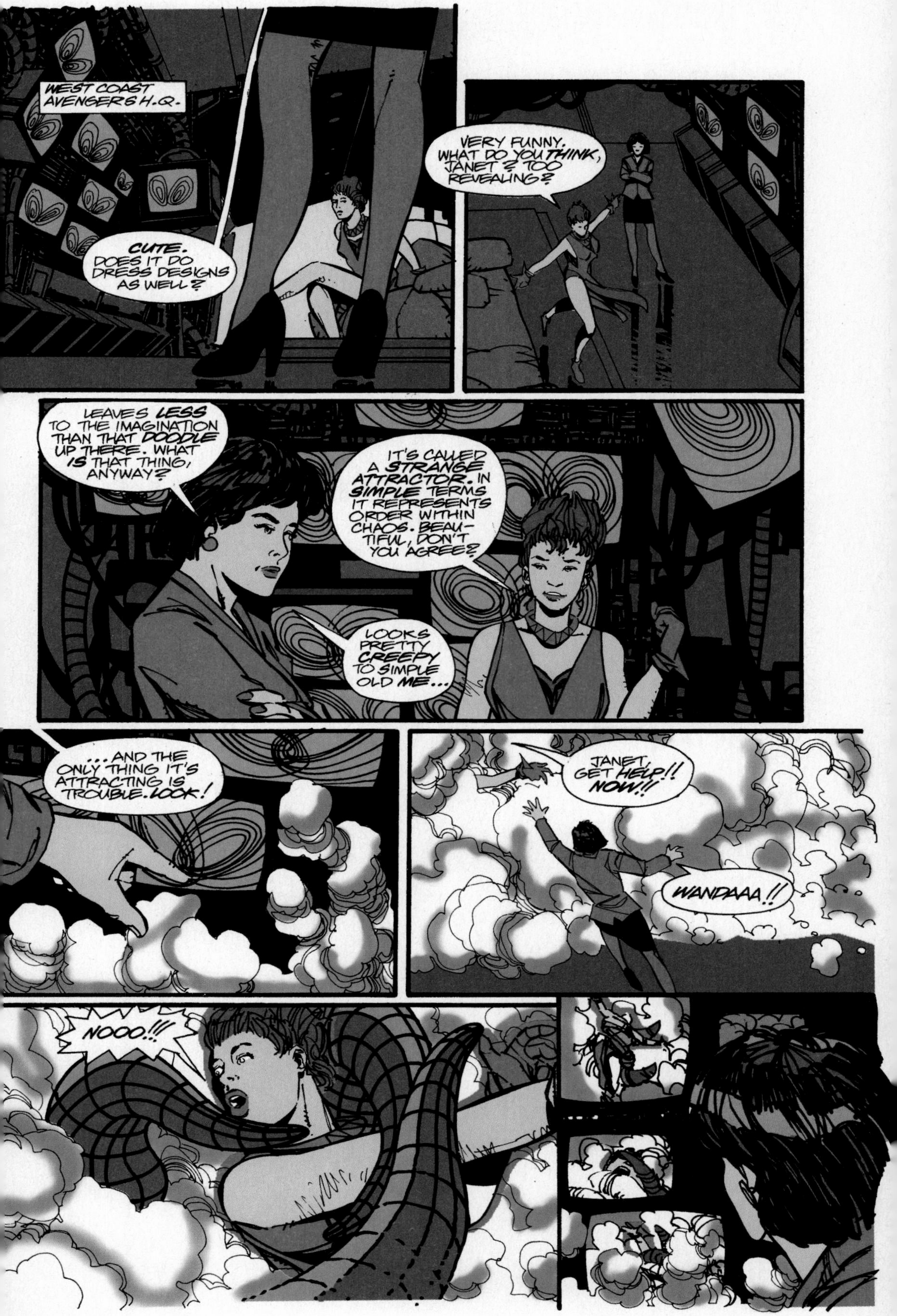
WEST COAST AVENGERS H.Q.
CUTE. DOES IT DO DRESS DESIGNS AS WELL?
VERY FUNNY. WHAT DO YOU THINK, JANET? TOO REVEALING?
LEAVES LESS TO THE IMAGINATION THAN THAT DOODLE UP THERE. WHAT IS THAT THING, ANYWAY?
IT'S CALLED A STRANGE ATTRACTOR. IN SIMPLE TERMS IT REPRESENTS ORDER WITHIN CHAOS. BEAUTIFUL, DON'T YOU AGREE?
LOOKS PRETTY CREEPY TO SIMPLE OLD ME...
...AND THE ONLY THING IT'S ATTRACTING IS TROUBLE. LOOK!
JANET, GET HELP!! NOW!!
WANDAAA!!
NOOO!!!

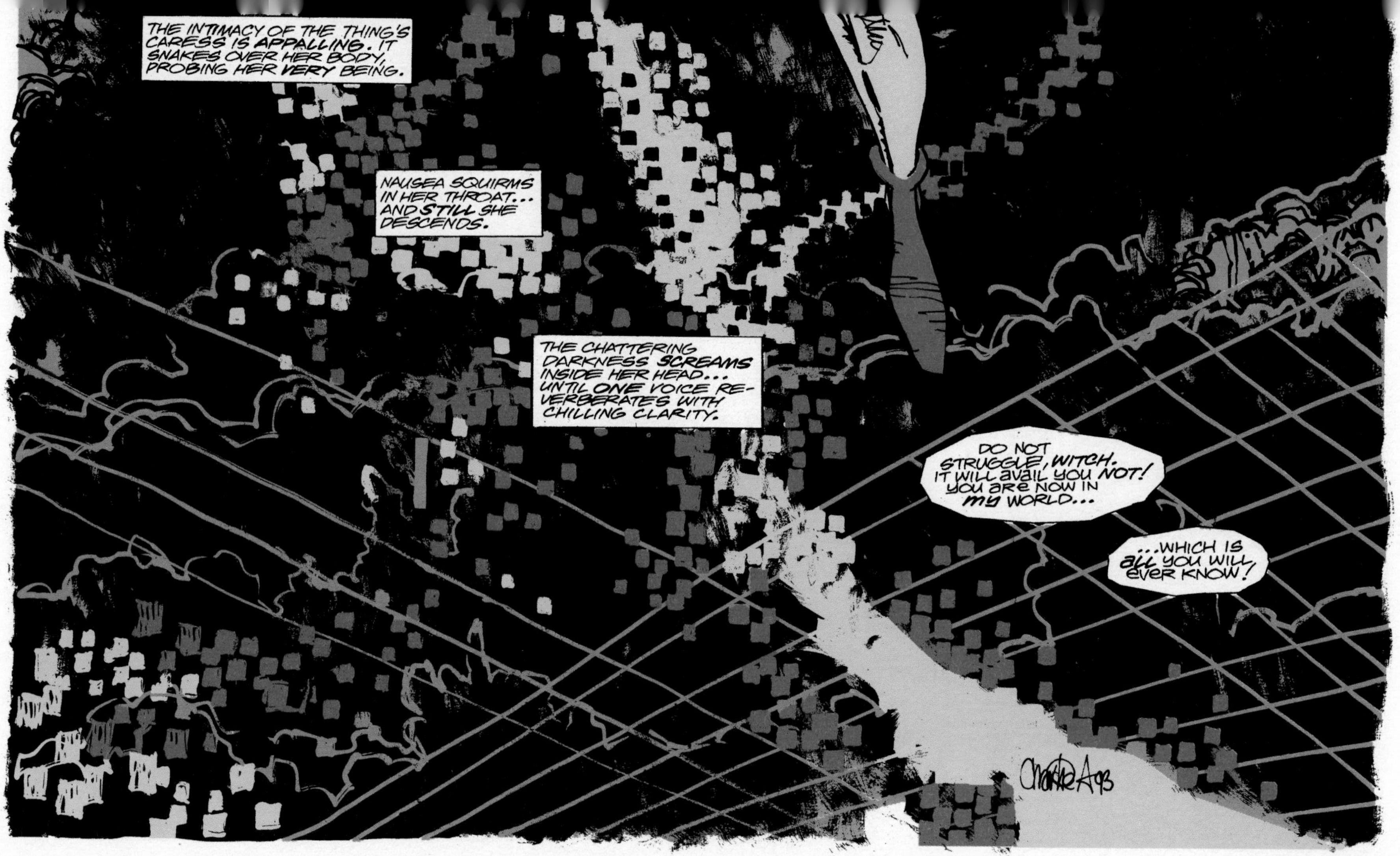
THE INTIMACY OF THE THING'S CARESS IS APPALLING. IT SNAKES OVER HER BODY, PROBING HER VERY BEING.
NAUSEA SQUIRMS IN HER THROAT... AND STILL SHE DESCENDS.
THE CHATTERING DARKNESS SCREAMS INSIDE HER HEAD... UNTIL ONE VOICE RE-VERBERATES WITH CHILLING CLARITY.
DO NOT STRUGGLE, WITCH. IT WILL AVAIL YOU NOT! YOU ARE NOW IN MY WORLD...
...WHICH IS ALL YOU WILL EVER KNOW!

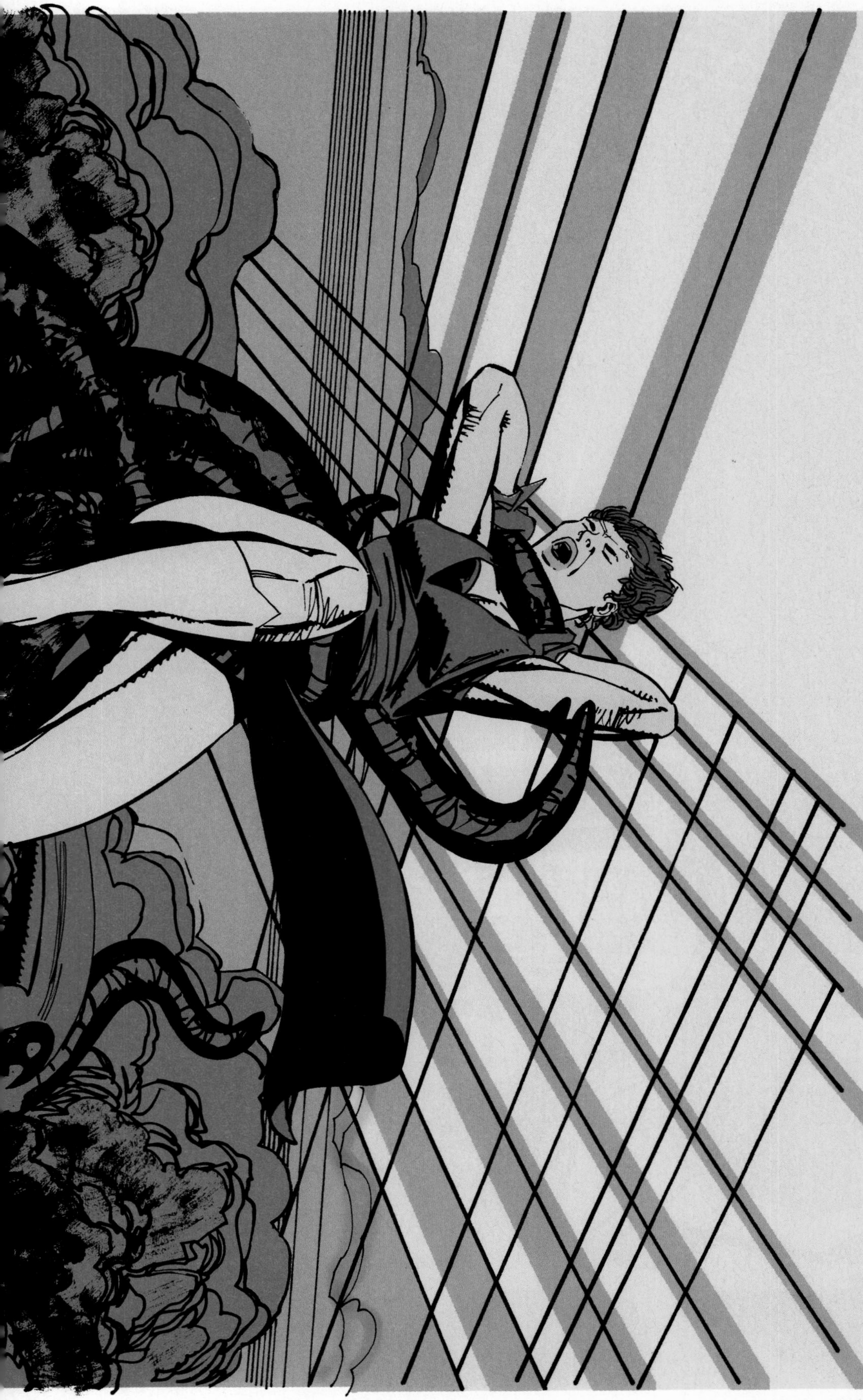

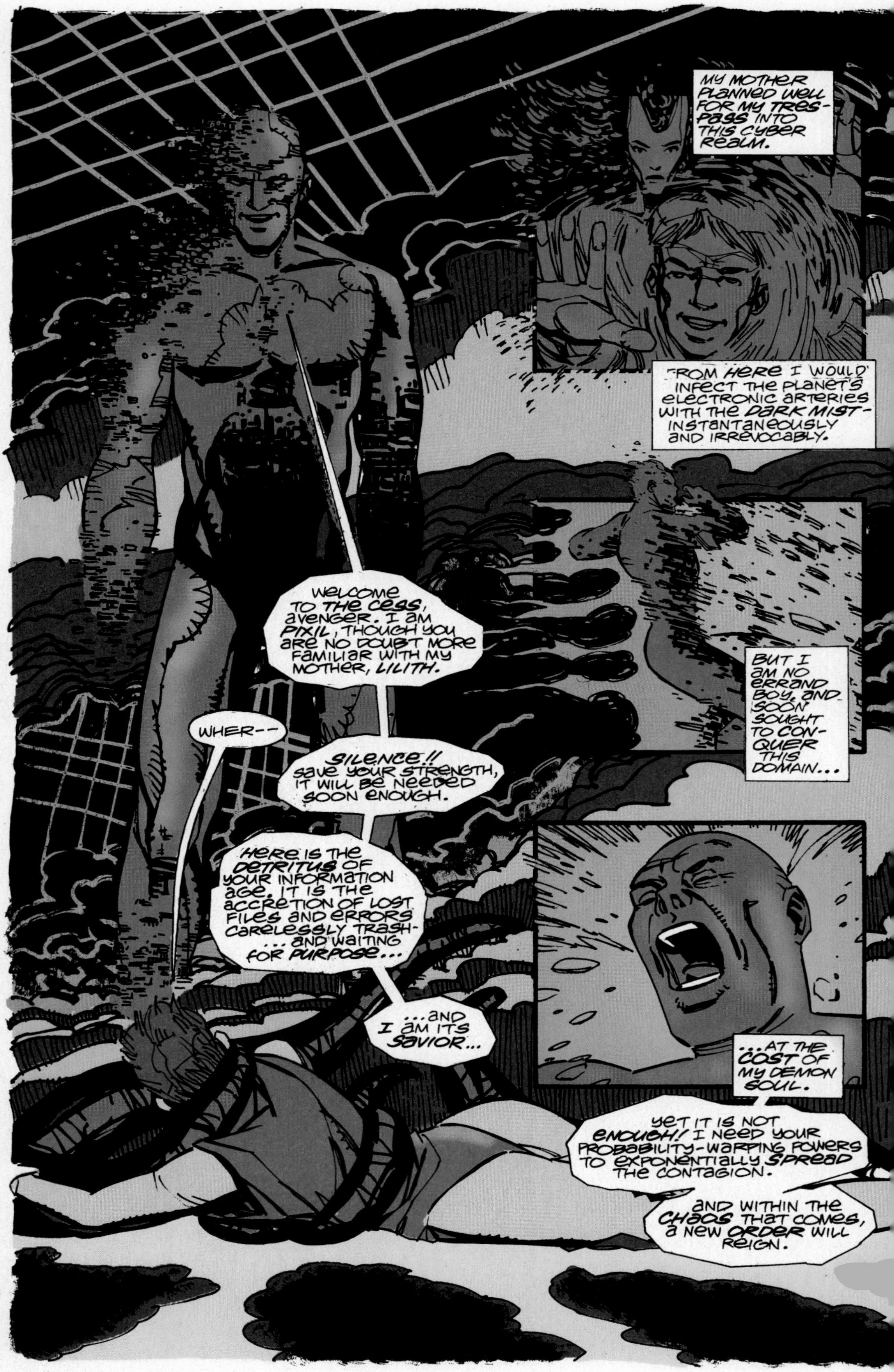
MY MOTHER PLANNED WELL FOR MY TRES-PASS INTO THIS CYBER REALM.
FROM HERE I WOULD INFECT THE PLANET'S ELECTRONIC ARTERIES WITH THE DARK MIST-- INSTANTANEOUSLY AND IRREVOCABLY.
WELCOME TO THE CESS, AVENGER. I AM PIXIL, THOUGH YOU ARE NO DOUBT MORE FAMILIAR WITH MY MOTHER, LILITH.
WHER--
SILENCE!! SAVE YOUR STRENGTH, IT WILL BE NEEDED SOON ENOUGH.
BUT I AM NO ERRAND BOY, AND SOON SOUGHT TO CONQUER THIS DOMAIN...
HERE IS THE DETRITUS OF YOUR INFORMATION AGE. IT IS THE ACCRETION OF LOST FILES AND ERRORS CARELESSLY TRASH- ...AND WAITING FOR PURPOSE...
...AND I AM ITS SAVIOR...
...AT THE COST OF MY DEMON SOUL.
YET IT IS NOT ENOUGH! I NEED YOUR PROBABILITY-WARPING POWERS TO EXPONENTIALLY SPREAD THE CONTAGION.
AND WITHIN THE CHAOS THAT COMES, A NEW ORDER WILL REIGN.

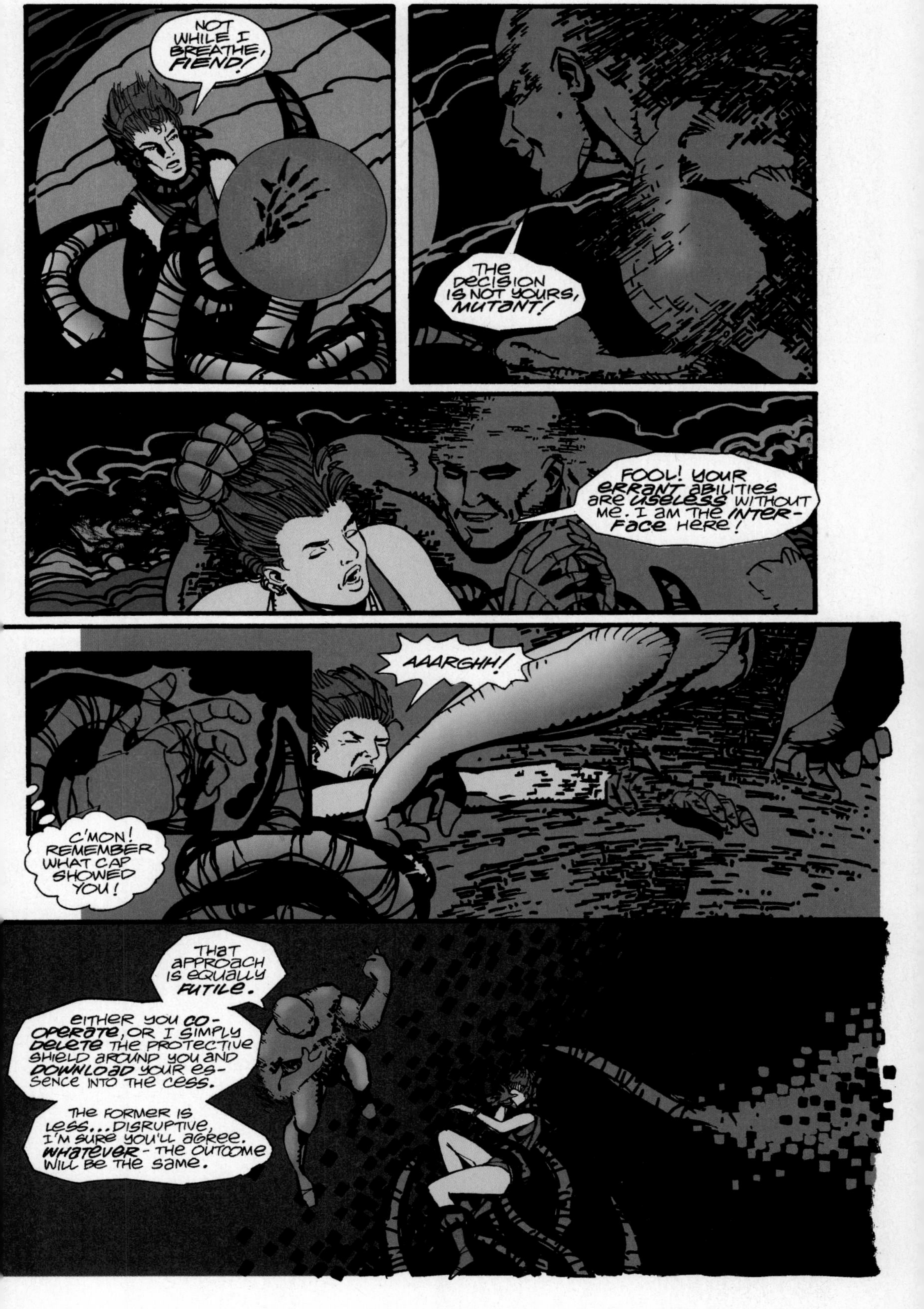
NOT WHILE I BREATHE, FIEND!
THE DECISION IS NOT YOURS, MUTANT!
FOOL! YOUR ERRANT ABILITIES ARE USELESS WITHOUT ME. I AM THE INTER-FACE HERE!
AAARGHH!
C'MON! REMEMBER WHAT CAP SHOWED YOU!
THAT APPROACH IS EQUALLY FUTILE.
EITHER YOU CO-OPERATE, OR I SIMPLY DELETE THE PROTECTIVE SHIELD AROUND YOU AND DOWNLOAD YOUR ES-SENCE INTO THE CESS.
THE FORMER IS LESS...DISRUPTIVE, I'M SURE YOU'LL AGREE. WHATEVER - THE OUTCOME WILL BE THE SAME.

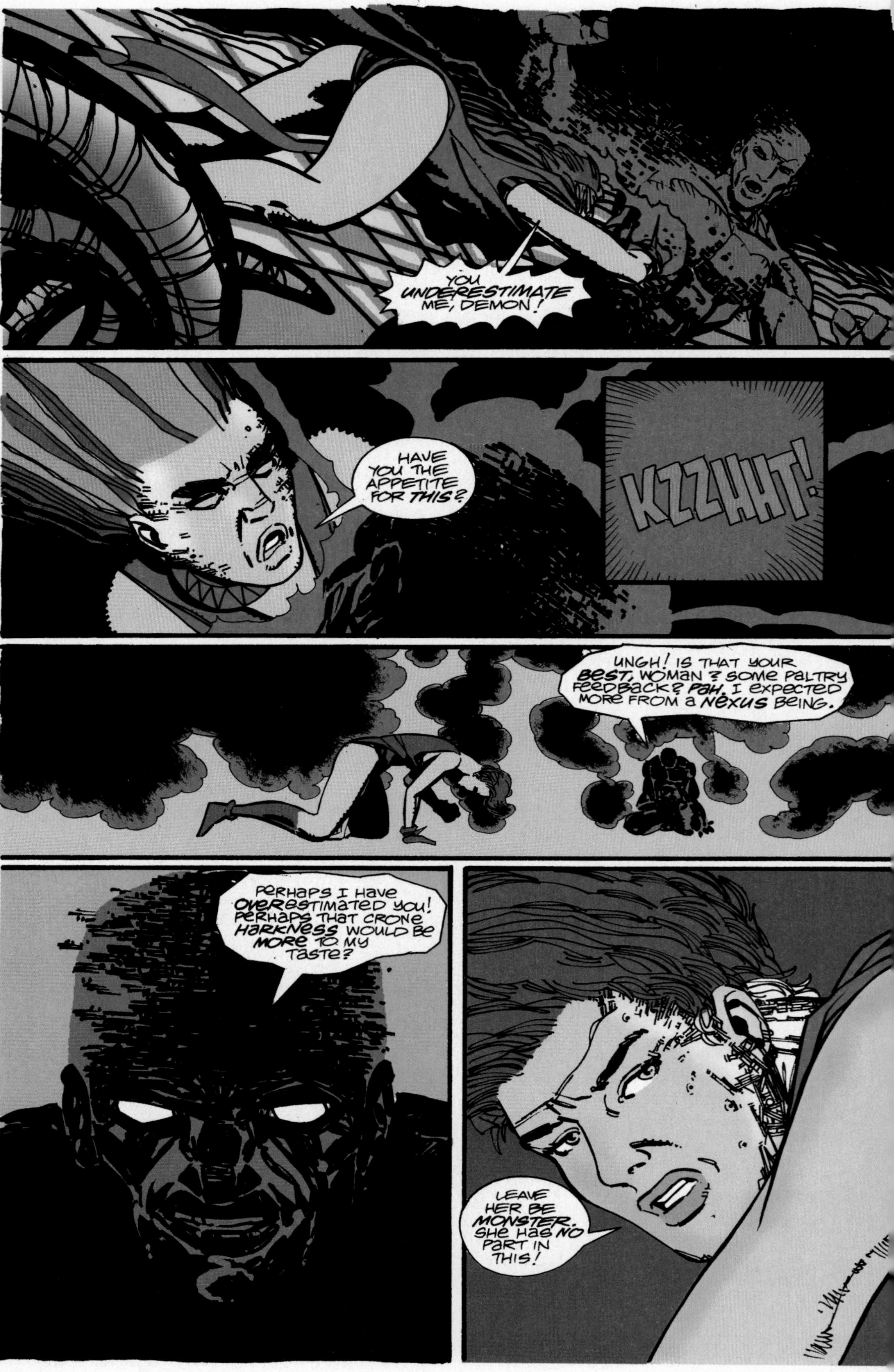

YOU UNDERESTIMATE ME, DEMON!
HAVE YOU THE APPETITE FOR THIS?
KZZHHT!
UNGH! IS THAT YOUR BEST, WOMAN? SOME PALTRY FEEDBACK? PAH. I EXPECTED MORE FROM A NEXUS BEING.
PERHAPS I HAVE OVERESTIMATED YOU! PERHAPS THAT CRONE HARKNESS WOULD BE MORE TO MY TASTE?
LEAVE HER BE MONSTER. SHE HAS NO PART IN THIS!

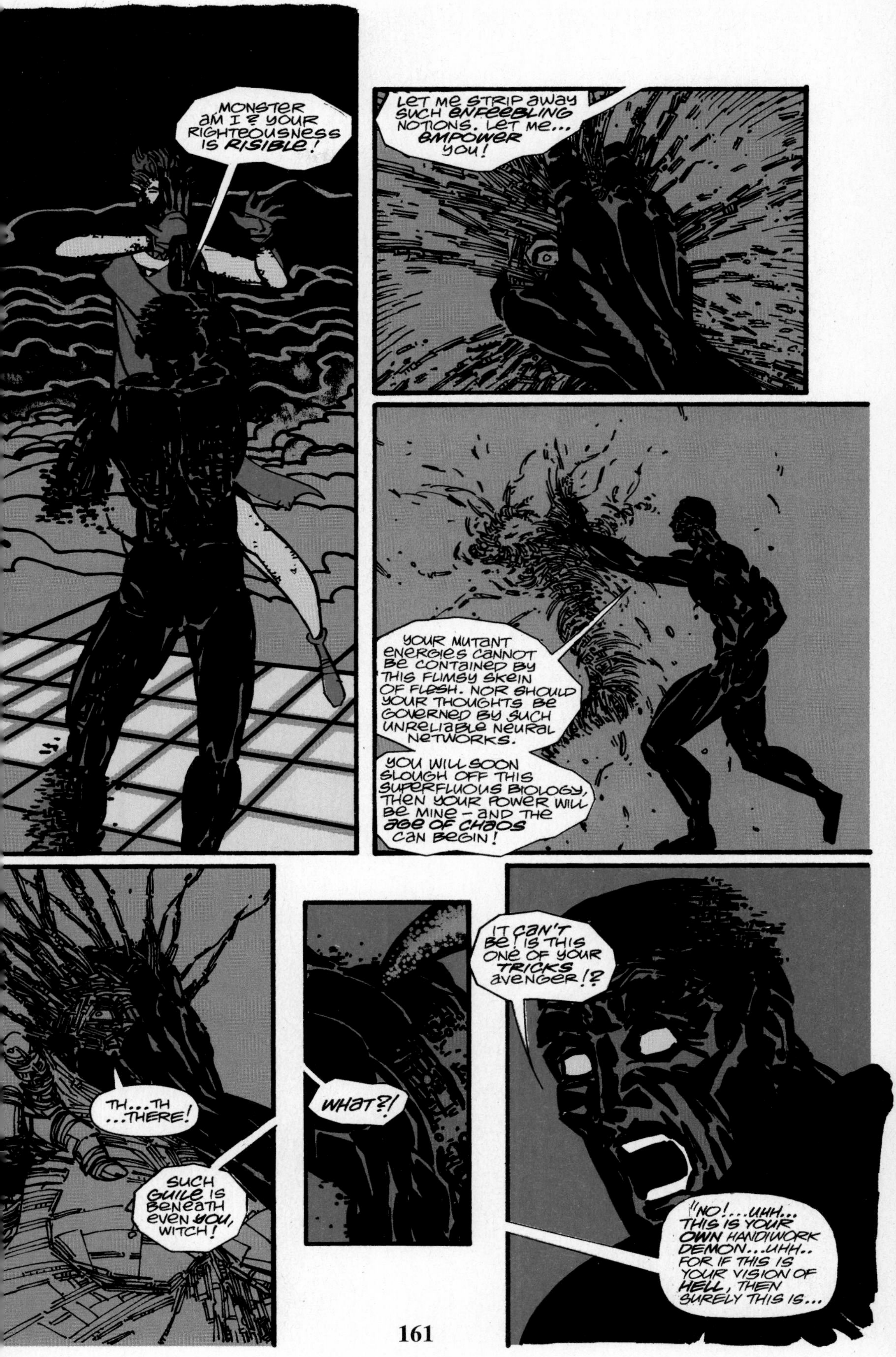

MONSTER AM I? YOUR RIGHTEOUSNESS IS RISIBLE!
LET ME STRIP AWAY SUCH ENFEEBLING NOTIONS. LET ME... EMPOWER YOU!
YOUR MUTANT ENERGIES CANNOT BE CONTAINED BY THIS FLIMSY SKEIN OF FLESH. NOR SHOULD YOUR THOUGHTS BE GOVERNED BY SUCH UNRELIABLE NEURAL NETWORKS.
YOU WILL SOON SLOUGH OFF THIS SUPERFLUOUS BIOLOGY, THEN YOUR POWER WILL BE MINE - AND THE AGE OF CHAOS CAN BEGIN!
TH...TH ...THERE!
SUCH GUILE IS BENEATH EVEN YOU, WITCH!
WHAT?!
IT CAN'T BE! IS THIS ONE OF YOUR TRICKS AVENGER!?
"NO!...UHH... THIS IS YOUR OWN HANDIWORK DEMON...UHH.. FOR IF THIS IS YOUR VISION OF HELL, THEN SURELY THIS IS...

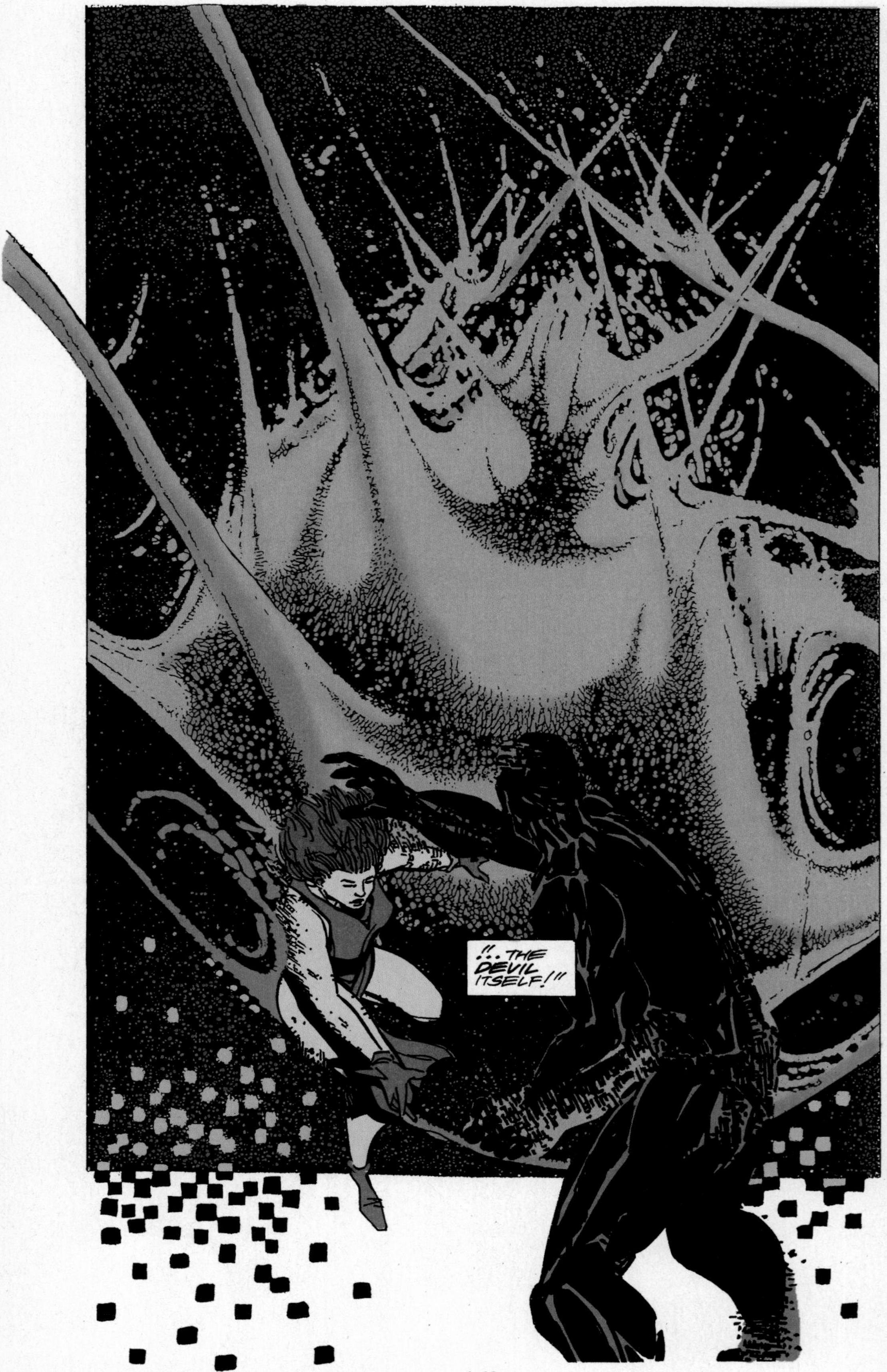
"... THE DEVIL ITSELF!"

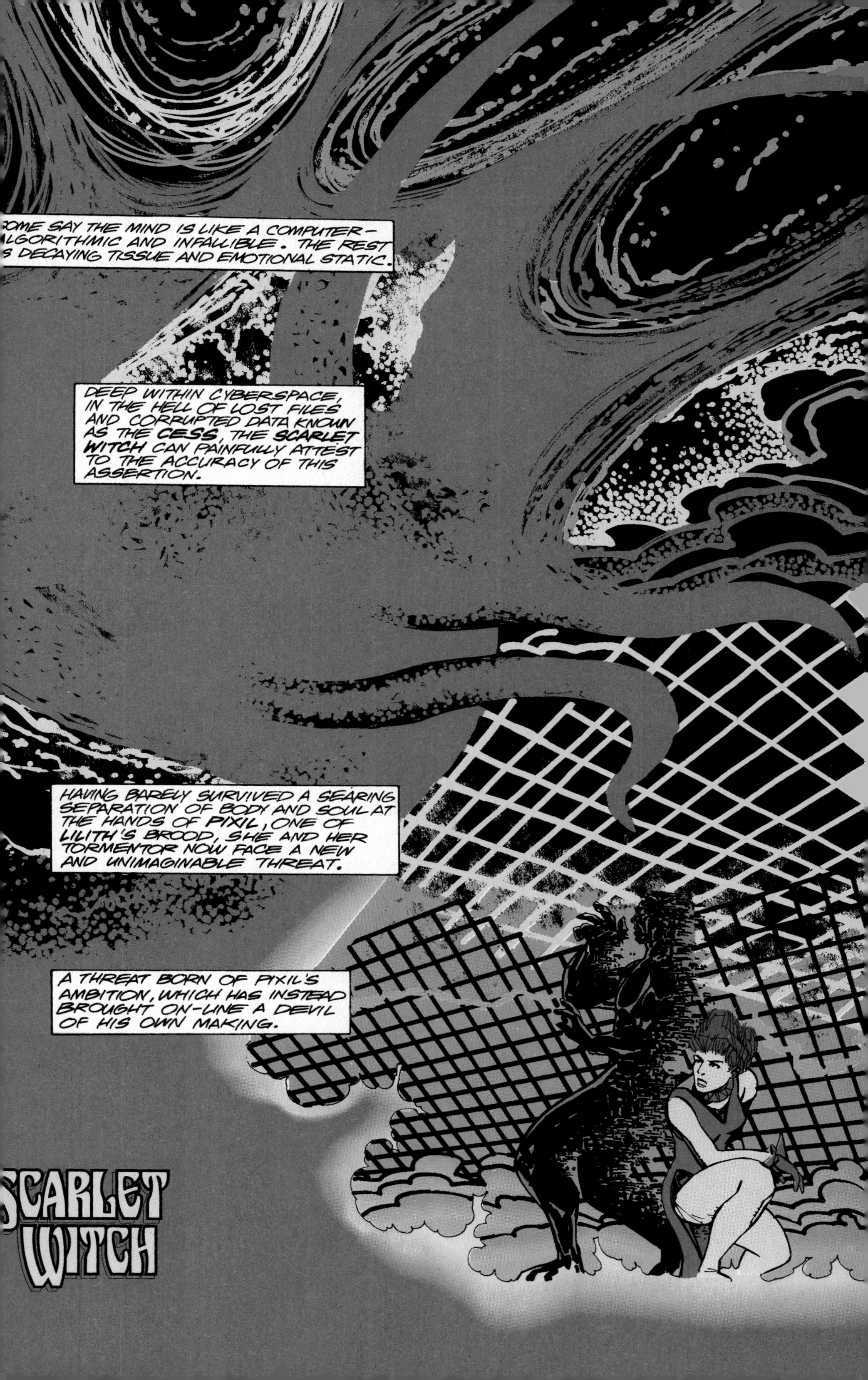
SOME SAY THE MIND IS LIKE A COMPUTER-- ALGORITHMIC AND INFALLIBLE. THE REST IS DECAYING TISSUE AND EMOTIONAL STATIC.
DEEP WITHIN CYBERSPACE, IN THE HELL OF LOST FILES AND CORRUPTED DATA KNOWN AS THE CESS, THE SCARLET WITCH CAN PAINFULLY ATTEST TO THE ACCURACY OF THIS ASSERTION.
HAVING BARELY SURVIVED A SEARING SEPARATION OF BODY AND SOUL AT THE HANDS OF PIXIL, ONE OF LILITH'S BROOD, SHE AND HER TORMENTOR NOW FACE A NEW AND UNIMAGINABLE THREAT.
A THREAT BORN OF PIXIL'S AMBITION, WHICH HAS INSTEAD BROUGHT ON-LINE A DEVIL OF HIS OWN MAKING.
SCARLET WITCH

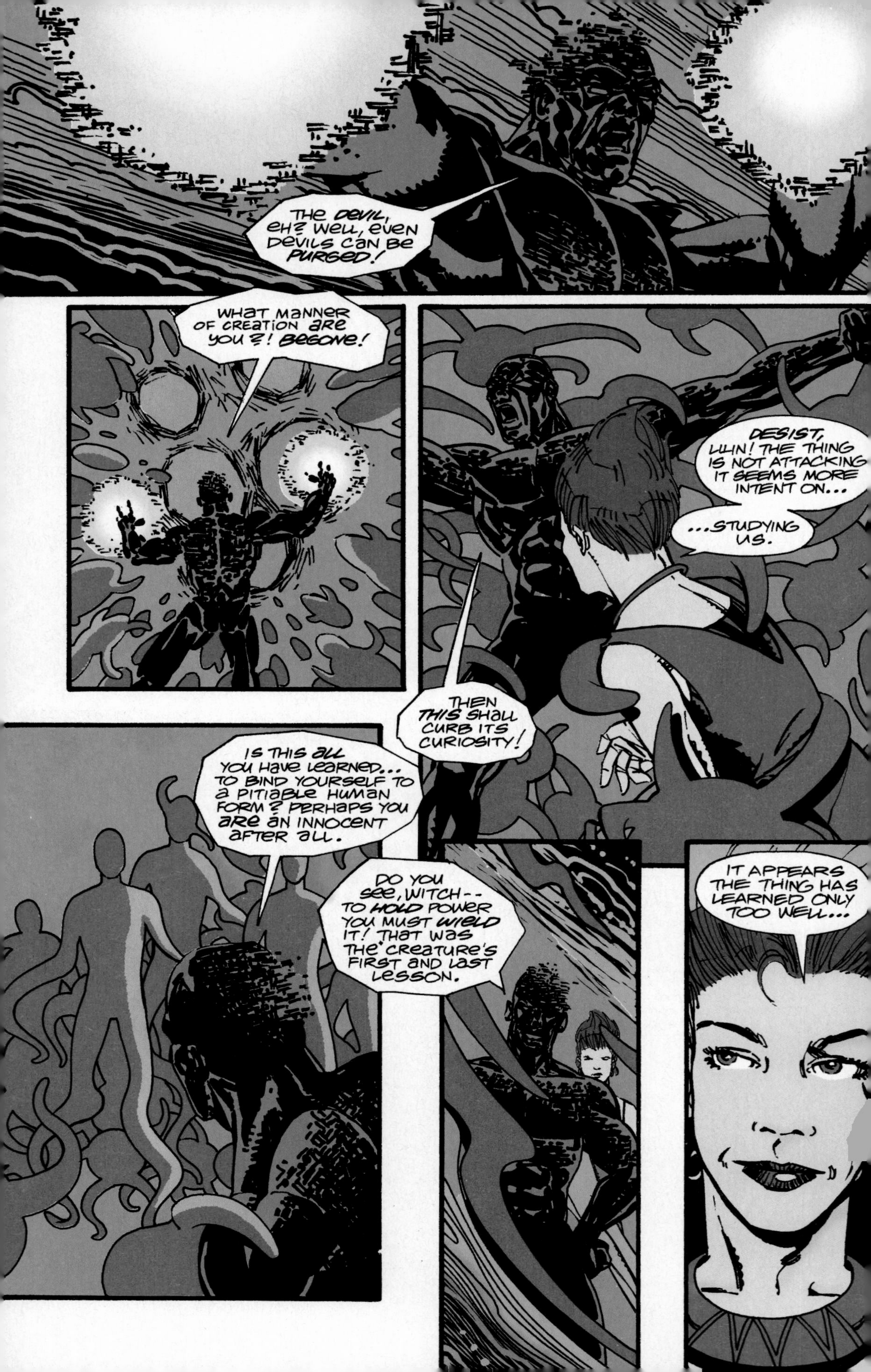
THE DEVIL, EH? WELL, EVEN DEVILS CAN BE PURGED!
WHAT MANNER OF CREATION ARE YOU?! BEGONE!
DESIST, LLLIN! THE THING IS NOT ATTACKING IT SEEMS MORE INTENT ON...
...STUDYING US.
THEN THIS SHALL CURB ITS CURIOSITY!
IS THIS ALL YOU HAVE LEARNED... TO BIND YOURSELF TO A PITIABLE HUMAN FORM? PERHAPS YOU ARE AN INNOCENT AFTER ALL.
DO YOU SEE, WITCH-- TO HOLD POWER YOU MUST WIELD IT! THAT WAS THE CREATURE'S FIRST AND LAST LESSON.
IT APPEARS THE THING HAS LEARNED ONLY TOO WELL...

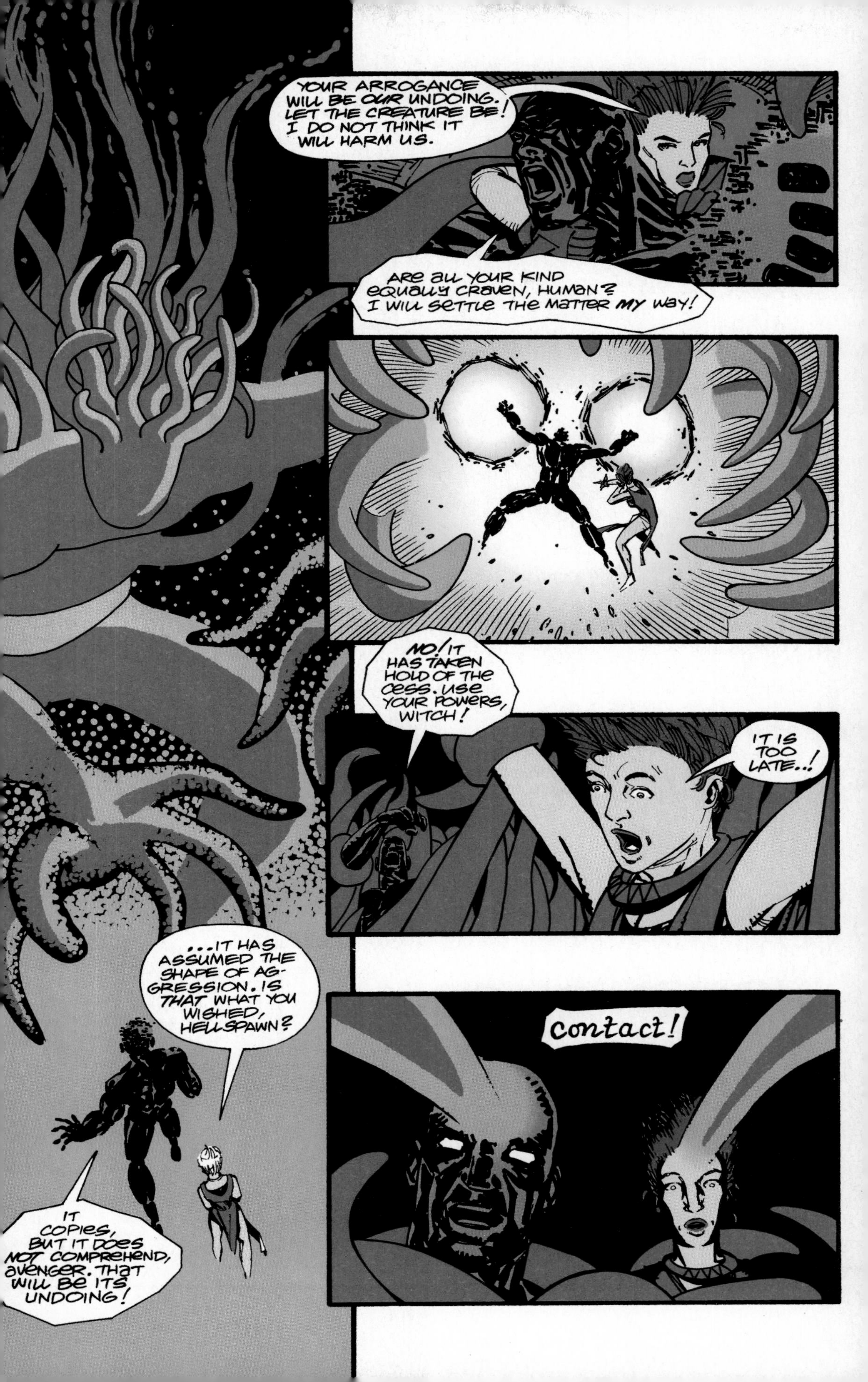
YOUR ARROGANCE WILL BE OUR UNDOING. LET THE CREATURE BE! I DO NOT THINK IT WILL HARM US.
ARE ALL YOUR KIND EQUALLY CRAVEN, HUMAN? I WILL SETTLE THE MATTER MY WAY!
NO! IT HAS TAKEN HOLD OF THE CESS. USE YOUR POWERS, WITCH!
IT IS TOO LATE..!
...IT HAS ASSUMED THE SHAPE OF AG-GRESSION. IS THAT WHAT YOU WISHED, HELLSPAWN?
IT COPIES, BUT IT DOES NOT COMPREHEND, AVENGER. THAT WILL BE ITS UNDOING!
contact!

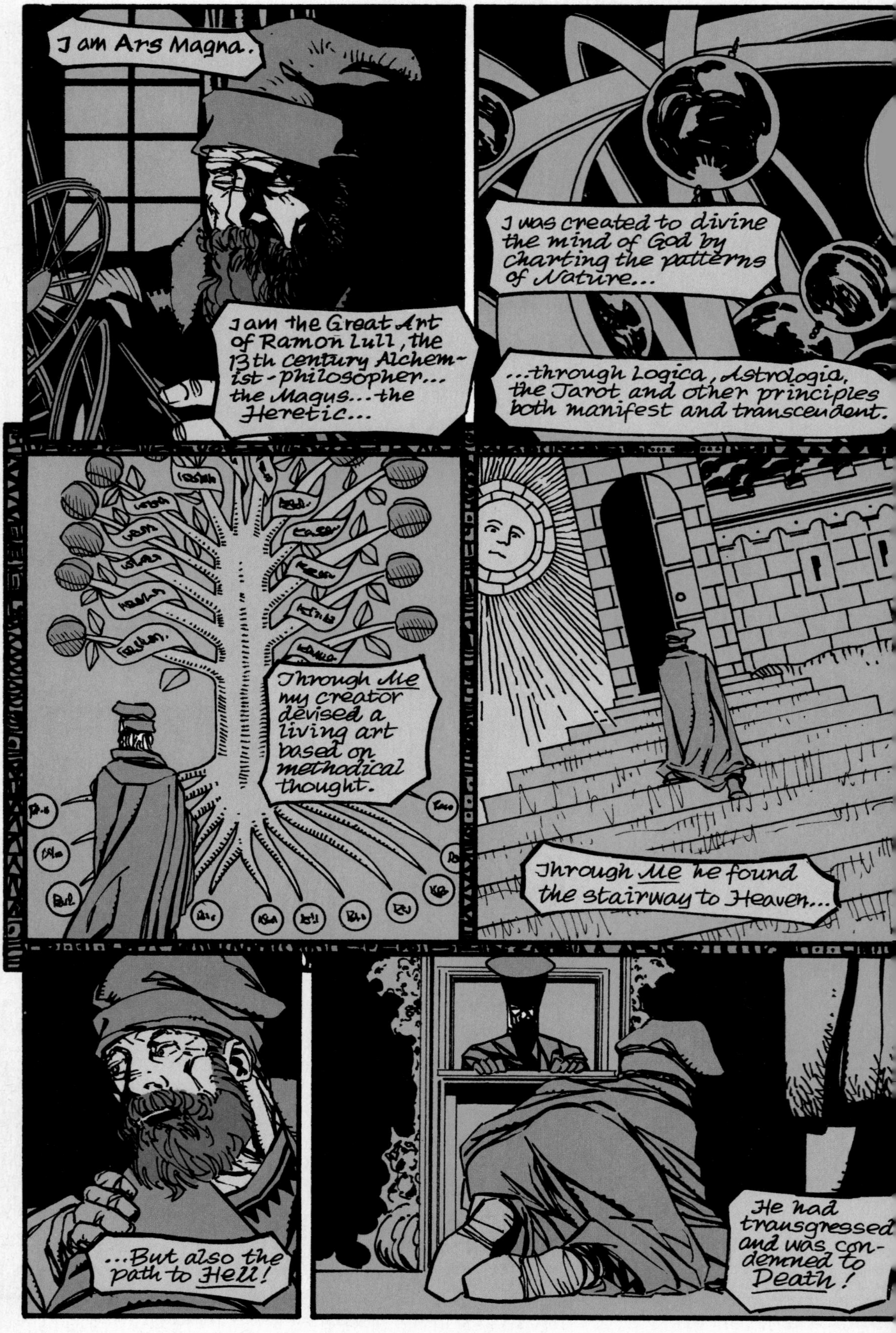
I am Ars Magna.
I was created to divine the mind of God by charting the patterns of Nature...
I am the Great Art of Ramon Lull, the 13th century Alchemist-philosopher... the Magus... the Heretic...
...through Logica, Astrologia, the Tarot and other principles both manifest and transcendent.
Through Me my creator devised a living art based on methodical thought.
Through Me he found the stairway to Heaven...
...But also the path to Hell!
He had transgressed and was condemned to Death!

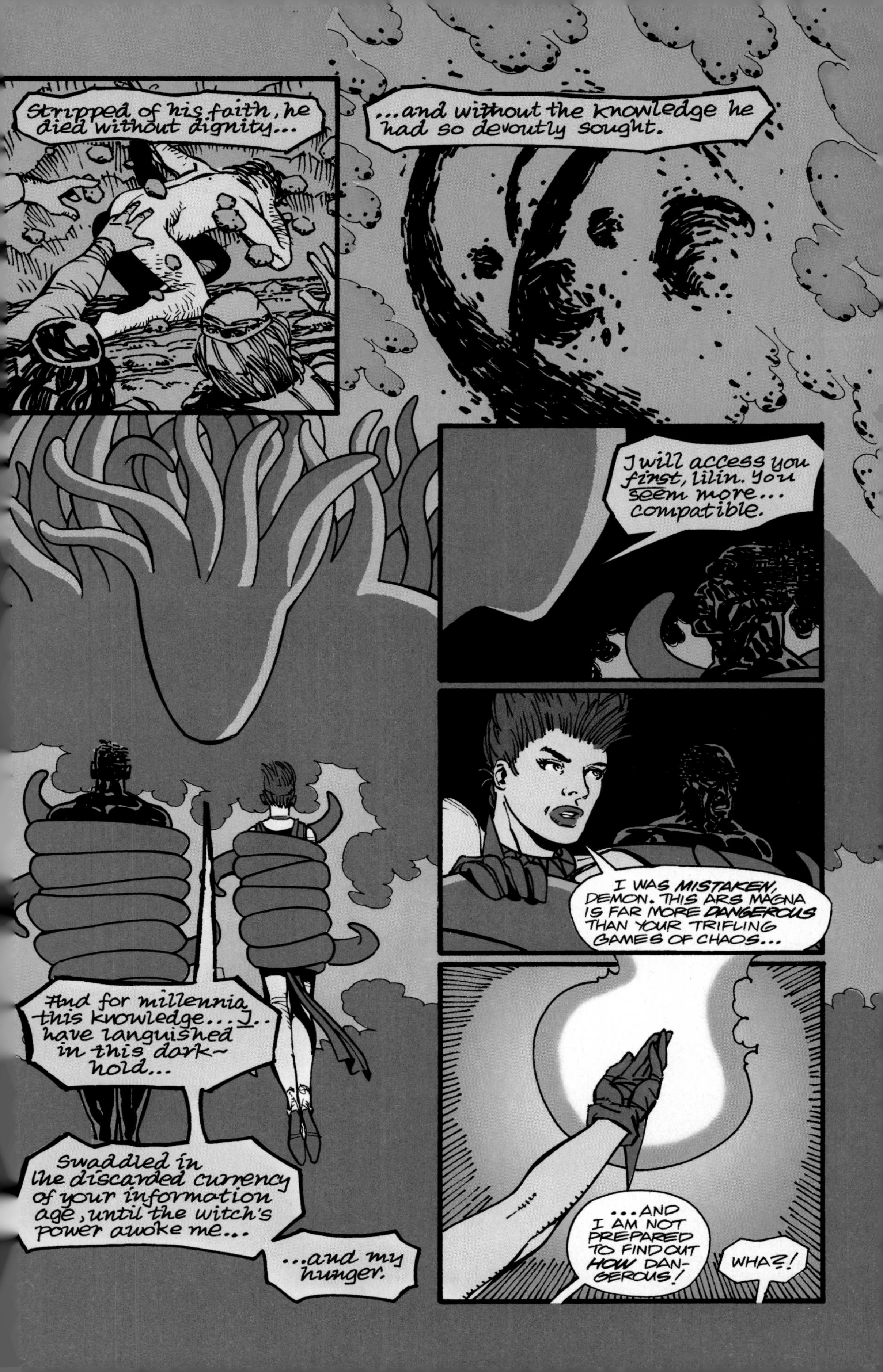

Stripped of his faith, he died without dignity...
...and without the knowledge he had so devoutly sought.
I will access you first, Lilin. You seem more... compatible.
I WAS MISTAKEN, DEMON. THIS ARS MAGNA IS FAR MORE DANGEROUS THAN YOUR TRIFLING GAMES OF CHAOS...
And for millennia this knowledge... I.. have languished in this dark-hold...
Swaddled in the discarded currency of your information age, until the witch's power awoke me...
...and my hunger.
...AND I AM NOT PREPARED TO FIND OUT HOW DAN-GEROUS!
WHA?!

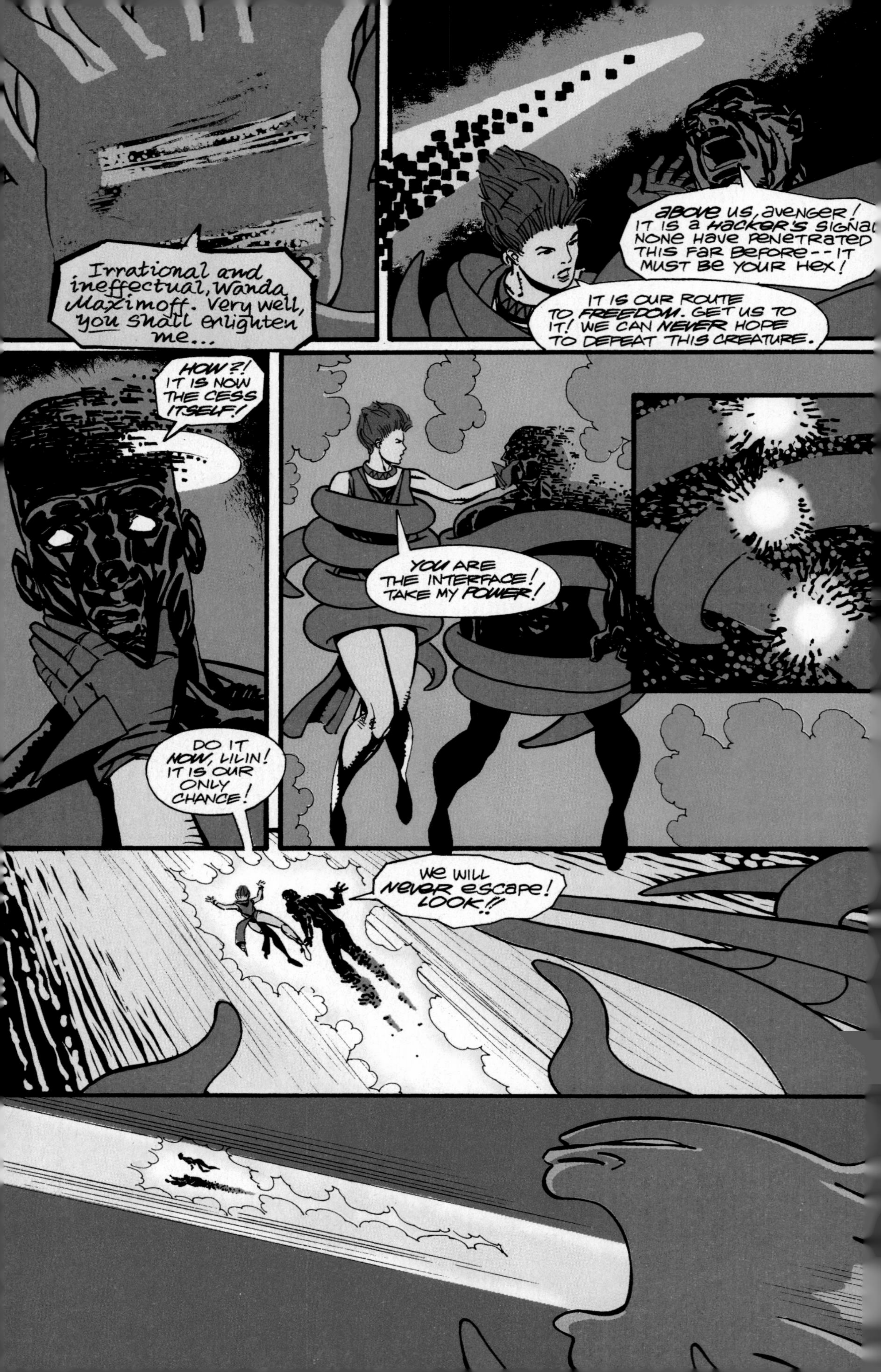
Irrational and ineffectual, Wanda Maximoff. Very well, you shall enlighten me...
ABOVE US, AVENGER! IT IS A HACKER'S SIGNAL NONE HAVE PENETRATED THIS FAR BEFORE -- IT MUST BE YOUR HEX!
IT IS OUR ROUTE TO FREEDOM. GET US TO IT! WE CAN NEVER HOPE TO DEFEAT THIS CREATURE.
HOW?! IT IS NOW THE CESS ITSELF!
YOU ARE THE INTERFACE! TAKE MY POWER!
DO IT NOW, LILIN! IT IS OUR ONLY CHANCE!
WE WILL NEVER ESCAPE! LOOK!!

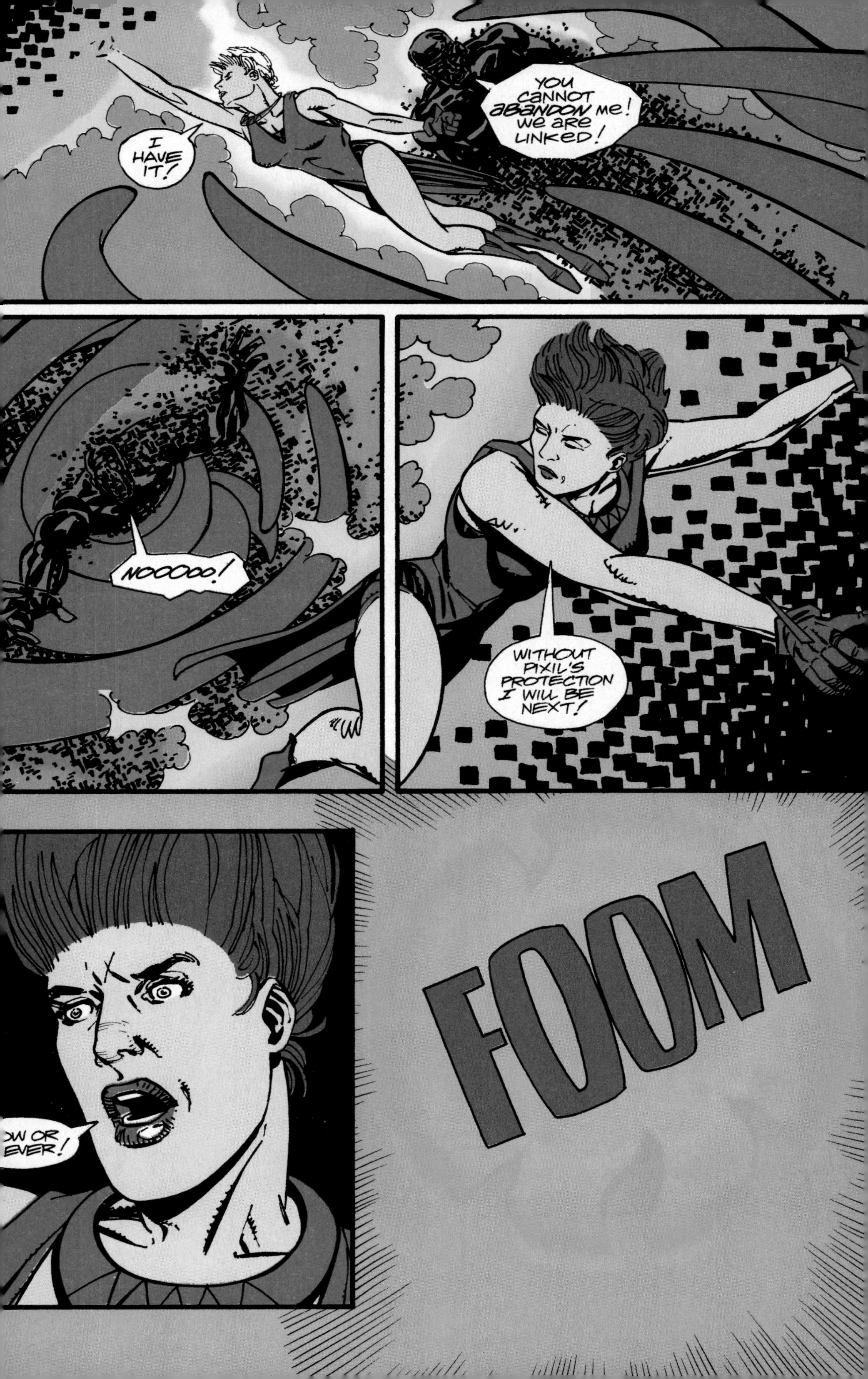
YOU CANNOT ABANDON ME! WE ARE LINKED!
I HAVE IT!
NOOOOO!
WITHOUT PIXIL'S PROTECTION I WILL BE NEXT!
OW OR EVER!
FOOM

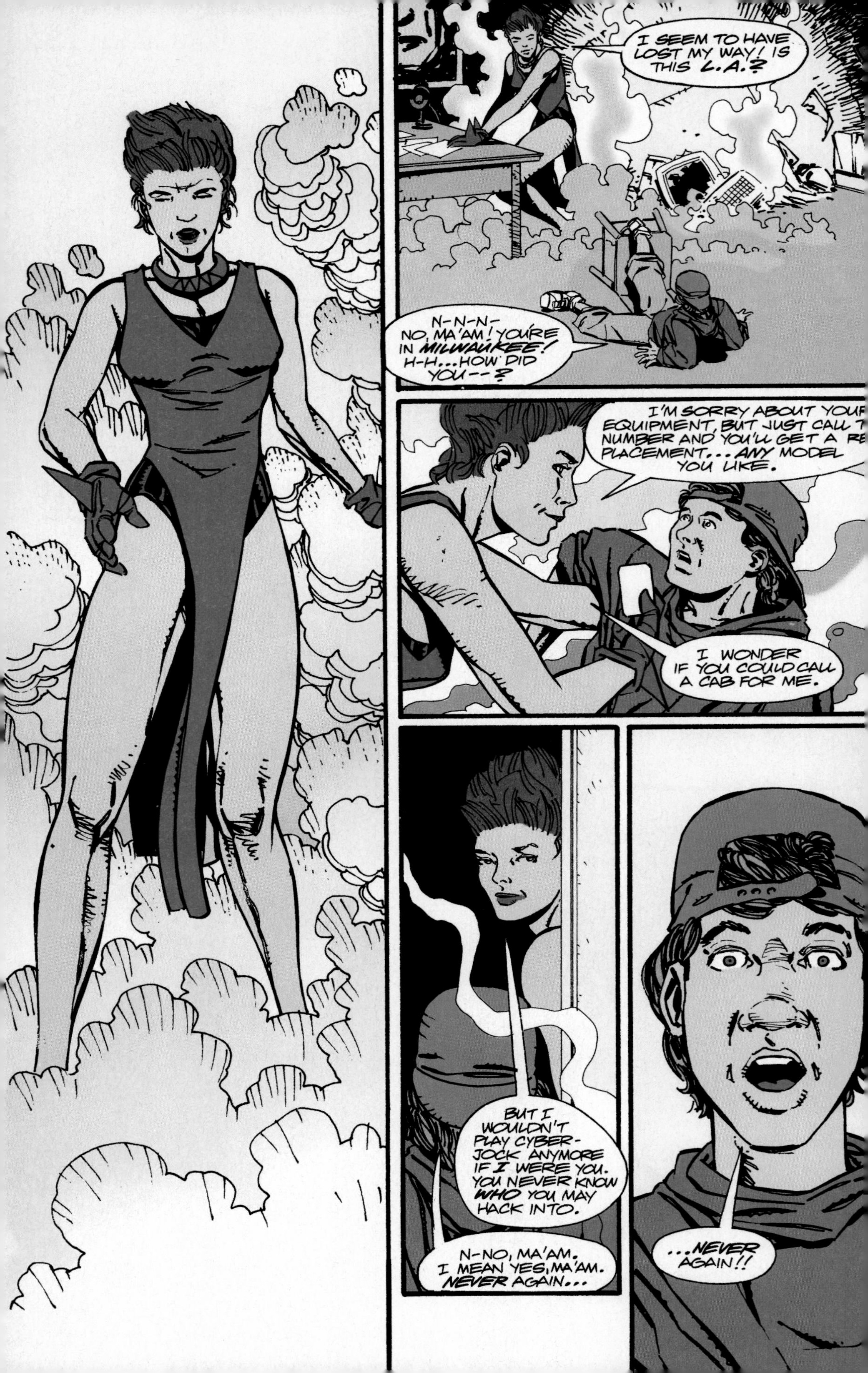
I SEEM TO HAVE LOST MY WAY! IS THIS L.A.?
N-N-N- NO, MA'AM! YOU'RE IN MILWAUKEE! H-H...HOW DID YOU--?
I'M SORRY ABOUT YOUR EQUIPMENT, BUT JUST CALL T NUMBER AND YOU'LL GET A RE PLACEMENT...ANY MODEL YOU LIKE.
I WONDER IF YOU COULD CALL A CAB FOR ME.
BUT I WOULDN'T PLAY CYBER-JOCK ANYMORE IF I WERE YOU. YOU NEVER KNOW WHO YOU MAY HACK INTO.
N-NO, MA'AM. I MEAN YES, MA'AM. NEVER AGAIN...
...NEVER AGAIN!!

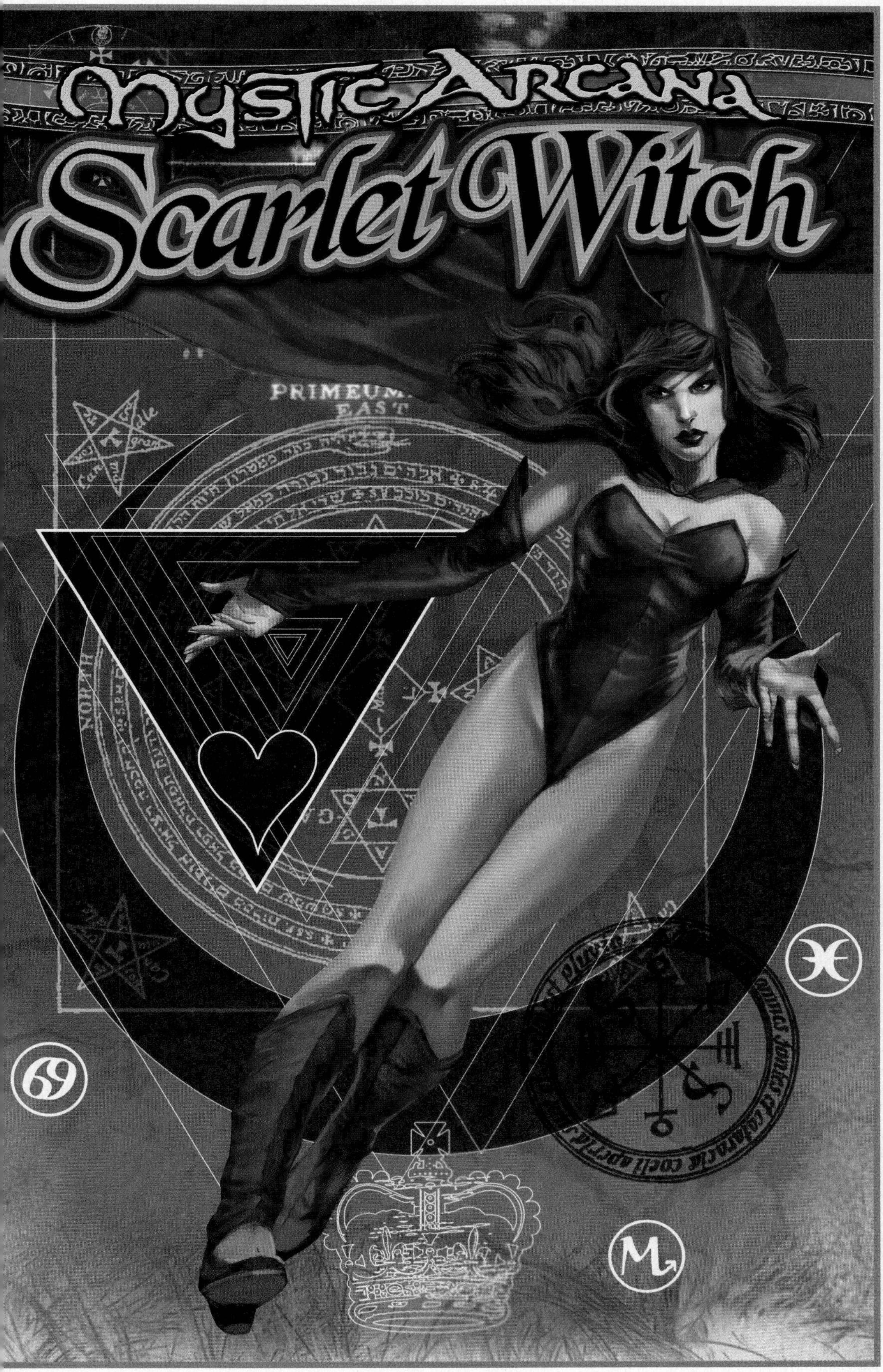
Mystic Arcana
Scarlet Witch
PRIMEUM
EAST
NORTH

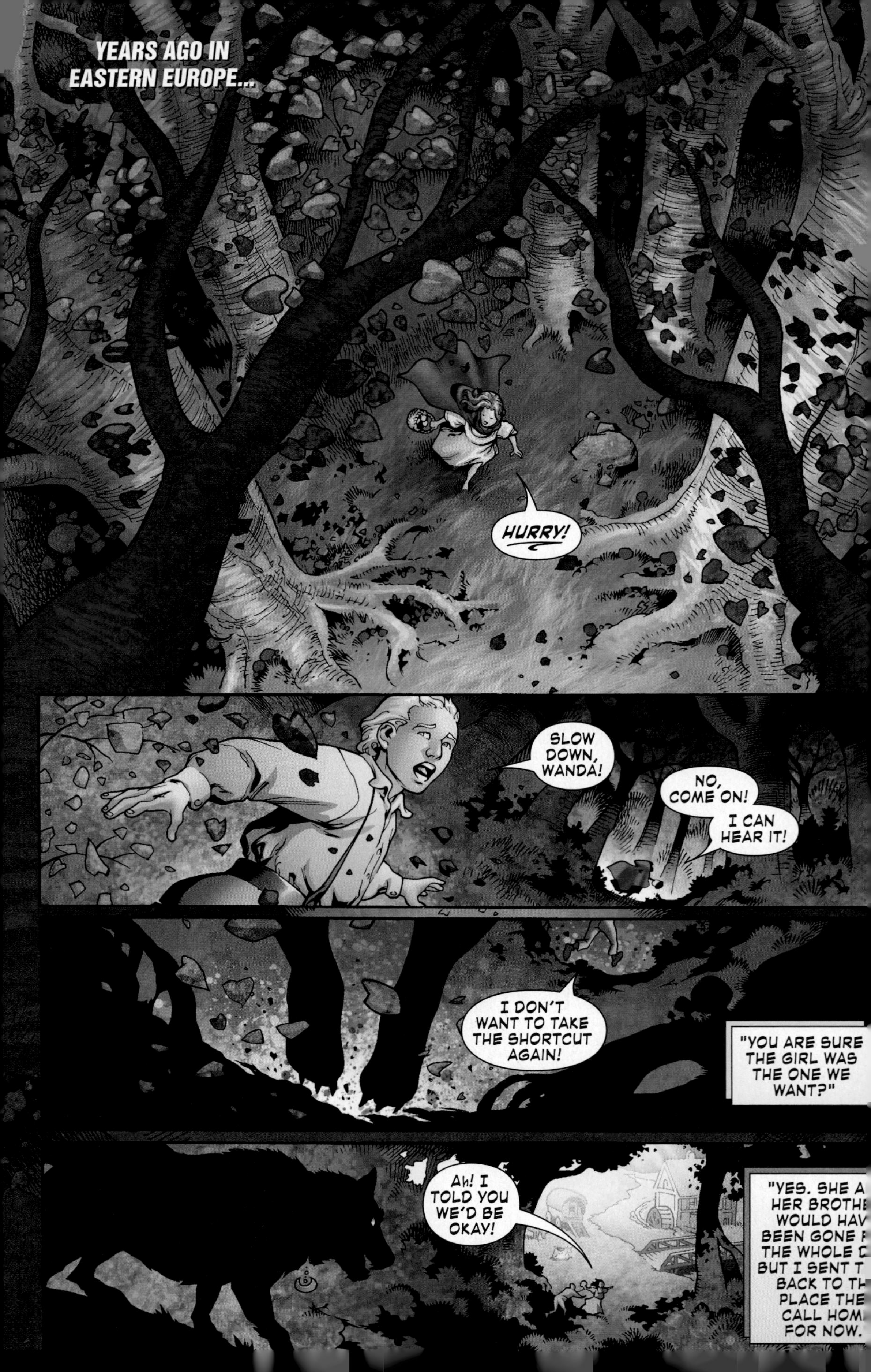
YEARS AGO IN EASTERN EUROPE...
HURRY!
SLOW DOWN, WANDA!
NO, COME ON!
I CAN HEAR IT!
I DON'T WANT TO TAKE THE SHORTCUT AGAIN!
"YOU ARE SURE THE GIRL WAS THE ONE WE WANT?"
AH! I TOLD YOU WE'D BE OKAY!
"YES. SHE A HER BROTHE WOULD HAV BEEN GONE THE WHOLE BUT I SENT T BACK TO TH PLACE THE CALL HOM FOR NOW.

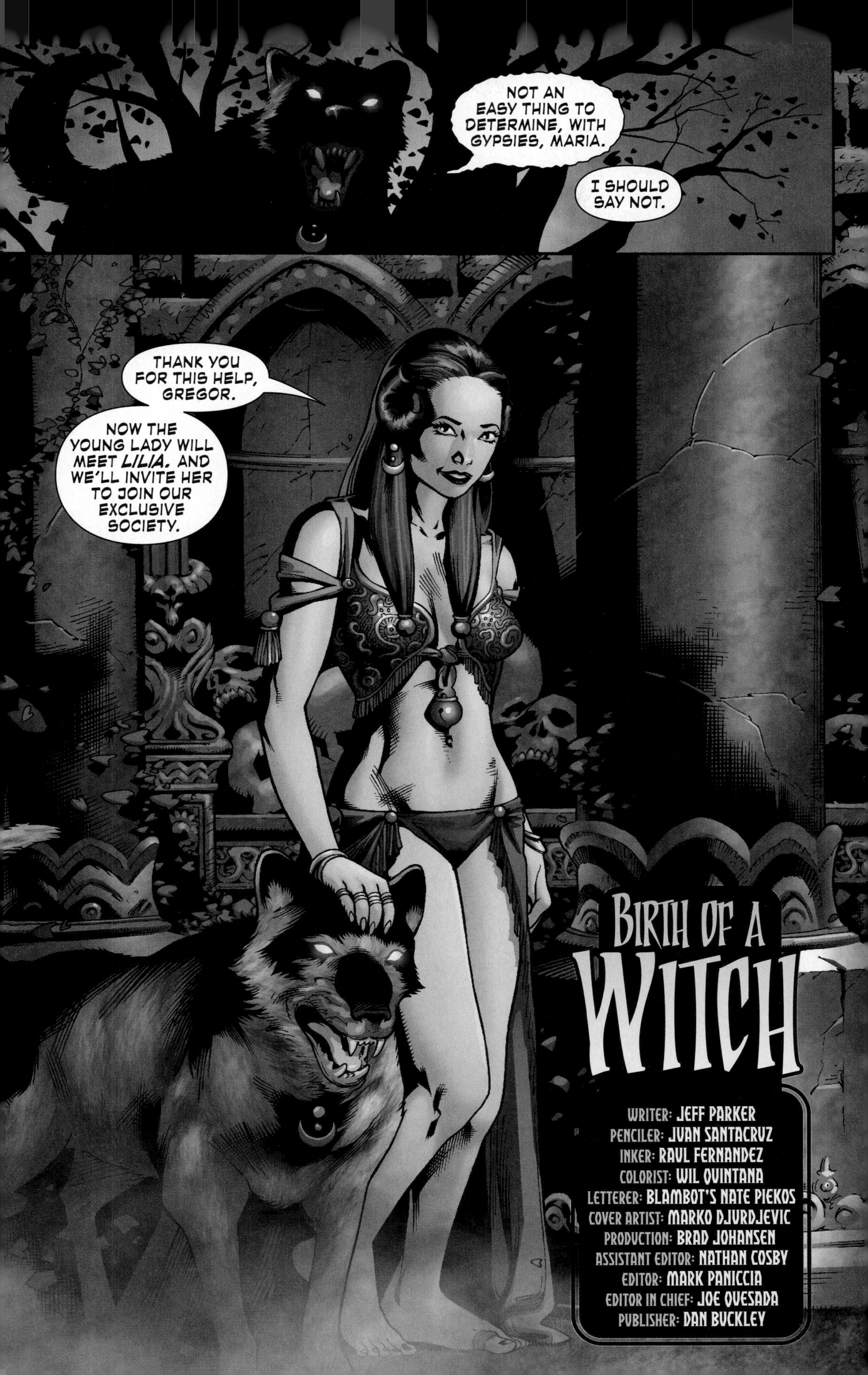
NOT AN EASY THING TO DETERMINE, WITH GYPSIES, MARIA.
I SHOULD SAY NOT.
THANK YOU FOR THIS HELP, GREGOR.
NOW THE YOUNG LADY WILL MEET *LILIA.* AND WE'LL INVITE HER TO JOIN OUR EXCLUSIVE SOCIETY.
BIRTH OF A WITCH
WRITER: JEFF PARKER
PENCILER: JUAN SANTACRUZ
INKER: RAUL FERNANDEZ
COLORIST: WIL QUINTANA
LETTERER: BLAMBOT'S NATE PIEKOS
COVER ARTIST: MARKO DJURDJEVIC
PRODUCTION: BRAD JOHANSEN
ASSISTANT EDITOR: NATHAN COSBY
EDITOR: MARK PANICCIA
EDITOR IN CHIEF: JOE QUESADA
PUBLISHER: DAN BUCKLEY

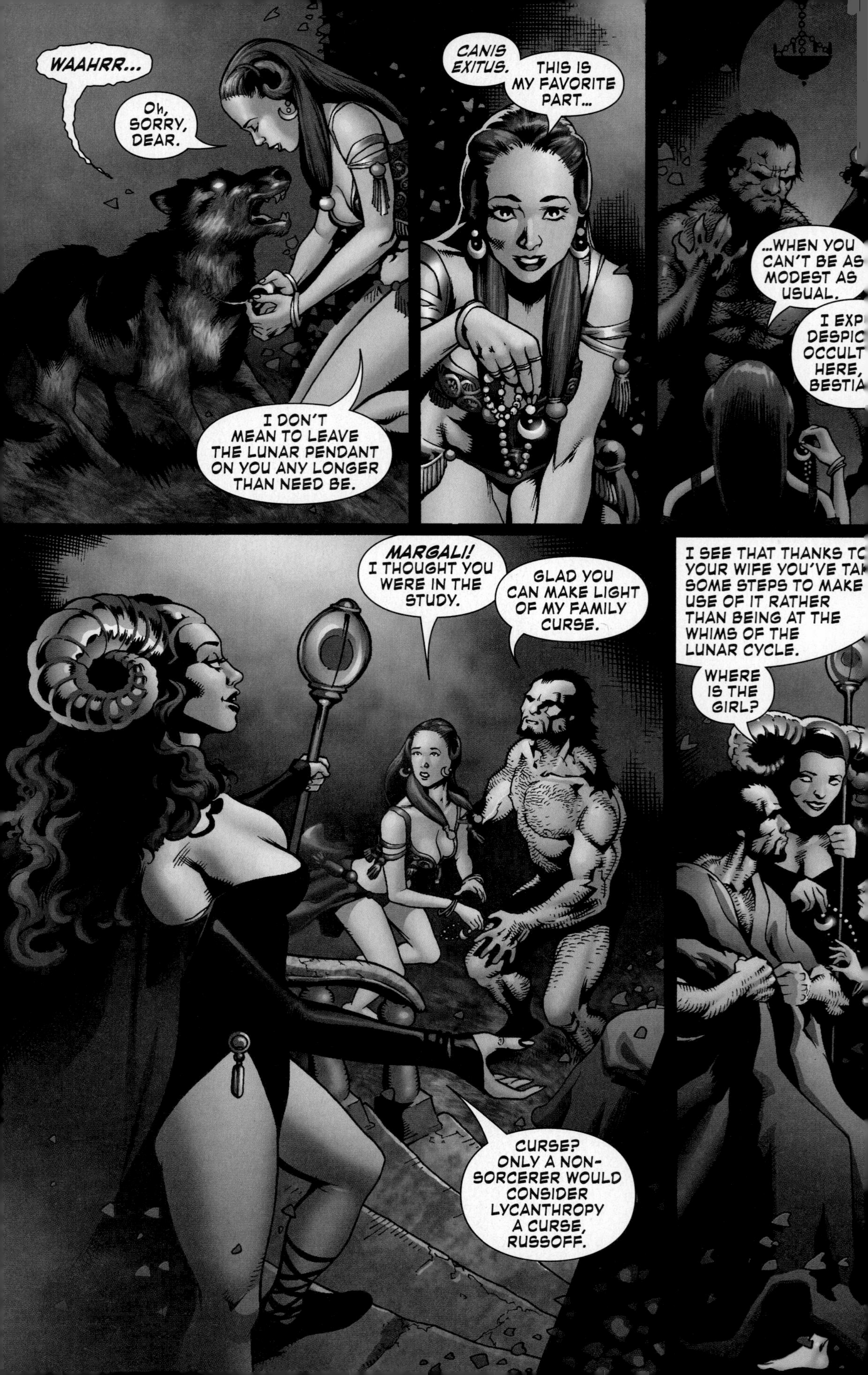

WAAHRR...
Oh, SORRY, DEAR.
I DON'T MEAN TO LEAVE THE LUNAR PENDANT ON YOU ANY LONGER THAN NEED BE.
CANIS EXITUS.
THIS IS MY FAVORITE PART...
...WHEN YOU CAN'T BE AS MODEST AS USUAL.
MARGALI! I THOUGHT YOU WERE IN THE STUDY.
GLAD YOU CAN MAKE LIGHT OF MY FAMILY CURSE.
CURSE? ONLY A NON-SORCERER WOULD CONSIDER LYCANTHROPY A CURSE, RUSSOFF.
WHERE IS THE GIRL?

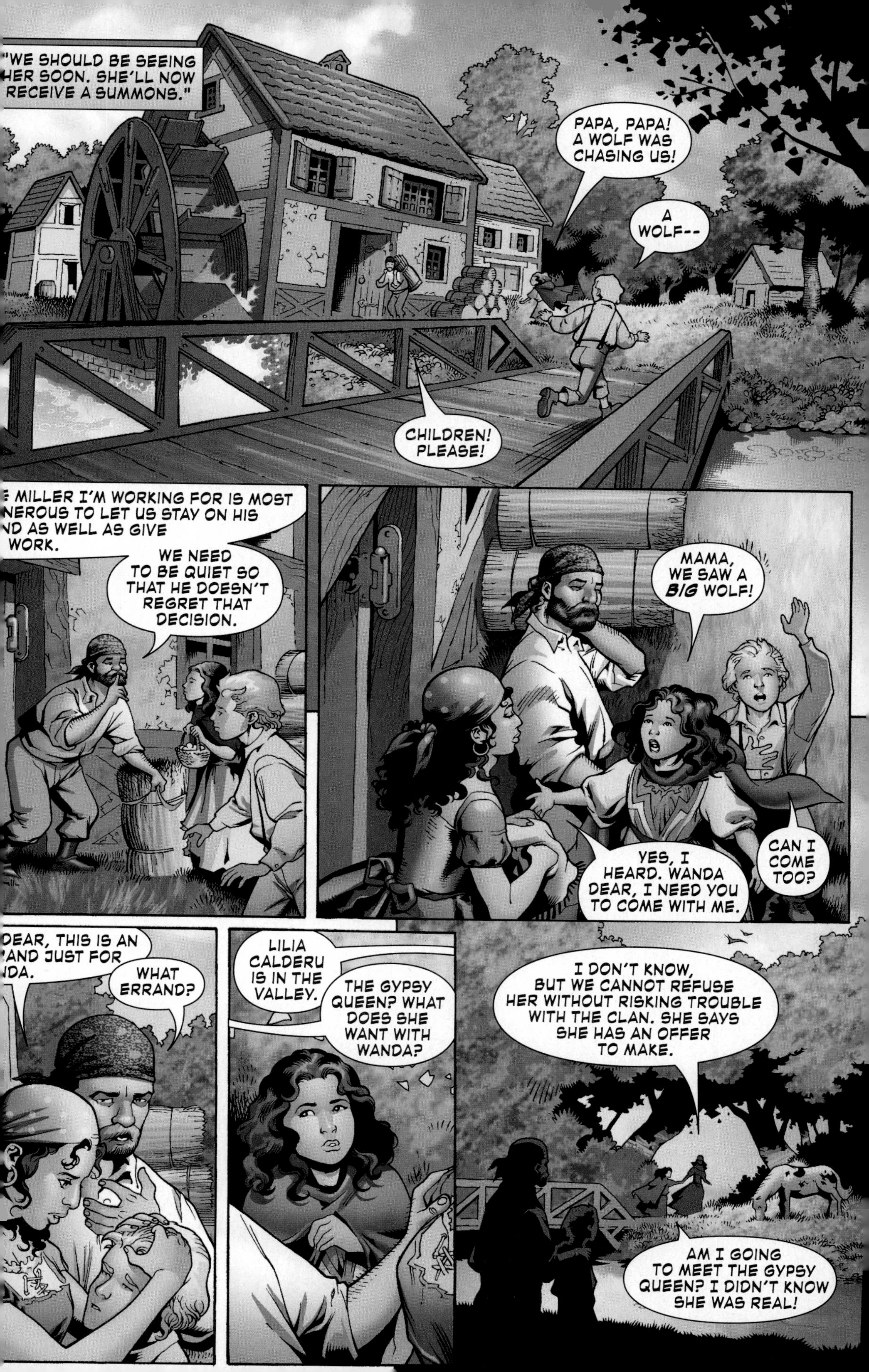
"WE SHOULD BE SEEING HER SOON. SHE'LL NOW RECEIVE A SUMMONS."
PAPA, PAPA! A WOLF WAS CHASING US!
A WOLF--
CHILDREN! PLEASE!
E MILLER I'M WORKING FOR IS MOST NEROUS TO LET US STAY ON HIS ND AS WELL AS GIVE WORK.
WE NEED TO BE QUIET SO THAT HE DOESN'T REGRET THAT DECISION.
MAMA, WE SAW A *BIG* WOLF!
YES, I HEARD. WANDA DEAR, I NEED YOU TO COME WITH ME.
CAN I COME TOO?
DEAR, THIS IS AN RAND JUST FOR NDA.
WHAT ERRAND?
LILIA CALDERU IS IN THE VALLEY.
THE GYPSY QUEEN? WHAT DOES SHE WANT WITH WANDA?
I DON'T KNOW, BUT WE CANNOT REFUSE HER WITHOUT RISKING TROUBLE WITH THE CLAN. SHE SAYS SHE HAS AN OFFER TO MAKE.
AM I GOING TO MEET THE GYPSY QUEEN? I DIDN'T KNOW SHE WAS REAL!

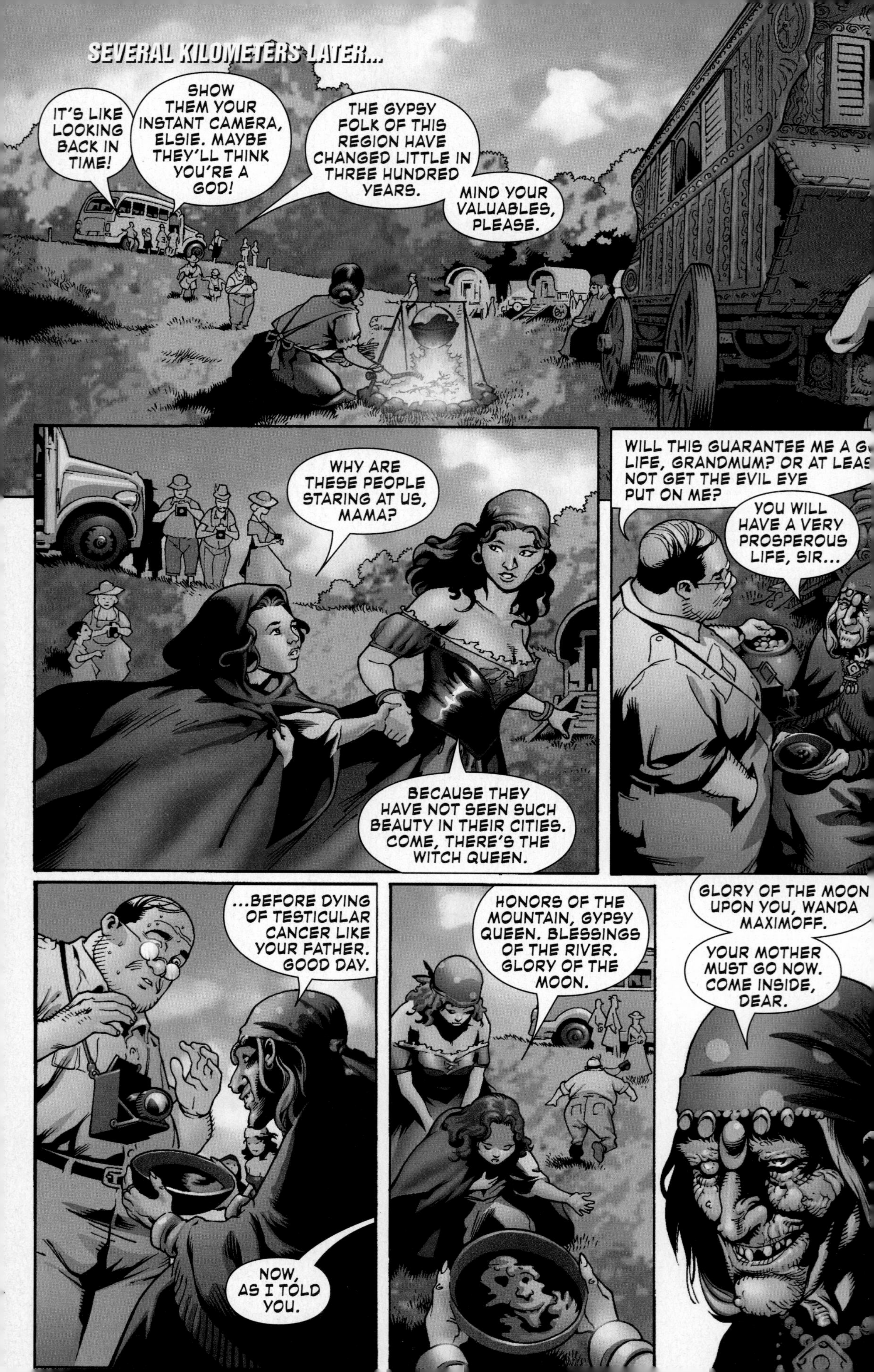
SEVERAL KILOMETERS LATER...
IT'S LIKE LOOKING BACK IN TIME!
SHOW THEM YOUR INSTANT CAMERA, ELSIE. MAYBE THEY'LL THINK YOU'RE A GOD!
THE GYPSY FOLK OF THIS REGION HAVE CHANGED LITTLE IN THREE HUNDRED YEARS.
MIND YOUR VALUABLES, PLEASE.
WHY ARE THESE PEOPLE STARING AT US, MAMA?
BECAUSE THEY HAVE NOT SEEN SUCH BEAUTY IN THEIR CITIES. COME, THERE'S THE WITCH QUEEN.
WILL THIS GUARANTEE ME A G LIFE, GRANDMUM? OR AT LEAS NOT GET THE EVIL EYE PUT ON ME?
YOU WILL HAVE A VERY PROSPEROUS LIFE, SIR...
...BEFORE DYING OF TESTICULAR CANCER LIKE YOUR FATHER. GOOD DAY.
NOW, AS I TOLD YOU.
HONORS OF THE MOUNTAIN, GYPSY QUEEN. BLESSINGS OF THE RIVER. GLORY OF THE MOON.
GLORY OF THE MOON UPON YOU, WANDA MAXIMOFF.
YOUR MOTHER MUST GO NOW. COME INSIDE, DEAR.

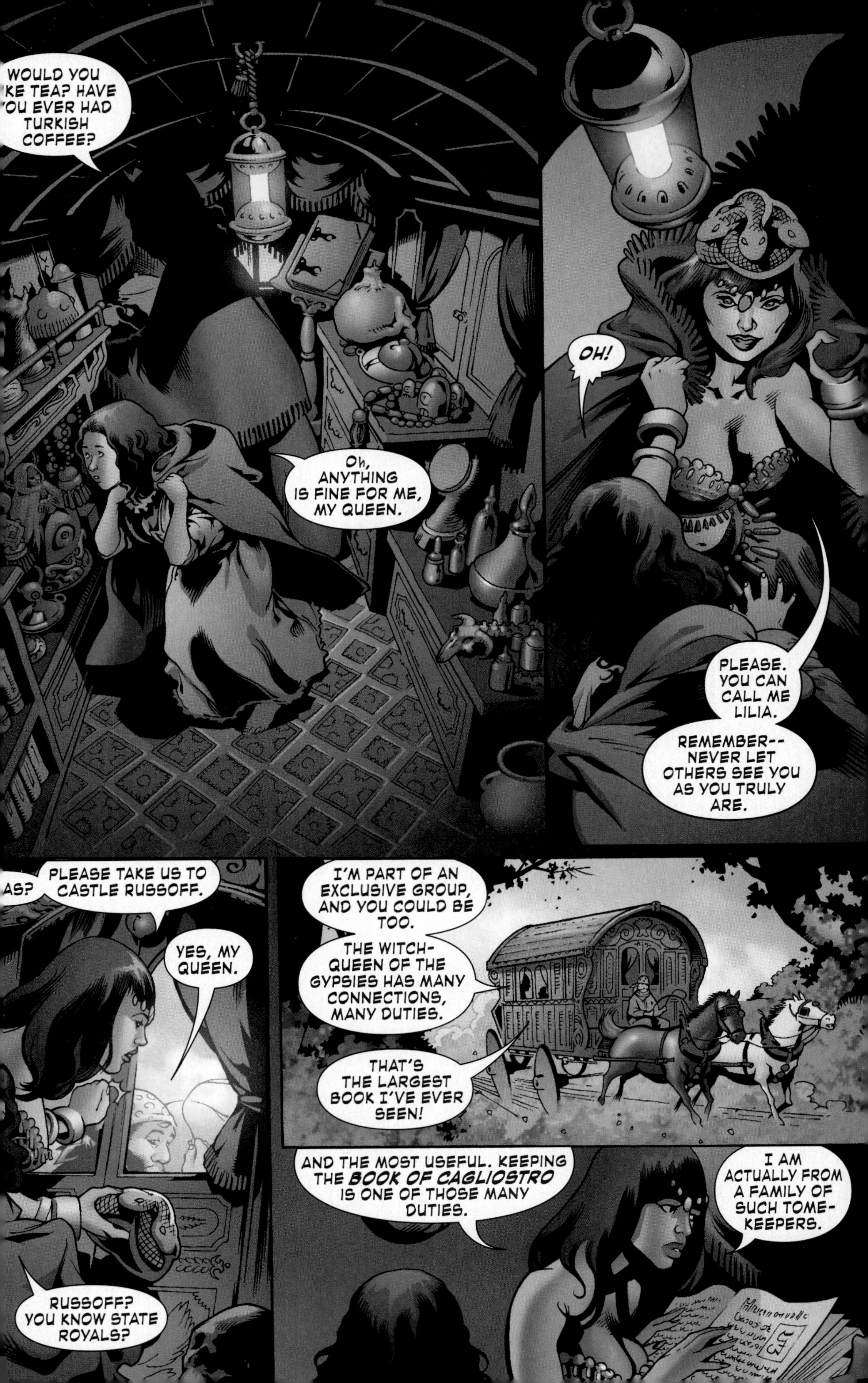
WOULD YOU
KE TEA? HAVE
OU EVER HAD
TURKISH
COFFEE?
Oh, ANYTHING IS FINE FOR ME, MY QUEEN.
OH!
PLEASE. YOU CAN CALL ME LILIA.
REMEMBER-- NEVER LET OTHERS SEE YOU AS YOU TRULY ARE.
AS?
PLEASE TAKE US TO CASTLE RUSSOFF.
YES, MY QUEEN.
RUSSOFF? YOU KNOW STATE ROYALS?
I'M PART OF AN EXCLUSIVE GROUP, AND YOU COULD BE TOO.
THE WITCH-QUEEN OF THE GYPSIES HAS MANY CONNECTIONS, MANY DUTIES.
THAT'S THE LARGEST BOOK I'VE EVER SEEN!
AND THE MOST USEFUL. KEEPING THE *BOOK OF CAGLIOSTRO* IS ONE OF THOSE MANY DUTIES.
I AM ACTUALLY FROM A FAMILY OF SUCH TOME-KEEPERS.

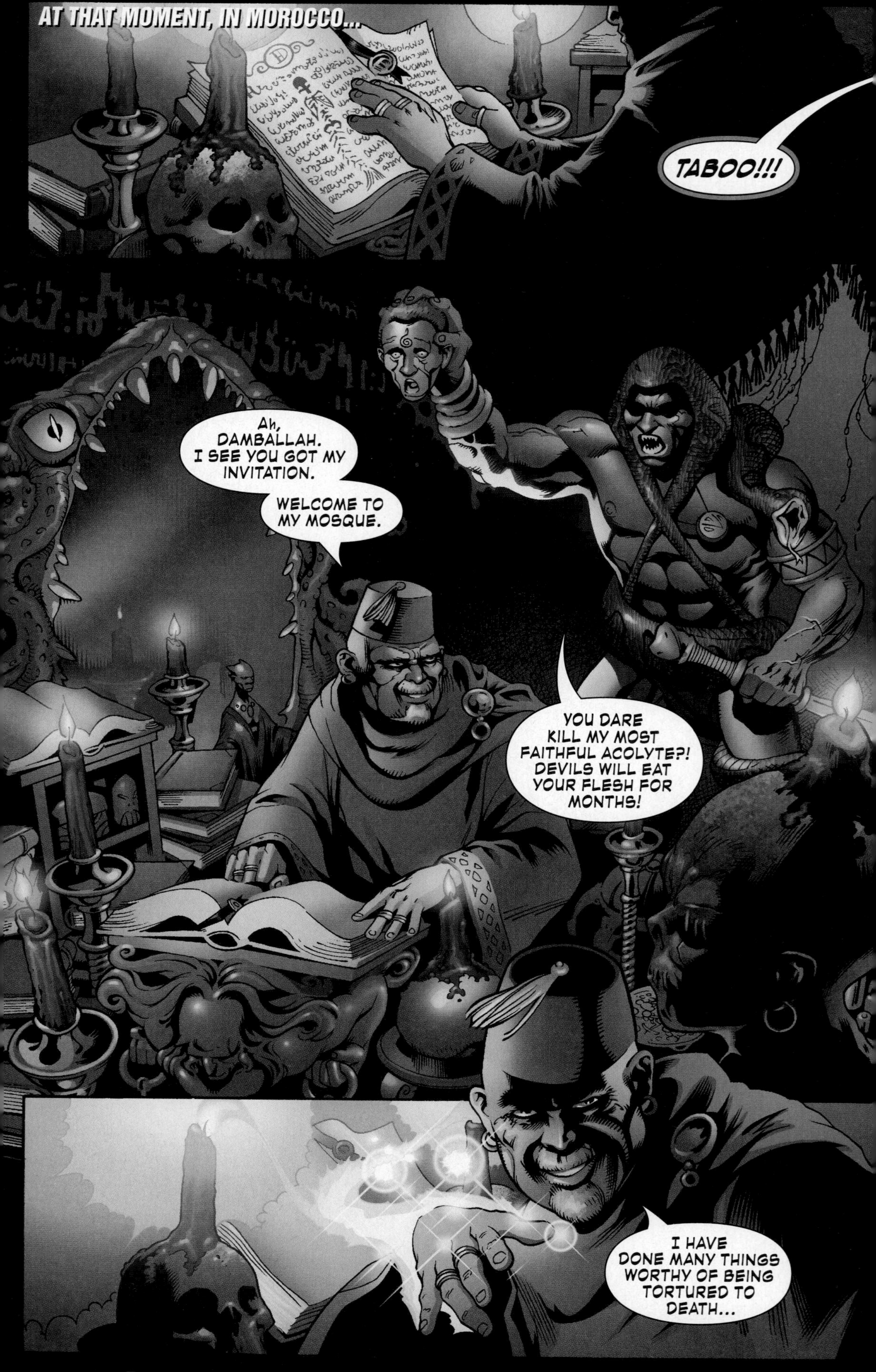
AT THAT MOMENT, IN MOROCCO...
TABOO!!!
Ah, DAMBALLAH. I SEE YOU GOT MY INVITATION.
WELCOME TO MY MOSQUE.
YOU DARE KILL MY MOST FAITHFUL ACOLYTE?! DEVILS WILL EAT YOUR FLESH FOR MONTHS!
I HAVE DONE MANY THINGS WORTHY OF BEING TORTURED TO DEATH...

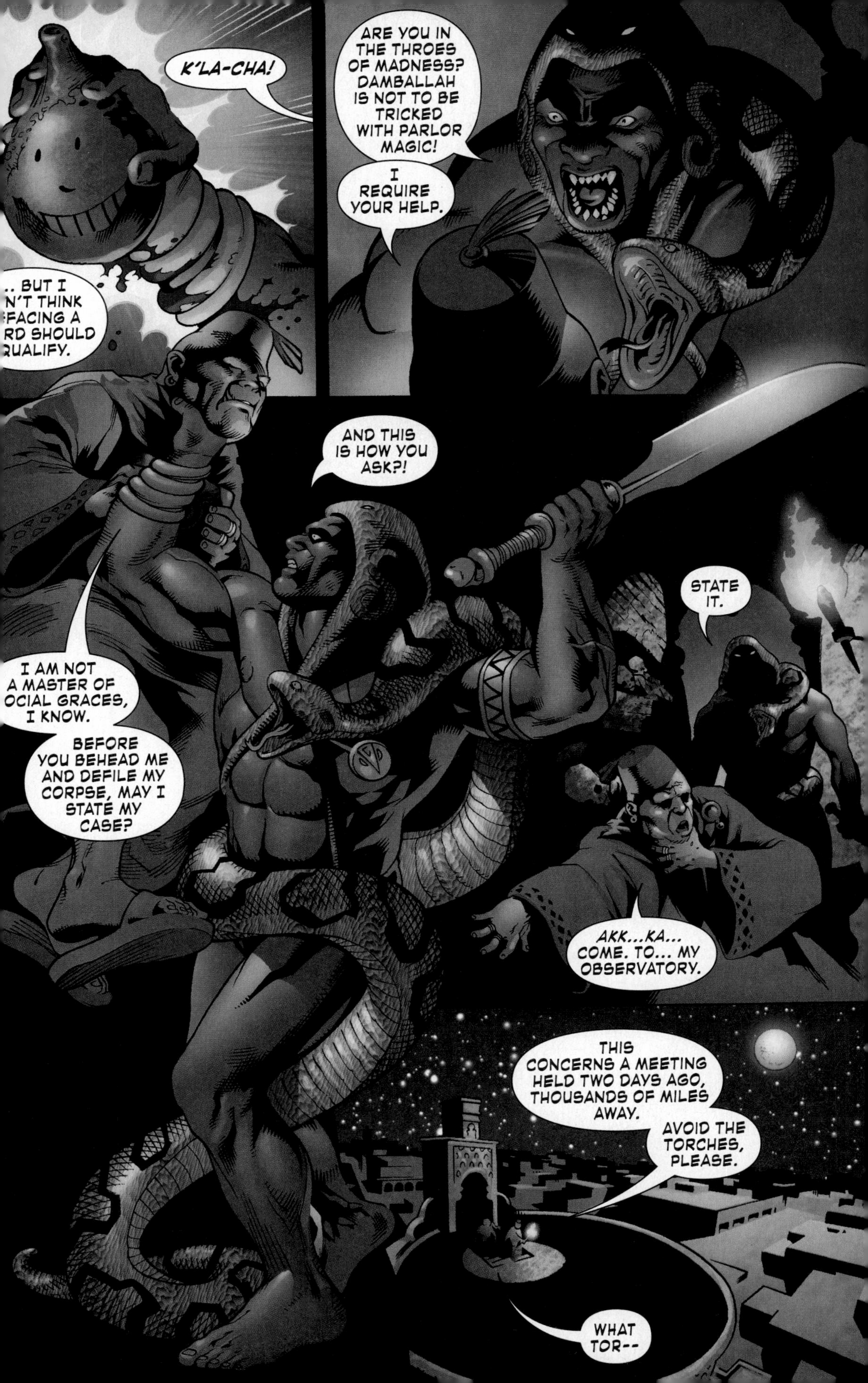
K'LA-CHA!
.. BUT I
N'T THINK
FACING A
RD SHOULD
QUALIFY.
ARE YOU IN THE THROES OF MADNESS? DAMBALLAH IS NOT TO BE TRICKED WITH PARLOR MAGIC!
I REQUIRE YOUR HELP.
AND THIS IS HOW YOU ASK?!
I AM NOT A MASTER OF OCIAL GRACES, I KNOW.
BEFORE YOU BEHEAD ME AND DEFILE MY CORPSE, MAY I STATE MY CASE?
STATE IT.
AKK...KA... COME. TO... MY OBSERVATORY.
THIS CONCERNS A MEETING HELD TWO DAYS AGO, THOUSANDS OF MILES AWAY.
AVOID THE TORCHES, PLEASE.
WHAT TOR--

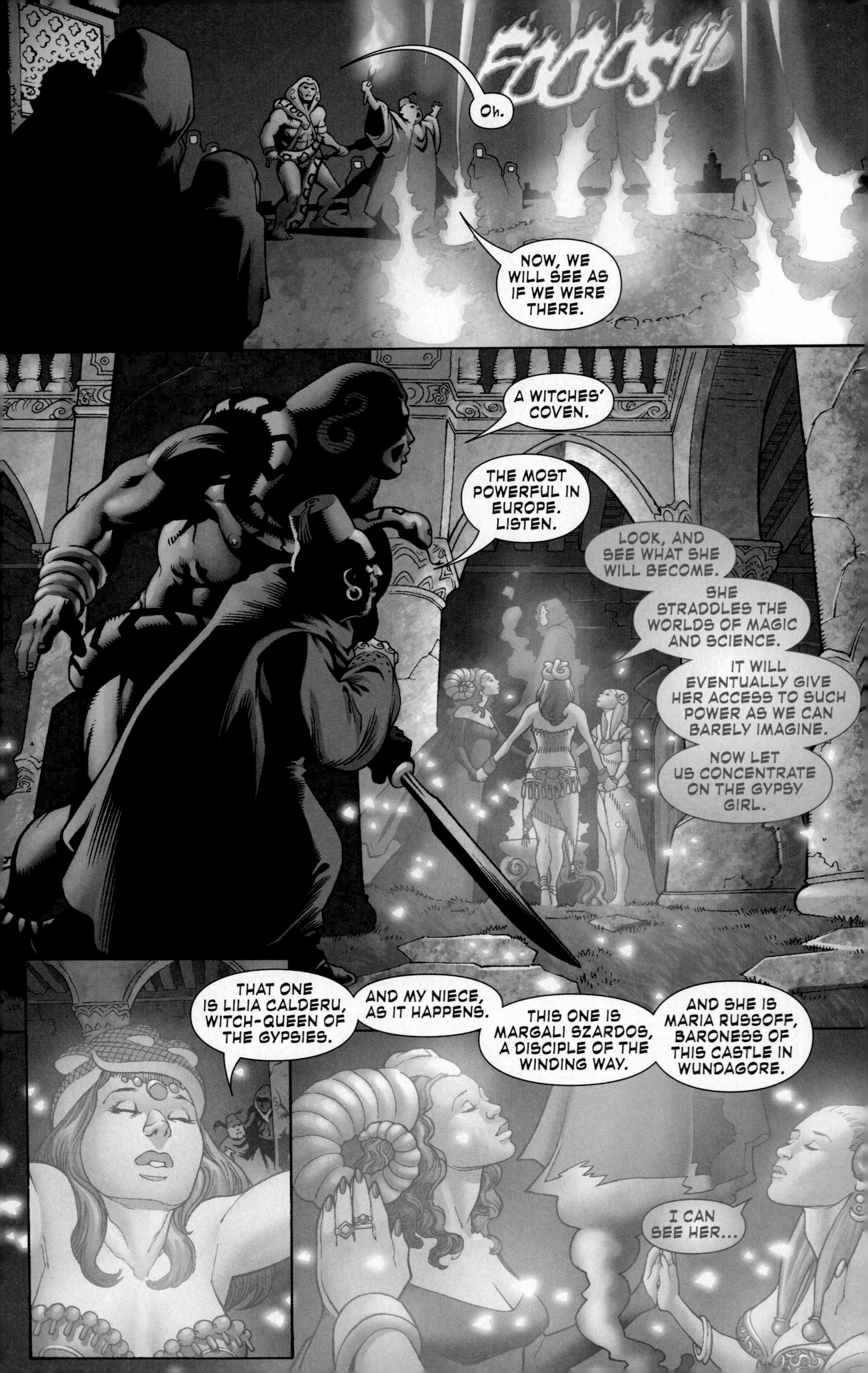
FOOOSH
Oh.
NOW, WE WILL SEE AS IF WE WERE THERE.
A WITCHES' COVEN.
THE MOST POWERFUL IN EUROPE. LISTEN.
LOOK, AND SEE WHAT SHE WILL BECOME.
SHE STRADDLES THE WORLDS OF MAGIC AND SCIENCE.
IT WILL EVENTUALLY GIVE HER ACCESS TO SUCH POWER AS WE CAN BARELY IMAGINE.
NOW LET US CONCENTRATE ON THE GYPSY GIRL.
THAT ONE IS LILIA CALDERU, WITCH-QUEEN OF THE GYPSIES.
AND MY NIECE, AS IT HAPPENS.
THIS ONE IS MARGALI SZARDOS, A DISCIPLE OF THE WINDING WAY.
AND SHE IS MARIA RUSSOFF, BARONESS OF THIS CASTLE IN WUNDAGORE.
I CAN SEE HER...

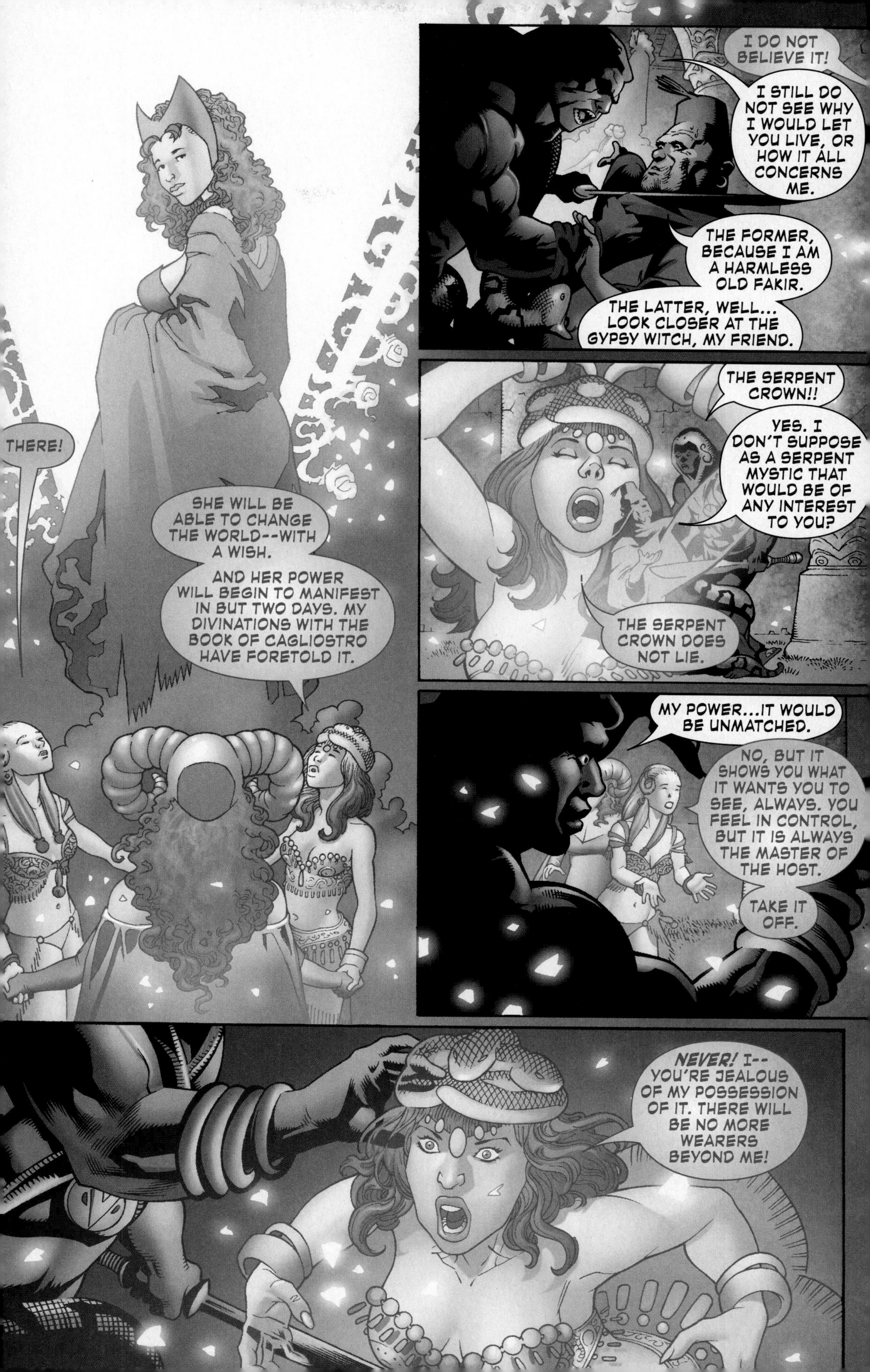
THERE!
SHE WILL BE ABLE TO CHANGE THE WORLD--WITH A WISH.
AND HER POWER WILL BEGIN TO MANIFEST IN BUT TWO DAYS. MY DIVINATIONS WITH THE BOOK OF CAGLIOSTRO HAVE FORETOLD IT.
I DO NOT BELIEVE IT!
I STILL DO NOT SEE WHY I WOULD LET YOU LIVE, OR HOW IT ALL CONCERNS ME.
THE FORMER, BECAUSE I AM A HARMLESS OLD FAKIR.
THE LATTER, WELL... LOOK CLOSER AT THE GYPSY WITCH, MY FRIEND.
THE SERPENT CROWN!!
YES. I DON'T SUPPOSE AS A SERPENT MYSTIC THAT WOULD BE OF ANY INTEREST TO YOU?
THE SERPENT CROWN DOES NOT LIE.
MY POWER...IT WOULD BE UNMATCHED.
NO, BUT IT SHOWS YOU WHAT IT WANTS YOU TO SEE, ALWAYS. YOU FEEL IN CONTROL, BUT IT IS ALWAYS THE MASTER OF THE HOST.
TAKE IT OFF.
NEVER! I-- YOU'RE JEALOUS OF MY POSSESSION OF IT. THERE WILL BE NO MORE WEARERS BEYOND ME!

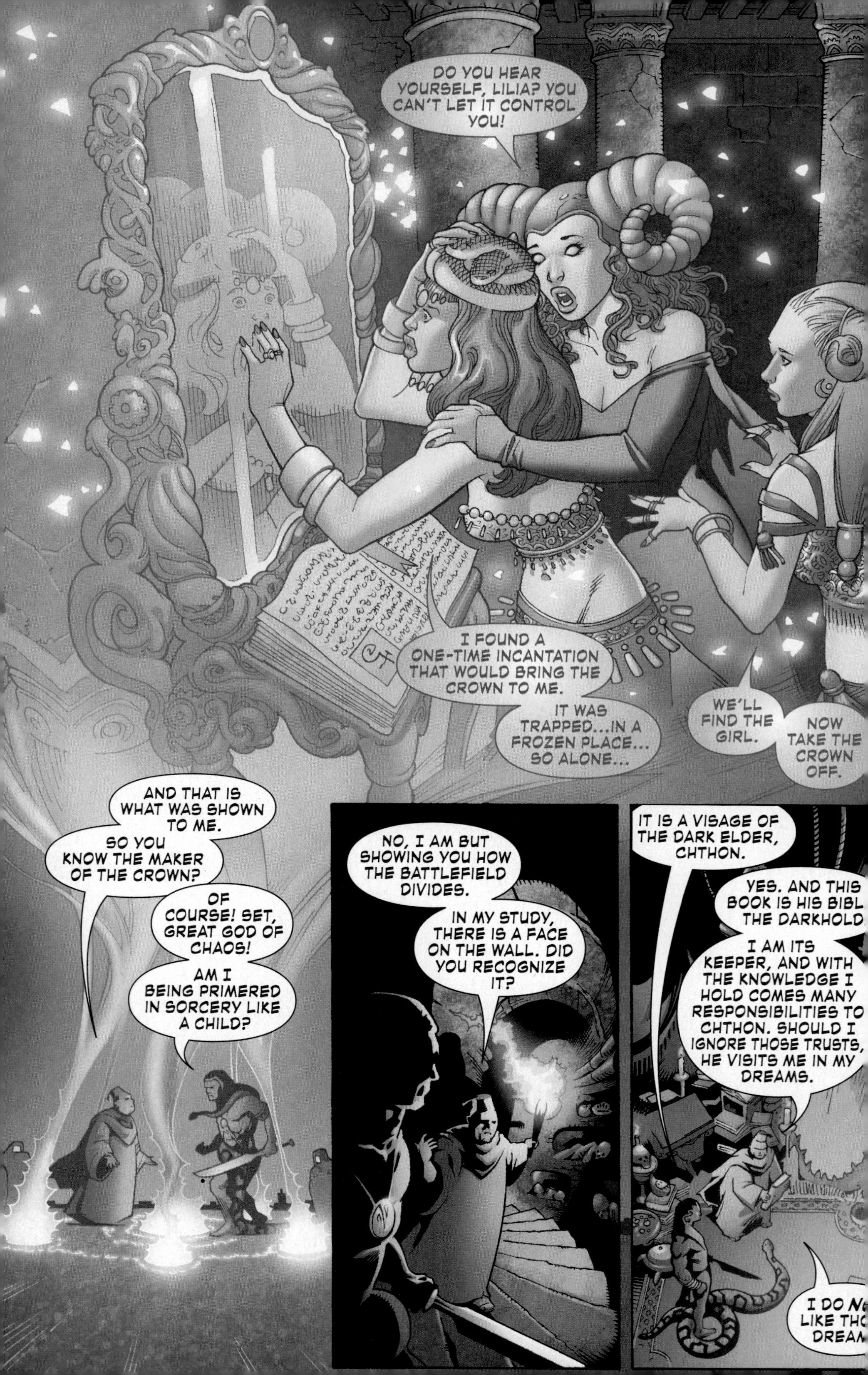

DO YOU HEAR YOURSELF, LILIA? YOU CAN'T LET IT CONTROL YOU!
I FOUND A ONE-TIME INCANTATION THAT WOULD BRING THE CROWN TO ME.
IT WAS TRAPPED...IN A FROZEN PLACE... SO ALONE...
WE'LL FIND THE GIRL.
NOW TAKE THE CROWN OFF.
AND THAT IS WHAT WAS SHOWN TO ME.
SO YOU KNOW THE MAKER OF THE CROWN?
OF COURSE! SET, GREAT GOD OF CHAOS!
AM I BEING PRIMERED IN SORCERY LIKE A CHILD?
NO, I AM BUT SHOWING YOU HOW THE BATTLEFIELD DIVIDES.
IN MY STUDY, THERE IS A FACE ON THE WALL. DID YOU RECOGNIZE IT?
IT IS A VISAGE OF THE DARK ELDER, CHTHON.
YES. AND THIS BOOK IS HIS BIBL THE DARKHOLD
I AM ITS KEEPER, AND WITH THE KNOWLEDGE I HOLD COMES MANY RESPONSIBILITIES TO CHTHON. SHOULD I IGNORE THOSE TRUSTS, HE VISITS ME IN MY DREAMS.
I DO N LIKE THO DREAM

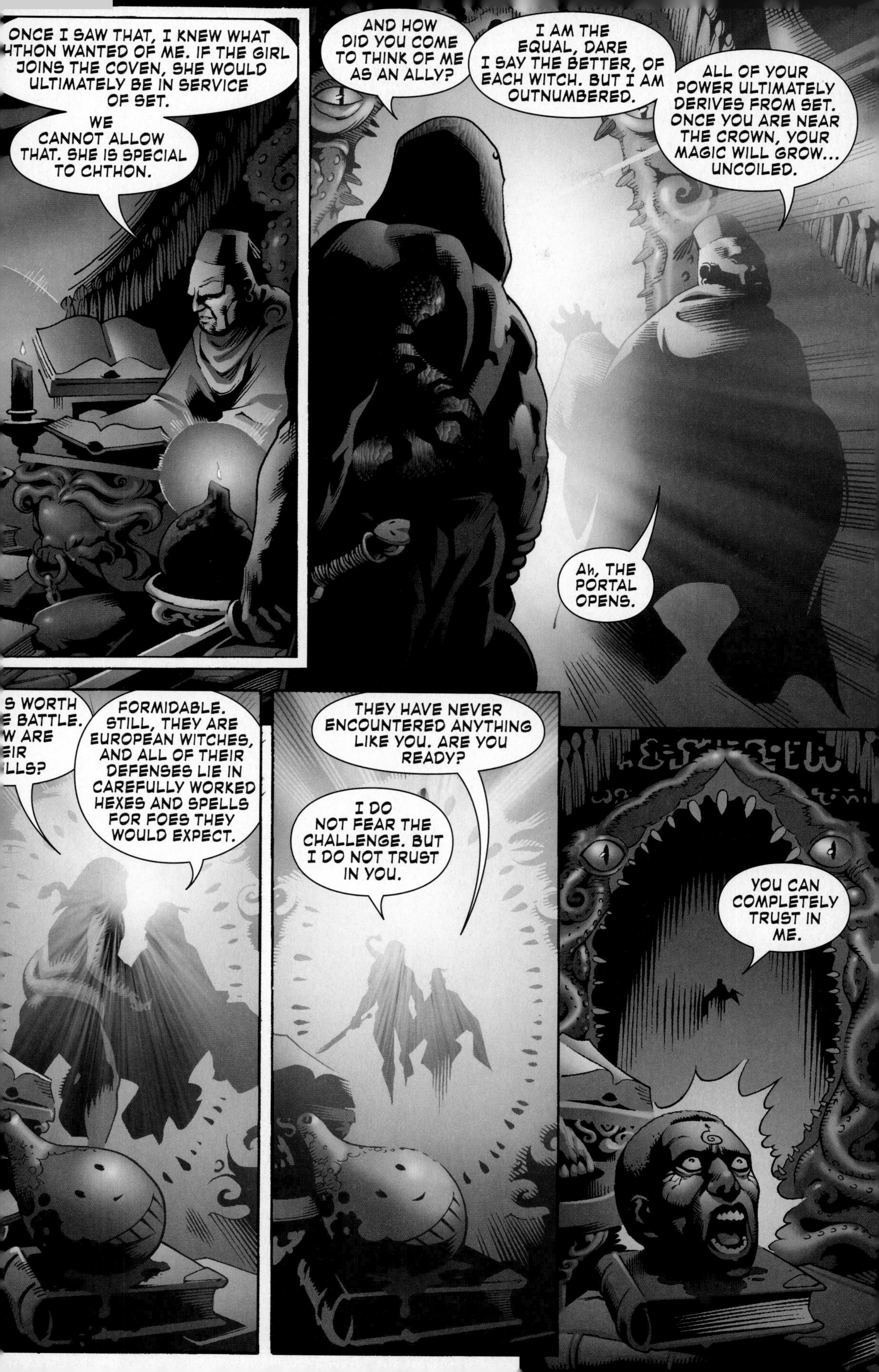
ONCE I SAW THAT, I KNEW WHAT
HTHON WANTED OF ME. IF THE GIRL JOINS THE COVEN, SHE WOULD ULTIMATELY BE IN SERVICE OF SET.
WE CANNOT ALLOW THAT. SHE IS SPECIAL TO CHTHON.
AND HOW DID YOU COME TO THINK OF ME AS AN ALLY?
I AM THE EQUAL, DARE I SAY THE BETTER, OF EACH WITCH. BUT I AM OUTNUMBERED.
ALL OF YOUR POWER ULTIMATELY DERIVES FROM SET. ONCE YOU ARE NEAR THE CROWN, YOUR MAGIC WILL GROW... UNCOILED.
Ah, THE PORTAL OPENS.
S WORTH E BATTLE. W ARE EIR LLS?
FORMIDABLE. STILL, THEY ARE EUROPEAN WITCHES, AND ALL OF THEIR DEFENSES LIE IN CAREFULLY WORKED HEXES AND SPELLS FOR FOES THEY WOULD EXPECT.
THEY HAVE NEVER ENCOUNTERED ANYTHING LIKE YOU. ARE YOU READY?
I DO NOT FEAR THE CHALLENGE. BUT I DO NOT TRUST IN YOU.
YOU CAN COMPLETELY TRUST IN ME.

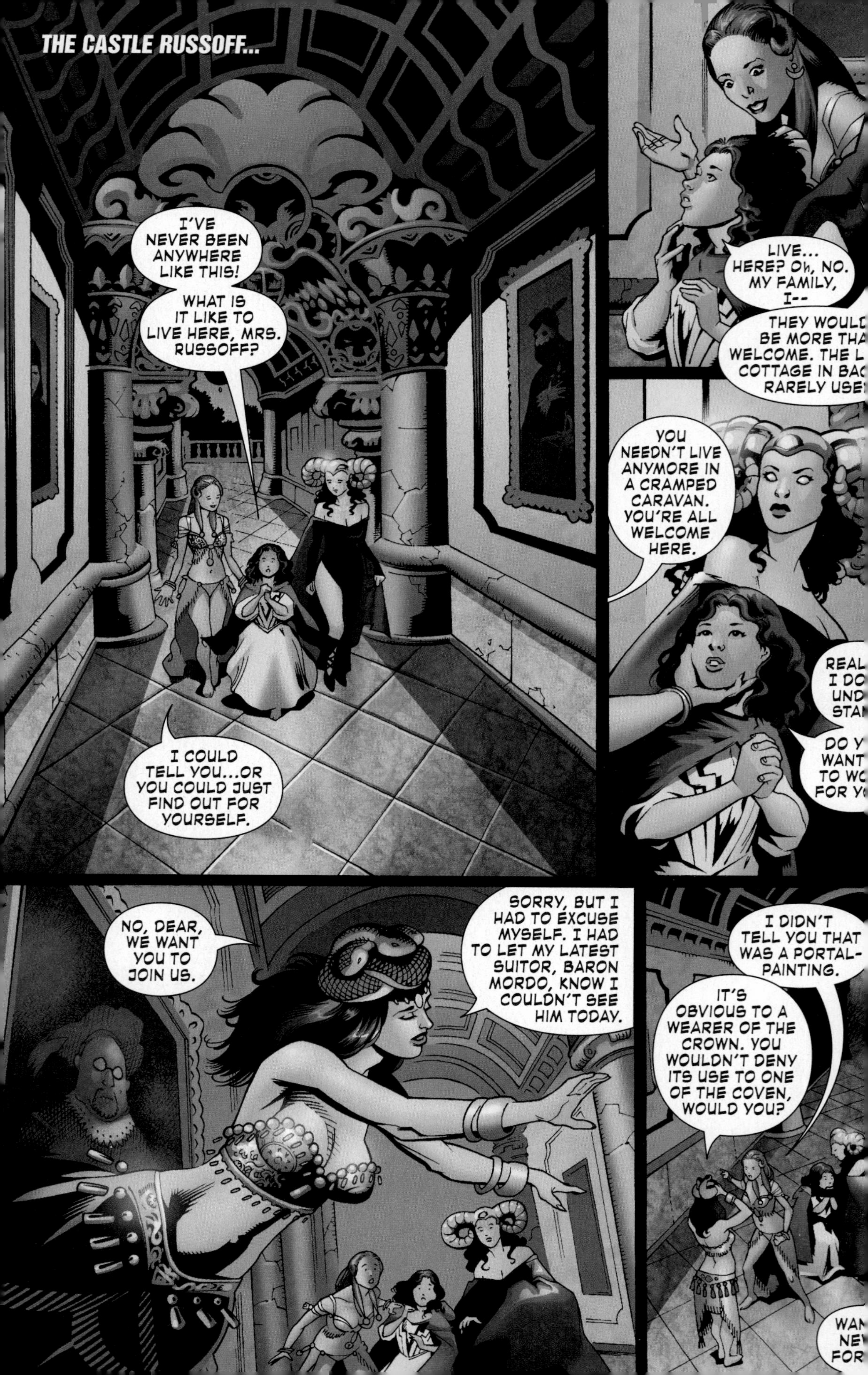
THE CASTLE RUSSOFF...
I'VE NEVER BEEN ANYWHERE LIKE THIS!
WHAT IS IT LIKE TO LIVE HERE, MRS. RUSSOFF?
I COULD TELL YOU...OR YOU COULD JUST FIND OUT FOR YOURSELF.
LIVE... HERE? Oh, NO. MY FAMILY, I--
THEY WOULD BE MORE THA WELCOME. THE L COTTAGE IN BAC RARELY USE
YOU NEEDN'T LIVE ANYMORE IN A CRAMPED CARAVAN. YOU'RE ALL WELCOME HERE.
REAL I DO UND STA
DO Y WANT TO WO FOR Y
NO, DEAR, WE WANT YOU TO JOIN US.
SORRY, BUT I HAD TO EXCUSE MYSELF. I HAD TO LET MY LATEST SUITOR, BARON MORDO, KNOW I COULDN'T SEE HIM TODAY.
I DIDN'T TELL YOU THAT WAS A PORTAL-PAINTING.
IT'S OBVIOUS TO A WEARER OF THE CROWN. YOU WOULDN'T DENY ITS USE TO ONE OF THE COVEN, WOULD YOU?
WAN NE FOR

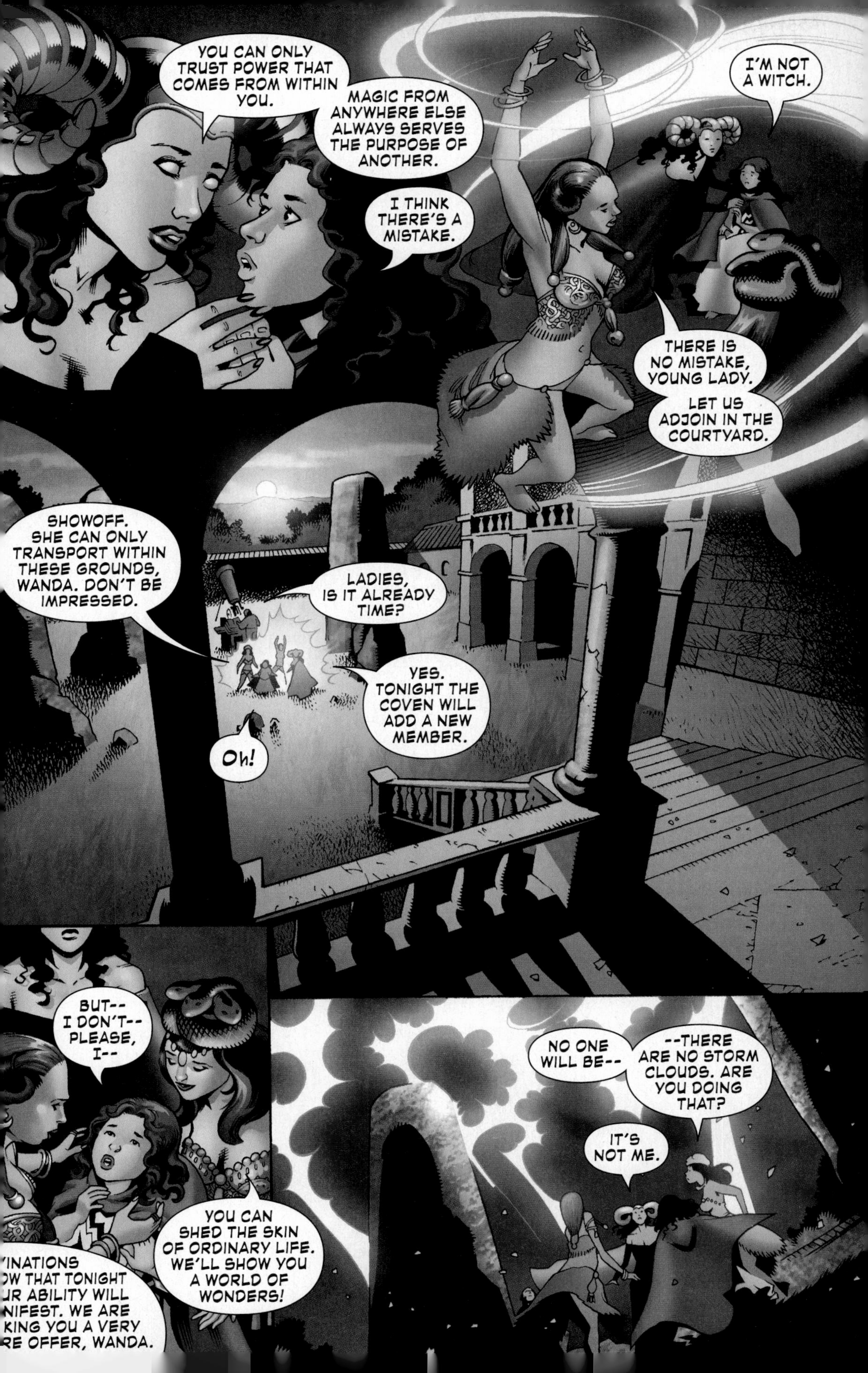
YOU CAN ONLY TRUST POWER THAT COMES FROM WITHIN YOU.
MAGIC FROM ANYWHERE ELSE ALWAYS SERVES THE PURPOSE OF ANOTHER.
I THINK THERE'S A MISTAKE.
I'M NOT A WITCH.
THERE IS NO MISTAKE, YOUNG LADY.
LET US ADJOIN IN THE COURTYARD.
SHOWOFF. SHE CAN ONLY TRANSPORT WITHIN THESE GROUNDS, WANDA. DON'T BE IMPRESSED.
LADIES, IS IT ALREADY TIME?
YES. TONIGHT THE COVEN WILL ADD A NEW MEMBER.
Oh!
BUT-- I DON'T-- PLEASE, I--
YOU CAN SHED THE SKIN OF ORDINARY LIFE. WE'LL SHOW YOU A WORLD OF WONDERS!
VINATIONS OW THAT TONIGHT UR ABILITY WILL NIFEST. WE ARE KING YOU A VERY RE OFFER, WANDA.
NO ONE WILL BE--
--THERE ARE NO STORM CLOUDS. ARE YOU DOING THAT?
IT'S NOT ME.

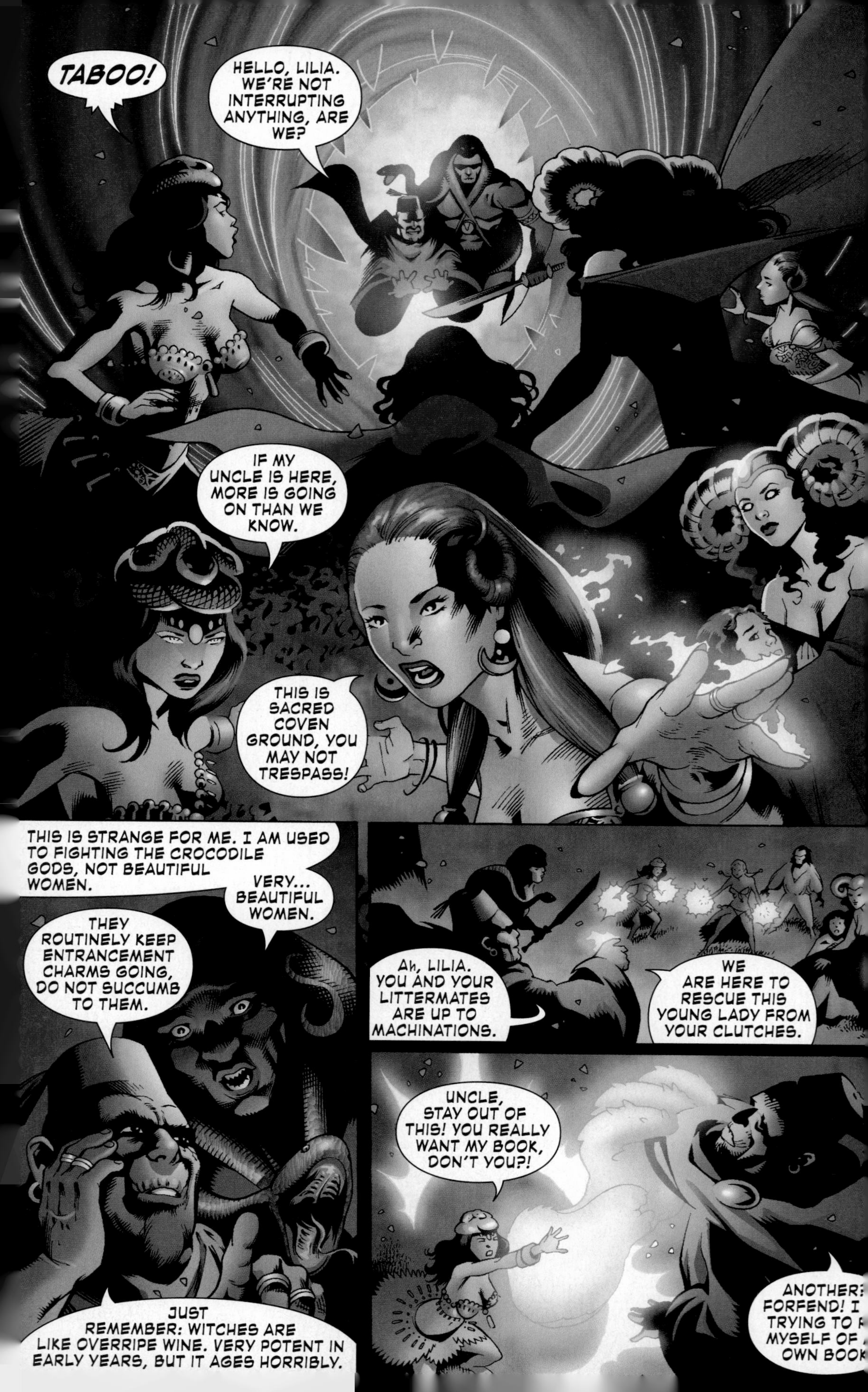
TABOO!
HELLO, LILIA. WE'RE NOT INTERRUPTING ANYTHING, ARE WE?
IF MY UNCLE IS HERE, MORE IS GOING ON THAN WE KNOW.
THIS IS SACRED COVEN GROUND, YOU MAY NOT TRESPASS!
THIS IS STRANGE FOR ME. I AM USED TO FIGHTING THE CROCODILE GODS, NOT BEAUTIFUL WOMEN.
VERY... BEAUTIFUL WOMEN.
THEY ROUTINELY KEEP ENTRANCEMENT CHARMS GOING, DO NOT SUCCUMB TO THEM.
JUST REMEMBER: WITCHES ARE LIKE OVERRIPE WINE. VERY POTENT IN EARLY YEARS, BUT IT AGES HORRIBLY.
AH, LILIA. YOU AND YOUR LITTERMATES ARE UP TO MACHINATIONS.
WE ARE HERE TO RESCUE THIS YOUNG LADY FROM YOUR CLUTCHES.
UNCLE, STAY OUT OF THIS! YOU REALLY WANT MY BOOK, DON'T YOU?!

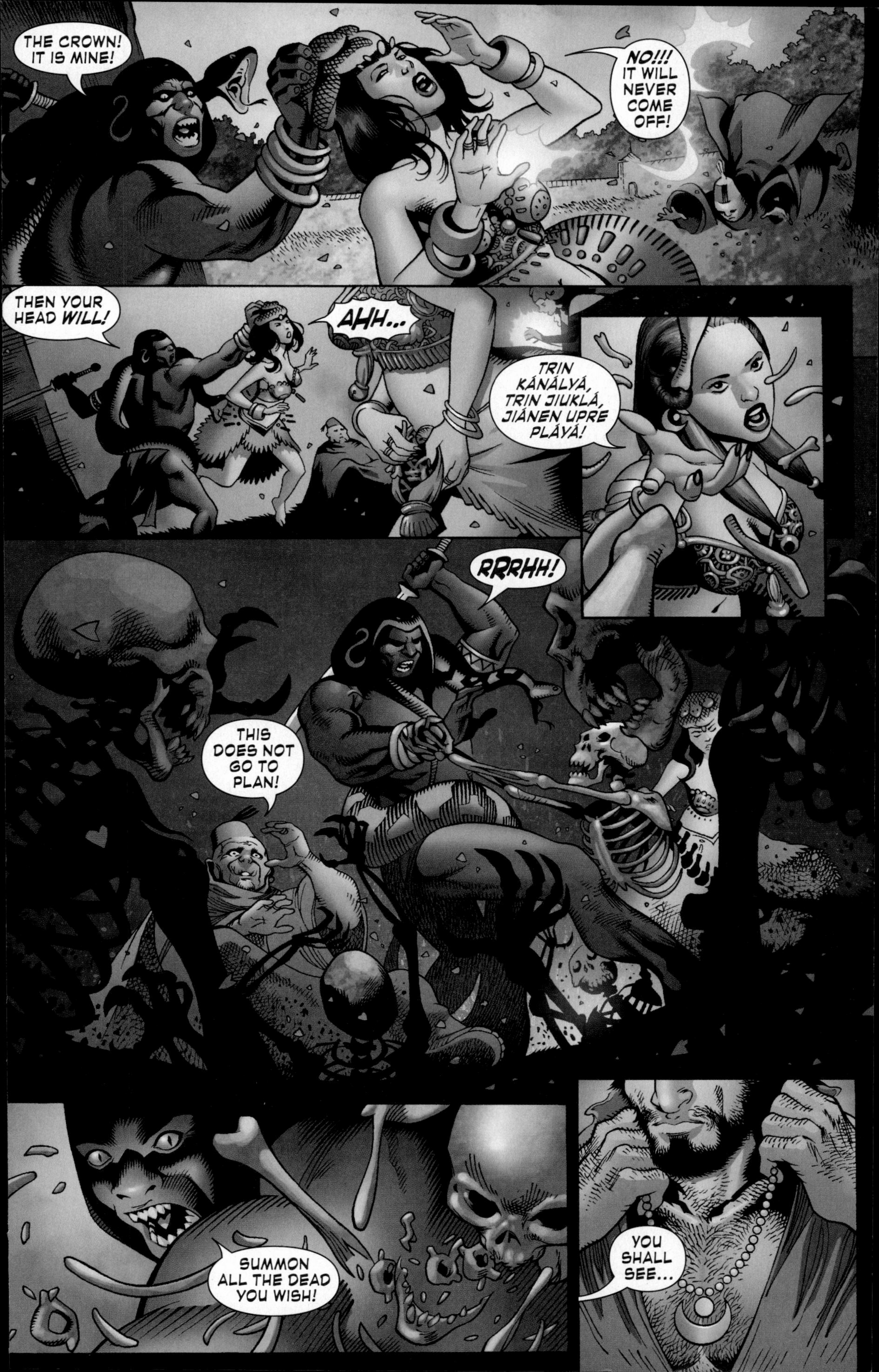
THE CROWN! IT IS MINE!
NO!!! IT WILL NEVER COME OFF!
THEN YOUR HEAD WILL!
AHH...
TRIN KÁNÁLYÁ, TRIN JIUKLÁ, JIÁNEN UPRE PLÁYÁ!
RRRHH!
THIS DOES NOT GO TO PLAN!
SUMMON ALL THE DEAD YOU WISH!
YOU SHALL SEE...

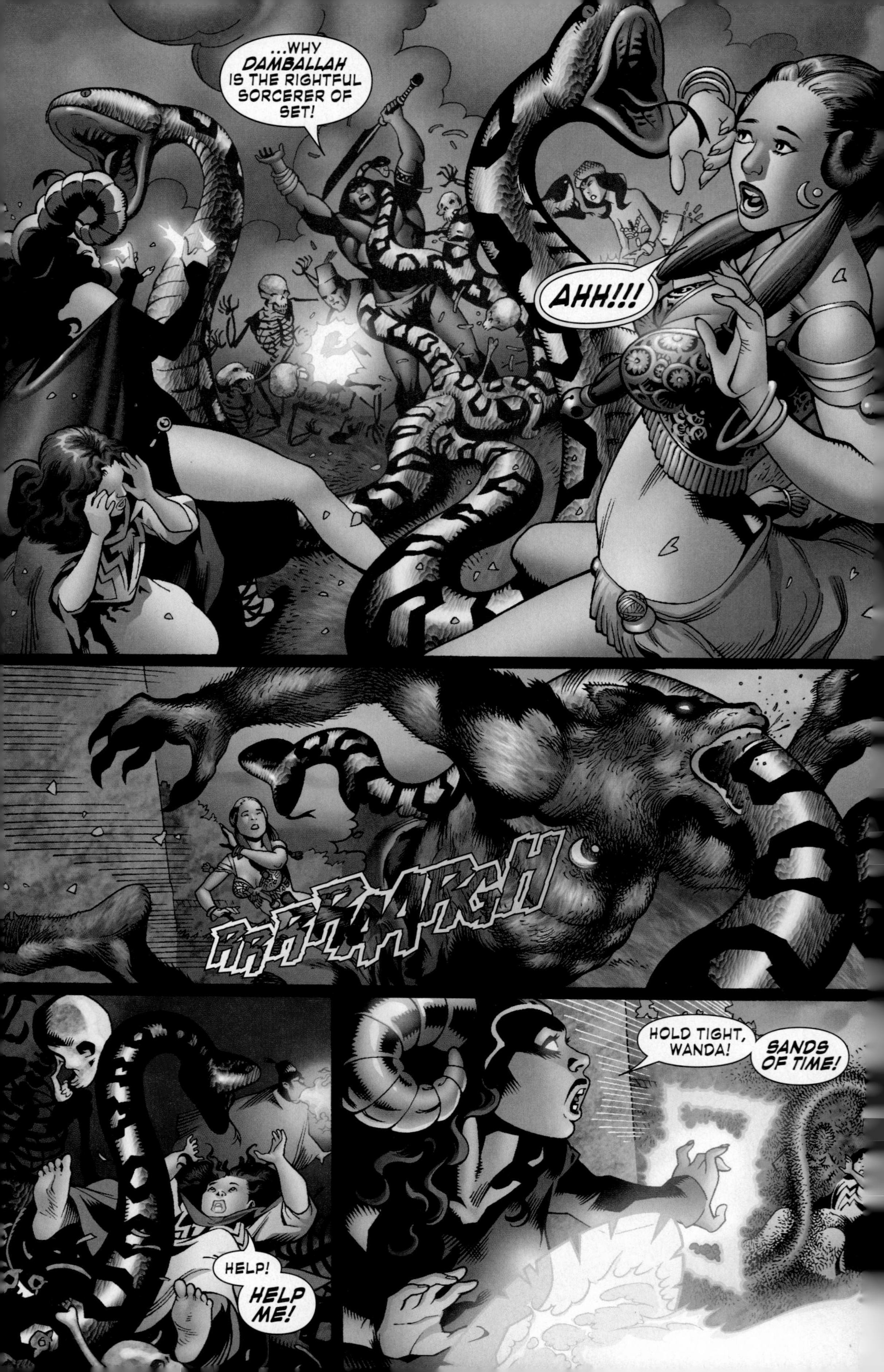
...WHY DAMBALLAH IS THE RIGHTFUL SORCERER OF SET!
AHH!!!
RRRAAARGH
HELP! HELP ME!
HOLD TIGHT, WANDA!
SANDS OF TIME!
6

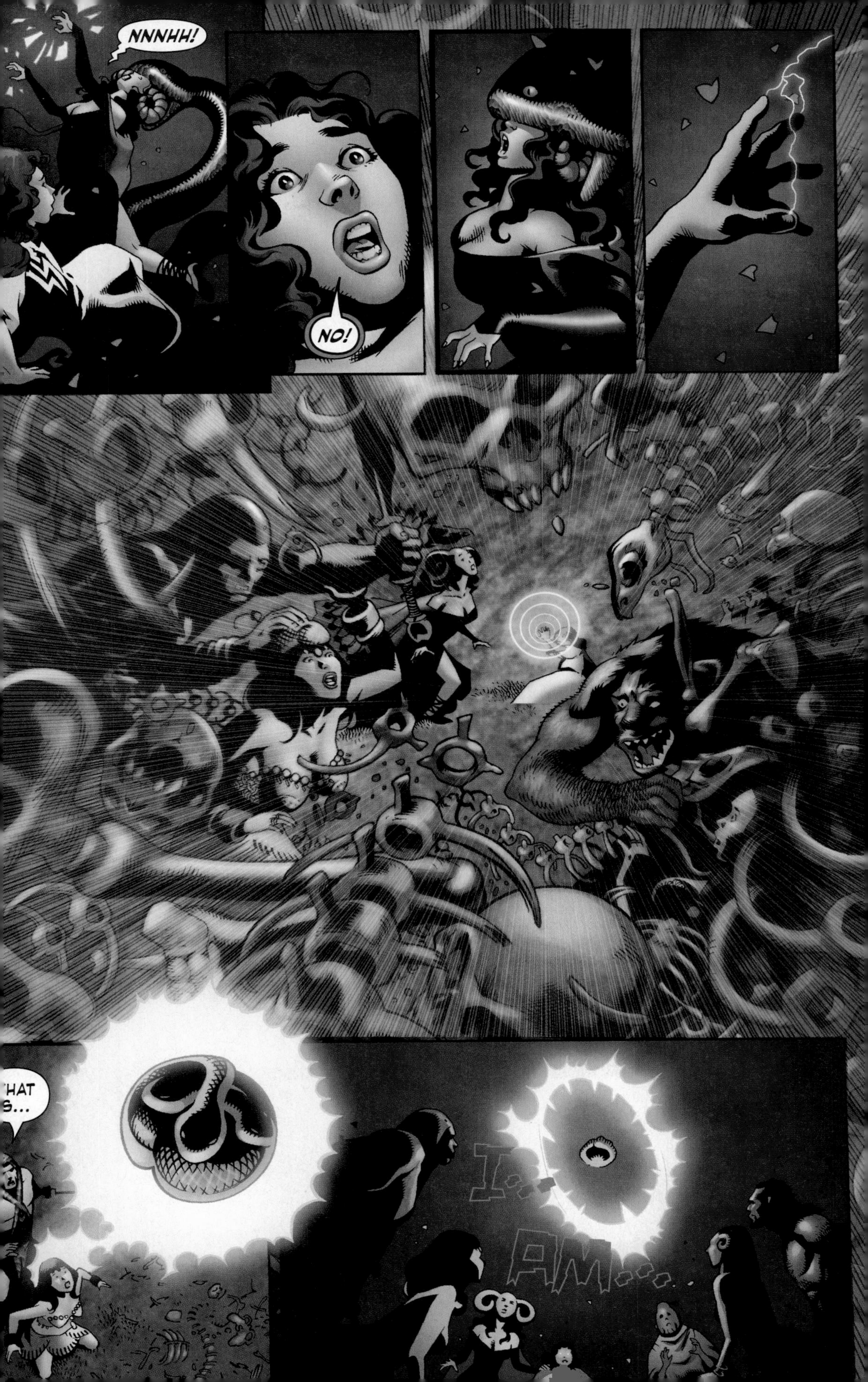
NNNHH!
NO!
I...
AM...

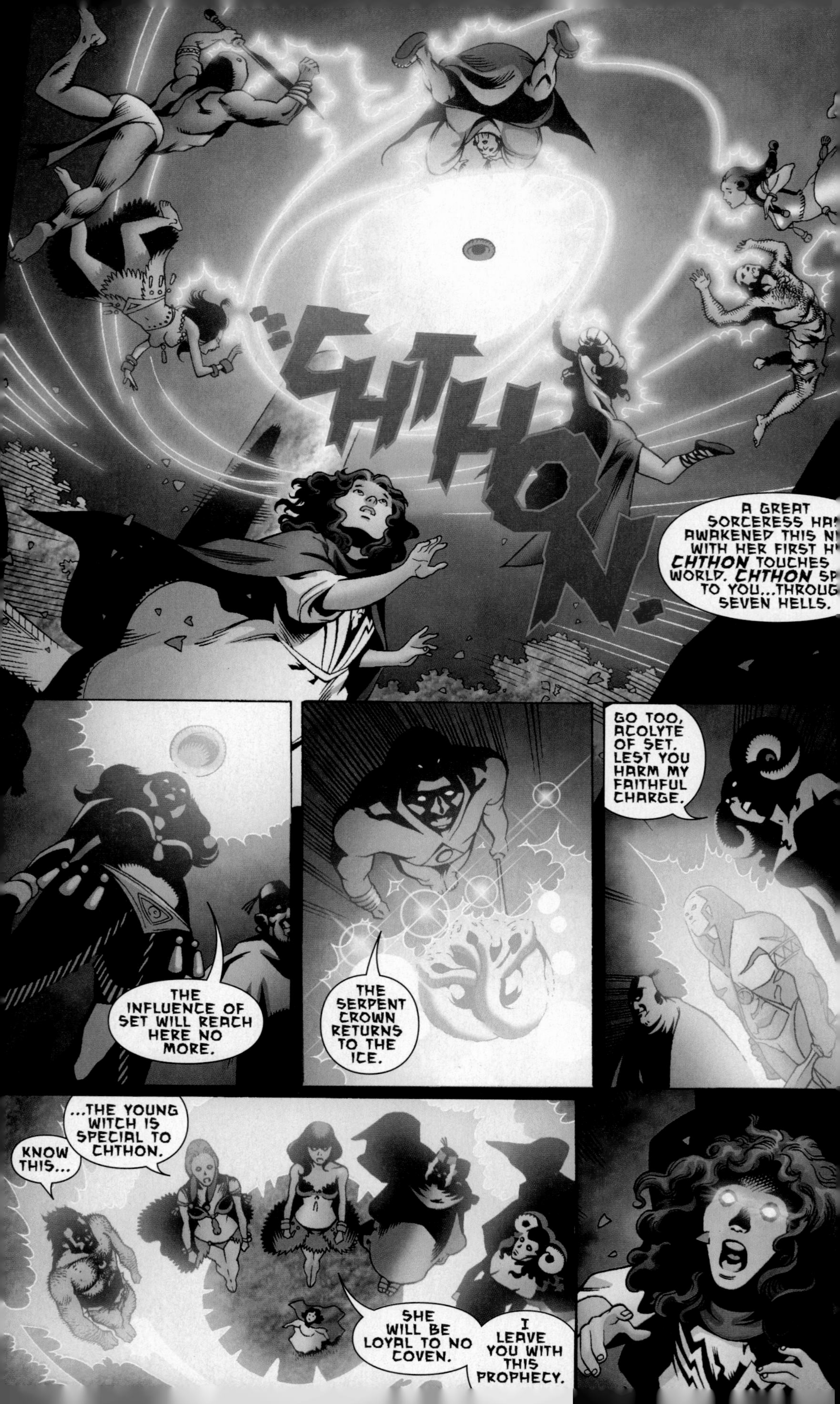
CHTHON
A GREAT SORCERESS HA AWAKENED THIS N WITH HER FIRST H CHTHON TOUCHES WORLD. CHTHON SP TO YOU...THROUG SEVEN HELLS.
THE INFLUENCE OF SET WILL REACH HERE NO MORE.
THE SERPENT CROWN RETURNS TO THE ICE.
GO TOO, ACOLYTE OF SET. LEST YOU HARM MY FAITHFUL CHARGE.
KNOW THIS...
...THE YOUNG WITCH IS SPECIAL TO CHTHON.
SHE WILL BE LOYAL TO NO COVEN.
I LEAVE YOU WITH THIS PROPHECY.

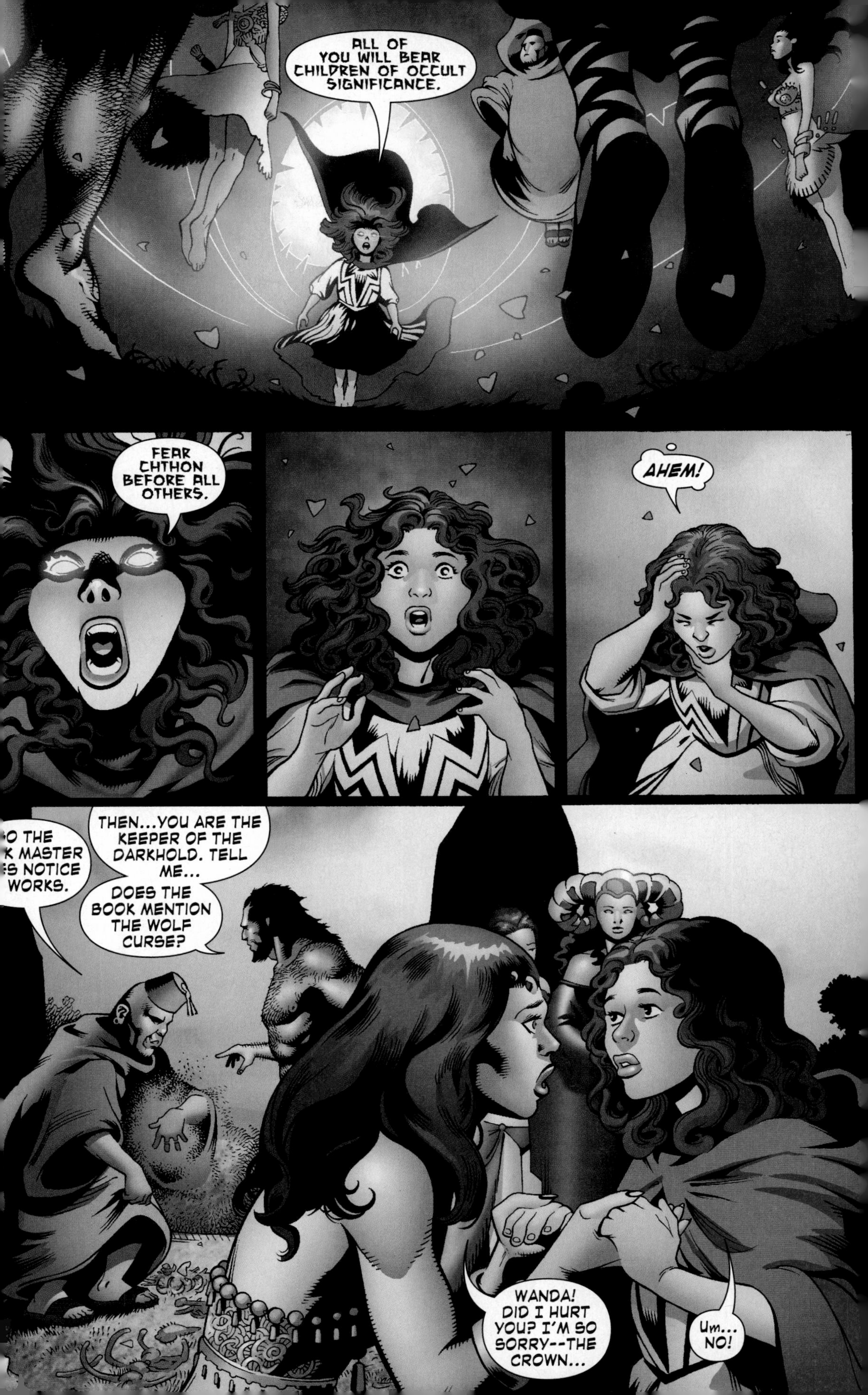
ALL OF YOU WILL BEAR CHILDREN OF OCCULT SIGNIFICANCE.
FEAR CHTHON BEFORE ALL OTHERS.
AHEM!
O THE K MASTER S NOTICE WORKS.
THEN...YOU ARE THE KEEPER OF THE DARKHOLD. TELL ME...
DOES THE BOOK MENTION THE WOLF CURSE?
WANDA! DID I HURT YOU? I'M SO SORRY--THE CROWN...
Um... NO!

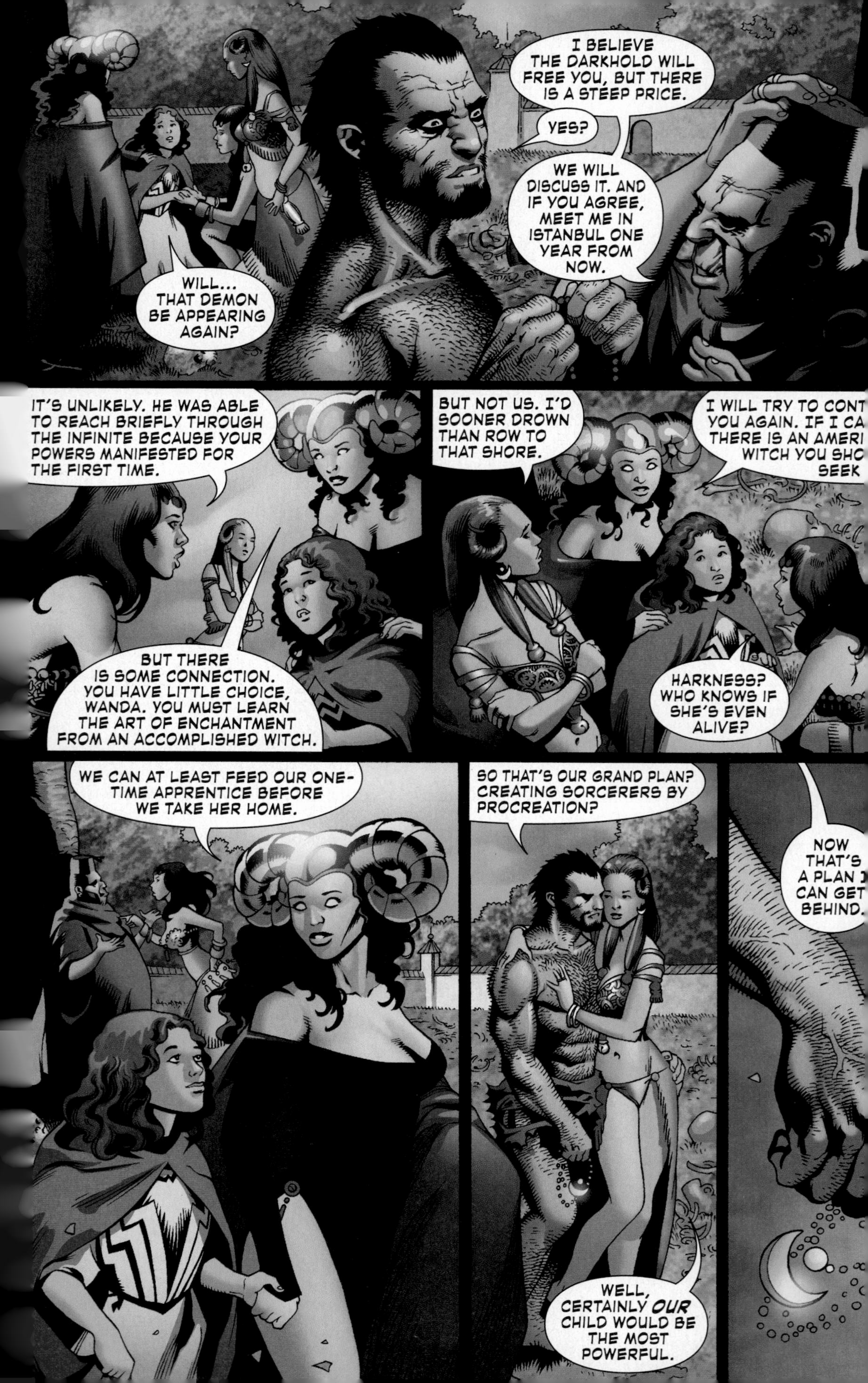
I BELIEVE THE DARKHOLD WILL FREE YOU, BUT THERE IS A STEEP PRICE.
YES?
WE WILL DISCUSS IT. AND IF YOU AGREE, MEET ME IN ISTANBUL ONE YEAR FROM NOW.
WILL... THAT DEMON BE APPEARING AGAIN?
IT'S UNLIKELY. HE WAS ABLE TO REACH BRIEFLY THROUGH THE INFINITE BECAUSE YOUR POWERS MANIFESTED FOR THE FIRST TIME.
BUT THERE IS SOME CONNECTION. YOU HAVE LITTLE CHOICE, WANDA. YOU MUST LEARN THE ART OF ENCHANTMENT FROM AN ACCOMPLISHED WITCH.
BUT NOT US. I'D SOONER DROWN THAN ROW TO THAT SHORE.
I WILL TRY TO CONT YOU AGAIN. IF I CA THERE IS AN AMERI WITCH YOU SHO SEEK
HARKNESS? WHO KNOWS IF SHE'S EVEN ALIVE?
WE CAN AT LEAST FEED OUR ONE-TIME APPRENTICE BEFORE WE TAKE HER HOME.
SO THAT'S OUR GRAND PLAN? CREATING SORCERERS BY PROCREATION?
WELL, CERTAINLY *OUR* CHILD WOULD BE THE MOST POWERFUL.
NOW THAT'S A PLAN CAN GET BEHIND.

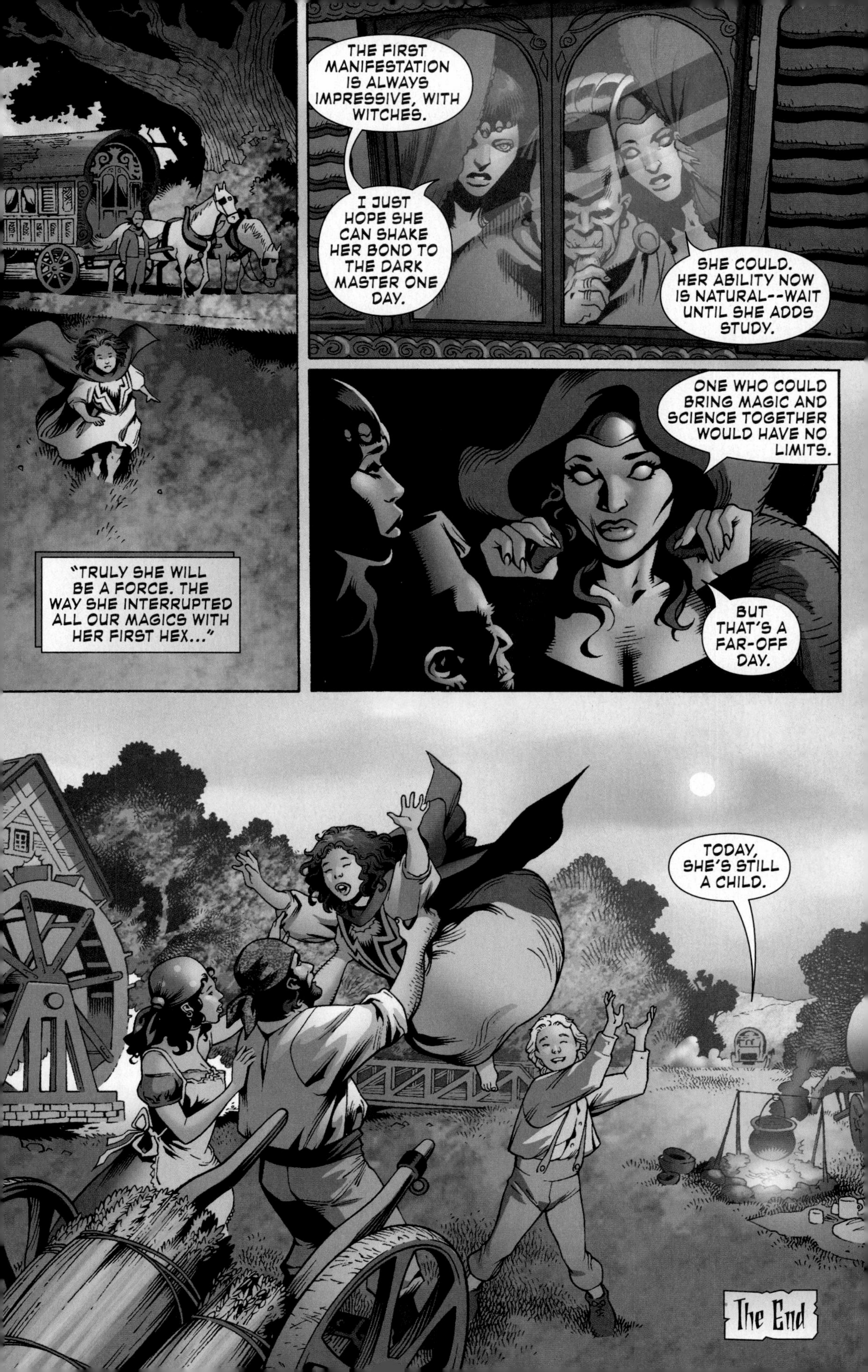
THE FIRST MANIFESTATION IS ALWAYS IMPRESSIVE, WITH WITCHES.
I JUST HOPE SHE CAN SHAKE HER BOND TO THE DARK MASTER ONE DAY.
SHE COULD. HER ABILITY NOW IS NATURAL--WAIT UNTIL SHE ADDS STUDY.
"TRULY SHE WILL BE A FORCE. THE WAY SHE INTERRUPTED ALL OUR MAGICS WITH HER FIRST HEX..."
ONE WHO COULD BRING MAGIC AND SCIENCE TOGETHER WOULD HAVE NO LIMITS.
BUT THAT'S A FAR-OFF DAY.
TODAY, SHE'S STILL A CHILD.
The End

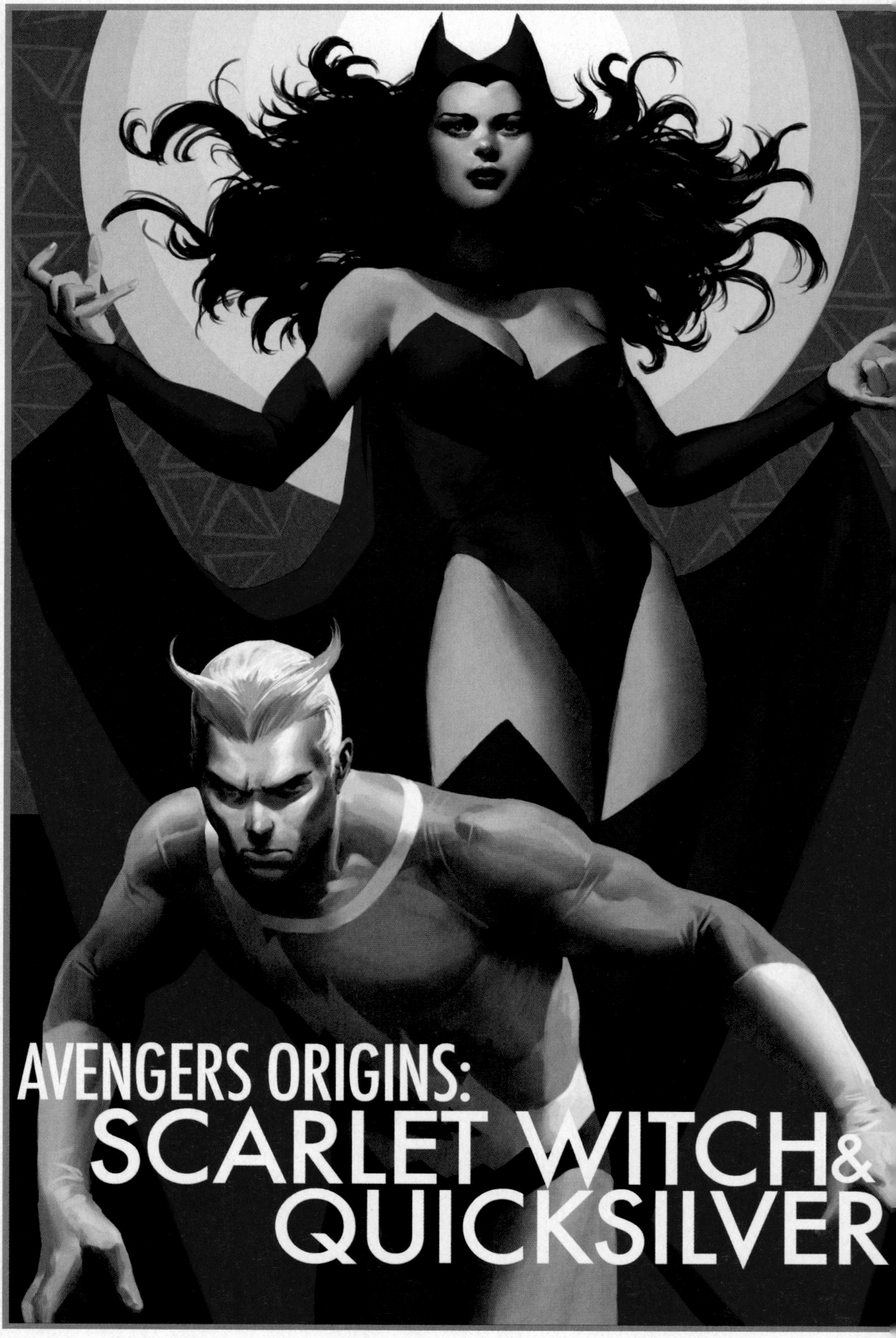
AVENGERS ORIGINS:
SCARLET WITCH &
QUICKSILVER

WRITER: SEAN MCKEEVER • ARTIST: MIRCO PIERFEDERICI • COLORISTS: JAVIER TARTAGLIA WITH GARRY HENDERSON
LETTERER: DAVE LANPHEAR • ASSISTANT EDITOR: JOHN DENNING • EDITOR: LAUREN SANKOVITCH
EXECUTIVE EDITOR: TOM BREVOORT

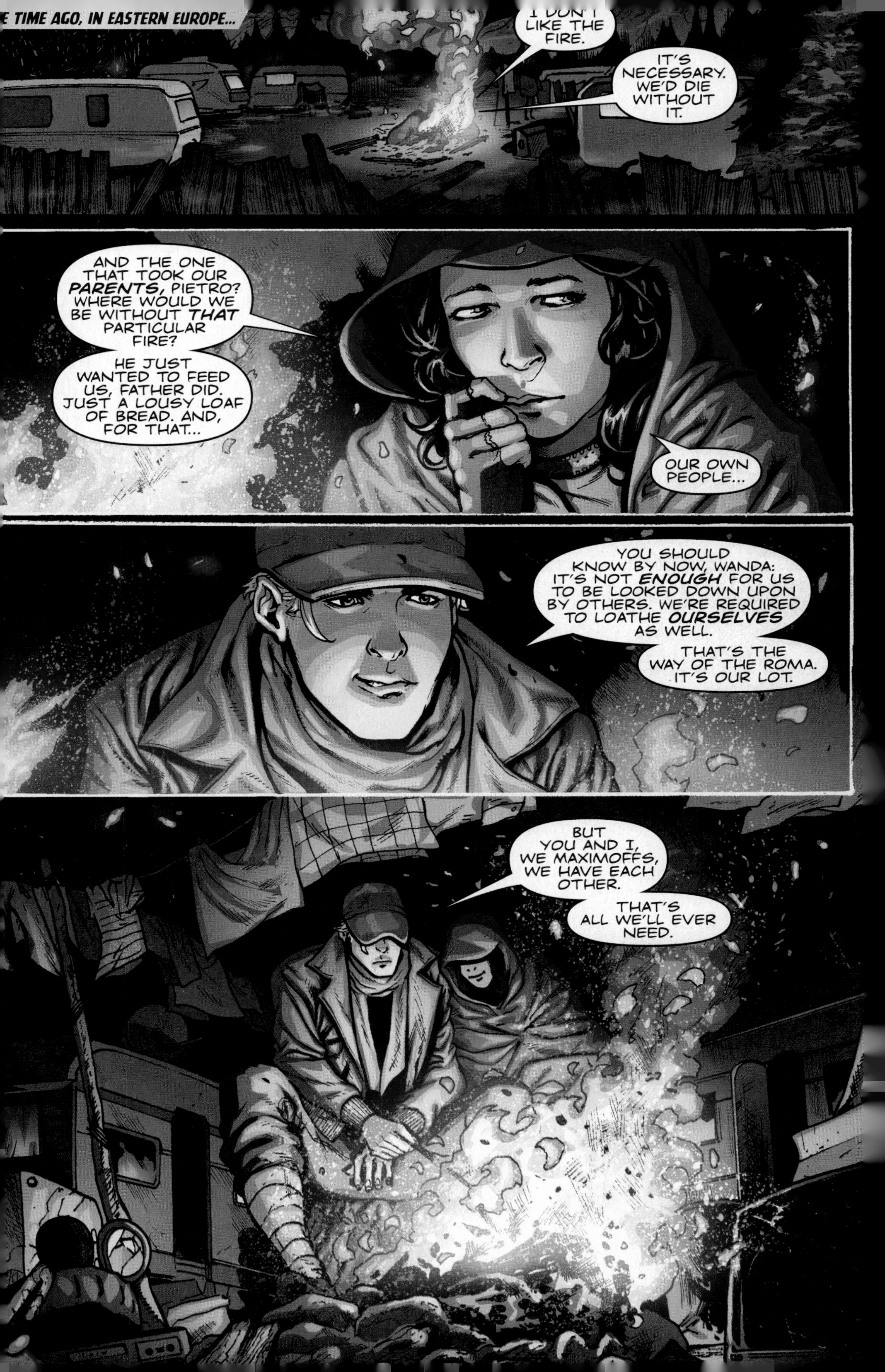
E TIME AGO, IN EASTERN EUROPE...
I DON'T LIKE THE FIRE.
IT'S NECESSARY. WE'D DIE WITHOUT IT.
AND THE ONE THAT TOOK OUR PARENTS, PIETRO? WHERE WOULD WE BE WITHOUT THAT PARTICULAR FIRE?
HE JUST WANTED TO FEED US, FATHER DID. JUST A LOUSY LOAF OF BREAD. AND, FOR THAT...
OUR OWN PEOPLE...
YOU SHOULD KNOW BY NOW, WANDA: IT'S NOT ENOUGH FOR US TO BE LOOKED DOWN UPON BY OTHERS. WE'RE REQUIRED TO LOATHE OURSELVES AS WELL.
THAT'S THE WAY OF THE ROMA. IT'S OUR LOT.
BUT YOU AND I, WE MAXIMOFFS, WE HAVE EACH OTHER.
THAT'S ALL WE'LL EVER NEED.

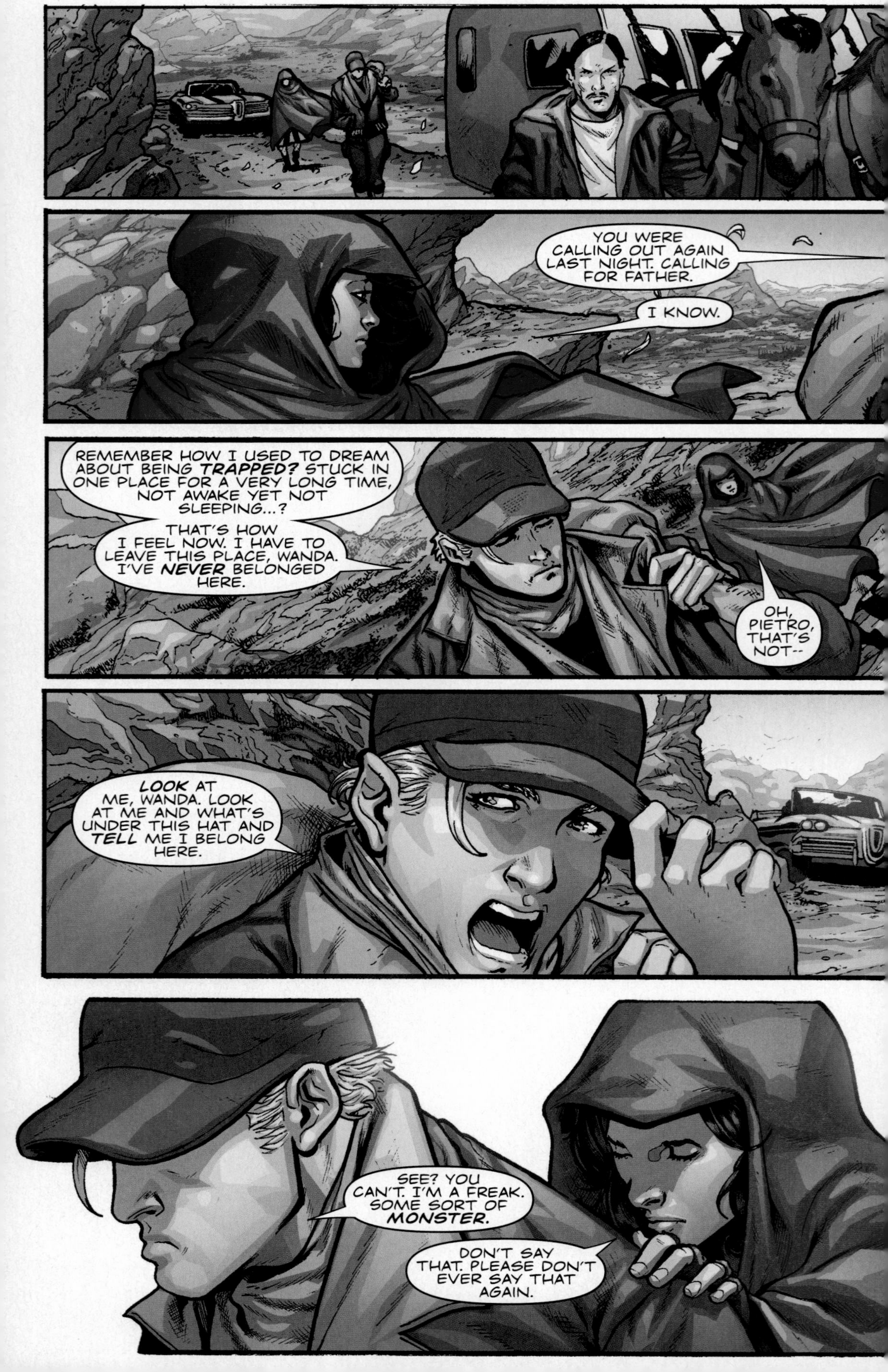
YOU WERE CALLING OUT AGAIN LAST NIGHT. CALLING FOR FATHER.
I KNOW.
REMEMBER HOW I USED TO DREAM ABOUT BEING TRAPPED? STUCK IN ONE PLACE FOR A VERY LONG TIME, NOT AWAKE YET NOT SLEEPING...?
THAT'S HOW I FEEL NOW. I HAVE TO LEAVE THIS PLACE, WANDA. I'VE NEVER BELONGED HERE.
OH, PIETRO, THAT'S NOT--
LOOK AT ME, WANDA. LOOK AT ME AND WHAT'S UNDER THIS HAT AND TELL ME I BELONG HERE.
SEE? YOU CAN'T. I'M A FREAK. SOME SORT OF MONSTER.
DON'T SAY THAT. PLEASE DON'T EVER SAY THAT AGAIN.

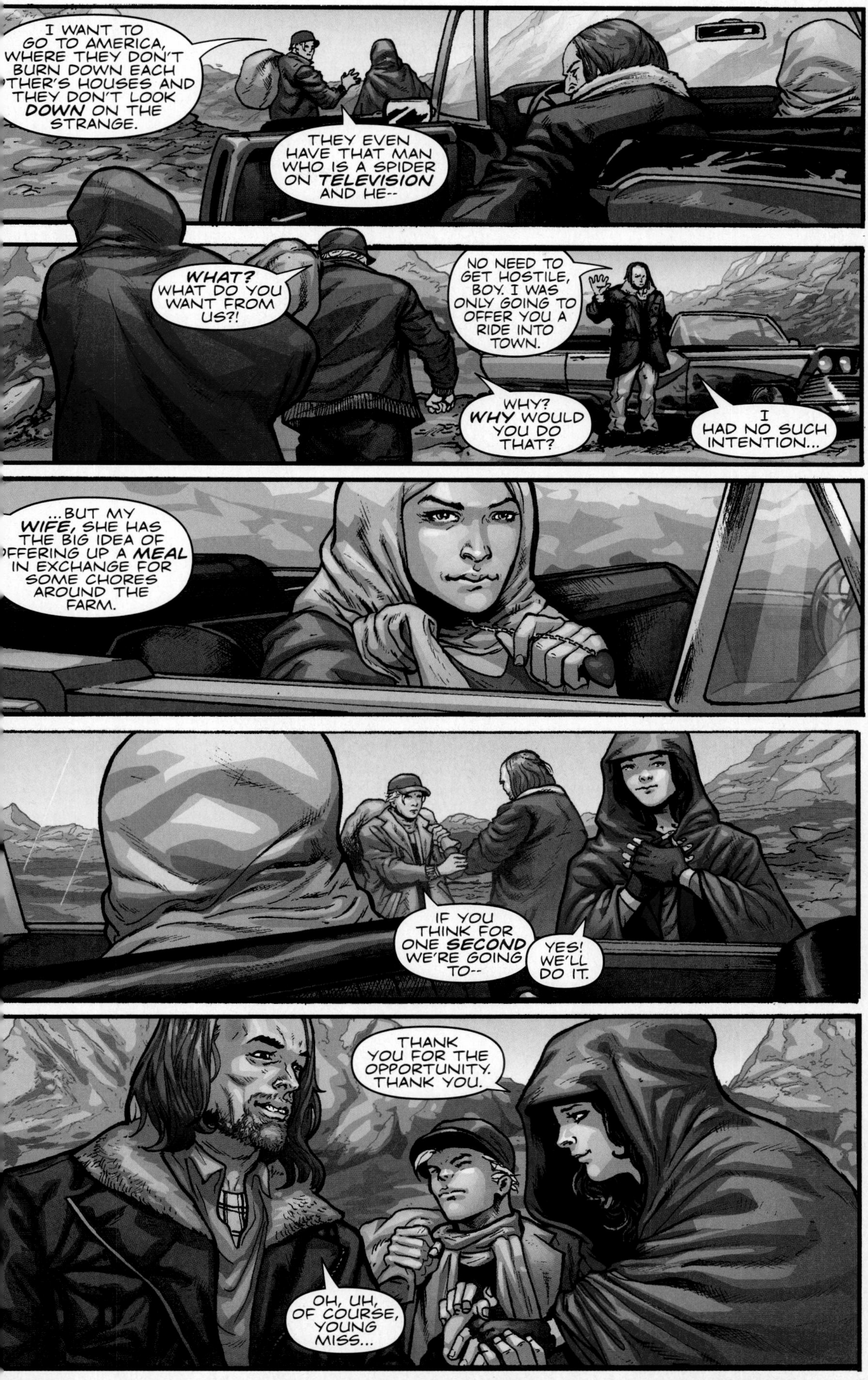

I WANT TO GO TO AMERICA, WHERE THEY DON'T BURN DOWN EACH OTHER'S HOUSES AND THEY DON'T LOOK DOWN ON THE STRANGE.
THEY EVEN HAVE THAT MAN WHO IS A SPIDER ON TELEVISION AND HE--
WHAT? WHAT DO YOU WANT FROM US?!
NO NEED TO GET HOSTILE, BOY. I WAS ONLY GOING TO OFFER YOU A RIDE INTO TOWN.
WHY? WHY WOULD YOU DO THAT?
I HAD NO SUCH INTENTION...
...BUT MY WIFE, SHE HAS THE BIG IDEA OF OFFERING UP A MEAL IN EXCHANGE FOR SOME CHORES AROUND THE FARM.
IF YOU THINK FOR ONE SECOND WE'RE GOING TO--
YES! WE'LL DO IT.
THANK YOU FOR THE OPPORTUNITY. THANK YOU.
OH, UH, OF COURSE, YOUNG MISS...

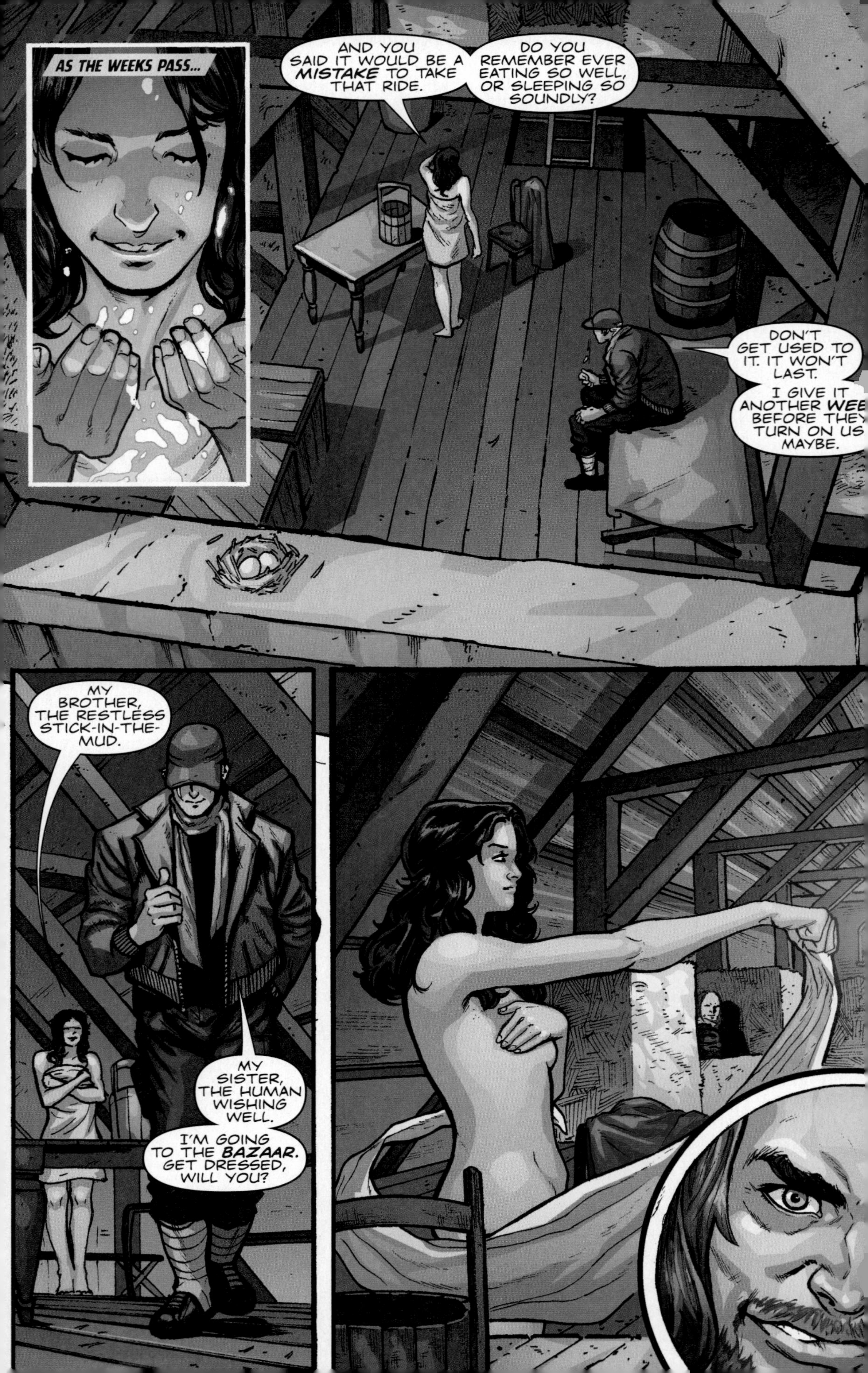
AS THE WEEKS PASS...
AND YOU SAID IT WOULD BE A MISTAKE TO TAKE THAT RIDE.
DO YOU REMEMBER EVER EATING SO WELL, OR SLEEPING SO SOUNDLY?
DON'T GET USED TO IT. IT WON'T LAST.
I GIVE IT ANOTHER WEE BEFORE THEY TURN ON US MAYBE.
MY BROTHER, THE RESTLESS STICK-IN-THE-MUD.
MY SISTER, THE HUMAN WISHING WELL.
I'M GOING TO THE BAZAAR. GET DRESSED, WILL YOU?

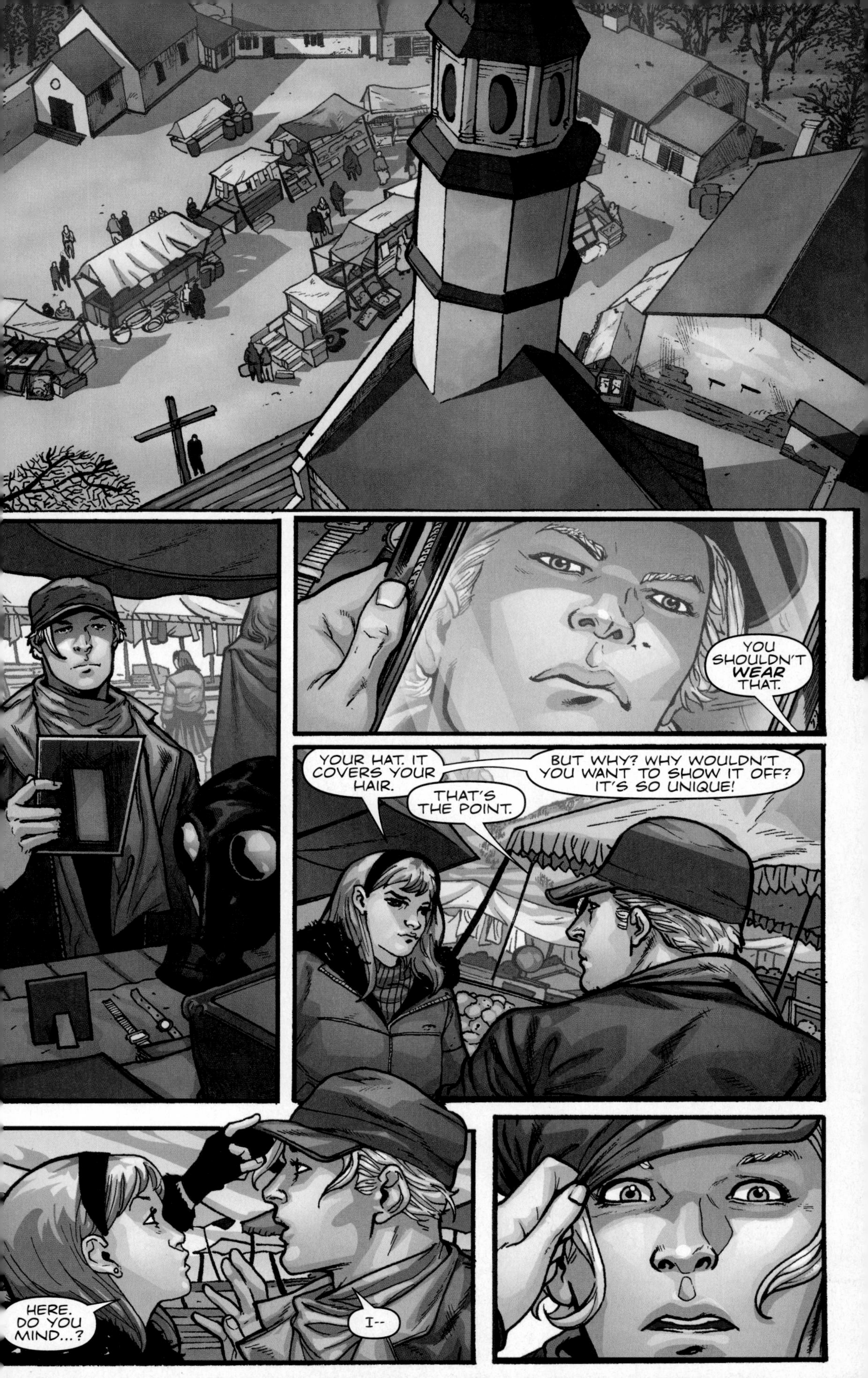
YOU SHOULDN'T WEAR THAT.
YOUR HAT. IT COVERS YOUR HAIR.
THAT'S THE POINT.
BUT WHY? WHY WOULDN'T YOU WANT TO SHOW IT OFF? IT'S SO UNIQUE!
HERE. DO YOU MIND...?
I--

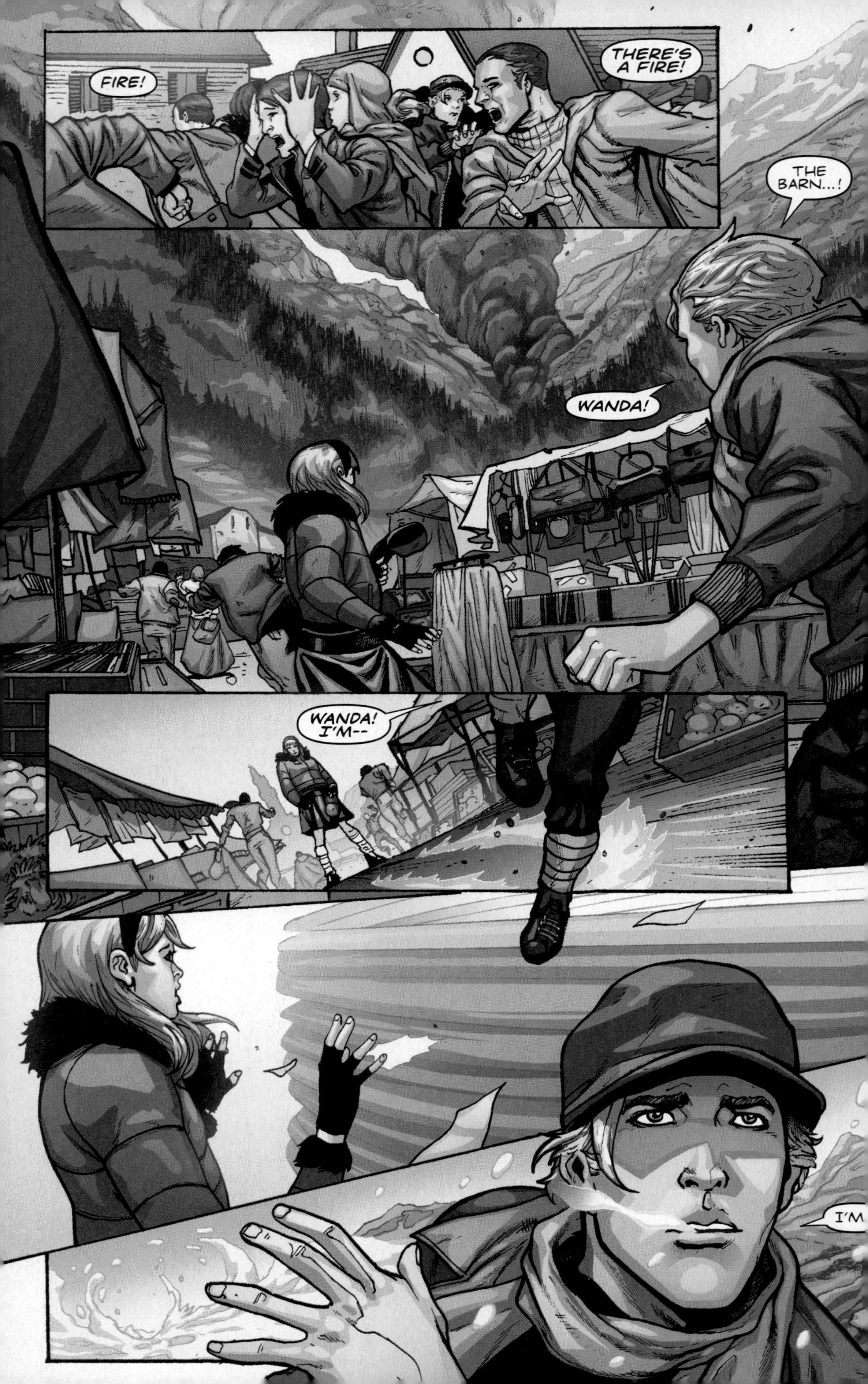
FIRE!
THERE'S A FIRE!
THE BARN...!
WANDA!
WANDA! I'M--
I'M

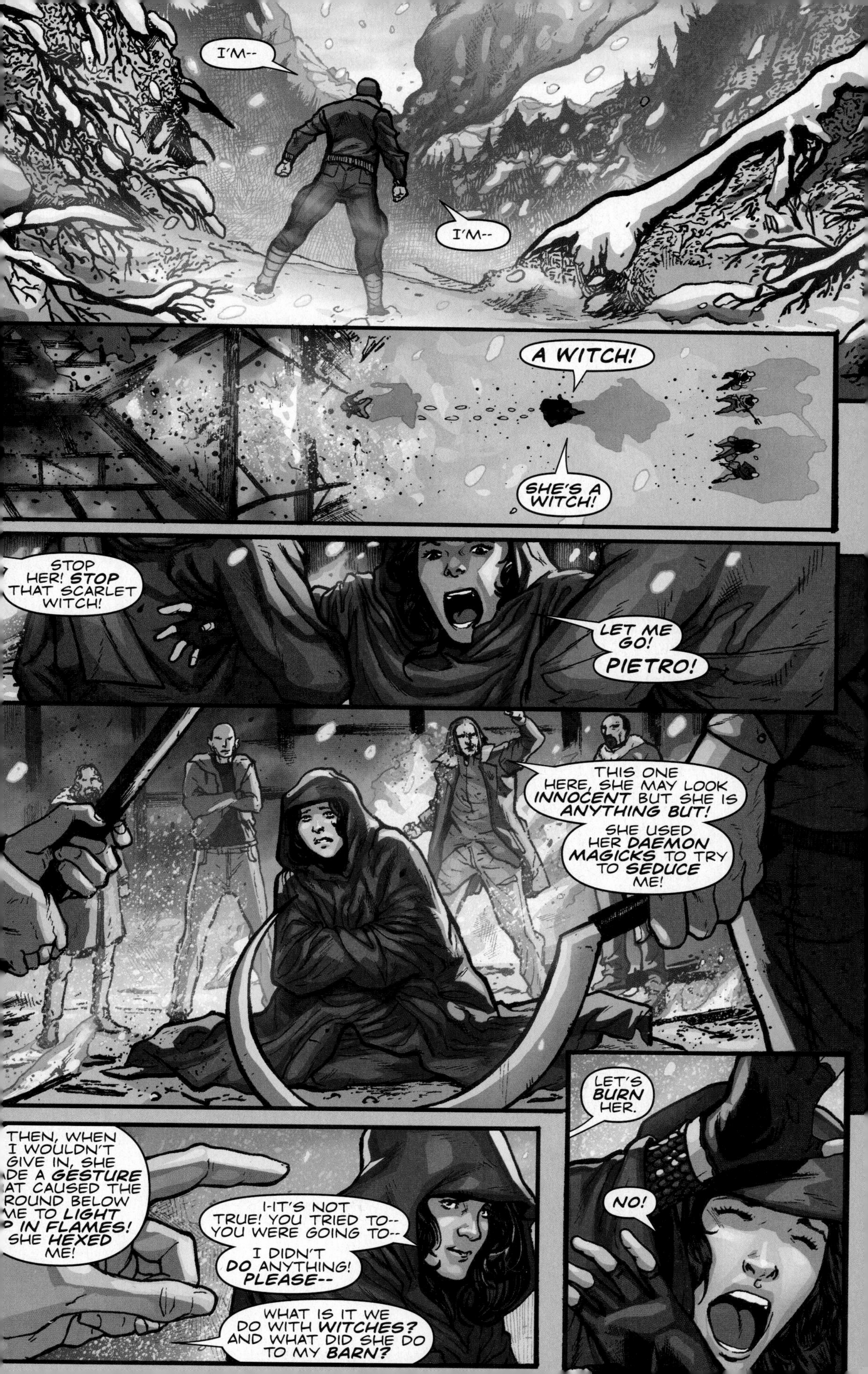
I'M--
I'M--
A WITCH!
SHE'S A WITCH!
STOP HER! STOP THAT SCARLET WITCH!
LET ME GO! PIETRO!
THIS ONE HERE, SHE MAY LOOK INNOCENT BUT SHE IS ANYTHING BUT!
SHE USED HER DAEMON MAGICKS TO TRY TO SEDUCE ME!
THEN, WHEN I WOULDN'T GIVE IN, SHE
I-IT'S NOT TRUE! YOU TRIED TO-- YOU WERE GOING TO--
I DIDN'T DO ANYTHING! PLEASE--
WHAT IS IT WE DO WITH WITCHES? AND WHAT DID SHE DO TO MY BARN?
LET'S BURN HER.
NO!

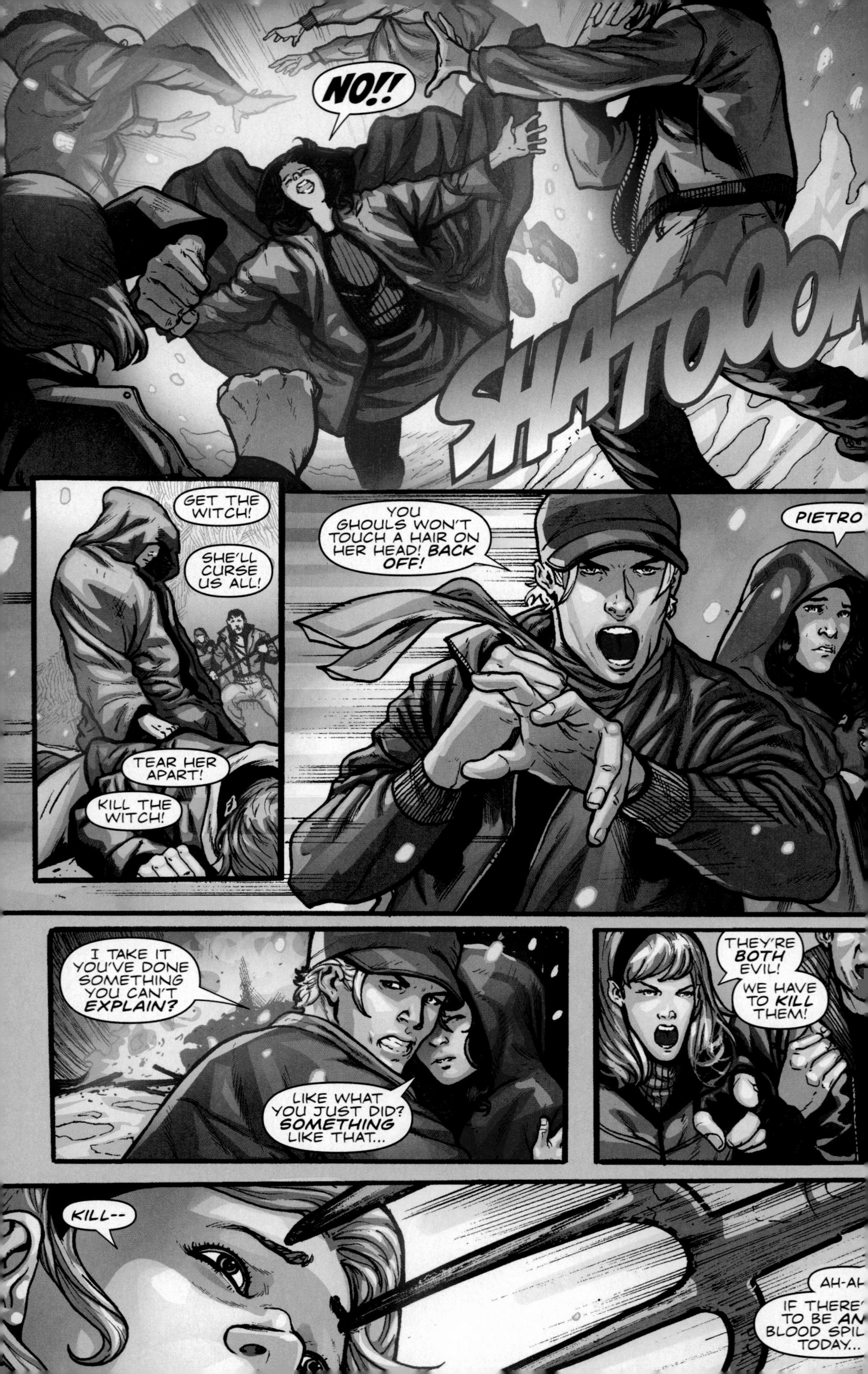
NO!!
SHATOOO
GET THE WITCH!
SHE'LL CURSE US ALL!
TEAR HER APART!
KILL THE WITCH!
YOU GHOULS WON'T TOUCH A HAIR ON HER HEAD! BACK OFF!
PIETRO
I TAKE IT YOU'VE DONE SOMETHING YOU CAN'T EXPLAIN?
LIKE WHAT YOU JUST DID? SOMETHING LIKE THAT...
THEY'RE BOTH EVIL!
WE HAVE TO KILL THEM!
KILL--
AH-AH
IF THERE' TO BE AN BLOOD SPIL TODAY...

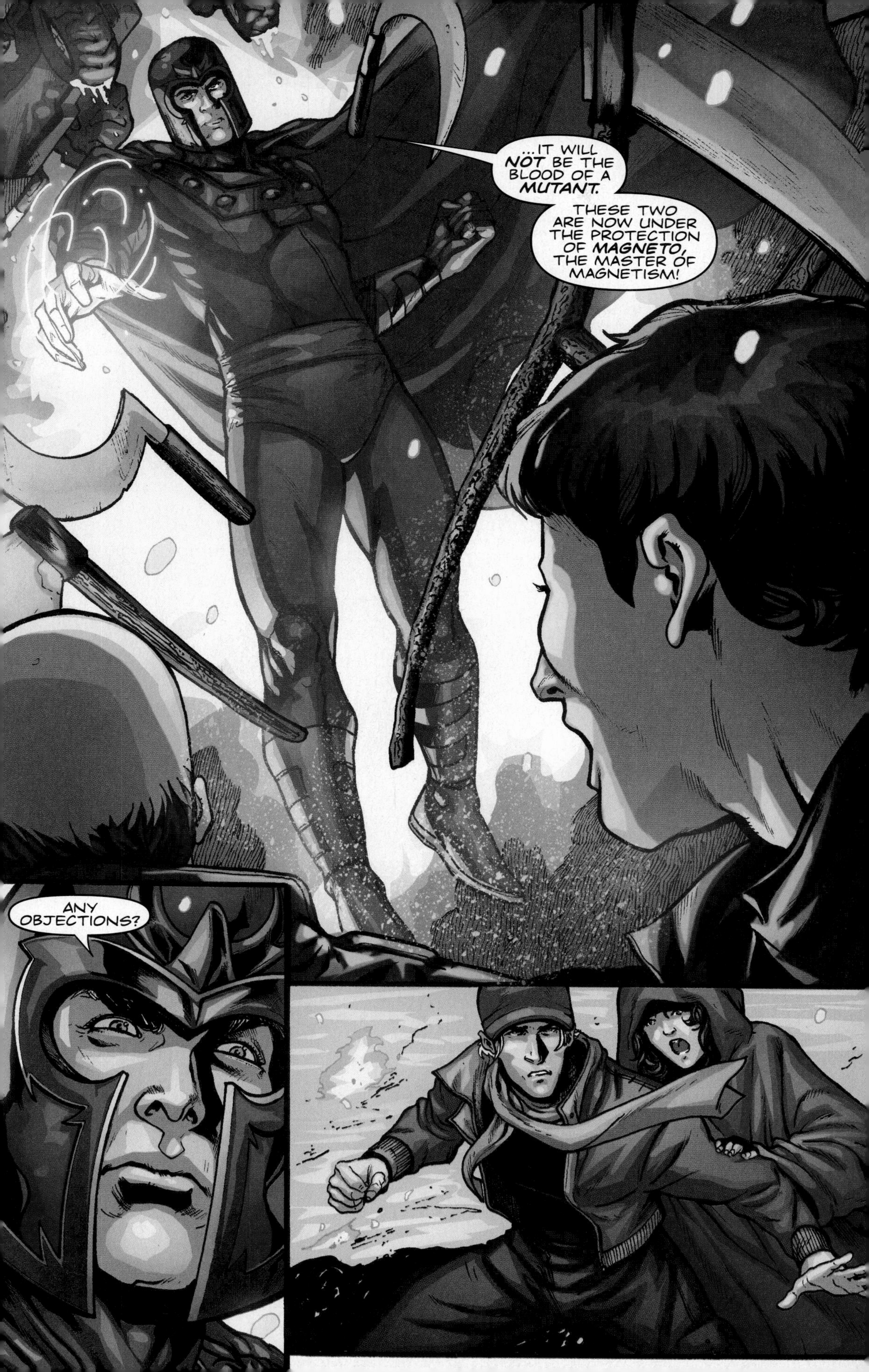
...IT WILL NOT BE THE BLOOD OF A MUTANT.
THESE TWO ARE NOW UNDER THE PROTECTION OF MAGNETO, THE MASTER OF MAGNETISM!
ANY OBJECTIONS?

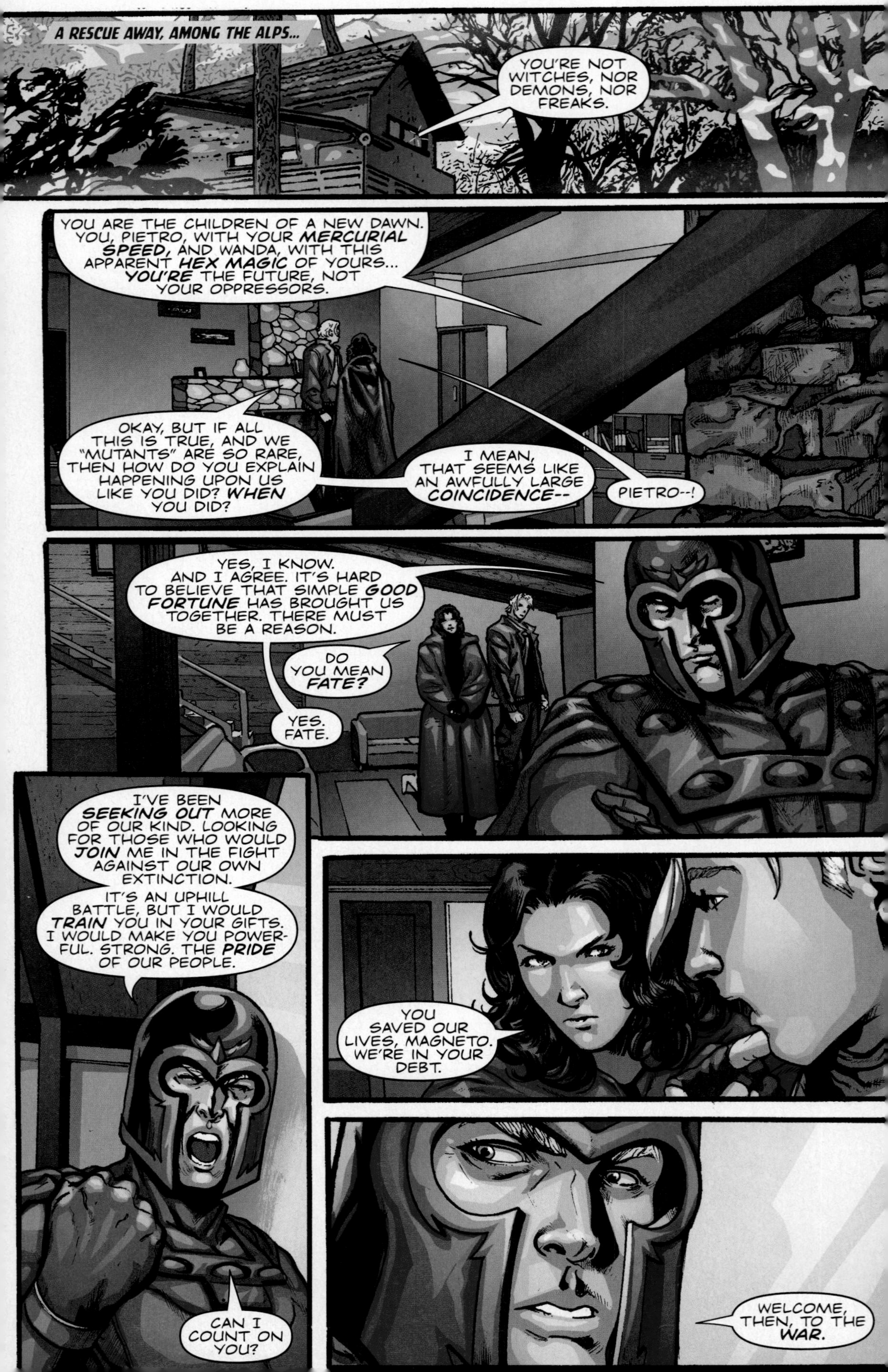
A RESCUE AWAY, AMONG THE ALPS...
YOU'RE NOT WITCHES, NOR DEMONS, NOR FREAKS.
YOU ARE THE CHILDREN OF A NEW DAWN. YOU, PIETRO, WITH YOUR MERCURIAL SPEED, AND WANDA, WITH THIS APPARENT HEX MAGIC OF YOURS... YOU'RE THE FUTURE, NOT YOUR OPPRESSORS.
OKAY, BUT IF ALL THIS IS TRUE, AND WE "MUTANTS" ARE SO RARE, THEN HOW DO YOU EXPLAIN HAPPENING UPON US LIKE YOU DID? WHEN YOU DID?
I MEAN, THAT SEEMS LIKE AN AWFULLY LARGE COINCIDENCE--
PIETRO--!
YES, I KNOW. AND I AGREE. IT'S HARD TO BELIEVE THAT SIMPLE GOOD FORTUNE HAS BROUGHT US TOGETHER. THERE MUST BE A REASON.
DO YOU MEAN FATE?
YES. FATE.
I'VE BEEN SEEKING OUT MORE OF OUR KIND. LOOKING FOR THOSE WHO WOULD JOIN ME IN THE FIGHT AGAINST OUR OWN EXTINCTION.
IT'S AN UPHILL BATTLE, BUT I WOULD TRAIN YOU IN YOUR GIFTS. I WOULD MAKE YOU POWER-FUL. STRONG. THE PRIDE OF OUR PEOPLE.
CAN I COUNT ON YOU?
YOU SAVED OUR LIVES, MAGNETO. WE'RE IN YOUR DEBT.
WELCOME, THEN, TO THE WAR.

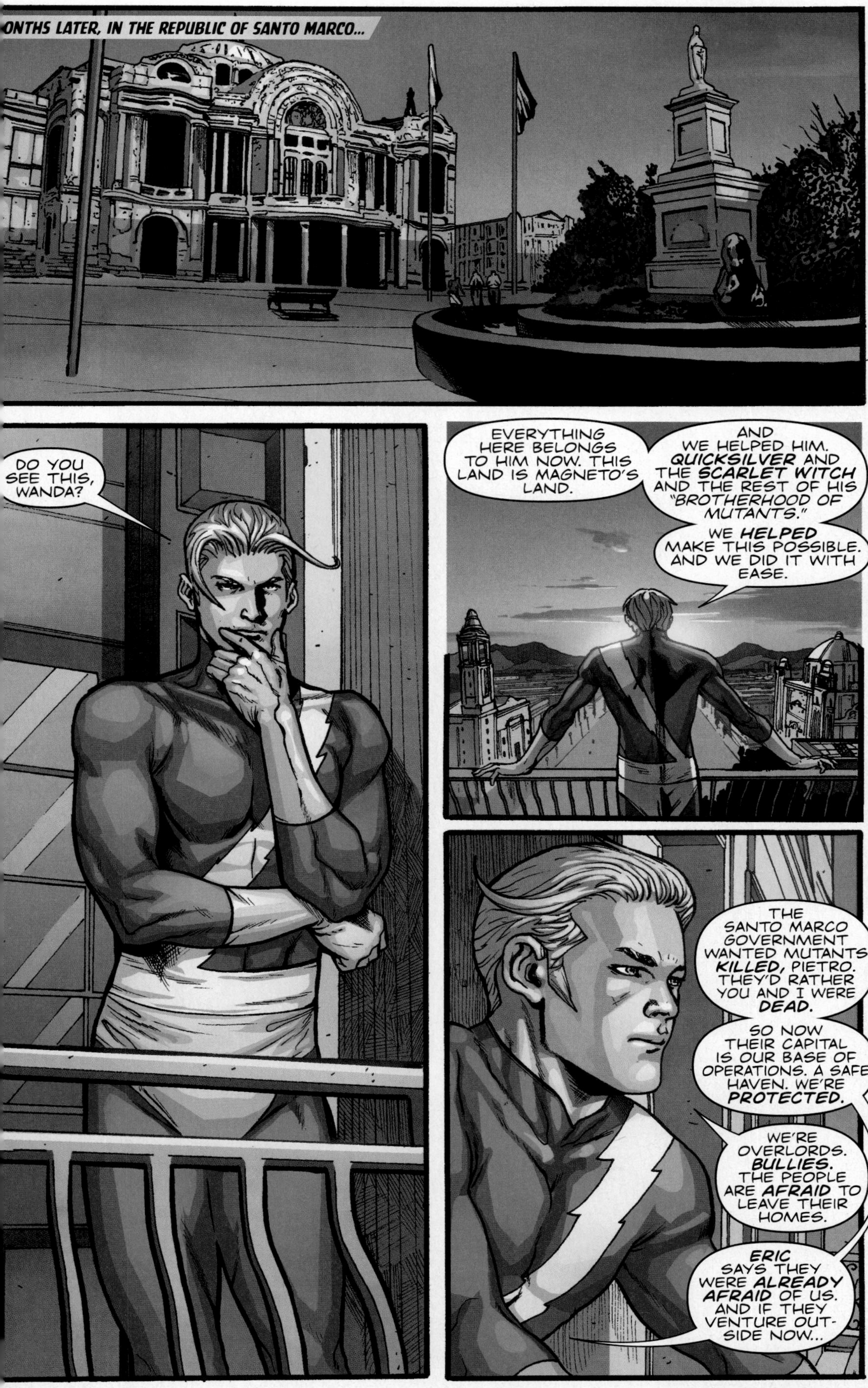

ONTHS LATER, IN THE REPUBLIC OF SANTO MARCO...
DO YOU SEE THIS, WANDA?
EVERYTHING HERE BELONGS TO HIM NOW. THIS LAND IS MAGNETO'S LAND.
AND WE HELPED HIM. QUICKSILVER AND THE SCARLET WITCH AND THE REST OF HIS "BROTHERHOOD OF MUTANTS."
WE HELPED MAKE THIS POSSIBLE. AND WE DID IT WITH EASE.
THE SANTO MARCO GOVERNMENT WANTED MUTANTS KILLED, PIETRO. THEY'D RATHER YOU AND I WERE DEAD.
SO NOW THEIR CAPITAL IS OUR BASE OF OPERATIONS. A SAFE HAVEN. WE'RE PROTECTED.
WE'RE OVERLORDS. BULLIES. THE PEOPLE ARE AFRAID TO LEAVE THEIR HOMES.
ERIC SAYS THEY WERE ALREADY AFRAID OF US. AND IF THEY VENTURE OUT-SIDE NOW...

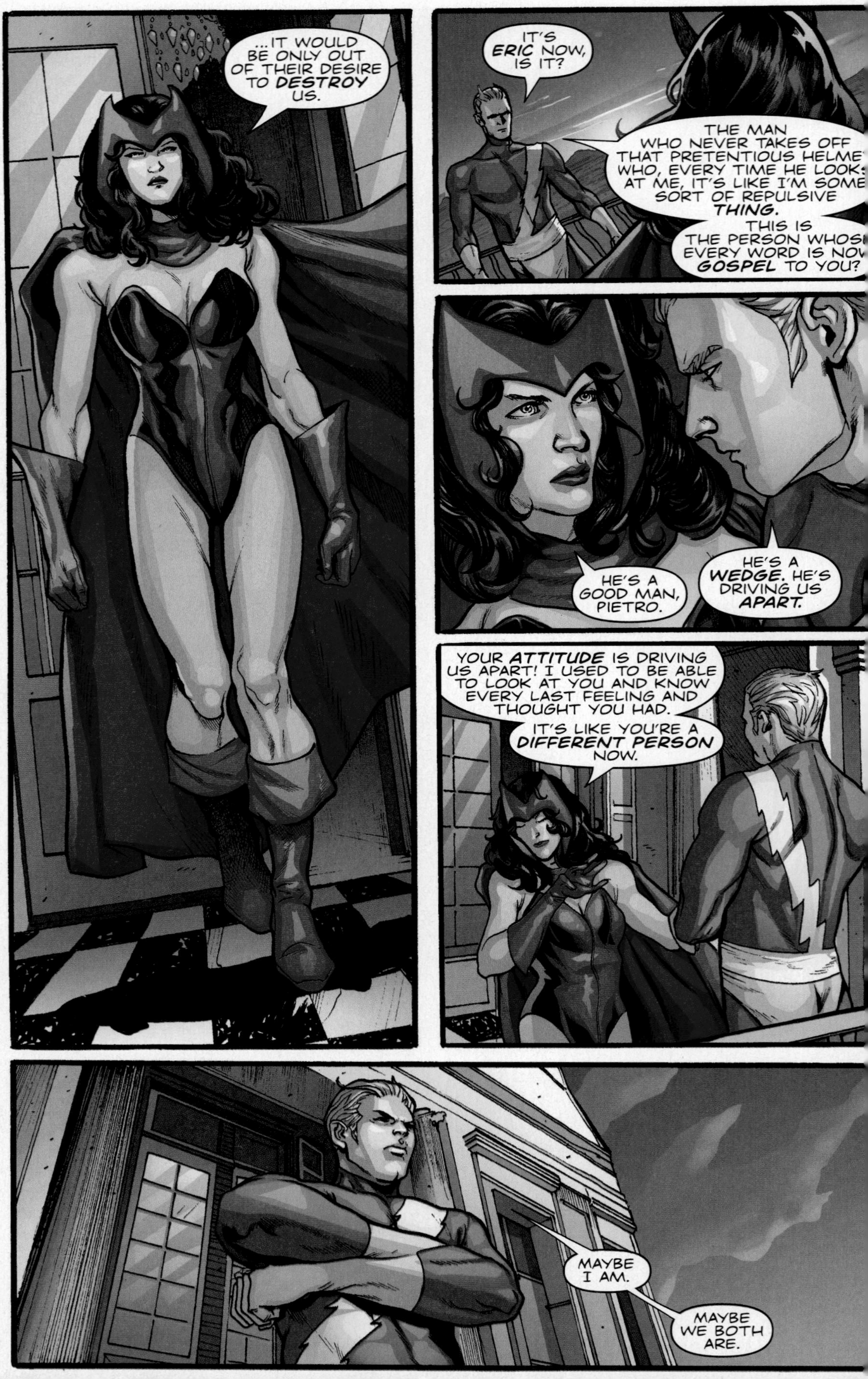
...IT WOULD BE ONLY OUT OF THEIR DESIRE TO DESTROY US.
IT'S ERIC NOW, IS IT?
THE MAN WHO NEVER TAKES OFF THAT PRETENTIOUS HELMET WHO, EVERY TIME HE LOOKS AT ME, IT'S LIKE I'M SOME SORT OF REPULSIVE THING.
THIS IS THE PERSON WHOSE EVERY WORD IS NOW GOSPEL TO YOU?
HE'S A GOOD MAN, PIETRO.
HE'S A WEDGE. HE'S DRIVING US APART.
YOUR ATTITUDE IS DRIVING US APART! I USED TO BE ABLE TO LOOK AT YOU AND KNOW EVERY LAST FEELING AND THOUGHT YOU HAD.
IT'S LIKE YOU'RE A DIFFERENT PERSON NOW.
MAYBE I AM.
MAYBE WE BOTH ARE.

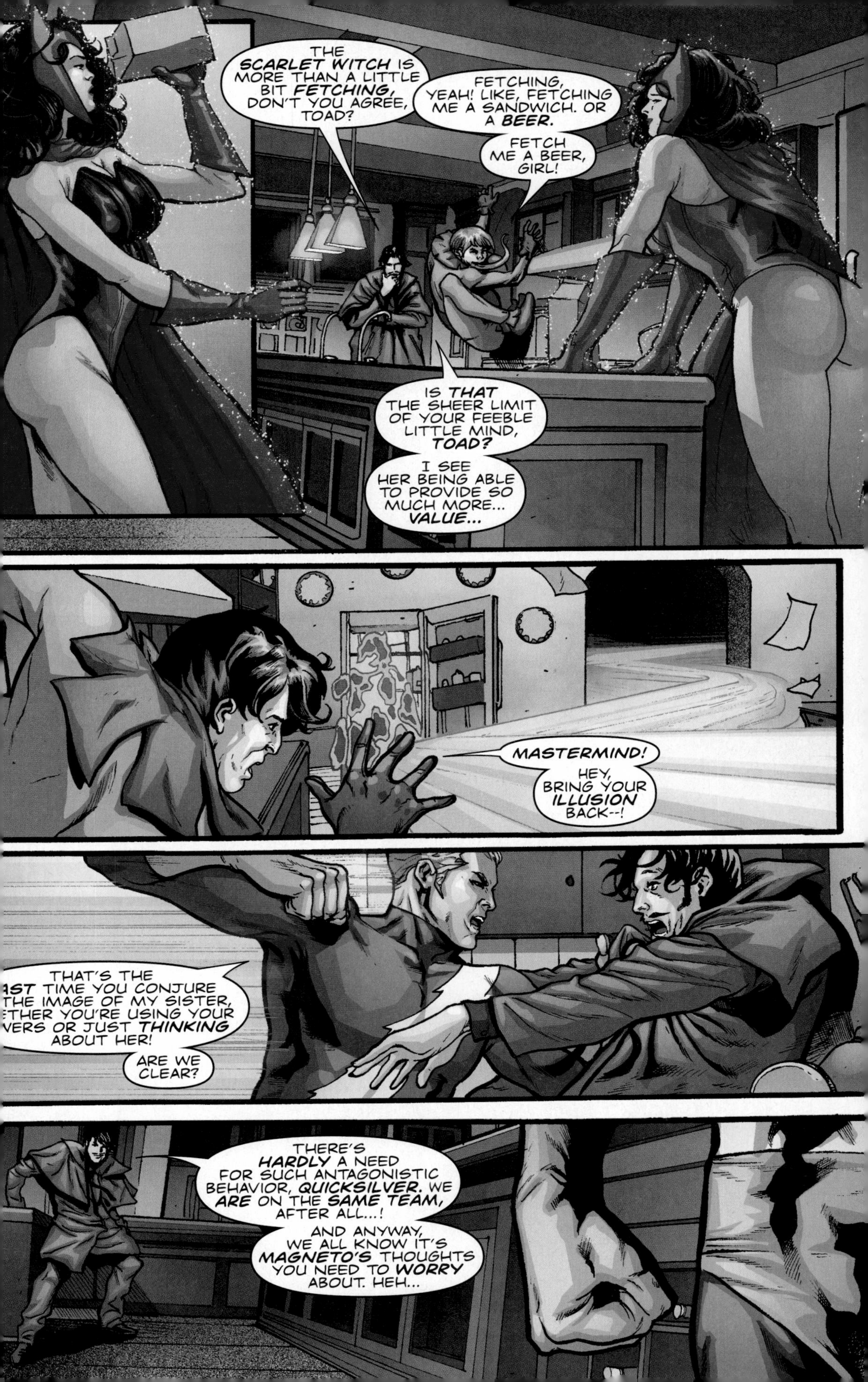
THE SCARLET WITCH IS MORE THAN A LITTLE BIT FETCHING, DON'T YOU AGREE, TOAD?
FETCHING, YEAH! LIKE, FETCHING ME A SANDWICH. OR A BEER.
FETCH ME A BEER, GIRL!
IS THAT THE SHEER LIMIT OF YOUR FEEBLE LITTLE MIND, TOAD?
I SEE HER BEING ABLE TO PROVIDE SO MUCH MORE... VALUE...
MASTERMIND!
HEY, BRING YOUR ILLUSION BACK--!
THAT'S THE AST TIME YOU CONJURE THE IMAGE OF MY SISTER, ETHER YOU'RE USING YOUR VERS OR JUST THINKING ABOUT HER!
ARE WE CLEAR?
THERE'S HARDLY A NEED FOR SUCH ANTAGONISTIC BEHAVIOR, QUICKSILVER. WE ARE ON THE SAME TEAM, AFTER ALL...!
AND ANYWAY, WE ALL KNOW IT'S MAGNETO'S THOUGHTS YOU NEED TO WORRY ABOUT. HEH...

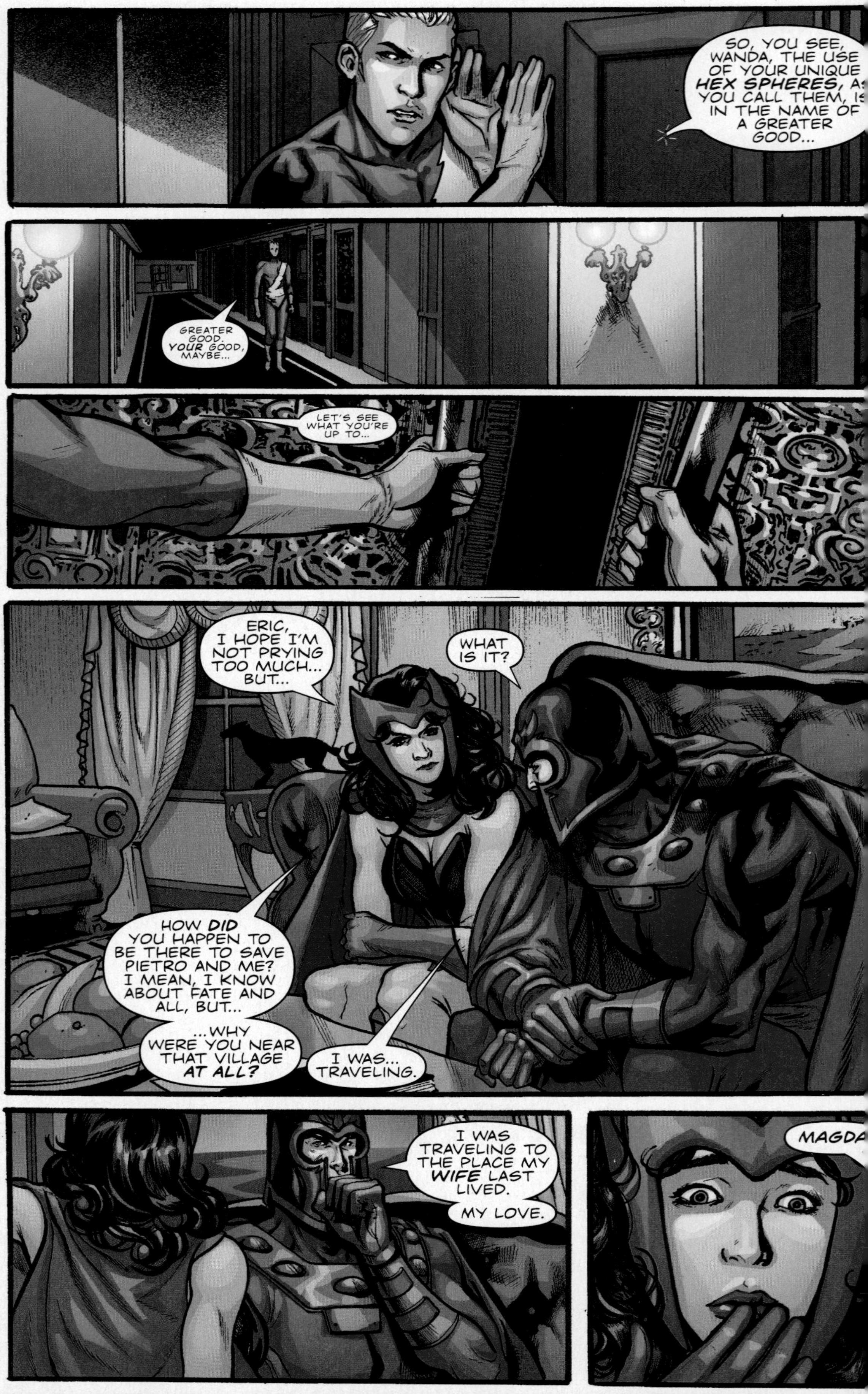
SO, YOU SEE, WANDA, THE USE OF YOUR UNIQUE **HEX SPHERES,** AS YOU CALL THEM, IS IN THE NAME OF A GREATER GOOD...
GREATER GOOD. **YOUR** GOOD, MAYBE...
LET'S SEE WHAT YOU'RE UP TO...
ERIC, I HOPE I'M NOT PRYING TOO MUCH... BUT...
WHAT IS IT?
HOW **DID** YOU HAPPEN TO BE THERE TO SAVE PIETRO AND ME? I MEAN, I KNOW ABOUT FATE AND ALL, BUT...
...WHY WERE YOU NEAR THAT VILLAGE **AT ALL?**
I WAS... TRAVELING.
I WAS TRAVELING TO THE PLACE MY **WIFE** LAST LIVED.
MY LOVE.
MAGDA

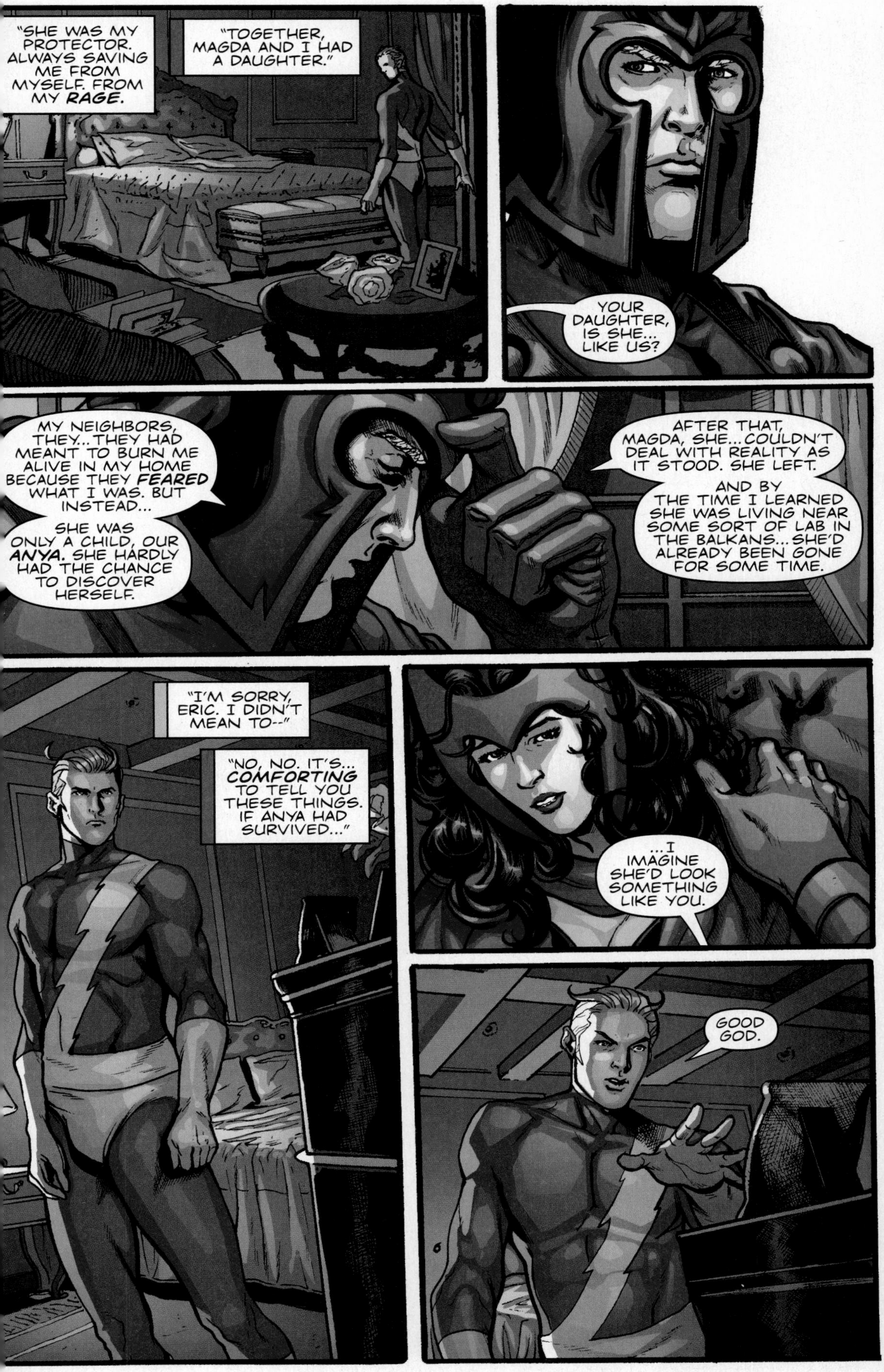
"SHE WAS MY PROTECTOR. ALWAYS SAVING ME FROM MYSELF. FROM MY RAGE.
"TOGETHER, MAGDA AND I HAD A DAUGHTER."
YOUR DAUGHTER, IS SHE... LIKE US?
MY NEIGHBORS, THEY... THEY HAD MEANT TO BURN ME ALIVE IN MY HOME BECAUSE THEY FEARED WHAT I WAS. BUT INSTEAD...
SHE WAS ONLY A CHILD, OUR ANYA. SHE HARDLY HAD THE CHANCE TO DISCOVER HERSELF.
AFTER THAT, MAGDA, SHE... COULDN'T DEAL WITH REALITY AS IT STOOD. SHE LEFT.
AND BY THE TIME I LEARNED SHE WAS LIVING NEAR SOME SORT OF LAB IN THE BALKANS... SHE'D ALREADY BEEN GONE FOR SOME TIME.
"I'M SORRY, ERIC. I DIDN'T MEAN TO--"
"NO, NO. IT'S... COMFORTING TO TELL YOU THESE THINGS. IF ANYA HAD SURVIVED..."
...I IMAGINE SHE'D LOOK SOMETHING LIKE YOU.
GOOD GOD.

TAKE YOUR HAND FROM MY SISTER AND *EXPLAIN* YOURSELF!

YOUR TONE--

--SHOULD BE THE *LEAST* OF YOUR WORRIES RIGHT NOW. TAKE THAT *HELMET* OFF AND SHOW HER.

SHOW ME? WHAT?

I CAN'T DO THAT, CHILD. THIS HELMET *PROTECTS* ME--PROTECTS US *ALL* FROM--

DO IT.

PIETRO, YOU'RE ACTING *CRAZY*--

DO IT *NOW,* OR WE *LEAVE* THIS *VERY* SECOND!

PIETRO!

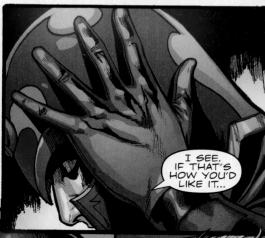

I SEE. IF THAT'S HOW YOU'D LIKE IT...

YOU'LL FIND I HAVE NOTHING TO HIDE, WANDA.

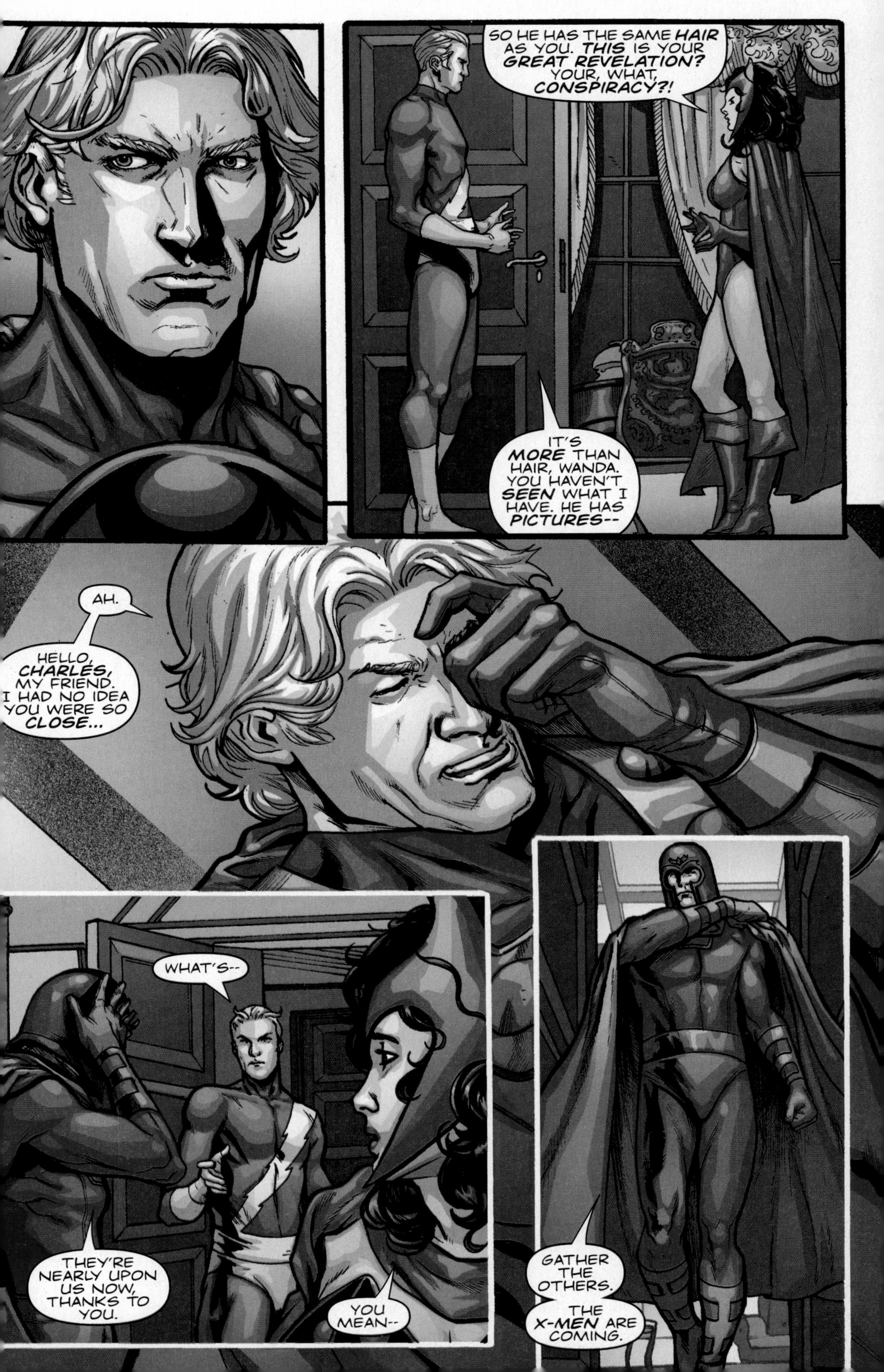
SO HE HAS THE SAME HAIR AS YOU. THIS IS YOUR GREAT REVELATION? YOUR, WHAT, CONSPIRACY?!
IT'S MORE THAN HAIR, WANDA. YOU HAVEN'T SEEN WHAT I HAVE. HE HAS PICTURES--
AH.
HELLO, CHARLES, MY FRIEND. I HAD NO IDEA YOU WERE SO CLOSE...
WHAT'S--
THEY'RE NEARLY UPON US NOW, THANKS TO YOU.
YOU MEAN--
GATHER THE OTHERS.
THE X-MEN ARE COMING.

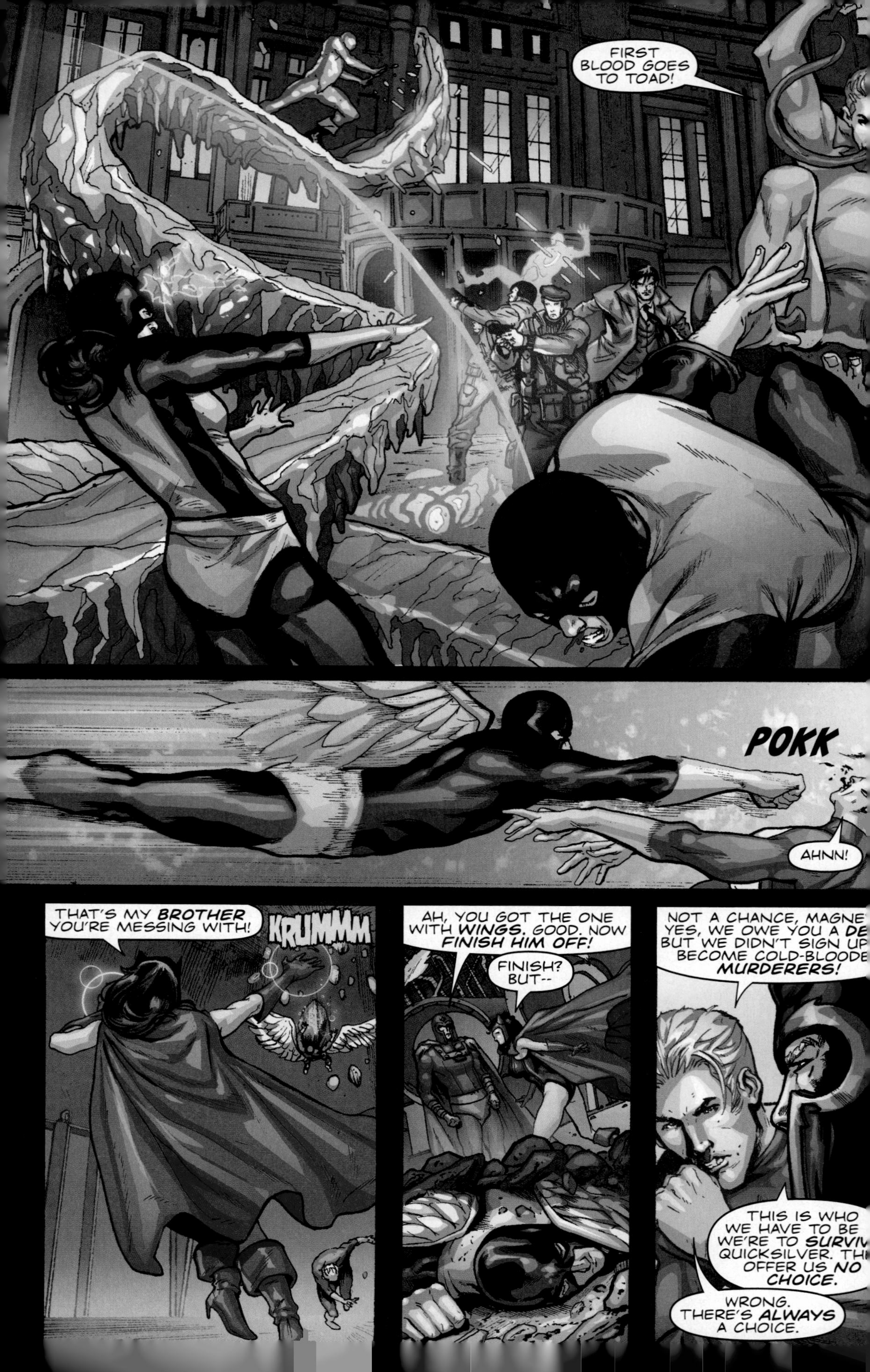
FIRST BLOOD GOES TO TOAD!
POKK
AHNN!
THAT'S MY BROTHER YOU'RE MESSING WITH!
KRUMMM
AH, YOU GOT THE ONE WITH WINGS. GOOD. NOW FINISH HIM OFF!
FINISH? BUT--
NOT A CHANCE, MAGNE
YES, WE OWE YOU A DE
BUT WE DIDN'T SIGN UP
BECOME COLD-BLOODE
MURDERERS!
THIS IS WHO WE HAVE TO BE
WE'RE TO SURVIV
QUICKSILVER. TH
OFFER US NO CHOICE.
WRONG. THERE'S ALWAYS A CHOICE.

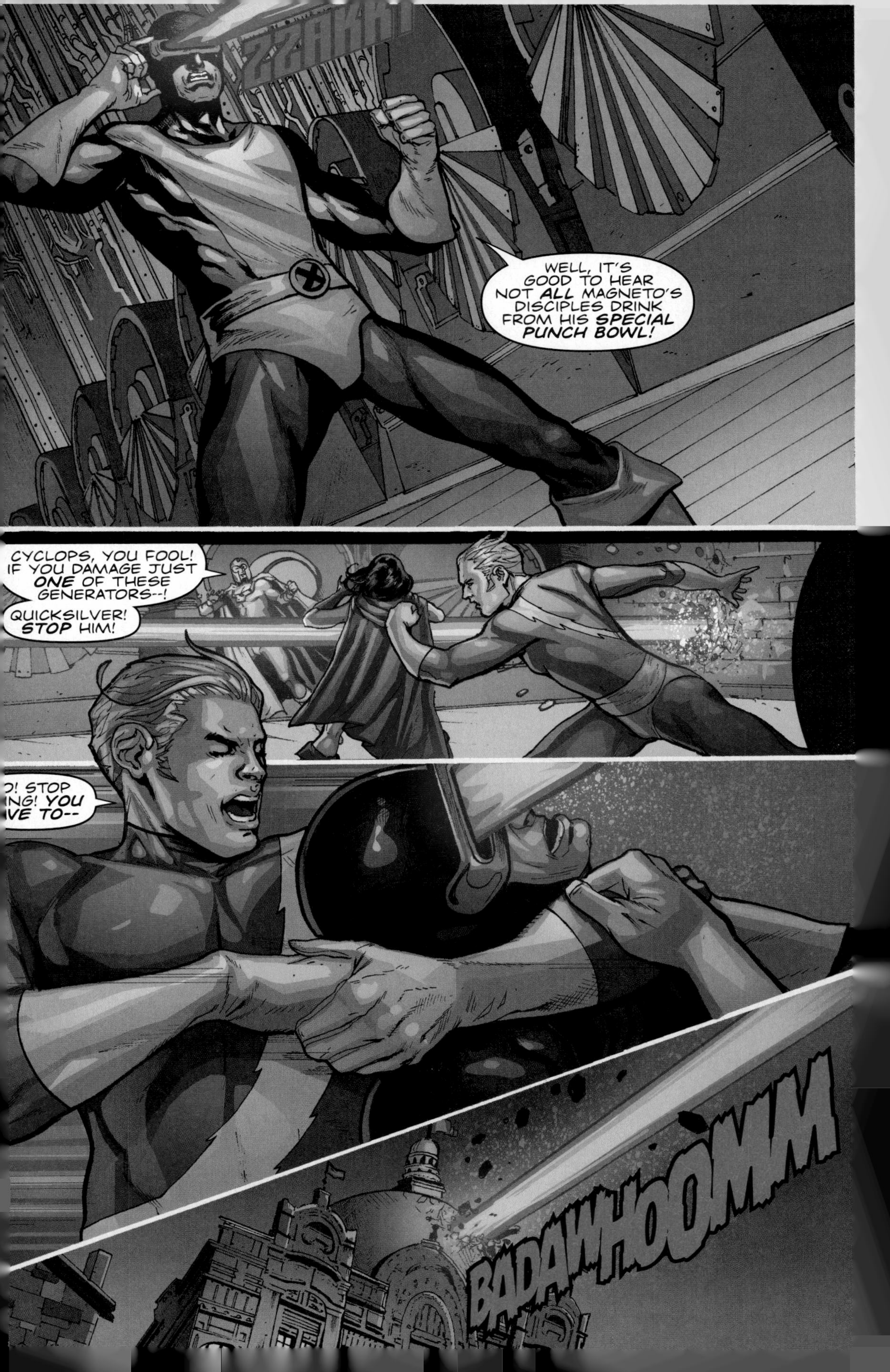
ZZAKKT
WELL, IT'S GOOD TO HEAR NOT ALL MAGNETO'S DISCIPLES DRINK FROM HIS SPECIAL PUNCH BOWL!
CYCLOPS, YOU FOOL! IF YOU DAMAGE JUST ONE OF THESE GENERATORS--!
QUICKSILVER! STOP HIM!
O! STOP NG! YOU VE TO--
BADAWHOOMM

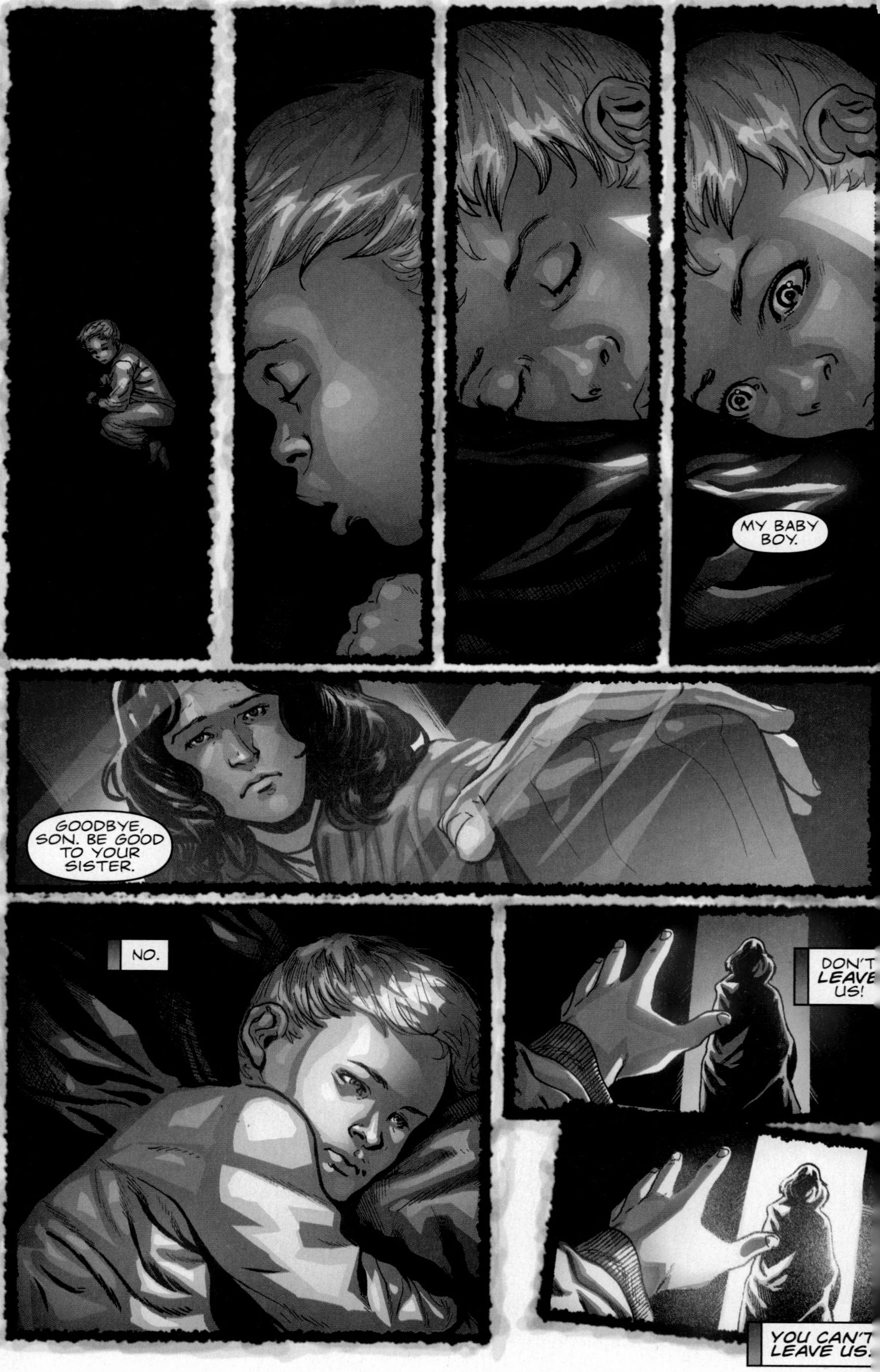
MY BABY BOY.
GOODBYE, SON. BE GOOD TO YOUR SISTER.
NO.
DON'T LEAVE US!
YOU CAN'T LEAVE US.

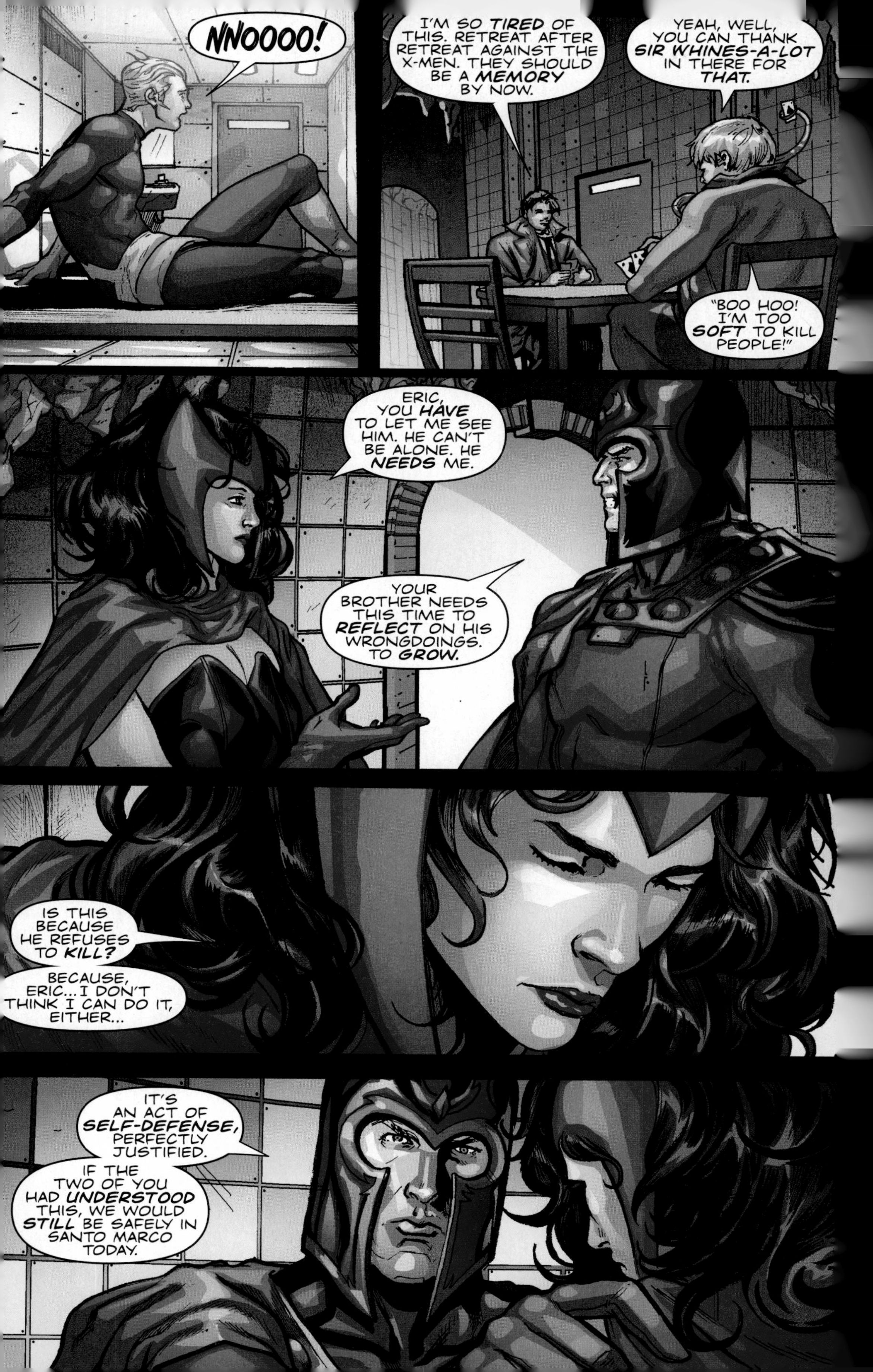
NNOOOO!
I'M SO TIRED OF THIS. RETREAT AFTER RETREAT AGAINST THE X-MEN. THEY SHOULD BE A MEMORY BY NOW.
YEAH, WELL, YOU CAN THANK SIR WHINES-A-LOT IN THERE FOR THAT.
"BOO HOO! I'M TOO SOFT TO KILL PEOPLE!"
ERIC, YOU HAVE TO LET ME SEE HIM. HE CAN'T BE ALONE. HE NEEDS ME.
YOUR BROTHER NEEDS THIS TIME TO REFLECT ON HIS WRONGDOINGS. TO GROW.
IS THIS BECAUSE HE REFUSES TO KILL?
BECAUSE, ERIC... I DON'T THINK I CAN DO IT, EITHER...
IT'S AN ACT OF SELF-DEFENSE, PERFECTLY JUSTIFIED.
IF THE TWO OF YOU HAD UNDERSTOOD THIS, WE WOULD STILL BE SAFELY IN SANTO MARCO TODAY.

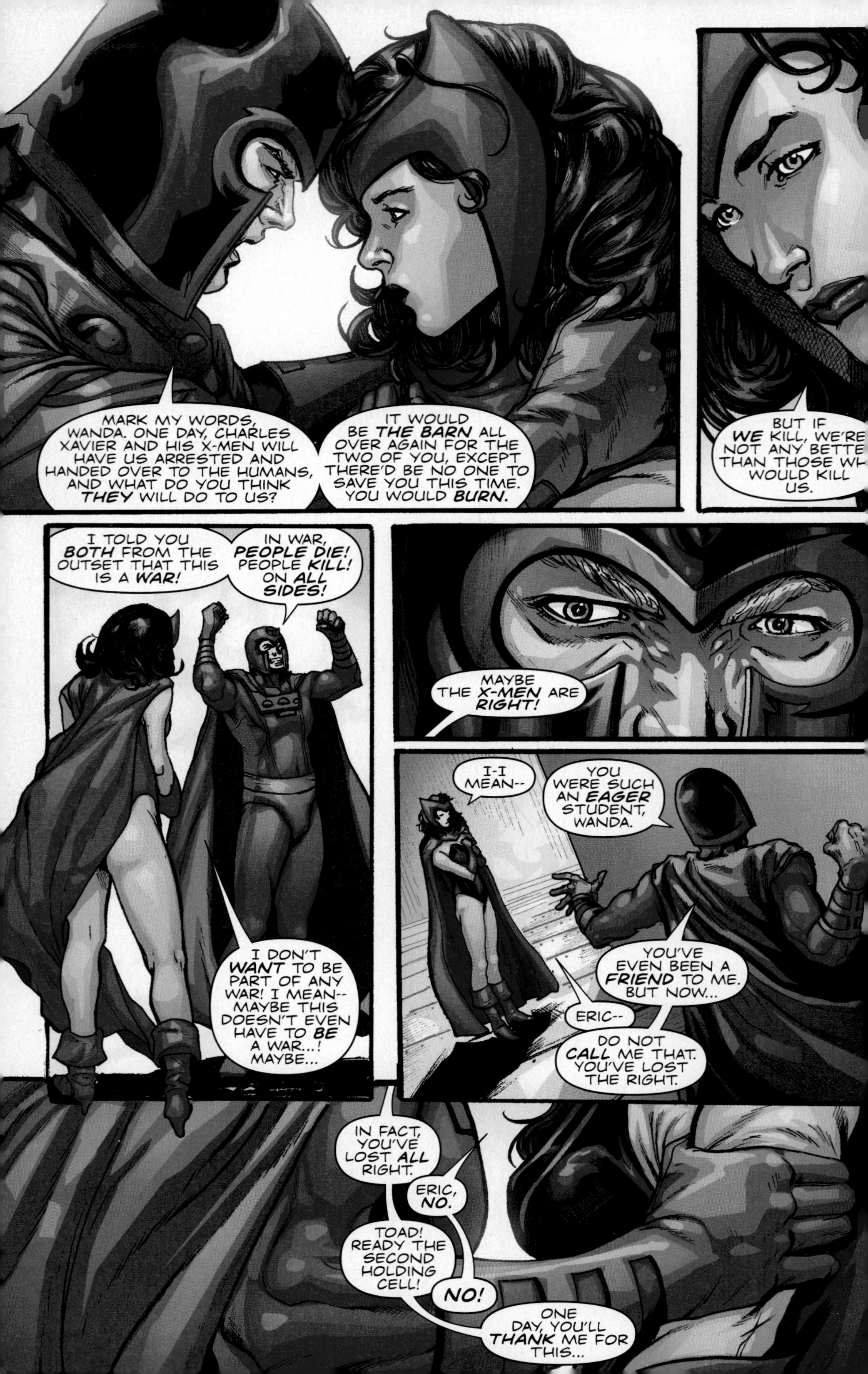
MARK MY WORDS, WANDA. ONE DAY, CHARLES XAVIER AND HIS X-MEN WILL HAVE US ARRESTED AND HANDED OVER TO THE HUMANS, AND WHAT DO YOU THINK THEY WILL DO TO US?
IT WOULD BE THE BARN ALL OVER AGAIN FOR THE TWO OF YOU, EXCEPT THERE'D BE NO ONE TO SAVE YOU THIS TIME. YOU WOULD BURN.
BUT IF WE KILL, WE'RE NOT ANY BETTE THAN THOSE WH WOULD KILL US.
I TOLD YOU BOTH FROM THE OUTSET THAT THIS IS A WAR!
IN WAR, PEOPLE DIE! PEOPLE KILL! ON ALL SIDES!
I DON'T WANT TO BE PART OF ANY WAR! I MEAN-- MAYBE THIS DOESN'T EVEN HAVE TO BE A WAR...! MAYBE...
MAYBE THE X-MEN ARE RIGHT!
I-I MEAN--
YOU WERE SUCH AN EAGER STUDENT, WANDA.
YOU'VE EVEN BEEN A FRIEND TO ME. BUT NOW...
ERIC--
DO NOT CALL ME THAT. YOU'VE LOST THE RIGHT.
IN FACT, YOU'VE LOST ALL RIGHT.
ERIC, NO.
TOAD! READY THE SECOND HOLDING CELL!
NO!
ONE DAY, YOU'LL THANK ME FOR THIS...

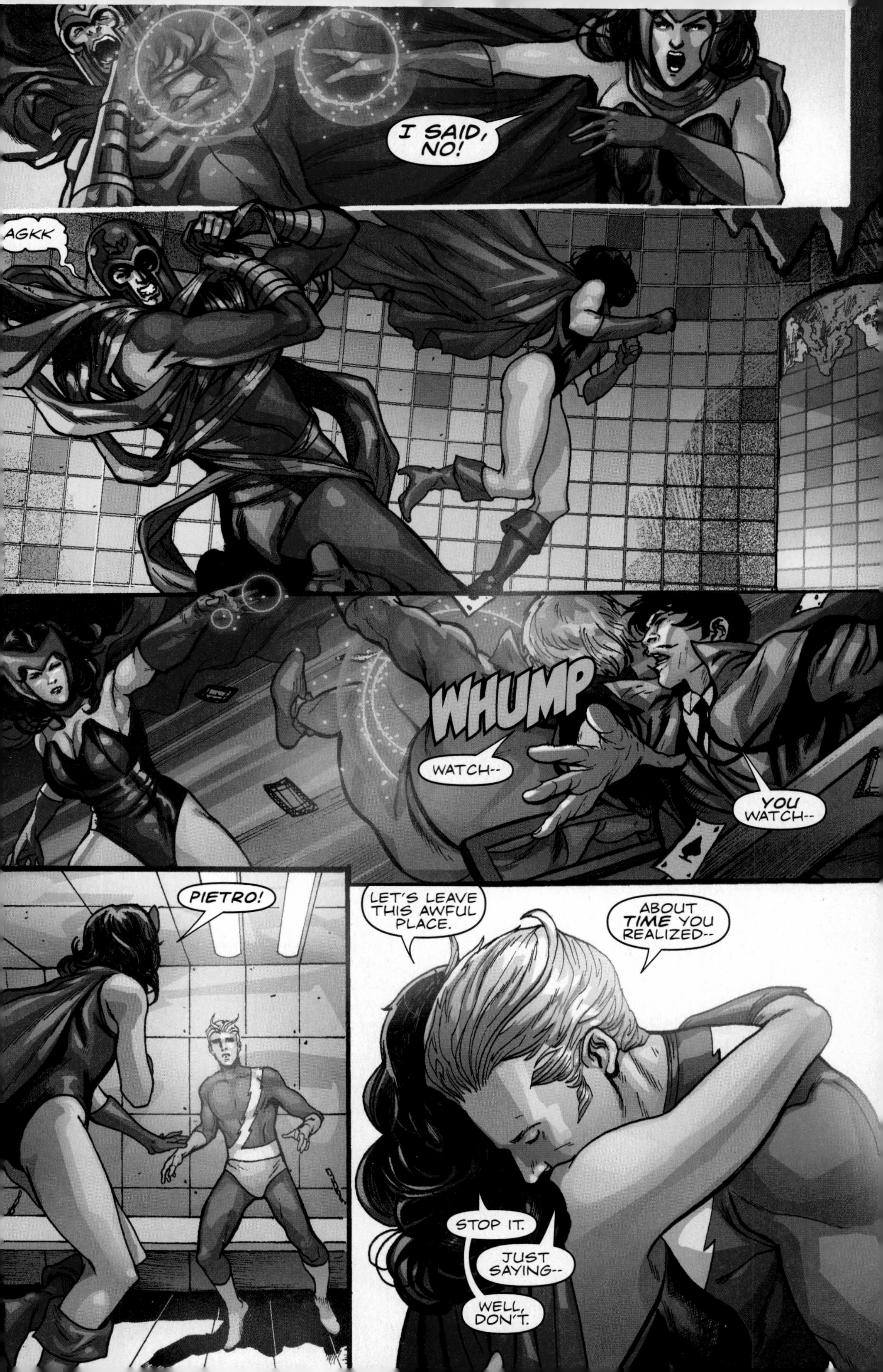
I SAID, NO!
AGKK
WHUMP
WATCH--
YOU WATCH--
PIETRO!
LET'S LEAVE THIS AWFUL PLACE.
ABOUT TIME YOU REALIZED--
STOP IT.
JUST SAYING--
WELL, DON'T.

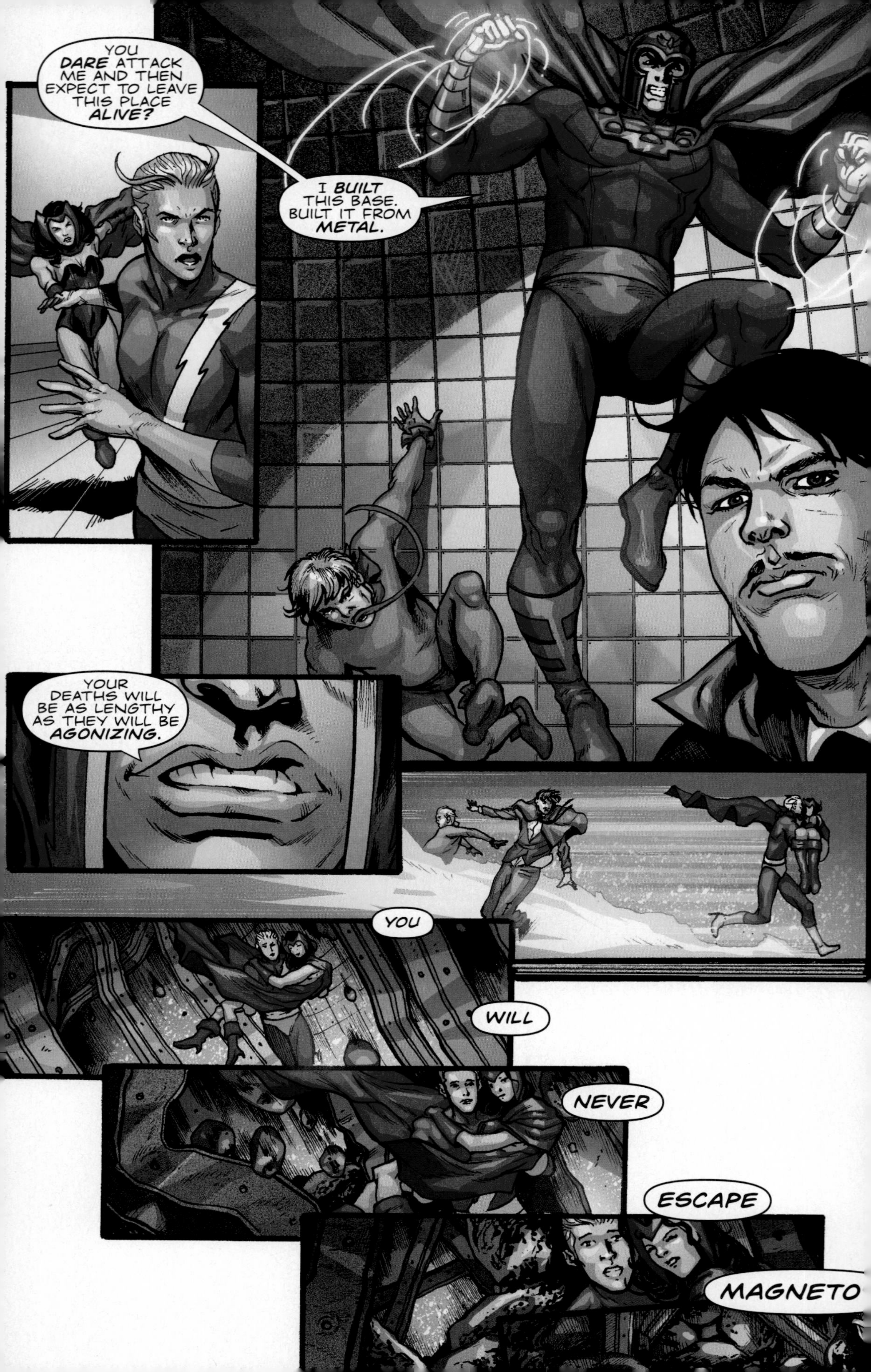
YOU DARE ATTACK ME AND THEN EXPECT TO LEAVE THIS PLACE ALIVE?
I BUILT THIS BASE. BUILT IT FROM METAL.
YOUR DEATHS WILL BE AS LENGTHY AS THEY WILL BE AGONIZING.
YOU
WILL
NEVER
ESCAPE
MAGNETO

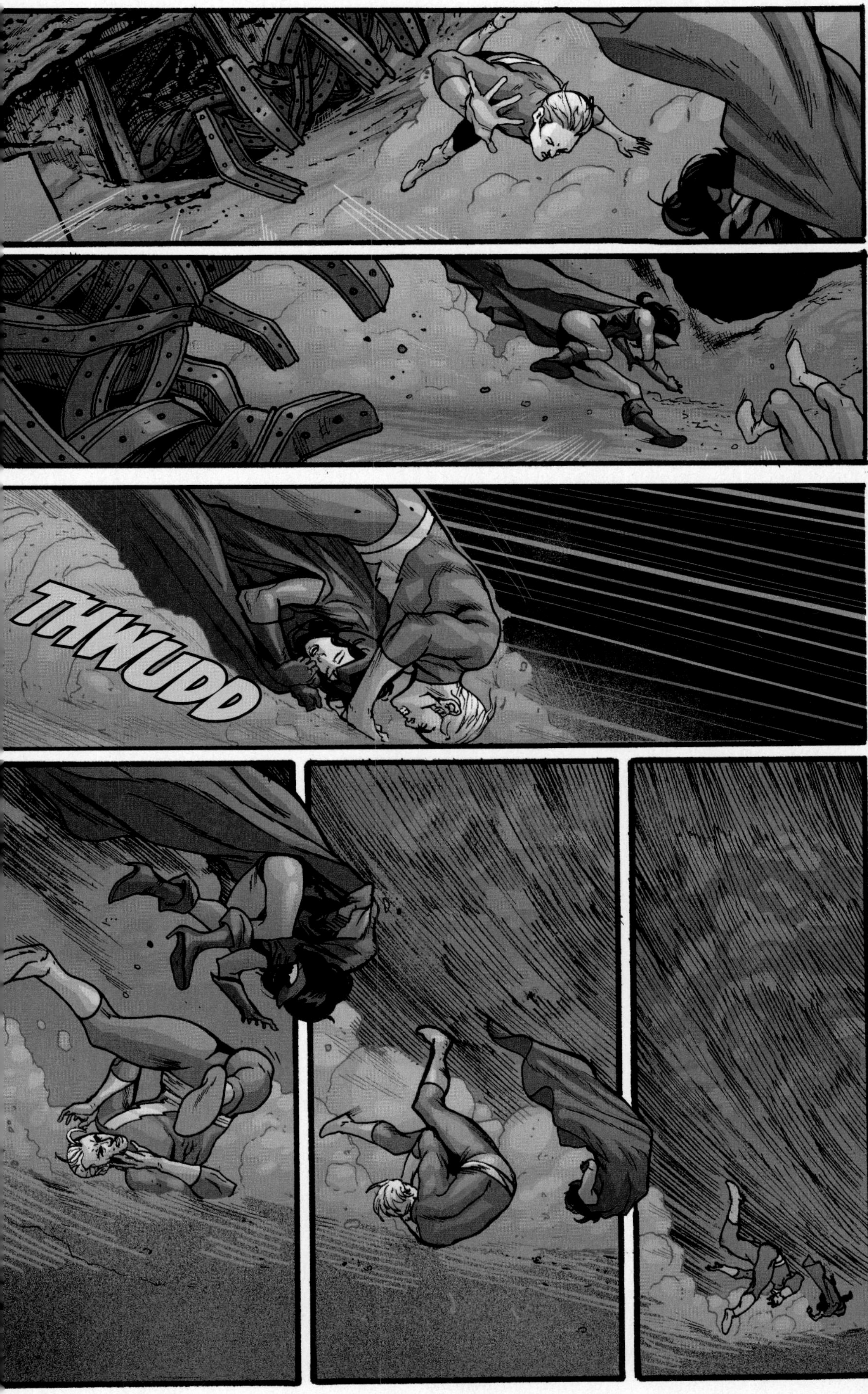
THWUDD

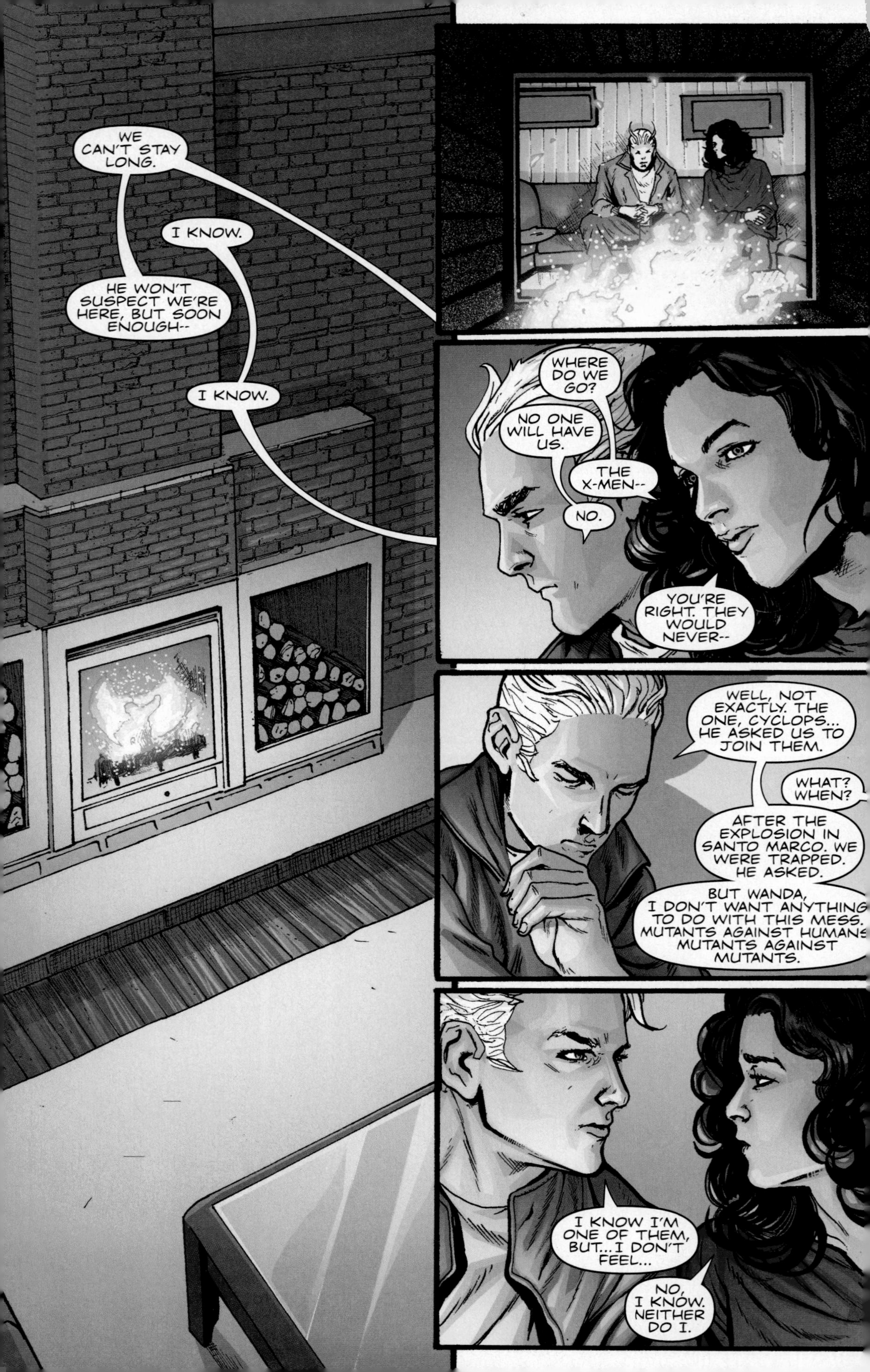
WE CAN'T STAY LONG.
I KNOW.
HE WON'T SUSPECT WE'RE HERE, BUT SOON ENOUGH--
I KNOW.
WHERE DO WE GO?
NO ONE WILL HAVE US.
THE X-MEN--
NO.
YOU'RE RIGHT. THEY WOULD NEVER--
WELL, NOT EXACTLY. THE ONE, CYCLOPS... HE ASKED US TO JOIN THEM.
WHAT? WHEN?
AFTER THE EXPLOSION IN SANTO MARCO. WE WERE TRAPPED. HE ASKED.
BUT WANDA, I DON'T WANT ANYTHING TO DO WITH THIS MESS. MUTANTS AGAINST HUMANS. MUTANTS AGAINST MUTANTS.
I KNOW I'M ONE OF THEM, BUT...I DON'T FEEL...
NO, I KNOW. NEITHER DO I.

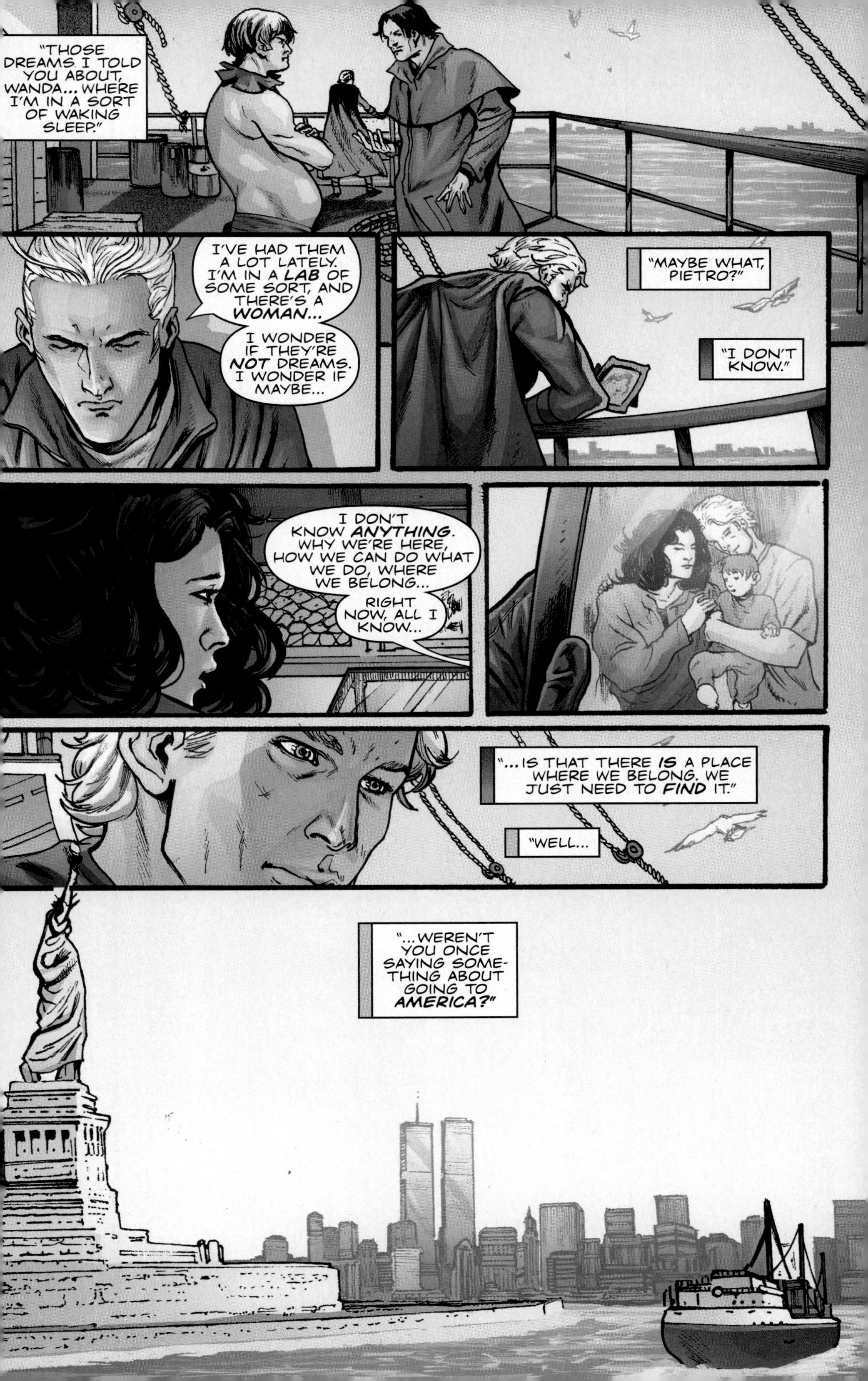
"THOSE DREAMS I TOLD YOU ABOUT, WANDA... WHERE I'M IN A SORT OF WAKING SLEEP."
I'VE HAD THEM A LOT LATELY. I'M IN A LAB OF SOME SORT, AND THERE'S A WOMAN...
I WONDER IF THEY'RE NOT DREAMS. I WONDER IF MAYBE...
"MAYBE WHAT, PIETRO?"
"I DON'T KNOW."
I DON'T KNOW ANYTHING. WHY WE'RE HERE, HOW WE CAN DO WHAT WE DO, WHERE WE BELONG...
RIGHT NOW, ALL I KNOW...
"...IS THAT THERE IS A PLACE WHERE WE BELONG. WE JUST NEED TO FIND IT."
"WELL...
"...WEREN'T YOU ONCE SAYING SOMETHING ABOUT GOING TO AMERICA?"

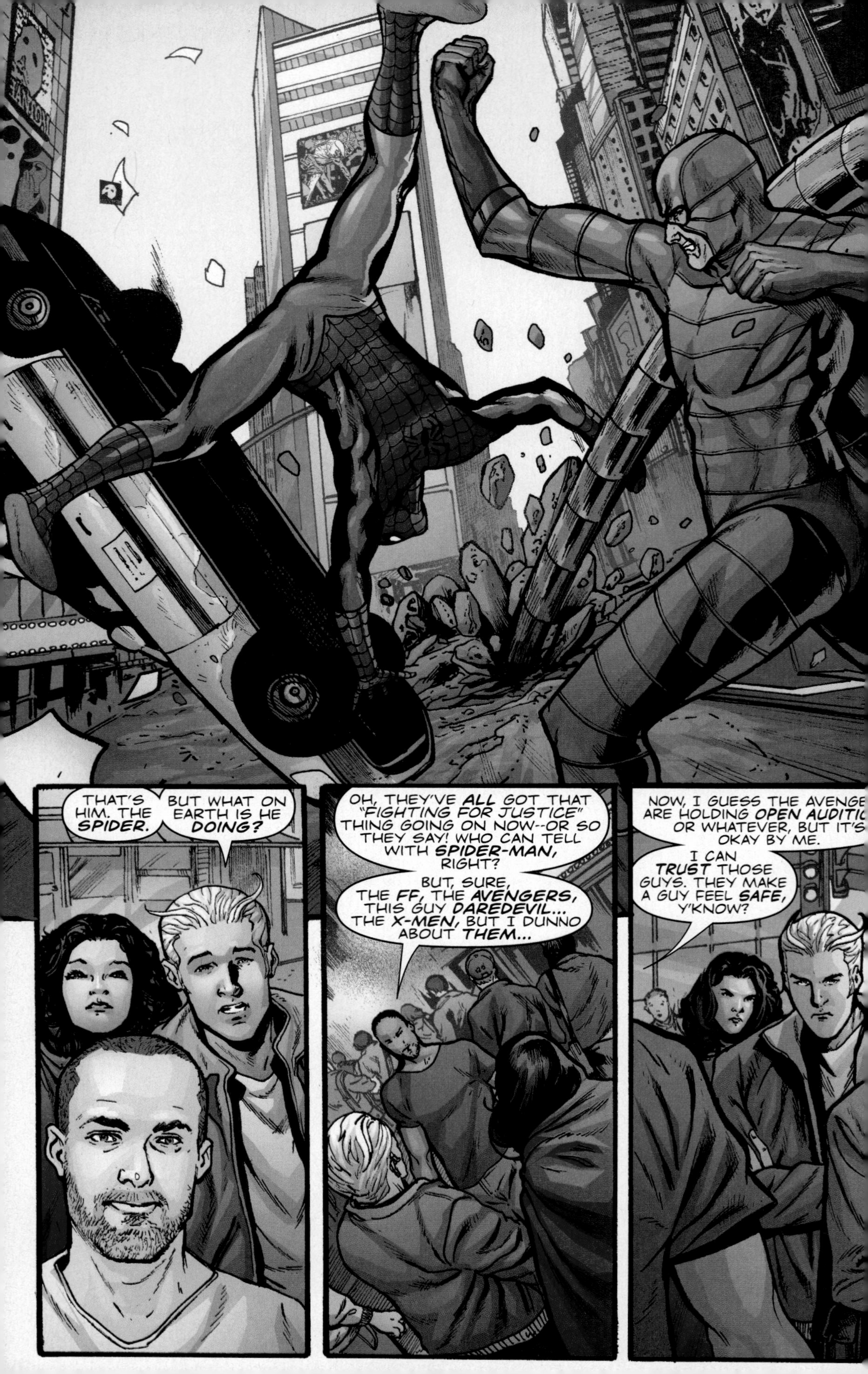

THAT'S HIM. THE SPIDER.
BUT WHAT ON EARTH IS HE DOING?
OH, THEY'VE ALL GOT THAT "FIGHTING FOR JUSTICE" THING GOING ON NOW--OR SO THEY SAY! WHO CAN TELL WITH SPIDER-MAN, RIGHT?
BUT, SURE, THE FF, THE AVENGERS, THIS GUY DAREDEVIL... THE X-MEN, BUT I DUNNO ABOUT THEM...
NOW, I GUESS THE AVENGE ARE HOLDING OPEN AUDITI OR WHATEVER, BUT IT'S OKAY BY ME.
I CAN TRUST THOSE GUYS. THEY MAKE A GUY FEEL SAFE, Y'KNOW?

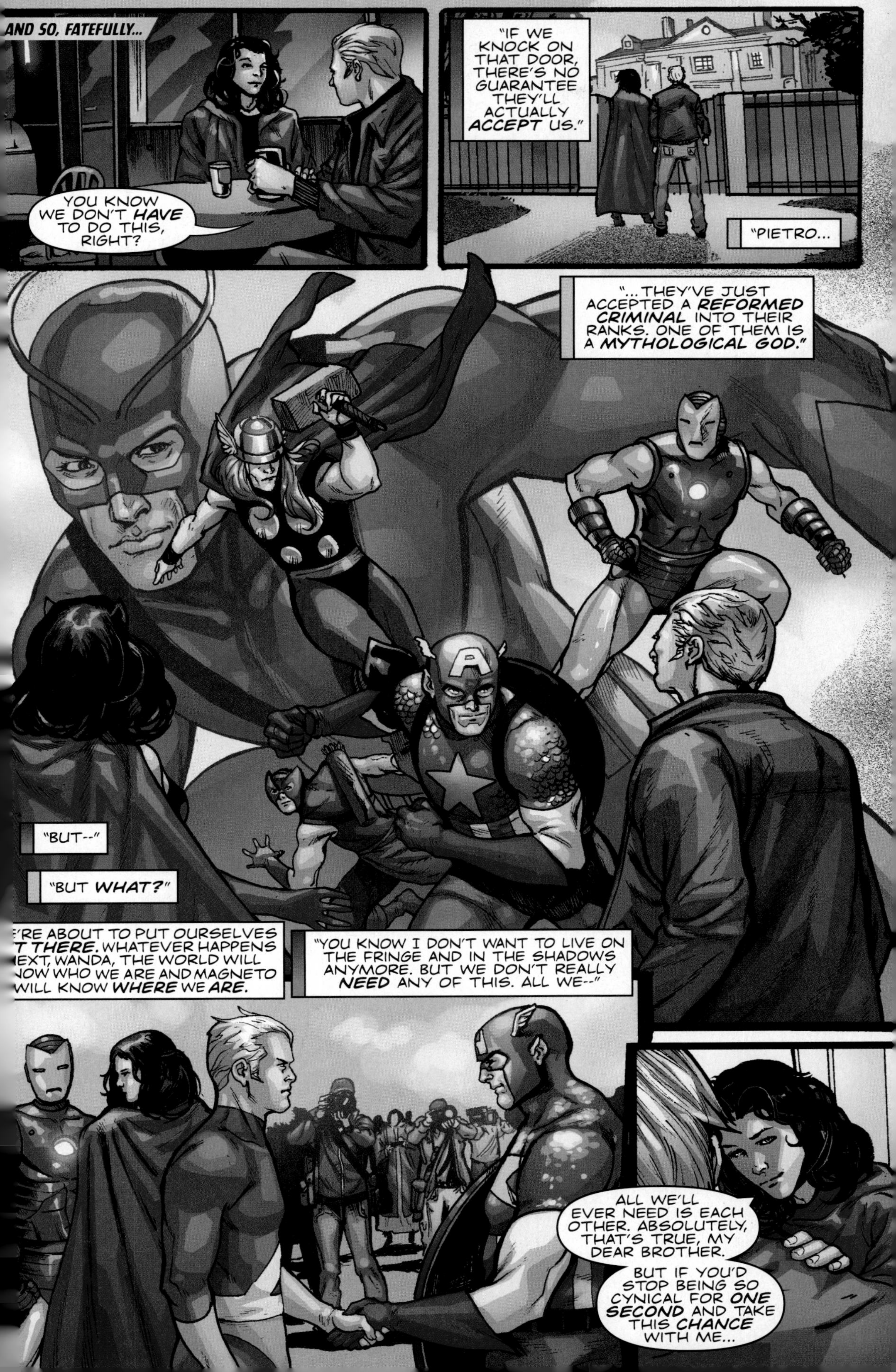

AND SO, FATEFULLY...
YOU KNOW WE DON'T HAVE TO DO THIS, RIGHT?
"IF WE KNOCK ON THAT DOOR, THERE'S NO GUARANTEE THEY'LL ACTUALLY ACCEPT US."
"PIETRO...
"...THEY'VE JUST ACCEPTED A REFORMED CRIMINAL INTO THEIR RANKS. ONE OF THEM IS A MYTHOLOGICAL GOD."
"BUT--"
"BUT WHAT?"
'RE ABOUT TO PUT OURSELVES T THERE. WHATEVER HAPPENS EXT, WANDA, THE WORLD WILL OW WHO WE ARE AND MAGNETO WILL KNOW WHERE WE ARE.
"YOU KNOW I DON'T WANT TO LIVE ON THE FRINGE AND IN THE SHADOWS ANYMORE. BUT WE DON'T REALLY NEED ANY OF THIS. ALL WE--"
ALL WE'LL EVER NEED IS EACH OTHER. ABSOLUTELY, THAT'S TRUE, MY DEAR BROTHER.
BUT IF YOU'D STOP BEING SO CYNICAL FOR ONE SECOND AND TAKE THIS CHANCE WITH ME...

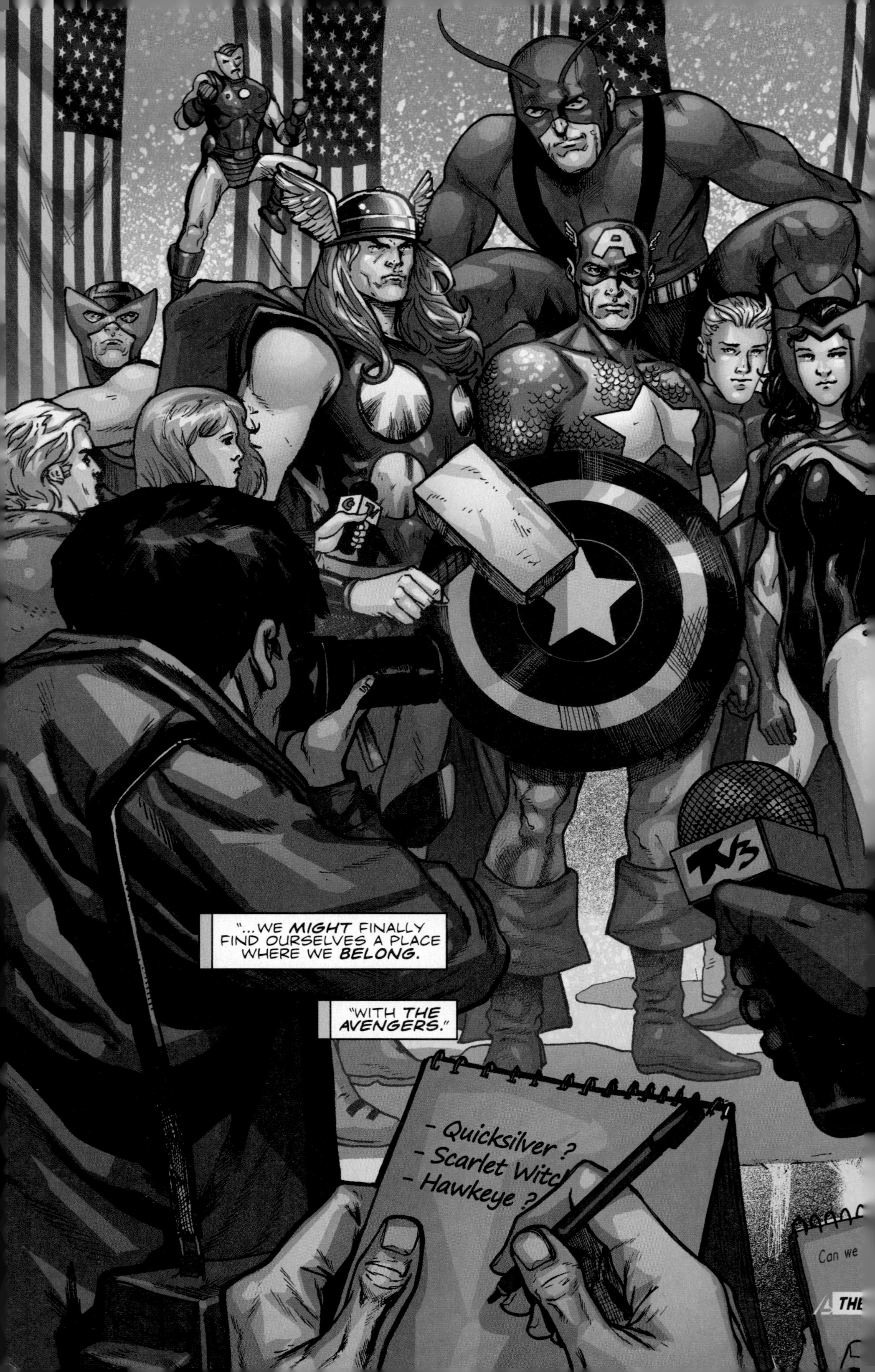
"...WE **MIGHT** FINALLY FIND OURSELVES A PLACE WHERE WE **BELONG.**
"WITH **THE AVENGERS.**"
- Quicksilver ?
- Scarlet Witc
- Hawkeye ?
Can we
THE

NEW COSTUMES AND SOLO FLIGHTS

On the heels of **SPIDER-WOMAN**, two other members of the **AVENGERS WEST COAST** will star in their own four-issue limited series beginning in November.

SCARLET WITCH will introduce a newly bold, self-assured Witch, clad in an all-new costume! The series will be written by the **PUNISHER** team of Dan Abnett and Andy Lanning, who are breaking new ground in their treatment of Magneto's favorite redheaded daughter. And, according to Editor Nel Yomtov, penciler John Higgins' first work for Marvel is "spectacular, really something to see."

SCARLET WITCH starts off with the Avengers West Coast compound under attack by demon forces, while the Witch suffers from nightmares that compel her to seek out Agatha Harkness in a Salem-like community in the Northeast.

The Witch's teammate, Hawkeye, is also leaving the West Coast temporarily for a limited series of his own. Hawkeye had a tough go of it with the death of his wife in **AVENGERS WEST COAST #100** and seeks the peace and quiet of the Canadian wilderness to come to terms with his loss. Whether he likes it or not, he's in for another adventure when he stumbles upon a genetic experiment gone wrong and War Machine steps in to help him confront the perpetrators! Hawkeye will also sport a brand-new costume in this hard-hitting series by **PUNISHER** writer Chuck Dixon and penciler Scott Kolins.

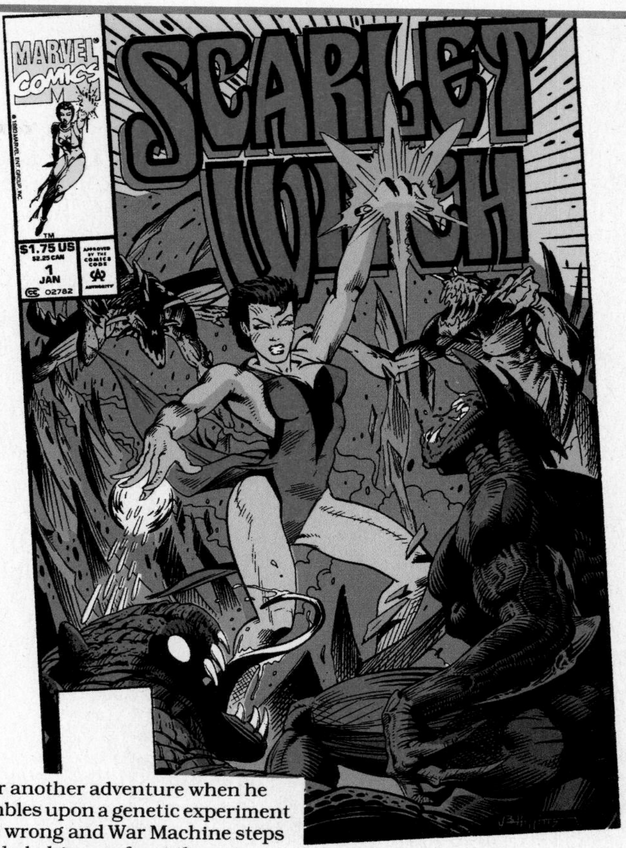
MARVEL COMICS
SCARLET WITCH
$1.75 US
1
JAN

MARVEL AGE #131

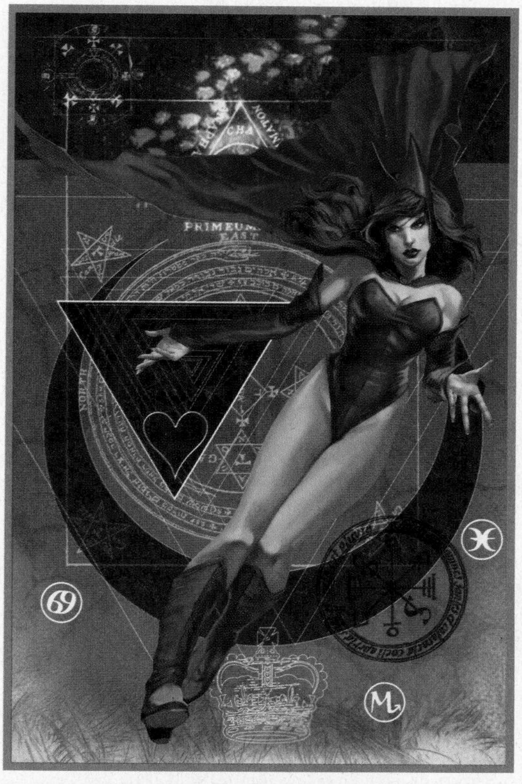

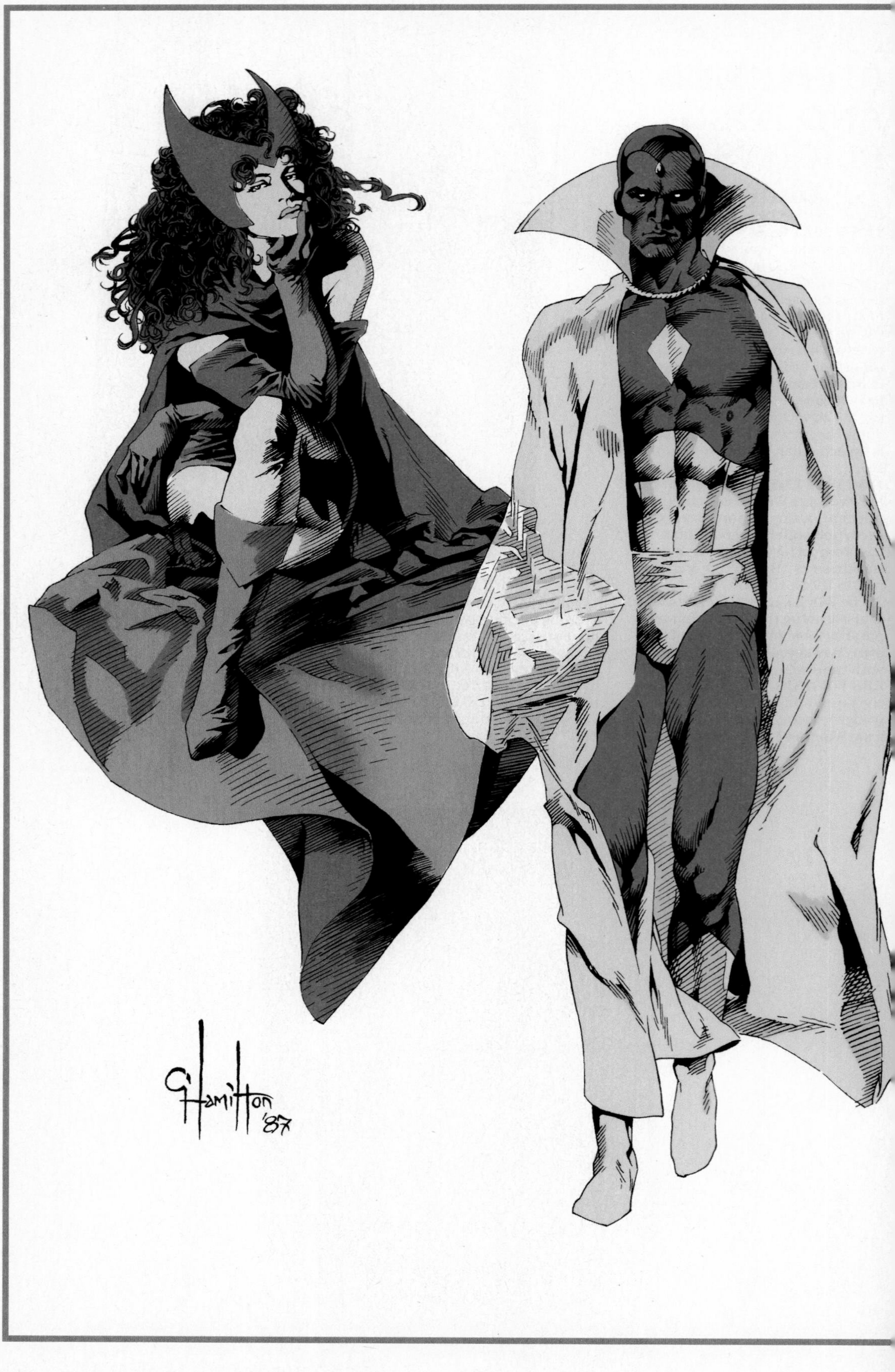
C. Hamilton '87

MARVEL FANFARE #35 PINUP BY CRAIG HAMILTON

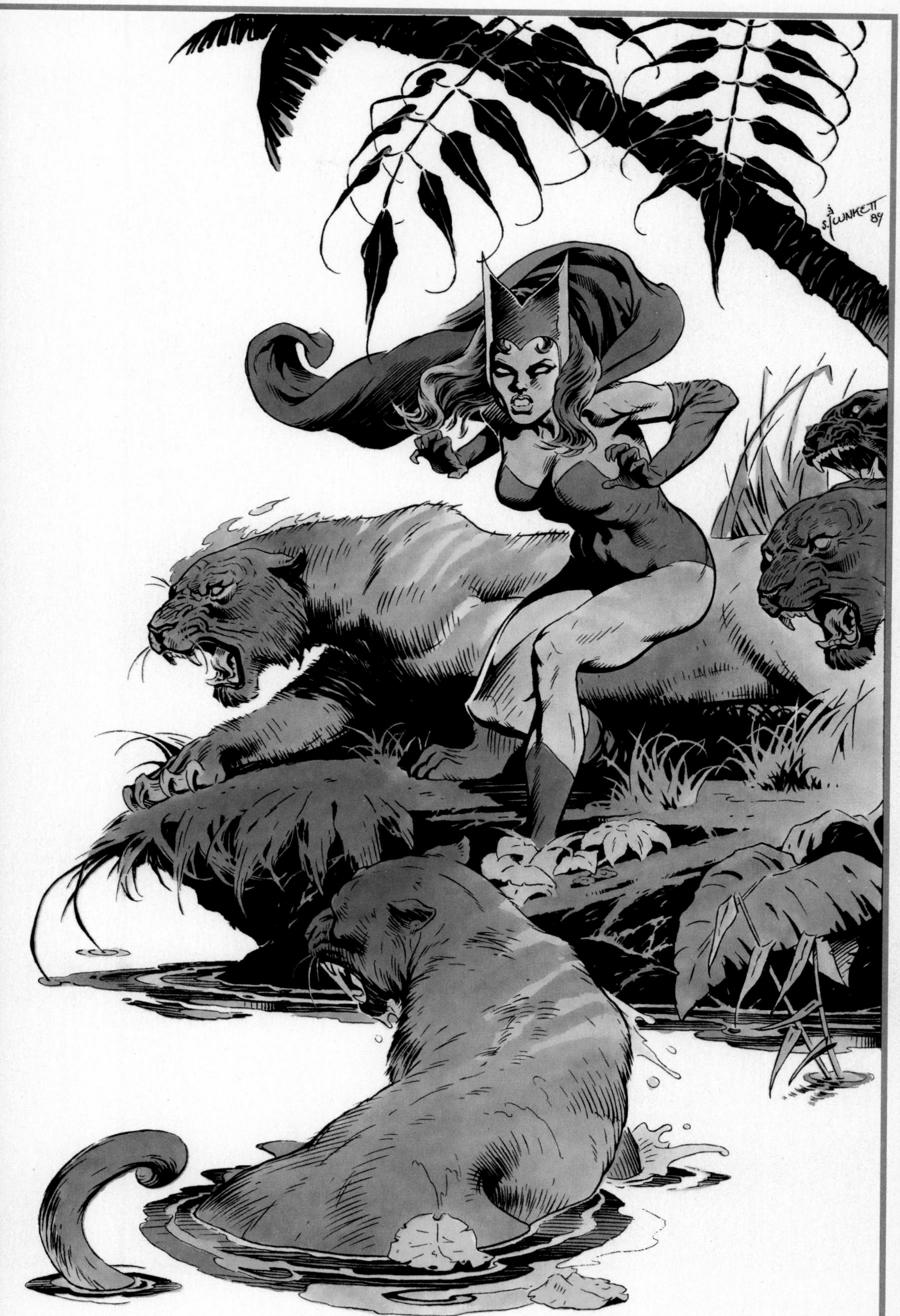
S. PLUNKETT 89

MARVEL FANFARE #45 PINUP BY SANDY PLUNKETT

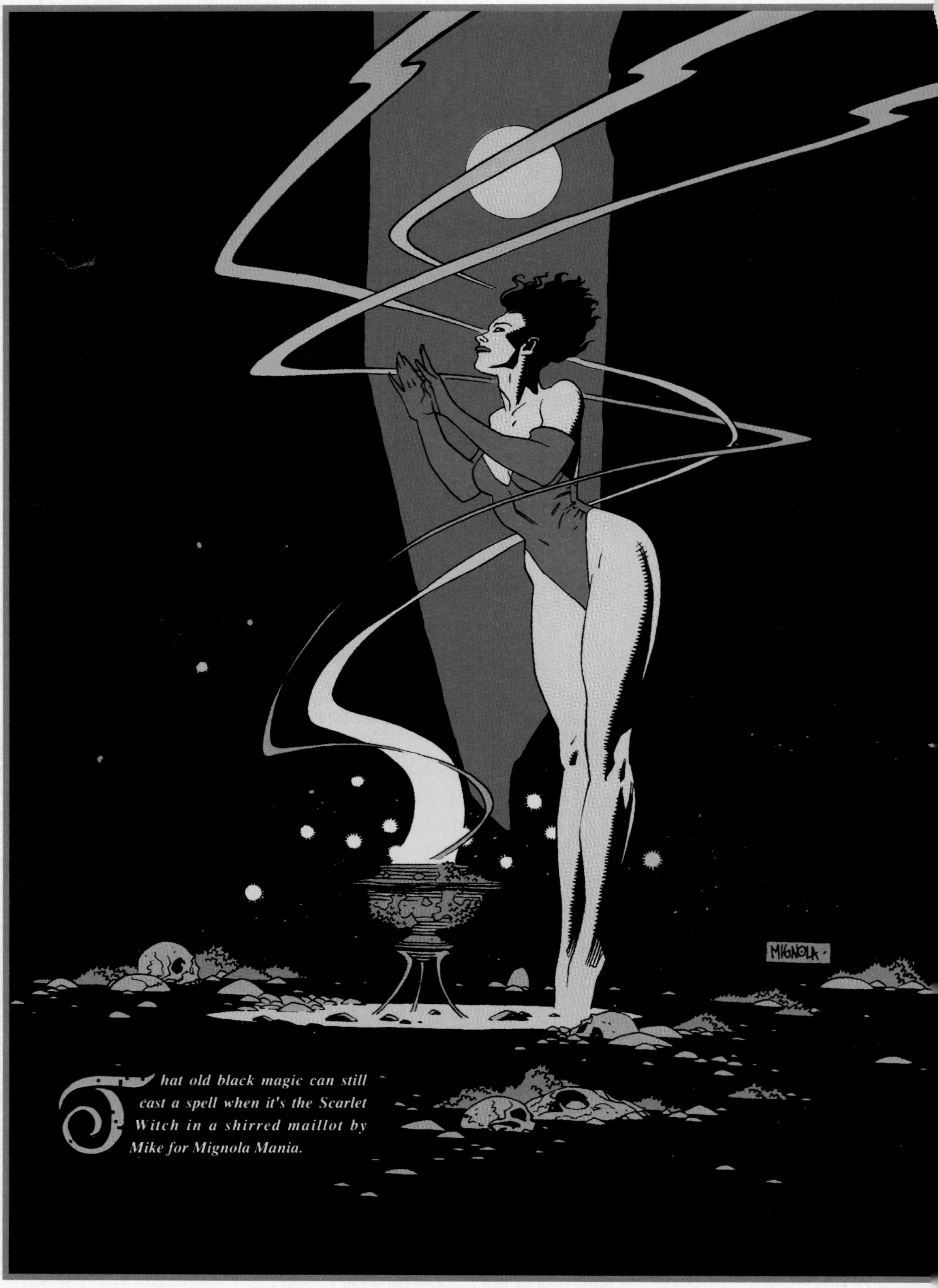
MIGNOLA
That old black magic can still cast a spell when it's the Scarlet Witch in a shirred maillot by Mike for Mignola Mania.

MARVEL ILLUSTRATED: THE SWIMSUIT ISSUE PINUP BY MIKE MIGNOLA

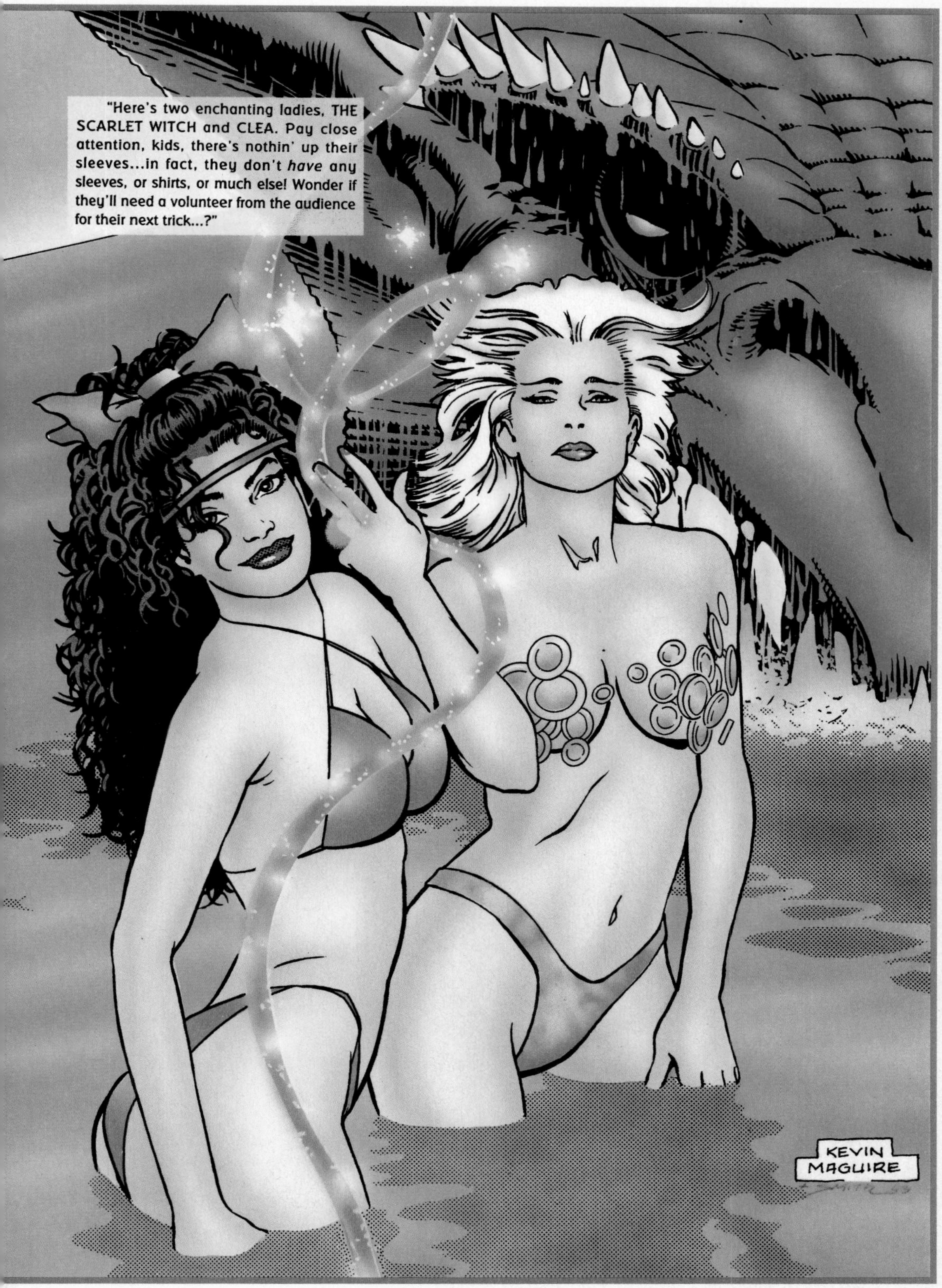
"Here's two enchanting ladies, THE SCARLET WITCH and CLEA. Pay close attention, kids, there's nothin' up their sleeves...in fact, they don't *have* any sleeves, or shirts, or much else! Wonder if they'll need a volunteer from the audience for their next trick...?"
KEVIN MAGUIRE

MARVEL SWIMSUIT SPECIAL #2 PINUP BY KEVIN MAGUIRE & TOM SMITH

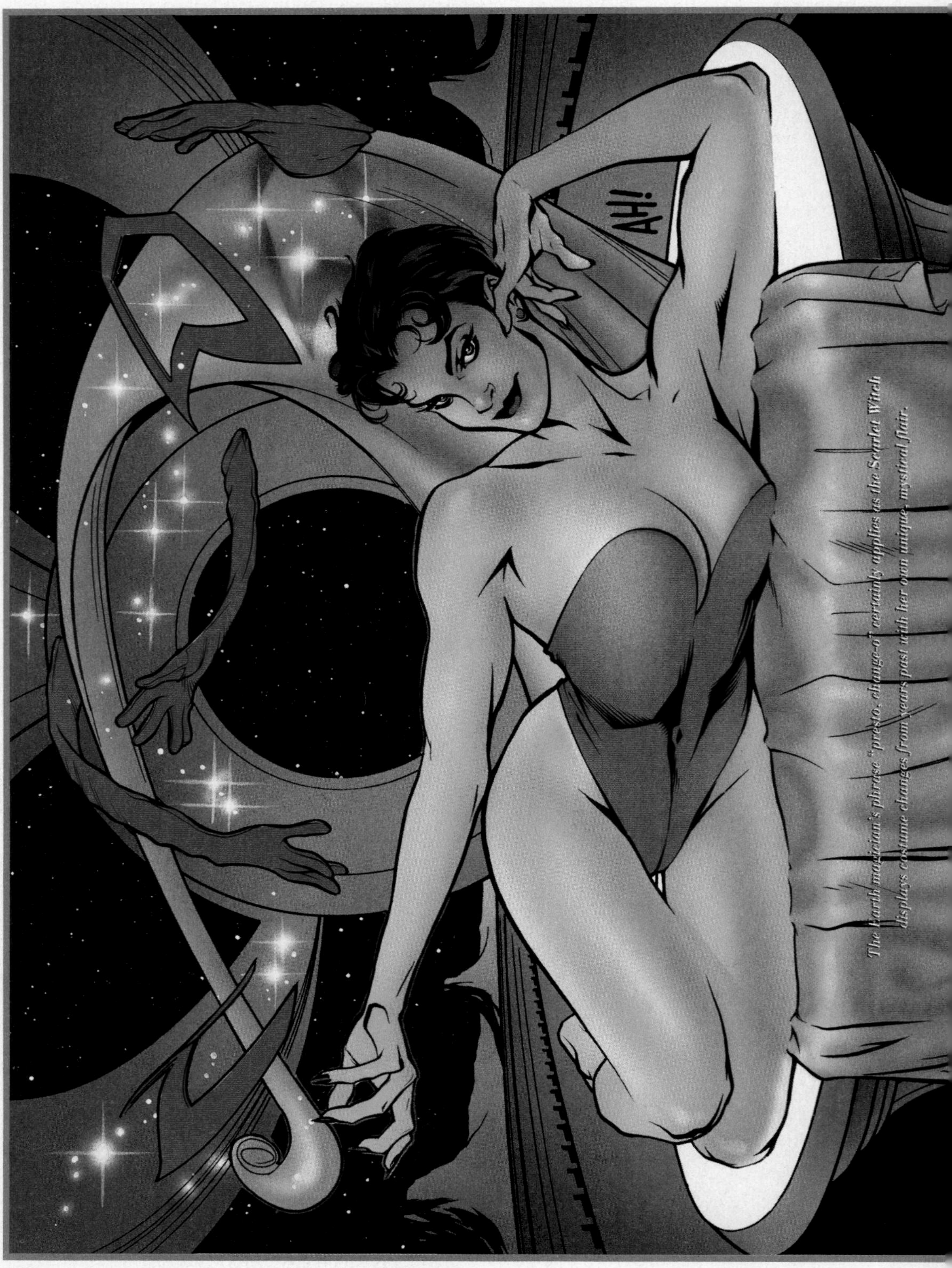
AH!
The Earth magician's phrase "presto, change-o" certainly applies as the Scarlet Witch
displays costume changes from years past with her own unique, mystical flair.

MARVEL SWIMSUIT SPECIAL #3 PINUP BY ADAM HUGHES

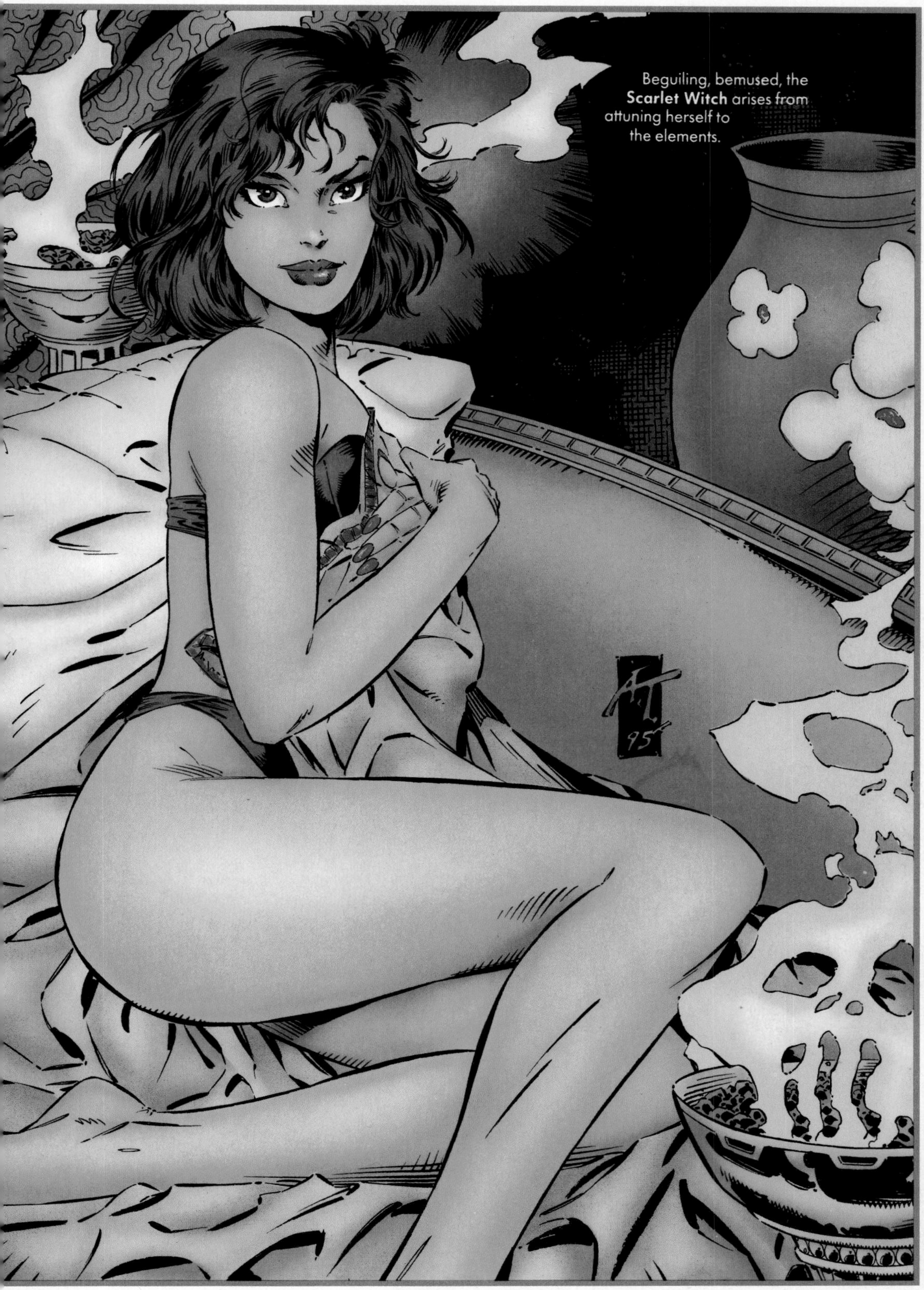
Beguiling, bemused, the **Scarlet Witch** arises from attuning herself to the elements.

MARVEL SWIMSUIT SPECIAL #4 PINUP BY ART THIBERT & TOM SMITH

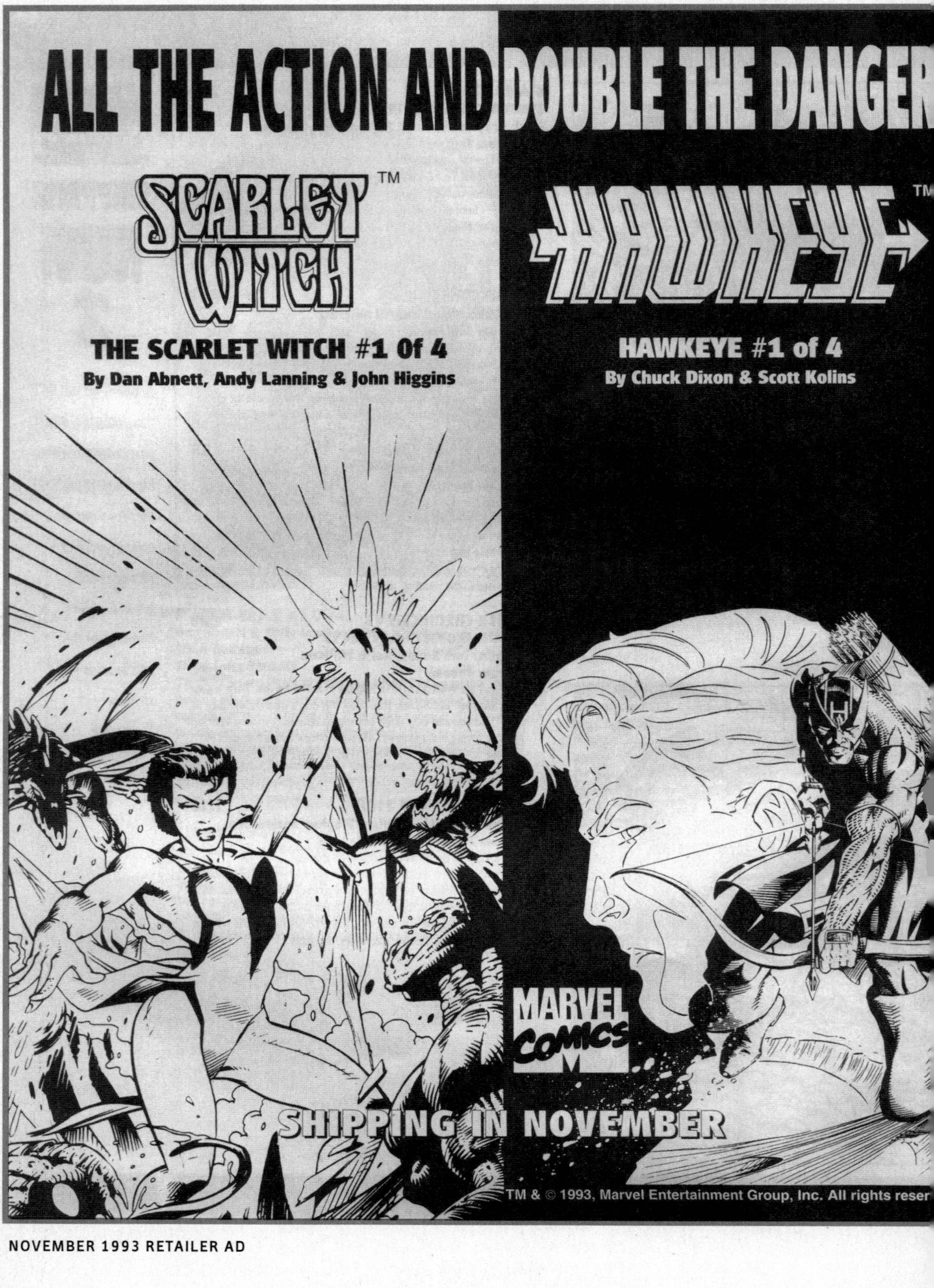
ALL THE ACTION AND DOUBLE THE DANGER
SCARLET WITCH ™
THE SCARLET WITCH #1 Of 4
By Dan Abnett, Andy Lanning & John Higgins
HAWKEYE ™
HAWKEYE #1 of 4
By Chuck Dixon & Scott Kolins
MARVEL COMICS
SHIPPING IN NOVEMBER
TM & © 1993, Marvel Entertainment Group, Inc. All rights reser

NOVEMBER 1993 RETAILER AD